THE PREHISTORIC SOCIETY

THE SOCIAL CONTEXT OF TECHNOLOGY

THE PREHISTORIC SOCIETY

The Social Context of Technology

Non-ferrous metalworking in later prehistoric Britain and Ireland

Leo Webley, Sophia Adams and Joanna Brück

Prehistoric Society Research Paper No. 11
2020

Project Funded by
The Leverhulme Trust

LEVERHULME
TRUST _____

THE PREHISTORIC SOCIETY
Series Editor: Michael J. Allen
Managing Editor: Julie Gardiner

 **OXBOW** | books
Oxford & Philadelphia

Published in the United Kingdom in 2020 by
The Prehistoric Society

and

OXBOW BOOKS
The Old Music Hall, 106–108 Cowley Road, Oxford, OX4 1JE

and in the United States by
OXBOW BOOKS
1950 Lawrence Road, Havertown, PA 19083

Hardcover Edition: ISBN 978-1-78925-176-0
Digital Edition: ISBN 978-1-78925-177-7 (epub)

A CIP record for this book is available from the British Library

Library of Congress Control Number: 2020937149

Printed in Malta by Melita Press

For a complete list of Oxbow titles, please contact:

UNITED KINGDOM
Oxbow Books
Telephone (01865) 241249
Email: oxbow@oxbowbooks.com
www.oxbowbooks.com

UNITED STATES OF AMERICA
Oxbow Books
Telephone (610) 853-9131, Fax (610) 853-9146
Email: queries@casemateacademic.com
www.casemateacademic.com/oxbow

Oxbow Books is part of the Casemate Group

Front cover: Experimental reconstruction of prehistoric copper smelting by Newcastle University students. Photo: Stephen Dann. Reproduced under Flickr CC licence Attribution-ShareAlike 2.0 Generic. CC BY-SA 2.0

Rear cover: Middle Bronze Age bronze palstave mould from Wiltshire (both sides of single valve). PAS: WILT-FFC218 CC BY 4.0

Early Bronze Age stone mould for axes and bars from Glenrinnes House, Duffown. Photo: Sophia Adams, courtesy of National Museum of Scotland

Late Bronze Age ingot hoard from Cranmere School, Esher, Surrey. Courtesy of Surrey County Archaeological Unit

THE PREHISTORIC SOCIETY
RESEARCH PAPERS

The Prehistoric Society Research Papers publish collections of edited papers covering aspects of Prehistory. These may be derived from conferences, or research projects; they specifically *exclude* the publication of single excavation reports. The Research Papers present the fruits of the best of prehistoric research, complementing the Society's respected *Proceedings* by allowing broader treatment of key research areas.

The Research Papers is a peer-reviewed series whose production is managed by the Society.

Further information can be found on the Society's website (www.prehistoricsociety.org)

THE PREHISTORIC SOCIETY

The Prehistoric Society's interests are world wide and extend from the earliest human origins to the emergence of written records. Membership is open to all, and includes professional, amateur, student and retired members.

An active programme of events – lectures, study tours, day- and weekend conferences, and research weekends – allows members to participate fully in the Society and to meet other members and interested parties. The study excursions cater for all preferences from the relatively luxurious to the more economical, including highly popular student study tours. Day visits to sites are arranged whenever possible.

The Society produces two publications that are included with most categories of membership: the annual journal, *Proceedings of the Prehistoric Society* and the topical newsletter, *PAST*, which is published in April, July and November. In addition the *Prehistoric Society Research Papers* are published occasionally on which members may have discount.

Further information can be found on the Society's website (www.prehistoricsociety.org), or via the Prehistoric Society's registered address: ℅ Institute of Archaeology, University College London, 31–34 Gordon Square, London, WC1H 0PY.

The Society is a registered charity (no. 1000567)

THE PREHISTORIC SOCIETY RESEARCH PAPERS

CONTENTS

LIST OF FIGURES AND TABLES

List of Figures

List of Tables

AUTHORS

SOPHIA ADAMS
Scottish Universities Environmental
Research Centre
Rankine Avenue
Scottish Enterprise Technology Park
East Kilbride
Scotland G75 0QF

JOANNA BRÜCK
School of Archaeology
University College Dublin
Belfield
Dublin 4
Ireland

LEO WEBLEY
Oxford Archaeology
Janus House
Osney Mead
Oxford
England OX2 0ES

ABSTRACTS

The Social Context of Technology explores non-ferrous metalworking in Britain and Ireland during the Bronze and Iron Ages (*c.* 2500 BC to 1st century AD). Evidence for bronze-working dominates the archaeological record, though the crafting of other non-ferrous metals – including gold, silver, tin, and lead – is also considered. Metalwork has long played a central role in accounts of European later prehistory. Non-ferrous metals were employed to make a wide range of tools and weapons as well as a variety of elaborate decorated objects, and they are thought to have played a significant role in economic, social and political change. Metalwork could be treated in special or ritualised ways, by being accumulated in large hoards or placed in rivers or bogs. But who made these objects? Prehistoric smiths have been portrayed by some as prosaic technicians, and by others as mystical figures akin to magicians. They have been seen both as independent, travelling 'entrepreneurs', and as the dependents of elite patrons. Hitherto, these competing models have not been tested through a comprehensive assessment of the archaeological evidence for metalworking. This volume fills that gap, with analysis focused on metalworking tools and waste, such as crucibles, moulds, casting debris and smithing implements. The find contexts of these objects are examined, both to identify places where metalworking occurred, and to investigate the cultural practices behind the deposition of metalworking debris. The key questions are: what was the social context of this craft, how was it organised, and what was its ideological significance? How did this vary regionally and change over time? As well as elucidating a key aspect of later prehistoric life in Britain and Ireland, this research contributes to broader debates on material culture and the social role of craft.

Résumé

Le contexte social de la technologie explore le travail des métaux non ferreux en Grande-Bretagne et en Irlande pendant les Âges du Bronze et du Fer (vers 2 500 av. J.-C. au premier siècle ap. J.-C). Les témoignages de travail du bronze dominent les archives archéologiques bien que le travail d'autres métaux non ferreux –y compris l'or, l'argent, l'étain et le plomb sont aussi examinés. La métallurgie a de longue date joué un rôle primordial dans les récits de la préhistoire européenne tardive. Les métaux non ferreux étaient utilisés pour fabriquer une grande gamme d'outils et d'armes ainsi qu'une variété d'objets élaborés décorés et ils sont supposés avoir joué un rôle important dans les changements économiques, sociaux et politiques. La métallurgie pouvait être traitée d'une manière spéciale, ou ritualisée en étant accumulée en grands résors ou placée dans des rivières ou des marécages. Mais qui fabriquait ces objets? Certains ont décrit les forgerons comme des techniciens prosaiques et d'autres comme des personnages mystiques proches des magiciens. Ils ont été considérés à la fois comme des 'entrepreneurs' indépendants, itinérants, et comme les dépendants d'une élite de mécènes. Jusqu'à présent ces modèles concurrents n'ont pas été testés par une évaluation apprpofondie des témoignages archéologiques de la métallurgie. Ce volume comble cette lacune avec une analyse concentrée sur les outils et les déchets de la métallurgie tels que les creusets, les moules, les résidus de coulées et les instruments de forge. Les contextes des découvertes de ces objets sont examinés à la fois pour identifier les endroits où se déroulait la métallurgie et pour enquêter sur les pratiques culturelles derrière; le dépôt de débris de métallurgie Les questions clés sont:quel était le contexte social de cet artisanat, comment était-il organisé et quelle en était la signification idéologique?, comment cela variait-il t selon les régions et comment cela avait-il évolué au fil du temps? En plus d'élucider un aspect clé de la vie préhistorique tardive en Grande-Bretagne et en Irlande, ces recherches contribuent aux débats plus étendus sur la culture matérielle et le rôle social de l'artisanat.

Zusammenfassung

Das soziale Umfeld der Technologie befasst sich mit der Buntmetallverarbeitung in Großbritannien und Irland während der Bronze- und Eisenzeit (ca. 2500 v. Chr. bis 1. Jahrhundert n. Chr.). Das archäologische Quellenmaterial hierzu wird von Belegen für Bronzeverarbeitung dominiert, es wird aber auch die Verarbeitung anderer Nichteisenmetalle – wie Gold, Silber, Zinn und Blei – behandelt. Metallverarbeitung spielt in Arbeiten zu den jüngeren Perioden der europäischen Urgeschichte seit langem eine zentrale Rolle. Nichteisenmetalle wurden zur Herstellung einer umfangreichen Bandbreite von Werkzeugen und Waffen sowie einer Vielzahl von kunstvoll verzierten Gegenständen verwendet, und es wird angenommen, dass sie eine bedeutende Rolle beim wirtschaftlichen, sozialen und politischen Wandel gespielt haben. Metallobjekte konnten auf besondere oder ritualisierte Weise behandelt werden, indem sie in großen Horten zusammengetragen oder in Flüssen oder Sümpfen deponiert wurden. Wer aber hat diese Gegenstände hergestellt? Prähistorische Schmiede wurden von einigen als prosaische Techniker und von anderen als mystische, magierähnliche Figuren dargestellt. Sie wurden einerseits als unabhängige Wanderunternehmer, andererseits als Abhängige von zur Elite gehörigen Auftraggebern angesehen. Diese konkurrierenden Erklärungsmodelle wurden bislang noch nie im Rahmen einer umfangreichen Untersuchung des archäologischen Quellenmaterials zur Metallverarbeitung überprüft. Der vorliegende Band schließt diese Lücke mit einer Analyse, die sich auf die Werkzeuge und Abfallprodukte der Metallverarbeitung wie z. B. Gusstiegel, -formen, -abfall und Schmiedewerkzeuge konzentriert. Dabei werden die Fundzusammenhänge dieser Objekte untersucht, um sowohl die Orte zu identifizieren, an denen die Metallverarbeitung stattfand, als auch die kulturellen Praktiken hinter der Deponierung von Metallverarbeitungsabfällen zu untersuchen. Die Schlüsselfragen sind: Was war das soziale Umfeld dieses Handwerks, wie war es organisiert und welche ideologische Bedeutung hatte es? Wie variierte dies regional und veränderte sich im Laufe der Zeit? Diese Untersuchung beleuchtet nicht nur einen Schlüsselaspekt der Lebensumstände während der späteren urgeschichtlichen Perioden in Großbritannien und Irland, sondern trägt auch zu breiteren Debatten zur materiellen Kultur und der sozialen Rolle des Handwerks bei.

Resumen

El Contexto Social de la Tecnología explora el trabajo del metal no ferroso en Gran Bretaña e Irlanda durante la Edad del Bronce y del Hierro (*ca.* 2500 BC y el siglo AD I). La evidencia de los trabajos metalúrgicos en bronce domina el panorama arqueológico, aunque también se toma en consideración el trabajo de otros metales no ferrosos –incluidos el oro, la plata, el estaño y el plomo-. Las actividades metalúrgicas han jugado un papel fundamental a la hora de abordar la Prehistoria Reciente en Europa. Los metales no ferrosos fueron empleados en la elaboración de una amplia gama de herramientas y armas, así como en una gran variedad de objetos decorados, y por ello se considera que han jugado un papel significativo en los cambios económicos, sociales y políticos. La metalurgia pudo ser tratada de manera especial o ritualizada, acumulándose en grandes depósitos o en ríos y ciénagas. Pero, ¿quién elaboró esos objetos? Los herreros prehistóricos han sido considerados por algunos como personas con un conocimiento técnico prosaico, mientras que otros los han considerado figuras místicas similares a los magos. Han sido considerados tanto como "emprendedores" independientes e itinerantes como dependientes de una élite de patrones. Hasta el momento, estos modelos opuestos no han sido comprobados a través de una evaluación exhaustiva de la evidencia arqueológica de la metalurgia. Este volumen llena este vacío, con un análisis centrado en las herramientas y desechos de la metalurgia, como crisoles, moldes, escorias de fundición e instrumentos de herrería. Se examinan los contextos de estos objetos, tanto para identificar los lugares de producción de la metalurgia, como para investigar las prácticas culturales detrás de la deposición de los desechos del trabajo del metal. Las preguntas fundamentales son: ¿cuál era el contexto social de esta artesanía, cómo estaba organizada, y cuál era su significado ideológico? ¿Cómo varía regionalmente y a lo largo del tiempo? Además de esclarecer un aspecto crucial en la vida de la Prehistoria Reciente en Gran Bretaña e Irlanda, esta investigación contribuye a debates más amplios sobre la cultura material y el papel social de la artesanía.

ACKNOWLEDGEMENTS

This project was kindly funded by the Leverhulme Trust with additional financial support from the Robert Kiln Charitable Trust and the Department of Anthropology and Archaeology, University of Bristol. Advice, assistance and information (including permission to reproduce site plans, artefact drawings and photographs) have been provided by many individuals and organisations including but not limited to:

The Ashmolean Museum; Paul Craddock, Neil Wilkin, Julia Farley, Jennifer Wexler, Gaetano Ardito and Marta Mroczek, British Museum; Dorset County Museum; Paul Thompson and Huw Jones, Herbert Museum; Sara Taylor, Hertford Museum; Malcolm Chapman, Hunterian Museum; Samantha Harris, Pernille Richards and Rebecca Arnott, Maidstone Museum; Jody Joy, Museum of Archaeology and Anthropology, Cambridge; Margaret Lannin, National Museum of Ireland; Fraser Hunter and Matt Knight, National Museum of Scotland; Adam Gwilt, National Museum of Wales; Keith Fitzpatrick-Matthews, North Hertfordshire Museum; Rose Nicholson, North Lincolnshire Museum; David Moon, Oxfordshire Museum Services; Shrewsbury Museum; Matthew Fittock, St Albans Museums; Greer Ramsey, Ulster Museum; Lisa Brown, Wiltshire Museum; George Children, Border Archaeology; Christopher Evans, Cambridge Archaeological Unit; Gabrielle Day, Cambridgeshire County Council; Peter Clark and Andrew Richardson, Canterbury Archaeological Trust; Stephen Coleman, Central Bedfordshire Council; James Gossip and Andy Jones, Sean Taylor, Cornwall Archaeology Unit; Neil Holbrook and Mary Alexander, Cotswold Archaeology; Chris Patrick, Coventry City Council; Essex Society for Archaeology and History; Tim Young, Geoarch; Paul Nichols and Toby Catchpole, Gloucestershire County Council Archaeology Service; David Jenkins, Gwynedd Archaeological Trust; Magnar Dalland and Candy Hatherley, Headland Archaeology; Karen Dempsey and Rob Lynch, IAC; Rebecca Peake and Yvan Pailler, Inrap; Andrew Mayfield, Kent County Council; Modern Records Centre, University of Warwick; Nick Crank, Milton Keynes Council; Alison Telfer, MOLA; Andy Chapman, MOLA Northampton; National Monuments Service Archive, Dublin; Heather Hamilton, Norfolk County Council; Mike Hemblade, North Lincolnshire HER; Hugh Winfield, North East Lincolnshire Council; Christine Addison, Northamptonshire County Council; Gill Hey, Oxford Archaeology; Penny Ward, Shropshire Council; Suffolk County Council; Rob Poulton, Surrey County Council; Peter Rowe, Tees Archaeology; Ges Moody, Trust for Thanet Archaeology; Patrick Clay, Richard Buckley, John Thomas and Lynden Cooper, University of Leicester Archaeological Services; Phil Andrews, Alistair Barclay, Pippa Bradley and Will Foster, Wessex Archaeology; Robin Jackson, Derek Hurst and Aisling Nash, Worcestershire County Council; Justine Bayley; Katharina Becker; Lindsey Büster; Richard Bradley; Mary Cahill; Nick Card; Edward Caswell; Kerri Cleary; Trevor Cowie; Jane Downes; Andrew Fitzpatrick; Jennifer Foster; Angela Gallager; Carlotta Gardiner; Barbara Garfi; Catriona Gibson; Colin Haselgrove; Mark Landon; Kevin Leahy; Marcos Martinón-Torres; Tobias Mörtz; Stuart Needham; Peter Northover; William O'Brien; Brendan O'Connor; Henrietta Quinnell; Lorenz Rahmstorf; John Sills; Mansel Spratling; Richard Tabor; Simon Timberlake; Simon Weller; Alan Williams; Fiona Wilson and

Ann Woodward. We also thank all those support staff and volunteers at museums, units, county services, the Portable Antiquities Scheme, university departments and archaeological societies who have made our research possible, often anonymously.

We are particularly grateful to Ben Roberts, Tim Champion and an anonymous referee for reading draft chapters of the text; to Fiona McGibbon for assessing the geological origins of the Scottish stone moulds; and to Anne Leaver for her work on the illustrations. Ana Jorge and Kostas Trimmis kindly assisted with other illustrations. This project has also greatly benefitted from unpublished research by Hilary Howard and Vanessa Fell exploring the social context of metalworking through refractory remains and tools.

1

Introduction: non-ferrous metals in context

Introducing the problem

Metals have long been central to accounts of social and economic change in later prehistory. Non-ferrous metalwork represents one of the most visible and impressive elements of the archaeological record of the Bronze and Iron Ages. During the Bronze Age, bronze was used not only to make a variety of tools and simple personal ornaments, but also elaborate decorated objects such as shields or cauldrons that can be regarded as masterpieces of craftworking skill. In the Iron Age, though bronze was increasingly replaced by iron for making some kinds of artefacts, it continued to be used for personal objects and intricate pieces of 'Celtic art', including weaponry, horse gear, and mirrors. During both periods, metal artefacts could be treated in apparently special or ritualised ways, for example by being deposited in hoards or in natural places such as rivers or bogs.

The introduction of metalworking is widely accepted to have had a significant impact on the character and organisation of later prehistoric society. Copper and gold were the first metals to be used in the Britian and Ireland: the earliest metal objects appear from *c.* 2450 BC and knowledge of metalworking technology was introduced from the near Continent at this time. Both copper and gold have restricted distributions as ores and in their native forms. Metal objects are found in regions far from metal sources from the beginning of the period and the uptake of metalworking is therefore thought to have resulted in a dramatic increase in trade and exchange. Early metal objects are often viewed as symbols of power and prestige, and the ability to access and display such items and to accumulate wealth through the control of trade and exchange is frequently linked to emerging social stratification. In some regions of Britain, for example south-east England and north-east Scotland, the earliest metal objects were associated with novel burial practices: the introduction of single inhumations with grave-goods including Beaker pots, gold ornaments, and copper daggers is thought to indicate that socio-political power was now predicated on access to exotic materials and new technologies. Recent research suggests that there may have been significant population movement into Britain during the second half of the 3rd millennium (Olalde *et al.* 2018) and the spread of metalworking and other innovations is often set within this context (Sheridan 2012).

Over the subsequent centuries, metals came to be used for an increasing range of objects, including new types of tools and weapons: the appearance of tools such as chisels, gouges, and sickles in bronze, for example, doubtless had an impact on agricultural activities and other crafts such as woodworking, while the production of weapons such as swords and spearheads is likely to have affected the character and organisation of later prehistoric conflict.

Given the importance of metals to later prehistoric societies, it is widely assumed that metalworking would have been a socially significant activity. This idea can be traced back to the work of Gordon Childe (1930), who saw the development of craft specialisation – and metalworking in particular – as key to the growth of social complexity. For Childe, Bronze Age metalworkers were important agents in creating new social conditions as they were independent, 'detribalised' entrepreneurs who moved from place to place. Childe's ideas are still influential, being echoed for example in a recent book by the anthropologist Jack Goody (2012), who argues that the development of metalworking during the Bronze Age was nothing less than the first step towards the modern world. The claim that metalworkers were itinerant and socially independent has also been repeated in recent work on both the Bronze Age and Iron Age (eg, Modarressi-Tehrani 2009).

An alternative view is that Bronze and Iron Age metalworkers were attached to elite patrons, whose control over the production and exchange of 'prestige' objects was a source of political power (eg, Vandkilde 1996; Kristiansen 1998; Earle 2002; Cunliffe 2005; Kristiansen & Larsson 2005). Complex metal objects such as gold gorgets and bronze cauldrons are thought to have been produced by highly specialised craftworkers. The appearance of specialists indicates emerging processes of social differentiation, as well as new forms of inter-dependency: full-time specialists cannot produce their own food and it has frequently been argued that they may have been supported (and controlled) by chiefs. In recent years, it has been claimed that metalworkers were mystical figures akin to magicians and that their craft was ritualised and symbolically charged (Budd & Taylor 1995; Haaland 2004; Goldhahn 2013). This may have

given significant social status to metalworkers or to those who could access their products. However, others have questioned whether prehistoric metalworking need have been a special or ritualised activity (Kuijpers 2008) and whether there was necessarily any link between metalworking and elites (Giles 2007; Kienlin 2013; Joy 2017).

The truth is that, although metalwork and metalworking have long played a central role in interpretations of the period, the organisation and social role of this craft remain poorly understood (Kienlin 2013, 431; Carey *et al.* 2019; see below for further discussion). One reason for this is the 'intra-disciplinary divide between archaeological scientists and socio-cultural archaeologists and anthropologists' that has long dogged research on prehistoric metalworking (Budd & Taylor 1995, 134; see also Kienlin 2013, 414–5). The former group have carried out scientific analyses of metal artefacts to elucidate the movement of metals from specific ore sources as well as technical aspects of the manufacturing process, but these studies are not always related to wider questions regarding the social organisation of metalworking. Thus, we have an increasingly detailed understanding of the circulation of metals and the practicalities of metal production, for example how different types of mould were used or how complex objects such as gold gorgets or bronze cauldrons were made. In contrast, other archaeologists have employed ethnographic and historical parallels to explore how metalworking may have been organised in prehistory, with studies of African ironworking playing a particular role. Such parallels – rather than archaeological evidence – have been the main source of many of the claims about the status and symbolic associations of this craft. Largely lacking is detailed work that investigates prehistoric metalworking practices within their *specific social context* (but see Baldwin & Joy 2017).

That issue is the subject of this book. The aim of the study is to explore the social context of non-ferrous metalworking in Britain and Ireland from the introduction of this craft in the mid-3rd millennium BC up to the time of the Roman conquest of southern Britain in the 1st century AD. Key questions include: what was the social significance of this craft, and what social roles did metalworkers play? How was metalworking organised? How did this vary regionally and change over time? A range of evidence will be drawn upon, but the main focus will be on the residues of metalworking recovered from excavated sites. This body of material is an under-researched resource which has been systematically collated for the first time here.

This introductory chapter begins by discussing previous debates around the social context of prehistoric metalworking. It then briefly sets out the chronology of prehistoric metal use and the availability of metal ores in Britain and Ireland. Finally, the scope of the present study and the methods employed will be outlined.

Previous discussion on the social context of metalworking

While questions surrounding the social roles of metals and metalworkers have been prominent in work on both the Bronze Age and the Iron Age, there are differences in the ways that these issues have been approached for each period. While bronze has often been seen as central to Bronze Age societies – playing a major economic role as well as having political, symbolic, and ritual significance – during the Iron Age its role as a key economic driver is assumed to have been taken over by iron. Bronze now largely ceased to be used to make tools and other everyday objects and was employed for a more limited range of artefacts including personal ornaments, horse gear, and feasting equipment. As such, *non-ferrous* metalworking has tended be seen as less central to Iron Age societies than to those of the Bronze Age and as primarily relevant to the spheres of ritual and prestige display. There are also further differences in traditions of scholarship, fostered by the fact that Bronze Age and Iron Age metalwork has generally been studied by separate groups of researchers. Work on fine Iron Age metalwork has been more strongly influenced by art-historical perspectives (eg, Megaw & Megaw 1989), in part because it can be elaborate in design and include figurative motifs and in part because of the perceived continuity of elements of 'Celtic art' styles into historical periods, most famously in illuminated Christian manuscripts. As a result, it has sometimes been implied that skilled Iron Age craftworkers would have operated in an analogous manner to artists of more recent times, an assumption reflected in

discussions of 'schools' of metalworkers (eg, Cunliffe 2005, 501), for example. References to the social position of craftworkers in medieval Irish and Welsh 'Celtic' law codes have influenced perspectives on Iron Age smiths, based on the premise that these documents fossilise aspects of older social arrangements (Gibson 1996; Cunliffe 2005). 'Celtic' and Norse mythology – in which smiths embody magical powers of creation and destruction and occupy a socially liminal position because of the transformative effects of their craft – has also had a significant impact on studies of Iron Age smithing (Green 2002; Haaland 2004).

Nevertheless, there are also strong similarities in how the social organisation of metalworking has been studied in the Bronze Age and Iron Age. There has in fact been significant cross-pollination of ideas between research on the two periods; for example, Childe's work on the mobility of Bronze Age metalworkers and on the relationship between craft specialisation and social complexity had a significant influence on interpretations of the Iron Age during the mid-20th century (see below). For both periods, a number of questions have recurred in the debates on the social role of prehistoric metalworkers, including:

- Were metalworkers itinerant, or settled within a community?
- Were they (always) full-time specialists?
- Did they have a special or elevated status, or did they operate under the patronage or control of elites?
- Were they (always) men?
- To what extent was their craft bound up with ritual and taboo?

The debates around each of these issues will be discussed in turn below.

Metalworkers and mobility
It has often been assumed (eg, Neipert 2006) that debates on the mobility and social position of prehistoric metalworkers originated in the work of Gordon Childe in the early 20th century, but in fact such issues had begun to be discussed already in the 19th century. French writers such as Fournet (1862) and Figuier (1870) suggested that at least some Bronze Age metalworkers may have been itinerant, based on the parallel of the travelling tinkers of their own day. Parenteau (1868, 23) specifically

interpreted a bronze hoard containing a mould from Port-Saint-Père in western France as the possession of a travelling smith. In Britain, these ideas were picked up by John Evans, who stated that:

> Though there appear to have been wandering founders, who, like the bell-founders of mediaeval times, could practise their art at any spot where their services were required, yet there were probably fixed foundries also, where the process of manufacture could be more economically carried on, and where successive generations passed through some sort of apprenticeship to learn the art and mystery of the trade. (Evans 1881, 477)

Aside from bronze hoards, moulds were also a source of speculation. For example, Callander (1904) suggested that an Early Bronze Age stone mould found at Foudland (Aberdeenshire) had belonged to an itinerant bronze founder, given its compact, portable form.

It was against this background that Childe formulated his ideas on the European Bronze Age smith. Working within the diffusionist paradigm dominant at the time, he argued that

> the diffusion of metallurgical knowledge … must be associated with an actual spread of initiates either as prospectors voyaging in quest of ore, or as perambulating smiths seeking their fortunes by plying their trade among barbarians, or as slaves or others who have secured initiation in the original centre or one of its offshoots, returning home. (Childe 1930, 10)

Childe further argued that metalworking was such a complex and time-consuming craft that it would have been an essentially full-time occupation and would have required a lengthy apprenticeship, with metalworkers perhaps initiated into a distinct caste. This combined with their itinerancy would have set metalworkers apart from the rest of society. They were thus 'detribalised', and free from the control of any patron (Childe 1930; 1940; 1958).

Childe's ideas were dominant for several decades. They also influenced work on the Iron Age, Bersu (1940) for example arguing that the sparse scraps of slag from the settlement at Little Woodbury (Wiltshire) evince occasional visits by wandering smiths. Studies of fine metalwork often attributed the spread of styles to the mobility of master craftsmen. Thus Hawkes and Smith (1957) argued that Irish smiths travelled to Continental Europe to learn to manufacture sheet bronze buckets and cauldrons, while Jope (1971) suggested that the Iron Age Witham shield had been made by a metalworker who had been trained on the Continent.

The first comprehensive critique of Childe's model came in an influential paper by Rowlands (1971), which is notable as the first detailed application of ethnographic parallels to the study of the social organisation of European prehistoric metalworking. Rowlands argued that 'the existence of a "free-travelling", itinerant smith divorced from any social context is rarely found in ethnographic contexts', noting that 'In the majority of ethnographic examples the smith is embedded in a particular social and cultural context, and, even if to some extent "itinerant", does not necessarily belong to a subgroup of distinct origin and cultural identity' (Rowlands 1971, 214). In fact, specialisation and restricted skills often heighten a craftworker's obligations and integration into the community.

Rowlands' paper has been widely taken to disprove the idea of the itinerant smith. Careful reading however shows that his target was not mobility *per se*, but rather the idea that metalworkers could have been 'detribalised', operating outside of society. In fact, in another publication from the following year, Rowlands argued that Bronze Age axesmiths 'could easily have travelled around the countryside', as they used reusable moulds, whereas swordsmiths 'are likely to have been much more static, probably having their own workshop', as they used single-use clay moulds and were thus restricted to areas where suitable clay was available (Moore & Rowlands 1972, 33). A decade later, a much more extensive survey of the ethnographic literature in Hilary Howard's PhD thesis (1983) showed that mobility of various kinds is far from rare for pre-industrial metalworkers, but this important work is little known as it was never published.

Another factor in the decline in the idea of the itinerant smith has been the excavation of large numbers of settlements with assemblages of metalworking debris. The large Iron Age assemblage of moulds and crucibles from Gussage All Saints (Dorset) for example, was interpreted by Spratling (1979) in terms of permanently settled craftworkers. In recent decades metalworkers have thus generally been envisaged as embedded within their community (though see eg, Foster 1980; 1995; Peltenburg 1982; Skowranek 2007 for contrary views). For the Iron Age in particular the relative ubiquity of iron in comparison to copper and tin has meant that it is usually assumed that there was little requirement for metalworkers to travel during this period.

Recently, interest in human mobility in later prehistory has increased again after a period of neglect, due in part to new isotopic and aDNA evidence (Leary 2014; Anderson-Whymark *et al.* 2015; Frei *et al.* 2015; 2017; Olalde *et al.* 2018; Parker Pearson *et al.* 2019). The mobility of metalworkers in particular has come back into focus with the discovery of the Beaker period 'Amesbury Archer' in Wiltshire. This individual was buried with a rich grave-good assemblage including putative smithing tools and isotopic evidence suggests that he may have been born in the Alpine region (Fitzpatrick 2011). The work of the anthropologist Mary Helms (1988; 1993) has also influenced recent research portraying Chalcolithic and Bronze Age skilled metalworkers as high-status voyagers (eg, Kristiansen & Larsson 2005). Helms argues that esoteric knowledge acquired from afar was viewed as divinely inspired and that those who had access to such knowledge were considered close to the gods.

Specialisation and the social status of metalworkers

Childe's identification of metalworkers as full-time specialists had significant implications, for increasing specialisation has been linked to social complexity. In more recent years, as the evidence for itinerant metalworkers has been questioned, it has been suggested that complex items such as bronze swords and shields may have been produced by full-time specialists dependent on chiefly patronage (Vandkilde 1996; Kristiansen 1998; Cunliffe 2005; Kristiansen & Larsson 2005). This has been supported by the recovery of metalworking debris from 'high-status' sites such as hillforts. Such social evolutionary perspectives posit that the ability of chiefs to control access to high-status objects and to use these to enhance their own social position resulted in increasing social differentiation. Recent interest in the cosmological significance of metalworking (see below) has also led to arguments that this would have linked it to chiefly power (Budd & Taylor 1995): the generative potency of smithing and the social and economic significance of metal objects

suggest that knowledge and control of this skilled craft may have been one source of enhanced social status (Helms 1988; 1993; Kristiansen & Larsson 2005). For the Iron Age, models in which skilled metalworkers were tied to elite patrons have been supported by citing medieval Irish and Welsh literature, based on somewhat questionable assumptions of historical and cultural continuity in the 'Celtic' west (Henderson 1991; Gibson 1996; Cunliffe 2005).

These arguments are not universally accepted, however. Many recent models of European later prehistoric societies posit heterarchical rather than hierarchical forms of organisation (eg, Crumley 1995; Hill 2012; Brück & Fontijn 2013; Dolan 2014; Currás & Sastre 2019), implying that metalworking would have been carried out without elite control, and that the production of 'high-status' artefacts may have been linked more to the prestige of communities than to that of individuals. Furthermore, studies of the ethnographic evidence suggest that the status of metalworkers in different societies can vary 'from fear, contempt and loathing to respect and awe' (Rowlands 1971, 216; see also Howard 1983), and that even highly skilled metalworkers are not always dependent on elite patronage (Costin 1991). Spielmann's concept of the 'ritual mode of production' (2002) provides an alternative possible context for skilled metalworking. For Spielmann, the requirements of rituals and festivities are key drivers for the crafting of elaborate objects, and thus 'craft production in small-scale societies [is] supported not by elites but by numerous individuals as they fulfil ritual obligations and create and sustain social relations' (*ibid.*, 197). This model has been applied to the Middle Iron Age of southern Britain by Joy (2017), who argues that the sophisticated bronze and iron cauldrons in the Chiseldon hoard (Wiltshire) were produced for use in communal feasts within the context of a heterarchical society.

Others argue that different forms of metalworking need not have been organised in the same way or had the same status connotations. Rowlands (1976), for example, notes that during the later Bronze Age certain categories of object (such as particular types of sword) have much wider areas of distribution than others (for example certain types of axe), and he suggests that this may be the product of more or less centralised modes of production. Objects, like swords, that required a high degree of technical proficiency may have been produced in regional centres where full-time specialists were based, while 'simpler' objects such as axes could have been manufactured locally by part-time smiths whose technical skills were of a lower standard. As such, Rowlands argues that different kinds of metalworkers may have operated in different social spheres: 'The socio-economic circumstances of the skilled craftsman attached to a high-status group need not be the same as the circumstances governing the position of the smith producing tools and weapons for the general population' (Rowlands 1971, 210–11). The identification of metalworking evidence on Bronze and Iron Age settlements – particularly 'ordinary' farmsteads – indicates that metalworkers (or at least those not involved in highly skilled work) need not always have been full-time specialists (Barber 2003; Kuijpers 2008; 2018; Dubreucq 2017; Sörman 2017), particularly where they were making or mending relatively 'simple' items. Instead, part-time farmer-smiths may have engaged in metalworking at quiet times in the agricultural cycle. Kuijpers (2008) argues, on the basis of experimental work, that the production of some of the most common bronze objects such as axes did not require a significant degree of knowledge and experience, although it is evident that this was not the case for more complex items such as cauldrons or swords. As such, there is no reason to suppose that metalworkers engaged in the production of simple objects such as tools would have enjoyed any special status (Kuijpers 2008; Kienlin 2013).

Of course, attitudes to smiths and smithing have an important impact on the spatial organisation of the craft, which may be centrally controlled (for example where smithing is symbolically associated with kingship, as in some west African societies) or geographically dispersed. Likewise, where smiths are feared or despised, the production of metal may be segregated or marginalised from other activities (Herbert 1994; Schmidt 1996). As we shall see below, the spatial location of metalworking has been a particular focus of interest in some recent studies.

Metalworking and gender

For all of the debates about the status of metalworkers, there has been much less attention to their gender. Assumptions that they must have been male have only rarely been challenged (though see Budd & Taylor 1995; Sørensen 1996). The androcentric bias of many accounts of the European Bronze and Iron Ages has meant that, as metalworking has been taken to be a highly skilled and often prestigious activity, it has been viewed as the domain of men rather than women. It has also been argued that women's involvement in child rearing and domestic tasks would have left them unable to dedicate the time to learning metalworking skills, or to see through lengthy procedures such as ore smelting. Here arguments used by Childe in the 1930s have persisted to the present day:

> Casting of bronze is too difficult a process to be carried out by anyone in the intervals of growing or catching food or minding her babies. It is a specialist's job. (Childe 1936, 9)

> It may have been more difficult, or simply not the best arrangement, for the biological sex responsible for children to conduct specialist craft activities which required extended blocks of continuous time. (Hurcombe 2000, 106)

> The reasons [for male dominance of metalworking] are predominantly cultural, as expressed through rules and taboos among other things, and can indeed reflect the commitment of mothers (and other female members of society) to other tasks including the care of children. (Barber 2003, 128)

It has also been argued that as most metalworkers recorded in ethnography are men, the same is likely to have been true in prehistory (Hurcombe 2000; Barber 2003; Haaland 2004). One influential cross-cultural study found that, of 86 societies for which data were available, metalworking was an exclusively male activity in 85 cases and predominantly male in the remaining case (Murdock & Provost 1973). Howard's (1983) survey of metalworking in almost 200 pre-industrial societies led her to conclude that metalworkers are almost always male.

Using ethnographic parallels as 'proof' that a practice did or did not exist in prehistory is problematic, however. Many exceptions to the pattern of male dominance of metalworking exist in the ethnographic record. In coastal Ecuador, both women and men have traditionally worked as bronze casters (Bruhns & Stothert 1999, 141–2). Despite the male associations of metalworking across Africa, women participated in iron smelting in some societies, such as the 19th century Njanja and Kalanga of Zimbabwe (Chirikure 2007, 81–4), and the Asirungu of Tanzania, where women also helped to build the furnaces (Howard 1983, 86, 159). Among the Chokwe the iron smelter's wife plays an important role in carrying out furnace fertility rites (Herbert 1984, 84). In a few other African case studies, women are recorded as playing a role in blacksmithing, by operating the bellows or assisting at the anvil (Howard 1983, 47–8). Even in African societies where smelting, casting, and smithing are entirely male activities, women and girls can be engaged in associated activities such as mining, gathering, processing and transporting ores; gathering fuel and producing charcoal for metallurgical activities; and bringing provisions to men engaged in smelting (Herbert 1984; Childs & Killick 1993, 327; Herbert 1994; Chirikure 2015). Such practices are easy to ignore as peripheral to metalworking but would have been essential to the process and would, in many cases, have required significant skill and investment of time. It is quite likely that female involvement in such tasks has been underplayed in many ethnographic accounts, given the evident bias towards focusing on male (assumed prestigious) activities in much of the ethnographic literature. There are also historical references to female metalworkers in the Roman Empire and medieval Europe, such as the woman blacksmith illustrated in the Holkham bible of *c.* AD 1327–1335 (Tschen-Emmons 2017, 65–6).

Metalworking and ritual

The potentially mystical nature of prehistoric metalworking was raised by Childe:

> Even more startling and mysterious were the transmutations involved in the extraction of the metal … What could be more startling than the evocation from these greenish or grey stones, crystalline or powdery in texture, of the tough malleable red metal! Here is a complete transmutation of the very nature of a material! … The possessors of these secrets would easily gain credit for supernatural powers among barbarians to whom all stones looked much alike. (Childe 1930, 5)

Although the myths and rituals associated with metalworking, both past and present, continued to be a focus of interest in other disciplines over subsequent decades (eg, Eliade 1971), most subsequent archaeological writers viewed metalworking in more functional terms, with discussion of the metal 'trade' and characterisation of particular traditions of metalworking as 'industries'.

Interest in ritual was renewed from the 1990s onwards. A seminal paper by Budd and Taylor (1995) put forward a generalising argument that ritual and magic are intrinsic to metalworking in pre-industrial societies, though few specific ethnographic or historical examples were given. Subsequent work has specifically drawn on ethnographic accounts of metalworking – and often African ironworking in particular – to argue that prehistoric metallurgy was a symbolically-charged and ritualised activity (eg, Hingley 1997; Creighton 2000; Aldhouse-Green 2002; Haaland 2004; Aldhouse-Green & Aldhouse-Green 2005; Giles 2007; Goldhahn 2013). Specifically, it has been argued that metalworking was viewed as a dangerous and powerful process because it involved the magical transformation of materials and objects via the medium of fire. This is one reason why metalworking skills and knowledge may be a source of power, but it also means that smiths can be viewed as marginalised and ambivalent figures: objects facilitate the maintenance of social categories so processes of transformation are inherently destabilising. This has impacted the interpretation of excavated sites. For the British Iron Age the evidence from some sites has been argued to show that ironworking was carried out in liminal locations because of its mystical or dangerous nature (Hingley 1997; 1999; Giles & Parker Pearson 1999). The possibility that metalworking residues could be deposited in a structured or ritualised manner has also been explored (Cunliffe 1995b, 33; Brück 2001; Barber 2003; Arnoldussen & Brusgaard 2015). For later British prehistory, it has been argued that metalworking was viewed as structurally and conceptually similar to other heat-mediated transformative processes, including ritual practices such as cremation (Brück 2006). Ethnographic studies indicate that the residues of metalworking are frequently considered a source of fertility because of their association with transformative processes. Similar symbolic links between metalworking and agriculture have been proposed for later British prehistory, for each involved cycles of regeneration and renewal (Hingley 1997; Brück 2001; 2006; Williams 2003; Giles 2007).

Whether prehistoric metalworking would *always* have been highly ritualised has, however, been queried by Kuijpers (2008) and Kienlin (2013), who criticise the fact that much of the work in this area has been based more on ethnographic parallels than archaeological evidence. So too new work on African ironworking in the recent past has challenged the extent to which it was always ritualised or involved restricted access to knowledge (Iles 2018). Ethnographic and historical parallels can play an important role in raising possibilities that might not occur to us if we remained in our modern Western mind-set. However, such parallels cannot 'prove' anything about prehistory. It should be remembered that many practices attested in European prehistory, such as the deposition of metal hoards, find no good parallel in the ethnographic record. We should also be aware that the ethnographic evidence that has been applied to the interpretation of prehistoric metalworking disproportionately comes from one region – sub-Saharan Africa – and relates to iron smelting and smithing, which are quite different processes to non-ferrous metal casting.

The use of metals in British and Irish prehistory: a brief overview

Although our understanding of the social context of non-ferrous metalworking remains a topic of considerable debate, studies of the finished artefacts themselves have revealed significant information on changing techniques and technologies. Copper and gold were worked in Britain and Ireland from *c.* 2450 BC. The earliest metal objects included simple ornaments of sheet metal as well as larger items such as flat axes. Tin was alloyed with copper to make bronze, a harder metal and therefore better suited for making objects such as bladed tools, from *c.* 2150 BC. Although the adoption of copper and gold metalworking took place much later than in many parts of Continental Europe, tin-bronze technology appeared at around the same time in Britain and Ireland as elsewhere. On average, bronze objects contained *c.* 10% tin, although some of the axes of the Earliest Iron Age contain a particularly high proportion of this metal which is likely to have rendered them unusable. The axes from the hoard at Langton Matravers

in Dorset, for example (Roberts *et al.* 2015), were high in tin and would therefore have been too brittle for use. Tin was occasionally used on its own to make small ornaments during the Early Bronze Age, for example the tin bead and braided bracelet of cow hair decorated with 32 tin studs from a cist on Whitehorse Hill in Devon (Jones 2016).

Very occasional use of lead for ornaments is also known from the Early Bronze Age, for example the lead bead necklace from West Water Reservoir in the Scottish Borders which dates to *c.* 2100–1600 BC (Hunter & Davis 1994; Hunter 2000). From the later Middle Bronze Age, lead was deliberately added to bronze, with relatively high percentages of lead being a particular feature of the Late Bronze Age (Rohl & Needham 1998). The addition of lead to bronze makes it softer but easier to cast and this would have made leaded bronze a particularly suitable material for the production of complex objects such as the horns and cauldrons of the Late Bronze Age. Leaded bronze largely disappears again in the Iron Age, however. A small number of lead objects are also known from the Late Bronze Age and Iron Age (Needham & Hook 1988; Coles & Minnit 1995), such as the lead axe from Mam Tor in Derbyshire (Guilbert 1996); this is likely to have been a non-functional object as it would have been too soft for use.

Ironworking may have occurred on a sporadic basis from the Late Bronze Age. At Hartshill Copse, Upper Bucklebury (Berkshire) an otherwise unremarkable open settlement produced abundant iron hammerscale, mostly from in and around a double-ring round-house (Collard *et al.* 2006). Radiocarbon dates suggest the site was occupied in the 10th century BC. Needham (2007, fig. 4) notes that the deposition of bronze reached a high point during the 9th century BC, after which the frequency of bronze objects decreases dramatically. This is not matched by a significant increase in iron objects, however. From the late 9th and early 8th centuries BC on, iron artefacts are sporadically found on settlements and other sites but the material was not used on a large scale until the mid-1st millennium BC (Ehrenreich 1985; Needham 2007, 51–2; Wallace & Anguilano 2010). At this point, the quantity of bronze artefacts also increased. However, bronze was used for a narrower range of object types than in the

Late Bronze Age, with most tools and weapon blades now made of iron.

Silver was first used in the Late Iron Age, mainly for coins but occasionally for other objects such as ornaments (Northover 1988b). The earliest occurrence of brass is the foil decoration on a sword from the Thames stylistically dated to the Middle Iron Age (Craddock *et al.* 2004), but otherwise brass ornaments first appear in southern Britain shortly before the Roman conquest. Brass is an alloy of copper and zinc that is both strong and ductile and was widely used in the Roman world: the appearance of this alloy indicates contact with provincial Roman groups on the near-Continent and probable importation of metal, though some production of brass in Britain during the mid-1st century AD is a possibility (Dungworth 1996; 1997; Davis & Gwilt 2008).

Ore sources in Britain and Ireland

Alongside work on the finished metal artefacts, there has also been significant research on the sourcing and extraction of non-ferrous metals, notably copper. Although gold and tin may have been acquired in their native form from alluvial deposits, copper and lead were obtained from deposits of ore that required smelting in order to extract the metal. Ore sources can be identified by examining the physical remains of mines or ore processing sites for evidence of early workings, or by elemental and isotopic studies of metal artefacts. Here we shall present a brief overview of knowledge of ore sources utilised in prehistoric Britain and Ireland. It should be stressed that metal imported from the Continent was an important source for metalworkers in Britain and Ireland during some periods of prehistory, and also that many metal objects would not have been made using 'virgin' metal, but rather by melting down and recycling old artefacts.

Copper

Chalcolithic and Bronze Age copper mining in Europe has been extensively discussed by O'Brien (2015). Unlike other parts of north-west Europe, a significant number of copper sources are known in Britain and Ireland, notably in north-west and south-west England, mid- and north Wales, western Scotland, and south-west Ireland. Copper was extracted from many of these sources during the historic period but evidence for use in prehistory is more restricted. The earliest identified mine in north-west Europe is Ross Island (Co. Kerry), active *c.* 2400–1900 BC, where a number of small workings were dug to exploit veins of mineralised rock (O'Brien 2004). An adjacent seasonal work camp was also identified where ore processing and smelting appears to have taken place. Metallurgical analyses show that Ross Island was a major source of copper for the earliest metalworking in Britain and Ireland (Northover *et al.* 2001). Subsequently, *c.* 1800–1400, production shifted to a series of smaller drift mines on the peninsulas of Co. Cork, the best known being Mount Gabriel, where a series of small tunnel-like workings have been identified (O'Brien 1994). There is less evidence for later copper production in Ireland, though it is attested at the 'trench mine' of Derrycarhoon (Co. Cork), *c.* 1300–1100 BC (O'Brien 2015, 135–7).

In Britain mining may have begun in mid-Wales *c.* 2100–2000 BC, at sites such as Copa Hill (Dyfed) where opencast mining was carried out (Timberlake 2009). Copper mining spread to north Wales from *c.* 2000 BC, at Parys Mountain on the Isle of Anglesey and Great Orme (Conwy), and to north-west England from *c.* 1900 BC, at Alderley Edge (Cheshire East) and Ecton (Staffordshire; Timberlake 2003; 2009; Timberlake & Prag 2005). Single finds of stone hammers near ore deposits at Bradda Head on the Isle of Man (Pickin & Worthington 1989) and Wanlockhead in southern Scotland (Timberlake 2009) also hint at mining or prospection. There is as yet no evidence for Early Bronze Age smelting from any of the mine sites in Britain but it is assumed to have occurred in the near vicinity. Most of these mines were only in use during the Early Bronze Age, but the Great Orme reached its peak *c.* 1600–1400 BC, and continued in use into the Late Bronze Age (Dutton *et al.* 1994; Lewis 1998; Williams & Le Carlier de Veslud 2019); the nearby small-scale smelting site at Pentrwyn dates to the latter period (Smith & Williams 2012; Williams 2013; Smith 2015).

Other sources of copper are also likely to have been employed. Lead isotope and chemical analyses of metalwork suggest that Cornish copper may also have been used throughout the Bronze Age (Rohl & Needham 1998; Bray & Pollard 2012; Ling *et al.* 2014), although the mines themselves have yet to be identified. An Early Bronze Age hearth and significant quantity of smashed quartz containing flecks of copper visible to the naked eye were found adjacent to an outcropping ore body at Roman Lode on Exmoor, Somerset, and it has been suggested that this may indicate the extraction of metal at this site (Juleff & Bray 2007). Chemical and lead isotope analysis of copper ingots from a Late Bronze Age (Ewart Park) hoard at St Michael's Mount (Cornwall), led Young (2015) to suggest an origin in the Shropshire/mid-Wales border area. From the late Middle Bronze Age (Penard period) onwards, however, metal analyses suggest that Britain was increasingly reliant on copper imported from the Continent, though some use of British sources is also possible (Northover 1982a; Rohl & Needham 1998; Williams & Le Carlier de Veslud 2019). The relatively homogeneous nature of the impurity patterns of Late Bronze Age metalwork indicates that recycling played an important role in maintaining the supply of bronze during this period (Bray & Pollard 2012; Northover 2013, 102). Many of the Bronze Age bronze objects from the well-known shipwreck sites at Langdon Bay in Kent and Salcombe in Devon had been fragmented (Needham *et al.* 2013). These artefacts date to the late Middle Bronze Age and their morphology indicates that most originate in northern France. Few certainly 'foreign' bronze objects are found in Britain, however, and it has been suggested that continental 'scrap' bronzes were imported to be recast in local form. Possible evidence for cross-Channel exchange of metal is also provided by the 258 copper ingots from the site of the Salcombe wreck or wrecks (Roberts & Veysey 2011; Wang 2018).

Much less is known about copper sources during the Iron Age, probably because of high levels of recycling, though Northover's work on the impurity patterns of bronzes suggests that multiple sources were used. One source may have been in south-west Britain, another in northern Powys (Northover 1984; 1988a; Musson *et al.* 1992). No copper mines of Iron Age date have as yet been identified, although tenuous evidence is provided by occasional finds of copper ingots of possible Iron Age date close to historic copper mines, for example the pair of plano-convex ingots

from the broch at Edin's Hall (Scottish Borders; Dunwell 1999).

The social context and organisation of copper mining will not be addressed in this volume for this has been considered in some detail by others (Timberlake 2009; O'Brien 2015). In many regions, mining appears to have been a relatively small-scale activity, particularly during the Chalcolithic and Early Bronze Age. At Mount Gabriel, O'Brien (1994, 196–7) calculated that the mines would have produced between 15 kg and 133 kg of metal per year, depending on the efficiency of the smelting process. This suggests that mining was not carried out on an 'industrial' scale and is unlikely to have been a full-time specialist activity. At Ross Island it has been suggested that farming communities living close to copper sources engaged in mining during quiet phases of the agricultural cycle (O'Brien 2004, 477). In Britain, too, it has been argued that the extensive network of shafts and galleries at the Great Orme was the result of small-scale, part-time mining over many centuries (Budd & Taylor 1995; O'Brien 2015). However, recent re-analysis indicates that the bulk of extraction activity took place between 1600 and 1400 BC, and that as much as 1–4 tonnes may have been produced per annum (Williams & Le Carlier de Veslud 2019). High levels of production are indicated also by the extensive distribution of metal from the Great Orme across Britain and Ireland and as far afield as Sweden, and Williams and Le Carlier de Veslud (2019) suggest that mining was undertaken on a large scale by full-time specialists.

Whether seasonal or full-time, mining may have involved most members of those communities: once the ore has been mined and brought to the surface, it must be crushed and sorted to extract the most mineralised pieces, a task that was carried out in the historic period by women and children. Indeed, the small size of some of the galleries at the Great Orme hints that children may have been directly involved in mining (O'Brien 2015, 252). The lack of evidence for copper ore or smelting at sites elsewhere in Britain and Ireland, and the identification of slag and other residues from smelting at Ross Island and the Great Orme, suggests that the communities engaged in mining were also involved in smelting the ore, although we do not know if these tasks were undertaken by the same people. There is little evidence that mining communities were particularly wealthy and many copper mines (for example those at Mount Gabriel) are located in areas that were relatively marginal in agricultural terms.

Tin

In Britain and Ireland, a rapid switch to tin-bronze occurred around 2150 BC, earlier than many other parts of Europe (Pare 2000). In recent centuries, Cornwall was the main source of tin in the British Isles (Penhallurick 1986; Quinnell 2017) but other sources are also known: tin is found in placer deposits in Co. Wicklow (Jackson 1991) but in such small quantities that it is unlikely to have been identified and used in prehistory (Budd *et al.* 1994). Larger quantities are present in the Mourne Mountains of Northern Ireland and Early Bronze Age tin extraction has also been suggested in that region (Warner *et al.* 2010). Metallurgical analyses indicate use of Cornish tin from the Early Bronze Age onwards (Rohl & Needham 1998; Haustein *et al.* 2010; Malham 2010; Ling *et al.* 2014). The earliest evidence for use of tin in this region is provided by six stone tools from Sennen (Cornwall) in contexts dated to *c.* 2300–2100 BC (see Chapter 3); pXRF analysis of these artefacts has identified tin residues suggesting that they were used to crush and grind cassiterite pebbles (a form of tin ore). Evidence of prehistoric tin mines or streamworks in the south-west peninsula has proved extremely elusive although an antler tool from 18th century streamworks in the Carnon Valley (Cornwall) has recently been radiocarbon dated to 1620–1460 cal BC (3269±27 BP; OxA-36336) (Timberlake & Hartgroves 2018), and a number of suggestive finds of Bronze Age artefacts have been made by tin streamers since the 19th century (Penhallurick 1986; 1997). Forty tin ingots (including one weighing more than 9 kg) were recovered from the Late Bronze Age Salcombe wreck(s), suggesting coastal or cross-Channel distribution of this material (Roberts & Veysey 2011; Wang *et al.* 2016). On the near-Continent, tin is also found in significant quantities in Brittany and tin smelting during the 14th–11th centuries cal BC is attested at St Renan (Finistère; Mahé-le Carlier *et al.* 2001).

Lead

Lead ores are more widely distributed than tin. In Britain, sources in Somerset, northern England, south-east Scotland, mid-Wales and the Welsh borders are known to have been exploited during the historic period, while in Ireland there were small-scale lead mining operations in the 18th and 19th centuries at a variety of locations from Co. Monaghan in the north to Co. Kilkenny in the south. Evidence for prehistoric extraction activities has been less easy to identify, however. The earliest claimed evidence for lead extraction is a large pit exposing galena deposits at Treanbaun (Co. Galway), radiocarbon dated to 2570–2140 cal BC (3883±75 BP; Wk-22715; Muñiz-Pérez *et al.* 2011). A cist burial dated 1930–1750 cal BC (3515±30 BP; Wk-22560) was later inserted into the backfill of the pit. The interpretation of this feature as a mine seems unlikely, however, given the absence of evidence for the metallurgical use of lead at this time and the remarkably regular circular, flat-based form of the pit. Lead and copper ores often occur in the same regions and the locations of some Early Bronze Age copper mines, such as Alderley Edge and Pwll Roman, mid-Wales (Timberlake 2004), were historically also exploited for lead. During the later Bronze Age, it has been suggested that the lead added to bronze derives from the British Isles, possible sources including Alderley Edge and the Mendips (Rohl & Needham 1998).

Exploitation of Mendip lead in the later Iron Age has been demonstrated by analysis of lead artefacts from the settlements at Glastonbury and Meare in the Somerset Levels (Ponting 2018) and Iron Age pottery from the Roman lead mine at Charterhouse-on-Mendip (Somerset) hints at a pre-Roman inception for the mining (Todd 2007). Radiocarbon dates allow the possibility of a Late Iron Age origin for the Roman lead smelting site at Erglodd (Ceredigion; Page *et al.* 2012). The digging of the ditch of the Middle Iron Age hillfort of Darren Camp (Ceredigion) exposed a silver-lead ore vein (Timberlake & Driver 2006), although it is not known if this was used.

Possible evidence for local lead mining and/or smelting during the Late Bronze Age and Iron Age is also provided by lead pollution records in peat bogs at Leadhills in southern Scotland and various locations in mid-Wales (Mighall *et al.* 2008; 2009; 2014). However, the interpretation of such data is complex as a variety of processes can cause a raised lead signature, including copper mining. Not enough evidence has been put forward to support claimed Early Bronze Age lead pollution signatures for mining in Lancashire (Barrowclough 2008).

Gold and silver

Like tin, gold occurs both in alluvial gravels that can be accessed through streamworking and as primary deposits that require mining. Historically, gold deposits have been identified and exploited in northern and western Scotland, west Wales, and south-west England, as well as in Northern Ireland and Counties Wicklow and Wexford.

Given the abundance of gold artefacts from Ireland in the Chalcolithic and Early Bronze Age, it has long been assumed that Irish gold was exploited in this period. Alluvial deposits in Co. Wicklow were long considered the most likely source (Jackson 1979; Eogan 1994, 10), though archaeological evidence for this has yet to be identified. Major element analysis suggests that the gold employed to make Irish Early Bronze Age objects such as lunulae may have come from placer deposits in the Mourne Mountains of Co. Down (Warner *et al.* 2010). Possible streamworkings and an extraction pit have been identified in this area although these remain undated. A recent study combining major element with lead isotope analysis has called this into question, however, arguing that Cornwall may have been the main source of gold for Irish Chalcolithic and Early Bronze Age objects (Standish *et al.* 2015). It has also been suggested that Cornish gold was used on the Nebra disc (Ehser *et al.* 2011).

There has been little work on the sources of later gold. It has been suggested that the Roman Dolaucothi gold mine in west Wales might have a pre-Roman origin but there is nothing to demonstrate this (Burnham & Burnham 2004). It is generally thought that the increased use of gold in southern Britain during the Late Iron Age derives from imported metal, much of it in the form of coinage (La Niece *et al.* 2018).

Silver, too, is found in Britain and Ireland, typically as lead–silver ores. There is evidence for silver extraction from the Middle Ages and later in many regions including the Pennines, Somerset, and Counties Clare and Tipperary (Claughton 2011; Claughton & Rondelez

2013). It is not known if silver from these sources was used in prehistory, however, and an analysis of Iron Age lead artefacts from Somerset has suggested that they were not produced from lead that had been desilvered (Ponting 2018). The evidence indicates that the appearance of silver in the Late Iron Age essentially results from the importation of metal from the Continent (Farley 2012).

The 'Social Context of Technology' project

Aims and objectives

In contrast to existing work, which has sought to understand the organisation of metalworking using ethnographic analogy or through detailed typological, technical, compositional, and metallographic analysis, this book will investigate non-ferrous metalworking practices within their specific social context by examining the *excavated contexts* in which the tools and residues of non-ferrous metalworking have been found. The relationship between metalworking and other aspects of social life can be explored by examining the spatial and depositional contexts from which metalworking remains have been recovered. The expansion of developer-funded excavation over the past 25 years has resulted in a dramatic increase in evidence for non-ferrous metalworking from excavated sites of the later prehistoric period, but this has not previously been brought together nor its significance evaluated. Our aim is to employ this evidence to improve our understanding of the organisation of metalworking, the social and conceptual significance of this craft, and the social role of metalworkers. This will help to illuminate the links between craft specialisation, political power and ritual in non-state societies. Some of the more specific questions that will be addressed include:

- Where was non-ferrous metalworking carried out? Was it associated with particular kinds of places, such as settlements, hillforts, ritual sites, or isolated locations in the landscape? Is it found at 'high-status' or ordinary sites? Was it restricted to specific parts of these sites – perhaps a marginal or boundary location – or integrated with them as a whole? Investigating these issues can inform us about the status and role of metalworking, such as whether it was linked to elites, or was subject to social control or taboos.

- Did different kinds of metalworking – such as making 'prestige' objects versus simple tools – occur in different locations or contexts? Were the residues of these processes treated in differing ways?

- What other practices took place at locations where non-ferrous metalworking was carried out? Was it associated with 'domestic' activities, or with other crafts such as ironworking? Ceramic and stone moulds were used in bronze casting, and there are composite objects that combine bronze with other materials such as iron: does this suggest that non-ferrous metalworkers worked alongside specialists in other materials, or perhaps undertook some of these other crafts themselves?

- Can we distinguish sites with relatively brief episodes of metalworking from those with more prolonged activity? This can address the question of whether craftworkers were peripatetic or tied to a particular community.

- Was metalworking a symbolically charged or ritualised activity? Can ritual practices be identified at locations where metalworking was carried out? Were metalworking tools and waste casually discarded after use, or were they carefully deposited in a 'structured' manner?

- What can graves containing metalworking tools tell us about the social personae of smiths and the ways that metalworking tools could be deployed to express identity?

- What can we learn about the social and conceptual associations of metalworking from the way objects associated with metalworking were treated at the end of their use lives? Is it possible to combine this information with existing studies on the production, exchange, and use of metalworking tools to understand the biographies of these artefacts?

- What evidence is there for regional and chronological variability in the organisation of metalworking and the social role of this craft and its practitioners? Are there particular developments over the Bronze Age to Iron Age transition, a period of social disruption and radical change to the significance of metal objects? How did the role of metalworking and its practitioners change in the context of wider social developments during the Late Iron Age including the emergence of proto-urban settlements and the use of new metal artefact types such as coins?

The scope of the project

The main emphasis of this book will be on the working of copper and its alloys. This was the only metal in wide use during both the Bronze Age and Iron Age, and it dominates the evidence for prehistoric non-ferrous metallurgy. The more elusive evidence for the working of other metals such as gold, silver, tin, and lead will, however, also be considered. Ironworking is not included, as it involves techniques that are rather different to those of non-ferrous metalworking and creates different kinds of residues. Iron Age ironworking in Ireland has been the subject of detailed study elsewhere (Dolan 2012; Garstki 2017; 2019). In Britain, very large numbers of Iron Age sites have produced iron smelting slag or blacksmithing waste and collating this evidence would require a separate project. However, the recovery of evidence for ironworking and for non-ferrous metalworking from the same or closely related contexts is noted where this occurs, and the relationship between these two crafts during the Iron Age is discussed in Chapter 5. The mining and beneficiation of metal ores is also outside the remit of the project, as this has been well studied by other researchers (eg, Timberlake 2003; 2009; O'Brien 2015).

The focus of the book will be on Britain and Ireland from the inception of metalworking in the mid-3rd millennium BC up to the time of the Roman conquest of southern Britain in the mid–late 1st century AD. For those areas that lay outside the Roman Empire, this is to some extent an arbitrary cut off, but in these regions too metalworking traditions came to be influenced by the Roman world, making it reasonable to exclude developments after the 1st century AD. Comparable sites on the near-Continent will be discussed briefly where relevant; these may help to interpret and contextualise finds from Britain and Ireland, notably for the Chalcolithic and Early Bronze Age where metalworking evidence is relatively sparse on these islands. The long chronological view taken by this book is unusual, as typically Bronze Age and Iron Age metalworking have been studied separately. This project has attempted to move beyond the artificial period divide in existing research by taking a long-term perspective on changes in the organisation of non-ferrous metalworking and the way in which the craft articulated with other arenas of social practice. Specifically, the changes that may have occurred in non-ferrous metalworking across the Bronze Age to Iron Age transition are of interest: it is commonly assumed that the introduction of iron technology had a major impact on existing traditions of metalworking, while differences in the types of objects made from bronze in the Bronze Age and Iron Age suggest that the social context in which the craft took place also changed significantly. Moreover, similarities in how metalworking has been studied in the two periods (see above) are such that it makes sense to study Bronze Age and Iron Age metalworking together.

Hitherto, the archaeological contexts from which metalworking tools and equipment have been recovered remain understudied. The assemblages from a few 'classic' sites – such as the Iron Age bronze casting site of Gussage All Saints (Dorset; Wainwright 1979) – tend to be cited time and again, even though these may not be representative of the evidence as a whole. The great increase in finds from development-led excavation since the 1990s means that a reassessment of the evidence is urgently needed and this is the primary aim of this study. Recent catalogues and discussions of metalworking equipment and waste are available for only a few regions of north-west Europe, namely the Bronze Age Netherlands (Kuijpers 2008), Late Bronze Age Ireland (Ó Faoláin 2004), Bronze Age Devon and Cornwall (Knight 2014), and Iron Age Scotland (Heald 2005). Elsewhere the issue has been neglected. For example, the last major work examining evidence for later Bronze Age and Iron Age metalworking in southern Britain was an unpublished PhD thesis that is now more than three decades old (Howard 1983; for a recent review of the gaps in our knowledge see Carey *et al.* 2019). A subsequent unpublished PhD thesis discussed technical aspects of bronze casting in England from the Late Iron Age to the medieval period, but only mentioned a few additional Iron Age sites and made little reference to finds context (Bayley 1992). A recent PhD thesis on British Bronze Age metalworking tools (Fregni 2014) focused

primarily on the technical aspects of their use through a programme of experimental research and did not consider their depositional context in detail. Ingots and finished artefacts have been subject to chemical and isotope analysis in order to understand the circulation of metals and aspects of the production process such as alloying and recycling (eg, Brown & Blin-Stoyle 1959; Coghlan 1975; Northover 1982a; Rohl & Needham 1998; Bray & Pollard 2012; Bray 2016), but such work has rarely been able to address the social context of metalworking in detail. Research examining the archaeological context of prehistoric metalworking finds is also scarce in other parts of Europe outside of the study region, though there has been significant work on Bronze Age Scandinavia (eg, Goldhahn 2007; Jantzen 2008; Melheim 2015; Sörman 2018).

A major focus of this book is examining the depositional context of metalworking tools and residues from archaeological sites. This includes a variety of objects and materials. Slag produced by the initial smelting of metal ores is occasionally found, usually close to mining sites. Much more widespread is evidence for the casting of metal artefacts in the form of crucibles, moulds, and casting waste. Evidence for the finishing of cast objects and for wrought metal working is provided by tools such as anvils, hammers, and files, although as we shall see, it is not always possible to link tools such as hammers to metalworking. For the purposes of this study, all such evidence from excavated sites has been recorded. For significant categories of object, such as stone moulds, that are mostly known as stray finds and have rarely been found on archaeological excavations, their broader landscape context will be considered. A large number of hoards containing broken objects that have been interpreted as scrap for recycling – and more occasionally tools – are known, but these are rarely from excavated sites. A detailed analysis of scrap hoards is therefore beyond the remit of this study and they are not catalogued here, although existing research on their landscape context will be discussed. Likewise, scientific analysis of objects such as casting waste and moulds did not form part of the project, but existing work on this topic has been incorporated wherever possible. Previous research on the form and function of particular metalworking tools (eg, Fregni 2014) provides the basis for our discussion of particular artefact types, although first-hand analysis of objects such as bronze moulds that have not yet been the subject of detailed study was also included as part of the current project. Coin pellet moulds are not discussed in detail in this study as they represent a distinct kind of metalworking technology very different to the casting techniques employed to produce other objects of non-ferrous metals; indeed, there has been significant recent research on these artefacts (e.g. Creighton 2000; Chadburn 2006; Leins 2012; Landon 2016; Talbot 2017).

To date, much of our information on the organisation of metalworking is derived from detailed technical and metallographic studies of the finished artefacts (eg, Armbruster 2000; 2017; Bridgford 2000; Stead 2006; Kienlin 2008; Uckelmann 2012; Bunnefeld 2016; Kuijpers 2017; Nørgaard 2018; Machling & Williamson 2018). This body of work forms an important backdrop to the current study, although our focus on the excavated context of metalworking tools and residues such as mould fragments and casting waste is quite different. Studies of the finished artefacts have revealed the operational sequences involved in the production of a range of different artefact types and have underlined the extraordinary level of technical proficiency required to produce items such as the gold collars and sheet-bronze shields of the Late Bronze Age. Visual and metallographic analysis of specific artefact types, such as Early Bronze Age axes in central Europe, demonstrate significant variability in the quality of the workmanship (Kienlin 2008; 2010; Kuijpers 2017). This suggests variation in the level of skill possessed by individual metalworkers that may help us to distinguish full-time from part-time smiths, although Kuijpers (2018) calls into question the assumption that a high degree of technical accomplishment always implies full-time specialisation. The sequence of actions required to produce a metal artefact can hint at possible divisions of labour, for example between those who performed more and less skilled tasks. The contribution of different craftworkers to single metal objects (for instance via the identification of different metalworkers' hands in the decoration of bronze ornaments) has been examined for the Nordic Bronze Age (Nørgaard 2018) and in some cases may indicate the work of apprentices. Detailed study of the techniques

used to make visually similar artefacts also reveals different traditions of practice that may reflect other aspects of social identity. Occasionally, the traces of individual tools can be identified, so that objects made by the same metalworker can be recognised (*ibid.*). The degree of innovation or conservatism in metalworking techniques can be assessed, facilitating a better understanding of the process and pace of technological change. The sharing of skills can also be examined: for example, the swift spread from the Carpathian Basin to Britain of the expertise required to make extraordinarily complex sheet-metal objects such as cauldrons and shields (Gerloff 2010; Uckelmann 2012) suggests that some metalworkers may have moved – though perhaps only temporarily – to learn new techniques (cf. Dietrich 2012; Nørgaard 2018); these artefacts could not have been reproduced merely by copying imported items. This has something interesting to tell us about the social networks in which smiths were enmeshed, for technical expertise is not usually shared with those with whom one has no existing social links.

Chemical and lead isotope analysis of the finished artefacts can also provide insights into practices such as alloying and recycling that may reflect particular traditions of metalworking and provide insights into skills sharing and technological change (eg, Northover 1988a; 2013; 2015; Bray 2012; 2016). Although existing technical, metallographic, and compositional analyses of finished artefacts will not be discussed in detail here, our assessment of the social organisation of non-ferrous metalworking will compare key results from these studies with the outcomes of our own research on metalworking equipment and waste from excavated sites.

Research methods
For this project, a database was created in 2014–2016 that systematically collated finds of non-ferrous metalworking equipment and debris from stratified prehistoric contexts in Britain and Ireland. For each site, details of the metalworking assemblages, their find context, and associated artefacts have been recorded. This includes slag, casting waste, hearth or furnace lining with metal residues, ingots, crucibles, moulds, tuyères, and smithing tools. A total of 416 published and unpublished

sites have been recorded (listed by modern administrative area in Appendix 1) and the full database has been made available online via the Archaeological Data Service (https://archaeologydataservice.ac.uk/archives/view/social_lt_2017/index.cfm). Single finds or hoards of metalworking tools or scrap metal that lack a good archaeological context have not been included in the database. For a few important sites that lack sufficient written documentation, the metalworking remains themselves have been examined where possible for macroscopic identification and quantification. Throughout this volume, the names of sites that formed part of the study are given in bold type; full references for each site are provided in Appendix 1. Radiocarbon dates have been calibrated by OxCal Version 4.3 using the INTCAL 13 calibration curve in December 2018 (Bronk Ramsey 2009). They are presented as a single range rounded out to the nearest ten years at 95% probability.

In order to collate this evidence, a systematic survey by country, region and county was undertaken. Published excavation reports, grey literature reports, unpublished PhD theses, and museum archives were all searched for information on the metalworking process and the character and context of metalworking remains. The unpublished material was accessed via the online Archaeology Data Service or was obtained through contact with Historic Environment Records or archaeological units. In Ireland, the archive of the National Monuments Service was consulted. The Portable Antiquities Scheme online database and the Bronze Age Index (held at the British Museum) were also examined for relevant finds and other information. Once sites with possible metalworking evidence were identified, it was necessary in many cases to access the full site records; even for published excavations, the exact nature and context of possible metalworking evidence was not always clear, and first-hand interrogation of the artefactual evidence and associated archives was often necessary.

It should be stressed that the purpose of the site analysis was not simply to find *in situ* metalworking workshops. In fact, few if any metalworking tools have been found literally in their position of use, in a 'Pompeii-like' situation. Nonetheless, through critical examination of the stratigraphic evidence and associated information such as geochemical analyses it is possible to identify sites and areas of sites where metalworking occurred. The fact that the majority of metalworking material was deposited in secondary contexts can indeed be informative in itself. Where and how people chose to deposit metalworking debris – and the other objects selected to accompany it – may have expressed ideas about the significance and conceptual associations of this craft. Over the past 30 years, much archaeological attention has been directed to depositional practice in British prehistory (Garrow 2012), and it is evident that the treatment of objects at the end of their use-lives can provide important information on the meanings and values ascribed not only to specific artefacts but to associated practices and people.

Although 'structured' deposition was originally thought to have been the result of purposeful ritual action (Richards & Thomas 1984), it is now widely recognised that a range of social and cultural processes are likely to have been involved (Brück 1999a; Brudenell & Cooper 2008; Garrow 2012). The location of deposits of metalworking debris, for example, may relate to the organisation of settlement space and the meanings ascribed to particular places. Of course, the spatial structuring of daily practice has important social implications, reflecting social distinctions (for example between gender groups) and hierarchies of value. The decision to deposit metalworking debris in particular locations is therefore likely to have been influenced by unexamined cultural norms relating not only to the meanings of such materials, but to the significance and associations of these places. There is no need to assume that patterning in choice of depositional context implies conscious decision-making, for cultural values are most effectively reproduced in the context of non-discursive daily practice. Yet, we should not discount the possibility that some highly selective deposits may be the result of deliberate, ritualised events, particularly where the objects themselves were considered to possess special powers. It should be noted, however, that some researchers have called into question the assumed dichotomy between ritual deposits and mere profane rubbish (Brück 1999a; Brudenell & Cooper 2008; Chadwick 2012), as in both cases the treatment of particular categories of object at the end of their use-life is likely to have been influenced by social norms and cultural values.

Often, the identification of possible ritualised acts of deposition has depended on the condition of the objects: complete and reusable bronze weapons found in rivers, for example, are generally interpreted as votive deposits. In this study, the condition of objects was recorded where possible, as this helps cast light on the biographies of different categories of artefact. Deposition is, of course, the end point (if sometimes temporarily) in an object's lifecycle, but it was often also possible to record information that illuminates other aspects of an artefact's use-life, for example evidence for the sequential addition of matrices (the negative shapes into which molten metal was poured) to stone moulds, or for the relining of crucibles. Such information raises interesting questions regarding, for example, the frequency of metalworking activities, the mobility of metalworkers, and the curation and changing significance of associated artefacts.

Structure of this volume

Chapter 2 will summarise existing work on the technology of non-ferrous metalworking in prehistory. The material evidence for non-ferrous metalworking will be described in detail focusing on the objects themselves, specifically metalworking tools and residues. This will draw on recent studies of particular artefact types where possible. Categories of evidence that have not been the focus of recent work will be subject to more detailed consideration. Issues with identifying metalworking evidence will also be addressed here. Chapters 3, 4, and 5 examine the finds context of non-ferrous metalworking debris for the Chalcolithic and Early Bronze Age, Middle Bronze Age to Earliest Iron Age, and Early to Late Iron Age respectively. These chapters examine the different types of site from which metalworking evidence has been recovered, with particular attention to the character of the evidence itself and the degree to which this varies by site type. The spatial locations and depositional contexts from which metalworking tools and residues have been recovered are a particular focus of interest. Chapter 6 provides a summary and detailed discussion of the results of the project, examining chronological change in the organisation and social context of non-ferrous metalworking in the Bronze Age and Iron Age.

2

Non-ferrous metalworking: techniques and materials

This chapter summarises the physical evidence for the production of non-ferrous metal objects, examining the materials and artefacts relating to the different stages of the process. There are very few known smelting sites of Bronze Age or Iron Age date and most of the evidence relates to the casting of metal artefacts, particularly those made of copper alloys. The finished objects themselves indicate that various forms of smithing were carried out, but these processes typically produce little or no waste material, and it can be difficult to distinguish tools used for non-ferrous metal smithing from those used for other crafts. There is also limited evidence for the production of precious metal objects, for several reasons. Precious metal artefacts were relatively rare and we might therefore expect the residues of their production to also be very rare. Gold may be worked cold, generating little waste and reducing the likelihood of traces of the metal being recognised on associated metalworking tools. Gold and silver are both volatile metals, meaning that they leave less of a chemical trace on moulds or crucibles than do base metals. It is also possible that casting waste or offcuts of precious metals would have been more carefully collected for recycling than the residues of base metalworking.

The following discussion summarises the stages of metalworking focusing on copper alloys; the materials required and what survives; and chronological variation in mould and crucible morphology and technology. It mainly draws on existing studies of prehistoric non-ferrous metalworking tools and residues. However, where particular metalworking tool types have not been a focus of previous study, some new observations will be offered. The aim is to provide a framework for the detailed contextual analysis of metalworking sites that is presented in the subsequent chapters.

Stages of non-ferrous metalworking

Metal artefacts have diverse and complex lifecycles. Simplifying greatly, the metalworking process can be divided into four broad stages (Fell 1990, 35; Fig. 2.1). The first comprises the extraction, processing and smelting of ores, resulting in the production of metal ingots. Stage 2 involves melting and casting metal to produce artefacts or 'blanks' for further working. The third stage, smithing and finishing, includes a wide range of different techniques including hot and cold working. Some cast artefacts would have required only

*Figure 2.1: Key stages in
the metalworking process*

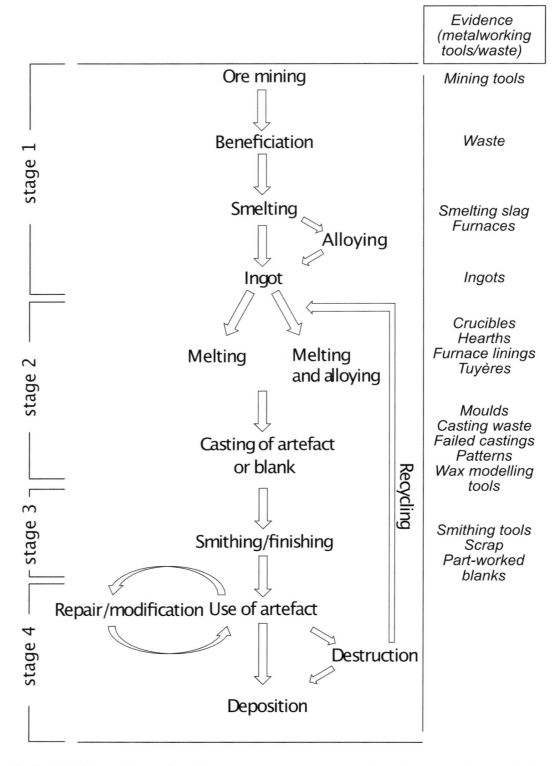

limited finishing while, at the other extreme, substantial work would have been needed to hammer out a sheet metal artefact from a simple cast blank. The final stage – use and reuse – does not represent the end of the story, as metal artefacts were often repaired or modified. At the end of their use lives many objects would have been melted down and recycled, thus rejoining stage 2.

Stage 1: extraction, processing and transport of metal

Mining and beneficiation

Our understanding of Bronze Age mines and mining has been significantly advanced by recent research (O'Brien 2015; Timberlake 2017). Excavations at Bronze Age mines in south-west Ireland, Wales, and north-west England in particular have cast light on the techniques involved in the extraction of ores during this period. Stone mauls and hammerstones are the most common finds, but waterlogged sites such as Mount Gabriel (Co. Cork) have produced organic artefacts including alder shovels and hazel and willow withies for hafting stone hammers (O'Brien 1994). The workings at Copa Hill (Ceredigion) were prone to flooding and a system of wooden launders (conduits) found in excavations at the site appear to have been designed to alleviate this problem (Timberlake 2017, fig. 3). The Great Orme mines (Conwy) have produced a large number of bone tools including cattle scapula shovels, although modified ribs and long-bones were most common (James 2008). The presence of pine chips and evidence of burning inside the workings at Mount Gabriel suggest that fires may have been built against the exposed rock face to help shatter the rock and extract the ore (O'Brien 1994). Once the ore was brought to the surface, probably in organic containers such as baskets, it was crushed and sorted to identify the most mineralised pieces. Working floors for the beneficiation of ore have been identified at **Ross Island** (Co. Kerry) and Mount Gabriel (Co. Cork; O'Brien 1994; 2004). While it appears that British ore sources were also exploited to some extent during the Iron Age (see Chapter 1), no mine workings or ore processing sites of this period have been positively identified.

Smelting

Although gold may have been acquired in its native form from alluvial deposits, copper, tin, and lead were obtained from deposits of ore that required smelting in order to extract the metal. Smelting involves the heating of copper ore together with a reducing agent such as charcoal to release the metal and separate it from waste materials. Evidence for smelting is very rare. The excavation of an Early Bronze Age 'work camp' immediately adjacent to the Western Mine at **Ross Island** has produced possible evidence for smelting (see Chapter 3). At **Pentrwyn** (Conwy) copper smelting slag and prills were found in and around a small charcoal-rich pit of Late Bronze Age date. This site was located on the east side of the Great Orme peninsula and trace element and lead isotope analysis of the smelting debris indicates that this was the product of local ores. To date, no certain evidence for the smelting of copper has been identified in the Iron Age.

In Devon and Cornwall, there is evidence for tin smelting from the end of the Early Bronze Age onwards (Quinnell 2017). Slag from the Early Bronze Age ring bank monument at **Caerloggas** (Cornwall) is indicative of small-scale, inefficient tin smelting. This find has been dated to 1700–1500 BC, providing the earliest direct evidence for tin smelting in Britain. The presence of cassiterite pebbles at a number of Bronze Age settlements may not, in itself, be evidence that the ore was smelted at these locations although a small globule of smelted tin was found in a deposit around a hearth at **Dean Moor** (Devon). Possible tin slag was also identified at a later Iron Age hillfort, **Castle Dore** (Cornwall), excavated in the 1930s, although this has not been subject to recent re-examination. Furnaces or hearths demonstrably used for tin smelting remain elusive.

Overall, the paucity of smelting evidence throughout the period suggests small-scale smelting employing relatively simple technology: it is likely to have been a low temperature process performed in shallow clay-lined pits that would create poorly reducing conditions and produce little slag (Craddock 1994). Pit furnaces of this sort are likely to have left little evidence in the archaeological record (Tylecote 1986, 181).

Ingots and the transport of metal

Once the metal was extracted from the ore it was transported to multiple places of production: as we shall see in subsequent chapters, much metalworking activity occurred in regions lacking ore sources. Our understanding of later prehistoric transport technologies has been significantly enhanced by recent discoveries of boats, trackways, and wheels, predominantly of Middle Bronze Age and later date (eg, Clark 2004; Van de Noort 2004; Moore 2008). Doubtless these facilitated the movement of a wide variety of different materials. Only

Figure 2.2: Plano-convex copper ingot of Late Bronze Age date from Boughton Malherbe (Kent) (photo: Sophia Adams courtesy of Maidstone Museum)

or to objects made by remelting metal – and alloying it if necessary – before casting it into any of a range of forms. Ingots of Early and Middle Bronze Age date are relatively rare and rib or ring ingots like those found on the Continent are entirely absent. Roughly circular cakes of raw copper are known from Early Bronze Age hoards in the southern half of Ireland (O'Flaherty 1995) and from the Morecambe Bay hoard in Lancashire (PAS: LANCUM-3BEC10). At least some of the Irish cakes were made of metal from the **Ross Island** mine (Northover 2004a). Middle Bronze Age examples take various forms, such as the putative 'hoof-shaped' ingots from the Hayling Island hoard (Hampshire; Lawson 1999; though these may in fact be casting jets), and the possible ingot, rectangular in plan with a plano-convex section, from the Wylye hoard (Wiltshire; PAS: WILT-038191).

In contrast, large numbers of circular plano-convex or 'bun' ingots of Late Bronze Age date have been found, particularly in hoards in southern and eastern England dating to *c* 1000–800 BC (O'Connor 1980; Northover 2015; Wang *et al.* 2018), for example at Boughton Malherbe (Kent; Fig. 2.2). This tradition extended across the Channel into north-west France, where research has shown that the term 'plano-convex ingot' conflates different categories of object (Le Carlier de Veslud *et al.* 2014). Small bronze examples seem to have been formed by melting metal in crucibles or ceramic vessels. Larger copper ingots were probably formed in shallow bowl-shaped features dug into the ground, as suggested by the rough, curved lower surfaces of these objects. The flat upper surfaces are typically pocked with holes suggesting that the cakes were the cast collection from the smelt. Complete plano-convex ingots are relatively rare and they were usually deposited in a fragmentary state. Lead isotope analysis indicates that plano-convex ingots were often transported for some distance: examples have been identified in south-eastern England that are likely to have derived from sources in western and northern Britain as well as on the Continent (Rohl & Needham 1998, 181; Northover 2015; Wang *et al.* 2018). Other forms of Late Bronze Age ingot are also known, for example a gold bar ingot from Brabourne, Ashford (Kent; PAS: KENT-ED8F86), but these are rare in British and Irish contexts. Forms common in other

the Bronze Age shipwreck sites at Salcombe (Devon) and Langdon Bay (Kent) provide direct evidence for the transport of metals, although the boats themselves did not survive at either site (Needham *et al.* 2013; Wang *et al.* 2016; 2018).

Indirect evidence for the transport of metals is provided by the discovery of ingots in regions far from the source of this material. The term ingot can refer either to a cake of raw metal derived directly from smelting,

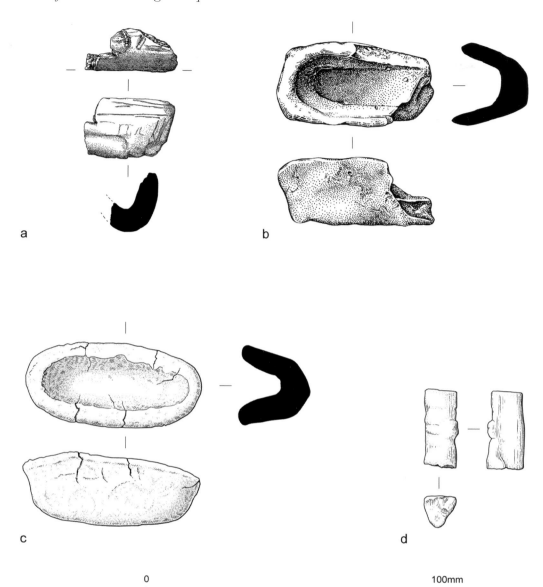

Figure 2.3: Later Iron Age billet or bar ingot moulds from a. Fison Way, Thetford (Norfolk) (after Gregory 1991, fig. 124.6); b. Weelsby Avenue, Grimsby (Lincolnshire) (drawing: Barbara Garfi, reproduced by kind permission; from Foster 1995, fig. 33); c. Broxmouth (Lothian) (after Armit & McKenzie 2013, fig. 10.67); d. bronze billet from Winklebury Camp (Hampshire) (redrawn by A. Leaver after Smith 1977, fig. 37)

a

b

c

d

0   100mm

parts of Europe, such as oxhide ingots, are absent in this region. Tin ingots of Bronze Age date are rarely encountered, though 40 plano-convex examples have been recovered from the later Bronze Age Salcombe B wreck site (Wang *et al.* 2016). A few small blocks of lead are known from Late Bronze Age contexts, though these could alternatively represent weights (see below).

Fewer ingots of copper or bronze are known from the Iron Age. Examples include small bar ingots with a triangular cross-section such as the high tin bronze fragment from **Winklebury Camp** (Hampshire; Fig. 2.3, d).

These would have been cast in open moulds such as the fragmentary clay examples recovered from the Late Iron Age enclosure ditch at **Weelsby Avenue** (North East Lincolnshire; Fig. 2.3, a). Rounder, flatter bars of tin bronze are also known, such as the Middle Iron Age ingot from **Gussage All Saints** (Dorset; Foster 1980, 228). A small number of stone moulds for casting the latter type have been found. The mould from the later Iron Age settlement at **Catterick Racecourse** (North Yorkshire) has two matrices for bar ingots of different lengths. One of the ingot moulds from the later Iron Age settlement at **Thorpe Thewles**

Table 2.1: Materials employed in later prehistoric non-ferrous metalworking

Material		Purpose	Evidence
Metals	Copper, tin, lead, zinc, gold, silver	Raw materials for metalworking Bronze also used to make moulds & smithing tools	Surviving evidence
	Iron	Smithing tools, tongs, pokers	Surviving evidence
Geological materials	Stone	Moulds, smithing tools, whetstones, touchstones	Surviving evidence
	Clay	Moulds, crucibles, tuyères, hearth & furnace linings	Surviving evidence
	Sand, crushed stone	Temper for clay moulds & crucibles, polishing finished artefacts	Surviving evidence for use as temper
	Glass, amber	Decorative inlay on composite objects	Surviving evidence
Organic materials	Wood	Mould patterns? charcoal, kindling	Surviving evidence
	Beeswax, tallow	Mould patterns (lost-wax casting)	Assumed
	Bone	Modelling tools for clay moulds or wax patterns	Surviving evidence
	Plant fibre twine	Binding bivalve moulds, manipulating crucibles	Possible impressions from clay moulds
	Textiles	Casting articulating parts of bronze objects	Evinced from impressions on lost-wax moulds
	Leather	Bellows	Assumed
	Grass, straw, chaff, hair	Temper for crucibles	Evinced from voids in refractory fabrics
Water		Mixing clay for moulds & crucibles; quenching hot metal	Assumed

(Stockton-on-Tees) was manufactured from local sandstone while another had been carved into a reused quernstone. Some of these items may have been cast as part of the production process for other finished artefacts rather than for the purpose of distribution or exchange, and Spratling (1979, 130, fig. 98.1) preferred the term 'billet' rather than ingot for such objects. In Ireland, an oval 'cake' and rod ingot or billet of bronze occur in the La Tène metalwork hoard from Somerset (Co. Galway; Raftery 1960).

Bars of other metals also occasionally occur in Iron Age contexts, for example the very small silver bar ingot with rounded edges from a late 1st century BC pit at **Hallaton** (Leicestershire: $15 \times 9 \times 5$ mm) and the lenticular lead ingot from an early 1st century AD ditch at **Bagendon** (Gloucestershire). An open clay mould for a bar from a Middle Iron Age deposit at **Broxmouth** (East Lothian; Fig. 2.3, c) retained traces of zinc and gold as well as copper. Other possible ingot forms have on occasion been recorded from Late Iron Age sites although generally towards the end of

the period. Examples include a bronze ingot of flat semi-circular form and a silver ingot, triangular in plan and plano-convex in section, from a deposit of early 1st century AD date at **Hallaton** (Leicestershire). The latter appears to be the result of melting silver coins in a crucible as indicated by the presence of two coins visible in the upper part of the object. Small gold alloy ingots of similar roughly triangular form were found in the Iron Age hoard at Essendon (Hertfordshire; eg, British Museum 1994, 0401.2).

Stage 2: melting and casting

To cast an artefact, a selected (and possibly weighed) amount of metal would be melted and alloyed in a crucible. The contents were poured into a mould and, after cooling, the finished, hardened object could be extracted. Our knowledge of the use of the various materials involved in melting and casting metals is derived from the finished objects, from the debris of the processes of production and from experimental work or analogies with more recent metalworking practices (Spratling

1979; Fregni 2014). Table 2.1 lists the range of materials employed in later prehistoric non-ferrous metalworking; in some cases, the materials themselves survive but in others their use is assumed or inferred from other artefacts and debris. The following summary focuses on the most common types of evidence for melting and casting recovered from the archaeological record.

Hearths and related equipment
Hearths and furnaces associated with melting and casting are often difficult to identify, as they need not necessarily retain any metallic residues, nor be particularly substantial (Barrett *et al.* 2000). Hearth linings that can be directly correlated with the working of non-ferrous metals are rare and mostly date to the Iron Age. For example, fragments of hearth lining yielding preserved copper prills were found in a Late Iron Age ditch at **Seaclean Wight Pipeline Site 32**, Havenstreet (Isle of Wight). A very small number of tuyères indicating the use of bellows have also been found. These include clay nozzle forms and plate-tuyères (also known as blow-holes and bellows guards) where clay was applied around the air inlet on a furnace. An example of the former type was found on a Middle Iron Age settlement at **Ballacagen Lough** (Isle of Man), while ED-XRF analysis of the plate-tuyère from a later Iron Age gully at **Fishers Road** East, Port Seton (East Lothian) found traces of copper and nickel on the vitrified outer surface. It is rare to find traces of non-ferrous metals on tuyères, however, and their presence need not definitively indicate non-ferrous metalworking. The rarity of tuyères in general may be due to problems identifying such objects, although the low firing of these items would have rendered them relatively fragile and less likely to survive.

Crucibles
Crucibles of clay with suitably refractory properties were employed for alloying and casting (Bayley & Rehren 2007). Crucible fragments have been found in both Bronze Age and Iron Age contexts but complete examples only in the latter. Crucibles are first evidenced during the Middle Bronze Age but they are particularly common on Iron Age sites. Both Bronze Age and Iron Age crucibles were open vessels that were heated from above. The metal charge was placed in the vessel on top of

which charcoal was heaped and burnt. Heating the vessels in this way meant they needed to be good insulators to keep the heat within. Their open form allowed as much fuel as possible to be fitted in and exposed to oxygen (Crew & Rehren 2002). Scientific analyses indicate that for the most part crucibles were employed for re-melting bronze. However, crucibles also appear to have been used for alloying. Analysis of the Middle Iron Age crucibles from **Coton Park**, Rugby (Warwickshire), for example, identified metal prills of pure copper, pure tin, and copper alloy, suggesting that these vessels had been used both for alloying copper and tin and for melting copper alloy prior to casting. SEM analysis of the interior vitrification deposit of one sample revealed small curved shavings of bronze; these can be interpreted as waste from trimming finished objects that had been collected for recycling. Preparation of other metals also occurred in crucibles. Gold residues have been identified in a Middle Iron Age crucible from the hillfort at **Pilsden Pen** (Dorset) while a crucible rim from the Late Iron Age settlement at **Dragonby** (North Lincolnshire) retained traces of silver.

LATER BRONZE AGE CRUCIBLES
Bronze Age crucibles were made using a variety of fabric recipes, with sand, crushed rock and/or organic material added to the clay as temper (Howard 1983; Sahlén 2011; 2013; Cotter 2012). Superficially at least, these fabrics may not always appear very different to those of ordinary pottery vessels, which can hinder identification of crucibles when only small fragments are present. No complete crucibles are known from Britain or Ireland and the majority of fragmentary examples have been recovered from Late Bronze Age contexts. Where they could be reconstructed from fragments they are typically thick-walled, with a rounded open bowl-shaped form and a pouring lip. Examples of this type have been identified as far apart as **Bestwall Quarry**, Wareham (Dorset), **Lough Gur** (Co. Limerick), and **Jarlshof** (Shetland) (Howard 1983; Sahlén 2011; Cotter 2012), and similar vessels also occur on the near Continent (eg, Queixalos *et al.* 1987). Such objects could be wide and shallow, for example the spouted vessel from the **Breiddin** (Powys; Fig. 2.4, a), or deeper and more rounded. The crucible from **Bestwall Quarry** (Fig. 2.4, b) was heightened at some

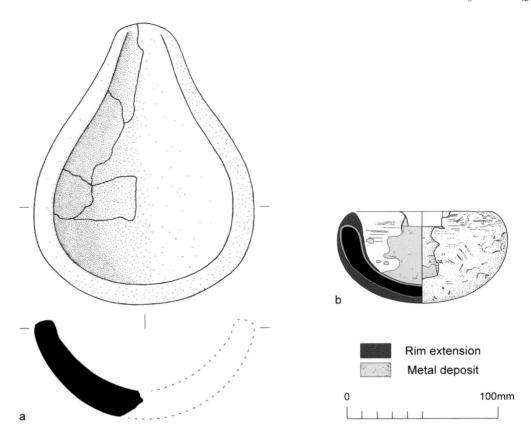

Figure 2.4: a. Proposed reconstruction of Late Bronze Age crucible from the Breiddin (Powys) (redrawn by Anne Leaver after Musson 1991, fig. 60.225); b. Middle Bronze Age crucible from Bestwall Quarry, Wareham (Dorset) (after Ladle & Woodward 2009, fig. 190.1)

Rim extension

Metal deposit

0   100mm

point during its life to create a vessel that was *c.* 46 mm deep and 95 mm in diameter. At the Late Bronze Age site of **Dainton** (Devon), one of the crucibles had three legs (Fig. 2.5) providing a stable base for the object. Bowl-shaped crucibles similar to Bronze Age examples continued in use into the Earliest Iron Age, as at **Dunston Park** (West Berkshire).

The absence of complete Bronze Age crucibles limits our assessment of the typical capacity of these vessels, but the small number that can be partially reconstructed indicate that they tend to be significantly larger than Iron Age examples. The crucible from **Dainton** had a diameter of *c.* 135 mm and a maximum surviving depth of 38 mm. This could have held over 450 ml of molten metal although, to avoid the metal flowing over the rim, the useable capacity of the vessel would have been slightly less. The crucible from **Bestwall Quarry** is a smaller vessel with a capacity of *c.* 200 ml. The volume of these Late Bronze Age vessels is significantly greater than that of most Iron Age crucibles (see below). Other Bronze

Age crucible sherds from incomplete vessels have thick walls and a curvature suggesting similarly large capacities.

Cast bronze artefacts of Bronze Age date are often significantly larger and heavier than those of Iron Age date, and this may explain differences in crucible capacity. For example, between *c.* 15 ml and 45 ml of bronze would have been necessary to cast each of the spearheads and axes in the Late Bronze Age hoard from Boughton Malherbe (Kent; Adams 2017). Larger objects required even more metal: the volume of bronze needed to produce a Late Bronze Age sword, for example, would have been in the region of 45–60 ml, while one of the bronze mould valves from Boughton Malherbe would have required *c.* 160 ml of metal. The largest known cast objects of Bronze Age date in Britain are the rare Middle Bronze Age ceremonial dirks such as that from Oxborough (Norfolk; Needham 1990a). This weighs 2.36 kg with an estimated volume of about 290 ml. Experimental archaeology has not yet attempted to replicate and use crucibles of Bronze Age form, but the challenges of

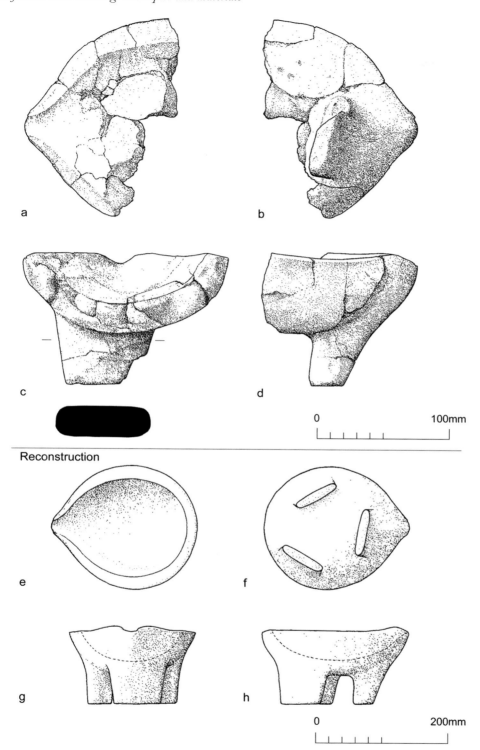

Figure 2.5: Late Bronze Age crucible from Dainton (Devon) (redrawn by Anne Leaver after Needham 1980, figs 4–5)

Reconstruction

manipulating a crucible containing well over 2 kg of bronze without the benefit of iron tongs suggests that more than one person must have been involved in the casting of such objects. Most Bronze Age tools and weapons are far smaller than the full capacity of the crucibles from **Dainton** and **Bestwall Quarry**, however, suggesting that these vessels may have been employed to cast multiple objects at once.

Relining and/or wall heightening of crucibles

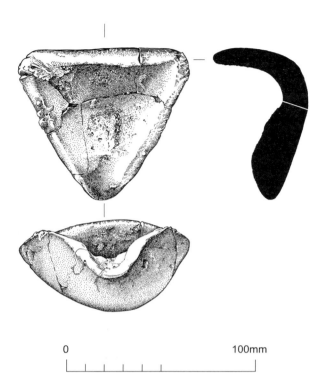

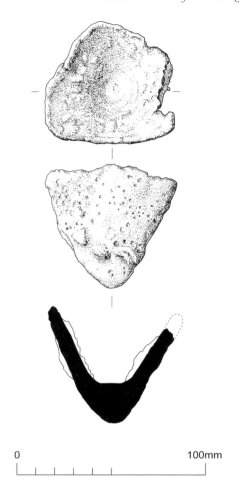

Figure 2.6: Shallow dished triangular-rimmed crucible of Late Iron Age date from Weelsby Avenue (Lincolnshire) (drawing: Barbara Garfi, reproduced by kind permission, from Foster 1995, fig. 32)

Figure 2.7: (right column) Deep conical triangular-rimmed crucible of Middle Iron Age date from Coton Park, Rugby (Warwickshire) (after Chapman 2019, fig. A1)

was particularly common in the later Bronze Age as observed on the **Bestwall Quarry** crucible (Fig. 2.4, b). This indicates that these objects saw more than one episode of use and that care was taken to maintain them (Howard 1983). A Late Bronze Age crucible sherd from **Runnymede Bridge** (Surrey) had evidence for relining, with alternating layers of unoxidised grey fabric and oxidised red fabric visible to the naked eye in the cross-section of the broken edge, as well as patches of what appear to be mixed deposits of metal. These suggest at least two episodes of relining the interior and at least one recoating of the exterior. As Bronze Age crucibles tend to be larger than their Iron Age equivalents, the parsimonious use of clay resources and manufacturing time is perhaps not unexpected. The success of the repairs suggests that these were carried out by individuals who were familiar with the crucible production process.

IRON AGE CRUCIBLES

More complete or near-complete crucibles are known from the Iron Age than the Bronze Age. In contrast to the preceding period where mould fragments dominate the record, they are now the most frequent indicator of non-ferrous metalworking on excavated sites (Table

2.2). Patching or relining is less common during the Iron Age although it has been identified on examples such as the crucible from **Westwood Campus**, University of Warwick, Coventry (Warwickshire; Fig. 2.9). If Iron Age crucibles had shorter use-lives, this may be one factor behind their increased frequency.

Iron Age crucibles from Britain differ significantly in form in comparison to their Bronze Age predecessors (Howard 1983; Heald 2005). They often have thinner walls, some exceptionally so, and in general they are altogether smaller. Previously unseen forms appear and crucibles of different types sometimes occur on the same site. The most common form of crucible from this period is shallow, thin-walled and triangular-rimmed. Such vessels dominate the evidence from southern Britain, where they occur from the Early Iron Age onwards, although they are most common in later Iron Age contexts (Fig. 2.6). They tend to have distinctive fabrics, densely packed with sand and/or charcoal (Howard 1983). The triangular rim provided three corners from which the molten metal could be poured although, on the shallower examples, the curvature of the base (often shallower on one side and deeper on the other) suggests that the corner on the shallow side was preferred. The arched sides of one of the reconstructed crucibles from **Gussage All Saints** (Dorset) would have successfully prevented the molten metal from spilling as it was poured into the mould via the shaped corner 'spouts'. Deep conical crucibles are also known from the Early Iron Age onwards, and some of these have triangular rims (Fig. 2.7). The crucibles from **Meare West** (Somerset) are all of this form; the examples from Glastonbury, just 5 km away, also have triangular rims but are shallow, bowl-shaped vessels, suggesting local traditions of craftsmanship. Triangular crucibles also occur in Scotland (Heald 2005), and possibly in later Iron Age contexts at **Tara** (Co. Meath; Crew & Rehren 2002). There is some evidence that the form remained in use into the 1st century AD and even post-Conquest in southern Britain: triangular crucibles have been recovered from post-Conquest deposits at **Marlowe Theatre Carpark, Canterbury** (Kent), for example.

Other types of crucible are also known. Crucibles with a rounded or conical base and a single square handle or lug (Fig. 2.8) are relatively rare finds and have been positively identified at only four sites, all hillforts. At **Danebury** (Hampshire), their use was restricted to the early phase (*c.* 550–300 BC) and they were subsequently replaced by triangular crucibles, but at **Llwyn Bryn-dinas** (Powys) they occur in contexts dating to the 3rd–2nd century BC. Bowl-shaped crucibles without a handle but often with pouring lips have been recovered only from Late Iron Age contexts, for example at **Kelk** (East Yorkshire) and **Silchester** (Hampshire). A unique spouted crucible from **Westwood Campus**, University of Warwick, Coventry (Warwickshire) is probably a variant of this type (Adams *et al.* 2018; Fig. 2.9). In Ireland, very small cup-shaped or hemispherical crucibles have been found at the later Iron Age sites of **Tara** and **Platin/Lagavooren 1** (both Co. Meath). Similar small 'thumb-pots' found at a number of sites in Britain may also have been used in metalworking, but metal traces have yet to be identified on these objects. In contrast

to crucibles of Bronze Age date, Iron Age crucibles from Britain and Ireland are quite different in form to those found on the other side of the Channel. Iron Age crucibles from northern France and the Low Countries are usually more closed in form, with an ovoid profile (Malrain & Pinard 2006, fig. 135; van den Broeke 2012, fig. 3.29; Zaour *et al.* 2014, fig. 4), though British-style triangular crucibles have been found at two sites in the Netherlands (van Heeringen 1987, pl. 45; van Renswoude & van Kerckhove 2009). This may imply that the casting technology used in Britain and Ireland differed from that on the near Continent.

Objects that appear to have functioned as crucible stands are exceptionally rare. A complete example and fragments of others were found in a Middle Iron Age pit at **Broom** (Central Bedfordshire). These were fired clay pedestals resembling an eggcup; a triangular crucible recovered from the same context fits snugly into the complete stand. As these objects are not heat affected, they are unlikely to have supported the crucibles during the melting process itself. Another possible stand of quite different form was recovered with hearth material of Early to Middle Iron Age date in **High Pasture Cave (Uamh an ard Achadh)** on the island of Skye (Highland). This was a flat fired clay slab with two cup-depressions in its upper surface; vitrification indicates that this object was used in a hearth or furnace.

Iron Age crucibles (Table 2.3) have a much smaller capacity than their Bronze Age counterparts, typically around 20 ml. A near-complete example from **Beckford** (Worcestershire), for example, would have held *c.* 20 ml of molten bronze when three-quarters full (Howard 1983, 329; note that Howard mistypes the volume of this object as 200 cc rather than 20 cc), while the deep triangular crucibles from **Fison Way**, Thetford (Norfolk) had a maximum capacity of 22 ml. This is in keeping with the size of objects cast during this period which tend to be smaller items of adornment (such as brooches and pins) or handles and other fittings for larger objects such as wooden buckets and iron swords.

	Bronze Age	Iron Age
Crucibles	44	188
Moulds	82	72

Table 2.2: Number of excavated sites from which moulds and crucibles (fragmentary & complete) have been recovered

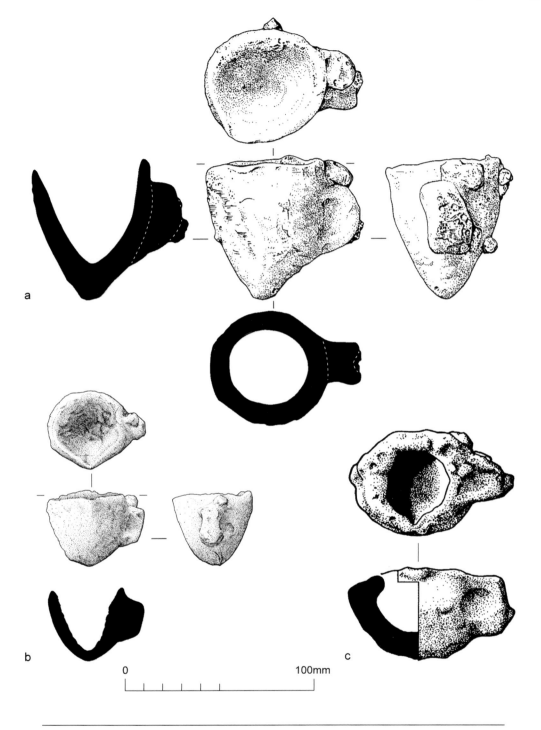

0   100mm

*Table 2.3: Number
of Iron Age sites with
crucibles (complete
or fragmentary) of
particular types*

Period	Shallow with triangular rim	Conical with triangular rim	Conical with circular rim	Triangular unspecified profile	Handled	Bowl-shaped (no handle)	Small incl. thumbpots	Extra large
Early Iron Age	0	2	2	5	0	1	2	0
Later Iron Age	26	14	1	8	5	16	11	4

The 'Arras' terret from Hod Hill (Dorset), for example, weighed 60.4 g and would have required just 8 ml of metal. As in the Bronze Age, the size of some crucibles suggests they could have been used to cast more than one object at a time and this raises questions regarding the organisation of production. One of the reconstructed crucibles from **Gussage All Saints** (Dorset) had a capacity of 47 ml (Spratling 1979, 130). This is greater than would have been required for any of the moulds (predominantly for equine equipment) found at this site, suggesting that it may have been used to cast linking components in succession, or to produce several non-linking pieces, potentially from different bridle sets. This would allow for a 'production line' method of casting and construction.

Moulds

Three main forms of mould technology were in use in prehistory: single-piece, bivalve, and lost-wax moulds (Tylecote 1986). The moulds themselves were variously made by being shaped in clay that was then dried and fired, carved in stone, or cast in bronze. The use of sand moulds is a further possibility, though these would leave no archaeological trace (Ottaway & Seibel 1998).

The use of single-piece moulds was the simplest method. The molten metal was poured into a matrix set into one face of the mould. These are often described as 'open' moulds, though it is possible that a flat slab was used to partially cover the matrix to avoid excessive oxidation of the metal (Hodges 1959). Objects cast using this method will often need extensive finishing, as the upper face of the casting will be flat and featureless. One-piece stone moulds for the production of axes and other objects are characteristic of the period from *c.* 2200–1900 BC (Needham 2004; Fig. 2.10). They then disappear from the archaeological record until the Iron Age, when one-piece moulds of stone or fired clay were used for casting small discs and bars (interpreted as ingots or billets).

Bivalve or two-piece moulds are formed of two interlocking halves, which may be made of stone, fired clay, or bronze (Fig. 2.11). A small opening or channel (known as a sprue or gate) is left between the two valves to allow ingress of the molten metal. A funnel-like 'sprue cup' made of clay may be attached to

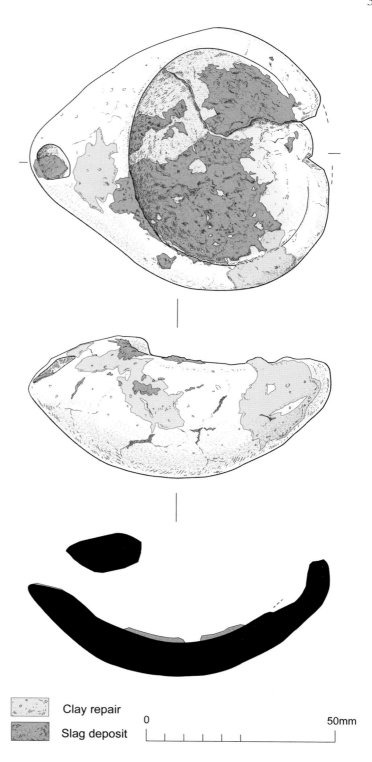

Clay repair

Slag deposit

0　　　　　　　　　　　　　50mm

the opening to avoid spillage when pouring the metal. Implements with hollow sockets can be cast in bivalve moulds by using a core placed between the two valves. Cores were normally made of clay, though Fregni (2014, 80) has

Figure 2.9: Unusual spouted Late Iron Age crucible from Westwood Campus, University of Warwick (Coventry) (drawing: Anne Leaver)

identified possible evidence for the use of cuttlebone cores during the Late Bronze Age. To ensure successful casting, the matrix of the mould may have been dressed with soot or fine clay, and the mould would have been heated immediately before use. The two valves may have been bound together with cords or twine to avoid slippage.

The form of some finished artefacts such as halberds indicates that bivalve mould technology was introduced from as early as the Chalcolithic (O'Flaherty 2002) but it was not until *c.* 1700 BC that the first bivalve moulds, carved from stone, appear in the archaeological record (Ó Faoláin 2004). Stone bivalve moulds continued in use throughout the later Bronze Age, though they were increasingly replaced by fired clay moulds (Fig. 2.12), and in southern Britain also by bronze moulds (Webley & Adams 2016; Fig. 4.25). In contrast to stone and bronze moulds, which can be used multiple times, later Bronze Age clay moulds were usually single-use: the two valves were encased in a coarser outer clay wrap before firing, which meant that the mould had to be smashed to release the casting within. Few moulds can be dated specifically to the Earliest Iron Age, due to the difficulties in distinguishing that period in many regions, but the use of bivalve clay and stone moulds continued, while those of bronze seem to have disappeared. Bivalve moulds appear to largely have gone out of use in southern Britain during the Early Iron Age (after *c.* 600 BC), when lost-wax casting became the dominant technology. However, clay two-piece moulds continued to be the norm through the Iron Age in Scotland and on the Isle of Man, examples including the ring-headed pin moulds from **Ballacagen** (Isle of Man). The few clay mould fragments known from Iron Age Ireland have yet to be studied in detail, and it is unclear whether they are from bivalve or lost-wax moulds.

Very different techniques were employed to make piece moulds of clay, stone, and bronze, and it is possible that metalworkers were dependent on other craftworkers for the production of some of these objects. The matrices in stone moulds were carved negatives of the object they were intended to cast whereas clay moulds were formed around a positive pattern (model) of the final object. Possible wooden patterns of Bronze Age

date are known (see below). The production of bronze moulds themselves involved several stages including use of a pattern and clay moulds (Webley & Adams 2016, fig. 8). Although the earliest stone moulds were often relatively simple in form, considerable care could be taken in the production of these objects: for example some bivalve moulds have holes for wooden dowels on their inner faces to ensure accurate registration of the two parts, for example. Significant skill and knowledge were also needed for the production of later Bronze Age clay moulds, in the selection of suitable clays and tempering materials. Making moulds for long objects such as swords was an especially lengthy and complex process (Howard 1983; Ó Faoláin 2004), with 2–3 weeks of drying time required between forming and firing the mould (Ó Faoláin & Northover 1998). The production of clay moulds for simpler objects such as axes may have been more straightforward (Kuijpers 2008), although ensuring that the clay core for a socketed artefact was correctly positioned required experience.

Lost-wax casting – also known as *cire perdue* or investment casting – involves the use of a clay mould formed around a wax model of the intended object. The wax is then melted to leave a cavity in the mould into which the molten metal may be poured. The metal object is extracted by breaking the mould, making these single-use items, although it is possible that patterns for preparing the wax models were used for repeated castings of the same form. Detailed analysis of some of the components of elaborate objects such as flesh hooks and cauldrons suggests that lost-wax casting was occasionally used during the Late Bronze Age (Stansby 1984; Beesley 2004; Bowman & Needham 2007), though no investment moulds of that period have been found.

The low level of use of the lost-wax method in Bronze Age Britain and Ireland contrasts with its much more extensive use in some other parts of Europe, notably Scandinavia (Jantzen 2008). Previous arguments that this was due to a lack of access to beeswax (Northover 1984; 1995b) now seem questionable. Honeybees have been found in Middle Bronze Age deposits at Perry Oaks (Greater London) and Late Bronze Age levels at Runnymede (Surrey); beeswax residues have been detected on Neolithic and Bronze Age pottery vessels from southern Britain; and the Dover boat of the 16th century BC

Figure 2.10: Early Bronze Age stone one-piece mould for flat axes and bars from Glenrinnes House, Dufftown (Moray) Note scale as Fig 2.11 (photo: Sophia Adams courtesy of National Museum of Scotland)

Figure 2.11: Earliest Iron Age stone bivalve mould for socketed axes from Stittenham, Rosskeen (Highland) (photo: Sophia Adams courtesy of National Museum of Scotland)

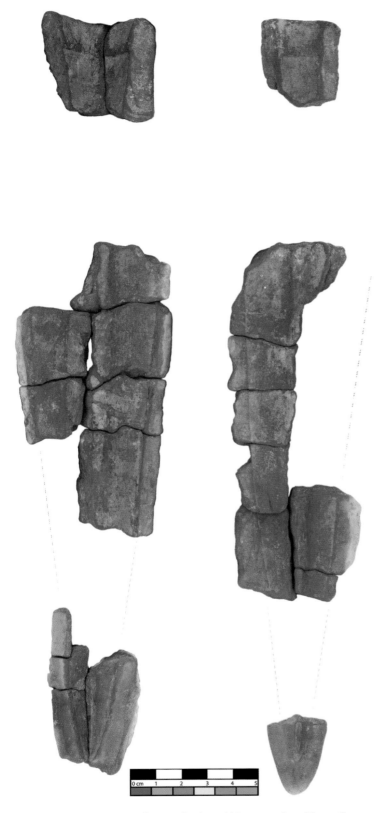

Figure 2.12: Late Bronze Age clay spearhead mould fragments from Maxey Quarry (Cambridgeshire) (photo: Sophia Adams courtesy of MOLA Northampton)

was caulked using beeswax and moss (Copley *et al.* 2005a; 2005b; Carreck 2008). A sheet-gold lock-ring from near Berwick-upon-Tweed (Northumberland) has also recently been shown to have a beeswax core (La Niece & Cartwright 2009). The lack of use of the lost-wax method during the Bronze Age may thus relate in part to the types of objects made and used in the British Isles and to the organisation of metalworking, but it may also be a matter of cultural choice. The lost-wax process subsequently became the dominant bronze casting technology in southern Britain during the Early Iron Age. Remains of investment moulds have been found at numerous Iron Age sites. These are often highly fragmented, which can hinder identification of the objects cast, though most known examples seem to be for horse gear or vehicle fittings (Fig. 2.13). Davey (2009, 150) has noted that although lost-wax casting enabled the production of elaborate three-dimensional forms, it was also often used to produce simpler shapes. In comparison with other casting technologies, it is well suited to the creation of smooth curved shapes; these were particularly favoured during the La Tène period (eg, Jope 2000).

When interpreting the relative numbers (Table 2.4) and distributions of different types of mould, the modes of recovery of these artefacts need to be taken into account. Virtually all clay moulds are from excavated sites, and they have only begun to be routinely recovered and recognised since the 1970s; hence their distribution reflects the pattern of modern fieldwork. Many stone moulds, in contrast, are old finds not deriving from excavations, often having been found during non-mechanised agricultural work. Bronze moulds occur only as stray finds or in bronze hoards; again many are old discoveries, though there have also been a number of metal-detector finds in recent decades. As such their distribution is influenced by patterns of metal detectorist activity (cf. Robbins 2013; Brindle 2014; Murgia *et al.* 2014).

One further type of mould unique to the Late Iron Age and early conquest period in southern and eastern England is the coin pellet mould (Landon 2016). The first production of coins in Britain occurred in south-east England from the mid-2nd century BC onwards (Haselgrove 1999). Two techniques were used: the casting of potin (high tin bronze) coins and the striking

	Britain				Ireland		
	Clay	*Stone*	*Bronze*		*Clay*	*Stone*	*Bronze*
EBA	–	27 (24)	–		–	10 (8)	–
Late EBA	–	2 (2)	–		–	9 (5)	–
MBA	(5)	29 (19)	15 (13)		(2)	76 (34)	1? (–)
LBA(–EtIA)	(58)	15 (13)	43 (37)		(20)	2 (–)	–
EtIA	(1)	4 (2)	–		–	3 (2)	–
EIA	(5)	–	–		–	–	–
MIA	(28)	17? (10)	–		(1)	–	–
LIA	(30)	>2 (2)	–		(2)	(1) 1	–
	(20) Cpm						

Table 2.4: Numbers of moulds from Britain and Ireland by period

Figures in brackets show the number of findspots (excluding moulds provenanced only to 'Ireland')
Questionable moulds are excluded.
Note that clay moulds includes both piece moulds and investment moulds.
Clay moulds are usually highly fragmented so it is rarely possible to specify the minimum numbers of moulds present. However, it is worth noting that in the Middle and Late Iron Age there are several thousand fragments concentrated in the most part at a few sites. Cpm = coin pellet moulds.

of gold, silver, and bronze coins. In some cases struck base-metal coins were plated with gold or silver foil (Cottam 2001). Potins were cast in strips or trees and then cut apart. From their surface characteristics it is argued that they were cast in bivalve clay moulds (Van Arsdell 1986). No such moulds have yet been found in Britain, though there is a possible fragmentary example from Le Grand Aunay, Sarthe in northern France (Vacher & Bernard 2003). In contrast, coin pellet moulds are relatively common finds. These were fired clay trays with a series of indentations in one surface (Fig. 2.14). They acted more as batteries of miniature crucibles than as moulds. A specific weight of gold, silver, or bronze was placed in each indentation before the trays were heated and the metal melted to form small pellets that could be struck with a die to create coins.

Very similar moulds were widely used across western and central Europe. Earlier scepticism that these could produce usable coin blanks has been allayed by more recent work (Gebhard *et al.* 1995; de Jersey 2009; Bucher *et al.* 2011), and similar coin blank moulds were used in historical periods in West Africa and elsewhere (Nixon *et al.* 2011). Indeed, pellets are occasionally found still stuck in coin pellet moulds from excavated Late Iron Age sites, as at **Turnershall Farm**, Wheathampstead (Hertfordshire). Variation in the shape of the trays as well as in the number, diameter, depth, and angle of the indentations may relate to the production of different denominations of coinage (Cowell & Tite 1982; Tournaire *et al.* 1982; Frere 1983; van Arsdell 1989; Farley

Figure 2.13: Fragment of clay lost-wax (investment) mould for the head of a Middle Iron Age linchpin from Gussage All Saints (Dorset) (photo: Sophia Adams courtesy of Dorset County Museum)

2012; Landon 2016), although this hypothesis is perhaps problematic given the variability both in the actual sizes of finished coins of the same denomination and in hole size in each tray.

Weights and scales
Scales might have played a role in weighing out small amounts of metal in preparation for alloying or casting (Pare 1999, 470; 2013; cf. Ialongo 2018). This may have been particularly important for making items such as Late Iron Age coins, or sheet objects such as lunulae where the size of the finished piece was dictated by the weight of the gold blank used. Scales could also have been used for many other purposes, including magical or ritual practices.

Two bone balance beams are known from

Figure 2.14: Fragment of Late Iron Age coin pellet mould from Standon (Hertfordshire) (PAS BH-95F015; CC BY-SA 4.0)

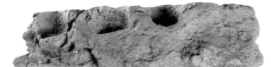

weights seem to have been used with balance beams during the later Bronze Age (Pare 1999; 2013). The only identified examples from Britain are two from the later Bronze Age Salcombe wreck site (Devon); one is decorated with a pattern of incised wavy lines that is directly paralleled on the Continent (Needham *et al.* 2013). A lead cone weighing 144 g from a 9th century BC context at **Cliffs End Farm** (Kent) is also fairly convincing as a weight. Small lead blocks dated to the Late Bronze Age from Fengate Power Station (Cambridgeshire), **Runnymede Bridge** (Surrey), and a few bronze hoards such as that from West Caister (Norfolk) could perhaps also have been weights, though they could equally have been small ingots (Needham & Hook 1988; Coombs 2001; West 2014). The small size of these examples hints that they may have been used for gold rather than for bronze (cf. Rahmstorf 2019). The rarity of such finds suggests that the kinds of weight systems postulated for bronze on the Continent (eg, Sommerfeld 1994; Lenerz-de Wilde 1995; Primas 1997) may not have been in operation in Britain and Ireland; certainly, there was considerable variability in the weight of plano-convex ingots (Wang *et al.* 2016; 2018).

Organic artefacts associated with casting

Organic objects and materials that were employed in melting and casting metals are particularly rare. A small number of possible wooden patterns for Bronze Age spearheads, axes and other objects are known, for example from Tobermore (Co. Derry), but despite the presence of wood-grain impressions on a few bronze swords, no definite wooden sword patterns have been found (Hodges 1954; Ó Faoláin 2004, 43–5, 81, 248, fig. 52). Wooden supports sometimes appear to have been used to reinforce clay moulds for swords, as indicated by the presence of longitudinal cavities between the inner wrap and outer wraps (Ó Faoláin 2004, 78–81, figs 5.3 1–3) or within the outer wrap itself. The carbonised remnants of a rod in a sword mould fragment from **Lough Eskragh** (Co. Tyrone; Ó Faoláin 2004, 43, 80, fig. 5.4, b) provides a rare instance where the 'stiffening-rod' was not removed before firing the mould (*ibid.*, 79-81).

Bone tools such as gouges and awls may also have been employed in metalworking, for example in creating and decorating wax models for investment casting. Bone objects

southern Britain: one from the Late Bronze Age/Earliest Iron Age midden at **Potterne** (Wiltshire) and a Late Bronze Age or Iron Age example from **Cliffs End Farm** (Kent), a site that was the focus of mortuary activities. Similar balance beams have been found in graves and caves in central France (Pare 1999; Peake *et al.* 1999). During the Middle and Late Iron Age a number of possible bronze or iron balances are known from sites in southern Britain (Van Arsdell 1993).

On the Continent, small rectangular bronze

with smooth spatula-like ends similar in shape to the plastic and wooden tools used for modelling clay, wax, and other mouldable materials today have occasionally been found. For the most part the function of bone tools is assumed rather than demonstrated, although where they are found in sealed contexts with other metalworking debris, we can suggest that they were used in the production process. Examples include four Middle Iron Age tools with spatula-like ends from layers of casting debris in a pit at **Gussage All Saints** (Dorset) and a similar Middle–Late Iron Age object found with an investment mould fragment for a bridle-bit in a pit at **Cadbury Castle** (Somerset). Textile impressions have been identified on some mould fragments for link pieces from **Gussage All Saints** (Foster 1980, 22–4); it has been suggested that these were wrapped around the side links of horse bits while the centre link was being cast in order to ensure that a suitable gap was maintained between the articulating components. Charcoal that presumably served as fuel for hearths or furnaces is also occasionally preserved with metalworking debris, particularly where the materials have been gathered together and deposited in pits soon after production ceased.

Metal casting waste, slags and residues
Casting waste is a relatively frequent find from Bronze and Iron Age metalworking sites. This includes small droplets or runs of the solidified molten metal where it has been poured from the crucible but missed the mould. Pieces of metal cut from the moulds after casting are also found, for example the sprues or casting jets where the molten metal has filled the gate and has then been cut off the object during the finishing process (Le Carlier de Veslud *et al.* 2014, fig. 5). In rare cases, entire miscast objects are found, such as the Late Bronze Age razor still partially encased in its clay mould found at **Runnymede Bridge** (Surrey). Slag of various forms is frequently assumed to indicate metalworking but it is only the high-density copper alloy slags that may be confidently associated with the casting of copper alloys; fuel ash slag is not a direct indicator of metalworking since it can be derived from a number of other high-temperature processes. Solid metallic residues from crucibles are also sometimes described as slag and are occasionally found separate from the crucible

in which they formed. These various forms of waste are often impossible to date unless they are stratified on excavated sites or found with other metal artefacts in hoards.

Remnant metal has also been identified within crucibles, as well as small prills of copper or traces of metal in the vitrification that occurs at the edges of these artefacts where they have been subjected to intense heat and the silica in the fabric has started to melt (Bayley 1985, 42). For example, a crust of copper alloy can clearly be seen adhering to the interior of a crucible fragment from **Runnymede Bridge** (Surrey), while traces of gold have been identified in a Middle Iron Age crucible from the hillfort at **Pilsden Pen** (Dorset). Small remnants of metals are also occasionally visible on mould fragments. Even where crucibles and moulds lack visible residues, metal traces can often be detected using XRF or electron microprobe analysis. Caution is needed when interpreting the results of XRF analyses of moulds and crucibles, however, as the proportions of metallic elements detected are unlikely to directly correlate to the composition of the original melt (Dungworth 2000; Kearns *et al.* 2010).

Stage 3: smithing and finishing
Smithing techniques can be evinced both by finds of smiths' tools and by visual or metallographic examination of the finished artefacts. As these techniques have been considered in detail by other researchers (eg, Maryon 1938; Spratling 1972; Northover 1984; Tylecote 1986; Cahill 1996; Bridgford 1998; Ó Faoláin & Northover 1998; Moyler 2007; Armbruster 2000; 2013; Gerloff 2010; Uckelmann 2012; Fregni 2014; Baldwin & Joy 2017; Nørgaard 2018), they will not be described exhaustively here. In summary, however, a range of techniques were employed in order to shape and finish different objects. Once a cast object had been removed from the mould, any excess metal from flashing and casting jets was trimmed. The edges of bladed weapons and tools were shaped, sharpened and hardened, a process that required repeated annealing and hammering of the metal (Britton 1963; Taylor 1980; Needham *et al.* 2015). Many of the most impressive metal objects are made of sheet metal and would have been formed by smithing rather than casting (Armbruster 2000; Cahill 2009; Gerloff 2010; Uckelmann

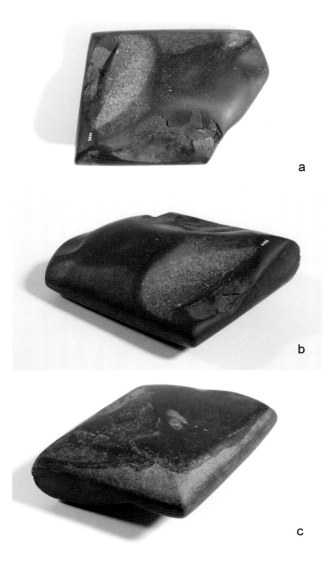

As non-ferrous metals are generally worked cold, the process does not normally produce waste metallic residues comparable to those generated by the hot working of iron. However, part-worked billets or blanks occasionally provide evidence for smithing on excavated sites (Fell 1990, 36). Scrap pieces of sheet bronze have been interpreted as off-cuts from sheet working (Northover 1984), but these can be difficult to distinguish from the broken remains of finished artefacts. Only a few smithing tools of Chalcolithic or Early Bronze Age date have been identified. The most distinctive are 'cushion stones': small blocks of hard, fine-grained stone, usually rectangular or trapezoidal in form, with carefully smoothed flat or concave surfaces (Fig. 2.15). These are believed to have been used as anvils and/or hammers for fine metalworking (Butler & van der Waals 1967; Freudenberg 2010; Needham 2011a; Drenth *et al.* 2013; Boutoille 2015a); copper and gold traces have been found on two examples from Hengelo-Elderinkweg in the Netherlands (Drenth *et al.* 2009), for example. Various other simple stone implements could have been used as smithing tools in this period, including hammers, anvils, grinding stones, whetstones, and polishers (eg, Clarke 1970; Lynch 2001; Armbruster 2006; Needham 2011a), but in the absence of contextual associations or metal traces a link with metalworking is often difficult to prove. A possible stone die or mould for making gold foil discs has recently been found at Hacketstown (Co. Waterford; Cahill 2016). Punches and riveting tools of Chalcolithic or Early Bronze Age date have yet to be recognised; perhaps they were made of materials such as bone or antler rather than metal. Experiments suggest that flint-tipped bow drills would have been best suited for drilling through copper and bronze (Bell 2016), and such drill bits would be difficult to identify in lithic assemblages.

Later Bronze Age smithing tools made of bronze have been discussed at length by Coombs (1971) and Fregni (2014). Socketed and tanged chisels of various forms are the most common type of tool that may have been used for metalworking, although they are also likely to have been employed for other tasks such as woodworking or leatherworking (O'Connor 1980). Some 'chisels' with flattened ends may have been used as metalworking punches (Fregni 2014, 79). Likewise, awls may also have

Figure 2.15: Cushion stone of Chalcolithic date from the grave of the Amesbury Archer, Wiltsthire (90.5 mm × 65 mm) (© Wessex Archaeology)

2012). Sheet metal objects were hammered out from ingots or blanks on metal anvils or over formers of wood or stone, then cut into shape and planished and polished to give them a smooth, shiny surface. Punches or drills were employed to create holes for rivets and other attachments, although components such as cauldron handles could be cast-on. The individual elements of composite objects could also be soldered together and other materials could be added such as bone handles or decorative glass inlay. Wire was produced by twisting sheet strips or bars, or by swaging (hammering into grooves on anvils). Bar-shaped castings were drawn out to produce objects such as gold torcs. Decorative techniques included chasing, embossing and repoussé.

been used in metalworking or in other crafts such leatherworking, textile production or the decoration of ceramics. Socketed hammers appear in the Middle Bronze Age, occurring in a range of forms and sizes that may have been used for different tasks such as working sheet metal and riveting (Fregni 2014). Bronze Age anvils and anvil-swages have been discussed by Ehrenberg (1981). These are small and suited to fine work, and it is likely that pieces of stone or wood were employed as anvils for the production of larger objects (Fregni 2014, 79). Jantzen (2008) listed 11 bronze anvils from Britain and Ireland but a number of further examples are now known (WANHS 1990; Needham 1993a; possibly Andrews *et al.* 2009, fig. 2.9; PAS KENT0278AC; PAS NMS-15E1DC; Fig. 2.16). There are gold traces on an anvil from Lichfield (Needham 1993a) and another (not certainly of later Bronze Age date) from Co. Sligo (Milligan 1886).

Three objects from the Late Bronze Age Isleham hoard (Cambridgeshire) have been interpreted as drawplates for making wire (O'Connor 1991, 238; Northover 1995a), though there is currently no evidence for drawn wire in this period (Cahill 2009; Armbruster 2013). Other smithing tools are equally rare. Fregni identifies a tool from the Lusmagh hoard (Co. Offaly) as a possible rivet snap, 'used to support a rounded rivet head while the shank end of the rivet is set and hammered flat' (Fregni 2014, 75), and there is a possible graver also from this assemblage. There is a possible vice from the Bishopsland hoard (Co. Kildare; Eogan 1983). An item identified as a pair of spring tongs is known from the Heathery Burn cave assemblage (Co. Durham; (Britton & Longworth 1968). These are quite flimsy, however, and may not have been suited to metalworking; the lack of other examples from the period suggests that Bronze Age crucibles may generally have been manipulated using wooden tongs or green withies. A tool from **Runnymede Bridge** (Surrey) has been identified as a drill bit (Fregni 2014, 75; BM cat. 1981,1101.4) but was originally published as a bradawl/tracer (Longley 1977). Experiments have suggested that bronze bits are not suitable for drilling copper or bronze (Bell 2016). Bronze saws have sometimes been suggested to be metalworking tools (eg, Rowlands 1976, 46) but are not hard enough for the purpose and are more likely to have been used in wood or bone working (Tylecote 1986, 102–3; Nessel 2010). Simple stone tools no doubt also continued to be used for smithing during the Middle and Late Bronze Age. Whetstones or grinding stones are fairly common finds from settlements but it is unclear how many of these may have been used for metalworking. On very rare occasions they also occur in metalwork hoards, as in the Late Bronze Age hoard from Donhead Clift, Dorset (Passmore 1931). Because of the difficulties in connecting objects such as whetstones, stone hammers, or bronze chisels with non-ferrous metalworking, no attempt has been made to comprehensively catalogue such items in this study.

For the Iron Age, a number of iron artefacts have been identified as smithing tools, including hinged tongs, pokers or smiths' rakes, files, chisels, sets, hammers, punches, and anvils (Fell 1990; 1997; 1998; Darbyshire 1995). The difficulty lies in determining whether these tools served for non-ferrous metal smithing, blacksmithing, or both. A key point is that while iron can be worked either hot or cold, non-ferrous metals are mainly suited to cold working (Fell 1990, 36). Fell's study of Iron Age smithing tools has identified some forms of hammer, chisel, and set that resemble tools historically used for cold working. These include a group of tools comparable to modern planishing hammers, used for removing prior hammer marks produced by the forging or raising of non-ferrous sheet metal (Fell 1990, 111). Cold working rarely leaves metal traces on smithing tools. There are, however, five Iron Age iron files with residues of non-ferrous metals in their teeth (Fell 1997). These include two fragments from **Fiskerton** (Lincolnshire) which may belong to the same object. The metal particles on one of these were identified as bronze, leaded bronze and lead. Two of the seven files from **Gussage All Saints** (Dorset) yielded a single particle of non-ferrous metal each; the composition of one of these particles has been analysed and has been found to be pure copper.

It is also likely that implements such as pokers and tongs were used for other high-temperature processes such as non-ferrous metal casting and glass working. Iron tongs were presumably used to manipulate crucibles as well as for blacksmithing; outside our study area at Rees-Haldern in western Germany a pair of iron tongs with a crucible between its jaws

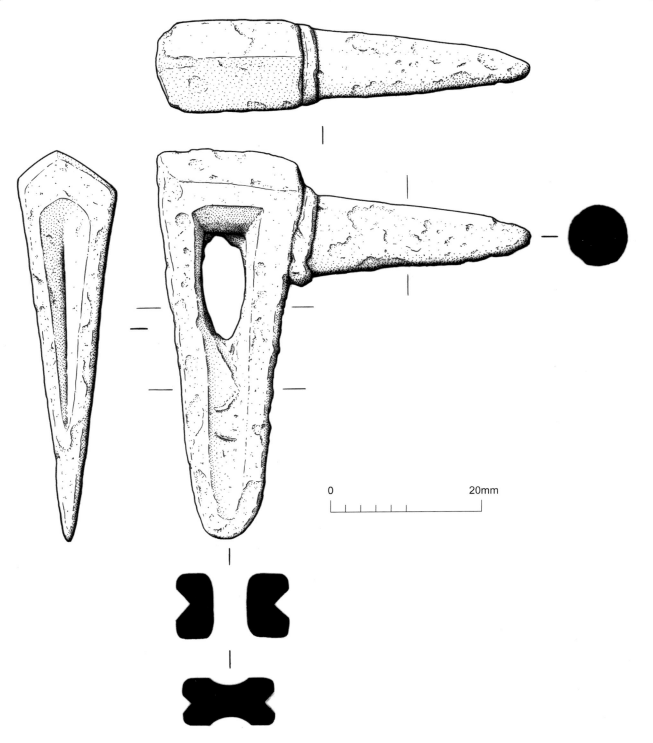

Figure 2.16: Bronze Age copper alloy anvil from Scarning (Norfolk) (drawing: J. Gibbons © Norfolk County Council Historic Environment Service)

was a placed deposit in a ditch surrounding a settlement of the 1st century BC (Schletter 2011). Other tools could have been used on organic materials: files and some forms of chisel may have been employed to work materials such as wood, stone, bone/antler, and horn (Darbyshire 1995), while small punches may have been used for activities such as leatherworking. Of course, these other crafts can be linked to non-ferrous metalworking, for example through the production of composite objects combining bronze with other materials.

Potentially a number of tools had a cross-craft purpose and this raises the possibility that non-ferrous metalworkers might also have made products in other materials. During the Late Iron Age, one new form of smithing tool appears that *can* be linked to a very specific form of non-ferrous metalworking. These are coin dies made of bronze, used to strike the gold, silver or bronze blanks that had been cast in pellet moulds (see Chapter 5).

Stage 4: use, reuse, and recycling

There is a long history of research on the use, reuse and deposition of finished metal objects of Bronze Age and Iron Age date. For example, analysis of the technical properties and use-wear evident on particular categories of objects has allowed the identification of some of the activities in which these were engaged (eg, Roberts & Ottaway 2003; Moyler 2007). Research on the final deposition of metal objects in graves and hoards has cast light on the social significance of non-ferrous artefacts as well as on aspects of funerary and ritual practice. Fully exploring the biographies of metal artefacts is beyond the scope of this study, but some aspects are directly relevant. Metalworkers' engagement with metal artefacts did not necessarily end with their initial manufacture. Many bronze objects had long use-lives and show signs of resharpening or repair. Some artefacts were considered more worthy of curation and repair than others; thus, Late Bronze Age swords sometimes had replacement handles cast on to them, while simpler implements such as axes rarely show any sign of repair (Coombs 1971, 400–1). Artefacts could also be modified or embellished in other ways. For example, Moyler (2007) argues that some Early Bronze Age flat axes had decoration added to them after they had already experienced a period of use (see Chapter 3). It may be unhelpful to view metal artefacts as being 'finished' at the point that they were first made; rather, they were continually in a process of becoming. At the end of their use-lives, many non-ferrous objects were melted down to be recast into new artefacts. Metallurgical analysis indicates that reuse or recycling of metal was common from at least the later stages of the Early Bronze Age (Rohl & Needham 1998; Bray & Pollard 2012). Other metal artefacts were not recycled but were selected for deposition in hoards, wet

places, or other landscape contexts, a practice that was especially common during the later Bronze Age. Deposition could be preceded by deliberate decommissioning, involving heating the objects before they were broken with a hammer and chisel. This may well have required the skills of smiths (Turner 2010; Fregni 2014; Knight 2018). It is possible that treating selected metal objects in this way was seen as an essential part of the metalworking cycle (see Chapter 4).

Conclusion

Prehistoric non-ferrous metalworking involved a wide variety of technologies and practices, which required differing skills and resources. These practices have also left differing archaeological signatures. Melting and casting is most conducive to leaving recognisable traces at excavated sites, in the form of casting waste, hearth lining with metal residues, and broken fragments of crucibles and moulds. While stone and bronze moulds could be used multiple times, clay moulds usually had to be smashed to release the artefact within, so that a single casting would produce multiple mould fragments. Friable fragments of clay crucibles and moulds would however be unlikely to survive unless they were deposited in the ground immediately, rather than being left exposed. The fragmentation of clay moulds can make it difficult to identify them, and to recognise the artefacts they were intended to cast.

Smithing is far less likely to leave recognisable waste at excavated sites. It can also be difficult to identify tools used for smithing non-ferrous metals, as objects such as hammers or chisels can be used for many purposes. Furthermore, while smithing tools made of stone or metal might be expected to have high survival rates, in practice it seems that they were rarely abandoned within metalworking areas at settlements. As we shall see, such artefacts were often deposited in the wider landscape, away from occupied places, something that also applies to bronze moulds. In some periods, smithing tools could also be placed in graves. These depositional practices may inform us about the meanings that metalworking had for prehistoric people. Nonetheless, they also create something of a contextual disconnect between the evidence for casting and smithing, complicating the task of understanding the spatial and organisational relationships between these two aspects of metalworking.

These caveats aside, prehistoric non-ferrous metalworking remains from Britain and Ireland provide a rich and diverse dataset that has yet to be fully explored. This provides the framework for the rest of this volume, which analyses the site context of the metalworking evidence and attempts to grasp the social significance of this craft.

3

The Chalcolithic and Early Bronze Age, *c.* 2450–1550 BC

The appearance of the earliest metal objects around 2450 BC poses a series of interesting questions regarding how and why metals came to be used in Britain and Ireland. Since Childe (1930, 2) first described prehistoric bronzeworking as the origin of '[m]odern science and industry', the status, significance, organisation, and impact of metalworking during the first centuries of its use have been topics of considerable discussion. Here, a number of key debates can be identified and an analysis of metalworking remains and their depositional context has the potential to contribute to several of these.

Childe's identification (*ibid.*) of Bronze Age metalworking as an 'industry' based on proto-Capitalist principles of innovation and technological progress can be considered particularly problematic in a Chalcolithic and Early Bronze Age context (Needham *et al.* 1989, 385; 2004; O'Brien 1994, 180–1; Bray 2012): the character of the earliest metal finds (often small items of personal adornment: Northover 1999) indicates that neither functional requirements nor a desire for economic gain can be considered the main drivers of early metal use. As Needham (2004, 218) puts it:

> Too often ancient metalwork production systems are described as 'industries' and conceived as cold technological innovation or modifications. This is tied to the idea that they were economically maximising systems, whereas the objective in the Early Bronze Age would have been rather to maximise prestige.

Although this is widely accepted, and although Chalcolithic and Earlier Bronze Age mining activities are recognised as relatively small-scale (eg, O'Brien 2004, 195–8), the mining and metallographic evidence – both key to our understanding of the organisation of Chalcolithic and Earlier Bronze Age metalworking – often continue to be figured in broadly functionalist terms. The 'trade' in metals from particular sources into areas without native copper or tin, for example, is often viewed as the inevitable result of the functional superiority of bronze over stone.

In contrast, research that has focused on the contexts of metal artefacts, for example finds from graves and hoards, has emphasised the social rather than the economic role of such objects (eg, Needham 1988; Needham & Woodward 2008; Fitzpatrick 2011). As we have seen above, this is often conjured as 'prestige' value (Thorpe & Richards 1984; Sheridan 2012), and this leads us to a second major question surrounding the adoption of metals in the 3rd millennium BC: were these inherently desirable? Recent discussion has accentuated the aesthetic properties of copper, gold, and tin: their eye-catching shine and luminosity, as well as their malleability, are considered to have been more significant than other 'technical' properties (such as hardness) during their first few centuries of use (Jones 2002; Ottaway & Roberts 2008, 214). The ability to transform dull ore to gleaming metal is argued to have been viewed as a magical skill that conferred status on the metalworker so that the symbolism of metal is thought to have been as important, if not more so, than its functionality during the first few centuries of its use (Cowie 1988; Needham *et al.* 1989, 385; Budd & Taylor 1995). Others have questioned the assumption that metals were valued more highly than other materials, arguing that they were just one of a range of visually-striking objects that were used to mark different social categories from the Late Neolithic onwards; as such, metals can be seen as a symptom rather than a cause of social change (Roberts 2009; Roberts & Frieman 2012). In particular, Roberts (2009) points out that the slow uptake of metalworking across Europe indicates that communities in many regions rejected metals, viewing them as uninteresting or undesirable for many centuries.

The extent to which the appearance of metals marks a genuine industrial or social revolution has therefore been questioned, at least for the Chalcolithic. Significant elements of continuity in social practice have been identified: in the Avebury and Stonehenge regions, for example, early Beaker pottery was deposited at existing monuments and was often treated in similar ways to Late Neolithic ceramics (Cleal & Pollard 2012). Yet, others have taken discoveries such as the burial of the 'Amesbury Archer', an early Beaker burial just 5 km from Stonehenge, to indicate dramatic and profound social change (Sheridan 2012). This unusually 'wealthy' adult male was accompanied by a large number of grave goods including six pots, two copper daggers, a pair of gold objects, basket-shaped earrings, and a cushion stone that may have been used for the working of metal (Fitzpatrick 2011). Both the quantity of grave goods and the presence of metals have been taken to indicate that this was an individual of particular wealth and status — an ideology of personal display at odds with

previous Neolithic practice. However, such an interpretation builds on the assumption that metals are intrinsically valuable which, as we have seen above, has been questioned by a number of researchers (Roberts & Frieman 2012); the essential correlation so often assumed between metals and status is equally problematic (cf. Brück 2004). The extent to which the introduction of metalworking can be considered a revolution of course raises questions regarding the mechanism by which metallurgy was introduced to Britain and Ireland, and the discovery of the **Amesbury Archer** contributes to these debates also, for the presence of the cushion stone has been taken to indicate that he may have been a metalworker (Fitzpatrick 2009). Stable isotope analysis has been argued to suggest that this man travelled to Wiltshire from central Europe around 2350 BC (Chenery & Evans 2011), reigniting longstanding discussion around whether metallurgical knowledge was brought by immigrants — perhaps even itinerant smiths — or was acquired by indigenous groups via exchange and other inter-regional connections. Recent aDNA analysis of Beaker burials suggests that there was significant population influx from the Continent at this time (Olalde *et al.* 2018); in many regions, the earliest metal objects have been found in Beaker graves, so it is possible that metalworking was introduced by immigrants. However, the scale of population movement and the processes involved have been the focus of much debate (eg, Carlin 2018; Furholt 2018; Frieman & Hofmann 2019; Parker Pearson *et al.* 2019); we may be looking here at the result of regular small-scale movement (for purposes such as marriage and exchange, for example, or as animals were brought to new pastures) rather than large-scale migration.

Much of what we know about metalworking during the Chalcolithic and Early Bronze Age derives from detailed typological and technological studies of the metal artefacts themselves, from metallurgical analyses, and from excavation of mines and associated 'work camps'. From *c.* 2450 BC, a variety of objects of copper and gold were produced. The earliest items were often small, decorative items of sheet metal, such as the copper rings from the burial of a child at Barrow Hills in Oxfordshire or the gold basket-shaped earrings that accompanied the burial of an adult male from the same site (Northover 1999). These were swiftly joined by tools and weapons of copper, such as flat axes, tanged knives and daggers, chisels, awls, and halberds (Britton 1963). From *c.* 2150 BC, tin-bronze rapidly replaced copper for the production of most objects (Needham *et al.* 1989), although it is possible that recycling of objects may obscure evidence for the use of bronze prior to this date (Bray 2012); from this point onwards, a remarkably standard 'recipe' for the production of tin-bronze was employed. The use of tin as a decorative inlay or coating on objects – such as the jet button from Rameldry in Fife (Baker *et al.* 2003) – found many miles from the likely source of this material in Cornwall suggests that metalworkers far from the south-west had access to tin, and that alloying did not only take place at primary production sites (Needham 2004, 235). Objects such as flat axes, tanged knives, and bars for the production of bracelets were cast in one-piece open moulds, while bivalve moulds were employed for the production of halberds from the Chalcolithic (O'Flaherty 2002), though no such moulds have yet been found. Later in the Early Bronze Age, bivalve moulds were more widely used for casting objects such as spearheads and flanged axes (Britton 1963). The practical steps required to craft these and other categories of object, for example the complex 'Wessex'-style goldwork of the early 2nd millennium BC (Taylor 1980; Needham *et al.* 2015), are increasingly well-understood.

The long history of metallographic analysis on objects of Chalcolithic and Early Bronze Age date (eg, Coffey 1901; Coghlan & Case 1957) means there is a growing body of information on the source of these metals, as well as alloying and recycling practices. Some of the early copper objects from southern and eastern England are composed of so-called Bell Beaker metal, the origin of which may lie in northern Spain (Needham 2002), although a Cornish source has also been suggested (Bray 2012, 60). However, the majority of copper objects and the earliest objects of bronze are made of 'A-metal', originally defined by Northover (1980; 1982a), and recognised now as the characteristic composition of copper from the mines at **Ross Island** (Co. Kerry; Northover *et al.* 2001; Northover 2004a). Interestingly, Ross Island copper comes from an arsenic-rich ore (known as 'fahlerz'). This

may have been chosen specifically for its high arsenic level: arsenic, like tin, renders copper stronger, less brittle, and easier to work. However, the processing of fahlerz ores is more complex than for secondary oxidised ores and it has therefore been suggested that the identification and mining of copper at Ross Island must have carried been out by individuals with pre-existing metallurgical knowledge (O'Brien 2004; 2012, 217–8). The excavation of Beaker pottery in association with ore processing debris and furnace pits for roasting and smelting the ore has been argued to indicate the presence of Beaker metal prospectors from the Continent – reflecting the enduring appeal of Childe's travelling metalsmith, and of culture-historical models that link the spread of technological innovations with the movement of people.

As we have seen in Chapter 1, a wider variety of copper sources were used after 2000 BC, and there has also been significant recent work on the likely sources of Chalcolithic and Early Bronze Age gold. Alongside work on sourcing, metallographic studies have cast light on significant aspects of manufacturing techniques, demonstrating, for example, that recycling was rare before *c.* 2200 BC (Bray 2012). The incidence of recycling gradually increases through the subsequent Early Bronze Age, although for most of the period this was carried out in a very particular way. Objects were not mixed to create new objects; instead, each new bronze artefact was manufactured from a single pre-existing artefact, creating a very clear form of linear object descent (*ibid.*).

Together, all this work has dramatically enhanced our knowledge of the technical and practical aspects of Chalcolithic and Early Bronze Age mining and metalworking. The social organisation of the craft remains elusive, however. Although, as we shall see below, metalworking remains have rarely been found in secure Chalcolithic or Early Bronze Age contexts, the existing evidence provides insights into many of the key debates discussed above. Discussion of the depositional context of metalworking-related remains will therefore form a particular focus of the remainder of this chapter. Just 16 excavated sites have produced metalworking tools or residues dating to this period (Fig. 3.1). Tools from excavated sites that may not have been employed exclusively for metalworking, for example hammerstones,

Figure 3.1: Distribution of excavated sites of Chalcolithic and Early Bronze Age date that have produced metalworking tools and non-ferrous metalworking residues

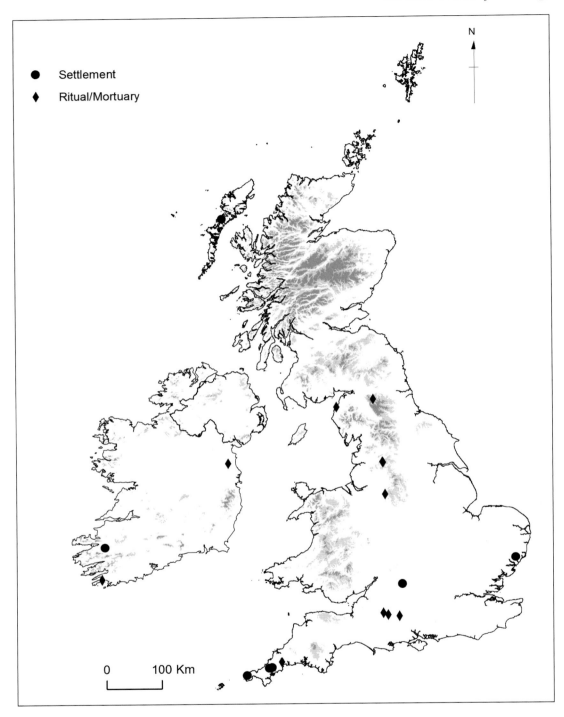

were not included in the database unless they bear traces of metal, although they are discussed briefly below. Other metalworking evidence, for example one-piece moulds and putative 'founders' hoards' will also be considered, although these have rarely been recovered from excavated sites.

Ore processing and smelting

The lack of evidence for copper smelting is one of the curious features of metalworking in Ireland and Britain throughout the period (see Chapter 2). Several fire-reddened pits yielding fuel ash, charcoal, crushed copper ore, and sand from a 'work camp' adjacent to the Western Mine at **Ross Island** (Co. Kerry) have been interpreted as furnaces. Fragments of roasted ore recovered from features near these pits indicate that they may have been used for roasting the ore to remove some of its sulphur content, although the sand may have been used as a flux in smelting. None of these features produced copper slag, although four fragments of copper slag, a droplet of copper, a runlet of copper, a small copper plate, and a small copper ingot were recovered from other contemporary features and deposits. Several stones next to one furnace pit had been carefully arranged, perhaps to act as a prop for a bellows while, elsewhere, a number of small stones were used to support a large boulder that may have served as an anvil. A small amount of copper smelting slag has also been recovered 4 km away at Ballydowny from a feature radiocarbon dated to 2120–1770 cal BC (3590±40 BP; Beta 168810) (Northover 2004a; Kiely & O'Callaghan 2010).

Although clearly a specialised site, the evidence from the Ross Island 'work camp' does not appear to indicate production on an industrial scale. The structural evidence comprises stake-holes, small post-holes, and a few foundation trenches, suggestive of light and probably temporary structures similar to those found on settlements of this date elsewhere in Britain and Ireland. One of the foundation trenches produced a fragment of human femur, hinting at the performance of small-scale ritual activities. Like other contemporary sites, the animal bone assemblage is predominantly composed of cattle; these animals appear to have been killed in the autumn or winter, indicating an element of seasonality to the activities undertaken at Ross Island. The lack of older animals suitable for breeding suggests that mining was carried out on a part-time basis possibly by people who farmed elsewhere in the local area at other times of the year. Certainly, there is nothing to suggest that the occupants of the site can be seen as wealthy or high-status, nor are there obviously intrusive finds or practices beyond the 'alien' activities of mining and metalworking themselves; the inclusions in the Beaker pottery, for example, indicate that it was locally made.

The evidence for copper ore processing at mine sites has been discussed in detail elsewhere (eg, O'Brien 1994) and will not be considered here. One other site has, however, yielded evidence for the processing of tin ore. At **Sennen** (Cornwall), pXRF analysis identified tin residues on six stone tools found in and around a small, oval, stake-built structure. Use-wear to their working ends suggested that these had been used to crush and grind cassiterite. The tools were associated with deposits of burnt material and areas of burning, and one was recovered from a hearth just outside the structure. It has been suggested that smelting of tin may have been carried out at this site: smelting in ceramic vessels over an unlined open hearth would leave minimal archaeological evidence. Radiocarbon dates place this activity in the period c. 2300–2100 BC, contemporary with the earliest use of tin-bronze. Other finds from the site include Beaker ceramics and flint artefacts, and the light-weight character of the oval structure suggests short-term occupation. Elsewhere in Cornwall, large numbers of cassiterite pebbles and a stone muller have been found in four pits dated to c. 2000–1600 BC at **Woodcock Corner**, Truro (Cornwall). Many of the pebbles from the pit containing the muller were crushed, and it is likely that these also indicate the collection and processing of tin ore. Cassiterite pebbles were also recovered from a post-hole dated to the Early Bronze Age at **Higher Besore and Truro College**, Threemilestone (Cornwall).

Casting

Very few excavated sites in Britain or Ireland have produced metal casting remains of this period. At the coastal settlement of **Northton** on the Isle of Lewis (Comhairle nan Eilean Siar), a small piece of bronze splash or spill was found within the stone wall of an oval house (Fig. 3.2), although the precise location of this object was not recorded. There was a hearth in the interior of this building and next to this lay a pit that produced a red deer antler and a complete badger skull: although this may be indicative of the performance of ritual activities in this building, special deposits of this sort are common in Bronze Age houses (Brück 1999b). Other finds from the house included Beaker pottery, worked bone and antler (some of these items may have been used for leather working or pottery production), flint and quartz tools, and a fragment of

Figure 3.2: Early Bronze Age house at Northton, Isle of Lewis (Comhairle nan Eilean Siar) (redrawn by Anne Leaver after Simpson et al. *2006, fig. 3.1)*

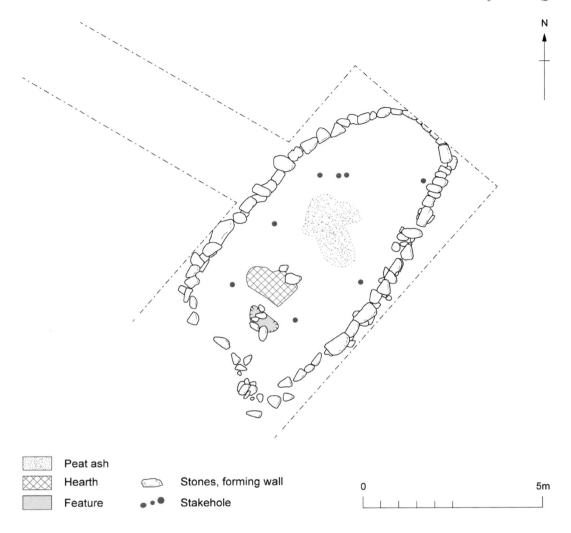

N

	Peat ash
	Hearth	Stones, forming wall
	Feature	• Stakehole

0   5m

human maxilla; it is not clear, however, if any of these derive from the same context as the bronze splash. A radiocarbon date of 2200–1760 cal BC (3604±70 BP; BM-706) was obtained on a fragment of animal bone from this phase of the settlement. Although highly unusual in a broader UK context, the house at Northton is part of a regional sub-tradition of building oval and subcircular stone houses that persisted in the Western and Northern Isles from the Neolithic through to the Iron Age, so despite the presence of Beaker ceramics, there is nothing to suggest that this was the settlement of immigrant metalworkers.

At **Sutton Hoo** (Suffolk), five bronze drips and parts of a bronze pin were recovered from a ditched field boundary. One drip and the pin fragments were found in the primary silt of the ditch and the remaining objects in later recuts. The feature produced Beaker and

Early Bronze Age ceramics as well as struck flint of Early Bronze Age date including a plano-convex knife, thumbnail scraper, and barbed-and-tanged arrowhead. A tiny fragment of clay mould was found during the excavation of Anglo-Saxon mound 5, which overlies the earlier boundary, and it is possible that this also derives from the ditch. Groups of pits and postholes on either side of the boundary produced Beaker and Early Bronze Age ceramics and a faience bead was recovered from a roundhouse 40 m north of the ditch, a rare find from a settlement. There is a radiocarbon date from one a pit of 2140–1930 cal BC (3650±35 BP; BM-3033). Pottery of Middle Bronze Age date was found in other features on this site and parallels elsewhere suggest that the boundary ditch is likely to date to this period. It is therefore possible that the metalworking residues derive from an Early Bronze Age pit that was later cut by a Middle Bronze Age ditch, although alternatively they may belong to the latter period. At **Roughground Farm**, Lechlade (Gloucestershire), two putative clay mould fragments were recovered from a pit forming a loose scatter of five Beaker pits. They were found with two incomplete 'cushion stones', four hammerstones, worked flint, pottery, animal bone, and other fragments of burnt clay. The identification of these as mould fragments is difficult to assess in the absence of any supporting information, and the cushion stones are questionable, as they are made of coarse sandstone. A single radiocarbon date from the pit calibrates to 2460–1880 cal BC (3710±100 BP; HAR-5499).

The sparseness of casting evidence is echoed on the near Continent. The most notable exception is Beg ar Loued (Finistère), a settlement on the small island of Molène off the coast of Brittany, with an oval stone house comparable to that at **Northton** (Pailler *et al.* 2014). A one-piece stone mould for a 'tapering bar' (perhaps actually a blank for a long narrow axe) was recovered, along with waste containing copper inclusions and five small broken objects made of sheet copper or copper alloy (*ibid.*, 124). An anvil, hammer, and several possible grinding stones from the site may also be associated with metalworking. Other finds include flint tools and Beaker and Early Bronze Age pottery, and the site is argued to span the transition from the 3rd to the 2nd millennium BC. The mould was found in slip from the external facing of the wall of the house (Pailler *et al.* 2008, 63); as at Northton, this object may originally have been deposited in the wall itself. The presence of a mould along with other metalworking debris from an apparent domestic site contrasts with the situation in Britain. Other sites include Val-de-Reuil 'les Florentins' (Eure), a Beaker occupation site alongside a palaeochannel of the Seine. Two small copper 'nodules' have been taken as evidence for metalworking. A hearth or oven elsewhere on the site was interpreted by the excavator as a pottery kiln (Billard 1991).

Life histories of one-piece stone moulds

In general, the settlement record throughout this period is patchy and ephemeral, perhaps reflecting a fairly mobile pattern of occupation (Brück 1999c), and this doubtless contributes to the paucity of stratified casting evidence. However, the absence of recognisable moulds or crucibles from excavated contexts in Britain and Ireland may also suggest that such objects were deliberately excluded from deposition at domestic sites, monuments, or cemeteries. In fact, at least 37 one-piece stone moulds for casting flat axes and other objects are known from Britain and Ireland (Appendix 2; Hodges 1959; 1960; Britton 1963; Needham 2004), but all are stray finds. They have mainly been found in northern and western parts of the British Isles, and in north-east Scotland in particular, corresponding to a concentration of contemporary metalwork in the same region (Britton 1963; Needham 2004; Fig. 3.3). A small number of moulds have been found in other regions, notably Ireland, Wales, and northern and south-western England. There is an outlying mould ascribed to the 'Suffolk Fens', but there is no record of its discovery and its provenance has long been regarded with suspicion (Britton 1963, 270).

Despite the lack of contextual evidence, one-piece stone moulds are our main source of evidence for metal casting, and aspects of their manufacture, use and deposition provide insights into the meaning and practice of metalworking. The British and Irish examples seem on typological grounds to date to a restricted period around *c.* 2150–1900 BC, when bronze had replaced copper for making axes (Needham 2004). The absence of surviving moulds from the centuries either side of this bracket may suggest that sand or fragile clay moulds were used instead. While one-piece moulds would have been sufficient for casting blanks for most metal artefacts of this period, objects such as certain types of halberd would have required the use of bivalve moulds already during the Chalcolithic (O'Flaherty 2002; Bray & Pollard 2012), though none of these has survived. Towards the end of the Early Bronze Age, around 1700 BC, a small number of bivalve stone moulds for casting weapons, tools, and ornaments appear in the archaeological record. As the technology and use of these moulds has more in common with the stone moulds of the Middle Bronze Age, these objects will be considered together with the latter in Chapter 4. The discussion below therefore focuses on one-piece moulds.

Figure 3.3: Distribution of Early Bronze Age one-piece stone moulds

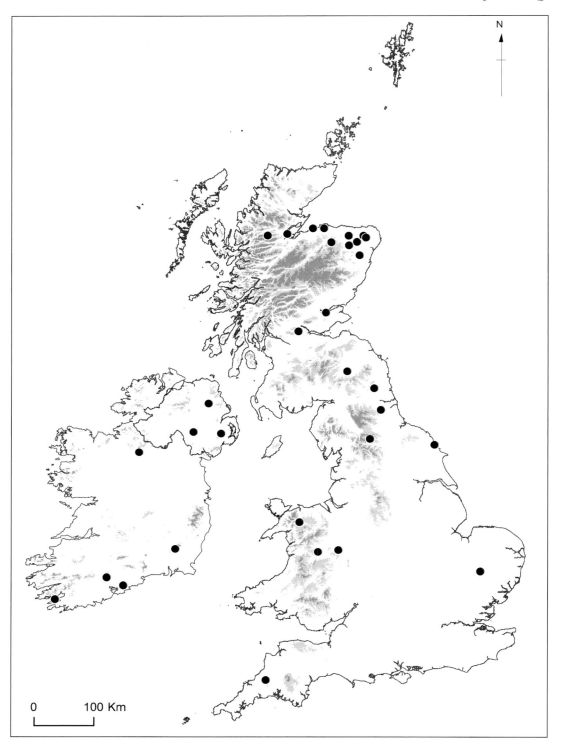

One of the most interesting aspects of one-piece stone moulds is that they were often used to cast more than one object. Most carry between one and four casting matrices (negative shapes in the mould for molten metal) on one or more faces of the mould, although moulds with up to nine matrices are known, such as the examples from Foudland, Insch (Aberdeenshire; 9 matrices: Callander 1904), and Ballyglisheen

	Axe	Chisel	Knife	Awl?	Bar	Ring	Dagger	Halberd
Axe	*	*	*	*	*	*	*	
Chisel	*	*			*		?	
Knife	*		?		*	*		
Awl?	*							
Bar	*	*	*		*		?	
Ring	*		*		*	*		
Dagger	*	?			?			
Halberd								*

Table 3.1: Associations of matrices on one-piece stone moulds

* = found together on one or more moulds

(Co. Carlow; 8 matrices: Prendergast 1958). Aside from a mould from New Mills (Powys; Green 1985) on which only halberd matrices can be identified, all the moulds were used for casting flat axes of particular styles (Migdale and Killaha types). Several of the axe moulds also carry matrices for other objects such as chisels, knives, possible awls, bars, and rings (Table 3.1), although these are relatively rare. The bars could have served as ingots or may have been worked into objects such as bracelets or penannular rings (Needham 2004). In total 83 axe matrices can be identified on the 37 known stone moulds in comparison with just 16 matrices for the casting of bars, seven for knives, and smaller numbers for other artefact types. Just one matrix for daggers can be positively identified, on a mould provenanced only to Ireland (Jones, C. 2002), suggesting either that these objects were generally cast using a different type of mould or that one-piece stone moulds for the production of daggers were not selected for deposition.

The combinations of matrices for different artefact types on individual moulds provides insights into the organisation of production: it suggests that metalworkers who cast flat axes also cast certain other kinds of tools and ornaments. However, similarities in the ways that different metal objects were produced do not seem to correspond neatly to patterns in the treatment of these objects at the end of their use-lives. In Britain, axes were usually deposited in hoards or as single objects in the landscape, whereas knives and daggers are mainly found in burials (Needham 1988). In Ireland, axes and daggers were treated in similar ways: they were predominantly deposited as single finds and in hoards, although some daggers were also placed in graves (Becker 2013). However, these two categories of object are rarely associated with each other; the hoard from Killaha East (Co. Cork), which contained four axes, a dagger, and a halberd (Harbison 1968, 52–3), is one of only a few exceptions. Yet, five axe moulds (all from Britain) have matrices for knives, and at least one (from Ireland) has a dagger matrix. Where matrices for the production of axes and knives are found together, these were often located on the same face of the mould, suggesting that the cultural categorisations that resulted in the differential treatment of these object types at the end of their use-lives did not operate in quite the same way when these objects were being manufactured. It is possible to read this to suggest that practical rather than symbolic concerns dominated the production process but, as we shall see, other evidence indicates that this is a somewhat problematic assumption.

The choice of stone (rather than clay or sand) for casting flat axes may simply reflect the fact that these artefacts were produced serially: axes are by far the most common metal object from the period and a durable, reusable casting medium that facilitated relatively high-volume production may therefore have been desirable. Even so, this is an observation that may be socially significant: it suggests that qualities of similarity, or repeatability, may have been valued over individuality for axes during this period (Jones 2015a, 83–5; though the subsequent addition of decoration could give these standardised objects greater individuality: see below). This has ramifications both for the meaning of the objects themselves and for their users, suggesting that the distribution of 'sibling' axes may have been one way of giving material form to interpersonal relationships. However, the selection of stone for the production of such objects might also embody a conceptual link between axes and this most durable material. Such a link may be suggested by carvings of axeheads on stone slabs forming part of funerary cists at Ri Cruin, Nether Largie, and Kilbride (Argyll & Bute) (Schmidt 1980; RCHMS 2008; Jones 2012; Needham & Cowie 2012). It is possible that these slabs originally formed part of other monuments before being reused in the cists (Jones 2006). The Ri Cruin carvings have been specifically identified as Killaha type axes, one of the types cast in the stone moulds; a halberd was carved on another stone from the cist (Needham & Cowie 2012). Interestingly, the axe carvings show these objects unhafted, perhaps visually referencing axe moulds rather than the finished objects. Jones (2015a, 86) has also commented on the similarities between the axe carvings and contemporary stone moulds arguing that '[t]he axe carvings embody and articulate some of the properties and processes of contemporary metalworking'. Carvings of two daggers and two flat axes have also been identified on a sandstone slab from a barrow at Badbury (Dorset; Piggott 1939); these were actually mistaken for moulds by one 19th century antiquarian. The slab may originally have formed part of a cist although the barrow was destroyed in the 19th century. Symbolic links between axes and standing stones have been suggested in the Neolithic (Tilley 2004, chap. 2), and it is possible that this persisted to the end of the Early Bronze Age, as indicated by the (Arreton-style) axe carvings on the sarsens at Stonehenge (Abbott & Anderson Whymark 2012); two carvings of stone axes or broad-butted flat axes also occur on the stone circle at Boscawen-ûn (Cornwall; Barnatt 1982). It seems possible that as the dangerous transformative power of metalworking came to be appreciated, metalworkers attempted to contain and control this through the use of a material that spoke of permanence and stability; this occurs just as alloying becomes more common and as multiple objects begin to be mixed in novel recycling practices.

The manufacture of one-piece moulds using stone and/or bronze tools would not have been a very lengthy procedure, as easily carvable stone such as sandstone was usually used; this perhaps suggests that the production of moulds was not a specialist activity. Fregni (2014, 138–9) cites an experiment in which a flat axe matrix was carved into a limestone block in five hours using bronze chisels. In some cases the disposition of the matrices suggests that they were added sequentially over time, and there are apparently unfinished matrices on a few of the moulds alongside the finished ones. The mould from Lough Scur (Co. Leitrim) has matrices for two Early Bronze Age flat axes and a Middle Bronze Age palstave, hinting that this object had a lengthy use life (Coghlan & Raftery 1961, 225). Some moulds also bear grooves or smoothed areas suggesting that they were used for grinding or honing metal artefacts, perhaps the objects cast in the moulds (Britton 1963; Ó Maoldúin 2014). Commenting on the mould from Doonour (Co. Cork), O'Kelly (1969) observed that the smoothed areas ran up to but respected the matrices, suggesting that the grinding occurred after the matrices had been carved but while they were still in use. Thus manufacture of these moulds was not a distinct stage preceding their use; rather they continued to develop through their life histories. Occasionally, there is evidence that moulds were made from stones that had previously been used for different purposes. It has been suggested that the mould from East Cruchie (Aberdeenshire) was made from a reused quernstone: the axe matrix was cut into a surface that had been pecked and smoothed by previous use (Cowie & O'Connor 2009, 317).

We have little insight into the possible mobility of the moulds and the metalworkers that used them. However, the moulds are generally made of locally available stone, usually sandstone or grit. A pilot study of ten Scottish moulds by Fiona McGibbon (pers. comm.) suggests that most could have been made of stone from the immediate vicinity of the findspot, and the same appears to have been the case in other regions: the mould from Ballyglisheen (Co. Carlow), for example, was manufactured from local millstone grit (Prendergast 1958). While some moulds have several matrices crammed onto fairly small, well-squared blocks, in comparison to later bivalve moulds they tend to have more bulk than is strictly necessary (Schmidt & Burgess 1981, 52). A few show no regard at all for portability, for example that from East Cruchie (Aberdeenshire), which has a single axe matrix on a boulder weighing 17.6 kg (Cowie & O'Connor 2009, 317). This particular object seems unlikely to have been part of the baggage of a 'wandering smith'. The careful dressing of some of these artefacts, for example the mould from the Walleybourne Brook, Longden Common (Shropshire; Thomas 1972), suggests an attention to aesthetics. The casting matrices themselves are often carefully arranged so that they share their orientation with other matrices on the same surface and with the edges of the mould itself: the mould from Foudland, Insch (Aberdeenshire; Callander 1904, figs 1–2), provides one such example.

Many of the moulds show blackening, metal traces, or thermal spalling to the matrices, demonstrating that they had been used. There have been claims that specific axes can in some cases be traced back to particular moulds. For Scotland, Coles (1971) suggests that 49 axes may derive from as few as five known moulds, and that in some cases mould and axe were separated by considerable distances (see also Jones 2012). Similarly, for Ireland Flanagan (1979) argues that multiple sibling axes can be identified for some known moulds and that moulds and their products ended up at opposite extremes of the island. However, such claims of refits between moulds and axes should be treated with caution, given the extensive smithing work required to turn a cast 'blank' into a finished axe, and the potential for further changes in the blade profile through the use and resharpening of the axe (Schmidt & Burgess 1981, 52–3).

All but two of the known moulds were deposited in a complete or near-complete condition, though some have damage to their matrices which would have rendered them unusable. The loss of a large flake from the edge of an axe mould from Glenhead Farm, Carron Bridge, near Denny (Stirling), for example, would have resulted in a matrix that was too shallow to allow effective casting (Cowie & O'Connor 2009, 319–20). The fresh condition of this mould suggests that this damage may have occurred during manufacture and that the object was never used. In contrast, a large portion of the mould from Easter Clunie, Abernethy (Perth & Kinross), is missing, so that four of its six matrices are incomplete (*ibid.*, 317–9); this is likely to have happened at a later point in the lifecycle of the mould. Evidence for the spatial context of deposition of the moulds is patchy, as many of them are old finds with no detailed findspot information. However, where the location is known, very few are from the vicinity of

known Early Bronze Age sites, monuments, or artefact finds. Despite the concentration of both moulds and contemporary metalwork in north-east Scotland, Needham (2004) suggests that at a local level they largely avoid each other. Most moulds are single finds, although there are three cases in which two moulds were found in the same locality (or have at least been ascribed the same provenance); two moulds from Mains of Corsegight, New Deer (Aberdeenshire), were found in the same field, although it is not clear whether they were actually deposited together (Cowie & O'Connor 2009).

The distribution of these objects therefore need not indicate locations of production and, as we shall see, many of them may rather have been deliberately deposited at selected points in the landscape. One case where we may have a plausible context of production is the Culbin Sands (Moray). Here one complete flat axe mould and a fragment of another (Black 1891) were recovered from an area of coastal sand dunes that was probably a peninsula during the Early Bronze Age (Bradley *et al.* 2016). The dunes have produced numerous Early Bronze Age finds including flat axes, a halberd, large quantities of lithics including debitage and numerous finished and unfinished barbed and tanged arrowheads, faience beads, and at least three cremation burials. Intensive lithic working is implied, which included reworking of Arran pitchstone (from 240 km away) and flint believed to be from Yorkshire (*c.* 550 km away). Faience production on the sands is strongly suspected based on slag finds and would have used beach sand, seaweed, or coastal plant ash, and copper or bronze as a colourant (Sheridan & Shortland 2004). The faience production may not, however, be directly contemporary with the axe moulds as British faience is argued to commence in the 19th century BC (*ibid.*), around the time that stone flat axe moulds seem to have gone out of use. There is also a Middle Bronze Age mould from the Sands hinting that this locality had a long-term association with metalworking and other crafts. The Culbin Sands may have been one of a number of coastal or estuarine beach sites in northern Britain and Ireland used as foci for production and maritime contacts during this period, perhaps associated with periodic or seasonal gatherings (Bradley *et al.* 2016). The liminality of this location – between land and sea, and at the interface between communities – may have made it an appropriate location for transformative activities such as metalworking. At the same time, the proximity of different crafts, at least some of which (such as lithic production) may not have been considered high-status, raises interesting questions regarding the relationship between metalworking and other activities; if casting took place at the Culbin Sands this was not a secluded occupation nor was it spatially segregated from other crafts.

Two further moulds have possible associations with monuments. That from Burgh Muir (Aberdeenshire) was reportedly found in a cairn, though there are no further details (Society of Antiquaries of Scotland 1855). This could refer to an Early Bronze Age funerary mound but, equally, the mould could have been incorporated into a later structure. The mould from Quarrywood (Moray) comes from the interior of an enclosure previously identified as a henge (Schmidt & Burgess 1981, 54). Recent excavations have suggested that the enclosure dates to the later Bronze Age but geophysical survey has identified a possible stone circle in the interior (Gordon 2012). This might provide a contemporary context for the mould; indeed, broad similarities in the distribution of one-piece moulds and recumbent stone circles have been noted in north-east Scotland (Needham 2004, 236).

The Quarrywood site lies on a south-facing hill crest overlooking the Lossie river valley. Several other moulds have comparable topographic locations on the crest of steep river valley slopes, as at Glenhead Farm near Carron Bridge (Stirling; Cowie & O'Connor 2009), Bwlch y Maen (Conwy; Williams 1924), New Mills (Powys; Green 1985), and Barf End, Gunnerside (North Yorkshire; Johnson 2014), with the caveat that the last of these was found reused in a dry stone wall. These locations were visible but perhaps peripheral to settlement. The moulds from Lyre (Co. Cork; O'Kelly 1975) and Mains of Corseight (Aberdeenshire; Inglis & Inglis 1983; Cowie & O'Connor 2009; Fitzpatrick 2015a) were found on gently sloping ground not far from streams. Two other moulds have watery contexts. That from Strathconon (Highland) was found in a peat bog in a remote glen (Britton 1963, 324; Schmidt & Burgess 1981, 54; though whether this was a bog in the Early Bronze Age is not known), while another comes from the bed of

the Walleybourne Brook (Shropshire), at a point where it passes through 'a miniature gorge' (Thomas 1972, 161). The mould from Doonour (Co. Cork; O'Kelly 1969) was found less than 150 m from the present shore line, while a mould from the Scottish Borders is described as either from Rubers Law or the Dunion – both prominent hills surmounted by later hillforts (Cowie & O'Connor 2009, 321–2).

Moulds have therefore been found in a range of topographical locations, but with the exception of Culbin Sands there is no clear evidence for an association with contemporary occupation or metal finds, and those associated with steep scarps or watery contexts seem unlikely to derive from settlements. It can be suggested that many mould finds may not represent actual locations of metalworking, but rather locations of deposition at selected points in the landscape. This mirrors the deposition of flat axes and other contemporary metalwork at significant, often visually striking places in the landscape, in bogs or streams, and overlooking bodies of water (Needham 1988; Cowie 2004; Becker 2013; cf. Yates & Bradley 2010a).

It should nonetheless be noted that moulds and metalwork were never deposited together and almost never in close proximity to each other (Needham 2004, 238). The deposition of moulds in such locations could suggest that the process of casting metal objects was not solely viewed in functional terms but was socially meaningful and ritualised. Many of these objects could have been reused but they were not; instead they were deposited in places which may have had a particular resonance in Bronze Age cosmographies. At least some of these (for example the mould from the bog at Strathconon) may have been deposited at a distance from contemporary settlement, hinting that access to metalworking-related objects (and perhaps knowledge of metalworking itself) was restricted. Alternatively, its transformative potential may have rendered it a socially hazardous occupation, the residues of which had to be disposed of in liminal spaces at a distance from the world of everyday activities. This interpretation, however, runs the risk of imposing contemporary views of places such as bogs onto the past. In fact, several moulds with a known provenance were found in locations that are likely to have formed part of the settled landscape, such as hillslopes overlooking streams: the moulds from East

Cruchie (Aberdeenshire; Cowie & O'Connor 2009, 317) and Easter Clunie (Perth & Kinross; Cowie & O'Connor 2009, 317–19), for example, were both found on gently-sloping farmland. Whatever the case, the deposition of moulds indicates that metalworking was not figured solely in terms of 'status' but evoked a range of other cultural values. Certainly, the fact that these objects were deposited as single finds speaks of small-scale rituals enacted without particular ostentation.

Smithing

Many of the most impressive metal objects of this period are made of sheet metal and would have been formed by smithing rather than casting. The skill required to, for example, shape out a lunula from a single gold ingot and then finely decorate it would have been much greater than that needed for casting an axe blank. This has raised questions regarding the possible existence of specialist metalworkers from the early part of the Bronze Age (Taylor 1980, 46–7). The blanks for flat axes and other objects cast in simple one-piece stone moulds would also have required extensive smithing work to produce the finished artefact. Elaborate engraved or punched decoration was added to some bronze flat axes, and a few were also 'tinned' to achieve a silvery finish, possibly through annealing in a reducing, cassiterite-rich hearth environment (Meeks 1986). This suggests that the aesthetic properties of early metal objects were often as important as their functionality. It has been argued that the colour of different materials including metals may have had symbolic significance during this period (Jones 2002; Woodward 2000, chap. 5). Needham (2004, 253), for example, suggests that the colour of tin may have symbolically referenced the moon: he notes the geographical congruence of early tin-bronze objects in north-east Scotland with recumbent stone circles and Clava cairns; these are monuments with astronomical orientations that suggest an interest in the lunar cycle (Bradley 2005a). The motivation to add tin to copper may therefore not have been solely technical. He argues that 'the use of the new alloy was at times flaunted by the application of a coating of precious tin' (*ibid.*, 235), although the precise relationship between metal, status and 'value' during this period remains unclear.

The act of decorating metal artefacts may have been significant in the biographies of these objects. Flat axes cast from a given mould would have been near-identical, but applying varied decorative patterns to some of them gave them a distinct identity or personality (Jones 2012). Possessing decoration may then have influenced the subsequent life course of the object. Decorated axes often seem to have been selected for deposition in striking locations (Cowie 1988; 2004), and in Ireland the ratio of decorated to undecorated axes is higher in hoards than among single finds (Ó Maoldúin 2014). Notably, in some cases decoration appears to have been added to axes after they had been used and become worn (Moyler 2007; 2008). This suggests that decoration could be used to mark significant events in the history of these objects and their users. As with the stone moulds used to cast them, these axes may never have been regarded as 'finished'; rather they could be engaged with and altered throughout their use lives. Interestingly, decorated axes are especially common towards the end of the Early Bronze Age. If decoration can be considered to indicate the social significance of an object (Braithwaite 1982), this suggests that the role of axes and those who used them may have become an issue of particular concern at this time; this may have had an impact also on the role of the smith or of smithing as practice. It is worth considering whether the skills required to decorate an axe might have been a source of admiration and wonder to others, although the extent to which the decorated axes were themselves always visible remains unclear: the decorated axe from Brockagh (Co. Kildare) was found unhafted in a leather sheath that would have hidden it from onlookers (Rynne 1963). In other cultural contexts, decorating an object is considered a magical act that imbues that item with agency (Gell 1998), and it may have been the potency of the Brockagh axe that meant it needed to be shielded in this way. This, of course, has implications for the perceived power of the metalworker in Early Bronze Age society.

The finished items indicate that a wide range of techniques for shaping, hardening and decorating metal objects had been developed by the Early Bronze Age. These included hammering, grinding, polishing, tracing, repoussé work with punches, perforation by punch, drilling, riveting, use of mandrels, work hardening, and annealing (Britton 1963). Despite this, only a few stone smithing tools have been identified (see Chapter 2), the most convincing being the 'cushion stones' particularly associated with the Beaker period. In general, stone tools that may have been used for smithing show a lack of standardisation, and where they have been provenanced, their source is not usually very distant (Drenth *et al.* 2013). This calls into question Childe's model of a distinct and specialist caste of full-time itinerant metalworkers. Nonetheless, cushion stones are finely worked objects that would have taken a substantial investment of time and effort to produce (around 80 hours in a replication experiment cited by Drenth *et al.* 2009).

Few recognisable smithing tools have been found in stratified contexts, and most of these are from burials (discussed below). No unequivocal examples have been found in settlement contexts in Britain or Ireland. At **Rainham** (Greater London), one of a group of Beaker pits contained a fragment of a rectangular siltstone object with smooth faces. This resembles a cushion stone but would be unusually small at only *c.* 2 cm thick. At **Newgrange** (Co. Meath), Beaker-period activity has been found adjacent to the Middle Neolithic passage grave, with occupation floors, hearths, and large quantities of artefacts. Near one hearth were found three stone tools suggested to be metalworking implements. These include a possible cushion stone, a 'hammer-like object' of quartzite, and an oval rubbing stone. It is entirely plausible that these could have been used in metalworking, though there is nothing to prove that they were. A putative 'anvil' stone and a bronze flat axe were found elsewhere on the site. While the Beaker activity at Newgrange was originally considered to be unproblematically domestic in nature, this is questionable on account of its association with the earlier passage grave and the presence of broadly contemporary pit- and post-circle monuments that can be interpreted as ceremonial spaces elsewhere on the site (Mount 1994; Carlin & Brück 2012). If the finds from Newgrange do indicate metalworking, then this was being carried out in the context of ceremonial activities at a site of longstanding ritual significance. The performance of metalworking at a location where other kinds of transformative, ritualised activities took place is perhaps significant, suggesting that the working of metals may also have been viewed as a magical process.

On the near Continent too, clear 'domestic' contexts for smithing tools are hard to find. In northern France cushion stones are known only as uncontexted finds (Boutoille 2015a). Further north, at Hengelo-Elderinkweg (Overijssel, Netherlands), an isolated pit contained two cushion stones and a grinding stone, each of which had traces of copper and gold. These formed part of a 'hoard' of stone objects including hammerstones, possible whetstones, two arrowshaft smoothers, and an axe. The pit cut another feature radiocarbon dated to 2290–2030 cal BC (3755±40 BP; UA-36482; Drenth *et al.* 2009; Drenth & Williams 2011). Another possible stone tool 'hoard' was found beneath a small boulder at Soesterberg (Utrecht, Netherlands). This contained a cushion stone, two hammerstones, two boars' tusks and a stone bracer (Drenth *et al.* 2013). The deposition of possible 'sets' of metalworking tools as 'hoards' is interesting, for it suggests that in certain contexts it may have been considered necessary to ritually decommission these objects, perhaps as the identities of their owners were transformed at particular stages in the lifecourse (cf. Fontijn 2005).

Metalworkers' burials?

A few Beaker burials from Britain contain stone tools that may have been used in metalworking. The most famous example is the so-called **Amesbury Archer**, a 35–45 year old man with a disability to one leg, buried near Stonehenge (Wiltshire) in the 24th or 23rd century BC (Fig. 3.4). A probable cushion stone had been placed behind his back (Fig. 2.15, above). This formed part of a lavish grave assemblage, including five beakers, a pair of gold ornaments, numerous flint arrowheads and other flintwork, three copper knives, and iron pyrites for fire making. Also possibly used in smithing were four boars' tusks that may have been employed for burnishing metals (Fitzpatrick 2011, 222): boars' tusks are often associated with metalworking tools in Continental graves (Moucha 1989; Bertemes & Heyd 2002, 217), and analysis of an example from a burial in the Czech Republic showed copper and silver traces (Peška 2016). The presence of early metal objects alongside items that may have been metalworking tools

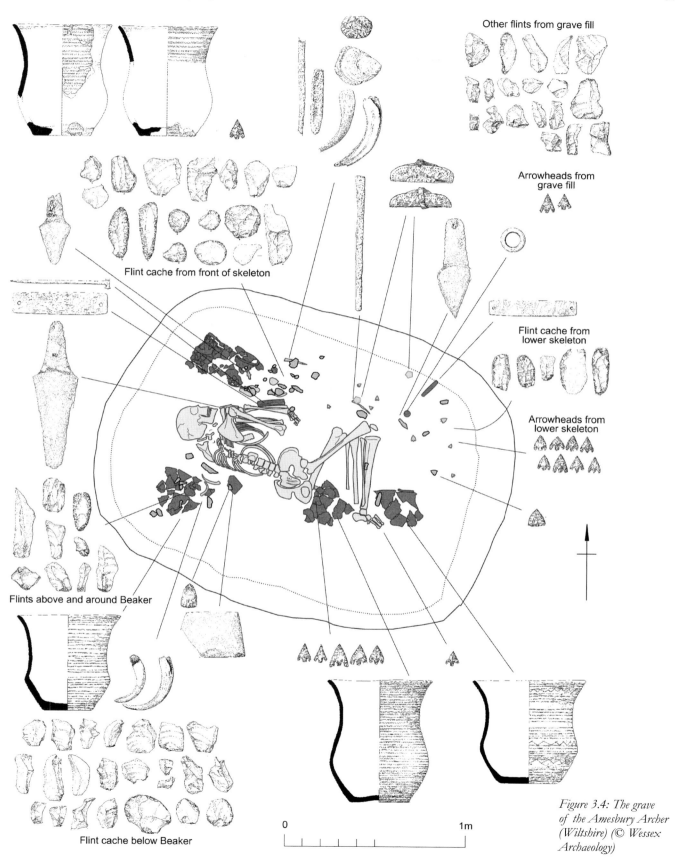

Other flints from grave fill

Arrowheads from grave fill

Flint cache from front of skeleton

Flint cache from lower skeleton

Arrowheads from lower skeleton

Flints above and around Beaker

Flint cache below Beaker

0   1m

Figure 3.4: The grave of the Amesbury Archer (Wiltshire) (© Wessex Archaeology)

has been used to suggest that this man was a smith. Isotopic analysis suggests that he had spent his early life overseas, perhaps in the Alpine region (Chenery & Evans 2011), and it has been suggested that he was accorded a special status in death because he had brought esoteric knowledge of metalworking from the Continent. As such, the find has been taken to support the supposed link between metals, wealth, and status (Fitzpatrick 2009; 2011; Sheridan 2012). It should be noted, however, that the cushion stone is made of lydite, a type of chert that would have been available 20–30 km away in north Wiltshire. Despite his 'foreign' origins, then, the cushion stone may have been a relatively local object, though whether it was brought to the Stonehenge area by an 'itinerant metalworker' or via local exchange networks is unknown.

Needham (2011a) has recently reviewed the evidence for other possible metalworking tools made of stone of similar date. There are few from excavated contexts, although similar polished stone tools from other Beaker burials may have been used in metalworking (Clarke 1970, 573–4). For example, a rectanguloid fine-grained polisher or hammerstone was found with the primary inhumation burial in Amesbury barrow G54 (Wiltshire): this item appears to have been placed at the feet of the body along with a Beaker pot and a flint dagger (Colt Hoare 1812, 163–4, pl. xvii). An inhumation burial at Winterbourne Monkton (Wiltshire) was accompanied by a greenstone hammerstone, along with two beakers, two jet buttons, a jet ring, and a flint knife (Cunnington & Goddard 1934, 26–9; Annable & Simpson 1964, 38, 89; Clarke 1970, 389, 445, 573–4). A carefully-shaped and semi-polished stone artefact from cairn 1 at **Kirkhaugh** (Northumberland) was originally identified as a cushion stone, but is more likely to be a hammerstone, as evidence for use is concentrated on one of the short edges rather than on its main faces. The cairn also yielded two gold basket-shaped ornaments similar to those interred with the **Amesbury Archer**, a beaker, two jet buttons, several flint arrowheads, a flint fabricator, flakes and cores, and iron pyrites. These artefacts probably originally accompanied a single burial although no human remains survived. The cairn is located on the edge of Alston Moor, a source of copper, lead, and silver during the 18th and

19th centuries, and it has been suggested that the individual buried at Kirkhaugh may have been a prospector. On the near Continent, the best-known example is a barrow burial from Lunteren (Gelderland, Netherlands), which contained two cushion stones, a hammerstone, a whetstone, flint arrowheads, a flint axe, a stone wrist guard, a copper awl, and two beakers. No human remains survived the acidic soil (Butler & van der Waals 1967; Drenth *et al.* 2013). It should be stressed, however, that metal traces have not been identified on the tools from any of these burials. Analysis of the Amesbury Archer's cushion stone, for example, showed no traces of metal (Cowell & Middleton 2011). Likewise, the lack of use-wear on the boars' tusks from the same burial suggests that they are more likely to have served as ornaments than tools (Woodward & Hunter 2015, 143), although they may nonetheless have been conceptually associated with metalworking given the association of such items with metalworking tools in burials on mainland Europe (Moucha 1989; Bertemes & Heyd 2002, 217).

A number of later burials of Early Bronze Age date also contain stone objects that might have been used as metalworking tools. At **Upton Lovell** (Wiltshire), a group of nine stone implements of various forms was found near the feet of the primary inhumation in barrow G2a (though there were difficulties in distinguishing the goods associated with this burial from those of a subsequent interment). These were first interpreted as metalworking tools by Piggott (1973). The most notable of these objects was a slate touchstone bearing gold streaks (Shell 2000). Other stones in the assemblage may have been hammers or anvils (Boutoille 2016). An extraordinary assemblage of other grave goods was also recovered, including boars' tusks, a large number of perforated bone points, a battle axe, flint axes, and four split hollow flint nodules. The boars' tusks and bone points are thought to have formed part of an elaborate costume (Piggott 1973) and a recent study of the latter indicates a strong preference for the use of the left hind leg of sheep/goats (Woodward & Hunter 2015, 105). Together, the unusual features of this burial has led to the identification of this individual as a high-status shaman or metalworker-shaman (Piggott 1962; Shell 2000). If so, the performance of smithing by

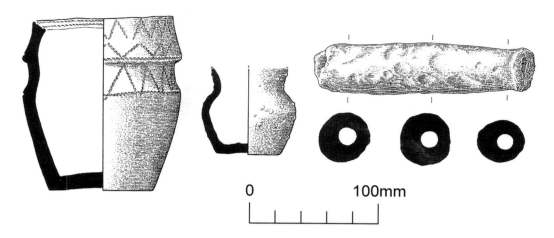

Figure 3.5: The grave goods from the cremation burial at Ewanrigg (Cumbria) (after Bewley et al. 1992, fig. 7)

0   100mm

a ritual specialist is interesting, for it suggests that in this case metalworking was viewed as a magical act, knowledge of which may have been restricted (cf. Herbert 1994). Shamans can traverse the boundary between this world and the next and between different states of being (Price 2011), and it would not be surprising if these abilities were considered essential to metalworking – a transformative and visually-striking act that conveyed life and efficacy to socially significant objects (cf. Gell 1998).

A fine-grained perforated stone with gold traces comparable to that from Upton Lovell has also been found amongst burnt bone contained in a Collared Urn cremation burial at **Arn Hill**, Warminster (Wiltshire); no other grave goods were identified. Of course, the use of touchstones need not necessarily be associated with the *manufacture* of gold artefacts. The Collared Urn cremation burial from Sandmill Farm, Stranraer (Dumfries & Galloway) is of a similar date: this contained two putative cushion stones (albeit made of sandstone) and a whetstone, along with a bronze razor or knife blade, a battle axe, and a bone pin (Anderson 1942; Clarke *et al.* 1985, 295–6), all apparently inside the pot. The battle axe was burnt and broken and appears to have accompanied the body onto the pyre, but it is not clear if this was also the case for the possible metalworking tools. Whetstones are recorded from a number of Early Bronze Age burials in Britain and Ireland (Waddell 1990; Woodward & Hunter 2015, 76–82), but they were presumably mainly for the maintenance of bladed tools and weapons rather than for

metalworking as such. On the near Continent too, a number of Early Bronze Age burials have produced stone implements such as hammerstones and whetstones that were possibly used for metalworking, though this is difficult to prove (eg, Nicolas *et al.* 2015a; 2015b).

Tubular fired clay objects identified as possible bellows components have been recovered from two Collared Urn cremation burials in the north-west of England. Neither is vitrified or has metal traces to support this identification, and a role in other high-temperature crafts – or perhaps even the cremation rite itself – cannot be excluded. At **Ewanrigg** (Cumbria) the burial was one of a number of satellite interments around a natural knoll. A clay tube identified as a rod to connect a bellows and tuyère was deposited beside a Collared Urn, which had been placed on its side (Fig. 3.5). The remains of an adult, possibly male, had been placed in the urn and these were radiocarbon dated to 2290–1750 cal BC (3640±90 BP; HAR-5959). Other grave goods comprised an accessory vessel and a burnt flint fragment, possibly a broken arrowhead. At **Gawsworth** (Cheshire East), a possible tuyère accompanied one of a group of satellite interments around a Beaker barrow. This was deposited with cremated bone and a burnt flint knife under an inverted urn; an accessory vessel was placed next to the urn. The osteological analysis was not conclusive, but it was suggested that it could include the remains of both a male and a female. Comparable tuyères have been found in burials and other contexts elsewhere in Europe (Lachenal *et al.* 2010).

Tools were not the only residues of metalworking deposited in mortuary contexts. Seven pieces of tin slag were found at the base of a ring cairn at **Caerloggas** (Cornwall) in turves laid to create a level surface for the construction of the monument. The barrow also produced a Camerton-Snowshill dagger dating to *c.* 1700–1500 BC, a fragment of amber, and a large number of quartz pebbles and crystals. No human remains were recovered, but it is possible that some, or all, of these objects were originally deposited with a burial. The ring bank itself was composed of yellow clay, a material that has been suggested to have been deliberately employed to reference the sun and its daily cycle (Owoc 2002); this calls to mind the symbolic links between the sun, fire, metalworking, and fertility that have been proposed in other parts of Bronze Age Europe (Goldhahn 2007).

Materials that may have been associated with metals in their unprocessed state have also occasionally been found. Galena crystals – a form of lead ore – have been identified in two Collared Urn cremation burials from the neighbouring sites of **Mosley Height** (1920–1690 cal BC; 3490±40 BP; SUERC-4431) and **Cliviger Laithe** (1880–1680 cal BC; 3455±35; SUERC-4436) (Lancashire). The latter burial contained the remains of 2–5 individuals. Barrowclough has argued that these were the graves of galena miners, the ore being exploited for metallurgical use (Barrowclough nd), but this is questionable given the paucity of evidence for the use of lead at this time. The crystals are more likely to have been collected for other purposes. Galena may have been valued for its attractive shiny appearance (a galena bead comes from the Neolithic chambered tomb at Quanterness (Orkney), for example: Henshall 1979), and it was also historically used to make pigments and cosmetics.

Quartz pebbles or fragments are known from many Early Bronze Age burials, as well as at other contemporary monuments such as stone circles, wedge tombs, and Clava cairns. A cremation burial in a Trevisker urn from Harlyn Bay (Cornwall) contained several quartz pebbles, a small amount of burnt animal bone, and a bronze pendant (Jones *et al.* 2011), while at Mains of Scotstown (Aberdeenshire), a Beaker burial had been placed in a cist with a floor of water-rolled pebbles, many of them quartzites (Ralston 1996, 124–5). At the stone circle at Cothiemuir Wood (Aberdeenshire), pieces of quartz were deposited on the old ground surface directly opposite the recumbent stone (Bradley 2005a). Many of the copper ores exploited in Britain and Ireland during the Bronze Age are associated with quartz deposits, and it has been suggested that quartz may have functioned as an indicator of the presence of copper deposits for early prospectors (Ó Nualláin 1975, 106; but see O'Brien 1994, 223–5). As such, quartz may have been revered as the bearer of metal, even if the pieces placed in burials did not actually come from mining sites. It is evident, however, that quartz was a material of particular symbolic significance long before the Bronze Age, for it is also found at many Neolithic monuments (eg, Lynch 1998; Cooney 2000, 176–8; Darvill 2002), and even in the Early Bronze Age it may have been valued for quite different reasons: the astronomical alignments of many recumbent stone circles in Scotland suggest an interest in the lunar cycle, and the frequent presence at these sites of quartz – a shiny, white stone – suggests that it may have been conceptually linked to the moon (Bradley 2005a).

For the Chalcolithic and Early Bronze Age of Britain and Ireland, then, there are few burials containing objects unambiguously linked to metalworking. Those items of probable metalworking equipment that do occur were mostly associated with smithing, specifically the shaping and finishing of fine objects of gold, copper, or bronze in the case of the cushion stones, while touchstones may have been used for testing the quality of gold. Objects directly involved in the casting process, such as moulds and crucibles, were not considered appropriate grave goods. This was not the case in all parts of Europe. Some Beaker and Early Bronze Age burials with moulds are known from central Europe, and in the North Pontic region there are burials from the 3rd millennium BC with extensive sets of metalworking equipment including moulds, crucibles, tuyères, hammers, and/or anvils (Bátora 2002; 2013; Nessel 2012; Martin 2014). In contrast to these Continental 'smith's graves', in Britain metalworking tools tend to form only a minor part of the grave assemblage. In the case of the **Amesbury Archer**, for example, the putative metalworking tools are far outnumbered by objects that reference other activities, such as warfare and/

or hunting, drinking, fire making, and flint working (Barber 2003). There is thus little sense that metalworkers were singled out in death as a discrete category of person, and there is considerable variability in the grave assemblages of which possible metalworking equipment formed a component.

Even if we accept that the stone tools discussed above were employed as metalworking implements (and in most cases that is not at all certain), it is simplistic to directly read off the identity of individuals from their associated grave goods, or to assume that everyone buried with a metalworking tool was involved in this craft. As Barber (2003, 128) puts it, the cushion stone buried with the Amesbury Archer 'no more makes him a metalworker than the Beakers make him a potter, the tools and flints make him a flint knapper, or indeed the arrows and wristguards make him an archer'. Although there is a tendency to assume that the grave goods accompanying the archer belonged to him during life (eg, Sheridan 2012, 44), this may not have been the case. Instead, they may have been used to create an idealised image of the deceased which may not have corresponded to the reality of his life. Fokkens (2012) argues that Beaker burial assemblages often contain a standardised selection of objects that represent a constructed ancestral identity and were not a representative collection of the possessions of the deceased. It is possible that the symbolism surrounding metalworking could have been appropriated by or ascribed to individuals not actually involved in this craft, as in some recent African societies where blacksmiths' tools form part of the regalia of chiefs (Herbert 1994). Thus Turek (2004) suggests that metalworking tools in Beaker period graves were symbols of a particular status more than an actual craftworker's toolkit. While many people may have been involved in smithing, only some may have had the right to be buried with the relevant tools.

The assumed link between particular types of object and status is nonetheless problematic, for the communication of social rank is not the sole concern of mortuary rites (Tarlow 1992). Objects perform a variety of roles in mortuary practices (Brück 2004; 2019; Fowler 2013). The items deposited in the grave may have been gifts from the mourners, signifying aspects of the relationship between the living and the dead: the Beakers, for instance, may have referenced the commensal ties between the archer and particular groups of kinsfolk or neighbours. Other objects, such as flint flakes and scrapers, may have been used during the mortuary rite (Barrett 1994, 116–18). The properties of particular artefacts may have been employed to comment symbolically on the circumstances or the impact of death – the flint knives or copper daggers, for example, perhaps speaking of the cutting of ties (Fowler 2005, 125). It is, in other words, problematic to assume that the cushion stone was owned and used by this man during life. Instead it could have been employed to prepare small quantities of substances of various sorts that might have been used (or ingested) as part of the mortuary rite, or if this was indeed a goldworking tool, to decommission one of the gold basket-shaped ornaments: this object had been carefully folded using a fine punch-like tool along the bottom of the 'basket' (Needham 2011b, 137). Alternatively, if we accept the cushion stone as an object used in smithing, the metaphors of 'working' or 'finishing' might have been usefully employed to comment on the productive life of a mature adult member of the community. More generally, the deposition of an object associated with the transformative act of metalworking may have functioned to symbolise the transition between life and death. It is interesting to note that one corner of the cushion stone was missing: it has often been suggested that the inclusion of broken objects in Early Bronze Age graves was a means of symbolising the social impact of death (Ashbee 1960, 96, 103; Woodward 2000, 107), though we might also note the similarities between this 'imperfect' object and the man himself who, missing a patella, would have walked with a noticeable limp (McKinley 2011).

If, on the other hand, we accept that the cushion stone belonged to the archer, and that he was indeed a metalworker, this raises questions regarding the status of smiths in Chalcolithic and Early Bronze Age societies. The examples of the **Amesbury Archer**, **Kirkhaugh**, and **Upton Lovell**, in which probable metalworking tools formed part of large assemblages of grave goods including goldwork, have encouraged an image of metalworkers as high-status individuals drawing power from their esoteric knowledge (eg, Shell 2000; Fitzpatrick 2011). Similar inferences have often been drawn from richly outfitted 'smith's graves' elsewhere in Europe (eg, Bertemes 2004; Brandherm 2009; Peška 2016). However, interpreting the social position of metalworkers from the burial evidence is not straightforward. Such readings of the evidence rely on two main assumptions: firstly that the quantity of grave goods is a direct reflection of wealth and status, and secondly that items such as gold ornaments are indisputable indicators of rank (cf. Brück 2004; 2019). Both of these assumptions are problematic, however, for the relationship between people and objects varies cross-culturally as indeed does the value ascribed to particular materials, including gold (eg, Saunders 2002). We can suggest that the Amesbury Archer was well-connected, for many people may have contributed to his grave assemblage; social connections and social status are not quite the same thing, however, though they are often linked. Alternatively, it is possible that the death of the archer provoked unusual concerns or anxieties, so that his identity and relationships with others required particularly careful definition (Thomas 1991). Such apparently 'wealthy' grave assemblages are, of course, not the only burials in which metalworking equipment occurs. As we have seen, there are other cases where probable metalworking tools occur in grave good assemblages that are otherwise fairly unexceptional, such as **Arn Hill**, Warminster (Wiltshire), or **Ewanrigg** (Cumbria). The burial from Ewanrigg, however, contained a tuyère – an item that would have evoked the working of a bellows. Such a task might have been allocated to an apprentice or assistant, so might indeed have been considered lower status than other aspects of metalworking such as casting or fine smithing.

Another inference that has been drawn from the burial evidence is that metalworkers were men (eg, Drenth & Williams 2011, 107). Of the burials discussed above, however, only three have been subject to modern osteological analysis: the **Amesbury Archer** (McKinley 2011), the cremation burial from Ewanrigg (identified as possibly male: Bewley *et al.* 1992), and the **Gawsworth** 'tuyère' burial which appears to have contained two individuals, possibly male and female (Rowley 1977). Nonetheless, both in Britain and on the Continent putative metalworking tools often occur in graves with weaponry and other objects that are conventionally associated

with men: examples from Britain include the flint dagger from **Amesbury G54** (Wiltshire; Colt Hoare 1812, 163) and the battle-axe from Sandmill Farm, Stranraer (Dumfries & Galloway; Anderson 1942), although the amber fragment from **Caerloggas** (Cornwall) could equally suggest the presence of a woman. Our understanding of the gendering of particular artefacts is, however, dependent in part on the assumptions of early excavators who frequently sexed burials on the basis of grave goods alone (Woodward & Hunter 2015, 518). On the Continent, a recently discovered Early Bronze Age burial of a woman aged 45–60 years at Geitzendorf (Niederösterreich) in Austria contained four stone tools argued to be associated with metalworking (Lauermann & Pany-Kucera 2013). An Early Bronze Age burial from Erfurt-Gispersleben (Thüringen) in Germany containing two tuyères has been identified as female, though it is not clear whether this is based on osteology or on the fact that the grave also contained a loomweight (Müller 1982). We need not follow Nessel's argument (2012) that this was a metalworker's daughter rather than a metalworker. The burials with metalworking equipment from the North Pontic region include a young woman aged 18–20 years and a boy of 12–13 years (Bátora 2002). Such exceptions may undermine the traditional image of the prehistoric metalworker, although we should recall here the argument above that grave goods need not necessarily reflect the social identity of the deceased.

Perhaps the best reading of the burial evidence is that in certain contexts, the ideals, values and associations conjured by metalworking – especially fine smithing work – could be usefully employed to comment on the lives of particular people, their relationships with others, the circumstances of their deaths, and their expectations of the afterlife. Whether the presence of possible metalworking equipment in graves indicates particular kinds of elevated male identities, and whether such idealised great men were representative of those actually involved in metalworking, is another matter.

Founders' hoards?

The argument that at least some prehistoric metalwork hoards represent the buried stock of metalworkers – either their finished products or scrap for recycling – goes back to the later

19th century (see Chapter 1). Such 'founders' hoards' are thought to have been buried for safekeeping in times of crisis or cached by itinerant smiths at strategic points along their routes of travel. Although most common in the Late Bronze Age, particularly in southeast England, this interpretation has also been applied to Irish Early Bronze Age hoards containing copper ingots (Bremer 1926; Herity & Eogan 1977, 122). Four hoards in the southern half of Ireland contain roughly circular ingots or ingot fragments along with one or more copper or bronze axes (O'Flaherty 1995). Analysis indicates that at least some of these ingots derive from Ross Island ore (Northover 2004). In Britain, a hoard from Morecambe Bay (Lancashire) contained three pieces of copper 'cake' and possible casting waste along with a tanged copper dagger of Chalcolithic date (PAS: LANCUM-3BEC10). Hoards containing damaged or broken metal objects have also been seen as scrap intended for recycling. Thus the hoard from the Maidens on the South Ayrshire coast, containing five worn and broken Migdale axes and a broken armlet, has been suggested to have belonged to 'an Irish smith who, having collected his quota of scrap, was awaiting ship back to Ireland' (Stewart 1955, 10).

Today there is scepticism over such interpretations, for they impose the kinds of economic rationalism more characteristic of contemporary society onto the past. It seems likely that most hoards of this period were buried with no intention of recovery (Bradley 1998). The contents of some hoards show careful arrangement, and striking locations were often chosen for their deposition (Needham 1988; Cowie 2004; Bradley *et al.* 2018). This includes some of the supposed 'founders' hoards'. At Carrickshedge (Co. Wexford) a hoard containing two or three ingots and four copper axes was placed on a rock shelf in a cave near a spring (Bremer 1926; Flanagan 1998, pl. 6), while the hoard from the Maidens was deposited in a crevice in a prominent rocky spur overlooking the sea (Coles 1971, 103). At **Toormore** (Co. Cork), a decorated bronze axe was carefully laid against the inner side of a large stone slab at the entrance to a wedge tomb (Fig. 3.6). Beneath the butt of the axe were two small copper ingots, one placed on top of the other. This deposit is likely to have been made during the main period of the use of this Early Bronze Age monument. Entry to this sacred space may have been restricted, and the hoard can be interpreted as a deliberate act to mark the point of transition from outside to inside the monument. The choice of copper ingots is interesting, for these referenced metalworking: the deposition of these items in such a liminal context – at the entrance to a location where the dead were encountered and transformed – hints that metalworking may have been viewed as a transformative, magical and dangerous activity (O'Brien 1999, 215). The combination of objects is equally intriguing: the axe blade is asymmetrically worn, indicating a long history of use, but the copper ingots had not yet been cast into artefacts. As such, the hoard brought together the new and the old – objects with quite different origins and histories that spoke of beginnings and endings, and of death and regeneration; it is not hard to see why such items might have been deliberately deposited in this monumental setting.

Of course, if hoards of used or broken objects were simply random accumulations of scrap for melting down, then we should expect a fairly representative range of metal artefacts of the period to be present. This is not the case, as some object types such as axes were recurringly selected for deposition in hoards while others were more often placed in contexts such as graves (Needham 1988). Although the wear on many of the axes deposited in Chalcolithic and Early Bronze Age hoards was the result of long use-lives (Moyler 2007), others were evidently deliberately broken. This need not have been in preparation for recycling, however: many axes were deliberately snapped in two across the middle in a manner that can just as plausibly be explained as an act of ritual decommissioning (Coles 1971). The presence in some hoards of both halves suggests that the destruction of these objects often happened immediately prior to deposition (Jones 2015a, 84).

The degree of wear to both complete and broken axes in individual hoards can vary dramatically. The hoard from the Hill of Finglenny (Aberdeenshire), for example, comprised seven axes, three of which had been snapped in half (Moyler 2007, section 6.3.10). The two axes with the most asymmetrical blades (and which had therefore had demonstrably lengthy use-lives) had been resharpened shortly

Figure 3.6: The hoard from the wedge tomb at Toormore (Co. Cork) (plan redrawn by Kostas Trimmis after O'Brien 1990, figs 73 & 76; artefact drawings courtesy of Angela Gallagher & William O'Brien)

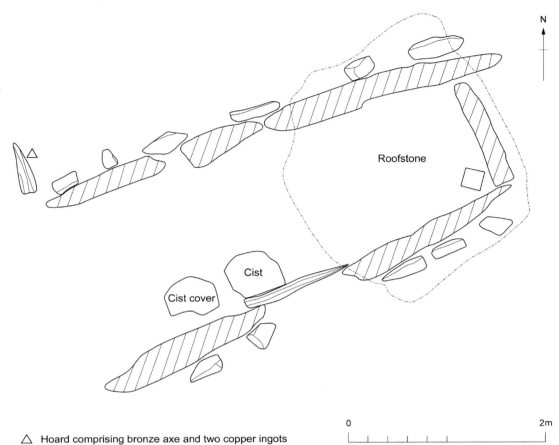

△ Hoard comprising bronze axe and two copper ingots

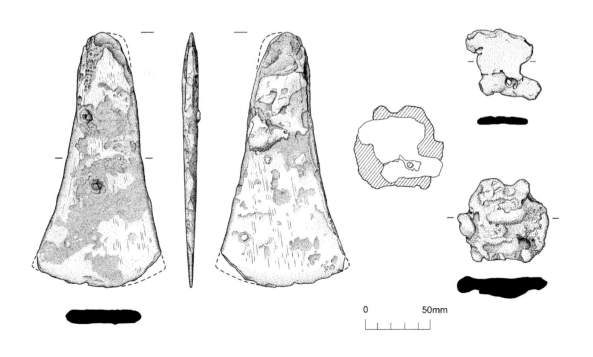

before deposition; these were clearly still considered usable objects. Another had been in use for a much shorter period of time but its edge was blunt. Both halves of the two broken axes were present but the blade and butt ends of these objects appear to have had different histories, with the broken edges of the axe butts in a much fresher condition than those of their matching blade fragments. As such, hoards containing broken bronze objects can be viewed not as caches of scrap metal for recycling, but as assemblages of objects with known and significant histories, brought together for deposition at special places in the landscape. It is nonetheless possible that practices such as the inclusion of ingots in hoards or the deliberate breakage of metal objects metaphorically referenced the metalworking process. The interpretation of scrap hoards and their relationship to metalworking will be discussed in more detail in relation to the later Bronze Age (Chapter 4).

Conclusion: the social organisation of non-ferrous metalworking in Chalcolithic and Early Bronze Age Britain and Ireland

Overall, the evidence presented here does not concur with the vision of Chalcolithic and Early Bronze Age metalworking as an 'industry'. Casting and smithing evidence is rare and certain types of artefact, notably crucibles, are as yet unknown during this period. The lack of evidence may simply reflect the sparse and ephemeral nature of the Chalcolithic and Early Bronze Age settlement record (Brück 1999c) and the difficulties in recognising metalworking tools from this period. However, it is also likely that the deposition of metalworking tools was deliberately separated from the domestic sphere. Early Bronze Age stone moulds are found away from known settlements and monuments and were instead almost always deposited as single finds. This pattern must be taken as a product of depositional practice and need not reflect the actual location of metalworking. Hence, although some moulds have been found in relatively inaccessible places in the landscape, this need not indicate restricted access to the practice or knowledge of metalworking itself. Patterns of selective deposition indicate that metalworking was

not viewed solely in practical terms. The ritual deposition of moulds at specific locations in the landscape suggests that metalworking and its residues had particular social and cultural resonance: objects that had been involved in the creation of particular social categories required careful decommissioning.

Metalworking residues are occasionally found in settlement contexts, suggesting that casting and smithing was (at least sometimes) carried out in domestic settings, even if moulds and smithing tools were then deliberately deposited elsewhere. Here, we can concur with Brodie's argument that metalworking was sometimes practised as a 'domestic' craft (Brodie 1997, 304), although this need not imply that it was a low-status activity or that it had no particular social significance. The association between Beakers and early metalworking posited on the basis of grave finds appears to be confirmed by the settlement evidence: all of the possible domestic contexts described in this chapter have produced Beaker pottery. Stone moulds of the period are found off-site rather than in settlement contexts; the size and weight of many of these suggest that some metalworkers were not itinerant or at least remained in one place of work for a significant time. Together, the evidence both from excavated settlements and from off-site deposits suggests that metalworking was a small-scale, sporadic and – for certain types of artefact at least – non-specialist activity.

Although there is little to indicate that the production of objects such as axes involved restricted access to knowledge, this may not have been the case for every type of metalwork: the extraordinary quality of Wessex goldwork, for example, has long been taken to indicate the existence of specialist goldsmiths. Unlike moulds, smithing tools that could have been used in such delicate work were sometimes deposited in graves. Some were accompanied by sizeable assemblages of other grave goods, such as gold ornaments and copper knives, and this has been taken to indicate that metalworkers were high-status members of the community. As we have seen above, however, this view depends on a very particular interpretation of the grave goods which sees them, firstly, as possessions of the deceased and, secondly, as primarily indicative of wealth and status. It also assumes that metals were inherently desirable, and that they were valued more highly than the other objects and materials in a grave. As we have discussed, there are a number of problems with this view, not least of which is the lack of microscopic traces of metal on the **Amesbury Archer**'s cushion stone, and the fact that other burials containing possible metalworking tools were not so well equipped. It is equally plausible to suggest that objects such as cushion stones were placed in the grave not to indicate the occupation and status of the deceased, but to convey other ideas relating to the 'finishing' or transformation of identity both for the living and the dead.

The presence of a slate touchstone and other possible metalworking tools in the 'shaman' grave at **Upton Lovell** is particularly interesting, however, for if we accept the view that these were the possessions of the deceased, they suggest that smithing was – in certain circumstances at least – viewed as a magical transformative activity carried out by those who held other kinds of specialist knowledge; specialist knowledge need not, of course, equate with high social rank. One of the key features of shamanism is that its practitioners can shape-shift, taking on the attributes of other beings, notably animals. They can cross the boundary between the world of the living and the spirit world, and they can move through hard surfaces such as stone (Lewis-Williams & Dowson 1990). If the man buried at Upton Lovell was indeed both a shaman and a metalworker, this tells us something important about how metalworking was viewed as a practice that facilitated shape-shifting and transformation.

It is therefore perhaps not surprising that metalworking remains are found in other liminal contexts. These include the mould from the bog at Strathconon (Britton 1963, 324), and the ingot fragments from the cave at Carrickshedoge (Bremer 1926) and from the entrance to the wedge tomb at Toormore (O'Brien *et al.* 1990). Each of these places may have been viewed as locations where one world met another, or where communication with spirits or ancestors could take place. Objects possibly associated with metalworking were deposited at **Newgrange** (O'Kelly & Shell 1979; O'Kelly *et al.* 1983), a site of ceremonial significance where communities came together to carry out ritual activities around a monument associated with the ancestors. Likewise, Culbin Sands was not a typical settlement but rather

a 'maritime haven' between land and sea that served as a focus for periodic gatherings, long-distance contacts, and a range of craft activities (Bradley *et al.* 2016).

What these sites have in common is their association with boundaries of various sorts – social, spatial, and conceptual. They may have been seen as suitable places in which to perform transformative activities such as metalworking. Alternatively, metalworking remains may have been considered appropriate offerings for deposition at such locations. In the case of hoards, well-worn artefacts – some of them deliberately broken – were combined with objects at the beginning of their lifecycle such as copper ingots. This suggests that it was the potential of items related to metalworking to signify ideas of transformation and rebirth that was significant. If so, then the presence of items such as tuyères or fragments of tin slag in graves or funerary monuments may have had more to do with the capacity of such objects to symbolise the transition from life to death than with signifying the identity of the deceased as a metalworker. Metalworkers may have been able to transfer magical qualities to the objects they made (Needham *et al.* 1989, 385), for example through the process of decorating an axe or a piece of goldwork, or simply by revealing the colour and lustre of metals; the consequent agency of these objects may be one reason why they had to be treated with such evident care at the end of their lives (Becker 2013).

The character and depositional context of different types of metalworking residues raise other interesting questions. Just as flat axe moulds were deposited in the landscape, so flat axes themselves mainly occur as off-site finds – either singly or in larger hoards – often in visually striking locations (Needham 1988; Cowie 2004). Other objects cast in these moulds, such as rings, also occur in such hoards (Britton 1963). By contrast, knives – which are one of the most frequent other artefact types represented on axe moulds – were instead mainly deposited in graves (Needham 1988). This suggests that objects made in the same way and by the same metalworker could subsequently be treated differently. Elsewhere, it is evident that different aspects of metalworking may have been ascribed different meanings or values. The striking distinction in the depositional context of moulds and smithing tools suggests that casting and smithing could have had different conceptual connotations and may even have taken place in different spatial or social contexts. This set a pattern that was to continue into the later Bronze Age and suggests that previous discussions of the role of 'the' Chalcolithic or Early Bronze Age smith may be too simplistic.

Moulds and hoards also invite comparison. Some moulds display just a single axe matrix, like the many single finds of axes. Others comprise matrices for complex assemblages of objects, often multiple axes differing in size and shape, but also axes and other objects, just as the objects themselves could be assembled into hoards. Use-wear analysis of axes and evidence for the addition of matrices to individual moulds over time indicate that both axes and moulds could have long and complex histories that doubtless rendered them socially meaningful. Attention was paid to aesthetics, both in the arrangement of finished objects in the ground, and in the composition of matrices on moulds. As a practice, then, metalworking was concerned with defining the significance and inter-relationship of social categories. Stone moulds were weighty objects, made of local materials and often of considerable age; they display a sensitivity to the social context of the objects produced and to the landscapes in which they were deposited that calls into question the idea of the itinerant smith.

Chalcolithic and Early Bronze Age metalwork is certainly dazzling, but it was just one of a range of potent and meaningful materials that played significant roles in social life, as recent work on jet, amber, and more 'lowly' materials such as bone also demonstrates (Woodward & Hunter 2015). The numbers of metal objects deposited during this period remained relatively small, and evidence for metalworking is sparse; although Kuijpers (2008, 53) argues that recycling is likely to have had an impact on the quantity of metal objects that reached the archaeological record, it is evident that recycling was rare before 2200 BC (Bray 2012). Some of the practices of which metal objects formed a component were novel (for example single burials with Beaker pottery), while others (such as the deposition of axe hoards and ongoing interest in locations such as **Newgrange**) indicate a significant element of continuity. Overall, there is little to suggest that the introduction of metalworking was the primary cause of social and economic change during this period (cf. Kienlin 2007; Bartelheim 2009). Nonetheless, it is evident that the practice of metalworking was socially significant, particularly for its ability to effect a variety of practical, social, and ritual transformations; as such, the range of cultural meanings ascribed to metals doubtless extended further than the simple indication of status.

4

The Middle Bronze Age,
Late Bronze Age and Earliest Iron Age,
c. 1550–600 BC

From *c.* 1550 BC onwards there was a significant increase in the scale of hoarding practices and a range of new types of metal artefact appeared. The amount of metal in circulation appears to have increased dramatically. Between 1600 and 1400 BC, high levels of production can be suggested for the Great Orme mine (Conwy), and this was the main source of copper in Britain during this period (Williams & Le Carlier de Veslud 2019). In contrast, analysis of Penard metalwork has revealed a sequence of distinct, new metal compositions that strongly indicates importation of copper or bronze from the Continent from *c.* 1250 BC on (Northover 1982a; Rohl & Needham 1998; Williams & Le Carlier de Veslud 2019); mining continued into the Late Bronze Age at the Great Orme but the scale of activity was much reduced. During this period, significant technological innovations were introduced from the Continent: the first socketed axes can be dated to around 1400 BC while bronze shields, cauldrons, and the earliest swords appeared around a century later (eg, Colquhoun & Burgess 1988; Bridgford 2000; Eogan 2000; Gerloff 2010; Uckelmann 2012). Both the quantity and character of the metalworking evidence also changes dramatically from *c.* 1550 BC on. An increasing number of excavated sites produce metalworking debris and a variety of new categories of metalworking-related finds appears.

This must be set in the context of broader social and economic change. Although Early Bronze Age settlements are hard to recognise, from the Middle Bronze Age onwards settlements comprising round-houses, pits, and other structures are a significant feature of the archaeological record (Ellison 1981; Brück 1999b; 2007; Ginn 2016). The large-scale, open-area excavations of the past 20 years, particularly in eastern and southern England, have uncovered densely-settled landscapes with small clusters of round-houses – sometimes open and sometimes enclosed – scattered amongst extensive field systems. Traditions of cremation burial continued, at least in some regions, but these were rarely accompanied by grave goods other than pottery, and large barrows were no longer built (Ellison 1980; Robinson 2007; Caswell & Roberts 2018). In the Late Bronze Age and Earliest Iron Age, other types of site also appeared. These include the first hillforts (large hilltop enclosures with earthen or stone ramparts), ringworks (smaller but nonetheless substantial circular enclosures), and extensive or monumental middens (Needham 1992a;

Brück 2007; O'Brien & O'Driscoll 2017; Waddington *et al.* 2019). Timber platforms were also constructed, at least some of which appear to have acted as foci for the deposition of metalwork into rivers, lakes and bogs (eg, Pryor 2001).

Many of these new types of site have produced rich and diverse finds assemblages, including significant quantities of metalwork and ornaments of amber, shale, and glass (eg, Lawson 2000). Briquetage, loomweights, spindle whorls, and a wide variety of stone and bone tools indicate that these were locations where a range of productive activities were carried out. The apparent 'wealth' of some of these sites has been read as suggesting that the Late Bronze Age saw the development of a settlement hierarchy mirroring increasing social stratification (eg, Grogan 2005; Yates 2007; O'Brien & O'Driscoll 2017), with open settlements at the bottom, sites such as ringworks (which despite their substantial defences have produced little metalwork or other 'exotic' finds) in the middle, and middens and hillforts at the top. Others have argued that middens and hillforts are better interpreted not as the residences of an elite, but as feasting and aggregation sites in which community identities and inter-group relationships were formulated (Hamilton & Manley 2001; Waddington 2009; Sharples 2010).

As we shall see in this chapter, metalworking was a common component of this settled landscape, particularly during the Late Bronze Age. The majority of metalworking residues from *c.* 1550–600 BC derive from the excavation of settlements (of various sorts) and their immediate environs. We will discuss the metalworking evidence in two period groups: the Middle Bronze Age (*c.* 1550–1150 BC) and the Late Bronze Age (*c.* 1150–800 BC) to Earliest Iron Age (*c.* 800–600 BC). The latter periods are discussed together in this chapter as the character of the evidence is similar and in many regions it is difficult to separate chronologically settlements from the two periods. Of course, this is not to say that the use of bronze remained static between 800 and 600 BC: for example, the deposition of bronze hoards reached a peak during the Ewart Park phase of the Late Bronze Age (1000–800 BC), after which the quantity of bronze objects that reached the archaeological record decreased dramatically (Needham 2007). Other changes

are also evident. The use of bronze for the production of tools and weapons appears to have been far less common in the subsequent Llyn Fawr phase (800–600 BC), although there is little evidence that this was a direct result of the adoption of iron; iron objects of any sort are extremely rare at this time (Collard *et al.* 2006; Needham 2007). The production of leaded bronze became frequent in the Late Bronze Age (Needham & Hook 1988; Rohl & Needham 1998), while new techniques such as lost-wax casting and casting-on were also now occasionally employed (Beesley 2004; Bowman & Needham 2007). Such changes in the production, use, and consumption of metals hint at significant changes also in the role and status of the smith.

One of the most significant questions in relation to metalworking in the period 1550–600 BC is the extent to which this was a specialist and centralised activity, for this relates directly to debates around the development of social stratification. Studies of technically sophisticated items such as gold ornaments and sheet-bronze objects have demonstrated the extraordinary levels of skill that some smiths possessed (eg, Armbruster 2000; Gerloff 2010; Uckelmann 2012) and it has often been argued that elites supported full-time specialist metalworkers to produce the objects they required for display, combat and exchange (eg, Kristiansen 1998; Earle *et al.* 2015). A two- or even three-tier system of production has been proposed, based partly on the distribution of different artefact types, with full-time specialists producing complex objects such as swords that were distributed from production centres over wide areas, while part-time metalworkers cast simpler items such as axes for local consumption (Rowlands 1976; Burgess 1980; Howard 1983; Northover 1988b). The existence of full-time specialists has been taken to indicate that Bronze Age societies were complex and hierarchical. Full-time craftworkers require the support or patronage of others, indicating that certain individuals in these communities may have been able to accumulate surplus wealth that could be employed to sponsor the production of prestige objects (cf. Earle & Kristiansen 2010). Specialisation has also been linked to the emergence of social inequality because it means that access to particular objects or products is no longer universal (Brumfiel &

Earle 1987; Wailes 1996). The application of social evolutionist narratives to the European Bronze Age has, however, been the focus of recent critique: it has been suggested, for example, that 'high-status' objects such as the Oxborough dirk may have been the inalienable possessions of kin groups rather than the property of chiefs or other wealthy individuals (Fontijn 2001; Brück & Fontijn 2013). The question of differential access to metalworking and control over its products is one area that the contextual evidence set out below will seek to address. The scale and spatial location of metalworking will also be considered, for this has a direct bearing on its organisation: societies in which household production is the norm are thought to exhibit lower levels of specialisation and social complexity than those in which special-purpose workshops are common (Arnold 1985; Costin 1991). As we have seen in Chapter 1, the mobility of metalworkers has also been a matter of debate, and this too will be discussed here.

Studies of well-contextualised metalworking remains have been few to date. Existing discussions regarding the organisation of metalworking during this period have, therefore, been based primarily on ethnographic parallels (eg, Barber 2003) or on technical, compositional and metallographic analysis of the finished objects themselves (eg, Bridgford 1998; Rohl & Needham 1998; Armbruster 2000; Bray 2016), with a smaller number of studies addressing subjects such as mould production technology (eg, Ó Faoláin & Northover 1998; Sahlén 2011). There has also been considerable discussion of the evidence provided by hoards. Smithing tools have predominantly been recovered from such assemblages (Fregni 2014) and, in contrast to some parts of the Continent, are not found in metalworkers' burials during this period. Ingots and casting waste also are frequent components of hoards, notably in south-east England during the Ewart Park phase (Turner 2010). The identification of 'founders' hoards' containing broken objects, casting waste and ingots, and of 'merchants' hoards' containing unfinished objects, were considered by Evans (1881) to indicate the mobility of those involved in the metal 'trade', while Rowlands (1976) employed ethnographic parallels to argue that the hoarding of broken artefacts supports a model of part-time specialisation, with the smith collecting broken

objects to be recycled at a later, quiet time in the agricultural cycle. Hoards of the Middle Bronze Age, Late Bronze Age, and Earliest Iron Age have been well-studied elsewhere, and will not be considered in detail here, although assemblages containing metalworking tools or debris (particularly those for which contextual evidence is available) will be discussed. Early interpretations of hoards were often framed in functional and economic terms but these have been a focus of detailed critique (Hansen 1991; Bradley 1998; 2017; Fontijn 2002; Becker 2013; but see Wiseman 2018) and it is now accepted that the contents of such assemblages may not provide a direct window into the organisation of metalworking.

One final important point is that because the archaeological record *c.* 1550–600 BC is dominated by settlements and field systems, research on the period has frequently focused on the 'practical' aspects of daily life (Brück 2000). The distinction between an earlier prehistory structured around ritual practice and later periods dominated by everyday concerns has been criticised, however, and since the 1990s, the significance and role of ritual in the later Bronze Age (particularly in the domestic sphere) has been a focus of considerable interest (Brück 1995; 1999a; Bradley 2005b). The metalworking evidence provides an interesting perspective on these discussions, for as we have seen in Chapter 1, reviews of the ethnographic evidence indicate that metalworking is often considered a magical process and is accompanied by ritual activities of various sorts. The possible ritualisation of metalworking will therefore also be a focus of interest in this chapter.

As discussed in Chapter 2, the majority of the remains from non-ferrous metalworking relate to the stages of melting and casting copper alloys, in particular crucibles, moulds, and metallic waste. Evidence for the primary smelting of copper ores is present only at one site, **Pentrwyn**, close to the Great Orme mines (Conwy), although a globule of smelted tin has also been recovered from **Dean Moor** (Devon). This chapter begins with an investigation of the life histories of moulds and crucibles. In contrast to smithing tools, which have been the subject of a recent synthetic study (Fregni 2014), these objects have been somewhat neglected. The evidence for the manufacture, movement, and use of moulds and crucibles has implications for the organisation of metal casting and the potential mobility of metalworkers during this period. Following this, we will discuss the finds contexts of metalworking tools and debris as well as chronological and regional differences in the character of the evidence. Casting residues including clay or stone moulds and crucibles have been found at many excavated sites, shedding light both on the spatial and social context of this activity, as well as on the structured deposition of associated remains. Bronze smithing tools, bronze moulds and ingots were, by contrast, deposited in metalwork hoards and other 'off-site' deposits, and the implications of these practices for the social significance of metalworking will be also discussed.

Life histories of moulds and crucibles: production, movement and use

Production and movement of crucibles

Studies of crucible fabrics have been carried out for several Middle and Late Bronze Age sites in England (Howard 1983), for Late Bronze Age sites in Scotland (Sahlén 2011; 2013), and for the Late Bronze Age hillfort at **Dún Aonghasa** (Co. Galway; O'Carroll 2012). These show that carefully selected local clays and temper were used, and that the recipes employed for the production of crucibles were highly variable, indicating that the producers of these objects had a detailed knowledge of the resources available to them in the local area. For England, Howard's analysis shows that sand or crushed rock were generally added to the clay to improve its refractory properties, although carbon temper was used at **Beeston Castle** (Cheshire West & Chester). On the whole there is little to indicate non-local resources, although a crucible from **Burderop Down** (Swindon) is argued to be made from non-local clay (Howard 1983, 439); a non-local stone mould was also found at this site (see below). Howard's review of the ethnographic evidence indicates that metalworkers usually make their own refractories and, if this was the case in the Bronze Age, it suggests that metal casters were usually settled members of the local community rather than itinerant craftspeople. The lack of standardisation hints at small-scale, decentralised patterns

of production rather than highly regulated or 'industrial' forms of manufacture. In Scotland, Sahlén suggests that coarse sandy clays were tempered with added rock and/or organic temper. Petrographic similarities with pottery from the same sites indicates similar clay sources and preparation techniques (Sahlén 2011; 2013). This suggests that pottery and crucibles may have been made by the same people, which has interesting implications for the involvement of different groups in the metalworking process, or that metalworkers drew on familiar traditions of ceramic manufacture in order to make casting equipment; in either case, this indicates that bronze casters were socially embedded in their local communities.

Production and movement of clay moulds

Significant skill was needed to produce clay piece moulds, especially moulds for long objects such as swords (Howard 1983; Ó Faoláin & Northover 1998; Ó Faoláin 2004). It was also a lengthy process: Ó Faoláin and Northover (1998) suggest that 2–3 weeks of drying time was required between forming and firing a sword mould. Most clay moulds had a two-layer construction in which the inner valves were enclosed with a coarser outer wrap; this made them single use, as they had to be smashed to release the casting. Howard (1983, 490) notes that in southern Britain there is a clear difference between the clays and tempering materials chosen for the production of moulds and those used to make crucibles; this distinction is also visible at **Dún Aonghasa** (Co. Galway). However, as for crucibles, local materials were generally used for Middle and Late Bronze Age clay moulds in England and Scotland, and the same clays were usually employed for both inner and outer layers (Howard 1983; Sahlén 2011). The same is true for Late Bronze Age Dún Aonghasa. The Late Bronze Age moulds from **Lady Graves, Fimber** (East Riding of Yorkshire) are different, with inner valves made from one clay type of probable local provenance, and outer wraps made from a different clay tempered with fragments of igneous rock derived from coastal erratics around 30 km from the site. There is no technological reason for the selection of this non-local rock, suggesting that it was a cultural choice (Howard 1983, 490). Use of non-local clays for some Late Bronze Age moulds has also been suggested at **Sigwells** (Somerset;

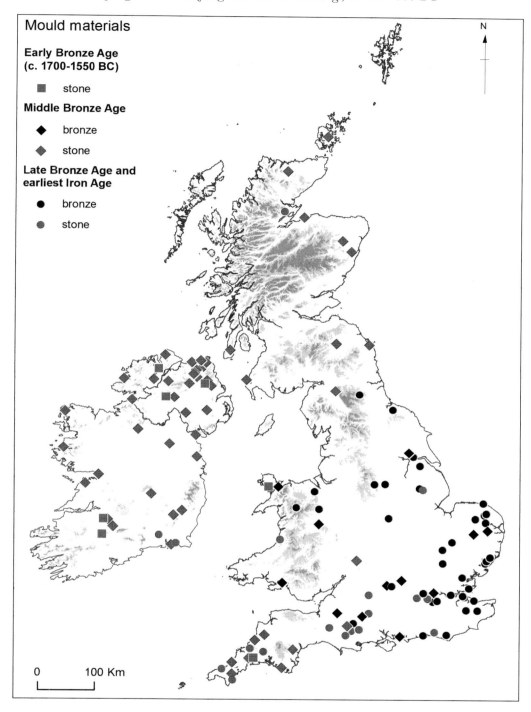

Figure 4.1: Distribution of bivalve stone and bronze moulds c. *1700– 600 BC*

R. Tabor pers. comm.). The significance of such non-local clays is difficult to assess, but it may of course indicate the movement of raw materials rather than metalworkers – either from special places, or from locations with which the local community had particular personal connections.

Production and movement of stone moulds

Whilst Early Bronze Age one-piece moulds were almost exclusively made from sandstones or grits, a much broader range of stones was used for later bivalve moulds (Appendix 3; Fig. 4.1). Various kinds of igneous or metamorphic rock are most common, but sandstone and even limestone were also used. Often fine-grained stone was favoured that would have allowed for crisper detail than coarse sandstones. The talc schist ('steatite') often used in Scotland and Ireland also had the advantage of being soft and easy to work (Forster & Turner 2009). Because of similarities in production techniques, use and deposition, bivalve moulds of the late Early Bronze Age (1700–1550 BC) will be included in the discussion in this section.

As we have seen in Chapter 2, Early Bronze Age one-piece moulds were normally made from stone available immediately locally. This was also true of some later Bronze Age moulds, but now there is clear evidence for moulds travelling significant distances from their source. Late Bronze Age moulds for south Welsh/Stogursey style socketed axes made from syenite or keratophyre from south Wales or the south-west peninsula have been identified at a variety of sites in south-central England, including **Everley Water Meadow** (Dorset); **Burderop Down** (Swindon); Bulford (Wiltshire); and **Petters Sports Field, Egham** (Surrey; Needham 1981). A fragment of worked syenite from the ditch of the Late Bronze Age enclosure at **Castle Hill, Little Wittenham** (Oxfordshire) might also come from a mould. Other types of stone from south-west England have also been found at some distance from their sources. For example, two Earliest Iron Age socketed axe moulds from **Ham Hill** (Somerset) were made of greisen from Devon or Cornwall, while a Late Bronze Age socketed axe mould from **Gwithian** (Cornwall) is made of non-local chlorite schist, possibly from the Start Bay area of south Devon. Further afield, a Late Bronze Age socketed axe mould in Fécamp Museum (Upper Normandy), believed to be a local find, is made from metamorphic stone probably from the Lizard in Cornwall (Marcigny *et al.* 2005). An unusual feature of this mould is a handle carved on the exterior, comparable to an axe mould from St Keverne on the Lizard peninsula (Knight *et al.* 2015, fig. 1). Stone from other sources also travelled. An ornament mould from **Downsview** (Brighton & Hove) is made of oolitic limestone that must come from Jurassic deposits at least 150 km to the west or north. In Scotland, a Middle Bronze Age mould from Aberdeenshire, a probable Middle Bronze Age mould from Strathnaver

(Highland), and two Earliest Iron Age moulds from Rosskeen (Highland) are made of talc schist ('steatite') that is definitely non-local and may derive from Catpund (Shetland; identification F. McGibbon). In Ireland, a number of Middle Bronze Age moulds described as being made of 'steatite' have been found some distance from the sources of steatite in the north-west of the island, though a proper programme of geological identification of the Irish moulds is required to confirm this.

Long-distance movement of stone moulds either through exchange networks or the mobility of metalworkers is thus indicated, a contrast to the predominantly local production of clay moulds and crucibles. Two stone mould hoards, one of Middle Bronze Age date from Ballyliffin (Co. Donegal) and the other of Late Bronze Age date from Helsbury (Cornwall), contained mould 'blanks' with no matrices carved into them; it may be that movement or exchange of moulds was sometimes in unfinished form (see below for discussion of stone mould hoards). Equally, the transport as far as Surrey of moulds of south-western or Welsh stone for Stogursey-style axes – which are concentrated in south Wales and the Bristol Channel area – would be consistent with movement of such moulds in their finished state. Howard (1983) argues that this indicates the existence of a distinct caste of itinerant metalworkers who travelled over very long distances. Stone moulds of this period were generally smaller and more portable than the one-piece moulds of the Early Bronze Age, though some were still quite heavy; for example, the Middle Bronze Age rapier mould from Inchnagree (Co. Cork) weighs nearly 7 kg. Eogan (1993) argues that the presence of stone mould hoards with a substantial combined weight suggests that smiths did not move far, though this assumes that such hoards were the 'tool kit' of an individual rather than an assemblage brought together for deposition. As we shall see below, the deposition of stone moulds in hoards indicates that these objects were themselves viewed as special; long-distance exchange was of course by no means unusual during this period, particularly for socially significant objects.

One aspect that distinguishes stone moulds from those of other materials is that they can be reworked. Some moulds (especially from the late Early Bronze Age and Middle Bronze

Age) have more than one matrix, and it seems likely that these were often added sequentially over a period of time. A Middle Bronze Age mould from Ireland (NMI 1882:88) has a rapier matrix significantly shorter than the length of the mould; it is probable that another longer rapier matrix was intended for the opposite face of the mould, which has been carefully smoothed flat. It is possible to read this evidence as indicating that these items belonged to mobile smiths who needed to use their tools as parsimoniously as possible, although it may also simply suggest that stone moulds were valued objects that were curated and reused over lengthy periods.

A few moulds were made from recycled older moulds. A Middle Bronze Age palstave mould from Lough Scur (Co. Leitrim) was made on a reused Early Bronze Age flat axe mould. Moulds from Lough Ramor (Co. Cavan) and the Omagh hoard (Co. Leitrim; late Early Bronze Age) were made from reworked fragments of spearhead moulds. On a second mould from the Omagh hoard, a matrix for a dagger or spearhead blade has been ground down and a matrix for a tanged spearhead carved in its place. On a Middle Bronze Age mould from **Trevalga** (Cornwall) it also appears that earlier matrices were ground down for reuse.

Production and movement of bronze moulds

The design and manufacture of bronze moulds have been discussed in detail elsewhere (Webley & Adams 2016). Bronze moulds from the Middle and Late Bronze Age (Appendix 4; Fig. 4.1) were made using an alloy composition typical for bronze artefacts of each respective period. In fact, analyses of the Hotham Carrs and Brough on Humber hoards (East Riding of Yorkshire) have shown that both the moulds and the axes actually cast in them shared a similar alloy recipe. The exterior surface finish of these objects shows that they were cast using clay moulds, though no such moulds have yet been discovered. The often remarkably close fit between the articulating surfaces of the two mould valves suggests that they were made in sequence, the second perhaps being cast directly against the first. In contrast to stone and clay moulds, we have no way of tracing how far bronze moulds moved from their place of production. It

has been argued that the Boughton Malherbe hoard (Kent), which contains end-winged axe moulds, was imported in its entirety from France (Matthews 2013), but this need not be the case (Adams 2017). End-winged axes are common finds in south-east England as well as in northern France, consistent with local production.

Some similarities can be seen between the design of bronze moulds and those of other materials. For example, some bronze and clay moulds share a similar method of registering the two valves, with raised tenons on one valve that fit into corresponding sockets on the other. Other characteristics are unique to bronze moulds, notably the fact that they were often decorated on the exterior. At least 25 moulds show cast decoration, mostly formed of raised ribs and pellets. In addition, a number of the plain moulds have a carefully smoothed exterior that suggests aesthetic concern, though some others had been left quite rough. Some moulds share similar decorative motifs, but the overall impression is of diversity. In a few cases the decoration may be skeuomorphic. This is most striking on a palstave mould from South Wiltshire, which has raised 'cords' around the exterior of each valve, evidently cast from impressions of actual cord or twine (Evans 1881; Clark 1905; Hodges 1960). These echo the cords that would have been bound around the mould when it was used for casting.

While some axes also have simple decoration formed of ribs and/or pellets, the specific designs on the moulds never correspond to features on the objects cast in them. In fact, the decoration on some moulds such as the South Wiltshire example is difficult to parallel on any other Bronze Age metalwork. The idiosyncrasy of the decoration gives the moulds an individuality, contrasting with the plain and generic nature of the implements that they were used to make. If the moulds were made by smiths for their own use, or the use of others in the same workshop, then they may not have been subject to the same strictures as objects such as axes which circulated widely and hence had to conform to certain culturally acceptable designs.

One possible inference to draw from the practice of decorating bronze moulds is that these were regarded as significant or prestigious objects. This suggests also that the process of casting was viewed as an important act that should be marked and made visible through the use of visually striking, technically complex, and valuable equipment. However, ethnographic case studies suggest that decoration is sometimes applied to objects not so much to emphasise their value as to confront their ambiguous, transgressive, or dangerous nature. For example, Braithwaite (1982) argues that among the Azande of Sudan decoration is applied to pots used in situations that may compromise the idealised distinctions between men and women. Denyer's survey (1978) of African traditional architecture similarly shows that decoration is often applied to points of potential social stress or ambiguity, as well as to elements at risk of structural failure. The decoration of Bronze Age bronze moulds may thus have been a means of dealing with the conceptual and physical dangers of metalworking and ensuring success in the casting process. It is tempting to suggest, for example, that the skeuomorphic cords around some of the moulds might have carried connotations of strength and security intended to aid successful casting.

Evidence for the use of moulds and crucibles

As we have seen, there is a marked difference between the use lives of clay, stone, and bronze moulds. Clay moulds were usually single use, as they had to be smashed to release the casting within, while stone and bronze moulds could in principle be reused multiple times. Clay crucibles too seem to have been deployed repeatedly. Relining or wall heightening of crucibles from several sites shows that they were used several times and that care was taken to prolong their use-lives (Needham 1980a; Howard 1983; O'Carroll 2012).

Metal residues on some clay and stone moulds, identified visually or though XRF analysis (eg, Needham *et al.* 1989; Young 2013; Jackson 2015), have confirmed that they were used for casting bronze artefacts. No moulds or crucibles for casting precious metals have yet been identified. Detecting bronze residues on a bronze mould is of course problematic. However, at least six bronze moulds for Late Bronze Age socketed axes contain the adhering remnants of lead castings. This has led to the suggestion that bronze moulds were used to cast lead patterns for investment casting – a so-called 'lost-lead' technique (Tylecote 1986,

92) – but there are serious practical difficulties with this idea (Foltz 1980). A few lead or lead alloy axes are known from southern Britain (Needham & Hook 1988; Guilbert 1996; PAS: LVPL-943AA3), but these could have served as ingots or as symbolic models of axes rather than being an intermediate stage in the production of bronze axes. There is little doubt that the main purpose of bronze moulds was the direct casting of bronze implements, whatever role they may also have had in lead casting (Webley & Adams 2016).

The repeated use of stone and bronze moulds has often left other visible traces on these objects. Many stone moulds, such as all five of those from the Omagh hoard (Co. Leitrim; Ó Faoláin 2004, 155), are blackened from exposure to heat, and bronze moulds can display wear or cracking that may have resulted from use (Webley & Adams 2016). A few stone moulds show more extensive thermal spalling damage that would have made them unusable. Such accidents would always have been a risk, though experimental work suggests that with care and luck these moulds could be reused indefinitely. Using a replica bronze mould, Drescher (1957) achieved 15 castings without any trace of damage, while Fregni has used the same bronze mould dozens of times (E. G. Fregni pers. comm.).

Relationships between moulds and their castings

Refits between moulds and individual artefacts that had been cast within them have rarely been identified. The only certain examples are cases where bronze moulds and their castings were deposited together in the same hoard, a practice that will be discussed further below. A bronze axe mould from the Roseberry Topping hoard (North Yorkshire) has tentatively been matched with a casting apparently found 40 km away at Forcett in the same county (Schmidt & Burgess 1981, 243). In Ireland, systematic examination of spearheads and stone moulds has thrown up only one possible match: a mould from Fethard (Co. Wexford) and a casting from Lough Erne (Co. Fermanagh), around 300 km away (Lineen 2017, 107). Due to their fragmentation, it is virtually impossible to match clay moulds to potential castings.

Moulds are known for most of the major types of cast bronze artefacts from Britain and Ireland, though not for some rarer forms.

Interior valve 1

Interior valve 2

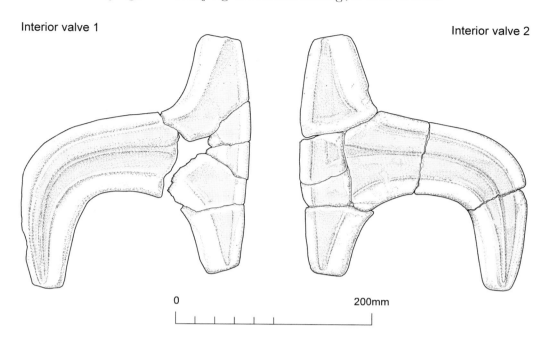

0   200mm

Figure 4.2: Stone sickle mould of Middle Bronze Age date from the Killymaddy hoard (Co. Antrim) (drawing: Anne Leaver after Coghlan & Raftery 1961, figs 37–9, & following observations & sketches by Leo Webley)

There are also moulds for object types that are otherwise unknown. For example, a stone mould from the Middle Bronze Age Killymaddy hoard (Co. Antrim) is for a sickle of unparalleled form with a widely splaying tang, similar to some halberds (Fig. 4.2). This object has previously been erroneously published as 3–6 incomplete sickle moulds (Coghlan & Raftery 1961; Boutoille 2015b) but the fragments clearly refit to form one virtually complete mould. A stone mould from Low Glengyre (Dumfries & Galloway) is for an unparalleled palstave-like implement (Childe 1948), though it has been suggested that this could be a fake (T. Cowie pers. comm.).

In other cases, moulds have been found peripheral to or outside the distribution of the object types they were used to cast. In Ireland, stone spearhead moulds often occur in locations at the edge of the distribution of the corresponding spearhead type (Lineen 2017). As we have seen, several stone moulds for Stogursey or South-Welsh style socketed axes occur outside the main distribution of this artefact type. The lithology of these moulds suggests that they had been transported away from their place of origin, but this does not apply in other cases. For example, a Middle Bronze Age mould from **Trevalga** (Cornwall) carries the only known matrix for triangular razors (*racloirs*), an object type

concentrated in western France with only a few examples from southern Britain, previously suspected to be imports. Yet this mould was made from stone probably fairly local to the findspot (Jones & Quinnell 2014). It also seems unlikely that fragile clay moulds would have been transported far, even if they were for casting objects little known in the local region. For example, the assemblage of clay moulds from **Lady Graves, Fimber** (East Riding of Yorkshire) included moulds for the production of various artefact types that are rare or unknown in northern England, being concentrated much further south (Burgess 1968). This suggests that the known distributions of Bronze Age metalwork are influenced by patterns of selective deposition and do not exactly correspond to their original areas of manufacture, circulation, and use (Bradley 2013, 129). Of course, the deposition patterns of moulds for different artefact types may also have been selective. Moulds that had travelled from afar, or that had been used to cast particular kinds of objects, could have been selected for special treatment that makes them more visible in the archaeological record.

As we have seen, the choice of material for making moulds varied between communities, both across space and through time. Cross-cutting these patterns, there is also a relationship between mould material and the objects cast

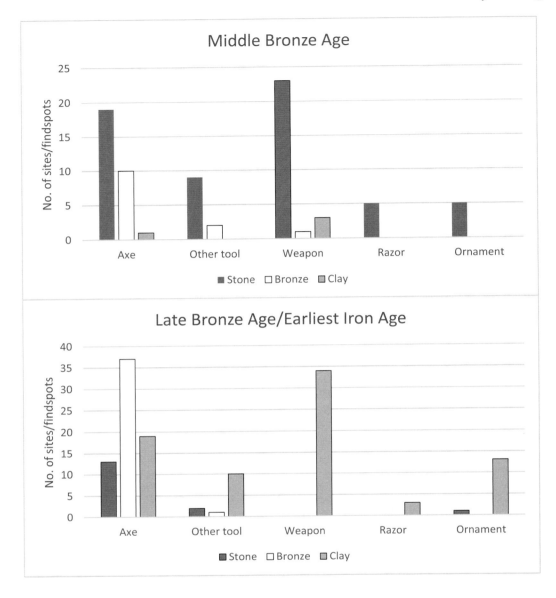

in the mould (Fig. 4.3). Stone moulds were used for a wide range of objects during the Middle Bronze Age, including weapons, axes, sickles, razors, ornaments, and craftworking tools such as chisels and punches. Moulds for the production of spearheads are particularly common in Ireland. With the reduction in the use of stone moulds during the Late Bronze Age and Earliest Iron Age they became restricted largely to the production of axes, though a few ornament moulds are also known. Bronze moulds were almost exclusively used for axes and very occasionally for other craftworking tools during both the Middle and Late Bronze Age, with just one spearhead mould known (Fig. 4.3). Clay

moulds were used during the Middle Bronze Age for spears, axes, rapiers and swords. In the Late Bronze Age and Earliest Iron Age they are attested for a wider variety of objects, including weapons, axes, craftworking tools, sickles, razors and ornaments (Fig. 4.3). However, clay moulds for spearheads, axes, and in particular swords were by far the most common during the period. In comparison, moulds for objects such as chisels, gouges, sickles, razors, and bracelets are very rare. As already noted, evidence from finished bronze objects indicates that the lost-wax method was used only during the Late Bronze Age for a limited number of 'prestige' or ceremonial objects, notably some of the components of flesh hooks, cauldrons, and horns, often to achieve effects not possible with piece moulds (Bowman & Needham 2007). Moulds for such items have not been found, however.

Some stone moulds have matrices for two or more objects. This practice declined over time, being found on 82% of late Early Bronze Age moulds (9 out of 11), 28% of Middle Bronze Age moulds (30 out of 108), 12% of Late Bronze Age moulds (2 out of 17), and no Earliest Iron Age moulds. Some multiple-matrix moulds are for different iterations of the same object type, but during the Middle Bronze Age there were also moulds used to make objects of differing kinds. This can inform us about the range of metal artefacts produced by individual metalworkers or workshops. By far the commonest matrix association is spearheads with razors, found on at least eight Middle Bronze Age moulds. The apparent link between the production of these two potentially male-associated implements is notable. A variety of other matrix associations do though occur, albeit less frequently. Each of the three broad categories of matrices – weapons, tools and ornaments – can be found in association with either of the others.

In the absence of any comprehensive survey of later Bronze Age metalwork from Britain, it is difficult to compare the abundance of particular artefact types with that of their moulds. For Ireland, data on metalwork is provided by Becker (2013). For the Middle Bronze Age, when moulds were overwhelmingly made of stone, rapiers/dirks and axes seem to be less commonly represented on moulds than they are in the metalwork corpus, while spearheads and tools other than axes are more commonly represented (Table 4.1). Strikingly, razor matrices are found on nine moulds, even though it is argued that the deposition of razors themselves essentially ceased in Ireland during the Middle Bronze Age (Becker 2013). Of course, we do not know how many castings may have been produced by different matrices. Comparison is harder for the Late Bronze Age, as clay moulds were now dominant; it is difficult to estimate how many moulds are present in fragmented assemblages, and some matrix types may be more readily identifiable from small pieces than others. With this caveat it can be noted that sword moulds are the most widely distributed mould type in Ireland (present at seven out of eight

	Metal finds	% metal finds	Stone moulds	% stone moulds
Axe	1180	46.84	27	34.62
Other tool	9	0.36	6	7.69
Spearhead	794	31.52	39	50.00
Sword	22	0.87	0	0.00
Rapier/dirk	501	19.89	3	3.85
Razor	0	0.00	9	11.54
Ornament	13	0.52	1	1.28
Total	2519	100.00	78	

Note that the table presents number of moulds not total number of matrices; the percentages for the moulds add up to more than 100% as some moulds have matrices for more than one object class

Table 4.1: Middle Bronze Age metal finds (information from Becker 2013) and stone moulds from Ireland

sites that have clearly identifiable matrices), with spearheads, axes, and pins the next most common. This does not closely correlate with the metalwork corpus, in which axes are by far the most common object type, and pins are not especially abundant (Becker 2013).

Caution is needed when comparing such different forms of data. Nonetheless, the evidence suggests that different materials were selectively employed to create moulds for different classes of object. It also may indicate that moulds for certain objects such as swords were more frequently selected for deposition than those for other artefact types. This latter point will be returned to below in the discussion of the evidence for casting from excavated sites.

Why different mould materials were selected for casting particular object types is an issue that deserves more attention. One factor may be the distinction between single-use and reusable moulds. While the manufacture of bronze and stone moulds required a certain investment of time, they could then be used repeatedly, with several castings per day possible. This made them particularly suitable for casting objects such as axes which were produced in large numbers during the later Bronze Age and were often quite generic in form. For objects only required in small numbers, single-use clay moulds may have been seen as more suitable. However, this does not explain why effort was expended in producing reusable stone moulds for a number of artefact types not represented among the bronze moulds.

Another part of the explanation may relate to the functional properties of mould materials. It has been argued that clay moulds were most suited to long, complex castings such as swords (Howard 1983). Yet, the choice of clay for the production of sword moulds is difficult to explain in purely functional terms: equally long rapiers were cast in stone as well as clay moulds during the Middle Bronze Age, and modern metalworkers have reported success in casting functional replica Bronze Age swords in both stone and bronze moulds (eg, McNally 1997, 12). Another possible factor is that bronze cast in moulds of different materials has a differing microstructure and thus different functional properties, as shown by experimental work (Staniaszek & Northover 1983; Jochum Zimmermann *et al.* 2003; Wirth 2003; Ottaway & Wang 2004). Thus Ottaway and Wang found that axes made in bronze moulds had a smoother surface finish and were harder than those cast in clay or sand moulds, and this could perhaps be partly behind the use of bronze moulds for axes and other tools. The differences in functional properties were only slight, however, and caution is needed as the experimental mould used in this instance was very different in design from actual Bronze Age examples. The smoothness and hardness of a completed implement will also very much depend on the smithing work carried out after casting. Furthermore, hardness was hardly likely to have been less of a concern when making bladed weapons such as spearheads, which were almost exclusively cast in clay or stone moulds during the later Bronze Age.

Arguably, it is likely that certain materials were considered appropriate or auspicious for casting particular artefact types partly for cultural reasons that are not easy for us to grasp today. It is also possible that stone, clay, and bronze had differing conceptual associations, perhaps relating to their contrasting origins, or to their sensory properties such as colour, feel, or sound. An ethnographic and archaeological study of Muisca metalworking in Colombia (Martinón-Torres & Uribe-Villegas 2015) has demonstrated that, in some cultural contexts, the performance of production and the materials used were as important as the final product (see also Sörman 2018). Thus the lost-wax process was employed to make ritual gold objects even when this does not seem the most logical method, and this preference is argued to relate to the cultural significance of wax and bees in this region of South America. Similarly, the choice of different materials for the production of moulds for Bronze Age swords and axes, for example, may have been influenced by the material properties and conceptual associations of clay, stone, and bronze. There are also differences in the performative aspects of using the three mould types. Thus in contrast to bronze and stone moulds, clay moulds usually had to be smashed to release the casting within. Perhaps this dramatic procedure was seen as particularly appropriate for the manufacture of certain object types, such as swords, which were themselves often deliberately fragmented before deposition. Swords were socially significant objects and may have been considered to possess their own life force (Kristiansen 2002; Pearce 2013; Melheim & Horn 2014). The decision to cast such objects in clay moulds that could not be reused may therefore relate to the perception of such items as animate artefacts with their own unique biographies. The use of clay may therefore be linked to the meanings ascribed to such objects and/or their context of production. Yet, clay moulds were also employed to make multiple near-identical bronze objects in some contexts: the Llyn Fawr-phase hoard from Langton Matravers (Dorset) included a minimum number of 382 socketed axes, over 90% of which were of Type Portland, but each axe was individually cast in a clay mould (Roberts *et al.* 2015). Reusing a stone mould might have been a more efficient and easier way of producing these objects, but that was not how the axes were made.

Treatment of metalworking tools and debris at the end of their use lives

The treatment of casting tools and debris at the end of their use-lives also related to the material they were made of (Fig. 4.4). Virtually all clay crucibles and moulds have been found at settlements or other excavated later Bronze Age sites, in other words locations where other 'domestic' and/or 'ritual' activities took place. These finds will be examined in detail below. Of course, such friable objects would have much less chance of survival and recovery had they also been used and/or deposited in the landscape away from contemporary sites. Possible exceptions include an assemblage of Late Bronze Age clay mould and crucible fragments deposited in the lee of a boulder at **Galmisdale** on the island of Eigg (Highland), though in the absence of wider excavation around the findspot it is unclear whether this lay in the vicinity of a settlement (see below).

Stone moulds could also be deposited at settlements and other excavated later Bronze Age sites, particularly in Ireland. However, most stone moulds are either surface finds not associated with any known later Bronze Age site or are old finds that have only a vague provenance. No doubt many of these objects do derive from Bronze Age sites. However, it is also possible that they were sometimes deposited at selected locales in the natural landscape, as argued for Early Bronze Age one-piece stone moulds. As well as single finds, there are a number of hoards of several stone moulds deposited together away from any known contemporary site. These mould hoards range in date from the late Early Bronze Age through to the Earliest Iron Age. The landscape context of stone moulds, including both single finds and mould hoards, will be considered later in this chapter.

Most bronze moulds were presumably melted down and recycled once their use-life was over, and we have only those whose biographies took a different path by being deposited in the ground. Bronze moulds are absent from excavated sites. Like most stone moulds, they were deposited in bronze hoards or as single finds in the wider landscape; again, their landscape context will be considered later in this chapter. Ingot fragments, casting jets, and waste can occur on settlements and other excavated sites, though most are found in bronze hoards. Where casting waste and ingot fragments are found on settlements, they tend to be more closely associated with complete and broken metal objects than with ceramic mould or crucible fragments. Single unstratified finds of such material away from excavated sites are difficult to date as specifically later Bronze Age. Bronze smithing tools occur predominantly in hoards or as single 'off-site' dry land finds, although two socketed hammers have been recovered from the Thames (Fregni 2014). In contrast to crucibles and moulds, smithing tools are essentially absent from excavated settlement contexts, suggesting that there was a significant element of selection in what objects reached the archaeological record and where and how they did so. Possible exceptions are tanged chisels and awls, which have been recovered from a number of

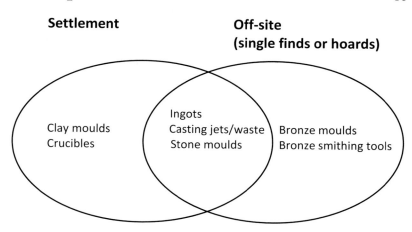

Settlement **Off-site (single finds or hoards)**

Clay moulds
Crucibles

Ingots
Casting jets/waste
Stone moulds

Bronze moulds
Bronze smithing tools

Figure 4.4: Key depositional contexts from which different types of later Bronze Age-Earliest Iron Age metalworking evidence have been recovered

excavated settlements and hillforts of the Late Bronze Age and Earliest Iron Age although, as noted in Chapter 2, many of these may have been employed in other crafts.

Such patterns indicate that there was an important element of selectivity to the deposition of different categories of metalworking remains. In the following sections, the finds contexts of clay and stone moulds, crucibles, and casting waste from excavated sites will be investigated in detail. The off-site deposition of stone moulds and bronze metalworking tools and waste will then be considered, focusing in particular on their landscape contexts, as this too has implications for the social significance of this craft.

The Middle Bronze Age: excavated evidence

In contrast to the Early Bronze Age, casting evidence has been recovered from a significant number of excavated sites of Middle Bronze Age date (26 sites: Fig. 4.5). These include 16 Middle Bronze Age sites from England, nine from Ireland, and one from Scotland. In England, there is a notable cluster of sites in the south-west. Twenty-two of these sites were settlements, including at least eight enclosed and 11 open settlements. However, the finds from four of these sites were from unstratified contexts or from contexts whose stratigraphy was difficult to interpret and, as such, they may not be contemporary with the other activities at these locations. Metalworking was also found at three earlier monuments (all in Ireland) and one other site that is more difficult to categorise (see below).

Figure 4.5: Distribution of excavated sites of Middle Bronze Age date that have produced metalworking tools and non-ferrous metalworking residues

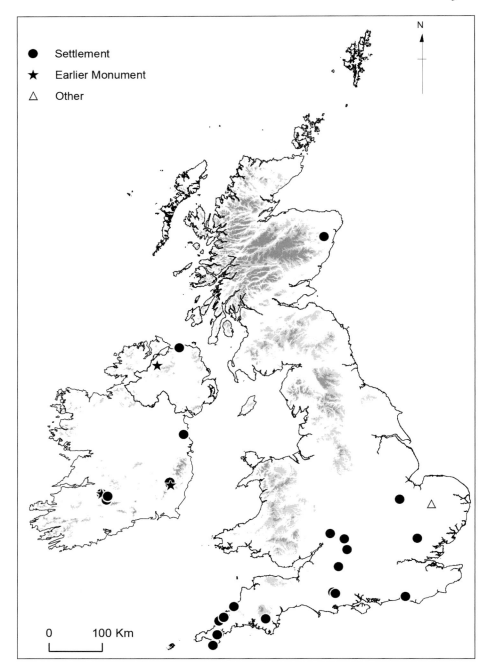

Evidence from settlements

Most settlements with metalworking evidence have produced only very small quantities of material. Even sites that are in other ways remarkable, such as the 'village' of 76 largely contemporary round-houses at **Corrstown** (Co. Antrim), have produced fairly modest assemblages of casting evidence – in this case, fragments of four stone moulds. There is little to indicate that the scale or character

of metalworking on enclosed and open settlements differed substantially and it is therefore difficult to relate the occurrence of metalworking debris to any kind of settlement 'hierarchy'. For example, the open settlement at **Trethellan Farm**, Newquay (Cornwall), comprised seven round-houses, constructed over at least two phases. Metalworking evidence from this site included a stone mould from what was interpreted as a 'ritual hollow', though as

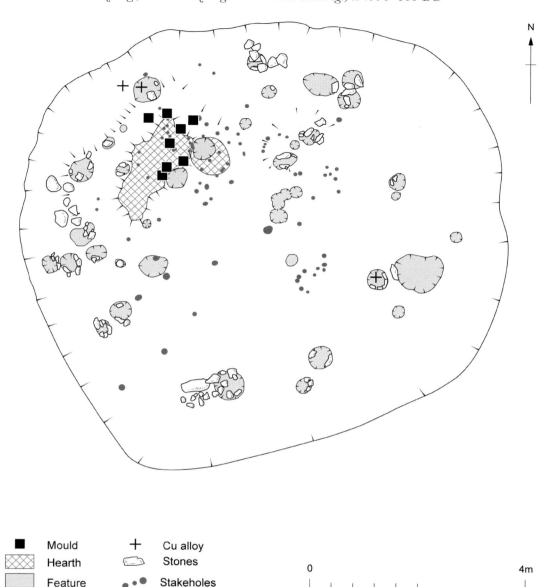

N

Figure 4.6: Middle Bronze Age round-house at Tremough (Cornwall) (redrawn by Anne Leaver after Jones et al. 2015, fig. 2.7)

■ Mould   + Cu alloy
▨ Hearth   ⬭ Stones
▦ Feature   •∙• Stakeholes

0   4m

only a small part of this feature survived it is possible that a building originally stood here. One of the round-houses produced bronze casting waste, clustered around a fire pit in a post-abandonment layer, indicating that craftworking took place here after the house had fallen out of use. At **South Lodge Camp** (Wiltshire), an enclosed settlement produced a single unstratified mould fragment. One case where a 'special' or 'high-status' location may have been associated with more intensive metal casting is the hillfort at **Rathgall** (Co. Wicklow). Much of the large metalworking assemblage from this site dates to the Late Bronze Age, and the hillfort itself is likely to

date to this period or later, but the presence of clay moulds for rapiers and palstaves suggests a Middle Bronze Age element. This site will be discussed below alongside other Late Bronze Age sites.

Very few settlements of Middle Bronze Age date have produced larger quantities of metalworking debris, or anything that resembles a 'set' of metalworking equipment. One exception is the small open farmstead at **Tremough** (Cornwall), where one of a pair of hollow-set round-houses produced fragments of nine stone moulds and one clay mould (Fig. 4.6). These were for a range of objects including axes, chisels, and pins. The stone moulds were found on the floor surface clustered around the hearth. Soil samples from the floor produced small droplets of copper alloy, and soil geochemistry showed high levels of copper and tin, indicating that bronze casting had taken place inside the building. The moulds themselves are from three different geological sources, at least one of them non-local (volcanic tuff possibly from the Lizard or Mount's Bay). There are also marked differences in the skill used to carve the moulds. One item may be an apprentice piece or a representation of a mould that was not intended for use: the matrix and imprecise scored decoration would have formed an object of approximate but unusable axe shape, while the absence of discoloration suggests that this mould was never subjected to the heat of bronze casting. Hence, despite the evidence for *in situ* metalworking in this building, it is possible that the moulds do not represent a single metalworker's tool kit but were brought together from several sources for deposition.

Middle Bronze Age casting evidence has been found in round-houses or other buildings from at least eight sites, mostly in Cornwall and Ireland. The metalworking evidence from settlements elsewhere in Britain tends to be sparser and scrappier – though this partly reflects the lack of use of durable stone moulds in south-east England – and associations with particular buildings are less evident. Aside from **Tremough** and **Trethellan Farm**, other examples of house associations include **Corrstown** (Co. Antrim), **Kilsharvan** (Co. Meath) (both discussed below in the section on the deliberate deposition of metalworking residues) and **Trevisker** (Cornwall), where a house produced a piece of copper alloy waste from one post-hole, and cassiterite pebbles from another. At **Trevalga** (Cornwall), a stone mould for a triangular razor (*racloir*) was found in a round-house close to the entrance, though it is unclear whether it had been left on the floor or was transported by post-occupation inwash. A crucible sherd with bronze residues was recovered from the upper fill of a penannular gully marking the outer wall of an unenclosed round-house at **Deer's Den**, Kintore (Aberdeenshire); this is the only excavated casting waste from a Middle Bronze Age settlement context in Scotland. With the notable exception of Tremough, it is not certain if metalworking was actually carried out in these

buildings. However, at **Chancellorsland** (Co. Tipperary), possible crucible fragments were recovered from a hearth within a D-shaped stake-walled structure, suggesting *in situ* bronze casting activities. This was one of a series of buildings inside an oval enclosure (60 × 50 m) defined by a palisade and ditch. Most residential structures of this date were round, so the form of this building may be one indication of its special purpose. Other finds from the site include human skull fragments and an amber bead and ring.

'Open air' settlement contexts outside of houses and other structures include pits (4 sites), hearths (2 sites), wells or waterholes (1 site), pathways (1 site), enclosure ditches (1 site) and field boundaries (1 site). In several cases, these include contexts at the margins of the settled area. At **Down Farm**, Gussage St Michael (Dorset), for example, three round-houses were enclosed by a fence, with a bank and ditch defining the eastern and southern sides of the site. A single lump of casting waste was found in the enclosure ditch. A small piece of casting waste was recovered from the fill of a ditched field boundary that formed part of an extensive field system at **Newark Road**, Fengate (Peterborough). A round-house, a second circular structure and a large number of pits and post-holes were found in the area partly defined by this ditch. At **Stansted Airport** (Essex) a number of crucible fragments were recovered from a waterhole in the south-eastern corner of a settlement comprising several round-houses set within a ditched and fenced enclosure. At **Bourton Business Park**, Bourton-on-the-Water (Gloucestershire), a pit containing a large deposit of clay mould fragments was located within and close to the entrance of a palisaded enclosure, although it is not clear if this was contemporary as other features of Late Neolithic–Iron Age date were also identified at the site. The pit contained substantial fragments of a clay mould for a Taplow-style sword dating to the Penard phase of the Middle Bronze Age, prefiguring the deliberate deposits of sword moulds that became more common during the Late Bronze Age. The inclusion of a fragment of stone mould in the cobbled roadway at **Corrstown** (Co. Antrim) is interesting too, for journeying – like metalworking – is a transformative process, although it is not possible to say with certainty that the mould was deliberately incorporated into this feature.

Such finds may, of course, have been deposited away from their original context of use and, as such, may not show the location of metalworking activities. Metalworking residues have, however, occasionally been recovered from hearths. At **Kynance Gate** (Cornwall), two joining fragments of a clay axe mould with apparent 'traces of copper sulphate' were found in a hearth of Middle Bronze Age date. This was one of a cluster of open hearths found at the site. A stone-lined trench attached to this hearth and linking it to a larger square hearth pit was thought to act perhaps as a flue. A single piece of casting waste as well as clay mould fragments for casting rapiers and spearheads were found in a hearth of possible Middle Bronze Age date at **Lough Gur (Knockadoon) Site F** (Co. Limerick) sealed beneath a later field bank.

Metalworking residues are occasionally found further from the settlement core. At **Tewkesbury** (Gloucestershire), the metalworking debris came from in and around a swathe of otherwise finds-poor pits set *c.* 300 m apart from the main settlement area, the latter incorporating a D-shaped enclosure (Fig. 4.7). Here, the upper fill of a small pit produced burnt stone, charcoal, clay spearhead mould fragments (possibly representing a single mould), and two bronze droplets. Nearby were found an unstratified scatter of four copper droplets, a piece of copper alloy (possibly a casting jet or miscast loop), and a number of fragments of fired clay incorporating copper corrosion products. The settlement was located on slightly higher ground, but the metalworking debris was found in an area today prone to seasonal flooding. This hints that metalworking at this site may have been a seasonal activity, although the presence of fragments from only one mould suggests a single episode. Its location well away from contemporary settlement and in a part of the landscape that itself underwent seasonal transformation may indicate that here there were particular rules regarding where metalworking could take place – rules that may have related to the perceived danger (both in practical and symbolic terms) of the activity.

The deliberate deposition of metalworking residues in settlement contexts

Although the finds from sites such as **Kynance Gate** and **Tewkesbury** may indicate an actual metal casting locale, this is not necessarily the case for finds from other sites. One of the four mould fragments from **Corrstown** (Co. Antrim) was found in the slot trench dug for the wall of round-house 8, while a second mould fragment was found in the upper fill of a post-hole located around 1 m north of round-house 1. It is not clear at what point in the history of these structures the mould fragments were deposited but it is possible that they represent offerings relating to the construction or abandonment of the buildings. If so, they may not indicate that metalworking took place at these locations: rather, mould fragments were viewed – presumably because of the social or cultural significance of metalworking – as objects suitable for marking out places and moments of transformation. Certainly, the mould from house 1 appeared to have a lengthy history, as three circular holes had been drilled through the matrix; these are unlikely to relate to the original use of the object since they would have compromised its integrity for casting. This indicates careful curation and reuse of this object, and it is possible that an 'ancestral' item of this sort may have been viewed as a suitable abandonment offering.

At other sites, the chronological context of deposition is more evident. At **Stansted Airport** (Essex), the waterhole in the south-east corner of the site was deliberately infilled (perhaps on the abandonment of the settlement) with material that included two crucible fragments, a human tooth and skull fragment, pottery, loomweights, polecat/ferret bones, tools of stone, flint and bone, and large quantities of burnt clay, stone, and charcoal. The finds from this feature prefigure similar (and more common) closing deposits from Late Bronze Age waterholes, as we shall see later in this chapter. At **Kilsharvan** (Co. Meath), a broken but near-complete stone mould for a Middle Bronze Age spearhead was found in the backfill of one of the curvilinear slot trenches that defined a possible round-house, indicating that this item was deposited at the end of the structure's life. The stone moulds from **Tremough** (Cornwall) had been placed on the floor of the round-house (Fig. 4.6), an act that appears to have formed part of ritualised closing events undertaken at this structure. When the house was abandoned, the posts were removed from the post-holes, and significant objects were placed in the

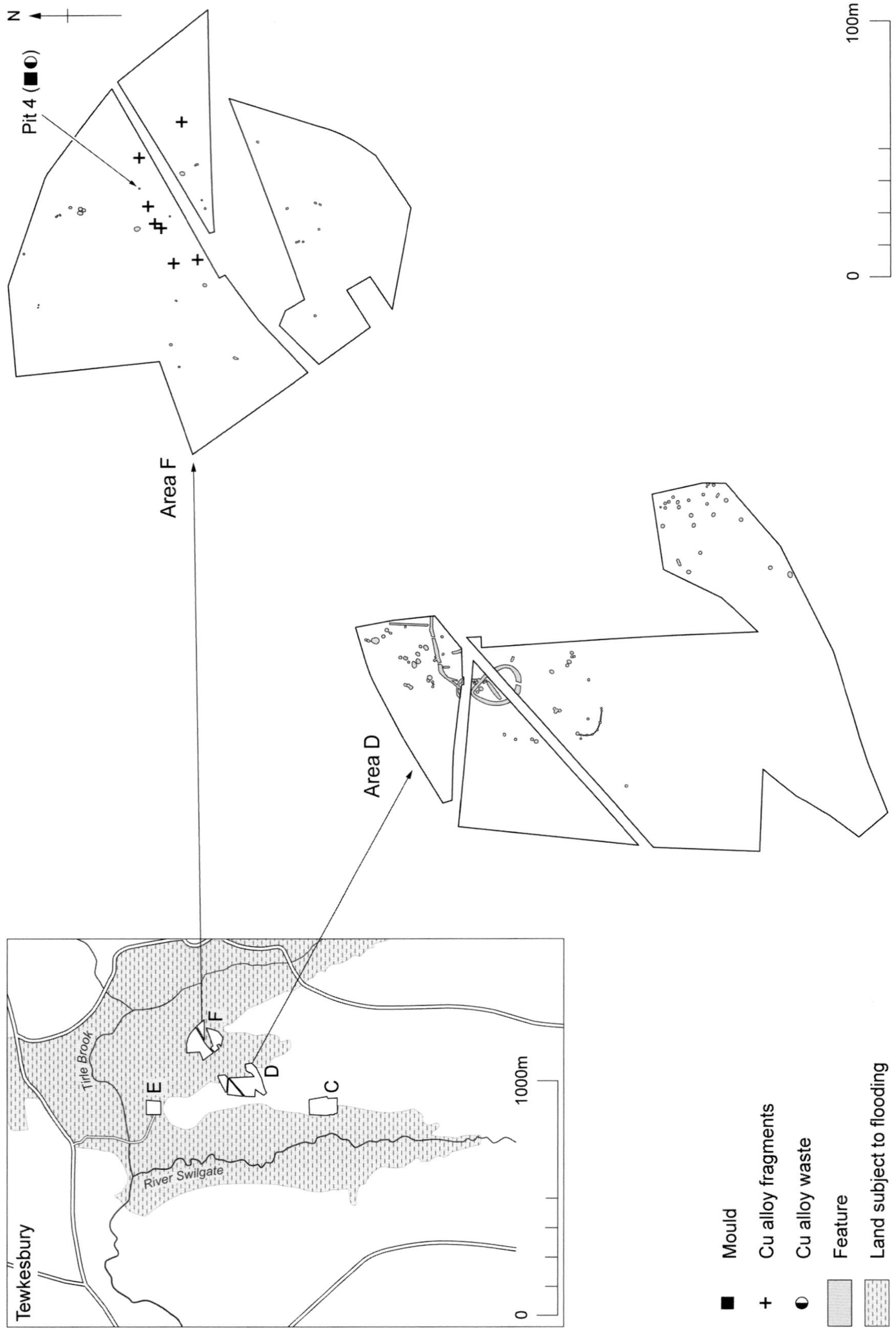

Figure 4.7: Areas of Middle Bronze Age settlement (D) and metalworking (F) at Tewkesbury (Gloucestershire) (redrawn by Anne Leaver after Walker et al. 2004, figs 4–6)

upper fills of several of these features. These included a copper alloy finger ring deposited in the upper fill of a post-hole near the entrance to the building, and a copper alloy pin in a post-hole diametrically opposite at the back of the house. The round-house was then deliberately infilled with a layer of soil containing significant quantities of pottery, stone artefacts, and other finds. All the moulds from the floor of the house were broken and fragmentary. They showed evidence for wear and some had been reworked, suggesting lengthy histories of use. In contrast to the finds from **Corrstown**, metalworking appears to have been carried out in this building, so that here there is a more evident link between the deposition of the moulds and the history of the round-house itself. The involvement of metalworking materials in house abandonment practices at **Tremough** and elsewhere may find contemporary parallel on the near Continent. At Tilburg-Tradepark Noord (Noord-Brabant, Netherlands), four pits within a Middle Bronze Age long-house contained metalworking remains, including a crucible with bronze residues and stone tools with copper alloy traces, and it has been argued that these objects were deposited following the abandonment of the house (Tol 2015).

Earlier monuments and other 'non-settlement' contexts

Middle Bronze Age metalworking debris has also been recovered from a small number of earlier monuments and other non-settlement contexts. At **Grimes Graves** (Norfolk), midden deposits rich in animal bone, pottery, worked flint, and other artefacts infilled the weathering cones of Neolithic flint mine shafts. The deposit in shaft X contained *c.* 150 clay mould fragments (though these are possibly from as few as three moulds) and a few crucible fragments. The moulds were for casting large 'ceremonial' or 'parade' spearheads. Bronze casting waste was also recovered from various contexts at this site, while several copper alloy awls may also have been used for metalworking. The midden material from Grimes Graves has been assumed to be rubbish from a neighbouring settlement but survey work failed to identify evidence for any such site. Instead we can suggest that this striking pockmarked landscape was selected as the venue either for particular activities

that produced these unusual accumulations or for the redeposition of midden debris – itself perhaps a symbolically significant material – from elsewhere. Equally, it is possible that the concave features of the partially infilled mine shafts would have provided a protected location for activities like copper alloy casting that required sustained heat.

In Ireland, Middle Bronze Age stone moulds have been found at three Chalcolithic wedge tombs. At **Loughash** (Co. Tyrone), a palstave mould fragment was incorporated into stones sealing one of the chambers. At **Moylisha** (Co. Wicklow), both halves of a spearhead mould were found outside the eastern end of the tomb and at the base of the cairn that overlay the monument. It is suggested that these may have been deposited when an outer kerb was added to the monument in the Middle Bronze Age. At **Lough Gur** (Co. Limerick), a spearhead mould fragment was found less than 3 m south of the entrance to the tomb and crucible fragments of probable Bronze Age date were found in the chamber. The deposition of these moulds may relate to ritual activity at these already ancient monuments, and need not imply that metalworking actually occurred here, though the presence also of crucibles at Lough Gur raises the possibility that it did. In either case, the discovery of casting debris at existing monuments tells us something interesting. We do not know how wedge tombs were viewed or understood in the Middle Bronze Age; however it is possible that they were recognised as locations associated with the dead, or that their astronomical orientation towards the midwinter sunset (O'Brien 1999, 216–17) was considered significant. If so, this suggests that in these cases bronze casting was symbolically linked with concepts of death and regeneration and that liminal spaces in which contact with the otherworld could take place were seen as appropriate places in which either to cast bronze or deposit the residues of this activity. No comparable deposits are known from Britain during this period, though at Plounevez-Lochrist in Brittany a stone palstave mould has been found associated with an older megalithic alignment (Le Roux 1975).

The Late Bronze Age and Earliest Iron Age: excavated evidence

This period sees a dramatic increase in the

Figure 4.8: Distribution of excavated settlements of Late Bronze Age and Earliest Iron Age date that have produced metalworking tools and non-ferrous metalworking residues

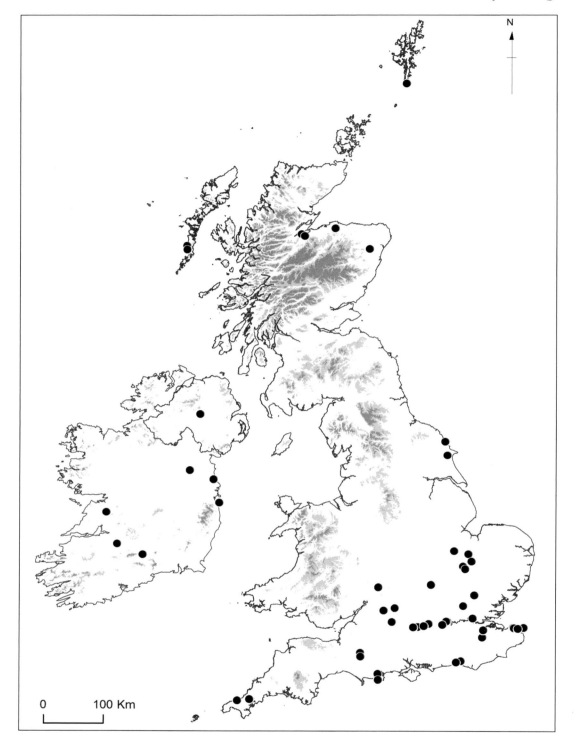

numbers of excavated sites with casting evidence. One hundred and twenty five sites dating to the period *c.* 1150–600 BC have been identified. Of these, 84 sites are in England (Figs 4.8 & 4.9), with a particular concentration in the south and east: a survey of published reports suggests that in this region around 40% of Late Bronze Age sites excavated since 1990 have produced casting evidence, compared to around a quarter of Middle Bronze Age sites. A significant number of sites have also been identified in Ireland.

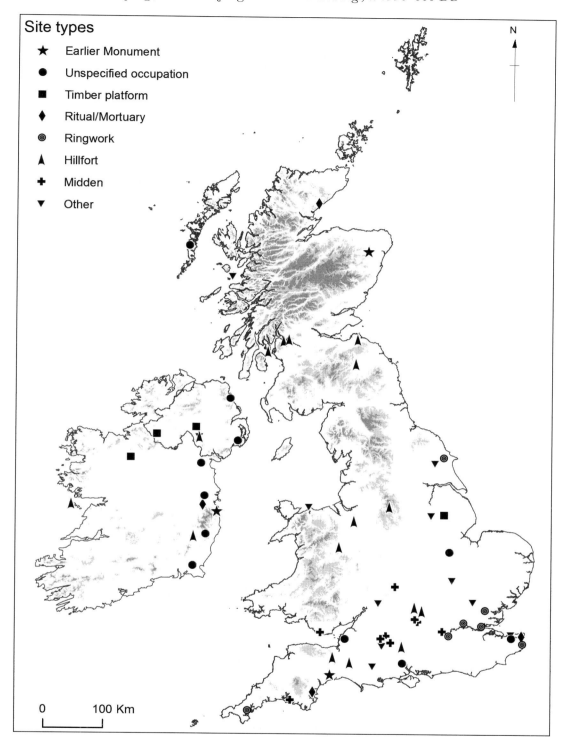

Site types

★ Earlier Monument
● Unspecified occupation
■ Timber platform
◆ Ritual/Mortuary
◎ Ringwork
▲ Hillfort
✚ Midden
▼ Other

0   100 Km

Figure 4.9: Distribution of other excavated sites of Late Bronze Age and Earliest Iron Age date that have produced metalworking tools and non-ferrous metalworking residues

In Scotland there is a dramatic increase not only in the number of sites with non-ferrous metalworking evidence but also the amount of material from those sites. Overall, despite the existence of particular regional concentrations, the evidence from this period is more widely distributed. In Britain, metalworking evidence from most sites falls into the period 1150–800 BC and cannot be dated more closely. At seven sites, the metalworking activity appears to date to *c.* 1150–1000/950 BC: four of these have produced Wilburton style moulds and there are early radiocarbon dates from three others. Metalworking evidence that can be dated to the latter part of the Late Bronze Age, *c.* 1000/950–800 BC, has been identified at slightly more sites: nine have yielded Ewart Park or Stogursey moulds and there are radiocarbon dates in this date range from four others. The finds from six sites can be specifically dated to the Earliest Iron Age. There is thus no clear evidence that the peak in metal deposition in south-east England during the Ewart Park phase (Needham 2007) was matched by a corresponding increase in production.

Casting evidence is now found at a more diverse range of sites, in line with the greater differentiation of site types seen in this period (Brück 2007) including, but not limited to, sites that have been interpreted as 'high-status' such as middens, timber platforms and hillforts (Fig. 4.10). As in the Middle Bronze Age, however, settlements remain the largest category. The quantity of metalworking debris is often much greater than at sites of Middle Bronze Age date (see below). The casting evidence itself also becomes more diverse (Fig. 4.11). More sites now have moulds for multiple different artefacts, and it seems that a range of weapons, tools and ornaments could often be produced at a single location. We also have the first stratified evidence for the casting of lead and gold. Clay moulds account for the greatest number of finds and are the most frequent form of evidence from any type of site. This is followed by crucible fragments and casting waste (Fig. 4.12); unlike mould fragments, which are often found in significant numbers (see below), sites tend to yield only one or two crucible fragments or pieces of casting waste. Copper ingots and stone moulds have sometimes been recovered from excavated sites but are more often found as single finds or in hoards. Possible smithing tools are rare outside of hoard contexts and have been recovered from only ten excavated sites in England, two in Scotland and one in Wales. These are predominantly tanged chisels which, as already discussed in Chapter 2, may have been used in metalworking, but might equally have been employed in a variety of other crafts.

There are some regional differences both in the types of sites that have produced metalworking remains and in the character of the evidence itself. In Ireland, casting evidence is more commonly associated with sites typically considered to be high-status or ceremonial sites, including hillforts, timber platforms and earlier monuments (ten out of 21 sites). As we shall see, hillforts in this region may have been foci for intensive or specialised metalworking. Despite the recent upsurge in developer-funded excavation, relatively few open settlements in Ireland have produced metalworking residues (seven sites, although a number of other sites that are difficult to interpret may also fall into this category). In Wales, only three sites of the period have been identified. In Scotland, metalworking debris has mostly been recovered from hillforts and open settlements (13 out of 17 sites). In England, metalworking evidence is frequently found on open settlements and in their environs (42 out of 84 sites): some of the largest and most diverse assemblages (eg, in terms of the numbers of different artefact types cast) are from otherwise apparently 'ordinary' sites, although metalworking evidence has also been recovered from possible high-status locales such as hillforts, middens, and ringworks. There are regional differences within England too. Given the general distribution of hillforts it is perhaps no surprise that casting evidence is more often found at hillforts in western and northern England than in eastern regions. Ringworks are mainly found in eastern England whereas middens have a south-central bias. A variety of types of sites occur in south-western England whereas in the south-east open settlements predominate.

Hillforts

Sixteen hillforts, predominantly in northern and western Britain and Ireland, have produced casting evidence of Late Bronze Age or Earliest Iron Age date. In several cases the metalworking residues appear to be from the latter stages of the Late Bronze Age: moulds of the Ewart Park tradition have been identified at three sites, while a radiocarbon date from a fourth also falls into this phase. However, it is often unclear whether the hilltops were already enclosed during this period, and the scale and character of the Late Bronze Age occupation is frequently poorly understood. Analysis of the distribution and context of the material within these sites is difficult, as in most cases only a very small proportion of the hillfort has

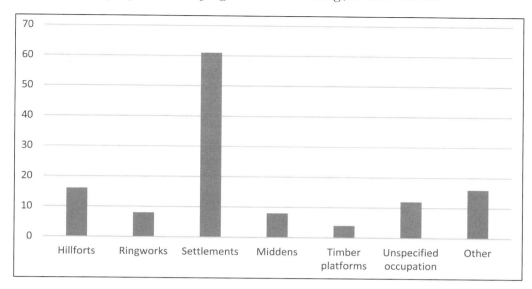

Figure 4.10: Number of excavated Late Bronze Age and Earliest Iron Age sites with metalworking evidence in Britain and Ireland, broken down by site type. The category 'other' includes a small number of earlier monuments, ritual/mortuary sites, linear boundaries, 2 palaeochannels, a glacial pingo, & several other unusual sites (see text)

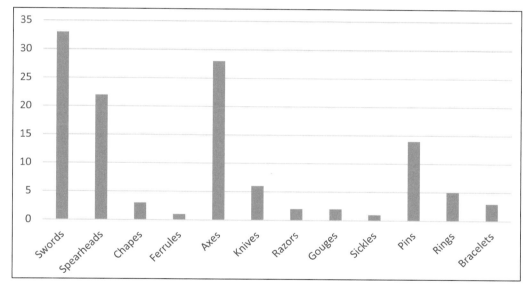

Figure 4.11: Number of excavated sites of Late Bronze Age and Earliest Iron Age date that have yielded casting evidence for particular types of artefact (note only moulds whose matrices could be identified with a reasonable degree of certainty are included)

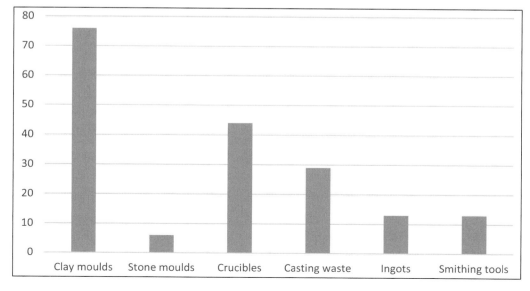

Figure 4.12: Number of excavated sites of Late Bronze Age–Earliest Iron Age date producing different types of metalworking evidence

been excavated, and often the Bronze Age contexts have been disturbed by later activity. Although it would be easy to assume that hillforts were high-status sites, the evidence is far from clear-cut. It is in hillforts that we find our most substantial assemblage of the period (**Rathgall** (Co. Wicklow)) and some of the most insubstantial remains (such as the single crucible sherd from **Mam Tor** (Derbyshire)). In some cases (as at the **Breiddin** (Powys)), the evidence may indicate the actual location of metalworking, while at other sites (such as **Norton Fitzwarren** (Somerset)) deliberate deposits of metalworking remains have been found that may be some distance from their original place of use.

The two largest and most diverse assemblages of Late Bronze Age casting debris come from hillforts in Ireland and these sites have also produced rare evidence for goldworking. The site at Rathgall (Co. Wicklow) is a multivallate hillfort and has produced the largest Bronze Age metalworking assemblage from Britain and Ireland, including some 4000 clay mould fragments, crucibles, a few pieces of scrap (although some of this may be medieval) and two small possible bronze bar ingots. The three outer ramparts at Rathgall (ramparts 2, 3, and 4) have not been dated directly and the earliest phase of silting in the ditch associated with the inner rampart (rampart 1) dates to the medieval period. However, the copious evidence for Late Bronze Age activity at the site suggests that the origins of at least some of the enclosing features lie in this period. Just inside rampart 1 at the centre of the site is a circular enclosure (ring-ditch 1), 34 m in diameter. This was defined by a ditch (possibly with an external bank, although this is unclear) and enclosed a substantial round-house. The cremation burial of an infant accompanied by a penannular gold ring was found in a pit inside this building. Outside and to the east of ring-ditch 1 was an area with thick charcoal-rich deposits containing the majority of the mould and crucible fragments from the site; thousands of sherds of coarseware pottery, querns, and whetstones (though these artefact categories are found in significant numbers elsewhere on the site too); and more unusual finds including 88 glass beads, shale bracelets, and amber, bronze, and gold objects. Moulds for the production of a wide range of tools, weapons, and ornaments are present, including

swords, chapes, spearheads, axes, sickles, knives, pins, and bracelets, with matrices for palstaves and rapiers indicating that activity at the site began in the latter part of the Middle Bronze Age. A piece of gold scrap suggests that goldworking may also have been carried out here.

Immediately adjacent to ring-ditch 1 but to the south-east was a smaller ring-ditch in which three cremation burials were found. A pit to the south of the central burial contained a sword blade fragment, a spearhead, and a socketed chisel. A number of mould fragments were found in other features interpreted as hearths or pyres within this ring-ditch, though these did not contain human bone. There were a few mould fragments and a piece of copper alloy waste from two further ring-ditches to the south of the hillfort, including from contexts interpreted as possible pyres. A trench through rampart 2 also yielded a small number of mould fragments from a pre-rampart context.

Bayesian modelling of radiocarbon dates from the site suggests a main phase of activity, including cremation and metalworking, from 1200–1000 BC. Ring-ditch 1 may date to this period, although it is suggested that the round-house at the centre of this enclosure dates to after 800 BC (and is hence later than the burial inside it). The similarity of ring-ditch 1 with its central round-house to the ringworks of eastern and southern England is notable. As we shall see below, several of these have produced metalworking debris from in or around their east-facing entrances – a spatial relationship that is not dissimilar to that visible at **Rathgall**. The close spatial link between cremation and metalworking – both heat-mediated transformative technologies – is interesting but unusual, and it is possible that the same specialists may have been involved in both processes.

A small number of other Irish hillforts have produced metalworking evidence. These include the stone-walled coastal cliff-top fort at **Dún Aonghasa** on the Aran Islands (Co. Galway) which produced a significant assemblage of crucible sherds from around five vessels, clay mould fragments for at least 16–21 cast objects including socketed axes, spears, swords, knives, pins, and bracelets, and a small quantity of bronze slag. Stratigraphy is poor, but most of these items were found in the innermost enclosure, particularly its southern part where it is argued that there was a single major episode of casting pre-dating the round-houses also found in that area. A cluster of relatively fresh pin moulds near a hearth close to the northern wall of the inner enclosure could suggest that this feature was used for metalworking. Other finds from the site include amber beads and 14 bronze artefacts. It has been suggested that a bronze bracelet from the site may have been cast in one of the recovered moulds. Both the hillforts that form the heart of the Navan complex (Co. Armagh) have produced metalworking evidence. Small-scale excavation within the interior of the earlier of the two, **Haughey's Fort**, produced both bronze and gold casting waste and object fragments from pits and post-holes. One pit with bronze casting waste is radiocarbon dated to 1230–900 cal BC (2877±60 BP; UB 3386), and radiocarbon dates from the inner ditch fall into the same date range. Two substantial double-ring post structures on the summit of the hill are too large to have been round-houses and a ritual or ceremonial role has been proposed for these (Mallory 1995). No moulds were found at **Haughey's Fort**, but sword moulds were deposited in the artificial pool known as the **King's Stables** just 300 m away (see below). One kilometre to the east of Haughey's Fort lies **Navan Fort**. Although the main *floruit* of activity at Navan Fort can be dated to 400–100 BC, and the hillfort itself can perhaps be assigned to this period, a 39 m diameter ditched enclosure in the interior has been dated to the Late Bronze Age. Inside this, a pair of conjoined circular timber structures (one larger than the other) were rebuilt on multiple occasions during the Earliest Iron Age. A few clay mould fragments of probable Late Bronze Age date were recovered, but contextual information is poor. Navan Fort is regarded as a so-called 'royal site' during the Iron Age and subsequent early medieval period and certainly functioned as a significant ceremonial centre from 400–100 BC. The significance of this landscape during the Late Bronze Age is further underlined by the discovery of the Tamlaght hoard with its rare bronze artefacts imported from the Continent deposited in a bog just 700 m south-west of Haughey's Fort (Macdonald & O Néill 2009).

In Wales the evidence from the **Breiddin** (Powys) is particularly interesting because of the rare association of non-ferrous metalworking with possible furnaces in a Late Bronze Age hillfort context. Here a timber-revetted rampart of stone and earth was constructed in the Late Bronze Age. The area enclosed by this feature is unknown, although if it followed the line of the later Iron Age hillfort, it may have been as large as 28 ha. Excavation was focused in the southern part of the hillfort interior. Clay moulds (*c.* 50 pieces) and crucible fragments were found across much of the excavated area (Fig. 4.13), with a particular concentration in and around a group of pits, hearths, and putative furnaces in the northern part of this area (Fig. 4.14). The possible furnaces were oval, pear-shaped, or waisted, with one end wider and deeper than the other. Some were stone-lined and had evidence of burning in their deeper ends and they produced small quantities of charcoal and metal slag. Two contiguous bands of yellowish clay and brown soil around the edge of furnace 5164B have been interpreted as the remains of a clay dome built over a light wooden frame (Fig. 4.14). It has been suggested that these features were used for the remelting and purification of bronze rather than primary smelting activities. One produced possible ferrous as well as cuprous slag, suggesting a spatial if not an organisational link between bronzeworking and early ironworking. A crucible fragment was recovered from a second excavated area in the northern part of the interior. There are several bronze objects from the site including a hammer, axe, knife, spearhead, portions of a sword, several pins, and part of a bracelet.

In contrast to the Breiddin, the evidence from **Norton Fitzwarren** (Somerset) is not associated with a defined area of metalworking activity. Here a hilltop enclosure was first laid out in the Early–Middle Bronze Age. A Middle Bronze Age hoard (comprising bracelets, palstaves, and axes) was deposited adjacent to the north side of the entrance. A pit (or possible ditch terminal) flanking the south side of the entrance contained deliberate deposits of Late Bronze Age sword mould fragments and two complete pots in its basal fill, suggesting that the earlier enclosure continued to be a significant element of the Late Bronze Age landscape. The mould fragments belong to the developed Ewart Park tradition of the 10th–9th centuries BC. The pit was later overlain by the hillfort rampart, probably in the Early Iron Age. At **Sheep Hill** (West Dunbartonshire), a timber-

Figure 4.13: Hillfort at the Breiddin (Powys) (redrawn by Anne Leaver after Musson 1991, figs 5, 8, 10, 15, & 31)

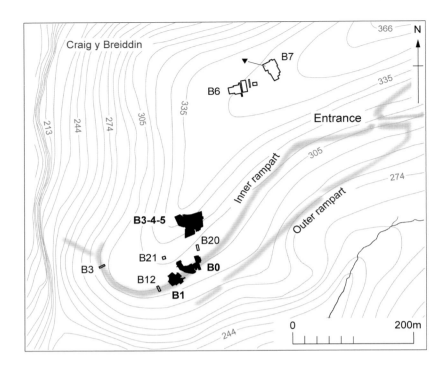

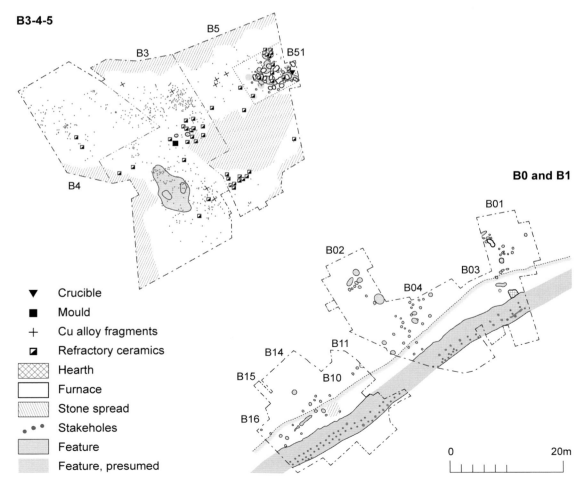

▼ Crucible
■ Mould
+ Cu alloy fragments
◪ Refractory ceramics
▨ Hearth
□ Furnace
▨ Stone spread
••• Stakeholes
▨ Feature
▨ Feature, presumed

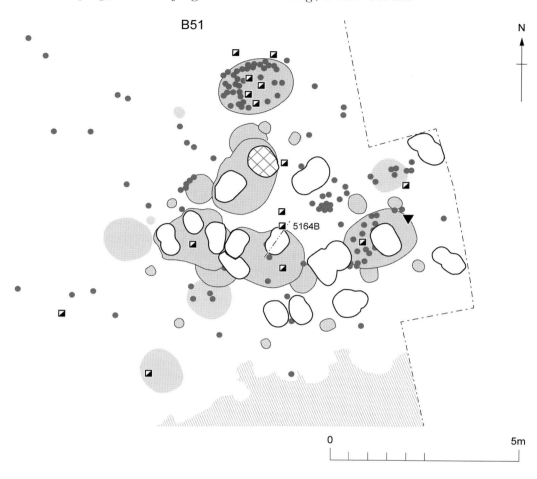

N

Figure 4.14: Area of most intense metalworking activity and cross-section of possible furnace at the Breiddin (Powys) (redrawn by Anne Leaver after Musson 1991, figs 32–3)

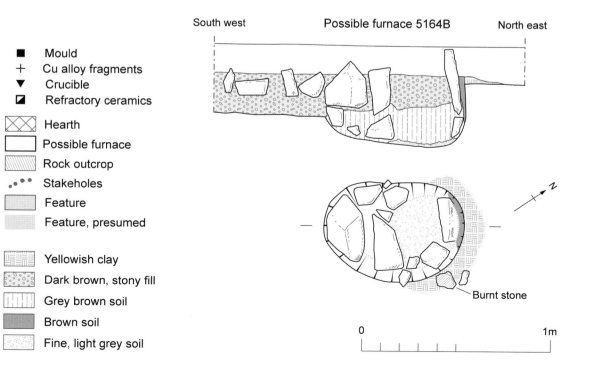

■ Mould
+ Cu alloy fragments
▼ Crucible
◪ Refractory ceramics
▨ Hearth
▭ Possible furnace
▨ Rock outcrop
⦁⦁⦁ Stakeholes
▨ Feature
▨ Feature, presumed

▨ Yellowish clay
▨ Dark brown, stony fill
▨ Grey brown soil
▨ Brown soil
▨ Fine, light grey soil

framed drystone enclosure on the summit of the hill was destroyed by fire and partly vitrified around 800 BC. A midden found outside this, and under the rampart of the later Iron Age fort, may either be associated with the Late Bronze Age enclosure or post-date it. It contained fragments of at least three clay moulds of the Ewart Park phase.

Contextual information for finds from other hillforts is in general poor. Oak charcoal from the timber-framed rampart at **Beeston Castle** (Cheshire West & Chester) yielded a wide date range in the Late Bronze Age (1260–830 cal BC; 2860±80 BP; HAR 4405), but the wood was mature and the sample is therefore unlikely to date the act of rampart construction. Moreover, the mould and crucible fragments from the site, as well as a plano-convex ingot fragment of possible Late Bronze Age date, were found redeposited in later contexts. The majority of the activity at **Traprain Law** (East Lothian) dates to the Roman Iron Age and later periods. However, the hillfort revealed evidence for Late Bronze Age metalworking although the context of these remains is poorly recorded. This includes clay mould fragments of the Ewart Park phase for the production of spearheads, swords, and axes; a bronze sprue; and three crucible fragments possibly from the same vessel. A hoard of four Late Bronze Age axes was also discovered on the cliff below the summit of the hill. Other finds of the period include bronze axes, knives, chisels, a gouge, armlet, and razor. Some of the pottery, amber beads, jet/shale armlets, and saddle querns found could also be associated with this phase. Other hillforts that have produced small-scale casting evidence of possible Late Bronze Age or Earliest Iron Age date include **Ham Hill** (Somerset), **Segsbury** (Oxfordshire), **Mam Tor** (Derbyshire), **Eildon Hill North** (Scottish Borders), **Craigmarloch** (Inverclyde), and **Little Dunagoil** (Argyll & Bute). The finds from most of these sites are unstratified, residual or have no context information, although in several cases (eg, **Eildon Hill North**) they have been recovered from within the later Iron Age defences, suggesting a possible association with the margins of these locations, as at **Norton Fitzwarren**.

It can also be noted that casting evidence has been identified at a number of hillforts on the other side of the Channel in northern France, most notably at Fort-Harrouard (Eure et Loire) where numerous moulds, crucibles, tuyères, casting waste, and bar ingots were found (Mohen 1984; 1989; Mohen & Bailloud 1987; Queixalos *et al.* 1987). There, the casting activity spans the Middle and Late Bronze Age and was in some cases associated with hearths or furnaces, providing a possible parallel for the **Breiddin**.

Ringworks

Metalworking evidence has been found at other enclosed sites of Late Bronze Age and Earliest Iron Age date, notably the ringworks of southern and eastern England. The term 'ringwork' has been applied to sites that actually vary significantly in size, form and associated material culture (Needham 1992a). Most of the classic excavated examples from around the Thames estuary have metalworking evidence within or outside them, though there are exceptions (eg, Kingsborough Manor (Kent); Allen *et al.* 2008). They have often been interpreted as high-status settlements because of the substantial circular earthworks that surround them, although their dense distribution across parts of the landscape of southern and eastern England and the relative paucity of 'exotic' finds calls this into question (Needham 1992a; Brück 2007). A ceremonial role has been suggested for some ringworks, for example **Paddock Hill**, Thwing (East Riding of Yorkshire): the circular timber building at the centre of the second phase enclosure at this site was 25 m in diameter and is unlikely to represent a 'normal' residential structure.

Metalworking evidence has been identified from at least seven and probably eight ringworks, mostly in south-east England but with one in the East Riding of Yorkshire and one in Cornwall. The mould fragments placed in two discrete deposits on the base of the enclosure ditch at **Springfield Lyons** (Essex) are perhaps the best-known example. These were placed in the northern terminals of the freshly-cut ditches at both the east and west entrances. They derive from the casting of at least ten swords, including both the clay moulds and crucible fragments. No other metalworking debris was recovered from the site and it is clear that these were deliberate and selective deposits, suggested to be foundation deposits. Other ringworks have also produced casting evidence from their enclosure ditches. At **Mill Hill**, Deal (Kent), a mould for an object decorated with

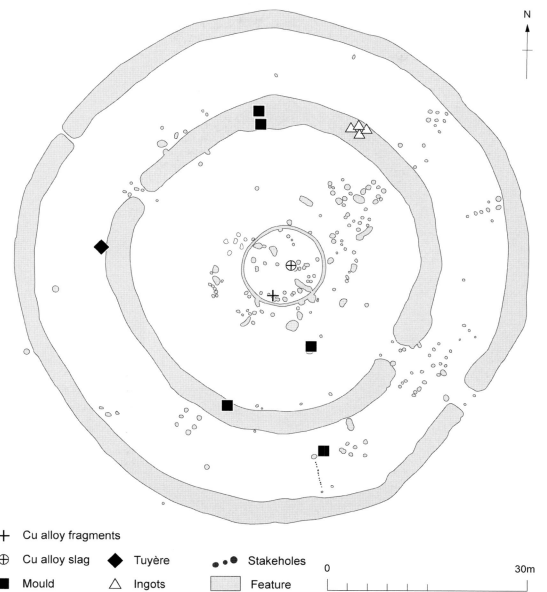

N

Figure 4.15: Late Bronze Age ringwork at Mucking South Rings (Essex) (redrawn by Anne Leaver after Evans et al. 2015, fig. 3.21)

+   Cu alloy fragments

⊕   Cu alloy slag   ◆   Tuyère   •●•   Stakeholes

■   Mould   △   Ingots   ▨   Feature

0   30m

concentric rings (possibly a plaque: Adams 2017, 49, 52) was recovered from the base of the enclosure ditch on its north-western side. Four clay mould fragments and a crucible fragment were found dispersed in various contexts in the enclosure ditch to the north of the east-facing entrance at **Mucking North Ring** (Thurrock). A piece of casting waste was also recovered from the butt end of the ditch to the south of the entrance. The nearby site of **Mucking South Rings** (Thurrock) is a double-ditched enclosure with a single central circular structure. The site was excavated in the

1960s and '70s so the context of the finds is not clear in every case. The inner ditch produced a clay mould fragment and several fragments of casting waste, although the exact location of the latter is unknown (Fig. 4.15). A cluster of four ingot fragments was found in the ditch on the northern side of the enclosure. Two further clay mould fragments may also originally have been deposited in the ditch and three more were found in pits inside the enclosure. A piece of casting waste and a fragment of copper slag came from the central structure. A possible tuyère was found within the enclosed area but

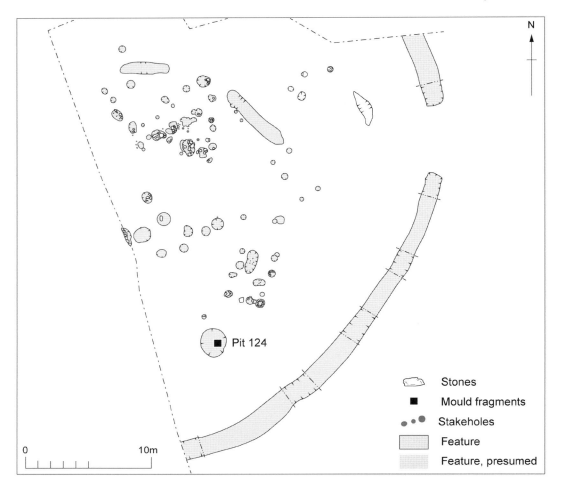

not in the ditches, and a further copper ingot was found elsewhere on the site. The mould fragments were for the production of swords and spearheads.

Slightly different patterns of distribution can be seen at other sites. A pit within a possible ringwork at **Tremough** (Cornwall) produced seven clay mould fragments, including a sword mould and possible axe and chisel moulds (Fig. 4.16). The pit was located towards the edge of the interior of the enclosure. Five further fragments were found in a hollow and a post-hole elsewhere in the enclosure. In some cases, metalworking debris was deposited just outside the entrance to ringworks. At **Oliver Close**, Leyton (Greater London), fragments of a crucible were found in a pit a short distance outside and to the south of the western entrance to the enclosure (Fig. 4.17). This feature also produced large amounts of pottery, burnt flint and burnt clay. A line of closely-set posts running out from the gateway

may have screened the environs of this pit from those entering the site. At **Paddock Hill**, Thwing (East Riding of Yorkshire), a possible metalworking area has been identified. This produced bronze droplets, crucible fragments and moulds and was located just outside of the earlier of the two enclosure ditches, some 20 m north of the south-eastern entrance. A burnt mound and trough were found inside the enclosure, suggesting that heat-mediated transformative activities of some sort also took place within the ringwork. Unfortunately, however, full analysis of the site is lacking. Comparable Late Bronze Age ringworks also occur in northern France, including Mathieu (Calvados), where fragments of crucibles and clay moulds for weapons and possibly ornaments came from the enclosure ditch and features within and just outside the enclosure. Abundant marine mollusc shell deposits in the ditch may be the residues of feasting (Giazzon 2013).

Figure 4.17: Late Bronze Age ringwork at Oliver Close, Leyton (Greater London) (redrawn by Anne Leaver after Bishop 2006, fig. 4)

N

Crucible

Fire pit

Feature

Feature, presumed

Feature, palisade

0   10m

Other enclosures

A small number of 'non-ringwork' enclosures have also produced metalworking debris, mostly in southern England. The ditched and palisaded subrectangular enclosure (B70) at **Highstead** (Kent) is interesting, for like the sites at **Oliver's Close** and **Thwing** described above, the metalworking evidence was recovered from a pit just outside the entrance. This feature produced six moulds, five of them near complete, for the production of disc-headed pins, as well as pottery of Earliest Iron Age date, a perforated clay slab, and a possible polishing stone. Two hearths were also identified in this area. Casting waste was found in several nearby features as well as in the enclosure ditch close to the entrance. At **Sigwells** (Somerset), clay mould fragments for the casting of swords, chapes, spearheads, rapiers, and socketed axes were found. Many of these were deposited in and around a round-house in the northern half of a rectangular enclosure. A scorched area in the western part of this building indicates the location of a hearth or furnace. Shallow scoops immediately outside the building were filled with burnt stone mixed with mould fragments and a droplet of casting waste. Two whetstones were found in the central post-hole of the round-house, and other post-holes yielded a 'perforated furnace spacer' and several human skull and mandible fragments; like the whetstones, hammerstones recovered from the building may have been used in metalworking. The saddle querns from the site were from at least four different sources and include two placed side by side in the enclosure ditch. A cooking trough in the southern part of the site yielded animal bone from at least one cow and three sheep/goats. Small pieces of slag were also recovered from environmental samples from the site. Both the enclosure ditch and most features associated with the building were backfilled after a short period of use. The excavator argues that the enclosure was the site of a short-lived craft fair at a neutral but visible location; survey work suggests a lack of Bronze Age occupation in the surrounding area. It is certainly possible that people from a wide area gathered at this site. However, finds such as human bone, non-local stone, and, as we shall see below, casting debris are frequently recovered from other Late Bronze Age settlements. Moreover, settlements of this period were venues where inter-group relations were forged and maintained: ceramic inventories from settlements of the Late Bronze Age and Earliest Iron Age include an increasing proportion of decorated pottery as well as new forms of vessel such as bowls and cups, suggesting that feasting may often have taken place in a domestic context (Barrett 1980; Brudenell 2012). As such, we should be cautious about drawing easy distinctions between 'normal' settlements and communal sites.

There is little metalworking evidence from other enclosed sites in Ireland. At **Stamullin** (Co. Meath), an enclosure defined by a curvilinear ditch 28 × 22 m in size was extended in its second phase with the construction of a larger outer ditch (*c.* 57 × 47 m). The enclosure contained pits, post-holes, hearths, and a four-post structure but no other recognisable buildings. A clay mould fragment was deposited in the fill of a recut of the outer ditch on the northern side of the enclosure. Portions of two human skullcaps and two abutting cattle skulls were found elsewhere in the outer ditch. Other finds from this site include spindle whorls, saddle querns, and possible fragments of briquetage.

Timber platforms and other watery contexts

Four crannógs or timber platforms at lakesides or in other wetland contexts have produced casting debris alongside other finds suggestive of high-status settlement. Three are in Ireland: at **Rathtinaun** (Co. Sligo), clay mould fragments were recovered from a Late Bronze Age crannóg on the eastern shore of Lough Gara, although details of their context remain unknown. At the edge of the platform, a wooden box containing bronze, tin and lead rings, amber beads, tweezers, a bronze pin, and boars' tusks was deposited in a pit marked by wooden stakes. This may represent a foundation deposit associated with the second phase of the site. A penannular gold ring was also found at the site. In the late 19th century, two clay mould fragments for the production of swords were found 'on the surface of an ancient crannoge associated with rude huts' at **Boho** (Co. Fermanagh). Finds from crannóg B on the eastern edge of **Lough Eskragh** (Co. Tyrone) included three crucible fragments and

eight clay mould fragments for the production of swords, socketed axes, and possibly knives or sickles. '[A] large stone which appeared to have been subjected to hammering' may also be connected with metalworking (Collins & Seaby 1960, 27).

In Britain, one timber platform site has produced metalworking debris: at **Washingborough** (Lincolnshire) two crucible fragments and three stone mould fragments for pin heads were recovered from peat deposits adjacent to a platform at the edge of the River Witham. Other finds from this context include a bronze pin and bar, pottery, a shale bracelet fragment, worked bone and antler, a quern fragment, human bone, and animal bone. Timber platform sites elsewhere in Britain – such as Flag Fen and Must Farm in Cambridgeshire or Shinewater in East Sussex – lack metalworking evidence (Woodcock 1999; Pryor 2001; Knight *et al.* 2019).

The presence of high-status and exotic objects including items of gold and amber, bronze weaponry, and feasting equipment, as well as finds such as skull fragments from other timber platforms suggests that these may have been high-status settlements or gathering places where a range of ritual activities were carried out (O'Sullivan 1997; Pryor 2001; Allen 2009). Their location in bogs and at lakesides is surely no coincidence: these were landscapes in which the votive deposition of metalwork took place – liminal spaces between land and water and between this world and the next where a variety of transformative processes including social transactions, rites of passage, and productive activities such as metalworking may have been carried out. Indeed, the visual impact of metalworking may have been enhanced by the reflection of fire in water. Water is required for quenching hot metals, so the location of metalworking near a water source may have also made sense from a practical perspective.

Associations with water can be seen at a number of other sites. The extensive mound of stone, baked clay, ash, charcoal, and burnt grain at **Killymoon** (Co. Tyrone) was located in an area of raised bog in a wetland context. This site produced two clay mould fragments alongside a variety of finds including a gold dress fastener, gold sleeve fastener, lignite bracelet fragment, perforated stone bead, bronze axe, stone spindle whorls, quernstones, hammerstones, textiles, and pottery. There were several hearths, as well as clusters of post-holes and stake-holes. No buildings could be identified and it is suggested that the post-holes and stake-holes represent the remains of fencing or screening. The purpose of this site is unresolved, though the excavators suggest that it could have had a ritual element. On **Dalkey Island** (Co. Dublin), a Late Bronze Age occupation layer on a small promontory produced crucible sherds, bronze slag, and clay mould fragments for spears, swords, knives, and pins, along with several bronze artefacts. The island is less than 300 m offshore at the very southern edge of Dublin Bay. Later, it was the site of an early medieval entrepôt and church, suggesting that this continued to be a location where social and cosmological boundaries were crossed. A mould has also been recovered as an uncontexted find on Burgh Island just off the coast of Devon (see below).

Late Bronze Age mould fragments have been found associated with palaeochannels close to burnt mounds at two sites. At **Sandy Lane**, Charlton Kings (Gloucestershire), a fragment of a clay spearhead mould was found in a layer sealing the palaeochannel, close to a burnt mound dated broadly to the later Bronze Age. At **Everley Water Meadow** (Dorset), where the burnt mound is dated to the Middle Bronze Age, finds include a syenite mould fragment and clay core for a socketed axe from a Roman period level in the palaeochannel, and a piece of copper ingot from an unspecified context. Despite occasional suggestions that burnt mounds themselves could have played a role in metalworking (Thelin 2007), there is little evidence to support this, and it is notable that none of the very large number of burnt mounds (*fulachtaí fia*) excavated in Ireland is associated with metalworking debris. It is, however, evident that burnt mounds are the product of heat-mediated transformative activities of one sort or another (Ó Néill 2009). This, along with their location in liminal places in the landscape, next to water courses, may have made them a suitable location for the deposition of metalworking debris in the two British examples.

Finally, excavations at the bottom of **Cathedral Hill**, Downpatrick (Co. Armagh) recovered significant quantities of bronze slag from the charcoal-rich fills of a group of pits and stake-holes. Until drainage operations in

recent times, the hill was virtually surrounded by a tidal estuary (Warner & Cahill 2012, 97), a striking landscape context not entirely dissimilar from other wetland and island sites. The excavator claimed that the site dated to the Bronze Age but the basis for this is not clear. There are, however, two hoards of Late Bronze Age gold ornaments from the hill and excavations close to one of these produced Late Bronze Age pottery (Proudfoot 1954; 1955; 1957), although Proudfoot's claim that the hilltop was defined by a Late Bronze Age enclosure has since been disproven and this feature is now thought to date to the early medieval period (Brannon 1988).

Middens

Alongside hillforts and other enclosures, a number of other possible 'high-status' sites have also yielded metalworking evidence. At least eight of the extensive – and often monumental – middens of the Late Bronze Age and Earliest Iron Age in southern Britain have produced metalworking debris. Only a few of these sites have yielded larger assemblages, and the quantity and variety of evidence from others is often little different to that from many 'normal' settlements (see below). Some of the best evidence comes from the **Runnymede Bridge/Petters Sports Field** complex (Surrey), although much of this was recovered from deposits that had been altered by river action after deposition. Finds from the area of the Late Bronze Age waterfront, for example, include a bronze sprue, two mould fragments, and a piece of furnace lining with attached droplet of bronze. Some of the many stone pounders, rubbers, burnishers, and whetstones recovered from the same area of the site may also have been used in the production of metalwork. Finds from other excavated parts of the complex include further clay mould fragments, a miscast razor in its mould, a stone mould, several crucible fragments, casting waste including a lead sprue, ingot fragments, as well as a 'scrap' hoard from a ditch (see below). Bronze tools from the site such as awls, a hammer and a chisel may have been utilised for metalworking.

At **Potterne** (Wiltshire), metalworking evidence includes 13 crucible fragments, three or four mould fragments, copper alloy and lead casting waste, a possible lead bar ingot, pieces of hearth lining, and slag with cuprous residues.

Iron slag was also found. Some of the stone rubbers or burnishers from the site may also have been used in metalworking. XRF analysis of crucibles indicates that they were employed for the casting of leaded bronze. The midden at **Whitchurch** (Warwickshire) stands out for the large assemblage of casting waste (>100 pieces) distributed across the site but this derives from extensive systematic metal detector survey, something not carried out at most sites. This may not all be contemporary with the midden as there is also later Iron Age activity on the site. Also found were two bronze bar ingots or billets, three punches, two chisels, and numerous broken bronze artefacts.

Most other midden sites have produced relatively small assemblages of metalworking debris. These include a single fragment of copper alloy ingot from **Llanmaes** (Vale of Glamorgan) and a crucible fragment from **Wittenham Clumps** (Oxfordshire). The latter site lay below a hilltop enclosure of Late Bronze Age date. Two pieces of casting waste were found at **Whitecross Farm**, Wallingford (Oxfordshire), alongside a possible Late Bronze Age bun ingot from a deposit of medieval alluvium overlying the site.

The fact that metalworking was carried out at midden sites is interesting, though it should be stressed that the metalworking assemblages are generally fairly modest in relation to the huge quantities of other finds recovered from these sites. Middens have produced an unparalleled variety and density of finds, including objects made of 'exotic' materials such as gold, amber, glass, and shale (Waddington 2009). Some of these sites are very large: the deposits at **Potterne** (Wiltshire), for example, were 2 m thick and extended over some 3.5 ha. Alongside metalworking a wide range of other craft activities was carried out at these locations, including spinning and weaving, pottery production, and the working of bone, shale, and stone. Ironworking occurred in the Earliest Iron Age levels at Potterne and **All Cannings Cross** (Wiltshire). Analysis of the animal bone assemblages found at midden sites suggests large-scale butchery and consumption, probably the result of feasting (Madgwick & Mulville 2015). Middens are often at focal points in the landscape. Seven linear ditches, a double-ditched avenue, and a pit alignment all converge at **East Chisenbury** (Wiltshire),

for example, while **Runnymede** (Surrey) and **Wallingford** (Oxfordshire) were located on islands in the Thames. There is evidence too for the performance of ritual activities at these sites. At Potterne, 139 fragments of human bone were recovered, and the preponderance of skull fragments suggests an element of selection and curation to the practices that resulted in their deposition at this site.

Middens, then, appear to have been locations where people congregated for a range of purposes, including feasting, craftwork, exchange, and ritual activities. It would be easy to assume that the presence of 'exotic' materials such as gold and amber indicates that these were 'high-status' sites located at the top of a settlement hierarchy. However, if we see these sites instead as places where communities gathered for socially significant activities, it is perhaps no surprise to find a variety of decorative items, for it seems likely particular attention might have been paid to the costumes worn at such locations. Alongside ornaments of exotic materials, Potterne also produced perforated dog, horse, and deer teeth, the bones of fur-bearing animals including beaver, polecat, and fox, and – although the site is 50 km from the sea – guillemot bones and the claw of a white-tailed sea eagle. It is tempting to imagine that these might have formed an element of the regional costumes (and perhaps even the ceremonial regalia) of those who gathered at the site. The positioning of middens at locations that may have been viewed as liminal, and the performance of ritual activities at these locations suggests that they may have been considered suitable places for other types of transformative practice. This may be one reason why such a wide range of crafts were carried out at these sites, for middens were locations in which both people and objects were made and unmade in practices that defined their place and significance in the order of things (Waddington 2009).

Open settlements

Although sites such as middens, hillforts and ringworks have often been viewed as high-status settlements, in fact metalworking evidence is frequently found at open settlements that in other ways look unexceptional, and *c.* 56 sites of this sort have been identified in the course of this project. The term 'open' is here used to describe sites without substantial boundary features that separate the settlement activity from the surrounding area although it must be born in mind that many of these sites are fairly extensive and the full limits have not always been revealed through excavation. Approximately half of the Late Bronze Age and Earliest Iron Age sites with metalworking evidence in Britain are open settlements compared to just under a third of the sites in Ireland. Material from open settlements has most commonly been recovered from pits and other features outside of buildings. For example, at **Bestwall Quarry**, Wareham (Dorset), two areas of open settlement were identified, each comprising two or three round-houses with associated pits. Two pits (one in each area) produced two crucible fragments and three clay mould fragments in total. Nineteen pieces of refractory material, including five mould fragments and a possible tuyère, were found in pits scattered across the site at **Tinney's Lane**, Sherborne (Dorset), although there was a concentration of finds from a cluster of pits outside one round-house. At **South Hornchurch** (Greater London), a substantial ringwork was identified. However, the metalworking evidence was not associated with this enclosure but was found elsewhere in the extensive contemporary settlement outside it. Most notably, fragments of a sword mould were deposited in a pit in a round-house that forms one of a group of three unenclosed structures around 100 m east of the ringwork. The chronological relationship between the pit and the round-house is unknown, however, and it is possible that the pit is associated with the linear ditch that cuts across and appears to pre-date the building (see below for other sites where metalworking debris is associated with field boundaries). Certainly, there is nothing to indicate that the round-house can be viewed as 'high-status'. A fragment of casting waste was also found in a pit to the west of unenclosed round-houses 2 and 3.

The scale of the metalworking activities at some open settlements appears to have been relatively substantial, calling into question the frequent assumption that sites such as ring-works or middens were particular foci for intensive metalworking. At **Bellfield Farm**, North Kessock (Highland), six crucible fragments and over 300 clay mould fragments for casting axes, sickles, gouges, knives, and a spearhead were found. These were mostly concentrated in a cluster of pits, although there were also a few fragments from two round-houses and a sub-rectangular post-built structure. The two mould fragments from one of the round-houses were found in a spread of burnt material around the hearth and in a pit towards the southern edge of the building, while the mould fragments from the other two structures were recovered from post-holes. Radiocarbon dates and the mould assemblage indicate a date in the Earliest Iron Age. At **Cladh Hallan**, South Uist (Comhairle nan Eilean Siar), an assemblage of more than 400 mould fragments was found. These were for casting a wide variety of objects, including swords, chapes, spears, pins, and razors. The majority of the moulds, together with a number of crucible fragments, were found in the central round-house in a row of three conjoined circular structures. The presence of metalworking debris in the three lowest floors of this building suggests the occurrence of several casting events over the life of the settlement. Most of the material was scattered in the entrance area of the building and the excavators suggest that these objects were deposited here from elsewhere. A bronze tanged chisel from one of the floor layers inside this building has been interpreted as an offering. The location of bronze metalworking on the site is unknown although several finds of mould fragments, slag, and other metallurgical debris from the western side of the settlement suggest that these activities were performed to the rear of the houses. The northernmost of the three round-houses shows evidence for metalworking after its abandonment, in the form of a tuyère fragment and copper casting waste. Reuse of abandoned buildings for metalworking has occasionally been identified at sites of both earlier and later periods (see also Chapter 5), suggesting that there was sometimes a preference for semi-derelict locations with particular histories.

A number of other round-houses have also produced casting debris, although in most cases it is likely that the objects in question formed part of special deposits of one sort or another and may not indicate the actual location of metalworking. At **Osprey Heights**, Boynds Farm, Uryside, Inverurie (Aberdeenshire), seven fragments of a pin mould were deposited in a ring-ditch defining a round-house, while another clay mould fragment was found in a

Figure 4.18: Late Bronze Age round-house at Ballylegan (Co. Tipperary) (redrawn by Anne Leaver after McQuade et al. 2009, fig. 3.18)

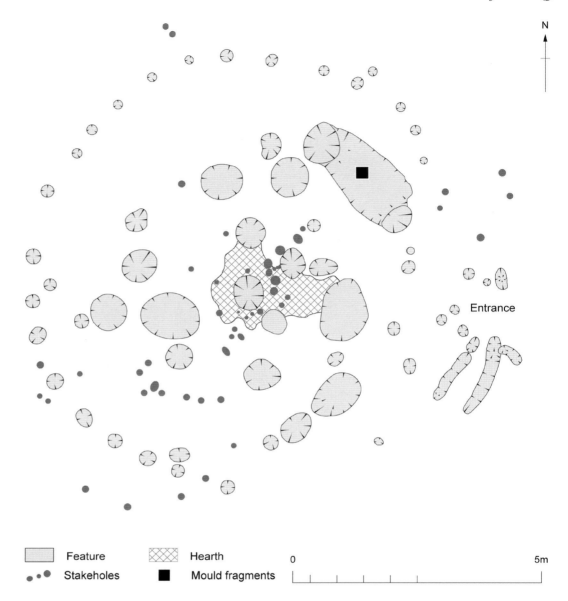

	Feature		Hearth
Stakeholes		Mould fragments	

0   5m

post-hole to the north of a second round-house. At **Gwithian** (Cornwall), part of a stone axe mould lay on the floor of round-house 1 by the hearth. A piece of the same mould valve was found by the hearth in House 4. The mould is of chlorite schist, possibly sourced in south Devon or the Lizard. The fragments of this object may represent formal abandonment deposits similar to those seen at Middle Bronze Age houses in Cornwall (Nowakowski 2001; Jones 2015b), and the deposition of parts of the same mould in two different houses may represent a link between the inhabitants of the buildings. Crucible fragments from a structural post-hole form

part of a series of abandonment deposits in the southern half of a large isolated round-house at **Dunston Park**, Thatcham (West Berkshire). The structure has been dated by its pottery to the 7th century BC and is one of the few sites of this period identified in the course of this project. Similar closing deposits have been identified in other large houses of this date in southern England (Webley 2007). Here, however, it is possible that mixed midden material was deposited in the post-holes, rather than the crucible being specifically selected. At **Ballylegan** (Co. Tipperary), a timber-lined trough containing burnt stone and charcoal-rich soil produced four clay mould fragments and a near-complete pot. This feature was located between the central post-ring and outer wall of a round-house to the right of the entrance (Fig. 4.18). The context is radiocarbon dated to 1120–920 cal BC (2854±33 BP; UB-7390). This is the only clear example from Ireland of a direct association between a Late Bronze Age round-house and metalworking debris, in contrast to the several examples of stone moulds in or near Irish Middle Bronze Age round-houses. It is, however, likely that this represents a special deposit made when the trough was backfilled and need not indicate that metalworking took place in this building; if metalworking was carried out here then only a small proportion of the remains were curated afterwards.

Most metalworking evidence from open settlements is, however, found in pits and other features outside of buildings. Clay mould and crucible fragments were found in four pits and a pond associated with a pair of round-houses at **Aldermaston Wharf** (West Berkshire), for example. Five different areas of settlement were identified across the contemporary complex of field systems and droveways at **Huntsman's Quarry**, Kemerton in Gloucestershire. These included round-houses, rectangular buildings, four-post structures, fences, pits, hearths, and waterholes. To the south of a row of three round-houses was a small fenced enclosure, *c.* 30 m in diameter. At the entrance to this was a pit that contained clay mould fragments for the production of spearheads, axes, and other bladed weapons, along with pottery, bone, struck flint, fired clay and burnt stone. At **Holborough Quarry**, Snodland (Kent), small numbers of refractory fragments were widely dispersed across the site, but the most substantial assemblages were found in two neighbouring pits (Fig. 4.19). These produced *c.* 250 mould fragments, the majority of which were from Wilburton sword moulds.

Only occasionally does the evidence appear to be directly associated with hearths or ovens that could be associated with metalworking. At **Cakestown Glebe** (Co. Meath), fragments of a mould for a straight-sided blade came from a post-hole that lay within an area defined by an arc of stake-holes (*c.* 3 × 2.5 m) open to the east. There was a hearth within this structure and it may represent a shelter for a working area. There are radiocarbon dates of 1000–830 cal BC from the hearth (2768±24 BP; UBA

12943) and 1120–930 cal BC from a stake-hole (2864±24 BP; UBA 12071). A small round-house lay a few metres away. Worked flint and carbonised cereals were also recovered from the site. Mould fragments for the production of swords and other objects were associated with a small double oven at **Halfhide Lane**, Turnford (Hertfordshire), although the site has not been fully published. The number of mould fragments from this feature was relatively low, however, in comparison to sites where the remains were deposited in pits.

Unenclosed settlements producing metalworking debris typically also have evidence for domestic activities such as food preparation and textile working. A spindle whorl made from a reused crucible sherd has been reported from Halfhide Lane. In a few cases, other crafts are evinced. At **Shorncote** (Gloucestershire), iron slag was found in the upper fill of a Late Bronze Age pit-well, 8 m from the well that contained socketed axe mould fragments, though the possibility that the slag was intrusive material of later date was not ruled out. As we have seen, potential associations between bronze casting and early ironworking have also been identified at the Late Bronze Age hillfort of the **Breiddin** (Powys) as well as in the Earliest Iron Age levels of the middens at **Potterne** and **All Cannings Cross** (Wiltshire). This is interesting in the light of arguments that bronze- and ironworking were conceptually distinct and organised in very different ways (for further discussion, see Chapter 5). This is not to say that these crafts invariably occurred together during this period; there was no evidence for non-ferrous metalworking at the putative 10th century BC ironworking site at **Hartshill Copse** (Berkshire) (Collard *et al.* 2006), for example. Links between pottery making and non-ferrous metalworking are also possible, given the use of clay to make moulds and crucibles, but pottery making sites are difficult to identify in prehistory. An exception is **Tinneys Lane**, Sherborne (Dorset), where numerous pottery wasters were found, some in contexts which also contained fragments of clay moulds. Sites with evidence for both bronze casting and shale working include **Bestwall Quarry** (Dorset) and possibly **Tuft Hill** (East Riding of Yorkshire).

Wells and waterholes
The deposition of moulds and crucibles in wells

Figure 4.19: Late Bronze Age settlement at Holborough Quarry, Snodland (Kent) (plan courtesy of Canterbury Archaeological Trust with highlighting by Anne Leaver)

★	Tool	▬	Sword mould
▼	Crucible fragments	■	Mould fragments
▨	Feature	▨	Feature, presumed

Larger symbols indicate multiple instances

0   50m

and waterholes occurs at a number of sites in southern Britain. A few crucible and mould fragments were found in a well at **Barleycroft Farm**, Needingworth (Cambridgeshire). This feature was located within a contemporary field system 30 m south of a ditched rectilinear enclosure that contained a substantial long-house – an unusual feature that may suggest

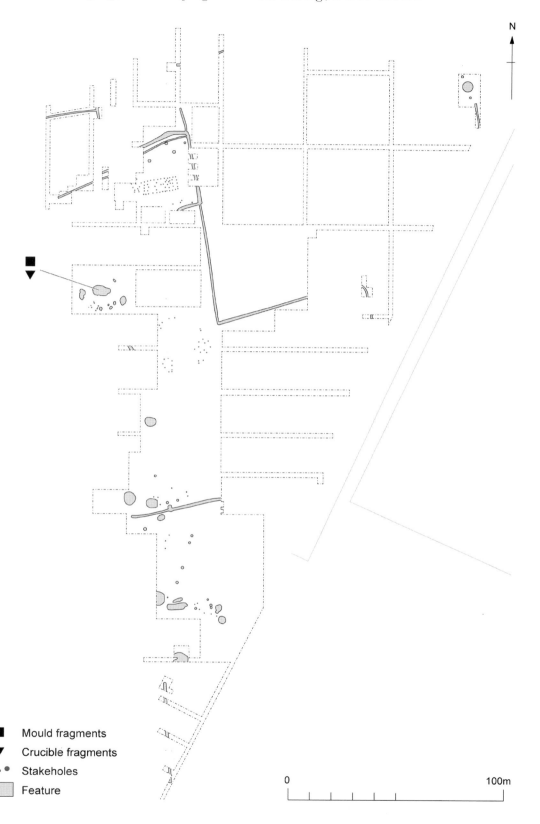

N

Figure 4.20: Late Bronze Age enclosure and fieldsystem at Barleycroft Farm, Needingworth (Cambridgeshire) (redrawn by Anne Leaver after Evans & Knight 1997, fig. 19)

■ Mould fragments

▼ Crucible fragments

· ·● Stakeholes

　 Feature

0　　　　　　　　　　100m

this was a high-status site (Fig. 4.20). There was also a relatively high proportion of deer and horse bone in the faunal assemblage, although the sample size was small. At **Cranford Lane**, Harlington (Greater London), several crucible and mould fragments, the latter possibly for the production of swords, were found in a well, one of a pair of such features flanking an entrance through a field boundary. This may parallel the associations with enclosure entrances seen at sites such as **Springfield Lyons** (Essex) and **Norton Fitzwarren** (Somerset).

At **Huntsman's Quarry**, Kemerton (Gloucestershire), mould fragments were recovered from three waterholes. One of these features produced a particularly interesting range of finds including parts of at least six loomweights, large quantities of pottery, a portion of a shale armlet, the lower section of a bone pin, and a fragment of human vertebra. Metalworking debris and human remains occur in waterholes at other sites, although they were not usually deposited together. An open settlement at **Striplands Farm**, Longstanton (Cambridgeshire), included a round-house, possible long-house, four-post structures, fencelines, pits, and waterholes. One of the waterholes produced a crucible fragment and possible mould fragment. Two unburnt skull fragments were found in another waterhole on the same site. At **Shorncote Quarry** (Gloucestershire), 20 fragments of a single clay axe mould were deposited in a well that formed part of an extensive open settlement comprising densely-packed round-houses, four-posters, pits, and waterholes; part of an unburnt human skull was also found in another waterhole.

At Shorncote Quarry, as at most sites, such finds occur in the upper fills of these features. The deposition of artefact-rich fills in wells and waterholes, especially in their upper fills, is seen more widely in southern Britain and may be a deliberate 'decommissioning' practice. In most cases the metalworking debris from these features is modest and it may be that it represents incidental inclusions in mixed deposits of midden-type material. On the other hand, the presence of a human vertebra fragment and part of a shale armlet alongside the mould debris at Huntsman's Quarry may suggest selection of specific objects for deposition. The deposition of metalworking debris in wells and waterholes may provide

another instance of the association of such material with watery places noted above.

Although a rather different kind of site, the **King's Stables** (Co. Armagh), located on lower ground *c.* 300 m east of **Haughey's Fort** and already mentioned above, shares some points of similarity with the waterholes that are such a common feature of the archaeological record in southern Britain. This is an artificial pool *c.* 25 m in diameter and up to 4 m deep, with a surrounding outer bank. Excavation of *c.* 5% of the pool produced clay sword mould fragments, animal bone (including much dog bone and deer antler), and part of a human skull. Votive deposition has been assumed, although the pool may also have served practical purposes including watering stock. Another unusual site that perhaps echoes the deposition of metalworking debris in waterholes is the large glacial pingo (a natural hollow) at **Greenfields** (Essex). Over 2 kg of Late Bronze Age clay sword mould fragments along with Middle and Late Bronze Age pottery were deposited in the lower fills of this feature. The moulds are suggested to derive from successive deposits rather than a single episode. There is a scatter of Middle and Late Bronze Age features close to the hollow, including a cremation burial. The pingo is 20 m in diameter and up to 2 m deep and may well have held water during prehistory. The selection of this hollow as a focus for deposition can perhaps also be compared with the reuse of the flint mine hollows at **Grimes Graves** (Norfolk) during the Middle Bronze Age, and caves (see below): such locations may have been viewed as entrances to the underworld.

Boundaries and isolated features

Systems of linear earthwork boundaries, sometimes extending over several kilometres, developed in parts of Britain from the Late Bronze Age onwards. Metalworking evidence is occasionally associated with these major landscape boundaries. Copper alloy casting waste was found in the middle fill of a double-ditched linear earthwork at **Breach Hill**, Tilshead (Wiltshire), while at **Lady Graves**, Fimber (East Riding of Yorkshire), a pit containing at least seven Late Bronze Age clay mould fragments for swords, chapes, and socketed axes, a complete core probably from a spearhead, pottery, and animal bone was cut into a linear earthwork bank.

Isolated pits containing significant quantities of mould debris have been identified at a few sites. A pit *c.* 150 m north-west of the enclosure at **Sigwells** (Somerset) produced fragments of moulds for casting between eight and 12 different objects, including swords, spearheads, and axes. At **Barford Road**, Eynesbury (Cambridgeshire), clay mould fragments in two different fabrics, including part of an axe mould, were found in a pit *c.* 90 m from a unique rectangular enclosure demarcated by pit alignments. This enclosure was aligned on an earlier cursus monument and hengiform ring-ditch on the flood plain of the River Great Ouse. The pit also produced worked flint and pottery. At **Maxey Quarry** (Peterborough), fragments of at least eight clay moulds for the production of spearheads and chapes were found in an isolated pit: extensive excavations at this site uncovered little other evidence of Late Bronze Age activity except for an unusual number of unstratified bronze finds including a ribbed blade, a socketed axe fragment, a sword blade fragment, the edge of an axe, and a knife blade; these finds are reminiscent of a dispersed hoard.

Quite different evidence for a possible isolated production site has been identified at **Galmisdale** on the island of Eigg (Highland), where clay mould fragments for at least two socketed axes, crucible fragments, a hammerstone, a polishing stone, fragments of possible furnace lining, and 'associated casting debris' were found in the lee of a large natural boulder that could have provided a measure of shelter for metalworking. Small-scale excavation did not reveal any associated structures. As only the immediate findspot has been excavated it is not known whether it lay in the vicinity of a settlement, though an undated hut circle lies *c.* 70 m away. The site is located on the slope below a prominent hill and above the main harbour on the island. Galmisdale provides a tantalising glimpse of a single or short-lived episode of production; it is possible that bronze casting occurred more frequently in the Late Bronze Age in association with other natural features though similar sites are so far unknown. However, it is interesting to note that the only known Bronze Age smelting site in Britain was found in a striking location at **Pentrwyn** on the Great Orme peninsula (Conwy). Here, copper smelting slag and prills were found in and around a small

Figure 4.21: Late Bronze Age smelting site at Pentrwyn, Llandudno (Conwy) (courtesy of David Jenkins & Gwynedd Archaeological Trust)

charcoal-rich pit of Late Bronze Age date. As we have already seen, the Great Orme was the location of extensive mining activities but these peaked several centuries earlier during the Middle Bronze Age (Dutton & Fasham 1994; Williams & Le Carlier de Veslud 2019). The pit was located on a natural terrace part-way down a series of sea cliffs on the east side of the peninsula (Fig. 4.21). This is a prominent landmark, and the choice of such a dramatic position for smelting activities is interesting; this calls to mind the deliberate siting of Neolithic axe quarries in inaccessible but often spectacular locations (Bradley & Edmonds 1993; Cooney 1998). There are a number of hut circles nearby, although the date of these remains unknown.

Earlier monuments and ritual or mortuary sites

Although metalworking debris has often been found in liminal locations of one sort or another, it is rarely directly associated with mortuary sites or pre-existing ceremonial monuments, although there are possible exceptions, as at **Rathgall** (Co. Wicklow) described above. At **Golspie** (Highland), the crouched inhumation of an adult male radiocarbon dated to 1000–830 cal BC (2761±31 BP; V-2172-16) was placed in a stone cist and accompanied by a deposit of burnt bone, a pumice pendant, and several clay mould fragments. At **Ballynakelly** (Co. Dublin) a dispersed cremation cemetery of the Middle–Late Bronze Age was located on a ridge with panoramic views. One possible token burial (containing 7 g of unidentified burnt bone) produced a clay mould fragment and crucible sherd, alongside one sherd of Late Bronze Age pottery, three pieces of unmodified quartz, a flint tool, and a chunk of burnt flint. This feature was radiocarbon dated to 1200–920 cal BC (2874±39 BP). A nearby pit produced a complete saddle quern.

At **Loanhead of Daviot** (Aberdeenshire), four refitting fragments of a clay sword mould were found laid against the inner side of a circular drystone enclosure surrounding an Early Bronze Age cremation cemetery. Next to the cemetery was a recumbent stone circle, probably also of Early Bronze Age date (Welfare 2011). Monuments of this class are known to have been remodelled and re-used in the late 2nd millennium, and a series of Late Bronze Age cremation burials had been inserted into the ring-cairn constructed at the centre of the stone circle. Late Bronze Age clay mould fragments for swords and other objects were recovered in the 19th century during the investigation of a mound of uncertain date at **Oldconnaught** (Co. Dublin). Small polished stone balls of a type characteristic of the Middle Neolithic were also found suggesting that this may have been a passage tomb (Eogan 1986, 144). An interest in earlier monuments may also be indicated by the discovery of four plano-convex ingot fragments under the kerb of a barrow, probably dating to the Early Bronze Age, at **Gittisham** (Devon).

Elsewhere in Devon, a substantial assemblage of mould, crucible, and other refractory fragments dating to the Wilburton phase of the Late Bronze Age was found in and around a pit next to a small stone cairn at **Stoneycombe Quarry**, Dainton. This is one of several scattered across a field system of probable Middle or Late Bronze Age date and is likely to have resulted from the clearance of stones from the fields. However, human bone was also recovered from the cairn; in northern Britain clearance cairns and funerary cairns are often indistinguishable in terms of their structure and contents, and Johnston (2008, 274–6) suggests this may relate to the role of the ancestors in maintaining links to the land. The moulds from Stoneycombe Quarry were for spearheads, ferrules, swords, and rings. They were made from two different

clays, both available in south-east Devon, and it is suggested that this indicates two distinct episodes of casting. The crucible sherds are from at least three vessels. The pit also contained a probable droplet of casting waste, a small bronze rod, and a few pottery sherds. An irregular nodular lump found close to the pit may be dross or waste metal.

The evidence from **Cliffs End Farm**, Ramsgate (Kent) is rather different. Here a series of Late Bronze Age inhumation burials, demonstrating interesting evidence for post-mortem manipulation and curation of human bone, was deposited in a pit at the base of a substantial linear depression that also formed a focus for Iron Age mortuary rites. Nearby were three Late Bronze Age enclosures; there were no buildings in these enclosures although evidence for substantial feasting activities was recovered, suggesting that they played a role in ceremonial activities at the site. Four copper plano-convex ingot fragments and a few pieces of casting waste were found in the ditch of the northern enclosure while a fifth ingot fragment formed part of a large deposit of feasting debris in a pit inside this enclosure. A further nine ingot fragments and a piece of casting waste were deposited in the ditch surrounding the central enclosure. A bronze sprue and part of another copper ingot were redeposited in an Iron Age ditch and a fragment of awl or chisel that may have been used in metalworking was found in the Iron Age levels of the linear depression.

Cremation deposits and – more occasionally – fragments of unburnt human bone have been found at several of the settlements and other sites described above, particularly in south-east England. We have already seen that mould debris and human bone fragments have been found in waterholes at several sites. At **Holborough Quarry**, Snodland (Kent), several cremation deposits were scattered across the main area of settlement, as well as to the north and south of the field boundaries that defined it. There were cremation deposits scattered amongst the waterholes, pits, and field boundaries at **Hampstead Lane**, Yalding (Kent), and in and around several of the round-houses at **South Hornchurch** (Greater London). Human cranial fragments were found in the primary fills of the main entrance terminals at **Mucking South Rings** (Thurrock) while the midden at **Potterne** (Wiltshire) produced both metalworking debris and a large quantity of unburnt and fragmentary human bone. However, only at **Huntsmans Quarry**, Kemerton (Gloucestershire), was the metalworking evidence directly associated with human remains. It is not unusual for human bone to be found on Late Bronze Age settlements and, in most cases, the presence of both metalworking debris and the remains of the dead may therefore be coincidental.

The scale of metal casting at Late Bronze Age and Earliest Iron Age sites

Assessing the scale and duration of metal casting at later Bronze Age sites is not straightforward. Much of the evidence consists of remains of clay moulds and crucibles, objects which are highly friable. The fragment count of an assemblage will depend on factors of deposition and preservation, for example, whether the material had been left exposed on a ground surface or has been disturbed from its original context. It does not directly relate to the numbers of moulds and crucibles originally present.

As we have seen, most Middle Bronze Age assemblages are very small, consisting of a single item or a handful of pieces of moulds, crucibles, and/or casting waste. The assemblage from **Grimes Graves** (Norfolk) is larger, with 150 clay mould fragments, but these may derive from as few as three spearhead moulds. Measured by the minimum number of individual moulds present, the largest assemblage is the group of ten moulds (nine stone and one clay) from the round-house at **Tremough** (Cornwall) (Fig. 4.6, above).

Late Bronze Age and Earliest Iron Age assemblages also tend to be small – in many cases consisting of fewer than ten fragments – but there are also some larger groups of material. The collection of around 4000 clay mould fragments from the hillfort at **Rathgall** (Co. Wicklow) is exceptional but, as this material is unpublished, the number of moulds represented is not known. At least a further 12 sites have assemblages in the range of *c* 100–500 fragments, including several open settlements, a hillfort **Dún Aonghasa** (Co. Galway), a ringwork **Springfield Lyons** (Essex), and one other non-settlement site, the pingo at **Greenfields** (Essex). The minimum number of moulds represented in these assemblages is not always clear but reaches double figures

in some cases, with around 20 at **Holborough Quarry**, Snodland (Kent) and **Jarlshof** (Shetland), 16–21 at Dún Aonghasa, 15 at **Bellfield Farm**, North Kessock (Highland) and 11 at Springfield Lyons (Essex). The most diverse mould assemblage appears to come from **Cladh Hallan** (Comhairle nan Eilean Siar), where at least nine different functional categories of objects were cast, including various kinds of weapons, tools, and ornaments (Needham & Bridgford 2013, 69). The numbers of crucibles represented in these large assemblages appears to be lower: around five separate vessels could be identified at Dún Aonghasa, and at least three at **Stoneycombe Quarry**, Dainton (Devon). This is to be expected, as crucibles could be reused, unlike clay moulds. The quantities of casting waste in these assemblages also tend to be small, generally amounting to no more than a few pieces. The exception is the collection of over 100 pieces recovered from surface survey of the **Whitchurch** midden (Warwickshire), but it is not certain that all of this material is contemporary with the Late Bronze Age– Earliest Iron Age activity. There are only slight hints of regional differences in the distribution of sites with different quantities of metalworking remains; a higher proportion of sites in Scotland appear to have produced relatively substantial assemblages, though the sample of sites in this region is small.

The site context and distribution of these assemblages may provide hints of the duration and intensity of the metalworking activity. At sites such as Holborough Quarry (see Fig. 4.19), Dún Aonghasa, or Bellfield Farm, North Kessock, where the material comes from several different features dispersed across the excavated area, it could be that these finds relate to numerous casting episodes. Other relatively substantial assemblages derive from one single deposit, as with the collection of clay sword moulds placed as an apparent foundation deposit at Springfield Lyons. Here we have evidence for only a single casting event.

Of course, the *minimum* counts cited above may be significantly lower than the actual numbers of clay moulds and crucibles present in these assemblages. It could also be that often only a small proportion of the waste generated by metalworking was deposited in the ground – perhaps a deliberately selected token amount (see below). Nonetheless, the impression given

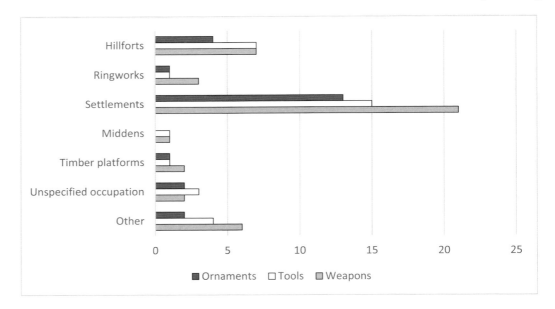

by the site evidence is that bronze casting was an activity that was widespread – being frequently found at sites of this date – but generally small-scale; this is reinforced by the rarity of metalworking hearths and furnaces. Only at Rathgall and possibly Whitchurch do we have sites where casting seems to have been a more intensive activity or took place over a more extended period.

Metalworking, status and depositional practice in the Late Bronze Age and Earliest Iron Age

It appears that the extent and intensity of the metalworking activity was not dictated by the character of the site. In Late Bronze Age Ireland, there are hints that hillforts such as **Rathgall** (Co. Wicklow) and **Haughey's Fort** (Co. Armagh) were a focus for more intensive or specialised metalworking. There is little sign of this in Britain, where relatively large assemblages come from a range of site types, not only those that might be considered 'special'. In fact, some of the largest and most diverse assemblages come from otherwise 'ordinary' unenclosed settlements such as **Bellfield Farm**, North Kessock (Highland). Interestingly, the production of items such as weaponry and ornaments was not restricted to what have conventionally been considered 'high-status' sites such as hillforts and ring-works (Fig. 4.22). Sword moulds have been found at a number of open settlements

including **Tinney's Lane**, Sherborne (Dorset), **Seafield West** (Highland), **Jarlshof** (Shetland), and **Holborough Quarry**, Snodland (Kent). The dispersed distribution of casting debris seen at some sites, with material found in features such as pits and waterholes across the settled landscape, does not suggest a concern to control access to metalworking and its residues.

This is not to say, of course, that the distribution of metalworking debris can be viewed as a direct result of its spatial or technological organisation, for there was evidently an important element of selectivity in what actually reached the archaeological record. Clay mould fragments for the production of weapons, especially swords, are more common than those for most other object types (Fig. 4.11, above), and some of the largest individual deposits (such as those from Holborough Quarry, **Springfield Lyons** (Essex) and **Norton Fitzwarren** (Somerset)) are composed predominantly of sword mould fragments. In some cases, these appear to be the result of single casting events, comprising multiple fragments from a small number of moulds, and it is possible to suggest that such deposits acted as a means of ritually decommissioning residues that were viewed as dangerous or ambivalent, or of commemorating the production of socially significant artefacts. In contrast, more 'everyday' objects such as axes are often represented by just one or two mould fragments.

The relatively small number of identifiable

mould fragments (including for 'high-status' artefacts such as weaponry) from middens (Fig. 4.22) is perhaps surprising but may also be the result of particular depositional practices: casting waste and ingots make up a greater proportion of the metalworking assemblages from middens than from contemporary settlements where it was predominantly mould fragments that reached the archaeological record. Waddington and Sharples (2011) have argued that the distribution of copper alloy casting waste on the hillside at **Whitchurch** (Warwickshire) indicates that metalworking was carried out in a highly visible location. While there is no evidence that prominent points in the landscape were generally preferred as locations for casting, it is possible that metalworking had a performative aspect (Sörman 2018). For anyone who has had the opportunity to watch bronze casting, the process has a magical quality as the metal is transformed between its glowing liquid and solid states. There is no reason to assume metalworking inspired the same feelings in Bronze Age people but the low quantities of casting residues at most sites suggest this was not an everyday task and the creation of objects such as swords clearly involved a significant element of skill (Ó Faoláin & Northover 1998). As such, the act of metalworking may have inspired awe in the audience; it might equally have been important to watch the making of the sword to ascertain its authenticity or quality or to strengthen the ties between those who produced and used these objects.

The remains of the metalworking process may themselves have been considered potent, particularly for socially significant objects such as swords, and the careful disposal of the resulting debris may therefore have been an important requirement (Mörtz 2014). If so, it is no surprise that mould fragments were often deposited in ways that suggest a degree of performance or ritualisation. The large deposits of sword mould fragments at sites such as **Norton Fitzwarren** (Somerset) or late Middle Bronze Age **Bourton-on-the-Water** (Gloucestershire) suggest that debris from the production of these objects was carefully disposed of soon after the casting event. At **Springfield Lyons** (Essex) the metalworking residues were deliberately placed at the main entrances to the site shortly after the enclosure ditch was recut, although in this case patterns

of abrasion and the presence of only portions of each valve suggest that a period of time elapsed between the casting event(s) and the deposition of this material.

The evidence from these sites indicates deliberate selection: clay refractory materials associated with sword production predominate and crucible fragments or metallic debris such as casting waste or dribbles of bronze are rare or absent. Such residues were presumably retained either for recycling or for deposition elsewhere; as we shall see below, casting waste predominantly occurs in hoards rather than in other excavated contexts during this period. At some other sites, such as **Holborough Quarry**, Snodland (Kent), sword moulds were not separated from other clay waste when they were deposited, but nonetheless seem to have been treated in a particular way. A pit at Holborough Quarry contained substantial portions of four sword mould valves (comprising two pairs), alongside a few fragments from three or four other such artefacts. This pit also yielded single fragments from moulds for several other objects (Table 4.2). The moulds for objects found elsewhere on the site were similarly fragmentary: moulds for artefacts such as a socketed hammer or chisel, a ferrule or socketed gouge, and several rings were each represented by just one or two pieces. This suggests that the sword moulds were gathered up and deposited in a more careful and deliberate way than the moulds used to cast other types of object. Importantly, the suggestion that large assemblages of sword mould fragments were the product of selective and ritualised depositional practices hints that some sites with significant quantities of metalworking debris – such as Springfield Lyons – may not in fact have been locations of production.

The deposition of Middle Bronze Age–Earliest Iron Age stone moulds in the wider landscape

Although the majority of stone and bronze moulds, as well as most hoards containing metalworking tools and debris, do not derive from controlled excavations, nonetheless their landscape context and associations may provide insights into the meaning and practice of metalworking during the period 1550–600 BC. Stone moulds have often been found at a distance from known Bronze Age

Table 4.2: The distribution of mould fragments across different features at Holborough Quarry, Snodland (Kent)

Feature	Mould type	Total weight sword moulds (g)	Total weight other moulds (g)
111	Socketed hammer or chisel	–	23
193	Ring	–	4
228	Spearhead (or razor) blade Ferrule or gouge Concentrically moulded disc Ornamental plaque? Flanged/moulded object Thin-edged blade/plaque	–	35
280	Double-ring razor handle?	–	8
328	Sword Axe blade? Ring Ring/concentrically moulded disc Sword Moulded ring/disc Object with raised triangular motif Object with curved depression Strip/thin tang	44	41
335	Sword (belonging to 7/8 different valves) Spearhead socket? Double-ring razor handle? Ring Concave-edged blade/plaque Rectangular sectioned blade? Sub-rectangular sectioned blade?	1831 (1642 g of which belong to just 4 valves)	52
358	Ring	–	5
436	Sword	4	–

Information from Needham (2014)

sites (Appendix 3). Some may have been deposited at significant places in the natural landscape. Suggestive locations for stone moulds include a palstave mould fragment from Burgh Island (Devon), a striking rocky offshore island, at present connected to the mainland by a sand bar only at low tide. At Chudleigh Knighton (Devon), two Middle Bronze Age rapier moulds were found at a location in the apex of the confluence of the rivers Bovey and Teign. They were reportedly found 20 ft (6 m) apart, each with their two valves fitted together. One set was deposited vertically in the ground while the other had been laid horizontally; each pair comprised one damaged and one complete valve. The location of this find echoes the riverine contexts often favoured for rapiers themselves (Bradley 1998; Becker 2013), and there is a concentration of

metalwork finds upstream of this point in the Bovey and Teign valleys (Pearce 1983, fig. 4.14), although the metal objects themselves were generally deposited in rather than near water. Stone moulds have rarely been found actually in wet contexts, although a Late Bronze Age chisel mould was recovered from a river bed at Abermâd (Ceredigion) and there is also a Middle Bronze Age mould purportedly from the River Bann in Ireland. Both valves of a stone mould for the production of palstaves, blades, and possible pin shanks were apparently deposited in a bog at Mountrath (Co. Laois), though no further details are available; Irish Middle Bronze Age palstaves and ornaments were also often deposited in bogs (Becker 2013).

Hoards comprising several stone moulds are known from nine other locations (not including the group of moulds from the round-house at **Tremough** (Cornwall) discussed above). At Helsbury (Cornwall), three Late Bronze Age axe moulds were found in the valley of the River Camel, reportedly 'beneath an oblique stone, which appeared to have formed the roof of a cave' (cited in Needham 1981). At Ballyliffin (Co. Donegal), at least two Middle Bronze Age palstave moulds and 13 mould valve 'blanks' were deposited 'under a shelving ledge of rock' (Bremer 1927, 64). The Helsbury and Ballyliffin finds are echoed by a number of stone moulds deposited in caves or rock clefts on the Continent (eg, Gomez de Soto 1996). At Killymaddy (Co. Antrim) three complete Middle Bronze Age moulds and single valves of three more had been placed close to a stream, on a ridge overlooking the Bann valley. At Toorglass (Co. Mayo), single valves of two Middle Bronze Age moulds were found *c.* 100 m from the present shoreline of Trawmore Bay. Other stone mould hoards are from near Omagh (Co. Tyrone; late Early Bronze Age), Sultan (Co. Tyrone; Middle Bronze Age), Culfin (Co. Galway; Middle Bronze Age), Campbeltown (Argyll & Bute; Middle Bronze Age), and Stittenham (Highland; Earliest Iron Age), but no details of their landscape context are recorded. Stone mould hoards are also found on the Continent, notably in the western half of France (Boutoille 2009). We should also note here that the clay mould fragments and other metalworking debris found in the lee of a large boulder at **Galmisdale** on the island of Eigg (Highland; described above) provide a possible parallel to some of the stone mould finds, for these too were deposited at a striking natural landmark away from any known contemporary settlement.

As most stone mould hoards incorporate moulds that are incomplete or otherwise unusable, they were perhaps not caches of equipment intended for future use by a metalworker. It may be more plausible to see these as hoards buried with no intention of recovery, analogous to contemporary metal hoards. The Killymaddy hoard (Co. Antrim) contained moulds from at least two different geological sources. As with the group of moulds from the round-house at Tremough, this may not have been the equipment of a single metalworker, but was perhaps brought together for deposition, in a comparable way to the contents of some metal hoards (see below). The moulds from hoards are for a range of different artefact types and as such it is not obvious that their incorporation into the hoards followed any consistent rules of selection.

Hoards and 'off-site' metalwork deposits and their relationship to metalworking

As this book focuses on the evidence from excavated sites, no attempt has been made to collate a list of metal hoards containing possible metalworking related tools and debris. Such finds and assemblages have already been a focus of other detailed studies (eg, Burgess & Coombs 1979; O'Connor 1980; Eogan 1983; Pearce 1983; Taylor 1993; Lawson 1999; Pendleton 1999; Maraszek 2007; Turner 2010; Becker 2013; Fregni 2014; Knight *et al.* 2015). Nonetheless, hoards and single finds, of relevant items require consideration. Bronze moulds and smithing tools are almost exclusively found in hoards or as single off-site finds, and ingots and casting jets are predominantly found in the same way. Such finds demonstrate a pattern of off-site deposition that mirrors most other categories of metal artefacts, though unlike some other types of metalwork they were very rarely deposited in watery contexts. Hoards containing 'scrap' metal – particularly common in Late Bronze Age southern Britain – have also been explicitly linked with metalworkers.

The assembly and composition of hoards with metalworking tools and residues

Where metalworking equipment is found in hoards it generally only represents a small proportion of a more diverse assemblage. Bronze moulds found in hoards can be combined with a range of other objects (Fig. 4.23), especially where they occur in large Late Bronze Age 'scrap' hoards, where they may be associated with ingots, craftworking and agricultural tools, weapons, ornaments, horse gear, and/or feasting equipment. Data presented by Fregni (2014, fig. 7.7) shows that bronze smithing tools were similarly combined with a wide range of other artefacts. There is therefore no obvious indication that metalworking tools or waste were preferentially combined with or separated from any other specific metal object types.

Figure 4.23: Number of hoards in which bronze moulds were associated with other artefact types

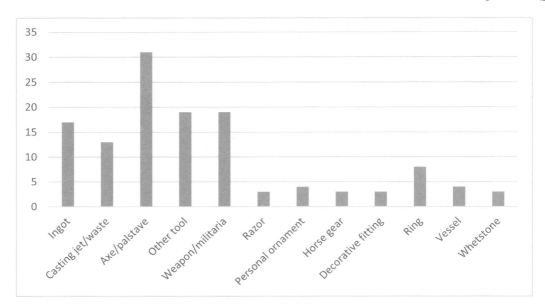

Figure 4.24: Late Bronze Age ingot hoard from Cranmere School, Esher (Surrey) (courtesy of Surrey County Archaeological Unit)

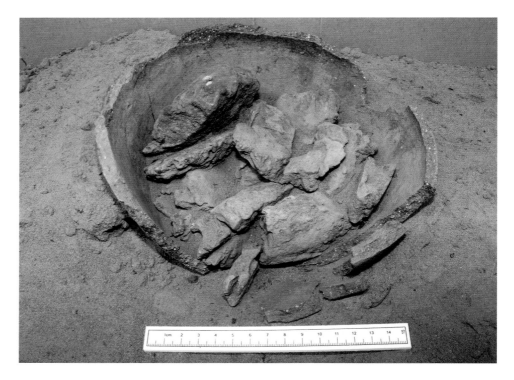

Some rare cases in which metalworking tools form a more prominent part of a hoard have been identified as metalworkers' tool kits (Hodges 1957, 53). The most frequently cited example is the Middle Bronze Age Bishopsland hoard (Co. Kildare), which contained three hammers, two chisels, a graver, an anvil, and a possible vice, but also several other objects not necessarily connected to metalworking such as axes, a saw, and tweezers (Ó Ríordáin 1946; Eogan 1983). The hoard was deposited on a steep slope overlooking the River Liffey (National Museum of Ireland files). On the Continent, the Late Bronze Age Génelard hoard (Saône-et-Loire) is the classic example, containing a mould, hammers, anvils, chisels/gravers, and stamps for decorating sheet metal, though again it also incorporated many objects not linked to metalworking such as ornaments and a spearhead (Thévenot 1998).

Figure 4.25: Bronze socketed axe mould and its castings from the Late Bronze Age Isle of Harty hoard (Kent) (photo courtesy of the Ashmolean Museum)

As such, the concept of the metalworker's tool kit as a discrete category of hoard must be open to question. The only hoards from Britain and Ireland that consist solely of items linked to metalworking are a small number of Late Bronze Age ingot-only hoards from south-east England, such as the 32 ingot fragments deposited within a pot at **Cranmere School**, Esher (Surrey) (Fig. 4.24), or the eight fragments also within a pot at Betchworth (Surrey) (Williams 2008).

While most discussion has focused on the composition of hoards and, more recently, also their landscape context (see below), one aspect that has received relatively little attention is the processes by which hoards were assembled. Although small hoards containing metalworking tools or scrap may have been produced by a single smith, large hoards such as the assemblage from Isleham (Cambridgeshire) with its *c.* 6500 items (Britton 1960a) were presumably collected from a variety of sources, perhaps taking an extended period of time to accumulate (see also Needham 1988). They can contain very varied ranges of objects, including weapons, agricultural implements, craftworking tools, feasting equipment, horse gear, and/or personal ornaments. It is unlikely that all members of the community would have owned or had equivalent access to each of these different object types and, as such, particular objects could have represented certain people or social roles. Some hoards also contain objects originating from widely separated regions (Bradley 2005b). This bringing together of objects from different people and places suggests that the collation of hoards may have embodied, reinforced or even dissolved social relationships within and between communities. The incorporation of metalworking tools and waste into such hoards may therefore represent smiths' social ties and obligations.

A small number of hoards containing bronze moulds also contain implements that had actually been cast in them, and these raise interesting questions regarding the histories and inter-relationships of objects and people, as well as the temporality of deposition (Webley & Adams 2016). The most striking example is the hoard from the Isle of Harty (Kent), containing three socketed axe moulds and castings from each of them (nine castings in total; Fig. 4.25). Other examples include the hoards from Isleham (Cambridgeshire) (palstave mould fragment and at least one casting), Hotham Carrs (East Riding of Yorkshire) (palstave mould and two castings), Hayling Island (Hampshire) (punch mould and one casting), Blewbury (Oxfordshire) (socketed axe mould and three castings, these objects comprising the entire hoard), and Brough on Humber (East Riding of Yorkshire) (two socketed axe moulds and one surviving casting from each). In addition, Greenwell and Clinch (1905, 204) state that some of the axes from the Heathery Burn cave 'were probably cast in the mould' found there, but this cannot be verified as many of the axes are now lost. The nine moulds known to have been deposited with their castings represent just under a quarter of all moulds from hoards. The practice may well have been more widespread than this, as several hoards containing moulds have not been examined for refits. Hoards with moulds and their castings are also known on the Continent, as at Vron (Picardy) (Agache 1968, 298–9) and Baiões (São Pedro do Sul, Portugal) (Armbruster 2000).

The evidence should not be pushed too far, and it should be stressed that most bronze moulds were *not* deposited with their castings. However, where such associations do occur we should not dismiss the possibility that they were meaningful. The Hayling Island example hints at this, as here the casting was actually nestled within and fused to one valve. Though there is a small possibility that this was a failed casting that could not be removed, it is more likely that the punch was placed back into the mould when it was deposited in the hoard and subsequently adhered to it through corrosion (S. Needham pers. comm.). This could suggest a desire to emphasise the connection between these two objects. The same practice might also have occurred in the Brough on Humber hoard. Few details are known about the discovery of this hoard – and most of it is now lost – but a tantalising near-contemporary account implies that the axes were found enclosed within their matrices (Briggs *et al.* 1987, 13).

How moulds and their castings came to be deposited together seems to have varied, however. In the case of the Blewbury hoard, the axes were recorded as having fresh, undamaged edges and casting seams. They may thus have been deposited together with the mould soon after they were cast – perhaps being made specifically for deposition – though it is also possible that they had been lightly used and then resharpened. If the casting of these objects and their deposition

did indeed happen in quick succession, this perhaps suggests that the act of placing these objects in the ground formed a significant element of the metalworking process itself. In this case, as for the large deposits of ceramic moulds discussed above, it seems possible that the deposition of bronze moulds and their products may have occurred relatively soon after an episode of casting, perhaps as part of rituals that surrounded the act of metalworking. In contrast, the Isle of Harty hoard is quite different, as here all nine of the refitting axes show varying degrees of use wear or damage. In other words, after casting each accumulated their own history of use, perhaps passing into different hands along the way, before they were reunited with their parent mould in the hoard. The three axes cast from one of the moulds show markedly divergent histories of use (Fig. 4.25). While two are in a reasonable condition, the third has a significantly shortened and splayed blade indicating repeated use and resharpening, and a large chip in its cutting edge. The ability to reunite a mould and its castings after some time hints that the metalworker was a permanent member of the community for whom the axes were made, and the act of bringing these objects together perhaps worked to give material form to significant inter-personal relationships.

Interpreting scrap hoards

So-called 'scrap hoards' are dominated by broken bronze objects, often also including ingot fragments and/or casting jets. Bronze moulds or smithing tools – either broken or complete – can be incorporated into such hoards, though only in a minority of cases. Hoards containing broken objects occur throughout the Bronze Age, but classic 'scrap' hoards are mainly a feature of the Late Bronze Age, particularly the Ewart Park phase and especially in south-eastern England and north-western France, where they can contain hundreds or even thousands of objects. They are less common in Scotland and Ireland; exceptions include the Roscommon hoard (Eogan 1983).

Scrap hoards have often been referred to as 'founders' hoards', based on the argument that they were the stock of smiths, intended for recycling. It is claimed that they were either buried for safekeeping in times of instability or warfare or cached by itinerant smiths at strategic points along their routes of travel and, for whatever reason, their owners failed to recover them. As we have seen in Chapter 1, this concept can be traced back to French writers in the mid-19th century, and in Britain Evans' distinction between founders', traders', and treasure hoards was influential (Evans 1881). The concept of the founder's hoard is still accepted by many today, either in a form essentially unchanged from Evans' day (Malim 2010, 39; Waddell 2010, 211), or with the caveat that their functional role could have been accompanied by a ritual significance (Davis 2015).

As several authors have pointed out (eg, Barrett & Needham 1988; Bradley 1998; 2013; Brück 2001; 2006; Barber 2003; Hansen 2016), there are a number of problems with the founder's hoard theory. In the first instance, it is not clear why Late Bronze Age smiths should so often have buried their stock of raw material but then not recovered it. If this was a means of safekeeping it seems to have been remarkably ineffective. Moreover, if these hoards were composed of randomly accumulated scrap, we should expect a random assortment of artefact types. In fact there seems to have been conscious selection of particular artefacts, with some others typically deposited in non-hoard contexts: weapons, for example, were most often deposited as single finds in rivers, whereas tools are more frequent components of scrap hoards (Bradley 1998; Fontijn 2002; Becker 2013). Furthermore, the sheer bulk of the largest scrap hoards arguably makes it implausible that these were the surplus stock of an individual smith or workshop. These were accumulations intended to impress through their size.

It is interesting to observe that when broken objects are recovered from contexts such as rivers and lakes where there was clearly no intention of recovery, a ritual interpretation is widely accepted. In many cases it is evident that such objects were deliberately broken, perhaps in an act of ritual decommissioning (York 2002). Similar types of breakage can be seen on items deposited in dryland hoards and it is not clear why different interpretations should be applied to broken objects from wet and dry contexts (Bradley 1998). Certainly, it is not self-evident that the breakage of bronze objects was in preparation for the melting pot. In some cases the breakage seems to have been

very violent, possibly suggestive of a ritual act (Nebelsick 2000). Often the aim seems have been more to render the object unusable than to break it into pieces suitable for recycling. For example, the blades of axes from the Carp's Tongue hoards of south-east England and north-west France have frequently been removed and, in some cases, their sockets have been deliberately filled with fragments of other artefacts (Turner 2010). It seems that some categories of object such as swords were more likely to be broken – or were broken into smaller pieces – than others (Taylor 1993; Gabillot & Lagarde 2008). Furthermore, there is typically either only a single fragment of a given object present, or multiple *non-joining* fragments, and certain parts of artefacts could be favoured for deposition over others (Bradley 2005b; Maraszek 2007; Turner 2010; Becker 2013). This is suggestive of systematic selection on a *pars pro toto* basis (Hansen 2016).

This patterning extends to the metalworking equipment that sometimes forms a component of scrap hoards. The bronze moulds occasionally incorporated into these assemblages are normally broken or otherwise unusable, suggesting that these were not intended for later use in recasting the scrap objects. In a few cases the breaks are irregular and could perhaps have resulted from accidental fracturing during use, but several others were clearly broken deliberately, such as the moulds from the Grays Thurrock (Essex) and Isleham (Cambridgeshire) hoards which have been quite cleanly chopped in half (Webley & Adams 2016). Smithing tools from these hoards such as hammers and chisels *are* often complete, but their presence may be due to their having been used to break the other objects in the hoard before deposition (Turner 2010). The types of fragmentation visible in scrap hoards (and indeed in other contexts such as rivers) required knowledge and experience of metalworking (Gabillot & Lagarde 2008; Turner 2010; Knight 2018): there was a degree of skill required, for example, to heat a socketed axe to the right temperature to allow it to be broken cleanly across the body. Such breakage would have been a dramatic way of ending the use stage of the lifecycle of these objects. Acts geared towards the deliberate decommissioning of socially significant objects or the creation of *pars pro toto* offerings may have been ritualised and sometimes it may therefore have been necessary to treat and dispose of the tools employed for such purposes in a particular way.

It therefore seems more plausible that scrap hoards were generally deposited without any intention of later recovery. The burial of this material transferred it to another realm, perhaps to the keeping of gods or spirits. This interpretation is consistent with the careful selection and arrangement of the contents of many hoards and the choice of striking landscape contexts for some deposits. While scrap hoards were thus probably not directly linked to metalworking in the sense that they were intended for recovery and recycling, the inclusion of broken objects, ingots and metalworking tools may imply that the rites involved in their collation and deposition made reference to the metalworking process. Smiths may have played an important role in these rites as their skills were needed for the systematic fragmentation of the metal objects. It is possible that the offering of scrap hoards (and metalwork more generally) was seen as an essential part of the metalworking process, perhaps as a *pars pro toto* offering to ensure the success of a particular smithing event or to maintain the supply of raw metal (Worsaae 1866; Brück 2001; 2006; Helms 2012; Bradley 2013).

The landscape context of deposits containing metalworking related material

It has long been noted that certain landscape contexts were preferentially selected for the deposition of metalwork, though the specific patterns vary regionally and through time (eg, Bradley 1998; Fontijn 2002; Becker 2013; Bradley *et al.* 2018). Some object types such as swords and rapiers tended to be placed in watery contexts such as rivers or bogs, while axes and other tools were mainly placed on dry land. In south-east England, many hoards were placed on valley slopes or low rises overlooking watercourses (Yates & Bradley 2010a), while in the East Anglian Fenland they often occur in still water or at the fen edge (Yates & Bradley 2010b). In other regions, locations such as prominent hills, rock clefts, mountain passes, or caves recur.

Corresponding with the general pattern for tools, bronze moulds are only ever found on dry land. The same applies to most bronze smithing tools (Fregni 2014) and ingots, although it has been suggested that the finds

from what are usually interpreted as shipwreck sites such as Salcombe (Devon), which includes a large number of tin and copper ingots, might in fact have been deliberately deposited in the sea (Samson 2006). Beyond this, it is not obvious that the landscape contexts selected for metalworking equipment vary significantly to those for metal deposits in general. Thus several hoard and non-hoard finds of bronze moulds (Webley & Adams 2016) and smithing tools from south-east England are on gentle slopes or rises overlooking rivers. For example, the Thorndon hoard (Suffolk) included a hammer and awl, and was found on a gravel terrace of the River Dove (Hawkes & Smith 1955), while the Leigh II hoard (Essex) contained two hammers and several ingots and was found immediately adjacent to the Prittle Brook (Turner 2010). Elsewhere, metalworking tools have been found in striking upland locations. The Roseberry Topping hoard (North Yorkshire) – which contained a mould, hammer, and chisel – was hidden in a rock cleft near a spring, half way up a tall hill with an unusual and dramatic profile (Pearce 2006). The Beacon Hill mould (Leicestershire) is also from a prominent rocky hill, crowned by a hillfort of uncertain date. The White Edge mould (Derbyshire) and Donhead Clift hoard (Dorset; containing a mould and hammer) were associated with steep scarps.

One unusual context for the deposition of metalworking debris was the Heathery Burn cave (Durham), located in a ravine formed by a small river. A range of Late Bronze Age finds was recovered from various locations within the cave during the 19th century, including metalwork, pottery, spindle whorls, animal bone, and human remains; traces of hearths were also observed. The metalwork included one valve of a bronze mould, a possible second mould (Harding & Young 1986), an ingot fragment, a casting jet, a socketed chisel, and tongs. While it is possible that metalworking actually took place within the cave, it may equally be that the metalworking artefacts were deposited in the cave as part of rituals perhaps carried out over an extended period. A possible parallel is Kent's Cavern (Torbay), where at least six copper ingots of uncertain date form part of a varied assemblage of finds ranging from the Late Bronze Age to the Roman period (Pearce 1974; Silvester 1986). There are also examples from the Continent of later Bronze

Age moulds or bronzeworking waste deposited in caves, as in the grotte du Quéroy and grotte des Perrats in Charente (Bourhis & Gomez 1985; Gomez de Soto & Kerouanton 1991; Gomez de Soto 1996).

While most metalwork deposits took place away from known Bronze Age settlements, recent excavation in south-east England has uncovered a few examples of Late Bronze Age hoards containing scrap, ingots and metalworking tools placed at the margins of settlements, and sometimes in associated boundaries. The Isleham hoard (Cambridgeshire), for example, contained large quantities of scrap metal as well as two hammers and a bronze mould fragment. This was deposited close to the terminal of a field boundary where it met the fen edge. A possible long-house was located immediately south of the hoard and boundary (Malim 2010). Five of the cluster of eight hoards on the Ebbsfleet peninsula (Kent) produced ingot fragments and one a possible anvil fragment. These were found on low-lying land towards the margins of the peninsula and at the edge of areas of contemporary settlement; in one of the latter, a single ingot fragment from a pit was also recovered (**East Kent Access**, Zone 4). Similarly, at **Tothill Street**, Minster in Thanet (Kent), a hoard containing two bracelets, two axe fragments and a spearhead fragment was found a short distance outside a settlement enclosure. Inside the enclosure, an occupation or midden deposit contained a single ingot fragment.

In some further cases, hoards and other (separate) evidence for metalworking have been found at the same sites. At **Ellington School**, Pysons Road, Ramsgate (Kent), a hoard containing copper and bronze ingots, axeheads, spearheads, sword blade fragments, and other objects was deposited in a pit within a Middle or Late Bronze Age field system and adjacent to a Late Bronze Age–Earliest Iron Age settlement complex; bronze droplets and 'slag' were recovered from pits within the settlement (Oxford Archaeology 2015). As we have already seen above, a group of four ingot fragments was recovered from the outer ditch of the Late Bronze Age ringwork at **Mucking South Rings** (Thurrock) (Fig. 4.15); other metalworking evidence was found elsewhere in the ditch as well as inside the site (see above). At **Petters Sports Field**, Egham (Surrey), a scrap hoard that included casting jets was found in the upper fill of a ditch terminal. This feature formed part of the wider Petters/Runnymede complex that produced a range of metalworking evidence including a stone mould, clay moulds, a crucible fragment, ingots, and casting waste. Very rarely, scrap hoards occur within settlements. The Llyn Fawr hoard from **Tower Hill**, Ashbury (Oxfordshire), is highly unusual in its association with a round-house that formed part of an extensive open settlement. The assemblage included eight casting jets, one possible piece of slag, and 19 small pieces of scrap, as well as socketed axes (22 complete, 24 fragmentary; a significant number of these were unfinished or part-finished), rings (6 complete, 5 fragmentary), parts of two bracelets, a piece of coiled strip, and fragments of a ring-headed pin and two rods (Coombs *et al.* 2003). The hoard had been placed directly on the natural chalk adjacent to the entrance of a round-house: here, an assemblage that symbolised a transformative process was deposited next to a transitional point in settlement space. A pit close to another round-house contained what is interpreted as a stone anvil, though it cannot be proven that this was used for metalworking.

The deposition of scrap or ingot hoards close to locales at which metalworking took place may support the suggestion made above that such deposits may have referenced metalworking, or that their burial was seen as an essential part of the metalworking process. It should however be stressed that the examples listed above are exceptional: the large majority of hoards containing scrap and/or metalworking equipment cannot be linked to any known metalworking locale. The landscape contexts chosen for such deposits were diverse. Some were found in what could be viewed as liminal contexts: locations such as rivers, caves, or prominent hilltops may have been viewed as places between this world and the otherworld. The deposition of metalworking debris in such contexts may have acted as a means of drawing attention to the dangerous and transgressive qualities of locations in which rituals of various sorts – including interaction with the dead – may have been performed. Equally, other deposits containing metalworking material were in apparently unremarkable lowland locations within settled and farmed landscapes. The transformative nature of the metalworking process could also have served as a metaphor for other moments of transformation in the lifecycles of people, livestock, or crops (Brück 2006; Turner 2010), and scrap hoards may therefore have been deposited in the context of calendrical rites or other *rites de passage*. It seems that no universal rules governed the placing of these deposits. This hints that metalworking residues could carry a variety of connotations and could be deployed to serve differing ends.

Conclusion: the social organisation of non-ferrous metalworking from the Middle Bronze Age to the Earliest Iron Age

Childe's work in the mid-20th century (Childe 1930; 1936; 1940; 1958) still casts a long shadow on the study of Bronze Age metalworking. Part of the attraction of Childe's arguments is their simplicity: he implied that a single model could explain the organisation of metalworking and the social position of the Bronze Age smith across the whole of Europe. This chapter has suggested that in fact there was significant variation in the social context of this craft even within Britain and Ireland. Regional variation in metalworking practices is clear from the kinds of metal objects produced in different areas and also from the use of differing tools and techniques. For example, the use of stone moulds appears to have been a cultural preference in certain areas such as south-west England (see Fig. 4.1). The evidence from excavated sites also suggests regional differences in the spatial and social organisation of metalworking. This is seen, for example, in the frequent occurrence of casting debris at 'ordinary' open settlements in south-east England but more rarely on these types of site in Ireland, though such evidence has as much to do with depositional practice as the location of metalworking *per se*.

It is also possible that there was variation in the organisation and significance of different *kinds* of metalworking, even within a given region. Certainly, the lack of smelting evidence from excavated sites and the discovery of the smelting site at **Pentrwyn** on the Great Orme (Conwy) close to contemporary mines suggests that the initial stages of metal processing

may have been carried out by a different set of craftworkers to those who undertook the alloying, recycling, casting, and smithing of metals. The possibility that casting and smithing could have been organised differently from each other also needs consideration. Excavated sites with casting evidence almost never produce smithing tools; instead, these occur in hoards or as single off-site deposits. For Ireland, Boutoille (2015b) has suggested that bronze casters and bronze smiths were separate specialisations, the tool kits of the former represented by hoards of stone moulds and those of the latter by bronze hoards containing smithing tools. This is a questionable distinction, however, as casting jets occur alongside smithing tools in bronze hoards in Ireland and elsewhere. Bronze moulds are essentially absent from Ireland, but in regions where they do occur they were placed in metal hoards, again sometimes in combination with smithing tools. The deposition of metalworking equipment was to a large degree governed by the material it was made from: while clay and stone artefacts could be deposited within settlements, the proper place for metal objects was usually elsewhere in the landscape. There is thus little basis to argue that casting and smithing were carried out by different sets of people, which is unsurprising given the close inter-relationship that must have existed between these two practices.

Another possibility is that the manufacture of particular artefact types could have been organised differently or had a different significance. For example, the production of simple tools need not have had the same connotations as the manufacture of more complex or prestigious objects (Kuijpers 2008; 2018). This is suggested by the different materials and techniques used to make different metal artefacts, choices not always fully explicable by functional imperatives. Certain types of mould were preferentially employed for certain types of object – bronze moulds were mainly for axes, for example, and swords were only made in clay moulds. During the 1970s and '80s it was suggested that there was a distinction in southern Britain between peripatetic axe or tool smiths using portable, reusable stone or bronze moulds and more settled metalworkers who cast weapons and other objects using single-use clay moulds and hence needed knowledge of local clay resources (Moore & Rowlands 1972; Northover 1982b; 1988b Howard 1983). More recent excavation has complicated the picture: matrices for axes and other tools are frequently found along with those for weapons and/or ornaments in Late Bronze Age clay mould assemblages. This does not suggest any rigid separation of production by artefact type. The same is implied by Middle Bronze Age stone moulds that have matrices for different artefact types and by the combinations of moulds seen in the stone mould hoards. Recent archaeometallurgical work also supports this view. Late Bronze Age swords, spearheads and axes from England and Wales generally share a similar alloy composition, throwing doubt on the idea that weapon makers operated in a separate sphere of metalworking (Bray 2016). Yet, the presence of large deposits comprised predominantly of sword mould fragments suggests that these may have been the product of particular casting events, even if they were made by the same people as other bronze objects.

The question of the mobility of metal-workers remains one of the hardest to address. There is no obvious way to decide whether a single small deposit of metalworking debris from a settlement represents a visit from a peripatetic metalworker or is all that survives from the sporadic activities of a settled part-time smith. The evidence for the long-distance movement of stone moulds is a notable contrast to the Early Bronze Age but could be the result of exchange rather than the movement of metalworkers. The combination of an exotic stone mould and an apparently non-local crucible at the Late Bronze Age settlement of **Burderop Down** (Swindon) is however suggestive. At other sites, clay moulds and crucibles were typically made locally. The evidence is equivocal, but need not be made to fit a single, simple model. Too often, a false dichotomy has been drawn between two opposing situations: settled, sedentary metalworkers versus the Childean notion of free-roaming detribalised smiths (Dietrich 2012). This in turn rests on questionable assumptions that sedentism was the norm for people in later prehistory and that anyone with greater mobility must have been a special individual set apart from the rest of society (cf. Webley 2015). It may be more realistic to envisage a situation in which metalworkers were typically based in a particular community but also had the potential for mobility over

varying scales, in a context in which people in general moved around more than is often assumed; this has implications too for ease of access to the raw materials.

The frequent occurrence of metal casting material at settlements shows that this craft was relatively common in a domestic milieu in the Middle and Late Bronze Age. This observation must be set in the context of the increasing amount of metal in circulation during the Middle and Late Bronze Age (Radivojević *et al.* 2018; Williams & Le Carlier de Veslud 2019; see also Pernicka *et al.* 2016). In some cases, we have evidence that metalworking actually took place within round-houses (as at **Tremough** (Cornwall)), though elsewhere this may have occurred after the abandonment of the house (for example at **Trethellan Farm** (Cornwall)). In many cases metalworking debris was deposited along with other 'domestic' material, for example in waterholes. The deliberate deposition of metalworking material within houses suggests that such residues were seen as appropriate for marking episodes in the life histories of these buildings and their inhabitants. It also suggests that the metalworkers at these sites were often members of the community rather than itinerant craftspeople. Nonetheless, despite the increase in metalworking evidence during this period, the craft may have been a more common activity at Middle and Late Bronze Age settlements than our database suggests. The recent discoveries at Must Farm (Cambridgeshire) (Knight *et al.* 2019) not only highlight the range and quantity of metal artefacts that constituted a normal household inventory but underline the scale of the material evidence that has undoubtedly been lost at other less well-preserved sites; refractory ceramics, for example, are very friable.

Alongside the settlement evidence, metal casting evidence also occurs at many sites that are not 'ordinary' settlements but may have played other social roles, for example as foci for gatherings or for ritual. This is particularly the case for Late Bronze Age Ireland, where hillforts and crannógs may have been centres for metalworking. This is less clear for Britain, but even so sites such as hillforts, middens, and ringworks form almost one-third of all sites with casting evidence, a higher proportion than might have been expected had this craft been evenly distributed across all categories of excavated site. Certain kinds of locales may thus have been more frequently used for metalworking than ordinary settlements. Whether such sites were particular foci for intensive or specialised metalworking is another matter. In most cases the metalworking assemblages from these sites are modest. For example, when one compares the three or four clay mould fragments and 13 crucible sherds from **Potterne** (Wiltshire) with the *c.* 100,000 sherds (1 tonne) of pottery and 134,000 animal bones recovered from this site it seems difficult to sustain an argument that metalworking was a key element of the activities carried out there. For England, at least, the link between metalworking and possible high-status sites is not absolutely clear. Even sites such as middens that have produced unusually large and diverse assemblages of non-metal items can perhaps be better interpreted as gathering places where a range of social, technological, and ritual activities were carried out, rather than high-status settlements.

Nor does it seem that particular kinds of metalworking were restricted to particular site types. Mould matrices suggest that swords, spearheads, tools, and razors were all cast at a range of sites, including settlement, non-settlement, and 'off-site' contexts. The relatively common occurrence of casting evidence for items such as swords and spearheads both at 'ordinary' open settlements and elsewhere across the wider landscape, for example in field boundaries, in isolated pits and near watercourses, suggests that even the production of 'high-status' objects was not a focus of elite control but was practiced in a wide variety of social contexts and settings (cf. Sörman 2018).

There are many examples where metal-working material was placed in formal or structured deposits, and this could occur in a range of contexts. There are several cases in which substantial numbers of sword mould fragments were specifically selected for this (Mörtz 2014). The deposits in the ditch terminals of the **Springfield Lyons** ringwork (Essex) are the most widely known example, but other examples include **Greenfields** (Essex), **Norton Fitzwarren** (Somerset), and **Bourton-on-the-Water** (Gloucestershire). Swords are thought to have been prestigious objects and their casting was a lengthy and highly skilled process (Ó Faoláin & Northover 1998). In most of these cases, the

metalworking debris may have been the product of a single casting event. This may suggest that metalworking was a rare and relatively small-scale activity at these sites, or that only certain metalworking events were commemorated through the process of deposition.

Equally, not all deposits of metalworking material can be assumed to have been deliberately placed (Needham & Bridgford 2013). Where a few fragmented pieces of metalworking debris are mixed with other 'domestic' material, as for example in the waterhole at **Striplands Farm** (Cambridgeshire), we may be dealing with the secondary deposition of midden material rather than the conscious deposition of metalworking residues; the presence of the latter may not even have been recognised (cf. Brudenell & Cooper 2008). The evidence from sites such as **Runnymede** (Surrey), where a variety of different types of metalworking debris were found spread throughout the midden, is also very different from the discrete deposits of sword mould fragments from sites such as Norton Fitzwarren. The former may represent the residues of *in situ* metalworking, much of which may have been incidentally incorporated into the midden, while the latter may have been brought from a distance for purposeful and ritualised deposition at a significant location. Of course, the fact that sites such as middens were viewed as suitable locations for metalworking is not without significance, for these were places in which a variety of materials, objects and people were brought together, assembled and transformed in a range of ritual and productive activities (Waddington 2009). Midden material – like metalworking debris – symbolised transformative processes.

The relatively large deposits of sword mould fragments in pits contrasts with the deposition of clay moulds for other types of object, such as axes, which tend to be found either as single fragments or as part of mixed assemblages comprising moulds for several different artefact types as at **Holborough Quarry** (Kent) described above. The singling out of sword moulds for 'special' types of deposition might hint that these were made by particular specialists, although as we have seen sword moulds also frequently occur as part of mixed assemblages, and, like other moulds, they can be found in round-houses. Even the largest deposits of sword mould fragments do not represent the production of more than a few objects. Many deposits represent the residues of just a few small-scale metalworking events rather than continuous production.

Although the round-house at **Tremough** (Cornwall) can perhaps be identified as a specialist workshop, the architecture of this building and its finds inventory (other than the metalworking debris) are little different to other 'domestic' buildings of the period. The rarity of possible discrete workshops may suggest that metalworking was not usually a full-time specialist activity but was undertaken alongside other tasks as part of the household economy by people who, for the most part, were fully embedded in their local and regional cultural contexts. The discovery of mixed assemblages of mould fragments even at small open settlements suggests that in regions such as southern England, part-time but nonetheless highly skilled metalworkers made objects for their local areas; there is little to suggest that these individuals were under the control of an elite and metalworking appears to have been a decentralised activity. In Ireland, in contrast, casting appears to have occurred more often at 'special' places in the landscape, such as lakesides and hilltops, although as we have seen it is not clear whether these should be interpreted as elite settlements or community gathering places.

Only very rarely – as at **Rathgall** (Co. Wicklow) – is there enough metalworking debris to suggest that full-time specialists may have been present over a prolonged period of time or that there was more than a single metalworker. It should be noted, however, that evidence for the production of objects that required the highest levels of technical accomplishment, notably gold ornaments and sheet-bronze objects such as shields and cauldrons, is extremely rare or absent entirely. Evidence for the working of sheet bronze cannot be identified with any certainty as the craft does not produce diagnostic waste.

Fragments of sheet bronze have occasionally been found on excavated sites (and in some hoards) but it is difficult to tell if these are offcuts from sheet working or the remains of discarded or scrapped artefacts. Some of the tools from bronze hoards may have been used to work sheet bronze but all are divorced from any excavated site context. Convincing evidence for goldworking is present only at **Haughey's Fort** (Co. Armagh), although the craft may also have been carried out at Rathgall; both of these sites are hillforts, although the ramparts at Rathgall may post-date the metalworking activity. It is therefore possible that the organisation of production for those objects that required the most specialised skillsets was very different to that for most other artefact types.

In the Late Bronze Age, in particular, some of the contexts in which metalworking debris was deposited can be described as liminal in one way or another. Metalworking debris has been found in field boundaries and enclosure ditches, in and near wet places such as lakes, rivers, and waterholes, and – occasionally – in locations such as pre-existing ceremonial monuments, a cave, and a glacial pingo. The occurrence of metalworking evidence in such contexts suggests that the activity of metalworking could be viewed as dangerous but productive and its tools and by-products could be employed to symbolise processes of transformation and rebirth. Certainly, this is a long way from Childe's model of Bronze Age metalworking as the foundation for the emergence of primitive capitalism. This is not to say that all acts of metalworking were ritualised or heavily freighted with symbolism: metalworking material was also often found within the settlement core, at a distance from locations that might be identified as liminal. The metalworking process had the potential to be a rich source of metaphor but this seems to have been drawn upon in differing ways in different times and places.

5

The Iron Age,
c. 600 BC–AD 100

Given that the very concepts of the Bronze Age and the Iron Age were initially defined in relation to metal, it is unsurprising that metalworking has been accorded an important role as a driver of social change during the 1st millennium BC. This can clearly be seen in the work of Childe, who drew a distinction between bronze and ironworking that remains influential to this day. As we have seen, Childe argued that metalworking in the Bronze Age lay in the hands of a discrete group of craft workers with esoteric knowledge and privileged access to copper and tin, resources that derived from just a few restricted sources. The introduction of ironworking at the beginning of the Iron Age was a 'democratising' force that shattered the old social order, as iron was much more widely and 'cheaply' available (Childe 1954, 183). These ideas have been echoed more recently by Kristiansen (1998, 410), who similarly argues that the development of ironworking during the Iron Age democratised the production of tools and weapons, thus shifting the focus of power from the control of bronze exchange networks to the control of land and its produce. In a British context, Ehrenreich (1991; 1995) draws a contrast between later Bronze Age bronzeworking and Middle Iron Age ironworking. The former, he argues, required complex technical knowledge and was therefore restricted to specialists and hierarchically organised, while the latter was more accessible and took place in a heterarchical context.

While it cannot be doubted that the introduction and development of ironworking technology had a profound social impact, since Childe's day it has become clear that these processes were lengthy and complex. As we saw in the previous chapter the first, very limited, use of iron in Britain occurred during the Late Bronze Age. The Earliest Iron Age saw a marked decrease in the use of bronze objects, or at least their deposition, but growth in the numbers and variety of iron objects was very modest. Thus, as Needham (2007, 58) puts it, the transition to the Iron Age was 'not so much about replacing bronze with iron, but rather, doing away with a social value system based heavily on bronze'. It was only from the 6th–5th centuries BC onwards, and particularly after *c.* 400 BC, that iron began to be produced in significant quantities in Britain and Ireland and was routinely used to make tools and other everyday objects. The production of bronze objects also increased again around the same time. The intensification of metalworking during the later Iron Age occurred in tandem with increasing population densities and the colonisation of new areas of the landscape (Bradley *et al.* 2015). Settlement reappears in Ireland in the last four centuries BC, having been largely invisible during the Early Iron Age (Becker *et al.* 2008; Corlett & Potterton 2012). In many parts of southern Britain, a dense pattern of settlement emerged in the later Iron Age, with increased enclosure creating a more ordered and bounded landscape. In certain parts of Britain, increased specialisation in the production of some other artefact types, such as pottery and querns, can be seen at around the same time as the later Iron Age upturn in metalworking (Morris 1996; Sharples 2010).

These developments were accompanied by changes in bronzeworking technology (see also Chapter 2). Alloy recipes after *c.* 600 BC tend to be very different from those of the Late Bronze Age with a much lower lead content (Dungworth 1996). Crucibles tend to be smaller than before, commensurate with a focus on casting smaller objects (see Chapter 2). In southern Britain, the bivalve mould technology of the Bronze Age and Earliest Iron Age seems to have been abandoned completely in favour of lost-wax casting, alongside the use of simple one-piece moulds for ingots or blanks for sheet working, though in Scotland and the Isle of Man clay bivalve moulds continued to be used for casting simple objects such as pins. As we have seen, the lost-wax method had been used in Britain on a small scale during the Late Bronze Age. Its wider uptake may be linked to the appearance of new artefact types such as brooches and La Tène objects with elaborate forms, as lost-wax casting is well suited to producing such objects. The La Tène metalworking tradition of the 5th–4th century BC onwards also involved skilful use of a range of cold working techniques, both to decorate and finish cast objects, and to form artefacts from sheet bronze (Jope 2000).

In contrast to the later Bronze Age, when metalworking in Britain and Ireland clearly formed part of wider 'Atlantic' traditions, the style and technology of metal objects during the Early and Middle Iron Age has been taken to indicate that there were only limited and sporadic contacts across the Channel. The adoption of the La Tène style in the 5th–4th century BC clearly demonstrates interactions with craft workers on the Continent, but distinctive insular variants of this soon developed. Arguably, however, a closer examination of metalwork and other evidence suggests that the extent of British insularity during this period has been exaggerated (Joy 2015; Webley 2015).

The majority of objects made from cast or beaten bronze during the Iron Age were small personal objects and decorated items that may have had a role in the presentation of personal or group identity. Most characteristic are dress accessories such as pins, brooches, and bracelets; horse gear such as bridles; and elements of wheeled vehicles such as linchpins and terrets (Dunning 1934; Spratling 1972; Raftery 1983; Palk 1991; Jope 2000; Becker 2008; Adams 2013; Booth 2014; Lewis 2015). Rarer items include mirrors; fittings for weaponry such as swords, scabbards, and shields; feasting equipment such as sheet bronze cauldrons and tankard handles; and possible ritual paraphernalia such as 'divination spoons' (Spratling 1972; Raftery 1983; Jope 2000; Stead 2006; Joy 2010; 2014; Horn 2015). Precious metals essentially went out of use during the earlier Iron Age, but gold was again used to make torcs from around the 3rd century BC onwards, especially in Ireland and Scotland (Becker 2012; Hunter 2018; La Niece *et al.* 2018). Lead was occasionally employed to make simple objects such as weights (Ponting 2018). In contrast to bronze or gold, lead may have had negative connotations in this period: at a Middle Iron Age settlement at Great Houghton (Northamptonshire) a woman was buried face-down and bound with a crude lead-tin alloy torc worn back-to-front around her neck, perhaps a deliberate statement of insult or disgrace (Chapman 2001; Aldhouse-Green 2004).

Contrasting with its ubiquity during the later Bronze Age, bronze now seems to have been preferentially deployed in a more limited range of socially significant activities. Metal objects may though have had a social role that went beyond their ostensible function. For example, some items of horse gear appear to have been non-functional (Palk 1991) and the deposition of objects such as terrets in large sets suggests that they circulated and had their own social life separate from any use as vehicle fittings (Sharples 2010, 142). It is likely that elaborately decorated metal objects had considerable social significance, given the skill, time, and resources required to produce them, though whether they expressed the prestige of individuals (Armit

2007) or that of larger groups (Sharples 2010; Hill 2012; Dolan 2014) is a matter of debate.

Many of the artefact types made in bronze also had counterparts in iron. There were also many composite objects in which bronze was combined in various ways with other materials such as iron, glass, coral, jet, horn, wood, or leather. The production of composite objects could be a lengthy and complex process (Stead 2006; Joy 2010). This emphasis on juxtaposing materials with contrasting appearances and sensory properties – and different geographical origins – contrasts with the situation in the later Bronze Age, when prestige objects such as the Oxborough dirk (Norfolk) and accumulations such as the Isleham hoard (Cambridgeshire) were designed to awe through their sheer volume of bronze. Another feature of Iron Age decorated metalwork is its bewildering variety – objects such as terrets, for example, have proved difficult to classify into coherent stylistic groups (Lewis 2015).

Different kinds of metal objects tended to be treated in differing ways at the end of their use lives (Becker 2012; Garrow & Gosden 2012). Bronze artefacts deposited at settlements are generally restricted to simpler items such as pins and brooches, though finer objects do occasionally occur. In some cases, the metal objects found in such contexts had clearly been deliberately placed in line with wider practices of 'structured' or ritual deposition. A well-known example is the collection of horse gear placed with other objects in a pair of disused storage pits within the hillfort at Bury Hill (Hampshire) (Cunliffe & Poole 2000). Objects such as ornaments, weapons and mirrors were also placed in graves, though accompanied burials were largely restricted to the later Iron Age in a few specific regions, notably Ireland, East Riding of Yorkshire, Cornwall, and Late Iron Age south-east England. Many other metal objects – especially the more elaborate decorated items – were deposited singly or in hoards in the wider landscape away from occupied sites. Some were placed in wet contexts such as rivers or the lake at Llyn Cerrig Bach (Anglesey), where objects made of iron, bronze, and other materials were deposited from the Middle Iron Age into the Roman period (Fox 1947; Macdonald 2007a). This separation from settlement contexts has made it difficult to relate fine metalwork to other aspects of Iron Age society. The problem

is compounded by the fact that decorated metalwork has traditionally been studied from an art historical perspective that is somewhat divorced from wider archaeological concerns (Macdonald 2007b, 333–5).

The same issues that dominate debates on the organisation of Bronze Age metalworking recur in discourse on the Iron Age (see also Chapter 1): were metalworkers itinerant or settled in their communities, and to what extent did they operate under elite control? There has been a particular emphasis on the evidence from a small number of metalworking sites, above all the Middle Iron Age settlement at **Gussage All Saints** (Dorset) with its large deposits of crucibles and moulds for equine equipment (see below). This impressive accumulation of material has been interpreted in contrasting ways: while some argue it must have been generated over a lengthy period by metalworkers permanently residing at the site (Spratling 1979; Gibson 1996), others envisage a single intense episode of production involving itinerant specialists (Foster 1980; Sharples 2010, 142). Conversely, at some other sites where only a limited amount of casting debris is present this has been taken as implying non-resident metalworkers (eg, Cracknell & Smith 1983, 35). Other commentators have regarded the question of the mobility of metalworkers as impossible to resolve (Howard 1983; Cunliffe 1995b; 2005, 501). Indeed, sites with small quantities of evidence are often neglected in existing discussions of prehistoric metalworking because of the expectation that distinct workshops should be present.

It has often been asserted that skilled metalworking would have been carried out under elite control or patronage, though the production of simpler items may have been less controlled (Fox 1958; Howard 1983; Henderson 1991; Gibson 1996; Cunliffe 2005). The concept of a patron–client relationship derives from accounts in medieval Irish and Welsh documents (Gillies 1981; Karl 2006), the assumption being that the hierarchical 'Celtic' social systems described by these sources had their roots in the pre-Roman Iron Age. In recent years the relevance of these much later sources has been questioned and it has been argued that many Iron Age societies had heterarchical forms of organisation (Ehrenreich 1995; Hill 2012; Dolan 2014), providing an alternative to the model of elite control of metalworkers.

It is routinely stated that skilled metal-workers were specialists, though it is not always clear whether *full-time* specialisation is implied. Non-ferrous metalworking has generally been seen as a separate specialism from blacksmithing and other high-temperature crafts, though it has been noted that composite objects imply some cooperative working (Spratling 1972, 355; Howard 1983, 538). It has also been suggested that different forms of non-ferrous metalworking – such as the casting of horse gear and the production of sheet metalwork – may have been carried out by distinct groups of specialists (Howard 1983; Northover 1984; 1988b; Hunter 2015, 235).

As divine smiths feature in 'Celtic' myth, it has long been suggested that skilled metalworking had a supernatural aspect during the Iron Age (eg, Wheeler 1954, 29–30; Aldhouse-Green & Aldhouse-Green 2005). Interest in the role of ritual and symbolism in metalworking has increased since the 1990s, with ethnographic parallels playing an important role. This can be seen in Hingley's discussion (1997; 1999) of ironworking in Iron Age Britain, which was strongly influenced by Herbert's work (1994) on African iron smelting and its associated taboos. Hingley argued that ironworking was symbolically associated with concepts of regeneration and transformation, supporting this with examples where smelting or smithing occurred at liminal locations at the boundaries or entrances of settlements and hillforts, or on the sites of much older monuments. This argument has been elaborated by others (Aldhouse-Green 2002; Giles 2007), with Giles and Parker Pearson (1999, 227) arguing that 'it is notable that crafts "unbound" by seasonal timing, such as metalworking, are often spatially distinct from dwellings, away from or at the margins of settlements … Debris from the process is almost unknown from household contexts'. The dominant role given to one particular set of African parallels in these accounts can perhaps be questioned, as can the implication that these parallels can be applied to all forms of Iron Age metalworking; iron smelting is, after all, a quite different kind of process to bronze casting or smithing. It should also be stressed that the argument that metalworking was carried out in liminal locations is based on a small number of selected Iron Age metalworking sites rather than a comprehensive overview of the evidence, a point that will be addressed in this chapter.

In southern and eastern England the Late Iron Age saw significant social change, with the emergence of new forms of political power and the reordering of contacts across the Channel from *c.* 150 BC onwards. Linked to these changes were developments in the manufacture and use of non-ferrous metalwork. There was a marked increase in the production – or at least deposition – of metal items, notably brooches and objects with La Tène decoration (Jundi & Hill 1998; Worrell 2007; Garrow & Gosden 2012). An influx of coins and other metal objects from Gaul and the Roman world facilitated an increase in goldworking, and the first appearance of objects made of silver and brass. Existing artefact types such as brooches became more diverse in style and some entirely new objects were adopted, such as cosmetic implements (Eckardt & Crummy 2008). The most important new artefact type was coinage, which was struck in gold, silver, or bronze, or cast in potin (silver-coloured high-tin copper alloy; Northover 1992). Although the production of coins will not be considered in detail here, the minting of struck coinage involved novel techniques originating on the Continent such as precision weighing, the production of blanks in pellet trays, die-cutting, and the striking of the blanks with dies, and it has been suggested that migrant specialists may have been involved in the spread of these technologies (Spratling 1972, 355; Chadburn 2006, 442). The purposes that Iron Age coins served are imperfectly understood, and it cannot be assumed that they represent 'money' as we understand it today (Farley 2012; Haselgrove & Webley 2016; Talbot 2017). It is, though, apparent that the production and circulation of coinage was bound up with the negotiation of new networks of power; some coins from the latter stages of the Late Iron Age bear the names of political rulers (Creighton 2000). These developments presaged the Roman conquest of southern Britain, which marks the end point of this study, though it should be noted that elements of 'native' metalworking traditions continued into the late 1st century AD and beyond on both sides of the new frontier; the frequency of deposition of 'Celtic art' actually increased in the decades following 40 BC (Garrow *et al.* 2010; Garrow & Gosden 2012).

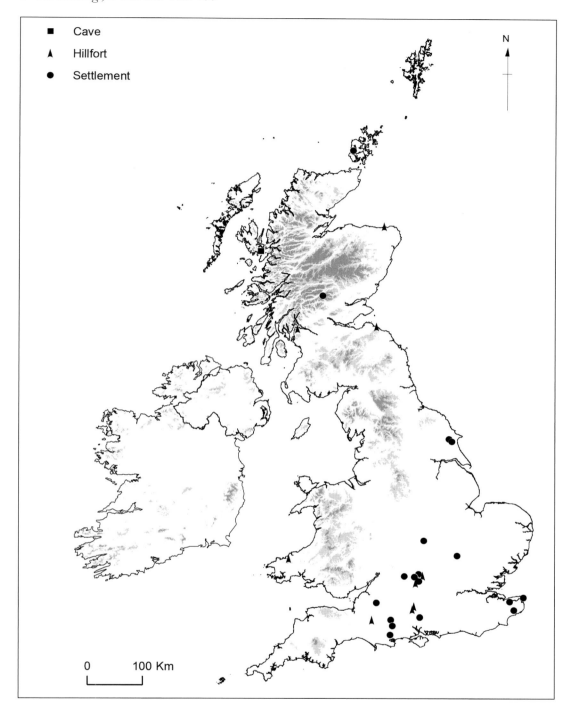

Figure 5.1: Distribution of excavated sites of Early Iron Age date that have produced metalworking tools and non-ferrous metalworking residues

The nature, distribution and chronology of the evidence

In this chapter, we will examine the range of non-ferrous metalworking evidence from excavated sites by region and by period to explore the contexts in which the craft took place as well as geographical and chronological variability in its organisation and significance. Some 205 individual sites in the project database have revealed non-ferrous metalworking evidence of Iron Age date including crucibles, moulds and/or casting debris and, in some cases, also possible smithing tools; however, not all of these could be more closely dated. Sixteen further sites have produced smithing

Figure 5.2: Distribution of excavated settlements of later Iron Age date that have produced metalworking tools and non-ferrous metalworking residues

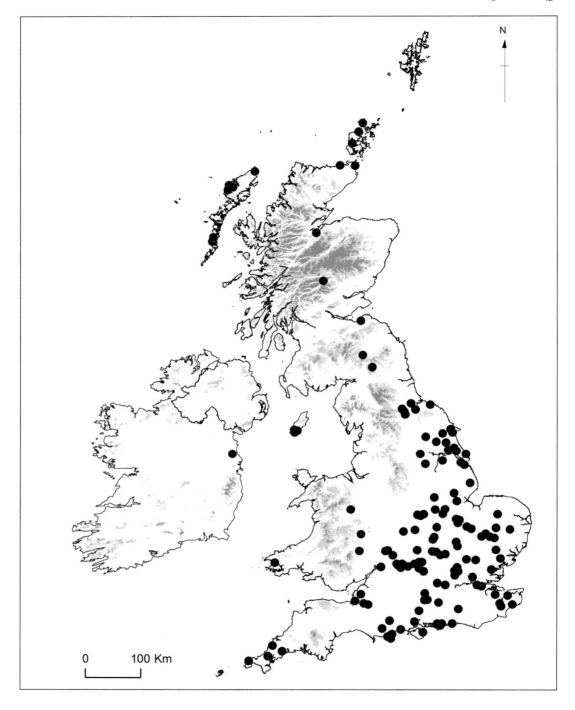

tools alone although, as noted in Chapter 2, these may have been employed in ironworking or other craft activities. These figures exclude sites from southern Britain which can only be dated broadly to a period spanning either side of the Roman conquest (29 further sites with non-ferrous metalworking evidence and four with smithing tools only).

The metalworking debris from Iron Age sites differs significantly from later Bronze Age assemblages. Fragments of crucibles are the most common remains of non-ferrous metalworking in Iron Age contexts, whereas moulds have been recovered from significantly fewer sites (see Table 2.2); as seen in Chapter 4, the opposite was the case in the later Bronze

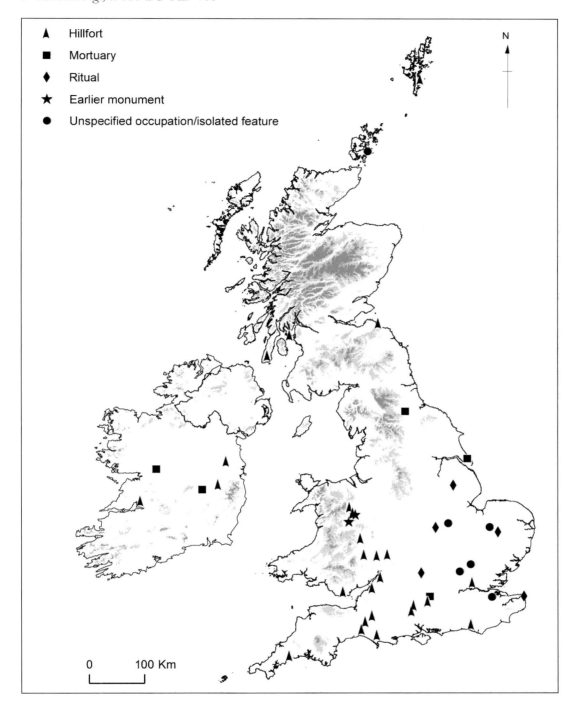

Age. In part this may be because Iron Age crucibles are easier to recognise than those of Bronze Age date because of their distinctive forms and fabrics. It is also possible that Iron Age crucibles had shorter use lives than those of the Bronze Age, and hence were produced and discarded in greater quantities (see below). In contrast, fragments of lost-wax moulds may be hard to recognise: many of the copper alloy objects produced at this time are small and, when the moulds were broken to extract the finished artefact, the resulting debris may be too fragmentary for identification. Evidence for smelting is limited to possible tin slag at **Castle Dore** and possible copper slag at **Trevelgue Head**, both in Cornwall (see Chapter 2).

Figure 5.4: Number of excavated Iron Age sites with non-ferrous metalworking evidence by period and by region (excluding sites that have yielded only smithing tools; some multi-phase sites have been included in both the Early Iron Age and later Iron Age totals)

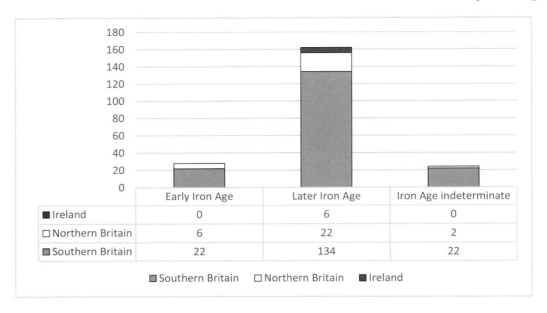

	Early Iron Age	Later Iron Age	Iron Age indeterminate
■ Ireland	0	6	0
□ Northern Britain	6	22	2
■ Southern Britain	22	134	22

■ Southern Britain   □ Northern Britain   ■ Ireland

Most of the Iron Age sites recorded for this project were settlements of one sort or another. Non-ferrous metalworking evidence has also been recovered from a number of hillforts. Finds from other types of site are rare: these include cemeteries, 'shrines', and older monuments. It is often difficult to distinguish evidence of non-ferrous metalworking from the remains of other activities. Site plans indicating the distribution of metalworking debris do not always differentiate ironworking and non-ferrous metalworking evidence and sometimes include fuel ash slag, a material that is commonly found on Iron Age sites in southern England but is typically not associated with metallurgy. Once undiagnostic evidence is separated, it is often evident that the non-ferrous metalworking debris is more restricted spatially than originally thought.

Sites yielding non-ferrous metalworking evidence of Iron Age date are widely distributed across Britain and Ireland although there are relatively few in Ireland despite increasing recognition of Irish Iron Age settlements (Becker *et al.* 2008) (Figs 5.1–3). There is a particular concentration of sites in southern and eastern England, at least partly the result of intensive developer-funded activity in those regions; in contrast, there is a lack of sites in areas such as central Wales and central Scotland. Overall, our study has yielded relatively few finds of Early Iron Age date (*c.* 600–400 BC), mirroring the paucity of non-ferrous metal artefacts from this period.

The majority of the evidence discussed in this chapter dates to after 400 BC (Fig. 5.4). For many sites, it is difficult to distinguish between finds of Middle Iron Age and Late Iron Age date, and for most of Britain and Ireland there is significant continuity over these periods.

Following a general discussion of the evidence for the manufacture and movement of metalworking tools, the site evidence for metalworking from excavated archaeological sites will be discussed by region. For southern Britain, Early Iron Age sites are discussed first, followed by those of 'later Iron Age' date (post-400 BC). Developments specific to the Late Iron Age in southern and eastern England (*c.* 150 BC–AD 50), such as the use of smithing tools as grave goods and the working of precious metals at sites identified as shrines and oppida, are treated separately as they suggest changes in the role of non-ferrous metalworking linked to the wider social transformations that occurred in this region in the two centuries preceding the Roman conquest. The smaller number of sites from northern Britain and Ireland are then considered. The concluding discussion considers issues such as the relationships between non-ferrous metalworking and other crafts.

Production and movement of crucibles and moulds

The developments in metalworking technology during the Iron Age altered the relationships between metalworkers, their tools, and the artefacts they produced. The use of reusable moulds – which easily allowed repeated production of identical castings – had already been on the wane during the Late Bronze Age, but in the Iron Age it ceased entirely, except for the production of simple ingots or billets. For all other artefacts a new clay mould had to be made for each casting, requiring fresh materials and a significant investment of time. As argued in the previous chapter, this is a different way of working not just in practical terms but also conceptually. The emphasis on the 'individuality' of each casting was greatest in southern Britain, where use of the lost-wax technique became the norm. With this method, not only did a new mould need to be made for each casting, but the pattern for each mould was individually crafted in wax.

Iron Age crucibles may also have had short use lives, as they rarely show evidence for repair. Exceptions include the crucible of unusual form from **Westwood Campus, University of Warwick** (Coventry), which has patches of clay applied to areas of cracking (Fig. 2.9). This stands in contrast to the more frequent evidence for relining and repair on Bronze Age crucibles (Howard 1983). Such a comparison may, however, be simplistic, as differences in fabrics and forms between Bronze Age and Iron Age crucibles would have affected their functional properties. Iron Age crucibles from southern Britain typically have fabrics densely packed with sand or carbon, or a mixture of the two (*ibid.*), and this could perhaps have given them better refractory properties than many Bronze Age crucibles, allowing them to withstand repeated use without the need for relining or repair. In the absence of any comparative experimental work, the question must remain open.

In southern Britain, it has proven difficult to tie refractory ceramics to particular source locations due to the character of the materials typically used as temper (namely sand and/or carbon for crucibles and sand and/or grog for lost-wax moulds). At the Somerset lake villages of **Glastonbury** and **Meare East** and **West**, clays used for moulds and crucibles are likely to derive from the Coal Measures deposits around 20 km to the north (Howard 1983). Meare West also produced an ingot mould made of Greisen that probably originated at least 150 km away in the South-West Peninsula. This use

of non-local materials is notable in the light of arguments that the Meare lake villages were seasonally-occupied productive sites or 'fairs' (see below). Elsewhere in southern Britain, Howard's petrological analyses (Howard 1983) suggest that moulds and crucibles were generally produced locally, though the fabric recipes were typically quite different from domestic pottery found on the same sites. She argued that 'as the standard formulae stipulated specific ingredients it was not necessary for the Iron Age smith to possess such an intimate knowledge of his environment [as Bronze Age metalworkers]. Iron Age bronze casters could, conceivably, have moved from area to area producing crucibles and moulds from locally available sands and clays' (*ibid.*, 506–7). In Scotland, Heald's petrological and SEM analyses (2005) of crucibles and moulds from **Culduthel Farm**, Inverness (Highland) and **Mine Howe** (Orkney) suggest use of local clays in both cases, though again there was no obvious technological link to domestic ceramics from the same sites.

The context of metal casting residues from excavated sites: southern Britain

For the purposes of this study, southern Britain is defined as the region south of Cumbria and Northumberland, and including Wales; sites in Yorkshire and Durham, for example, tend to have more in common with those to the south than those in the northernmost counties of England or in Scotland.

Early Iron Age (c. 600–400 BC)
Evidence of non-ferrous metalworking is relatively uncommon in southern Britain during the Early Iron Age. Twenty-two sites have produced finds that can be dated to this period, including six hillforts and 16 settlements. Most of the material consists of crucibles or casting waste. Moulds are exceptionally rare: the only example from a secure Early Iron Age context was a fragment of clay mould found in a pit at **Gravelly Guy**, Stanton Harcourt (Oxfordshire). Too little of this survived to discern the object type cast. One settlement and three hillforts yielded smithing tools. A poker was found in a storage pit on the settlement at **Fairfield Park** (Central Bedfordshire), for

example; this had been deliberately bent back on itself. At two of the hillforts, the only other metalworking evidence recovered was for the production of iron objects, so the tools may not indicate that non-ferrous metalworking was carried out at these sites.

The majority of the evidence is small-scale and scattered. Some Early Iron Age sites have produced finds from just a single feature. For example, at **Covert Farm**, Crick (Northamptonshire), three crucible fragments, one with copper alloy traces, along with iron smithing debris were found in a round-house gully. At **Broom** (Central Bedfordshire), a pit contained pottery, a single crucible sherd, a smithing hearth bottom, and a large quantity of burnt stone. Elsewhere, small amounts of evidence are scattered across Early Iron Age settlements. At Gravelly Guy, crucible fragments, hearth- or furnace-lining fragments and a single piece of clay mould were recovered from seven different Early Iron Age pits spread over an area of *c.* 100 m (Fig. 5.5). In four of these features, only single fragments were present, although another yielded a complete and intact 'thumbpot' crucible. A further crucible fragment and two fragments of hearth-lining were recovered from two pits and a post-hole of Early–Middle Iron Age date. There is nothing to indicate that any of these pits had a metalworking function, although the presence of furnace-lining material suggests that metalworking hearths were once present at the site. Northover (2004b, 353) has interpreted the material from Gravelly Guy as indicating a 'small, intermittent workshop'. The non-ferrous metalworking debris is too dispersed to suggest the existence of a single workshop area, however. Ironworking slag including fragments of smithing hearth bottoms was also widely scattered across the site.

Evidence from Early Iron Age contexts in hillforts is also sparse. A single small lump of 'copper or bronze slag' was found in an Early Iron Age occupation layer to the rear of the rampart at **Balksbury** (Hampshire), while the earliest evidence from **Danebury** (Hampshire) dates from the late 5th century BC if not later (see below). The assemblage from **Cadbury Castle** (Somerset) is slightly more substantial and much of this was concentrated in one part of the site. The earliest stratified material consists of crucible fragments and copper-stained hearth lining recovered from a shallow hollow lined with stone slabs towards the centre of the hillfort. A few metres east of this feature was a small group of spreads of burnt stone, cobbles, and hearth or oven features, or possibly small furnaces or kilns. This may have been a metalworking area although none of the features retained positive evidence for the craft. The main distribution of finished metal objects of Early Iron Age date coincides with the area around the hearths, although bronze objects were also found elsewhere on the site. Bronze casting waste was also recovered from an area of cobbling 10 m east of the shallow hollow; the dating of this material is not clear, although some is likely to be Early Iron Age.

Some Early Iron Age metalworking evidence forms part of assemblages of items that may have been deliberately selected for deposition; special deposits in pits are a phenomenon that is widely attested in this period (Cunliffe 1992; Hill 1995a; Chadwick 2012). As such, the distribution of metalworking-related finds need not directly reflect the location where the craft itself was carried out. A pit at **Cresswell Field/Worton Rectory Farm**, Yarnton (Oxfordshire), contained not only four crucible sherds (half the total assemblage belonging to this phase of the site), copper alloy slag, and a tuyère fragment but also an almost complete articulated sheep skeleton with one forelimb replaced with that of another animal; the feature also yielded further disarticulated animal bone, ceramics, several copper alloy fragments, an iron nail, and a cut piece of antler. Another pit at this site contained a dog skeleton and other disarticulated animal bone, ceramics, possible furnace debris, two or three crucible sherds and tuyère fragments, a bone gouge, and another bone object. A third pit contained the articulated remains of a dog laid on a bed of burnt stone, an articulated horse leg, over 2 kg of pottery, a piece of copper alloy slag, and a quantity of iron slag; the burnt stone may be the product of metalworking or of other activities such as cooking.

It is difficult to be certain whether the inclusion of metalworking residues in these features was accidental or deliberate, but both the character and quantity of other finds is suggestive of processes of selection. What the remains do show is that non-ferrous metalworking remains were not spatially segregated from the residues of other everyday

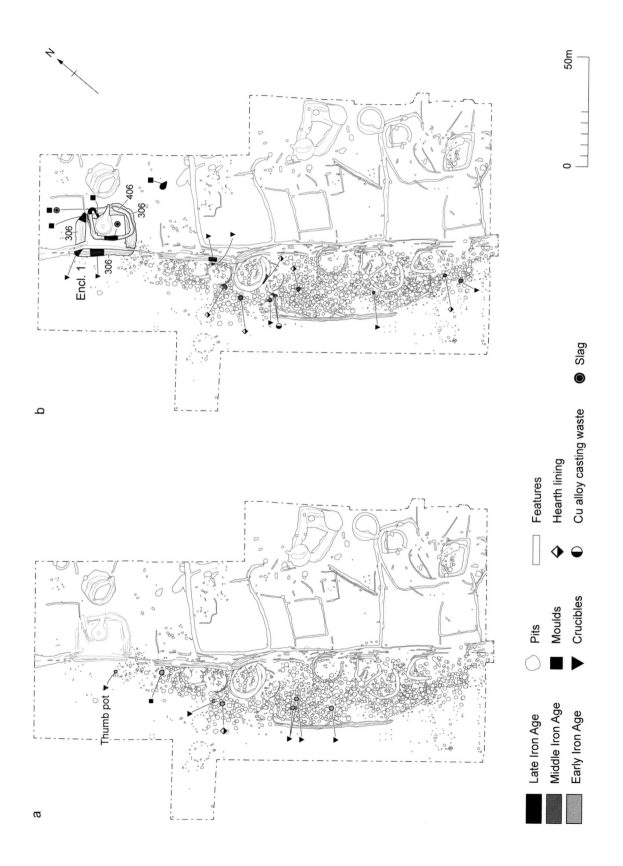

Figure 5.5: a. Early Iron Age features and b. Middle and Late Iron Age features at Gravelly Gay, Stanton Harcourt (Oxfordshire) (redrawn by Anne Leaver after Lambrick & Allen 2004, figs 1.4 & 4.2, with additions)

practices, even if metalworking was not carried out on a daily basis. There is little to suggest that the tools or residues of the craft were treated differently to other things during this period, and a wide variety of different types of objects and materials were incorporated into deliberate deposits in Early Iron Age pits. There are no recurrent associations between metalworking debris and other classes of artefact in these contexts, and the general impression is of considerable inter- and intra-site variability in depositional practice.

Overall, the finds from Early Iron Age sites suggest that non-ferrous metalworking was generally a small-scale and rare event during this period, with little to suggest intensive or specialist production. The paucity of metalworking evidence reflects the low numbers and relatively narrow range of finds from Early Iron Age settlements in general, as well as the low-density character of Early Iron Age occupation in many regions. In cases where several pieces of metalworking debris have been recovered, these residues do not cluster in particular areas of these sites, and this mirrors the scarcity of evidence for clear spatial structuring on settlements of this period in many regions. It also echoes patterns in the contemporary metalwork. It was rare for either ferrous or non-ferrous metalwork to reach the archaeological record during this period: hoards are virtually unknown and iron objects and ironworking sites were still relatively uncommon. It is possible that there was a decrease in the production of metal objects. Alternatively, changing depositional practices may reflect new social and political conditions that impacted the way in which metal objects were employed to negotiate social relationships: Sharples (2010) has argued that the homogeneity and lack of decoration that characterise many Early Iron Age artefacts in southern England reflect a heterarchical society. In general, sites with more abundant evidence such as **Gravelly Guy** (Oxfordshire) and **Cadbury Castle** (Somerset) have also produced metalworking tools and residues of later Iron Age date, suggesting that the character of the Early Iron Age activity impacted the subsequent history of these sites.

Later Iron Age (c. 400 BC–AD 50)

In southern Britain, there is a significant increase in the range and quantity of non-ferrous metalwork of Middle Iron Age and especially Late Iron Age date. Some of these items – notably those associated with the creation of high-status martial identities – were highly decorated in styles shared with Continental metalworking (Hunter 2008; Garrow & Gosden 2012; Farley & Hunter 2015). Fine metalwork was mostly deposited in hoards or as single finds in rivers, lakes, and bogs, although it is also found in burials and at Late Iron Age 'shrines' and other focal sites. There is a considerable increase in the number of settlements that can be dated to the later Iron Age. Both open and enclosed settlements are common. In some regions, extensive settlement complexes have been identified including both open and enclosed elements, with significant numbers of round-houses suggestive of emerging population clusters. Many later Iron Age settlements appear more ordered than those of Early Iron Age date, with evidence for zoning of different activities (Bradley *et al.* 2015, 284–5). Hillforts continued to be constructed and used into the Middle Iron Age. In Wessex, fewer hillforts were in use than during the Early Iron Age, suggesting that each was associated with a larger territory, and those that remained were more heavily fortified (so-called 'developed' hillforts). Both in Wessex and in some other areas, hillforts had largely been abandoned by the Late Iron Age (Cunliffe 2005; Harding 2012). Debate continues regarding whether hillforts were the apex of a settlement hierarchy or focal places for dispersed and heterarchically organised communities (Hill 1995b; Cunliffe 2005; Sharples 2010). In southern and eastern England, new types of focal site appear in the Late Iron Age, notably the so-called oppida. Characterised by finds of Continental imports, these sites have been interpreted as political centres with possible proto-urban features, although the dispersed and polyfocal character of settlement and other activities within these extensive complexes is very different to the Roman towns that in some cases succeeded them (Pitts 2010; Moore 2012). These distinctive Late Iron Age sites will be treated separately below.

Inter-site comparisons and the role of hillforts
The later Iron Age evidence dominates the later prehistoric record of non-ferrous metalworking, both in terms of the number of sites and the quantity of remains from some of

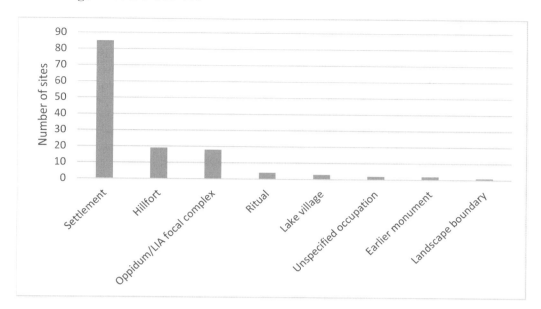

Figure 5.6: Excavated later Iron Age sites with non-ferrous metalworking evidence from southern Britain, categorised by site type (note that settlements & hillforts that have yielded only smithing tools have been excluded from the count)

these locations: 134 sites in southern Britain have produced evidence for the craft, excluding those with smithing tools only. In contrast to the artefacts themselves, evidence for the production of non-ferrous metalwork occurs mostly on settlements (Fig. 5.6). These vary in form from single enclosures and small open farmsteads to large complexes of houses, pits and other structures with no distinct boundary features. Non-ferrous metalworking evidence has also been recovered from 19 hillforts and 18 sites associated with oppida or other Late Iron Age focal complexes, as well as smaller numbers of other types of site including three possible 'shrines' and two other ritual sites, three 'lake villages', two earlier monuments, and a linear landscape boundary. Smithing tools have been found as components of larger assemblages of metalwork deposited in three wetland locations but only in one case was there a conclusive link with non-ferrous metalworking. The majority of later Iron Age sites have produced fewer than ten finds that relate to non-ferrous metalworking, with just a handful yielding larger assemblages in the hundreds (counts included mould and crucible fragments, casting waste, and tools). Two sites have yielded exceptionally large quantities of metalworking residues comprising several thousand fragments of moulds and crucibles alongside other finds. This suggests that casting activity was widespread but, in most cases, was only small-scale or intermittent or that its residues were not subject to activities

that resulted in their incorporation into archaeological deposits. The larger assemblages may indicate intensive or prolonged production. Most come from enclosed lowland settlements (Northover 1984); these will be considered in detail below.

A key question in discussion of the southern British Iron Age has been the role of hillforts, and how the activities at these sites may have differed from those at 'ordinary' settlements. Much of the debate has been dominated by the 'developed' hillforts of Middle Iron Age Wessex. For Cunliffe (2005), these sites were centres of power, dominating their surrounding territories, and had a significant role in the production and redistribution of goods. Hill (1995a) argues against this hierarchical model, and instead, emphasises the role of hillforts as centres for communal rituals and festivals. More recently, Sharples (2010) has suggested that the construction of hillforts in Wessex can be seen as an expression of community identity. The issue is complicated by the fact that sites labelled as hillforts are diverse in character, with significant variation in the areas enclosed and in the monumentality and defensive capabilities of the ramparts. While some hillforts contained substantial permanent settlements, as at **Maiden Castle** (Dorset), others may have been venues for seasonal or temporary gatherings.

Both settlements and hillforts have produced a similar range of casting evidence, almost always for equine equipment where the

*Figure 5.7: The
distribution of later Iron
Age smithing tools and
non-ferrous metalworking
evidence by site type*

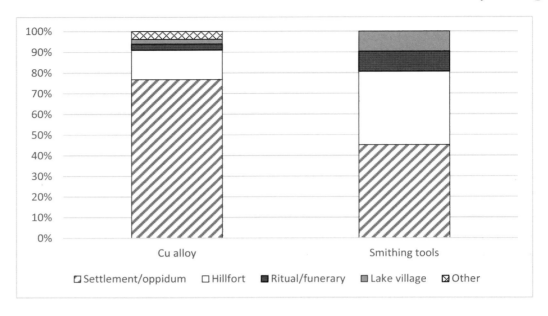

mould matrices can be identified. In contrast, smithing tools are more common at hillforts and other 'non-settlement' sites (including ritual sites) although, as we shall see, deposits of such artefacts may not indicate the actual location of the craft. The only evidence for the working of precious metals outside of Late Iron Age south-east England is a Middle Iron Age crucible fragment with gold residues from a hillfort: **Pilsdon Pen** (Dorset). In general, however, there is little to suggest that hillforts were particular foci for non-ferrous metalworking. At **Danebury** (Hampshire), for example, relatively little non-ferrous metalworking evidence has been recovered from the hillfort despite extensive and long-running excavations and a lengthy history of occupation. Finds include a complete crucible, 15 crucible sherds, and a collection of bronze filings or turnings: traces of a leather pouch were identified in the mineralised surface of the filings, suggesting that they were the accumulated debris from working small bronze items. A tuyère fragment, fragments of seven possible bellow's guards, and iron tools including two anvils, a hammer, two files, three chisels, and a possible punch may relate to bronzeworking or ironworking. Low density slags containing iron and copper are likely to be furnace linings. Fragments of sheet bronze were also recovered although, as we shall discuss below, it is not clear if these indicate the production of artefacts.

Other hillforts have yielded even less

evidence. **Ham Hill** (Somerset) has seen extensive recent excavations as well as sporadic earlier investigation but the only finds from later Iron Age contexts are a possible clay mould fragment and a fragment of bronze slag. A crucible sherd and some further pieces of slag from the site were unstratified, as were several iron tools (including two hammers, a punch, a file, and a chisel) that may have been employed in metalworking or other craft activities. The indications here are that the site was only occasionally the location of copper alloy casting in the later Iron Age. Most other hillforts have seen only small-scale excavation and evidence for metalworking is often minimal. The only find from **Old Oswestry** (Shropshire) was a single complete crucible, while excavations at **Winklebury** (Hampshire) yielded just a few crucible sherds and a single bronze ingot fragment.

Nonetheless, it has been suggested that certain specialist metalworking activities may have been concentrated at hillforts. Northover (1984; 1988b) has argued that hillforts were centres for sheet metalworking, indicated by finds of sheet 'scrap', rivets, and iron smithing tools from sites such as **Maiden Castle** (Dorset) and **Cadbury Castle** (Somerset). This is questioned by Sharples (2010, 145–6) who argues that the presence of sheet metal fragments may relate to the use of metal vessels such as cauldrons in communal feasting activities at these sites. Finds of scrap metal may indicate recycling of vessels rather than the production of such artefacts, for fragments of bronze sheet are found only in small numbers. Alternatively, sheet metal fragments may indicate the deliberate decommissioning and deposition of special objects after feasting episodes (cf. Baldwin & Joy 2017). At Maiden Castle the association of sheet metal fragments with evidence for casting suggests that metalworkers may have been involved in this process.

Iron smithing tools such as anvils, hammers, chisels, punches, files, tongs, and pokers have been found at 31 later Iron Age sites, of which 18 also have diagnostic evidence for non-ferrous metalworking while 13 do not. A number of sites with smithing tools have also produced ironworking debris. Smithing tools have a different distribution pattern to other non-ferrous metalworking evidence. While settlements and oppida account for 77% of sites with non-ferrous metalworking, for sites with smithing tools the figure is just 45% (Fig. 5.7). Hillfort contexts are proportionately much more common for smithing tools than for non-ferrous metalworking, and smithing tools also occur at a notable number of ritual sites, including burials, watery contexts and the possible shrine at **Woodeaton** (Oxfordshire) (these sites will be discussed separately below). However, the presence of smithing tools at hillforts and ritual sites need not indicate metalworking activities. It is clear that many of the finds from these sites are deliberate deposits. At several hillforts they form an element of larger ironwork hoards containing objects such as currency bars, non-metalworking tools and horse gear. As we shall discuss further below, whether in hoards or as single finds, smithing tools were often deposited in or around the ramparts or entrances to these sites, a pattern common to deposits of iron objects in general across much of western and central Europe (Hingley 1990; 1997; Haselgrove & Hingley 2006; Buchsenschutz & Ralston 2007; von Nicolai 2009). It is rare for smithing tools to be found in close spatial association with other metalworking remains. Exceptions include **Uphall Camp**, Ilford (Greater London), where an iron file was found in the ditch of a penannular enclosure 10 m from a round-house that produced crucible fragments (Fig. 5.8). There are no smithing tools from definite pre-Roman Iron Age contexts in Scotland or Ireland, suggesting deliberate selection of such artefacts for deposition in southern Britain. As such, the presence of smithing tools need not indicate the actual location of non-ferrous metalworking.

Metalworking on settlements: major assemblages
The largest assemblages of casting evidence derive from enclosed lowland settlements such as **Gussage All Saints** (Dorset), **Weelsby Avenue**, Grimsby (North East Lincolnshire) and **Coton Park**, Rugby (Warwickshire). Within the Middle Iron Age settlement enclosure at **Gussage All Saints** (Dorset; Fig. 5.9), a disused storage pit (pit 209) yielded over 600 crucible fragments (several of which could be refitted to make complete crucibles); more than 7000 mould fragments (probably comprising parts of several hundred moulds); tuyères; casting waste; fuel and other hearth debris; a bronze billet; pieces of 'scrap' metal including a worn fragment of a bronze-plated iron bridle bit; tools including iron files, a hot chisel, and two possible cold sets; and bone tools that may have been used for shaping the wax models around which the clay was moulded. Substantial quantities of ironworking slag were also recovered from this feature. These finds were deposited in the lower fills of the pit; the upper fills contained material of a more 'domestic' character, although they also yielded a human skull fragment. Radiocarbon dates indicate that the lower fills were deposited some time between the mid-4th and 2nd centuries cal BC (Garrow *et al.* 2010).

The metalworking residues from this pit provide evidence for the production of multiple sets of horse-gear and vehicle fittings: mould matrices are for terrets, bridle bits, linchpin terminals, strap unions, button-and-loop fasteners, and for casting the bronze feet of linchpins onto the iron shank. The assemblage contains residues from every stage in the metalworking process (Wainwright 1979; Spratling 1979; Spratling *et al.* 1980; Foster 1980). The organisation of production has been a particular focus of discussion. Some have viewed it as the assembled remains of several phases of activity spread over many years (Spratling 1979, 145; Howard 1983, 407–13; Gibson 1996); metalworking residues may have gradually accumulated in the pit itself or they may have been gathered for deposition after a period of time. Others suggest that the deposit is the result of a single intensive

Figure 5.8: Middle Iron Age hillfort at Uphall Camp, Ilford (Essex) (redrawn by Anne Leaver after Telfer 2004, figs 1 & 5)

★   Iron tools
●   Iron slag
■   Mould fragments
+   Cu alloy fragments
▼   Crucible
.·˙ Postholes
◗   Smithing hearth debris
▢   Feature
▨   Feature, presumed

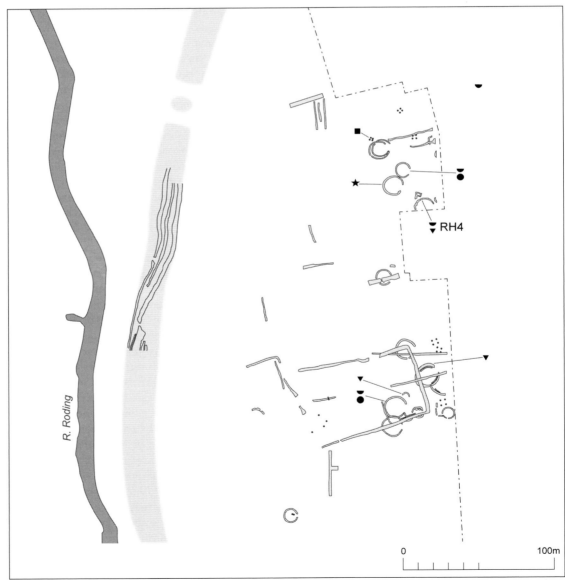

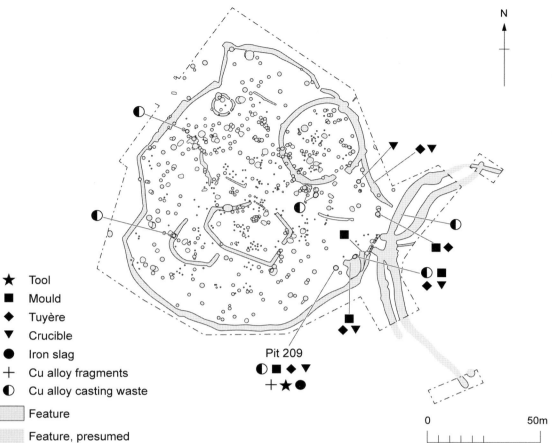

N

Figure 5.9: Later Iron Age settlement at Gussage All Saints (Dorset). Above: site plan; below: section of pit 209 (redrawn by Anne Leaver after Wainwright 1979, fig. 96 & Garrow & Gosden 2012, fig. 8.5. Note features from all three phases are shown)

★ Tool
■ Mould
◆ Tuyère
▼ Crucible
● Iron slag
+ Cu alloy fragments
◐ Cu alloy casting waste
▨ Feature
▨ Feature, presumed

Pit 209

0   50m

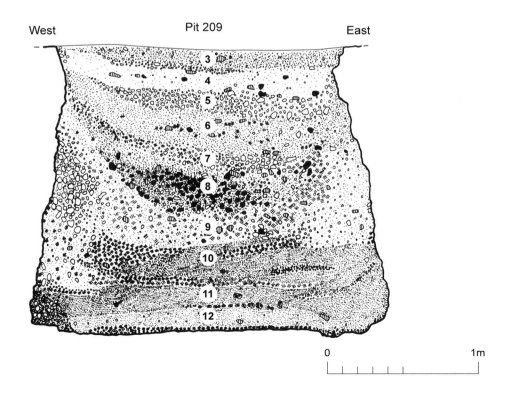

West   Pit 209   East

0   1m

episode of metalworking (Wainwright & Spratling 1973, 124–6; Foster 1980; Sharples 2010, 142; Garrow & Gosden 2012, 273–6): the mould and crucible fragments show little sign of abrasion, with precise refits possible across different layers in the pit (Foster 1980, 37). The latter scenario is favoured here, as we made similar observations on re-examining the material first-hand.

It has been argued that the order in which the mould fragments entered the pit at **Gussage All Saints** reflects the order in which the different objects were cast, with multiples of individual object types being manufactured at the same time (Foster 1980, 33). This implies that the production process was well-organised and involved an accepted sequence of activities. This included making wax models of the objects to be cast; forming clay moulds around these models; alloying the metal; casting the objects; extracting them from the moulds; and finally finishing them by smithing and polishing. It is possible that one person undertook all these steps, or that different individuals were responsible for successive stages of the production. Despite the abundant evidence for production, the finished cast products are absent from the site. This implies that the products were used, displayed, and deposited elsewhere. Likewise, the scale of production hints that these items were not being made solely for the occupants of this site: Spratling (1979, 144) suggested that the assemblage represents the production of at least 50 artefact sets.

Although the assemblage from pit 209 has understandably dominated discussions of metalworking at the site, it should be noted that metalworking remains, albeit in much lower quantities, were found in a number of other features (Fig. 5.9), although they are rarely mentioned in the literature. These include refractory ceramics, metallic debris such as slags and casting waste, iron tools that could have been used for smithing (Fell 1988), and two balances perhaps for weighing out metal. Some of these features were in the vicinity of pit 209 but others were elsewhere on-site. The small number of finds from the latter is more typical of the low-level evidence that dominates the record for this period. These finds indicate that metalworking was carried out in all three phases of occupation and suggest that pit 209 represents just one specific

but socially important event where multiple sets of horse-gear and vehicle fittings were produced, and the debris of production was selected for deposition; the material from this context is therefore perhaps best considered in the wider context of special deposits in storage pits in the Iron Age (Cunliffe 1992; Hill 1995a).

The character, scale, duration, and organisation of metalworking suggested for **Gussage All Saints** (Dorset) can be usefully compared with the evidence from other enclosed settlements that have produced large assemblages of non-ferrous metalworking debris. The material from a small enclosed settlement at **Weelsby Avenue**, Grimsby (North East Lincolnshire) comprised approximately 5000 crucible fragments, over 3000 fragments of clay investment moulds, a tuyère fragment, a large quantity of ferrous slag, casting waste, eight possible bone modelling tools, and iron tools including five files, a chisel, and a punch. There was also a large amount of material described as furnace debris although this has not been subject to detailed investigation, as well as charcoal and fuel ash slag which may derive from metalworking activities. The matrices of about 2500 of the 3000 mould fragments could be identified. Of these, around 80% were for casting terret rings while the remainder were for the production of strap unions, horn caps, linchpins, and bridle bits – all items for horses or the components of horse-drawn vehicles. There was also a single billet mould suggesting that preparation of alloys may have taken place at this location.

The finds from Weelsby Avenue derive from four deposits of metalworking debris recovered from the enclosure ditch (Fig. 5.10). Stratigraphic evidence suggests these deposits are roughly contemporary and date to the final phase of occupation in the 1st century BC. Two round-houses were identified inside the enclosure and finds of a domestic character, including animal bones and pottery, were recovered. It is not clear whether these are contemporary with the metalworking evidence, and the stratigraphic position of the latter has led some to argue that the enclosure may have been occupied solely for metalworking after the round-houses fell out of use (Ellis *et al.* 2001). There is a clear distinction between the character of the deposits on the eastern and western sides of the site and it is possible that they relate to two different types or episodes

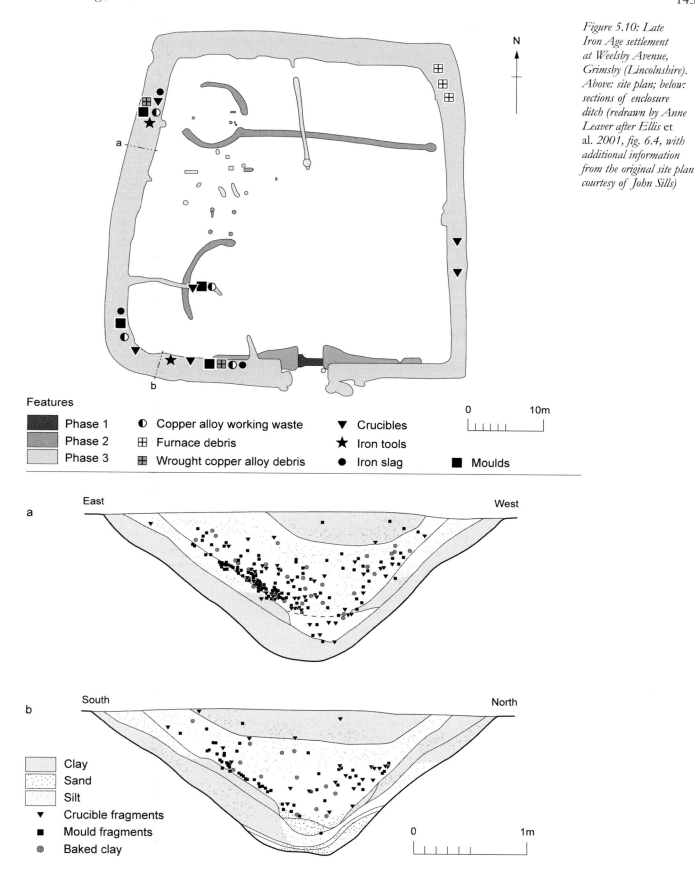

Figure 5.10: Late Iron Age settlement at Weelsby Avenue, Grimsby (Lincolnshire). Above: site plan; below: sections of enclosure ditch (redrawn by Anne Leaver after Ellis et al. 2001, fig. 6.4, with additional information from the original site plan courtesy of John Sills)

Features

Phase 1	
Phase 2	
Phase 3	

◑ Copper alloy working waste
⊞ Furnace debris
⊞ Wrought copper alloy debris

▼ Crucibles
★ Iron tools
● Iron slag
■ Moulds

0   10m

a   East   West

b   South   North

Clay
Sand
Silt
▼ Crucible fragments
■ Mould fragments
● Baked clay

0   1m

of metalworking activity. Those on the east form two distinct deposits: the deposit at the southern end of the ditch consists solely of crucible fragments, while that to the north consists entirely of hearth debris. The crucible fragments include vessels of various types and sizes, suggesting the production of a range of different artefact types. It is not yet known if there are traces of metal on the hearth debris, however, as the assemblage has yet to be fully investigated. The two deposits on the west comprise a wider range of finds: they include clay mould and crucible fragments, iron slag, iron tools, copper alloy debris, and other possible metalworking related items such as bone tools and lead weights. These deposits in particular are similar to those described above from pit 209 at Gussage All Saints (Dorset): the form and capacity of the crucibles from the deposits in the western ditch at Weelsby Avenue are very similar to those from Gussage All Saints, for example, although there is a higher percentage of terret moulds in the former assemblage. As at Gussage All Saints, this material may indicate one or two intensive episodes of metalworking in which large numbers of artefacts were produced.

Other settlements have produced smaller but still significant metalworking assemblages. At **Coton Park**, Rugby (Warwickshire), 153 fragments of crucibles, 460 mould fragments, and six pieces of copper alloy casting waste were found in and around a penannular gully and neighbouring rectilinear enclosure that formed part of a larger Middle Iron Age settlement (Fig. 5.11). Most of the mould matrices cannot be identified but there are two matrices for bridle bits as well as an incomplete open mould for bars. Parts of at least 14 crucibles are present. These include both smaller, thin-walled and larger, thick-walled examples which may have been employed for the production of different types of object or for different stages in the production process. Scientific analysis indicates the vessels were used for alloying copper and tin, and for melting copper alloy prior to casting. Antler and bone-working debris was also recovered in the area. At **Castleview Road** (Slough) (Figs 5.12–5.14), a Late Iron Age penannular enclosure and two neighbouring hollows flanking a trackway produced 125 crucible fragments, three possible mould fragments (including one for a terret ring) and several

pieces of copper alloy working waste as well as ironworking slag, hammerscale, and smithing hearth bottoms. Much of this material was from the upper fills of the enclosure ditch, suggesting that metalworking may have taken place over a relatively short timescale. The enclosure was located *c.* 160 m away from the core of the Middle–Late Iron Age settlement. A Late Iron Age enclosure at **Kelk** (East Riding of Yorkshire) has produced an assemblage of 11 crucible sherds and 34 mould fragments, probably for casting bridle bits. While this is a relatively modest quantity of material, it derived from several different contexts from a very limited test excavation (*c.* 1% of the site), suggesting that this may be another example of a later Iron Age enclosure with substantial deposits of casting debris from horse gear production. Although the site has yet to be fully published and detailed contextual information is lacking, interim reports from **Beckford** (Worcestershire) suggest the presence of a substantial non-ferrous metalworking assemblage including fragments of crucibles, clay moulds and tuyères as well as casting debris, scrap metal, and an iron poker. In contrast to some of the other sites described here, these finds appear to derive from both Middle Iron Age and Late Iron Age contexts, suggesting multiple casting events over a relatively long timeframe.

The Somerset 'lake villages', **Glastonbury** and **Meare East** and **West**, are another distinct category of settlement that has produced non-ferrous metalworking evidence in some quantity although, at these sites, the evidence was not associated with enclosures. It has been suggested that Meare may have been a seasonally occupied 'fair' or production site, while Glastonbury may have been more permanently occupied (Coles & Minnit 1995). Although detailed contextual information is lacking, the 'lake village' at Glastonbury yielded 16 fragments of small triangular crucibles, several 'thumbpots' that may have been crucibles, and one fragment of a much larger vessel. Other finds include a possible casting gate, four pieces of casting waste (three of copper or copper alloy and one of tin), a tin and lead lump, a piece of galena, and a possible piece of lead 'ore' or product of metal refining; the working of Mendip lead is a distinctive feature of these sites. Six or seven iron files, an iron hammer head, two

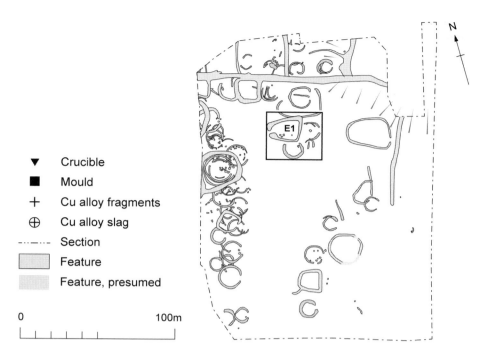

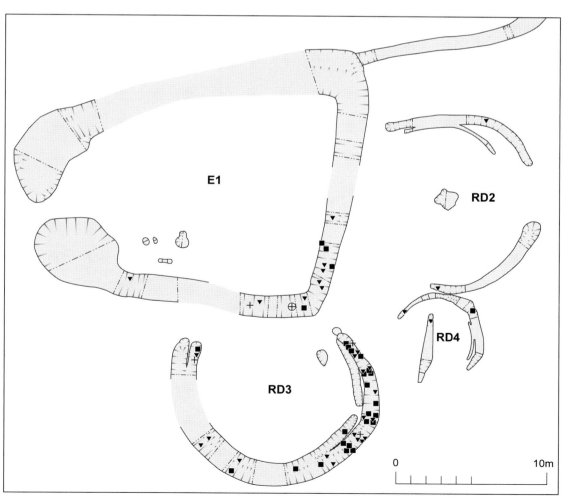

▼ Crucible

■ Mould

+ Cu alloy fragments

⊕ Cu alloy slag

—·—·— Section

  Feature

  Feature, presumed

0   100m

Figure 5.12: Late Iron Age settlement at Castleview Road, Slough (Berkshire) showing the penannular enclosure and neighbouring hollows (© Wessex Archaeology)

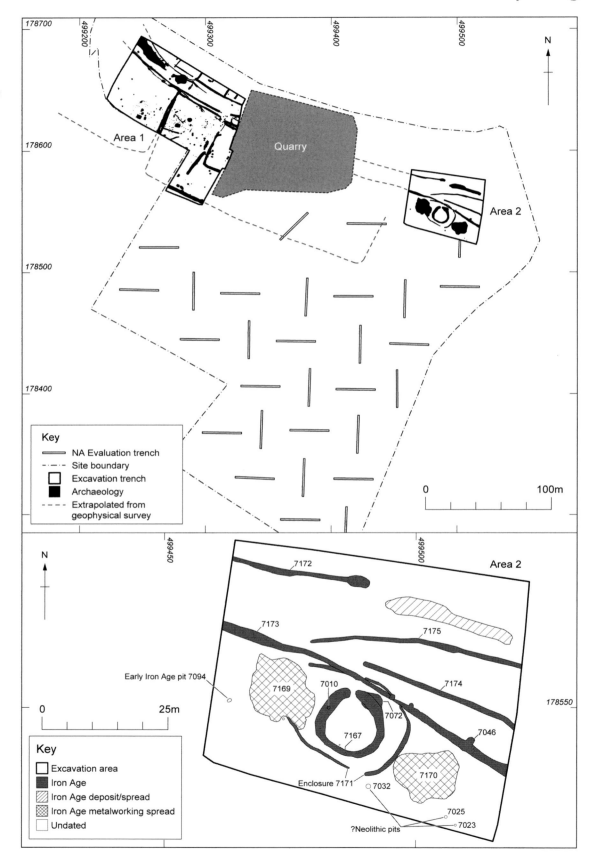

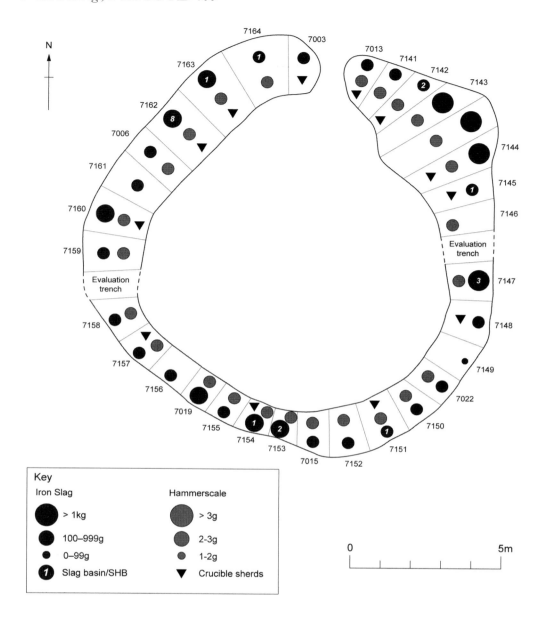

Figure 5.13:
Distribution of ferrous
and non-ferrous
metalworking debris in
the penannular enclosure
ditch at Castleview Road,
Slough (Berkshire) (©
Wessex Archaeology)

hot chisels, and three possible wax modelling tools of bone or antler were also found. Other crafts are also in evidence, including iron smithing, bone- and antlerworking, and small-scale shaleworking. Despite the number of finds, however, the evidence suggests that non-ferrous metalworking at this site was relatively small-scale, with sporadic activity over a relatively long period of time. The finds were widely distributed across the settlement, with just four concentrations of material: three of these represent short-lived episodes of activity, with evidence present at only one point in the stratigraphic sequence. A similar range

of metalworking activity was present at Meare, including galena, bronze and lead casting waste, crucibles, stone moulds, and iron smithing tools, along with evidence for glassworking. Contextual evidence is again limited but there are no signs that the material was concentrated in particular areas.

The casting of equine equipment and the significance of the horse

As noted above, the particularly large assemblages from **Gussage All Saints** (Dorset) and **Weelsby Avenue**, Grimsby (North East Lincolnshire) are dominated by moulds for

Figure 5.14:
Distribution
of ferrous and
non-ferrous
metalworking debris
in the hollows on
either side of the
penannular enclosure
at Castleview Road,
Slough (Berkshire)
(© Wessex
Archaeology)

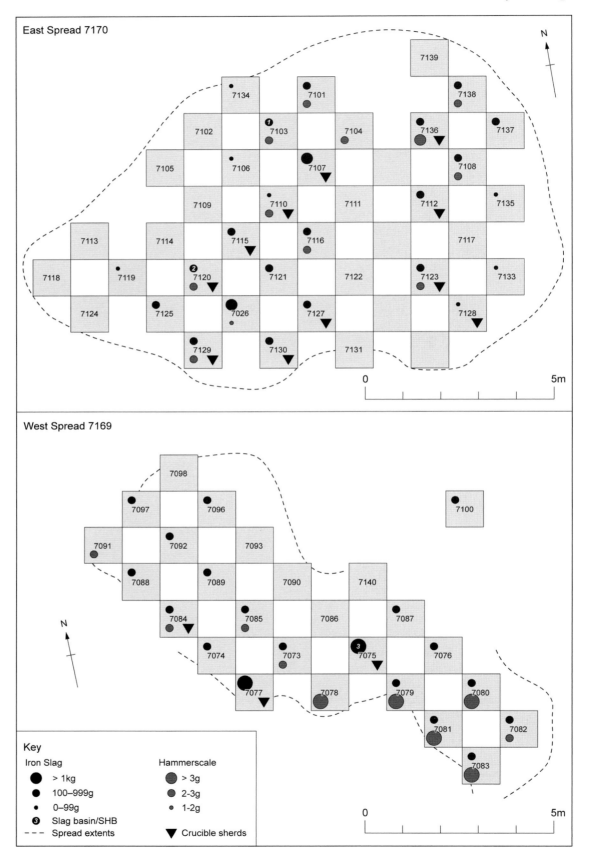

the production of artefacts such as terrets, linchpins, and bridle bits. It is remarkable that almost all lost-wax moulds excavated from Iron Age southern Britain are specifically for horse gear and vehicle fittings. Equine equipment forms a prominent element of the Iron Age metalwork repertoire from southern Britain, but not to the extent that it dominates mould assemblages. A few one-piece billet or ingot moulds are known, for example from **Coton Park**, Rugby (Warwickshire), but rarely have other moulds been identified. There is also a possible fibula mould from **Ketton** (Rutland), for example, while at **Silchester** (Hampshire) moulds for equine equipment have been found in combination with fragments of others for penannular brooches and spiral bracelets/ rings. No moulds have been recognised for categories of artefact such as fittings for weaponry, vessels or mirrors, even though these seem to have typically been produced in the same manner using the lost-wax technique.

The apparent over-representation of moulds for equine equipment could be explained in different ways. It may suggest that the organisation of production for equine equipment was different to other artefacts. Mass production of multiple sets of horse gear and vehicle fittings in a single episode of metalworking may have resulted in large deposits of waste, for example. This is perhaps supported by the fact that objects such as terrets were themselves sometimes deposited in large sets. Mass production of such artefacts could be interpreted as indicating the existence of specialist workshops, although there is little to suggest that casting equine equipment was carried out on a full-time basis; as we have seen above even the largest assemblages are suggestive of intensive but short-lived episodes of production. It should be noted, however, that moulds for equine equipment are also found on sites that have yielded only small non-ferrous metalworking assemblages. At **Billingborough** (Lincolnshire), for example, two conjoining fragments of a mould for a horse bit were the only finds, although an iron poker from the site may also have been used for bronzeworking. This indicates that not every casting event entailed production of equine equipment on a large scale.

Alternatively, moulds for equine equipment may have been deliberately selected for deposition. The large deposits at Weelsby Avenue and Gussage All Saints suggest that the production of equine equipment may sometimes have been a socially significant practice, the residues of which needed to be treated with care. This included deposition even of items that could be used again, such as iron tools and complete crucibles, suggesting that the residues of this craft may have been viewed as particularly special or dangerous. It is possible that the production of horse gear and vehicle fittings may have been a special event. When the objects had been made, the residues of production were formally deposited, perhaps to mark the occasion, to safeguard those involved in casting or to ensure that the items produced remained unique. This practice must be viewed in relation to the wider traditions of structured deposition that formed such an important component of Iron Age social and religious life (Cunliffe 1992; Hill 1995a; Chadwick 2012).

The careful disposal of tools and residues relating to the casting of equine equipment may be a reflection of the cultural significance ascribed to horses and vehicles at this time. Metal horse gear and vehicle fittings were often elaborately decorated, and are often found as components of hoards and as single finds of metalwork in the landscape (Palk 1991; Garrow & Gosden 2012; Lewis 2015). Horse gear was sometimes deposited at hillforts, for example the bronze terret and strap union from **Bury Hill** (Hampshire), although there is little to suggest that it was produced at these sites. A linchpin formed part of the large assemblage of metalwork deposited in the River Witham at **Fiskerton** (Lincolnshire), while complete or dismantled chariots were also placed in graves in Yorkshire and at Newbridge (Lothian) (Carter *et al.* 2010; Giles 2012). In some cases, horse gear seems to have been symbolic rather than functional. For example, the Stanwick hoard (North Yorkshire) contains examples that were miscast and unusable, yet effort was still taken to inlay them with enamel, and it has also been suggested that some bridle bits were designed to be displayed flat, perhaps by being mounted on a wall (Palk 1991). The decoration, display, and deposition of equine equipment suggests that horses, equine travel, and associated activities such as exchange and warfare were of particular ideological significance during this period (Creighton 2000; Lewis 2015). Horses were widely used for riding or pulling vehicles in the southern British Iron Age; horse bone is much more abundant in Iron Age faunal assemblages compared to those of the Bronze Age, and most analysed Iron Age horses show bitting damage (Bendrey 2010). There are also artistic depictions of horses, most notably on coins (Creighton 2000). The careful deposition of objects employed in the production of horse gear must therefore be placed in this wider social and ideological context.

The context of metalworking within settlements and hillforts

Substantial settlement complexes became more common during the later Iron Age, and some of these have been extensively excavated, providing greater opportunities to explore the spatial distribution of metalworking remains. In some cases, the material is dispersed across the site, or at least across the excavated area. For example, at the Middle Iron Age site of **Thorpe Thewles** (Stockton-on-Tees), 11 crucible fragments and two bar ingot moulds were found widely distributed across the 0.58 ha excavated area; these derive from ring-gullies, a ditch, and various other contexts. At **Mucking** (Thurrock), a settlement complex that originated in the Early Iron Age but is mainly of later Iron Age date extended over an area of more than 600 m. The distribution of crucible and mould fragments extends across much of this area, though there is a concentration around a group of round-houses in the northern part of the settlement.

Elsewhere, metalworking activities appear to have been more clearly concentrated in particular areas or set apart from other activities. At **Latton Lands** (Wiltshire), a linear Middle Iron Age settlement with round-houses and small enclosures extended over a distance of 375 m. The metalworking evidence was restricted to an area *c.* 150 m across at the northern end of the settlement, deriving from features including irregular subcircular gullies, boundary ditches, and a waterhole. Crucible fragments with copper corrosion products from melting copper alloys were recovered from one of the gullies, while a pit adjacent to this feature yielded crucible fragments, fragments of copper oxide, and casting waste. The presence of boneworking debris and a piece of worked antler, thought to be an unfinished toggle, suggests craftwork

of various sorts was carried out on this part of the site. At a few later Iron Age sites, most or all of the metalworking residues were associated with a single, fairly small enclosure and associated features within a larger settlement complex, as for example at **Coton Park**, Rugby (Warwickshire), or **Castleview Road** (Slough), discussed above. It is not always clear that such enclosures were solely or even primarily for metalworking, however. At **Cresswell Field/Worton Rectory Farm**, Yarnton (Oxfordshire), two discrete areas were excavated within a Middle Iron Age settlement extending over a total area of *c.* 450 m. Though an ingot mould was found in a gully elsewhere on the site, crucible fragments were restricted to a single circular enclosure 20 m in diameter (Fig. 5.15). The enclosure surrounded a single round-house, and other finds from the site included crop processing debris, animal bone and ceramics, indicating that here metalworking occurred amongst regular settlement activity. At **Gravelly Guy** (Oxfordshire) (see Fig. 5.5), the metalworking activity appears to have become more spatially circumscribed over time: whereas metalworking debris of Early and Middle Iron Age date was recovered from pits dispersed across much of the site, in each period extending over an area of around 100 m, the majority of the evidence of Late Iron Age date derived from features in and around a multi-phase rectangular enclosure measuring 21 m across. At **Ferrybridge** (Wakefield) in West Yorkshire, a 7 ha excavation has uncovered an extensive Late Iron Age to Roman field system containing settlement enclosures. Small-scale metalworking evidence in the form of crucibles and casting waste was concentrated in one of the settlement enclosures, and was absent from a second adjacent enclosure and a third enclosure 120 m away.

Most hillforts have seen only small-scale excavation so it is difficult to assess evidence for the distribution of non-ferrous metalworking activities. At **Danebury** (Hampshire), non-ferrous metalworking residues were relatively dispersed, although some small groups of finds could be identified. One complete crucible and fragments of seven others were found in a quarry hollow just inside the inner rampart on the southern side of the hillfort. Two other crucible fragments were recovered from a nearby pit and post-hole, and a pouch containing bronze filings or turnings was

Figure 5.15: Middle
Iron Age settlement at
Yarnton (Oxfordshire):
a. Cresswell Field; b.
Worton Rectory Farm
(redrawn by Anne
Leaver after Hey et al.
2011, figs 6.35–36)

N

▼ Crucible

△ Ingot mould

▨ Feature, Middle Iron Age

0   100m

found in the same area. A further cluster of finds was recovered from an area of dense pits on the north-western side of the hillfort between road 4 and the rampart. This included a few crucible fragments, a tuyère fragment, and pieces of furnace lining. At **Cadbury Castle** (Somerset), evidence for the craft was recovered from a number of different locations inside the hillfort. Metalworking was carried out in and around an area of cobbling at the east end of the central plateau. Finds included copper casting waste, iron slag, and an iron

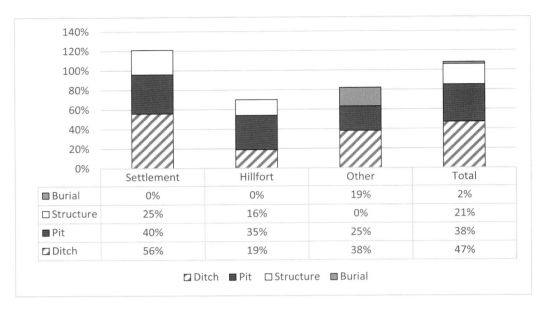

	Settlement	Hillfort	Other	Total
▣ Burial	0%	0%	19%	2%
☐ Structure	25%	16%	0%	21%
▪ Pit	40%	35%	25%	38%
◪ Ditch	56%	19%	38%	47%

◪ Ditch ▪ Pit ☐ Structure ▣ Burial

smelting furnace. Towards the western end of the plateau, a pit adjacent to a round-house contained crucible fragments and hearth lining with copperworking residues. At the north-eastern edge of the plateau, a group of three pits contained moulds for four terrets, a bridle bit, and a possible horn cap, plus other finds including a tuyère or bellows plate and a bone modelling tool. Another pit in the same area contained a crucible and copperworking hearth material. Around 45 m further to the north-east, and off the central plateau, pits within the floor of another round-house contained copper alloy casting waste. A small number of other metalworking related finds were recovered from elsewhere on the site.

Metalworking and boundaries
As we have seen, it has been argued that Iron Age metalworking was associated both spatially and conceptually with settlement boundaries and other liminal contexts (Hingley 1997; 1999; Giles & Parker Pearson 1999). Certainly, ditches are the most common feature type in which the by-products of metalworking are found (Fig. 5.16), with evidence recovered from such contexts at 47% of all southern sites. Examples include a single crucible sherd from a ditched droveway at **Wales Street**, Kings Sutton (Northamptonshire) and five crucible fragments from an enclosure ditch at the eastern edge of the settlement at **Tattenhoe Park** (Milton Keynes). Perhaps the largest later Iron Age assemblage of

non-ferrous metalworking debris from a boundary feature derives from the trapezoid ditch enclosing the site of **Weelsby Avenue**, Grimsby (North East Lincolnshire) discussed above (Fig. 5.10). Occasionally, the deposition of metalworking-related finds concentrated in or around the entrances to settlements. The large assemblage of casting debris from **Gussage All Saints** (Dorset), discussed above, was found in a pit just inside the entrance to this enclosed settlement (Fig. 5.9). Other metalworking evidence was recovered from the ditches on either side of the entrance and from other pits in this area, although further material was found in a number of features elsewhere on the site. It should be noted, however, that many of the ditches that have yielded metalworking evidence from later Iron Age sites lie *within* settlement complexes rather than marking the outer boundary of the settlement. It also needs to be acknowledged that on many sites of this period, ditches are the largest features and collect the greatest quantities of material culture of all kinds, not just metalworking debris. We must be careful, therefore, not to overstate the link between metalworking debris and boundaries.

A comparison between settlements and hillforts indicates that non-ferrous metalworking evidence has been recovered from ditches at 56% of the settlements in our study compared to only 19% of hillforts (Fig. 5.16); pits are the main context from which such material has been recovered at the latter sites.

This is surprising, given that excavations at hillforts have most often focused on their ditches and ramparts. However, metalworking appears to have been carried out immediately behind the ramparts at some hillforts. At **Walesland Rath** (Pembrokeshire), one of the few extensively excavated fortified settlements in Wales, fragments of at least six crucibles were recovered from deposits located against the inner edge of the bank and associated with neighbouring structures dating to the 3rd–2nd centuries BC. In addition, portions of four further crucibles were recovered from deposits dating to the 1st century BC in the terminal of the southern ditch. At **Llanymynech** (Powys), copper alloy droplets adhering to vitrified clay were recovered from charcoal layers, two hearths, and a pit just inside the eastern rampart. Similarly, at **Llwyn Bryn-dinas** (Powys), a terrace cut into the rear of the rampart has been interpreted as a metalworking floor used for both copper alloy and ironworking (see *Cross-craft interaction* below). However, at both **Llanymynech** and **Llwyn Bryn-dinas** a small area adjacent to the rampart was the only part of the hillfort that was excavated and we know nothing about the activities conducted within the interior of the site. Elsewhere, too, hillfort excavations have tended to focus on the defences rather than the interiors, so the association of metalworking related finds with locations in or around hillfort boundaries may be the result of excavation strategy and may not reflect either the spatial organisation of this craft or the structured deposition of its residues (Moore 2006).

Metalworking and buildings

Although metalworking residues have been found in settlement enclosure ditches and around hillfort defences, they are also often found at the heart of settlements where they are routinely associated with finds of more 'domestic' character such as pottery and animal bone. Around 21% of southern British later Iron Age sites recorded for this project yielded metalworking evidence from features or layers directly associated with round-houses and other buildings (Fig. 5.16). Often, these look little different from 'ordinary' domestic dwellings. Many round-houses of this period are represented only by the gully surrounding the building; there may be structural post-holes but rarely is there any trace of a floor

or internal fixtures. As such it is difficult to ascribe a function to individual buildings and it may be that 'round-houses' were used for a variety of differing purposes. It is also possible that the activities associated with particular buildings changed over time, for example on a seasonal basis.

In most cases (24 out of 38 sites with evidence from in or around buildings: 63%), these have produced just one or two metalworking related finds. At **Storey's Bar Road**, Fengate (Peterborough), for example a single vitrified crucible rim was found in the fill of a round-house gully. This indicates only that casting took place within the general vicinity of this building and it is not possible to identify it as a workshop. A crucible fragment with traces of gold was recovered from an occupation layer just outside a round-house in the hillfort at **Pilsdon Pen** (Dorset). Often, artefacts of a domestic character are recovered alongside metalworking evidence. At **Collfryn** (Powys), round-houses 7 and 9 each yielded a few crucible fragments, while part of a possible clay mould was recovered from the gully surrounding round-house 8. Other finds from these buildings include a spindle whorl, quern fragment, ceramic salt containers, and animal bone.

Some buildings have produced more evidence for metalworking. At **Wardy Hill**, Coveney (Cambridgeshire), 30 crucible fragments as well as pieces of hearth lining and fuel ash slag were found in the gullies of two neighbouring round-houses and adjacent ditches. Magnetic susceptibility survey of the topsoil in the area of the northern of the two buildings produced unusually high readings which may be the result of metalworking activity in or around this structure. In most cases, however, because metalworking waste is derived from negative features such as gullies and post-holes, it is not clear if the craft took place within these structures or if the metalworking debris was redeposited from elsewhere.

Maiden Castle (Dorset) has provided rare evidence for internal deposits indicative of *in situ* metalworking activities in buildings. Here, the non-ferrous metalworking remains were concentrated in 1st century BC features and deposits within two adjacent round-houses and a small rectangular structure within the south-western edge of the hillfort near the ramparts. Crucible fragments, copper alloy casting waste and sheet metal fragments, fragments of a possible tuyère and bellows guard, hammerscale, iron welding slag, and iron tools were recovered from these buildings, and one crucible was associated with a clay oven within the small rectangular structure. Magnetic susceptibility survey of the western round-house suggested that metalworking may have taken place in this building: relatively high readings were yielded by deposits within the southern part of the structure. However, neither the two pits within the eastern side of the round-house from which the main deposits of debris were recovered, nor the hearth at its centre, exhibited enhanced magnetic susceptibility. 'Copper alloy working waste', sheet metal fragments, and iron hammerscale were also recovered from one of the floor layers in the building.

The buildings discussed above are similar in architectural form to round-houses identified as domestic dwellings at the same sites. Others, however, look different. The majority of the metalworking related debris from **Coton Park**, Rugby (Warwickshire) (Fig. 5.11. above) was recovered from a penannular gully of *c.* 13 m diameter with an opening to the north. It is not clear if there was a building inside this and, if so, which way its doorway faced, but its northerly opening contrasts with the east-facing round-houses elsewhere on this site. At **Latton Lands** (Wiltshire), the metalworking evidence was recovered from a number of irregular subcircular gullies which may represent open-sided shelters.

The deliberate deposition of smithing tools
It is possible that some of the finds from settlement enclosure ditches and other boundary contexts were deliberate deposits, as suggested for the assemblage from pit 209 at **Gussage All Saints** (Dorset). We noted above that the deposition of smithing tools at hillforts can often also be interpreted in this way. Smithing tools were often deposited in or around the ramparts or entrances to these sites. At **Madmarston Camp** (Oxfordshire), for example, an assemblage of ironwork comprising a poker, 12 currency bars, a shaft-hole axe, a sickle, and two bridle bits was found beneath a cobbled floor behind the rampart on the northern side of the hillfort. Five iron hammer heads and a file were found at **Bredon Hill** (Worcestershire); their

context is unclear but they appear to derive either from the area behind the rampart or from the paving in the entranceway; the latter also yielded other metalwork including bronze shield fragments, seven iron spearheads, and several bronze ornaments. Probable deliberate deposits of iron tools also occur within hillfort interiors, as at **Bury Hill** (Hampshire) where two neighbouring storage pits each contained an iron file in their basal fill; one of these pits also produced a bronze terret and strap union from its upper fill. Deliberate deposition of smithing tools seems likely in some settlement contexts too. At **Garton Slack** (East Riding of Yorkshire) two iron pokers and a pair of tongs were placed on the base of a Middle Iron Age storage pit, while at **Billingborough** (Lincolnshire) a poker had been snapped in half and the two halves laid out parallel with each other in a ditch. There are resonances between the latter find and the Early Iron Age poker from a pit at **Fairfield Park** (Central Bedfordshire) which had been deliberately bent back on itself.

Smithing tools have been found at three watery sites but they form only a minority of larger assemblages at these locations (only one of these sites was subject to archaeological excavation, however). At **Fiskerton** (Lincolnshire), two hammer heads, four files, two possible punches, and a possible anvil were deposited beneath and around a timber causeway, dated to the 5th–4th century BC, in the River Witham. As noted in Chapter 2, residues of non-ferrous metals were identified in the teeth of two of the files, indicating a clear link with this craft (Fell 1997). A variety of other iron and copper alloy objects including swords, spearheads, axeheads, and a linchpin, as well as bone spear points, pottery, a jet ring, and amber beads were also found, indicating deposition from the Iron Age into the Roman period (Field & Parker Pearson 2003). At Llyn Cerrig Bach (Anglesey) two pairs of tongs were recovered, one decorated with a La Tène style design (Steele 2012), a very unusual feature for an item of metalworking equipment. This formed part of an assemblage of at least *c.* 170 iron and copper alloy objects, mostly weaponry and vehicle fittings, the only other tool being a sickle (Fox 1947). The assemblage was probably formed through repeated offerings in a lake. Most objects date from the 4th–3rd century BC to the mid-1st century AD, with some others probably from the late 1st century AD or later; radiocarbon dates on animal bone suggest that deposition began before *c.* 200 cal BC (Macdonald 2007a). At Waltham Abbey (Essex) it is argued that the artefacts were placed in shallow water at the edge of the River Lea (Manning 1980; 1985). There were 13 smithing tools (five tongs, three anvils, three pokers, a hammer-swage, and a file), along with six carpenter's tools, a billhook, a sword, vehicle fittings, a lead lump, and a whetstone. The pokers and tongs had been deliberately bent before deposition, echoing the deliberate destruction of iron tools at Billingborough and Fairfield Park above. The material has been interpreted as a single hoard of the Late Iron Age or conquest period, but successive deposition is also possible. The deposition of smithing tools in wetland contexts and at hillforts may have referenced concepts and ideologies linked to metalworking. Equally, though, the fact that these deposits often contained a mix of different object types may imply that the important common element was simply the fact that these objects were made of iron.

Four Late Iron Age burials contain smithing tools. In three cases these are probable male burials also containing weapons (see below). Finally, at **Woodeaton** (Oxfordshire), an iron file and possible punch were recovered from Middle Iron Age deposits. These overlay a Late Bronze Age/Early Iron Age midden; as we have seen in Chapter 4, such sites have often been interpreted as gathering places where a variety of social, economic, and ceremonial activities were carried out. Later, a Romano-British shrine was constructed at the site. An unusually large number of Middle Iron Age brooches have also been found, as well as many other pre-Roman bronze objects, suggesting that the site may have been a location of longstanding ceremonial or ritual significance.

The deliberate deposition of casting debris

Although there has been much research on structured deposition in Iron Age settlements and hillforts, including artefacts and residues relating to ironworking (eg, Hill 1995a; Hingley 1990; Haselgrove & Hingley 2006; Smith *et al.* 2018), very little attention has been paid to whether non-ferrous metalworking residues played a role in these practices. The deliberate deposition of crucible fragments as well as

iron slag has been noted in the Netherlands, however (Arnoldussen & Brusgaard 2015). In southern Britain too, casting residues also appear to have been incorporated into special deposits of one sort or another. At **Winnall Down** (Hampshire), a chalk bar mould was recovered from a storage pit adjacent to a round-house. This was in a deposit of daub in the lower fill of this feature. Finds from the upper fills included articulated pig and dog skeletons and part of a rotary quern. A pit on a settlement at **Gilcross** (East Riding of Yorkshire) yielded three crucible fragments and a single mould fragment. These were found in fills that overlay the skeleton of a possible adult female. Other finds from the same fills included bronze objects (sheet fragments, a brooch spring, and a bar-toggle), briquetage, and pottery. Elsewhere, distinctive spatial structuring hints at practices of deliberate selection: for example, the mould fragments from the Late Iron Age enclosure at **Gravelly Guy**, Stanton Harcourt (Oxfordshire) (Fig. 5.5, above) were deposited around its entrance, whereas crucibles were found at the rear of the enclosure.

Although such deposits have been widely interpreted as evidence of ritual practice, it should be noted that in many instances the metalworking residues were not treated differently to other finds, including objects relating to 'everyday' activities of various sorts. At **Blaise Castle** (Bristol), for example, a saddle quern was placed faced down at the bottom of a pit, over which was a deep layer of broken limestone. Above this was a deposit containing 3–4 droplets of bronze, 317 sherds of pottery, two copper alloy bow brooches (already of some antiquity when they were buried), three weaving combs, an antler handle, a bone point, an iron pin, a stone spindle whorl and disc, a rubbing stone, a hammerstone, two hones, flints, a clay sling bullet, and about 300 pieces of animal bone. In this case, although it can be suggested that items such as the brooches were deliberately selected for deposition, objects such as the potsherds, animal bone, and the bronze droplets may have formed part of undifferentiated accumulations of refuse or midden material scooped up for redeposition in this pit. Of course, this does not mean that this material – as the residues of socially significant domestic and craft activities – was not considered significant in and of itself. The incorporation of metalworking residues into such general 'refuse' matrices indicates they were not consciously kept separate from other domestic material. This counters the argument that metalworking was always framed as dangerous or liminal and was therefore set apart from other activities.

The difficulties involved in identifying evidence for deliberate inclusion of particular types of material is illustrated by the finds from Middle Iron Age pits at Gravelly Guy. Three of these pits produced metalworking residues together with human bone, an association which could be taken to indicate deliberate selection of meaningful materials. The uppermost fill of one feature, for example, produced a crucible sherd and the fragmentary remains of an infant, while the lower fill of another pit yielded casting waste and the crouched burial of another infant. It should be noted, however, that roughly a quarter of the pits at this site contained human remains (predominantly infants), so the association with metalworking debris may be incidental (cf. Brudenell & Cooper 2008). Overall, our analysis indicates that there are no recurring associations between metalworking evidence and other particular categories of find. Metalworking tools and residues are associated with a wide variety of artefacts and materials but that does not mean that there was no significance to these links.

Metalworking in off-site contexts
Although the majority of non-ferrous metalworking residues of later Iron Age date have been recovered from settlements and hillforts, metalworking material has occasionally been found at a distance from contemporary occupation. We have already described the tools deposited in the River Witham at **Fiskerton** (Lincolnshire). A single crucible fragment and pieces of a clay mould for casting brooches were recovered from a linear triple-ditched landscape boundary at **Ketton** (Rutland). Evidence for non-ferrous metalworking has also been documented at two earlier monuments in the Welsh Marches. At **Sarn-y-bryn-caled** (Powys), ten pieces of bronze casting waste were recovered from the uppermost fill of a pit at the centre of an Early Bronze Age timber circle. Two Early Bronze Age cremation burials were found in the lower fills of this feature, but charcoal

associated with the metalworking residues yielded a radiocarbon date of 370–50 cal BC (2160±60 BP; BM-2830) and scientific analysis of the casting waste itself indicated that its composition was consistent with other Welsh bronze objects of Iron Age date. No further Iron Age finds or features were identified at the site, suggesting that it was located away from other contemporary activity. At **Four Crosses** (Powys), two crucible fragments of characteristically Iron Age form were found in the upper silts of a Bronze Age ring-ditch. Nearby were two pits and a hearth; the latter yielded a radiocarbon date of 370–1 cal BC (2130±60 BP; CAR-766).

Late Iron Age developments in southern and eastern England
Much of southern and eastern England underwent a marked social transformation during the Late Iron Age, from *c.* 150 BC onwards. Cross-Channel interactions and exchanges became more prominent, novel artefact types such as coinage came into use, and social differentiation was more clearly expressed through practices such as burial rites. Another important development was the appearance of 'proto-urban' settlements and various other kinds of 'focal' places, which provided new contexts for the working of metals.

During the early 1st century BC, cross-Channel exchanges were focused on a few coastal 'port' sites, most notably **Hengistbury Head** (Dorset). This site lay on a headland cut off by ramparts of uncertain date and may have been situated at a cultural boundary zone (Sharples 1990). It was already occupied during the Middle Iron Age, when copper alloy working is indicated by a small amount of casting waste. The period from *c.* 120–50 BC saw an influx of imports, including Mediterranean amphorae and Gaulish ceramics and coins. During this phase there was also a range of craft activities, including copper alloy working (represented by a crucible fragment and casting waste), glassworking, shaleworking and salt making. During the period 50 BC–AD 50, the volume of imports decreased but craft activity continued. The evidence included nine further crucible fragments and waste suggesting the production of bronze. Evidence for the cupellation of silver probably derives from the Roman period, while a touchstone with gold streaks is undated.

While the role of Hengistbury Head may have been specifically focused on craft working and maritime exchanges, a wider range of activities is attested at the so-called oppida – a problematic term that has been applied to a range of Late Iron Age sites with diverse characteristics (Haselgrove 2000; Pitts 2010; Moore 2017). In essence, oppida are extensive sites that are often argued to have had 'proto-urban' characteristics, or to represent a form of 'low-density urbanism' (Moore 2017). A key characteristic used to define these sites is the presence of imported goods from Gaul and the Roman world, such as amphorae and fine tableware pottery, which were in some cases placed in richly furnished burials. The impression that oppida were centres of political power during the Late Iron Age is further supported by the fact that several of these places developed into cantonal capitals during the Roman period.

Oppida are distributed across much of southern and eastern England, with an outlier at **Stanwick** (North Yorkshire). Some began to be occupied in the early 1st century BC, though the heyday of most lay in the late 1st century BC to mid-1st century AD. Many of the larger oppida were polyfocal, with a series of discrete areas used for settlement, ritual, or burial dispersed over areas of many hectares. In some cases – the so-called 'territorial oppida' – these different areas of activity were situated within extensive complexes of linear earthwork dykes that were intended to channel movement and define areas of the landscape rather than forming a continuous defensible enclosure. Examples of territorial oppida include **Silchester** (Hampshire), **Verlamion**, St Albans (Hertfordshire), **Colchester** (Essex), and **Bagendon-Ditches** (Gloucestershire). Also often classed as oppida are a group of more nucleated sites that lack associated earthwork complexes. Examples of this category include **Braughing-Puckeridge** (Hertfordshire), **Heybridge** (Essex), and **Old Sleaford** (Lincolnshire).

The form of metalworking most clearly associated with oppida is coin minting. While detailed discussion of 'Celtic' coin production is beyond the scope of this book (see, for instance, Creighton 2000; Landon 2016; Talbot 2017), its relationship to other kinds of non-ferrous metalworking must be considered. Fragments of pellet moulds used to produce coin blanks have been found in significant quantities at a number of oppida, including Silchester, Verlamion, Braughing-Puckeridge, Colchester, and Bagendon-Ditches (Appendix 5). Moreover, a few coin issues were inscribed with the names of oppida: VERLAMIO for Verlamion, CAMVL for Camulodunum (Colchester), or CALLE for Calleva (Silchester). Pellet moulds have, however, also been recovered away from oppida, including unstratified surface finds from locations in eastern England where there are no other indications of the presence of a major Late Iron Age site, as at Scotton and Torksey in Lincolnshire (Appendix 5). Oppida did not, therefore, have a monopoly on coin production. It should also be noted that many pellet mould assemblages are from contexts of early Roman date. This includes most of the material from the **Sheepen** site at Colchester (Essex), which is often held up as a key example of a Late Iron Age industrial site and mint. A recently discovered assemblage from **Scotch Corner** (North Yorkshire) is not only clearly post-conquest in date but also lies outside the main zone of Iron Age coin circulation. While some of these late pellet mould finds are no doubt residual, it seems likely that the use of such moulds continued after the conquest, in the production of either 'Celtic' coins or copies of Roman coins (Landon 2016).

While pellet production was carried out at many oppida we have no direct evidence for whether the other stages of coin production – hammering of the pellets to produce usable blanks and the striking of the blanks to make coins – also took place at these locations. Coin dies have not been found at any oppida, and in fact the only die finds from Britain are for early coin types that pre-date the heyday of the oppida (Sillon 2015; Table 5.1). All the dies have been recovered by metal detecting away from any known Late Iron Age sites, which could imply that striking coins was a specialised or ritualised activity that was kept separate from settlement areas. Alternatively, the deposition of these objects could have formed part of wider traditions of metalwork deposition in the landscape, rather than relating to their actual locations of use. Unstruck pellets or blanks are also widely distributed away from oppida, with a number recorded by the Portable Antiquities Scheme; they were also occasionally incorporated into coin hoards (de Jersey 2014,

Table 5.1: Iron Age coin dies and related objects from southern Britain

Location	County	Coin type	Date (century BC)	Comments	References
Bredgar	Kent	Gallo-Belgic A stater	Late 2nd		PAS: KENT-2EEAF0; Rudd 2014; Farley & Hunter 2015, 110
Rotherwick	Hampshire	Gallo-Belgic A stater	Late 2nd	Gold flecks adhering. May (2006) suggests actually a coin weight	May 2006
Near Alton	Hampshire	Gallo-Belgic BB stater	Late 2nd		Williams *et al.* 2007
Near Andover	Hampshire	Sussex lyre	Mid-1st	Positive image of coin: punch for making dies?	Rudd 2014

43). It is possible that pellets or blanks could sometimes circulate as objects in their own right without the intention that they would later be struck.

Other non-ferrous metalworking evidence from oppida is patchier. The best evidence for copper alloy casting comes from **Silchester** (Hampshire). Excavation of an area at the centre of this site later occupied by the Roman forum-basilica uncovered a roadside pit containing the skeleton of an adult male (see discussion of 'metalworkers' burials' below) and an assemblage of crucibles, fragments of investment moulds, and one piece of a coin pellet mould. The investment moulds were largely for horse gear and vehicle fittings, and perhaps also penannular brooches. This was clearly a deliberate deposit, occupying a prominent location at the heart of the oppidum. A number of further coin pellet mould fragments were recovered from other features in this excavation area. By contrast, a second excavation area (insula IX) lying further out from the centre, *c.* 100 m from the forum-basilica, produced only a negligible amount of evidence for copper alloy casting, none of it from certainly pre-conquest contexts. Coin pellet moulds were present but at lower frequencies than in the central area. Older excavations and surface survey have recovered further coin pellet moulds and handmade crucible fragments from the outer areas of the oppidum (Corney 1984, fig. 85).

Dispersed metalworking evidence is a feature of several other territorial oppida. At Colchester (Essex) the evidence comes from the **Sheepen** site, located alongside part of the dyke complex. This is usually described as a Late Iron Age–Roman occupation and industrial site, and possible port on the River Colne, though Willis (2007, 121–2) suggests that it may have also been a venue for feasting and ritual, given the rich finds assemblages and the later presence of Roman temples here. The evidence from Sheepen is difficult to interpret as much of it comes from excavations carried out in the 1930s. Two main concentrations of coin pellet moulds have however been identified, *c.* 120 m apart, with more dispersed finds giving a total distribution extending over *c.* 700 m. The contexts for these are largely early Roman in date with one large pit assemblage argued to represent the post-conquest clearance of a Late Iron Age mint. Some crucibles were also recovered from this pit but, otherwise, the crucibles from this site appear to be associated with post-conquest activity.

At Verlamion coin pellet moulds have been found at eight locations dispersed over an area of 1.8 km (Niblett & Thompson 2005, fig. 3.1), though there is a particular concentration around the 'central enclosure', which may have had a ritual or ceremonial purpose. At one location (insula XVII) the coin pellet moulds were found in a Late Iron Age context associated with possible crucibles. Copper alloy working evidence has been found elsewhere in this oppidum complex at the Late Iron Age–Roman settlement at **Gorhambury**, but this appears to be essentially post-conquest in date. Metalworking evidence has been found at both of the main occupation foci within the Bagendon-Ditches oppidum complex (Gloucestershire). At **Bagendon**, excavation just within the rampart produced several crucible fragments and large numbers of coin pellet moulds. At **Ditches**, 3.5 km away, an enclosure that later became the site of a Roman villa has produced a crucible fragment, copper alloy casting waste, and further coin pellet moulds.

The Chichester Dykes complex of linear earthworks in West Sussex is often thought to have formed part of a territorial oppidum though as yet no major focus of Late Iron Age settlement has been identified in the area. Close to the Dykes at **Westhampnett Bypass**, a tuyère with copper alloy traces was found in an apparently isolated Late Iron Age pit, which lay at the edge of an earlier Middle Iron Age settlement and 1 km from a major Late Iron Age cemetery and ritual site. Coin pellet moulds have been found 4 km away in a Late Iron Age enclosure ditch at the eastern terminus of the Dykes complex at **Ounces Barn, Boxgrove**.

Standing somewhat apart from the other territorial oppida, both geographically and in terms of its character, is the site at **Stanwick** (North Yorkshire). The heyday of this site lay in the mid-1st century AD, when the earthwork dyke complex reached its greatest extent and significant numbers of imports reached the site for the first time. Modern excavations have focused on the interior of a 6 ha enclosure known as the Tofts, where the metalworking evidence predominantly comes from an earlier period, *c.* 80 BC–AD 40. Fragments from up to 13 crucibles, pieces of copper alloy casting waste, a stone mould with two cup-shaped matrices, and a failed casting of copper alloy finger ring were all recovered, dispersed across the excavation area. There is no evidence of coin production from this site.

Turning to the unenclosed, 'nucleated' oppida, at **Braughing-Puckeridge** (Hertfordshire) nine separate coin pellet mould assemblages have been recovered from a 500 m length of the valley of the River Rib; only at one site (**Wickham Kennels**) were these associated with other metalworking evidence, in the form of crucibles and a piece of bronze waste. Elsewhere in the Braughing-Puckeridge complex, the settlement site at **Skeleton Green** lacks coin making evidence but has produced a possible piece of copper alloy casting waste and what may be a tuyère. At **Old Sleaford** (Lincolnshire), a very large assemblage of coin pellet mould and crucible fragments was recovered, mostly from a single deposit in a ditch dated to the early 1st century AD, but with further finds dispersed

up to 150 m away. A possible ingot mould or annealing vessel with an adhering silver droplet was also found. Analysis showed that many of the crucibles and pellet moulds showed traces of silver alloys, and it is possible that all the non-ferrous metalworking activity at this site was geared ultimately to the production of silver coinage. At the **Marlowe Theatre and Car Park** site at Canterbury (Kent), a settlement area broadly dated to *c.* 50 BC–AD 80 produced crucible fragments with copper alloy traces, and a piece of a coin pellet mould from a different feature. Winchester (Hampshire) is another possible unenclosed oppidum site which later developed into a Roman cantonal capital, though the character of the Late Iron Age activity here is poorly known. Debris from copper alloy casting in the form of a crucible fragment and casting waste was deposited during the Late Iron Age in an upper ditch fill of the Middle Iron Age enclosure known as **Oram's Arbour**. A stray coin pellet mould fragment has been recovered elsewhere in Winchester at Cathedral Green. At **Elms Farm**, Heybridge (Essex), during the late 1st century BC and early 1st century AD a series of enclosed plots was arranged around a confluence of roadways with a shrine at the centre of the site. Several fragments of crucibles and clay moulds were recovered from features in one part of the site, to the south of a roadway that separated this area from the shrine to the north. There is no evidence for coin pellet production. At **Baldock** (Hertfordshire), the evidence consists solely of three unfinished Colchester brooches, only one of which is from a pre-conquest context.

It is not clear how best to interpret the association of crucible fragments and coin pellet moulds from a number of the oppida discussed above: the crucibles may have been involved in coin production or used to cast other objects. It is thought that coin pellet moulds were themselves used as miniature crucibles in which metal, in granular or powder form, was melted. The associated crucibles might have been employed at an earlier stage in the coin production process, although it is not clear what this might have been. Alternatively, other forms of precious metal working may have been carried out alongside coin making, while copper alloy casting of La Tène style objects may have taken place elsewhere, although this cannot be proven.

Aside from settlement and craft, ritual was clearly an important element of the activities occurring at oppida. Several of these complexes – including Verlamion, Heybridge, and Baldock – incorporated buildings or enclosures identified as 'shrines'. Similar shrines were also established during the Late Iron Age elsewhere in the landscape, away from oppida or other settlement foci (Smith 2001). Such shrines could be foci for the deposition of offerings of objects including coins or metalwork. Metalworking was not normally directly associated with these sites, with two important exceptions. At **Hallaton** (Leicestershire), dating to around the time of the Roman conquest, an open-air hilltop shrine was defined by a polygonal enclosure ditch and was associated with offerings including numerous coin hoards and a Roman cavalry helmet. Metalworking was indicated by droplets and sheet fragments of gold, silver, and copper alloy from the enclosure ditch and ploughsoil. The ditch also contained a bronze ingot and silver ingot, the latter clearly formed by melting coins in a crucible, while one of the coin hoards incorporated a further silver ingot. Though not associated with offerings of metalwork, the enigmatic Late Iron Age–early Roman site at **Fison Way**, Thetford (Norfolk), is also thought to have had a ritual or ceremonial role. This is based on the low quantities of 'domestic' material recovered from the site and its extraordinary form during the post-conquest period, when a large rectangular enclosure with multiple concentric palisades surrounded a monumental circular building and other structures. During the Late Iron Age phase, when the site consisted of a group of more irregular enclosures, crucible and investment mould fragments were concentrated in two areas *c.* 50 m apart (Fig. 5.17). Analysis of the crucibles showed that they had been used to melt copper alloy. In the immediate post-conquest period a concentration of material was found in an enclosure ditch just to the north of the main ceremonial enclosure, though it is unclear whether these metalworking deposits slightly pre-dated the ceremonial enclosure or were contemporary with it. Here coin pellet mould fragments were found along with further crucibles and investment moulds.

Discussion

Intrinsic to the social changes of the Late Iron Age was the forging of new links across the Channel. During the earlier 1st century BC, the site at **Hengistbury Head** (Dorset) had a privileged role in these maritime contacts and exchanges and it is notable that it was also the venue for an unusually wide range of craft activities, including copper alloy working. The quantities of non-ferrous metalworking debris are not particularly large, but it is significant that evidence for the primary production of copper alloys, rather than just their melting, has been identified. Sharples (1990; 2010) has argued that Hengistbury Head occupied a cultural border zone, and it may have had an ethnically mixed population, with large quantities of Armorican pottery suggesting the permanent or seasonal presence of people from across the Channel. The diverse and complex craft activities seen at Hengistbury Head may thus reflect its role as a liminal place, not subject to the usual social strictures, where skilled artisans from different communities could congregate (*ibid.*).

After the heyday of Hengistbury Head as a maritime hub, the late 1st century BC and early 1st century AD saw the rise of the diverse range of focal sites that have been labelled as oppida. Given the clear links between the issuing of coinage and the development of new power relationships during the Late Iron Age (Creighton 2000), it is unsurprising that debris from the production of coin pellets is often associated with oppida. Coin pellet moulds have though also been found away from such sites, especially in eastern England. Furthermore, within several oppida complexes pellet moulds have been found dispersed across wide areas extending over several hectares. It is not clear whether multiple locations of production within a single oppidum would have operated at one time, or whether we are dealing with separate episodes of production that occurred sequentially in different places. Seasonal production is one possibility, with Landon (2016) highlighting examples of grain and chaff impressions on some moulds which could suggest that they were made around harvest time. In any case, the fact that coin pellet production was not restricted to a few closely circumscribed locations has implications for the organisation of this activity, and the levels of political control imposed on it. This may call into question assumptions that Iron Age 'mints'

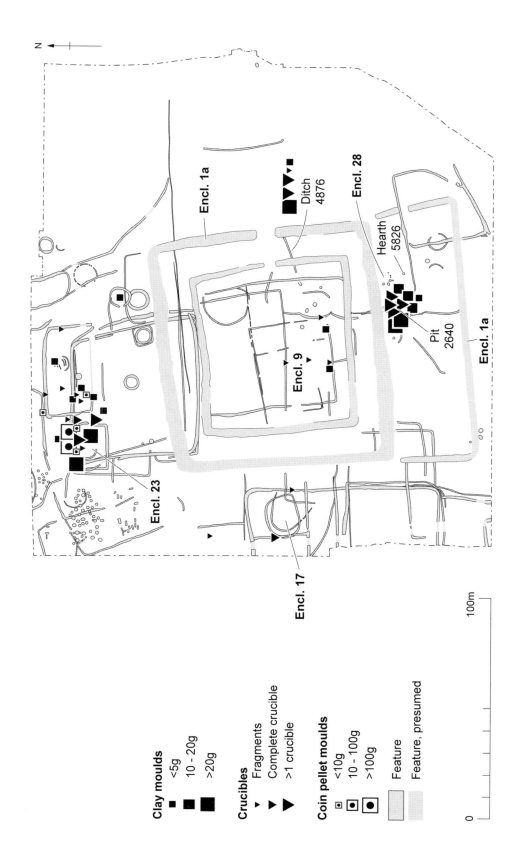

Clay moulds
- ■ <5g
- ■ 10 - 20g
- ■ >20g

Crucibles
- ▸ Fragments
- ▶ Complete crucible
- ▶ >1 crucible

Coin pellet moulds
- ⊡ <10g
- ⊙ 10 - 100g
- ● >100g

Feature

Feature, presumed

Encl. 1a

Encl. 28

Hearth 5826

Ditch 4876

Pit 2640

Encl. 9

Encl. 1a

Encl. 23

Encl. 17

N

0   100m

Figure 5.17: Features of Late Iron Age and post-conquest date at Fison Way, Thetford (Norfolk). The early Roman 'shrine' (enclosure 1a) post-dates the deposits of metalworking debris around enclosure 28 and ditch 4876, and may either post-date or be contemporary with the deposits around enclosure 23 (redrawn by Anne Leaver after Gregory 1991, figs 7 & 37)

were analogous to the state-controlled mints of historical periods.

Evidence for other forms of non-ferrous metalworking at oppida is patchier. Few of these sites have produced significant assemblages of crucibles and investment moulds for copper alloy casting, with a lack of the accumulations of moulds for the casting of equine equipment seen at some smaller settlements of the Middle and Late Iron Age (see above). The exception is the pit deposit from **Silchester** (Hampshire), containing a number of crucibles and moulds, largely for horse gear and vehicle fittings. Uniquely, this assemblage had been deposited along with the body of a man, and it had been placed in a prominent position at the centre of the site, later the administrative focus of the Roman city. This was clearly a 'structured' deposit, and as such it can be compared to other deliberate deposits of waste from casting equine equipment such as the much larger Middle Iron Age pit group from **Gussage All Saints** (Dorset).

Silchester aside, it seems clear that oppida did not generally take on a role as centres for the casting of copper alloy objects. It is not obvious that this is linked to any general downturn in the production of copper alloy objects in south-east England during the late 1st century BC and early 1st century AD, or to a lack of interest in La Tène style metalwork among the communities inhabiting the oppida. It is true that deposition of fine metalwork in the La Tène style seems to have fallen across Britain as a whole in the period *c.* 20 BC–AD 40, roughly corresponding to the heyday of the oppida (Garrow & Gosden 2012, figs 3.9–3.11). However, the objects that were deposited at that time were largely concentrated in south-east England (*ibid.*), and they include items placed within rich burials at oppida such as **Verlamion** (Hertfordshire) and **Colchester** (Essex). The casting of equine equipment at smaller Late Iron Age settlements can rarely be given a more precise date within this period, though at **Weelsby Avenue**, Grimsby (North East Lincolnshire), a date range of *c.* 100 BC–AD 25 has been suggested.

The production of coins and cast copper alloy artefacts may thus have been carried out in different social contexts. The new political centres known as oppida provided the normal venue for the minting of coins, which were objects closely linked to the negotiation of new power relationships, made using novel technologies imported from the Continent. Meanwhile, the longer-established craft of casting copper alloy objects in the La Tène style was able to continue at smaller settlements. The one oppidum with significant evidence for both crafts is Silchester, and even here the debris from the production of coin pellets and equine equipment was largely kept separate in their contexts of deposition.

The association of crucibles and moulds with a burial at Silchester raises questions of the relationship between metalworking and ritual during the Late Iron Age. As noted above, ritual was an important element of the activities carried out at many oppida, and metalworking debris has been found close to putative shrines at **Heybridge** (Essex) and Verlamion. Away from oppida, the ritual sites at **Hallaton** (Leicestershire) and **Fison Way**, Thetford (Norfolk), have also produced metalworking remains. In these cases, formalised ritual spaces were deemed to be appropriate venues for metalworking, though this was not the norm as most sites identified as Late Iron Age shrines show no evidence for craft activities. It is possible that metalworking was carried out in the vicinity of shrines in order to produce objects used in the rituals that took place there, or in order to melt down and recast the metal offerings that had been placed at the shrine. The clearest indications of such direct links between metalworking and ritual come from Hallaton, where offerings of thousands of local silver coins and other precious metal objects were accompanied by metalworking evidence including silver and gold droplets and a silver ingot that had evidently been formed by melting down coins.

Metalworkers' burials and the identity of the smith in the Late Iron Age

Human remains were often deposited in Iron Age settlements, either as complete burials or as disarticulated bones. Some features containing human remains have also produced metalworking tools or debris, although as noted above it is not always clear whether the association was deliberate or meaningful. The burial of a possible adult female from the pit at **Gilcross** (East Riding of Yorkshire), described above, was not directly associated with the metalworking residues from this feature. As such, it should perhaps be interpreted not as a 'metalworker's burial' but as part of the wider tradition of Iron Age pit deposits in which a variety of special objects (including human remains) were deposited during rituals that may have been geared towards maintaining human and agricultural fertility or community well-being (Wait 1985; Cunliffe 1992; Hill 1995a; Chadwick 2012; 2015).

'Formal' inhumation and cremation burials interred with grave goods are a rarity during the Early and Middle Iron Age but became more common in the Late Iron Age in parts of southern and eastern England. Smithing tools were included as grave goods in four burials and there are also two examples of burials directly associated with refractory ceramics. The graves containing smithing tools all come from larger cemeteries. Two extended inhumation burials of 1st century BC date from the cemetery at **Makeshift**, Rudston (East Riding of Yorkshire), contained tools; both were young adults, possibly male. One of these contained a pair of tongs laid alongside the torso, a hammer placed by the hips, and a coupler (for clamping the tongs) close to the head, as well as a sword, two spearheads, and a possible wooden shield. A second burial contained a hammer and an iron dagger. Based on the form of both hammers, Fell (1990, 112) has identified them as metalworking tools, the former perhaps used for small decorative work and the latter for shaping pieces of metal. At **Whitcombe** (Dorset), the most richly equipped burial in the cemetery was a male aged 25–30 years, interred in the early 1st century AD with a hammer and file, as well as a sword with scabbard, a spearhead, a copper alloy brooch, and a chalk disc or spindle whorl. Despite his young age, this individual had osteoarthritis throughout his spine, raising doubts over whether he could actually have engaged in heavy smithing work. A hammer also accompanied the cremation burial of an adult at **King Harry Lane**, within the **Verlamion** complex (Hertfordshire), which dated to *c.* AD 30–55 and contained a fine imported ceramic beaker. A second burial with a hammer from this cemetery post-dates the Roman conquest.

By contrast, the burials associated with refractory ceramics were not from formal cemeteries but were interred in pits or ditches at oppida. At **Stanwick** (North Yorkshire),

three crucible fragments were found with the tightly crouched inhumation burial of an adult female. The burial was placed in a sub-rectangular grave cut into a ditch and has been dated via Bayesian modelling to *50–1 cal BC* (Hamilton 2010, table 4.3.1). The body was laid on its right side on a similar axis to the ditch and with its head to the east. A cattle jaw was found at the feet and there was a cobble between the skull and the edge of the grave, thought to have been deliberately placed there to keep the head in position. At **Silchester** (Hampshire), as we have seen, non-ferrous metalworking remains were found in an elongated pit next to a road; finds from the pit indicate a date range of *c.* 15 BC–AD 40/50. The inhumation burial of a young adult male was found in the upper fill of this feature. This individual showed evidence of heavy physical labour and malnutrition, which does not suggest that he enjoyed a high-status in life. The metalworking remains do not appear to have been deposited as individually placed grave goods but were found in several of the pit fills; the large majority came from a fill below the burial, with small quantities occurring in the layers containing the skeleton and above it. Finds included 0.8 kg of crucible fragments (including one near-complete vessel), parts of around 100 recognisable moulds, along with gate and sprue cup fragments, a coin pellet mould fragment, and *c.* 1 kg of probable bronze slag, as well as animal bone and unusual imported pottery. The investment moulds were for the production of a variety of objects including terrets, rings, linchpins, openwork harness decorations, strap unions, and possibly penannular brooches.

All the burials described above are of adults. Only males or possible males were associated with smithing tools, while casting evidence was found with both sexes. The inclusion of smithing tools as grave goods at sites such as Whitcombe, Makeshift, and King Harry Lane indicates an increasing concern to employ metalworking tools to define the social identities of specific individuals, suggesting that the smith was now – in certain cases at least – a recognised and distinct social category. The appearance of small numbers of graves with metalworking tools (again often in combination with weapons) is a phenomenon seen more widely across much of temperate Europe during the late pre-Roman Iron Age (Henning 1991). It is interesting to note that some of the burials that produced smithing tools also contained items (such as swords) that have often been interpreted as markers of social and political status; this may reflect the esteem in which smithing and smiths were held. The two burials associated with refractory ceramics are different in character, and at Silchester these remains were not all found in direct association with the inhumation burial. Here, depositional activities may have centred around the formal disposal of metalworking residues; the body placed in the pit may have been of secondary importance and this individual may not himself have been a metalworker.

Even for sites such as Whitcombe and Makeshift, we are, however, faced with the same issues as for the Chalcolithic and Early Bronze Age 'smiths' graves' discussed in Chapter 3. Some of these objects may have been gifts from the mourners and may not have been owned or used by the deceased. Metalworking tools may have been emblems of a particular status or social role, a persona taken to the afterlife. Likewise, the symbolic potential of such objects may also have been employed to comment metaphorically on the social impact and transformative process of death. The presence of weaponry in three of the burials suggests that metalworking was only one element of the social roles or statuses displayed through the funerary rite. As Giles (2012, 162–3) argues in her discussion of tools in burials in East Riding of Yorkshire:

> whilst these may represent real gender differences in craftwork, and such items could be read as the personal possessions of the 'smith' or 'spinner', they also evoked a series of qualities which helped construct gender relations … Such tools may have been included in funerary rituals to structure ideas about death, identity and transformation: the making of new persons as ancestors – but they drew upon the model of power which was appropriate to each sex.

However we interpret these burials, it is pertinent to note that representations of smiths are also known on coins from the 1st century BC, suggesting that the identity of the smith was of increasing interest at this time. Two Late Iron Age coin types depict possible smiths or, following Allen (1958), a smith god equivalent to the Gallo-Roman Sucellus. A silver coin of Dubnovellaunus (Kent), dated *c.* 20 BC–AD 10 (Van Arsdell 1989, no. 178), shows a bearded, possibly naked male seated on a stool and brandishing a 'hammer'. A

struck bronze of Cunobelin, dated *c.* AD 10–40 (Van Arsdell 1989, no. 2097), shows an individual seated on a chair, apparently beating a vessel with a 'hammer'. This person is wearing a hat and has their hair held back in a bun; it has been assumed that this is a male, though this is not obvious. Of course, we need to be cautious about viewing these images as realistic representations of Iron Age metalworkers in action. The 'hammers' do not resemble the iron shaft-hole hammers attested in later Iron Age southern Britain (cf. Fell 1998). As with many other Iron Age coins, the images are probably classically inspired, and can be compared with depictions of seated smiths hammering helmets on gems (Henig 1972) and Greek vases (Mattusch 2008, fig. 16.1). Alternatively, Creighton (2000) has proposed a quite different interpretation of these coins as scenes of Roman-style sacrificial rites. The maleness of at least one of the metalworkers meanwhile needs to be seen in the context of the general scarcity of recognisable depictions of females on British Iron Age coins (Van Arsdell 1989). Hence, though the burial and coin evidence provide a sense that smithing had ideological associations with males of a certain status, and with martial prestige, how far this in reality represents the typical Iron Age metalworker is a different matter.

The context of metal casting residues from excavated sites: northern Britain

We will turn now to examine the evidence from Scotland, the Isle of Man, Cumbria, and Northumberland from the Early Iron Age through to the end of the 1st century AD. This will be considered more briefly than the evidence from southern Britain, partly because there are many fewer well-stratified finds and partly because most of the material has already been discussed in Heald's (2005) thesis on non-ferrous metalworking in Iron Age Scotland.

Settlement patterns in Scotland show a number of differences to those further south. Alongside open and enclosed round-house settlements and hillforts, in northern and western Scotland from the later pre-Roman Iron Age onwards there are various forms of massive stone-built 'Atlantic round-houses', including brochs and wheelhouses. The social role of these has long been a focus of debate (eg, Armit 1997; Sharples & Parker Pearson 1997); they have often been seen as the homes of an elite but others dispute this, not least because in some areas (such as North Uist) other forms of settlement are difficult to identify. Crannógs are another site type found in Scotland: these have again been seen as elite residences, but it appears that not all were domestic settlements, and rather they could fulfil a range of functions including ritual and craftworking activity (Cavers 2010).

There are some challenges in assessing the significance of metalworking-related finds from this region. Often, older excavations have yielded poor contextual information and in many areas there has been relatively little recent archaeological investigation. The extended time-span of the Scottish Iron Age (into the late 1st millennium AD) and the difficulties of dating many sites to specific horizons within this period mean that it can be challenging to identify evidence for change over time. Although the parameters of this project exclude material dating to after the end of the 1st century AD, many of the sites examined here were long-lived and were occupied well beyond this time-frame; it can often be difficult to distinguish finds that fall on either side of the cut-off date of AD 100. The complex palimpsests of activity within many long-lived Atlantic round-houses can be particularly difficult to interpret (Armit 2006). Nonetheless, some comparisons with southern Britain can be made. Many of the same themes emerge but there are also some striking differences. Moulds for the production of horse gear and vehicle fittings are completely absent, for example; instead, most identifiable matrices are for the casting of personal ornaments and ingots.

Only six sites have yielded evidence of demonstrably Early Iron Age date: **High Pasture Cave** (Highland), **Oakbank** crannóg (Perth & Kinross), a round-house or broch at **Bu 'Navershaw'** (Orkney), and the hillforts at **Cullykhan** (Aberdeenshire), **Craigmarloch** (Inverclyde), and **Broxmouth** (East Lothian). Twenty-two sites can be dated to the later Iron Age, including three settlements on the Isle of Man and one in Northumberland. The Scottish sites include four hillforts, four or possibly five brochs, two crannógs, one or possibly two wheelhouses, and three other settlements

as well as activity at an earlier monument and next to an unusual subterranean site.

As in southern Britain, the scale of the evidence is highly variable. In most cases, finds are sparse. Excavations at Oakbank crannóg, and at **Crosskirk broch**, Caithness (Highland), yielded just two crucible fragments each, for example. At **St Boniface**, Papa Westray (Orkney), three fragments of lost-wax moulds, two pieces of tuyères, and a vitrified clay fragment from a hearth were found on a stone floor in the corner of a rectilinear structure. Other sites produced slightly larger assemblages. Occupation deposits lying on a cobbled surface beneath the rampart on the north-western side of the coastal promontory fort at Cullykhan yielded hearth lining fragments with traces of copper alloy on the surfaces, ironworking slag, a bronze tanged chisel, five or six crucible fragments, three mould fragments, and dense pockets of ash and fire-cracked stones. These deposits were located adjacent to a rectangular building. A complete cup-shaped handled crucible was found next to a hearth in the same area, although the precise location of this is not described in the published report.

Small quantities of non-ferrous metalworking evidence were recovered from Early and Middle Iron Age contexts at Broxmouth (East Lothian). The hilltop was initially surrounded by a palisaded enclosure; a crucible fragment and part of a mould were recovered from features associated with a large round-house overlying this feature. Later, the site became a hillfort; another crucible fragment, copper casting waste, and waste with traces of silver and gold were found in the metalled surface of the hillfort's western gateway. The final phase of settlement at the site was unenclosed. A single crucible fragment was recovered from the floor of a round-house belonging to this phase while the hearth of the same building yielded a complete mould for the production of bar ingots; analysis of the latter item yielded traces of copper, zinc, and gold.

Some of the best-preserved and most extensive evidence for both ferrous and non-ferrous metalworking was found at **Culduthel Farm**, Inverness (Highland), an open settlement of 17 round-houses dating to the 2nd century BC–2nd century AD that yielded casting waste, 72 crucible sherds, 60 fragments from at least ten clay moulds, and a quernstone that had been reused as a mould with matrices for bar and dish-shaped objects. Most of the non-ferrous metalworking debris was derived from two areas paved with flagstones, one defined by four post-holes, just south-east of a substantial round-house. The majority of the refractory fragments were relatively unworn, indicating that they were deposited soon after use. If so, then this may be the location where metalworking was carried out. It is important to note that this was no ordinary settlement, however. Some of the round-houses were unusually large, and metalwork finds included weaponry and an imported Roman brooch. There is also rare glassworking evidence alongside large-scale iron smelting and smithing.

As in southern Britain, non-ferrous metalworking debris has often been recovered from inside buildings, although these vary in form. At **Jarlshof** (Shetland), three crucible fragments were recovered from a complex stone-built round-house of Early Iron Age date that has been interpreted as a workshop; two were found close to hearths in this building while the other was recovered from a possible furnace. At **Ballacagen Lough** (Isle of Man), 64 crucible fragments and 23 clay mould fragments were found in two round-houses. Only three of the mould matrices were identifiable and these were for the production of pins. Glassy residues on some of the moulds and crucibles suggest that they may have been used for working glass; alternatively, the ceramics may have become vitrified through over-heating during the metalworking process. A crucible and moulds for the casting of ingots and chain link were recovered from the 'guard chamber' at the entrance to the broch at **Ness** (Highland). There were crucible fragments from both the main broch and a subcircular annexe at **Dun Bharabhat**, Lewis (Comhairle nan Eilean Siar), although the precise location of these is not recorded. At **Fishers Road East**, Port Seton (East Lothian), an enclosure complex containing a number of round-houses was identified (Fig. 5.18). A u-shaped gully - possibly the foundation trench for a shelter - was located between the inner and outer ditch of an enclosure containing a round-house. This feature produced 11 crucible sherds from four vessels, fragments of a tuyère, fired clay, and iron slag.

It is not always clear whether such finds

indicate the location of metalworking or the deposition of the resulting residues, however. Some of the best evidence for *in situ* metalworking activity comes from the settlement at **Billown Quarry** (Isle of Man). Here, metalworking remains were found in and around a round-house defined by a penannular ring-groove. This feature was 6 m in diameter and had a north-north-west facing entrance. Inside, a roughly central hearth had been heated to over 1150°C suggesting that it was not used solely for cooking. Finds from the building included cuprous and iron smithing slags, copper alloy casting waste, vitrified hearth lining (some pieces with the remains of blow-holes), crucibles, and moulds. These were concentrated around the hearth and in the ring-groove, especially near the entrance. Crucible fragments and casting waste were also found in a pit in a cluster immediately north-west of the building. Magnetic susceptibility survey and extensive soil chemistry analysis demonstrated that both copper alloy working and ironworking took place within this building, with evidence for the production of non-ferrous objects concentrated just inside the doorway. With its north-north-westerly orientation, the sun would not have shone directly into this building. This would have made it easier for the smith to see the changing colour of the metal as it reached the correct temperature for working. The presence of crucibles and casting waste outside the structure suggests that elements of the casting process may have occurred outside too, or that some debris was removed from the building for deposition in external pits. The lack of copper inclusions in the iron smithing slags suggests the two metals were worked at different times, but it seems likely nonetheless that these activities were carried out by the same people, or at least by people with knowledge of each other's craft.

Sites such as **Culduthel Farm**, Inverness (Highland), and Billown Quarry indicate that, where more extensive evidence survives, this is often concentrated in one particular area of a site, in or around one building, or even in a specific room within that building, although elsewhere, as at **Broxmouth** (East Lothian), evidence is more dispersed. In general, metalworking debris is found within the settlement core, close to other domestic and craft activities. On some sites, however, the metalworking activity appears to belong to the

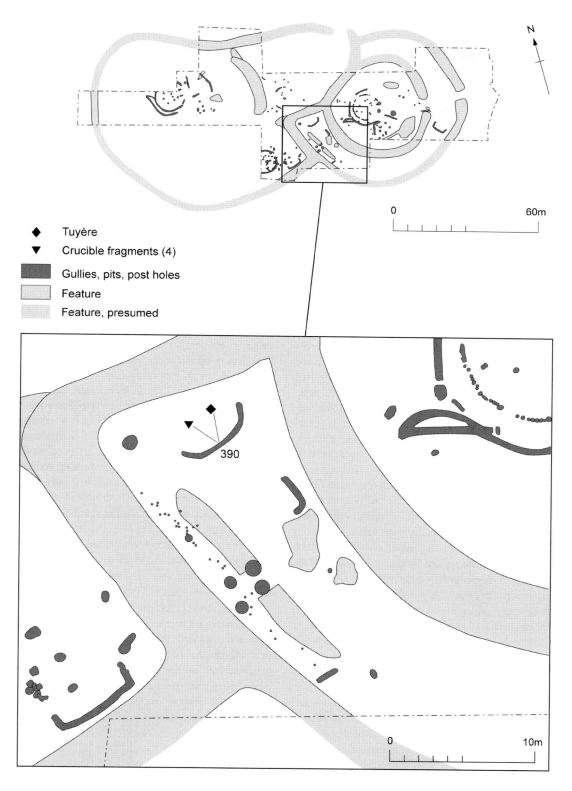

Figure 5.18: Late
Iron Age settlement at
Fishers Road East, Port
Seton (East Lothian)
(redrawn by Anne
Leaver after Haselgrove
& McCullagh 2000,
fig. 33)

◆ Tuyère

▼ Crucible fragments (4)

▮ Gullies, pits, post holes

▮ Feature

▮ Feature, presumed

0   60m

390

0   10m

abandonment or post-abandonment phases rather than the main period of occupation. For example, four clay pin mould fragments found in sandy layers within the side bays of a wheelhouse at **Cnip** (Comhairle nan Eilean Siar) date to the final phase of occupation when the building was falling into disrepair. Part of a crucible was recovered from silt that built up after the substantial stone-built round-house at **Bu** (Orkney) went out of use. Subsequently, a souterrain was built into the wall of the round-house and this yielded part of another crucible and fragments of a tuyère.

Although the majority of the evidence from northern Britain comes from settlements and hillforts a small number of sites hint at possible links between metalworking and underground spaces. **High Pasture Cave**, located in a valley on the Isle of Skye (Highland), has yielded six crucible sherds, a possible crucible stand, two fragments of vitrified ceramic with non-ferrous residues, and three tuyère fragments. Most of these were found in burnt spreads and other occupation deposits outside the cave, although fragments of one crucible and two tuyères were recovered from midden material inside the cave itself, while another crucible sherd came from deposits in a stone stairwell that was constructed to access the underground spaces. The activity began in the 8th–5th centuries BC and continued into the second half of the 1st millennium BC. A significant quantity of ironworking debris was also found inside and outside the cave. Analysis of the distribution of the hammerscale suggests that this activity was undertaken just outside the entrance, with the residues subsequently deposited underground. As well as metalworking, the site seems to have been the focus of feasting and ritual activities; there are a number of human burials from infill deposits in the stairwell, as well as a range of artefacts from the cave itself that have been interpreted as votive offerings. Cave 2 at **Covesea** (Moray) has also produced crucible fragments provisionally dated to the Iron Age; this cave, located on the shore of the Moray Firth, was previously a focus for the deposition of human bone in the Late Bronze Age.

At **Mine Howe** (Orkney), a stairwell and series of galleries led down into a corbelled stone chamber or cistern built deep in a natural mound. It has been suggested that this was a ritual space constructed to access supernatural powers associated with a watery underworld, possibly in the late 4th or early 3rd century BC. Surrounding the mound was a ditched enclosure and outside of this was a small circular stone building identified as a workshop for the production of copper alloy and iron objects. Bayesian modelling suggests that the main phase of use of this structure was *60 BC–AD 50*, with activity focused around a central hearth and a clay-lined bowl furnace to its south-east. Geochemical analysis of soil samples indicates that non-ferrous metalworking took place inside this building and finds include a large number of crucible fragments, at least 262 pieces of casting waste, fragments of furnace lining, and a few moulds. Working of sheet metal is indicated by the presence of sheet fragments and offcuts, as well as rivets and washers, some of them unused and unfinished. An ingot of pure copper and a steatite ingot or billet mould suggest that alloying may also have taken place in the building, while hammerscale and iron smelting slag provide evidence for ironworking. Bone and antler offcuts are likely to derive from the production of components of composite objects such as handles. Several stone settings to the north and west of the central hearth held anvils or workbenches of wood, stone and whalebone: geochemical analysis of one wooden plank yielded traces of copper and iron, indicating that it had been used for the working of both metals.

At the end of the main period of metalworking activity, the inhumation burial of a young adult female was interred below the floor. There were two copper alloy rings on her toes and a small object of antler with six drilled holes lay on her chest; the grave fill contained several crucible fragments, four pieces of copper sheet, pottery, and hammerstones. Midden deposits built up outside of the workshop in the centuries after the main phase of use of the structure and these produced moulds for the production of pins, rings, ingots, and spearbutts; most of these are likely to fall outside of the date-range for this project. A pit cut into one of the midden deposits contained the unaccompanied inhumation burial of an adult male who had suffered a violent death. Both this individual and the young adult female showed evidence for a lifetime of heavy manual labour including heavy lifting and repeated periods of bending, and it is tempting to interpret these as the burials of the metalworkers.

Discussion

Some similarities in the evidence from northern and southern Britain can be discerned but there are also interesting differences. There are few sites of earlier pre-Roman Iron Age date and most can be assigned to the last few centuries BC and 1st century AD. As in southern England, the evidence for non-ferrous metalworking is typically small-scale and there is considerable diversity in the types of site from which it has been recovered. Metalworking was often carried out in and around buildings. Some of these, as at **Mine Howe** (Orkney), may have been specialist workshops, although most yielded a variety of other finds including artefacts that can be considered more 'domestic' in character. Even for a given site type, there is variability in where the metalworking remains occur: at some broch sites, for example, the finds were recovered from the broch tower itself, while at others, as at **Midhowe**, Rousay (Orkney), they come from the outbuildings surrounding it. Heald (2005) has argued that the metalworking evidence from Scotland tends to be found at sites such as hillforts, complex Atlantic round-houses, and crannógs that he sees as having elite associations. However, as noted above, it is not certain that these kinds of sites were in fact the pinnacle of a settlement hierarchy, and metalworking also occurs at unenclosed settlements. Sites such as hillforts, brochs, and wheelhouses dominate the archaeological record from western and northern Scotland and have traditionally been the focus of excavation. The apparent preponderance of evidence from such settlements may therefore be the result of particular histories of research rather than of actual patterning in productive activities. Even in the Scottish lowlands and neighbouring counties in northern England, there has been relatively little development-led activity in comparison to parts of southern Britain, and very few sites have produced non-ferrous metalworking evidence. While most sites have produced only small quantities of metalworking remains, quite different was the craftworking centre at the unenclosed settlement at **Culduthel Farm**, Inverness (Highland), which produced substantial non-ferrous metalworking evidence along with glassworking and intensive iron smelting and smithing. This site shows contacts with the Roman world and provides an insight into social changes at the end of our period. Another notable feature of the Scottish evidence is the link between metalworking and subterranean spaces with possible ritual connotations, as at **Mine Howe** (Orkney), **High Pasture Cave** (Highland), and **Covesea** (Moray).

Ireland

Despite a significant upsurge in developer-funded archaeology over the past 20 years, only six Irish sites have yielded evidence for non-ferrous metalworking. All date to the 3rd century BC and later, although sites dating to the last few centuries of the Irish Iron Age (up to AD 400) are not included in this project. Until recently little was known about domestic settlement in Iron Age Ireland, but recent excavation and radiocarbon dating have changed the picture. While sites from the early part of the period are still rare, an increasing number of 'ordinary' unenclosed settlements are now known from *c.* 400 BC onwards (Becker *et al.* 2008; Corlett & Potterton 2012; Dowling 2014). A number of sites have produced iron smelting or smithing slag (Dolan 2014; Garstki 2017; 2019); often this is the only artefactual evidence on sites attributed to the Iron Age through radiocarbon dating. However, these sites rarely also produce non-ferrous metalworking evidence.

In most cases, non-ferrous metalworking seems to be associated with sites that are not ordinary domestic settlements. At **Ráith na Ríg**, Tara (Co. Meath), fragments of crucibles and moulds, iron slag, and possible glassworking debris were found together in a charcoal layer beneath the rampart of a hilltop enclosure. They are thought to derive from a neighbouring hearth. The date of the rampart itself has been modelled at *145–50 cal BC*. The significant group of prehistoric monuments on the Hill of Tara, including a passage tomb, palisade enclosure and a large number of barrows, indicates that this location was an important ceremonial centre from at least the Middle Neolithic; it figures in medieval literary sources as a royal inauguration site, and there is a cluster of early medieval monuments here too (Bhreathnach 1995; Schot 2018). A second 'royal site' at **Knockaulin** (Co. Kildare) has also yielded metalworking evidence. Excavations revealed three successive phases of circular timber structures, probably unroofed, inside the hilltop enclosure; these have been interpreted as ceremonial rather than domestic in purpose. Finds included copper alloy casting jets, two further possible pieces of casting waste, and two small copper alloy bars (possibly ingots); iron slag and waste glass were also found. The context of the metalworking related finds is not recorded in the published volume, however, and they are only broadly dated to the later 1st millennium BC to early 1st millennium AD.

At **Mooghaun South** (Co. Clare), a Late Bronze Age hillfort was reused during the Iron Age for bronze casting, ironworking, and rotary quern production. Finds from buried soil layers and a number of hollows include three clay mould fragments and two mould or crucible fragments, 'small globules of waste bronze', and iron slag. The character and context of the metalworking activity is unclear although the excavator argues that it was not domestic occupation (Grogan 2005). There is a radiocarbon date for this activity of 50 cal BC–cal AD 130 (1963±35 BP; UB-4314), although the context of the dated material is not clear, so it is unknown if this relates directly to the metalworking evidence. At the lowland settlement of **Platin/Lagavooren 1** (Co. Meath), 14 crucible fragments, a mould fragment, a tuyère fragment, and 7 pieces of hearth-lining were found in features associated with a putative working shelter defined by a series of gullies immediately to the east of a round-house (Fig. 5.19). Most of the finds were recovered from the western end of one of a pair of long linear features just east of the working shelter. These features ran parallel to each other and were roughly aligned on the same axis as the round-house and working shelter. Burnt animal bone from one of these produced a date of 160 cal BC–cal AD 60 (2025±30 BP; SUERC-31938). The site also produced red glass beads possibly imported from the Continent. Possibly just overlapping with the end of our period is a circular palisaded enclosure at **Baysrath** (Co. Kilkenny), radiocarbon dated to cal AD 70–220 (1880±25 BP; UB-10703). A clay mould, copper fragments, three tuyères, and iron slag were recovered from the palisade trench. At least three successive round-houses lay within the enclosure, and outside was a bowl hearth dated to 50 cal BC–cal AD 60 (1989±23 BP; UB-10693). An iron spearhead of possible Romano-British origin again suggests integration into wider networks (Dowling 2014). As none of the mould fragments from Baysrath or the other sites discussed in this section is diagnostic, we have no indications of what object types were cast at these locations.

At two further sites, metalworking debris is associated with funerary contexts, though the chronology is problematic. Crucible fragments and two copper alloy globules were found in a 'token' cremation burial pit radiocarbon dated to 210 cal BC–cal AD 10 (2080±40 BP; Beta-241006) at **Cross** (Co. Galway). However, as this feature also contained Bronze Age pottery sherds, it is possible that the metalworking debris is residual. At **Ballydavis** (Co. Laois), a crucible fragment and iron slag were recovered from the fill of a ring-ditch surrounding a high-status Iron Age burial; the burial was accompanied by an unusual bronze box, bronze brooch, and glass beads. There was a second crucible fragment from a group of neighbouring 'furnaces'. These features contained burnt clay, charcoal, and iron slag, though dating evidence from these contexts is lacking.

Cross-craft interaction

Interactions between metalworking and other crafts are not prominent during the later Bronze Age. The use of clay and stone moulds raises the question of links between metalworking, ceramic production, and stoneworking and, as we have seen in Chapter 4, there are a number of sites with evidence for metalworking and other crafts. There are also objects that combine metal with other materials, such as tools with organic handles. However, most 'prestige' objects of bronze or gold derived their power from the visual effect of the metal itself and the skill invested in crafting this material. The accumulation of bronze in hoards further emphasises the distinct social role of metal.

In contrast, a feature of later Iron Age fine metalwork across both Britain and Ireland is the significant number of composite objects in which bronze is combined with iron or is inlaid with materials such as glass (sometimes confused with enamel), coral, amber, horn, shell, bone, or clay – something much less common during the Bronze Age. This may suggest that bronze smiths worked in association with other craft workers, or themselves worked in different materials. There are also significant overlaps in some of the technical processes involved in the production of ferrous and non-ferrous metal objects, as well as in crafts such as pottery production; if the craftworkers were not one and the same people, then this

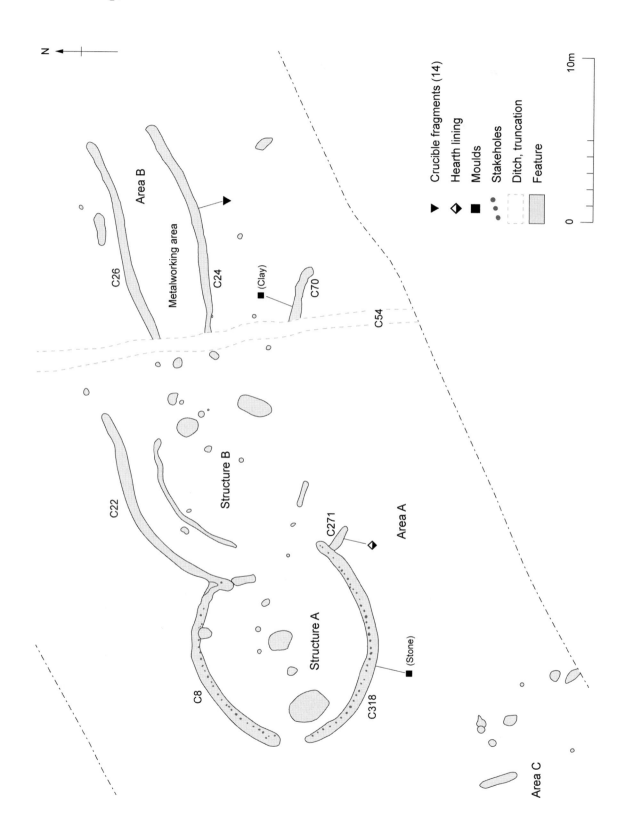

Figure 5.19: Developed Iron Age settlement at Platin/Lagavooren 1 (Co. Meath) (redrawn by Anne Leaver after Lynch 2012, fig. 4)

suggests that knowledge was shared, or that those involved drew on common practices and cultural tropes such as the use of fire to effect material transformations. There are particularly strong contextual links between non-ferrous metalworking, ironworking, and glassworking. Evidence for the production of bone and antler artefacts is also known from the same sites and contexts as non-ferrous metalworking debris. The association of non-ferrous metalworking with other crafts such as pottery production, shaleworking, and salt making will also be examined in this section.

Ironworking

It has often been assumed that during the Iron Age ferrous and non-ferrous metalworking were two quite separate crafts: very different technological processes organised in different ways and with different conceptual associations. Howard (1983) made this argument based on ethnographic parallels. Ehrenreich (1995) suggests that in Iron Age southern Britain, bronzeworking 'would have been restricted to specialists because of the complex technical knowledge required', as shown by the 'production for export' of horse trappings at **Gussage All Saints** (Dorset). 'Iron Age ironworking was not limited by the need for advanced technical knowledge, however' (*ibid.*, 38), and the raw material was easily available, and hence it had a heterarchical organisation. Garrow and Gosden (2012) highlight the different properties of bronze and iron and emphasise the differences in their working, such as the fact that the former can be liquefied for casting. They thus question 'whether [bronze and iron] both existed in the same categories for Iron Age peoples, even though today we class them both as metals' (*ibid.*, 89), though they do acknowledge that the evidence for the two crafts can occur on the same site.

The differences between iron and non-ferrous metalworking technologies should not be exaggerated, however. It is true that only non-ferrous metals can be melted down and cast. However, cast objects would almost always undergo subsequent smithing work to finish them. For sheet objects, casting only provides a billet or blank and almost ubiquitously most of the metalworker's effort and skill would have gone into smithing work. Smithing of iron and bronze would require

essentially the same skills and there is significant overlap in the range of tools that would have been used (Fell 1990). Iron files, for example, have generally been viewed as blacksmithing tools, but as we have seen already, there is direct evidence that some were used on non-ferrous metals. Composite items with elements in two metals become relatively common from the Middle Iron Age (Stead 2006; Joy 2010; 2014): these include copper alloy cauldrons with iron rims and handles, iron brooches with copper alloy rivets and torsion mechanisms, linchpins with an iron shank and copper alloy ends, horse bridle bits with copper alloy mouthpieces and iron cheek rings, and swords with iron blades and copper alloy hilts. Occasionally, bronze plating of iron has been identified, as for example on the bridle bit from Gussage All Saints.

Analysis of the excavated evidence from Iron Age sites across Britain and Ireland indicates that bronzeworking debris very often occurs on sites that have also yielded iron smithing evidence, though conversely many ironworking sites do not have non-ferrous evidence. Furthermore, bronze and ironworking waste can be found in the same areas of a site and even deposited in the same contexts. This may be a wider pattern, as it has also been noted that copper alloy working almost invariably occurs on sites with ironworking in Iron Age northern France (Vauterin *et al.* 2011; Mathiot 2012; Zaour *et al.* 2014). The implication is that either bronze and ironworking were occurring together, or that waste from these two activities was brought together for deposition, which may suggest a conceptual association between the two crafts. For example, the gully of a later Iron Age round-house at **Higher Besore and Truro College**, Threemilestone (Cornwall), contained pieces of a small crucible, some copper alloy residues, iron smithing slags, and undiagnostic hearth lining fragments. At **Llwyn Bryn-dinas** hillfort (Powys), a terrace cut into the rear of the rampart and covered with a thick layer of charcoal dated to 390–40 cal BC (2160±70 BP; CAR-708) has been interpreted as a metalworking floor. Features identified included three bowl hearths, two other hearths, and two possible anvil/forge sites (defined by stone settings and iron slag concentrations). Finds included crucible fragments, copper alloy waste, furnace lining, iron slag, hammerscale, and a stone pebble pounder. At **Broom**

(Central Bedfordshire), the upper fill of a Middle Iron Age pit yielded a complete crucible, several crucible fragments, parts of four crucible stands, and copper-alloy casting waste and scrap, along with ironworking waste in the form of smithing hearth bottoms and hammerscale.

In the Broom example, the absence of copper in the smithing slags suggests that copper alloy and ironworking were undertaken sequentially rather than at the same time. In contrast, at **Havenstreet** (Isle of Wight) Late Iron Age clay hearth material contained both copper and iron residues and has been interpreted as evidence that both ferrous and non-ferrous metalworking were carried out using the same hearths. Similarly, at the hillfort of **Danebury** (Hampshire) low-density slags contained both iron and copper residues, and it is argued that 'the most likely explanation is that they were furnace linings from furnaces used both to forge iron and melt copper-based alloys' (Cunliffe 1984, 437). In some other cases, there is direct evidence that both crafts were conducted on the same spot, suggesting that bronze and iron smiths worked together or were one and the same. As we have seen above, soil geochemistry and magnetic susceptibility analyses indicate that iron and copper alloy working occurred within the same Middle Iron Age round-houses at **Maiden Castle** hillfort (Dorset) (Slater & Doonan 2014) and **Billown Quarry** (Isle of Man) (Darvill 2001). The association of copper alloy casting waste, crucible fragments and hammerscale in the floor deposits of the workshop building at **Mine Howe** (Orkney) suggests that both crafts were practised here.

Glassworking

Glass was often used to inlay bronze and iron objects during the Iron Age, as well as being used in its own right for objects such as beads. Glassworking was a pyrotechnology that used crucibles similar to those used for non-ferrous metals, and glass beads were made in clay moulds, possibly including the use of the lost-wax technique (Henderson 1987). Furthermore, metal oxides were used as colourants and opacifiers for coloured glass (Henderson 1989) and it has been argued that yellow glass was produced in northern Europe by addition of lead stannate to imported clear glass deriving from the Mediterranean (Tite *et*

al. 2008). Aside from Woodham Walter (Essex), where excavation was small scale (Buckley *et al.* 1987), all the few Iron Age sites with evidence for glassworking also produced non-ferrous metalworking debris, as for example at **Meare East** and **West** (Somerset) and **Knockaulin** (Co. Kildare). Crucible fragments, bronze casting waste and finds of raw purple glass were recovered from Late Iron Age contexts at **Hengistbury Head** (Dorset). As we have seen, this site also yielded evidence for a range of other craft activities during the Late Iron Age and its location on a prominent headland on the south coast of England suggests that it may have been a centre of production and exchange.

Unfortunately, the contextual information is limited from many of these sites, although there is some evidence to suggest that bronzeworking and glassworking took place in close proximity. The arc of four post-holes defining the south side of an area of flagstones at **Culduthel Farm**, Inverness (Highland), produced part of a clay mould, 13 crucible sherds, copper alloy casting waste, and a possible iron file as well as 26 fragments of glassworking debris. At **Ráith na Ríg**, Tara (Co. Meath), small-scale excavations recovered crucibles, moulds, iron slag, and possible glassworking debris including two fragments of curved glass rods, one red and one purple, and several splinters of blue glass. These were found together close to a hearth that may have been the focus for a variety of different craft activities. Scientific analysis of the refractory ceramics yielded no evidence for the production of glass and it is possible that this material was brought to the site ready-made as rods or finished artefacts and then broken into smaller pieces and reused to decorate metal objects cast and forged here.

Other crafts

The production of bone, horn, and antler artefacts is associated with non-ferrous metalworking evidence at a small number of sites. Two pits immediately adjacent to a round-house at **The Park**, Guiting Power (Gloucestershire), contained three fragments of clay moulds. One of these features also produced an antler tine on which saw marks were identified. A second sawn piece of antler was found in another nearby pit. A large quantity of bone and antlerworking debris was recovered from in and around the group of features that produced the majority of the casting evidence from **Coton Park**, Rugby (Warwickshire).

Many types of bronze objects would have required handles and these were often undoubtedly made of such materials. Fittings or other components of bone, horn, or antler may also have formed elements of composite objects: four bone discs were used to decorate a terret from Garton Station (East Riding of Yorkshire), for example (Stead 1991a, 47). Shaleworking has also been found on the same sites as non-ferrous-metalworking in a few cases, as at **Glastonbury** (Somerset) and **Hengistbury Head** (Dorset). Evidence for textileworking, in the form of spindle whorls or loomweights, is fairly ubiquitous at Iron Age settlements across much of Britain, both those with metalworking and those without. Overall, there are no indications of any particular recurring associations between metalworking and the working of organic materials or shale, though it is possible that some individual cases where they occur together relate to the production of composite objects.

The use of clay to make crucibles and moulds may suggest some overlap between non-ferrous metallurgy and the manufacture of pottery and fired clay objects, with the sharing of basic skills and knowledge of clay sources. As we have seen, however, in southern Britain the manufacture of crucibles followed a limited range of standardised forms and fabrics that owes nothing to the varied local traditions of domestic pottery (Howard 1983). It may be that the manufacture of refractory ceramics was in the hands of metalworkers rather than potters, as is usually the case ethnographically (*ibid.*). As locales for pottery making are very difficult to identify in the Iron Age, it is unclear whether there was any spatial association between this craft and metalworking. However, one possible link between potting and ironworking is that crushed iron slag was occasionally used as pottery temper in later Iron Age Yorkshire (Roberts *et al.* 2001; Roberts 2005; Dent 2010, 78).

Like the production of pottery, salt making involved the use of hearths, ovens, and clay moulds. Briquetage has been found on some sites with non-ferrous metalworking evidence. We have already noted the association between briquetage, mould fragments, and crucible fragments at **Gilcross** (East Riding of Yorkshire) above; these were found in a pit in layers overlying the burial of a possible adult female. At **Eaton Camp** (Herefordshire), the upper fill of a ditch terminal produced briquetage and two crucible fragments. Salt circulated in ceramic containers, however, so these finds from inland sites indicate patterns of consumption and exchange rather than production. In general, actual salt production sites seem to be specialised to this one activity and separated from settlements; many were probably seasonally used (Kinory 2012).

Conclusion: the social organisation of non-ferrous metalworking in Iron Age Britain and Ireland

Discussion of Iron Age metalworking has been dominated for many years by the evidence from a few sites, notably **Gussage All Saints** (Dorset). This chapter demonstrates that in fact a very large number of sites, particularly from the later part of the period, have yielded metalworking residues, albeit often in small quantities. As such, non-ferrous metalworking is likely to have been a widespread activity undertaken in a variety of social and spatial contexts. The sorts of events that resulted in large dumps of metalworking debris, as at Gussage All Saints, may in fact have been relatively unusual. As we have seen, it has been suggested by a number of authors that crafts such as bronzeworking were carried out under elite patronage. The excavated evidence does not generally bear this out, however. In southern Britain, in particular, the residues of non-ferrous metal casting are not restricted to 'high-status' sites but commonly occur on settlements; these range in form from small single farmsteads to extensive settlement complexes and include open and enclosed sites. There is little to indicate that hillforts were centres of metal production and the largest assemblages of non-ferrous metalworking waste derive from non-hillfort settlements. The suggestion that the production of sheet-bronze objects was focused on hillforts is difficult to sustain: scraps of sheet metal found at such sites can be interpreted in other ways, for example as evidence for the decommissioning of objects such as cauldrons that may have been used in feasts at these locations. As such, there is little to suggest that non-ferrous metalworking and its products were controlled by a political elite.

In Scotland and Ireland, however, the situation may have been different, for there non-ferrous metalworking debris has been recovered primarily from sites that have been identified as political and ceremonial centres such as brochs and hilltop enclosures. In Ireland, the increase in developer-funded excavation over the past 20 years has resulted in the identification of a significant number of Iron Age settlements, many of which have produced evidence for ironworking (Dolan 2012). In contrast to southern Britain, however, these sites have not yielded non-ferrous metalworking remains, suggesting that there were significant regional differences in the organisation of the craft. In Ireland, bronze casting was associated with special places that in some cases were arenas for the exercise of status and power (Schot 2018). Often it was also associated with other crafts. In Scotland, the recovery of metalworking evidence from sites such as brochs and wheelhouses is more difficult to read, however. In many parts of northern and western Scotland, archaeological investigation has focused on these visible monuments and it is not clear whether they represent the 'ordinary' domestic dwellings of the majority of the populace or the apex of a settlement hierarchy. In either case, it should be noted that sites such as hillforts or wheelhouses have often yielded minimal evidence. Across both Britain and Ireland, almost all the evidence relates to the production of copper alloy artefacts and it is possible that the working of precious metals was organised in a different way.

In southern Britain, there is significant variability in the scale of the evidence from individual sites. There is little evidence of Early Iron Age date, and most of this is small-scale and scattered. Some of the larger assemblages of this date formed components of 'special' pit deposits and are unlikely to indicate the location of the craft itself. In the later Iron Age there is a spectrum of evidence from sites that yielded very small quantities of non-ferrous metalworking debris – usually just a few crucible sherds – to those that have produced more substantial assemblages including mould fragments. It should be noted that the vast majority of sites of this date fall into the former category, while sites that have

yielded large quantities of metalworking debris are highly unusual. This suggests that there may have been a distinction between different types of metalworking, for example, 'ordinary' low-level production and repair and 'special' events involving large-scale production of sets of equine equipment. It should be noted that some small assemblages include mould fragments; these are often also for equine equipment, indicating that there was no simple correlation between the scale or organisation of production and the type or sophistication of the objects produced. In general, however, Iron Age non-ferrous metalworking assemblages are small, suggesting that casting copper alloy objects was an intermittent activity at many settlements and hillforts. This could support the argument for itinerant smiths who travelled from one site to another to carry out repairs or produce new objects for their occupants. Alternatively, it could suggest that most metalworking was small-scale, irregular, and undertaken by craftworkers who were not full-time specialists. In the latter instance, these individuals are likely to have been primarily occupied in other activities, carrying out occasional repairs, replacing components of existing objects, or casting simple objects, probably close to where they lived. On the other hand, the relative paucity of metalworking debris may suggest that it was not treated and disposed of in a way that is archaeologically visible. This does, however, beg the question of why some exceptionally large assemblages of metalworking debris survive.

For the small number of sites with larger assemblages, it can often be difficult to assess whether these are the result of repeated acts of production over a long period of time or single large-scale events. As we have seen, the material from pit 209 at **Gussage All Saints** (Dorset) is more suggestive of the latter, although this is not the only non-ferrous metalworking evidence from the site; here, high-quality equine equipment was made in large quantities over a short period of time. It is possible that resident craftworkers produced these items when resources were available or demand was sufficient. Alternatively, where metalworking was a sporadic activity that occurred on a significant scale, it may have been carried out by skilled craftspeople who visited the site for the duration of a specific casting event. The innate theatricality of such an occasion may have been a significant component of the production of such special objects and the mass deposition of the residues of this event may have been one way in which value came to be ascribed to the metal objects themselves.

The scattered nature of the non-ferrous metalworking evidence at most sites means it is rarely possible to identify 'workshops', and structures with clear metalworking functions are scarce. However, magnetic susceptibility and geochemical analysis of buildings yielding unusually large amounts of metalworking evidence at **Maiden Castle** (Dorset), **Billown Quarry** (Isle of Man), and **Mine Howe** (Orkney) indicate *in situ* copper alloy and ironworking. The presence of such workshops suggests that metalworking may have been carried out on a frequent if not a full-time basis at these sites, possibly by resident metalworkers. It is important to note the very different character of these three sites. Hillforts have been interpreted on the one hand as centres of elite authority and on the other as focal places where community identity was reasserted through programmes of building and ceremony. The intensity of occupation at Maiden Castle is suggestive of permanent occupation, but whatever the role of the site, metal objects are likely to have been central to the construction of both personal and group identities at this location. The site at Billown Quarry, on the other hand, appears to have been a small open settlement, while the workshop at Mine Howe was located just next to an unusual subterranean ritual space.

As noted earlier in this chapter, these are not the only sites where non-ferrous metalworking debris was associated with buildings. Fragments of crucibles and moulds are frequently recovered from contexts in and around round-houses, albeit usually in much smaller quantities. Of course, metalworking may not have actually taken place within these buildings: some of these finds may have been deposited in the context of event-marking rites of foundation or abandonment, as suggested in Chapter 4 for metalworking debris from Middle and Late Bronze Age buildings. At other sites, metalworking residues come from irregular or incomplete gullies that may relate to other kinds of structures such as windbreaks or may have defined unroofed working areas.

The recovery of metalworking residues from the settlement core and in contexts associated with other 'domestic' activities challenges the argument that this activity was restricted to liminal locations (cf. Hingley 1997; 1999; Giles & Parker Pearson 1999). Although there is no indication that the location of non-ferrous metalworking was consistently separated from the domestic sphere, however, there may still have been particular occasions and circumstances in which it was considered appropriate to do this. The deposition of metalworking tools and residues in settlement enclosure ditches and hillfort ramparts as well as in more unusual locations such as earlier monuments, wet places, and subterranean ritual spaces hints that in some contexts, at least, the transformative power of metalworking gave it particular symbolic significance. Liminal spaces may have been viewed as appropriate locations for this craft; alternatively, the residues of metalworking may have been viewed as dangerous and powerful materials that needed to be deposited away from other activities. This may be why, at some Scottish sites, non-ferrous metalworking appears to be associated with the abandonment or post-abandonment phases. Nonetheless, we must not push the evidence too far: we have already noted, for example, that excavations at hillforts have tended to focus on their defences. So too, Iron Age depositional practices involved placing objects of many kinds in ditches, and it is therefore difficult to clearly demonstrate that metalworking remains were treated differently to other classes of artefact.

On some settlements in southern Britain, there seems to have been an increasing impetus to physically define spaces for casting activity in the last two centuries BC, as at **Gravelly Guy** (Oxfordshire). The creation of defined workspaces for metalworking may indicate an increase in the scale or intensity of this activity, an attempt to control metalworkers' activities, or to restrict access to their knowledge, skills, and products. As we have seen, however, this trend is far from universal: metalworking evidence at Late Iron Age focal sites is often widely dispersed, for example. Even where metalworking took place inside specific buildings or enclosures, this need not indicate that smiths worked in secret: metalworking evidence was found both inside and outside the 'workshop' at Billown Quarry (Isle of Man), suggesting that some parts of the process may have taken place outside of this building or that the smith moved in and out of the round-house to dispose of metalworking debris; in either case, the activity was not entirely invisible.

Whatever the case, it is evident that the presence of casting waste and smithing tools need not directly indicate the location of non-ferrous metalworking, for processes of selective deposition have shaped the character of the archaeological evidence. Smithing tools such as tongs, pokers, and files are most commonly recovered from hillforts, often as a component of hoards of iron objects from the ditches or entrances to these sites; they are also found in watery sites and graves. Although many different types of object were made using non-ferrous metals in the Iron Age, moulds for casting most of these are rare or entirely unknown. In contrast, investment moulds for the production of horse-gear and vehicle fittings are relatively common, but only in southern Britain, and most of these come from large deposits that may represent the residues of particular casting events. It is possible that the symbolic significance of the horse was such that the production of associated items may have been a special occasion, possibly witnessed by the wider community; the residues of such events may have been imbued with particular potency, and it may have been important to dispose of these in a careful and even ritualised manner. As we have seen, there is little to indicate that the production of such items took place only on high-status sites, and this raises interesting questions regarding ownership of these artefacts.

The paucity of evidence for the production of gold and silver artefacts is notable, given the significant number of sites that have yielded bronzeworking residues. Only 16 sites have yielded direct evidence for the working of precious metals, such as the silver ingots from **Hallaton** (Leicestershire) or the traces of gold identified on a crucible from **Elms Farm**, Heybridge (Essex). Most are focal sites or possible shrines of Late Iron Age date, and the majority are in south-east England. Much of the evidence for precious metalworking from Late Iron Age south-east England is associated with the production of coinage and this is rarely found together with debris from the casting of copper alloy objects, suggesting that these two forms of metalworking were

organised in different ways. Other than coins, few artefacts of silver are known and some of these are imports. Talbot's recent analysis of Icenian coins suggests that there may have been several million in circulation in East Anglia alone (2017); this hints at production on a large scale, although evidence for silverworking is sparse. It is thought that coin pellet moulds were used to produce blanks of silver and gold, though only a small proportion have been subject to scientific analysis; if they acted as miniature crucibles, with metal weighed into each indentation in granular or powder form (Gebhard *et al.* 1995; de Jersey 2009; Bucher *et al.* 2011), then the casting of such objects may have resulted in little waste other than the pellet mould fragments themselves. Gold was, of course, used for other types of objects, notably personal ornaments such as torcs. Although some may be continental imports, the distribution and form of many torcs, as well as the techniques employed to make them, suggests local manufacture (Jope 2000; Machling & Williamson 2018). It is intriguing that no evidence of the production of such artefacts can be identified although gold ornaments are of course rare. As we have seen in Chapter 2, the working of precious metals is intrinsically less likely to leave detectable traces than the working of copper and other base metals. Nonetheless, it is also possible that the organisation of production of gold ornaments was different to that of other high-status metal artefacts, or that the residues of the craft were not selected for deposition.

Finally, we need to address the question of the identity of the smith. In general, there is little to suggest that the activities of smiths were controlled. Although some may have been residents of the sites described in this chapter, others may have been visitors for the duration of short-term metalworking events. Crucibles were made from locally available clays and tempers but there was significant standardisation in form and fabric across southern Britain and it is therefore difficult to assess just how mobile Iron Age smiths might have been. The close spatial and contextual associations between fragments of moulds and crucibles and finds such as hammerscale and smithing hearth bottoms suggests that far from being quite separate crafts, iron and non-ferrous metalworking shared much in common. It is probable that bronze and iron smiths often worked together or were one and the same. So too, the same individuals may have been skilled in the working of other materials such as glass. This calls into question modern, western ways of categorising different materials. The scale of the non-ferrous metalworking evidence rarely suggests full-time craft production although, if the same craftworkers made both bronze and iron artefacts, it is possible that this required full-time work; the casting of items such as sword hilts, mirrors, or terrets required very significant skill.

The appearance of possible smiths' graves in the Late Iron Age is interesting, suggesting that metalworkers may have been identified as a discrete category of person during this period. However, smithing tools are not the only grave goods in these contexts, suggesting that metalworking was only one facet of the identity of the deceased; indeed, the presence of weapons in some burials may suggest that smithing was associated with status and power. On the other hand, the presence of smithing tools need not indicate that the deceased was a smith and it may have been their symbolic potency and transformative potential that rendered them suitable for inclusion in the grave. Notwithstanding this point, it is interesting to note that burials containing iron smithing tools are all those of males or possible males, although the bodies of both men and women were associated with casting debris. Intriguingly it was the body of a woman that was deposited in the workshop at **Mine Howe** (Orkney). It is, of course, not known if she was a metalworker although, as noted above, she wore copper alloy rings on her toes.

6

Conclusion: the social context of non-ferrous metalworking in later prehistoric Britain and Ireland

This volume has attempted to understand the social organisation of non-ferrous metalworking in Bronze Age and Iron Age Britain and Ireland. A detailed analysis of the spatial and depositional context of metalworking tools and residues has allowed us to re-examine existing models, many of which have been based on ethnographic parallels supported by a limited selection of archaeological examples. There are significant changes to the character of the evidence over these periods but there are also elements of commonality. In this chapter we will attempt to address the series of research questions set out in the introduction to the volume.

The location of non-ferrous metalworking

This project has brought together the evidence for non-ferrous metalworking from excavated sites, including the very large number of sites investigated in the context of developer-funded work over the past 25 years. Our research indicates that evidence for non-ferrous metalworking is relatively widespread during the later Bronze Age and Iron Age, although few excavated sites of Chalcolithic or Early Bronze Age date have yielded evidence for the

craft. Over 400 excavated sites have produced metalworking residues, the majority of which date to the Late Bronze Age and later Iron Age. This calls into question the idea that knowledge of metalworking was restricted, particularly for these periods. Previous interpretations of later prehistoric metalworking have tended to focus on a small number of well-known sites, such as **Springfield Lyons** (Essex) and **Gussage All Saints** (Dorset). The perceived rarity of the evidence and the significant size of the assemblages from these sites has led many authors to argue that metalworking was a specialist activity taking place at only a handful of select sites, but our study here calls this into question. Sites with small quantities of evidence have often been neglected in existing discussions of prehistoric metalworking because of the expectation that distinct workshops should be present. As shown in this volume, non-ferrous metalworking evidence is commonly recovered from excavated sites of Bronze Age and Iron Age date, even though buildings that can be identified as workshops are extremely rare. The large number of sites in south-east England reflects the frequency of developer-funded excavation in this area. Other regions, such as Ireland, have also seen a dramatic upsurge in excavation since the 1990s. Yet, this has not always resulted in a significant increase in evidence for non-ferrous metalworking. This suggests that the distribution of metalworking residues from excavated sites is not solely due to recovery bias but reflects regional differences in the organisation of this craft.

The presence of metalworking tools and residues need not, of course, indicate *in situ* metalworking activity. We have noted, for example, that Early Bronze Age stone moulds and Late Iron Age coin dies are often single finds recovered at a distance from other contemporary sites. As we shall discuss below, such finds may be the result of deliberate and selective deposition and are unlikely to signal the location of metalworking itself. The same argument can be made for many of the finds from excavated sites, such as the spearhead mould from the gully of a round-house at **Kilsharvan** (Co. Meath), or the poker found beneath a cobbled floor behind the rampart at **Madmarston Camp** (Oxfordshire); we have suggested that such items may have been deliberately deposited to mark important locations in space or significant points in the lifecycle of the site such as foundation or abandonment. Yet, clay moulds and crucibles are friable, and fragments of casting waste are often small, and in many cases the working assumption can be made that metalworking took place elsewhere on the sites where such items found, even if not always at the location of deposition itself. As previous chapters demonstrate, although a significant proportion of the evidence may result from practices of selective deposition rather than directly indicating where the craft was carried out, there are nonetheless significant inferences that can be drawn from these finds regarding the organisation and significance of non-ferrous metalworking.

There are interesting patterns in the types of sites at which metalworking residues have been found. In Ireland, during both the Late Bronze Age and later Iron Age, metalworking evidence is most frequently recovered from sites that have been interpreted as political and ceremonial centres, such as hillforts, crannógs, and 'royal' sites – locations that later medieval texts and oral traditions identify as the inauguration sites of early medieval kings. It is problematic, however, to impose models derived from later accounts (that

often have their own political agendas) onto much earlier periods and some have argued that sites such as hillforts might be better interpreted as community foci rather than seats of political power (Hill 1995b; Hamilton & Manley 2001; Sharples 2010). During the later Iron Age in Atlantic Scotland, locations such brochs and wheelhouses have produced metalworking evidence, but because relatively few archaeological excavations have been carried out in this region in comparison to other areas, it remains unclear whether these should be interpreted as 'normal' or high-status settlements.

In contrast, in southern England, metalworking evidence is widely dispersed across the settled landscape and is not restricted to particular categories of site. Although metalworking residues have been recovered from sites such as Late Bronze Age ringworks, which have sometimes been interpreted as local political centres, they are also often found on settlements that, in other ways, look unexceptional. A significant proportion of ordinary settlements have produced evidence for small-scale metalworking activities in the form of occasional mould or crucible fragments. Particularly large deposits of metalworking debris (including mould fragments for the casting of 'high-status' objects such as Late Bronze Age swords and later Iron Age horse gear) are not restricted to 'special' sites such as middens or hillforts and have been found in a variety of settlement contexts ranging from small open farmsteads of Late Bronze Age date to more extensive later Iron Age settlement complexes. Iron Age hillforts may have been foci for the ritual decommissioning and deposition of metalwork but there is little to suggest that the scale or character of metalworking activities at these sites differed from those at ordinary settlements. Substantial deposits of Late Bronze Age sword mould fragments have also been found in isolated pits at a distance from contemporary sites, suggesting that metalworking was not spatially confined as might be expected if this activity was centrally controlled.

Although most evidence comes from settlements of one sort or another, both for the Bronze Age and the Iron Age, metalworking debris has occasionally been found at sites of possible ritual significance. This includes earlier monuments: Middle Bronze Age mould fragments have been found at three wedge tombs of Chalcolithic date in Ireland, for example. A small number of caves have produced metalworking evidence of Late Bronze Age and Iron Age date. In the Late Iron Age, metalworking residues have been found at sites that have been interpreted as possible shrines, such as **Hallaton** (Leicestershire); here, metal objects may have been made specifically for votive deposition. Cremation burials are sometimes found on sites that have produced metalworking evidence, but rarely from the same (or even closely-linked) contexts. Although both can be viewed as heat-mediated transformative processes, no strong links between metalworking and the deposition of human remains can be discerned, in contrast to Bronze Age Scandinavia (Goldhahn 2007); we will discuss the occasional inclusion of metalworking tools as grave goods below.

Consideration of the intra-site distribution of metalworking evidence is highly informative and suggests a degree of variability in where the craft was carried out. Metalworking residues have frequently been found in and around later Bronze Age and Iron Age round-houses that are, in other respects, identical to contemporary domestic dwellings, often in close association with evidence for domestic activities of various sorts; if metalworking was carried out within the household, this has interesting implications for the transmission of knowledge. As suggested above, however, these finds need not indicate *in situ* metalworking, although geochemical and magnetic susceptibility analysis of the floor layers from a small number of round-houses, for example at **Tremough** (Cornwall) and **Maiden Castle** (Dorset), indicate that in some cases these buildings were the venue for metalworking activities. Only occasionally do these structures differ from other contemporary round-houses: we have seen, for example, that the round-house at **Billown Quarry** (Isle of Man) faced north-west and we have discussed possible reasons for this in the previous chapter. At many larger sites metalworking evidence is quite dispersed: this is the case, for example, at putative Late Iron Age 'tribal capitals' such as **Verlamion** (Hertfordshire), suggesting that metalworking was a relatively decentralised activity, with little evident concern to control the craft through spatial regulation. Elsewhere, particular areas may have been set aside for metalworking, for example at **Coton Park**, Rugby (Warwickshire), where a large quantity of mould and crucible fragments were found in and around a penannular gully and neighbouring rectilinear enclosure just east of the main group of round-houses. On some settlements, for example **Gravelly Guy**, Stanton Harcourt (Oxfordshire), metalworking activities appear to have become confined to a particular part of the site during the Late Iron Age, perhaps implying increasing specialisation or greater control of the craft over time.

The organisation of production

Technical analysis of non-ferrous metal objects has revealed the extraordinary levels of skill required to produce certain Bronze and Iron Age metal objects (eg, Ó Faoláin & Northover 1998; Armbruster 2000; Stead 2006; Gerloff 2010; Uckelmann 2012; Machling & Williamson 2018). Kuijpers' detailed examination of the techniques employed to produce Early Bronze Age axes in central Europe has demonstrated that even artefacts that look very similar can be shown to have been made by people with different levels of technical proficiency (2017; 2018), and he argues that it should be possible to distinguish the products of amateurs, common craftspeople, master crafters, and virtuosos. He has also demonstrated through close technical examination that people of varying levels of skill may have been involved at different stages in the production of individual artefacts (see also Nørgaard 2014; 2018). As we have seen in Chapter 1, it has long been suggested that the organisation of production may have differed for different types of object, with artefacts that demonstrate the greatest degree of skill, such as the gold gorgets of the Irish Late Bronze Age or the composite swords of Middle Iron Age Yorkshire, being produced by full-time specialists under elite patronage. In contrast, simpler items such as axes or knives might have been made by part-time specialists who for most of the year were engaged in farming and other subsistence activities alongside other members of their communities (eg, Rowlands 1976; Northover 1982b; Gibson 1996; Garrow & Gosden 2012, 276).

With a few possible exceptions, such as the extraordinarily large assemblage of metal-working evidence from the hillfort at **Rathgall** (Co. Wicklow), there is little evidence for elite control of production. As described above, metalworking residues have been recovered from a wide variety of settlement contexts in both the later Bronze Age and the Iron Age. In the Late Bronze Age moulds for the production of high-status and finely crafted weaponry such as swords have been recovered from the same sites as moulds for objects that could be made more easily, such as axes, suggesting that the same craftspeople were sometimes involved in casting different types of artefact. This is supported by metallurgical analysis demonstrating that similar alloy recipes were used for a wide range of objects during this period (Bray 2016). So too, Early and Middle Bronze Age stone moulds often include matrices for different artefact types.

Nonetheless, some key differences in the organisation of production can be discerned. Many settlements have yielded just a few crucible or mould fragments. These may have been the places where Kuijpers' 'common craftspeople' worked, repairing objects or making simpler items, although it should be noted that some of the smallest assemblages include moulds for elaborate objects such as later Bronze Age swords, the use of which would have required a significant degree of technical skill. In contrast, as we have seen above, a smaller number of sites have yielded substantial deposits of mould debris from a single feature or group of features. These are predominantly for the production of 'high-status' artefacts such as swords (in the Late Bronze Age) and horse gear and vehicle fittings (in the later Iron Age). This hints at two different modes of production although, in practice, these may have formed two ends of a spectrum of variation in the organisation of metalworking. On the one hand, small-scale 'everyday' metalworking appears to have often occurred within a domestic context. The relatively dispersed distribution of finds from some sites may suggest a low level of metalworking over a prolonged period of time, in many instances including the manufacture of both utilitarian and 'high-status' artefacts. In these cases, such smiths are likely to have been members of these local communities. The lack of evidence for centralised control and the recovery of metalworking residues from round-houses that have also yielded finds of a domestic character suggest that the craft was not usually undertaken on a full-time basis.

In contrast, there are a small number of sites with evidence for more intensive episodes of production. The scale and frequency of this latter mode of production deserves consideration. Although they include large numbers of mould fragments, many of the most substantial assemblages appear to result from the casting of a relatively small number of artefacts. The majority of the clay mould fragments from the two most productive (and neighbouring) features at **Holborough Quarry**, Snodland (Kent), for example, were from two near-complete sword moulds. Such deposits may therefore represent the residues of single casting events, or a small number of such events. Even the enormous assemblage of mould fragments from **Gussage All Saints** (Dorset) appears to represent just one episode of metalworking activity, although in this case as many as 50 sets of horse gear and vehicle fittings may have been made. What we may be seeing at such sites is not long-term or 'industrial' production, but the residues of socially significant and highly theatrical short-term events, perhaps occasions at which people from the wider region assembled to produce (or witness the production of) important classes of artefact. It is clear that the metalworkers involved were highly skilled, yet the craft does not appear to have been undertaken on a full-time basis at these locations. The possible infrequency of such events hints that smiths may not always have been resident at the sites in question but may have travelled from a distance for specific casting events. This need not imply the existence of itinerant smiths; instead, there may have been small numbers of master craftsmen within each region who could visit neighbours, kinsfolk, or political allies when their skills were required. Importantly, there is little to suggest that such significant casting events took place solely or even predominantly at 'high-status' sites. At sites such as Gussage All Saints, non-ferrous metalworking residues have been recovered in small quantities from other features, suggesting that residents may also have carried out repairs or casting of simpler items on a small scale over a more extended period.

Selective deposition

Of course, it is possible that the deposition of mould fragments for the casting of swords or horse gear does not indicate different modes of production but differences in depositional practice. Practices of deliberate selection are clearly in evidence. In the Early Bronze Age, for example, smithing tools have mostly been found in burials, while stone moulds are generally found as off-site single finds. In the late Early Bronze Age and Middle Bronze Age, a number of hoards of stone moulds have been documented; hoards of metal objects are often thought to be votive deposits and it is possible to interpret stone mould hoards in a similar way. During the Late Bronze Age, copper alloy waste and metalworking tools have predominantly been recovered from bronze hoards while clay mould fragments were deposited on settlements: the majority of the latter were for weapons rather than tools or ornaments, suggesting that these may have been chosen for deposition. Crucibles dominate the Iron Age evidence, and moulds for objects other than horse gear and vehicle fittings are very rare. The large deposits of clay mould fragments for horse gear and vehicle fittings discussed above are, moreover, a particular feature of the southern British record, although the finished objects occur elsewhere (eg, Raftery 1983). The dominance of moulds for equine equipment contrasts with the greater diversity of objects in the metalwork record in this region. Moulds for other relatively common artefact types such as brooches and bracelets are rare or unknown, suggesting patterns of deliberate selection. Relatively few moulds are known from northern Britain; here, matrices for pins and other small ornaments are more common than moulds for equine equipment. Unlike crucibles, which are commonly recovered from settlements, Iron Age smithing tools are more common on hillforts, and are occasionally found at ritual sites such the timber causeway at **Fiskerton** (Lincolnshire), or in graves.

Together, this suggests that finds such as crucible and mould fragments cannot be interpreted as incidental refuse – the by-product of an activity that was simply disposed of close to where the craft itself was carried out. Instead, the meanings and values ascribed to particular categories of evidence – clay moulds versus stone moulds, for example – may have governed how and where such items entered the archaeological record. Certainly, evidence for culturally regulated processes of selection are evident in the choice of materials

used to make different moulds. Objects such as swords were only produced using clay moulds but stone, clay, and bronze were all employed to make moulds for axes. This cannot be explained solely by the differing technical properties of mould materials, for the equally lengthy blades of Middle Bronze Age rapiers were cast in stone moulds. We have already suggested that some of the finds discussed in previous chapters may have been deliberately deposited: the stone moulds from the floor of the Middle Bronze Age round-house at **Tremough** (Cornwall) or the clay mould fragments found with other unusual items in the upper fills of Bronze Age waterholes may represent the residues of abandonment rituals, for example. Bronze Age hoards are widely interpreted as votive deposits and the inclusion of ingots and fragments of copper alloy waste in such assemblages suggests that such materials were not valued solely in economic terms but were carefully selected for their particular symbolic connotations. So, too, the deposition of Iron Age metalworking tools in the ditches of hillforts may have acted to mark out socially significant boundaries. This is not to say, however, that metalworking took place at such locations.

The implications of these points for the large deposits of moulds for weapons, horse gear, and vehicle fittings discussed above are significant. They suggest that these items may have been deliberately selected because of the particular social or cultural meanings ascribed to them. Items such as Late Bronze Age swords and Middle Iron Age horse gear are frequently viewed as socially significant objects. This is evident not only from the skill required to produce them. Swords, for example, are usually found as components of votive deposits in rivers (eg, Becker 2013). Horse gear and vehicle fittings were deposited in bogs and rivers, in dryland hoards, in pit deposits on settlements and hillforts, and as grave goods in some of the wealthiest Iron Age burials (eg, Lewis 2015). Horse gear and vehicle fittings were also often decorated with the characteristic motifs of La Tène art, and this may have imbued them with supernatural potency (cf. Giles & Joy 2007; Garrow & Gosden 2012). The act of making such powerful objects may have been imbued with ritual and it is possible that the residues of the production process had to be treated in special ways. If, as suggested above, communities may have come together to watch and marvel at the skill involved in casting such items, it is possible that the breakage and subsequent deposition of the moulds may also have been a dramatic and ritualised act, for it was the act of destruction that allowed the gleaming metal to emerge; the choice of clay for the production of sword moulds may have enhanced the performative aspect of this stage of production.

The meaning of metalworking

The incorporation of metalworking tools and debris into 'special' deposits of various sorts and the deliberate deposition of the residues of specific production events suggests that metalworking may sometimes itself have been a symbolically charged or ritualised activity. However, not all deposits of metalworking residues can be linked so directly to particular casting events and it is possible that other finds speak more of the social and cultural meanings ascribed to casting and smithing than of specific metalworking episodes. The selective and deliberate deposition of metalworking residues in contexts ranging from hoards to round-houses suggests that items such as mould fragments and dribbles of copper alloy waste were incorporated into particular depositional contexts because of their ability to reference significant cultural values. We have discussed current models of Iron Age ironworking in previous chapters and suggested that the argument that metalworking took place in liminal contexts does not entirely fit the evidence for the production of non-ferrous metal objects. The deposition of mould and crucible fragments in and around round-houses and in pits and other features scattered across Bronze Age and Iron Age settlements suggests that the production of non-ferrous metalwork often took place alongside other domestic activities. Of course, this need not indicate that metalworking was viewed solely as a practical activity: the evidence presented in this volume suggests that practical and spiritual concerns were interlinked in the production of non-ferrous metalwork and the deposition of its tools and residues.

Yet, it is evident that not all metalworking debris was deposited in or around round-houses. In Chapters 4 and 5 we have noted finds from the enclosure ditches surrounding settlements and from close to the entrances to these sites. Small numbers of finds have been recovered from earlier monuments (locations where encounters with the ancestors or the otherworld may have been possible), as well as field boundaries, caves, and watery places of various sorts. What these locations have in common is their liminal quality: they are places between worlds or between different social and political domains. It is possible that metalworking debris was deposited in these contexts for its ability to conjure concepts of social and material transformation. Indeed, even finds from the settlement core – for example mould fragments from house floors or waterholes – may have been deliberate deposits made to mark significant points in the lifecycle of the settlement such as the construction or abandonment of a round-house. These, too, were moments of transformation, points in time (rather than space) between different social conditions.

This interpretation does have its short-comings, however. First, enclosure ditches are often the largest features on settlements and collect the greatest quantities of material culture of all kinds. Ditches were, moreover, foci for deposition in general, and things ranging from complete pots to loomweights and animal remains are recovered from such contexts. Against such a background, it is unclear whether it was their particular symbolic properties that rendered it appropriate to deposit metalworking residues in these locations, or whether the meanings ascribed to the margins of the settlement meant that enclosure ditches were suitable receptacles for 'refuse' of any sort. This is countered, perhaps, by the clear evidence for selectivity in what entered the archaeological record and it is no surprise that other materials associated with ideas of transformation (notably human remains) are also found in contexts such as enclosure ditches, caves, and watery places. Yet, the selectivity of the depositional process also calls into question generalised interpretations that link metalworking with ideas of liminality and transformation. In the Bronze Age, for example, there are differences in the treatment of things such as stone and ceramic moulds, or smithing tools and crucibles, suggesting that the different elements of the metalworking process may have evoked different meanings and values. Hence, the kinds of metalworking residues that could be deposited in a hoard were not the same as those chosen to mark the abandonment of a round-house. Partly, this may be explained by the meanings of the different artefacts produced (swords versus axes, for example) or the different materials from which metalworking equipment was made (stone, clay, and metal), but activities such as casting and smithing may also have had different connotations for they perform different functions in relation to the form of the finished artefact. In the Iron Age, smithing tools were treated differently to other metalworking residues at the end of their use-lives, although processes of selection relating to the material character of the remains are less evident (refractory ceramics and copper alloy waste were frequently deposited together, for example). These observations cast doubt on previous arguments which posit a single generalising model for the significance of prehistoric metalworking or for the role of the prehistoric smith.

Who were prehistoric smiths?

This is not to say, of course, that different people were involved in casting and smithing; as we have seen, the tools and residues of both processes are sometimes found together, for example in scrap hoards. The paucity of smelting evidence, however, and the location of the few known smelting sites close to contemporary mines, suggests that the primary processing of metal ores is likely to have been carried out by mining communities at a distance (in spatial, temporal, and social terms) from those who undertook the later stages of casting and smithing.

In general, the evidence suggests that smiths were members of the communities for which they produced metal objects: the copious evidence of metalworking from settlements and especially from round-houses can be read in this way, for example. Early Bronze Age one-piece moulds were often large and heavy and were usually made of local stone, suggesting that their users are unlikely to have moved far, although the smaller stone and bronze moulds of the Late Bronze Age would have been more portable. As we have seen, the clays and tempering materials employed for ceramic moulds and crucibles suggest intimate knowledge of local landscapes and resources.

However, the regionality evident in Iron Age pottery forms and fabrics is not visible in contemporary clay moulds and crucibles, suggesting that while refractory production drew on local ceramic traditions it was probably not carried out by the same individuals. To date, it has not been possible to identify whether different 'recipes' for the production of bronze were employed on different settlements, partly because of the prevalence of recycling, particularly during the Late Bronze Age, which resulted in the production of bronze objects with relatively homogeneous chemical compositions, and partly because the evidence from most settlements takes the form of refractory ceramics rather than copper alloy waste.

Detailed appraisal of the evidence therefore makes it difficult to uphold Childe's model of the itinerant metalworker. Although some objects, such as Late Bronze Age stone moulds, appear to have travelled a considerable distance, this may have been via exchange rather than the movement of smiths: certainly, the treatment and deposition of such objects at the end of their lives suggests they were socially significant and it is possible that they may sometimes have been viewed as suitable items for circulation in gift exchange networks. Nonetheless, the degree of skill and the level of technological innovation required for the production of some of the most complex artefacts suggests forms of technological transmission that are likely to have involved some degree of mobility: craftspeople may have had to travel to learn the most specialised techniques, for example. Yet, there is increasing evidence that particular individuals sometimes moved considerable distances in their lifetimes (eg, McKinley *et al.* 2014; Parker Pearson *et al.* 2019; cf. Hamilton *et al.* 2019) and mobility at a local and regional scale may have been relatively common. The idea that later prehistoric settlements should be viewed as isolated islands whose social makeup was unchanging is overly simplistic; skills and knowledge are likely to have flowed via a variety of social transactions between communities that involved mobility over a range of scales. In this context, it is possible that the large deposits of moulds for Late Bronze Age swords or Iron Age horse gear may represent the residues of events where people, some of whom had specialist knowledge, travelled over some distance to take part in the production of special objects. Interestingly, although the majority of Bronze Age and Iron Age mould fragments are for casting objects such as swords and terrets that required a high level of skill, there is extremely little excavated evidence for the production of the most technically sophisticated items such as Late Bronze Age sheet metal objects or Late Iron Age gold torcs. As previously noted, however, sheet working leaves little or no recognisable waste while the greater volatility of gold means that it is less likely to leave detectable traces on moulds and crucibles than copper.

As already discussed, it is extremely difficult to identify excavated evidence for full-time metalworking despite the evident technical proficiency required to make certain types of object: the evidence is mostly small-scale and dispersed or indicative of single intensive episodes of production. Very few possible workshops have been identified; examples include the buildings at **Tremough** (Cornwall), **Billown Quarry** (Isle of Man), and **Mine Howe** (Orkney). It should be noted here, however, that 'workshop' is a problematic term that means different things to different people: here, it is employed simply to indicate a building in which we can be confident that casting was carried out. In the case of Tremough at least, other domestic activities also appear to have taken place in the building, so the evidence from this site cannot be taken to indicate a 'workshop industry' where a significant portion of the producer's income is derived from their craft, and household and workshop are spatially distinct (Peacock 1981; van der Leeuw 1984; Costin 1991). The small number of possible workshops identified to date hints that there may have been significant regional differences in the organisation of production, a point to which we will return below.

However, even if we assume that specialist metalworkers were full-time, whether based at permanent workshops or moving from site to site for the duration of particular casting events, there is little to indicate that they were under the patronage of elites: sites such as Tremough and **Gussage All Saints** (Dorset) look little different to other contemporary settlements. This suggests that the circulation of their products did not only take place among an elite, a point reinforced by the discovery of a large number of bronze objects including tools, weapons, and ornaments at the extraordinarily well-preserved Late Bronze Age settlement at Must Farm (Cambridgeshire) (Knight *et al.* 2019); bronze artefacts may have been more common than we often assume. As suggested by Spielmann (2002), the large-scale production of socially valued artefacts may have been undertaken to meet widely held social and ritual obligations rather than to bolster the status of an elite minority. As we have seen, however, the very rare evidence for the working of precious metals has predominantly been recovered from hillforts and from Late Iron Age focal sites, hinting that this craft may have been organised in a different way to the production of copper alloy artefacts, and may have been subject to greater social control. Although evidence for coin production within individual Late Iron Age oppida is often dispersed, calling into question the idea that these sites were the location of tightly controlled mints, it is widely accepted that there was a link between coin production and political authority in certain regions at least. However, it is not clear whether this was exercised through control of the metal supply, coin minting, or coin distribution and use.

We have already noted the close spatial and contextual links between bronze and ironworking at many of the Iron Age sites examined for this project, and the same hearths were sometimes used for both activities. This suggests that bronze smiths and iron smiths could be one and the same people. Although bronze artefacts were cast in moulds while iron objects were not, the production of both requires pyrotechnical and smithing skills. The occurrence of clay refractory fragments alongside hammerscale from the production of iron objects suggests that the same individuals had knowledge of both casting and smithing; this has implications too for the organisation of non-ferrous metalworking. The few sites with evidence for glassworking have also very often produced non-ferrous metalworking debris: the 'workshop' area at **Rathgall** (Co. Wicklow), for example, yielded the largest collection of glass beads in Britain or Ireland alongside the most extensive assemblage of metalworking evidence. As noted in Chapter 5, however, the production of composite objects combining bronze with other materials such as glass, bone or iron could indicate that bronze smiths were skilled in the working of other materials. Alternatively, it may suggest that those for whom these objects were made were able to bring together and display the expertise of different craftworkers who collaborated closely, for example in carefully pushing copper alloy rivets through bulbs of glass to secure them to bronze objects. Of course, it is far from clear how specialists were defined at this time: they may have been distinguished by the materials they worked, the skills they employed, or in other ways that remain difficult for us to elucidate.

Objects such as Early Bronze Age stone moulds were relatively easy to make, and the evidence for the gradual addition of matrices for different artefacts over the course of the lifespan of such items suggests that metalworkers probably often produced, maintained, and modified their own equipment. Yet, in later periods, the recovery of non-ferrous metalworking debris from a significant number of settlement contexts reminds us that this craft did not take place in a vacuum and involved the efforts of more than just a lone smith. As we have seen, some Bronze Age crucibles were very large and would have been difficult to manipulate by a single individual if full. The variety of resources required – clay, wood, wax, water, and so on – suggests that metalworking was a community enterprise that involved the productive activities of a significant number of people. So too those involved in short-term but intensive casting events such as the production of multiple sets of horse harnesses at **Gussage All Saints** (Dorset) required others to provide them with food and drink. Hence, although smiths may have been drawn from particular age or gender groups, the involvement of members of the wider community in the process was also important. Detribalised itinerant smiths, as envisaged by Childe, would doubtless have found it difficult to establish and maintain the social networks required to resource the craft.

The identification of possible smiths' graves may also cast light on the identities of metalworkers. Although a number of potential examples can be identified in the Early Bronze Age, in fact analysis of the artefacts identified as metalworking tools has very rarely yielded actual traces of metal. We have argued also that the inclusion of metalworking tools may not indicate that the individual was a smith and that instead such items may have referenced idealised identities or significant

cultural values and social processes, such as the forging of relationships or the transformation of the living to the dead. Although where they have been sexed, such burials tend to be male, that is not universally the case. Likewise, some graves have yielded other high-status artefacts, but others have yielded few or no other grave goods. Certainly, the rarity and variability of possible smiths' graves suggests that metalworkers were not a distinct social category. The same may apply to the graves with metalworking tools dating to the later Iron Age.

The interpretation of the identity of the Early Bronze Age individual buried at **Upton Lovell** (Wiltshire) as a 'metalworker-shaman' has potential implications for the social status of prehistoric smiths. It has often been argued that smiths were esteemed for their knowledge of the visually striking and apparently magical process of metalworking. The decoration of metal objects – an act that may have imbued them with agency – doubtless also elicited admiration for those who had these skills. In the later Bronze Age and Iron Age the selective deposition of residues from the production of artefacts that demonstrated particular technical prowess suggests that certain types of metalworking activity continued to be regarded with awe. So too the recovery of metalworking accoutrements and debris from liminal contexts such as ditches, bogs, and caves hints that it was viewed as a powerful transformative process associated with social and supernatural dangers because of its role in both the definition and transgression of boundaries. Hence, it has been argued that prehistoric smiths may have been feared and revered in equal measure. Yet, it is clear that this is only a partial reading of the evidence, for metalworking debris has also been found in and around settlements and in burials that, in other respects, look unremarkable. As we have already noted, it is easy to assume that metal artefacts were scarce and inherently valuable and that this had implications for the status of the smith. The relatively widespread and dispersed distribution of metalworking evidence in the later Bronze Age and later Iron Age suggests that this was not always the case; as we have already noted, there may have been more metal in circulation than has often been assumed (Williams & Le Carlier de Veslud 2019), and metalworking skills may have been relatively common.

Regional and chronological variation in the organisation of metalworking

There is evidence for significant regional and chronological variability in the organisation of metalworking and the social role of this craft. We have already noted above, for example, that non-ferrous metalworking residues are found more often on 'high-status' sites in Ireland than in England and this may support the idea that, in this area at least, the production of metal objects was controlled by those in positions of political power. Metalworking evidence is very rare in Wales throughout the period; that is doubtless in part the result of the relative paucity of excavations in comparison to areas such as south-east England, but Bronze Age mines are well-documented, particularly in north-west and mid-Wales. Cornwall in contrast which, like Wales, was a significant source of non-ferrous metals in prehistory, has produced a considerable amount of metalworking evidence from excavated settlements, even though this region has seen less developer-funded excavation in recent years than south-east England. There are differences in the distribution of particular artefact categories too that may hint at regional variation in the organisation and significance of metalworking: as we have seen, Early Bronze Age one-piece moulds are found predominantly in north-east Scotland, while differences in the distribution of clay, stone, and bronze moulds in the later Bronze Age suggest that both the social networks and patterns of working of those who produced and used these items varied significantly.

The rarity of excavated evidence of Chalcolithic and Early Bronze Age date may suggest that metalworking was less common or differently organised; knowledge of the craft may have been more restricted, for example, although we have questioned whether this necessarily indicates that its practitioners enjoyed special status. Alternatively, its residues may have been subject to different forms of depositional practice during those periods. In the later Bronze Age and Iron Age, most metalworking evidence derives from settlement contexts and the paucity of archaeologically identifiable settlements of Chalcolithic and Early Bronze Age date (Brück 1999c) may go some way towards explaining the disparity. In general, the amount of excavated metalworking evidence increases over time. The frequency of evidence at excavated sites peaks in the Late Bronze Age, although it is also common in the later Iron Age. There are changes in the kinds of artefacts that reached the archaeological record too: moulds, for example, are the most common category of metalworking-related find from excavated sites in the Late Bronze Age, while crucibles are more frequent in the Iron Age. This is unlikely to be the result of differences in casting techniques. Instead, it is possible that the larger crucibles of the Late Bronze Age may have had longer use-lives while Iron Age crucibles were replaced more often, perhaps because knowledge of how to make these artefacts was now more common. Alternatively, patterns of selective deposition may indicate that the meanings and values ascribed to particular metalworking artefacts changed over time.

Some useful points can also be made regarding the nature of the evidence at times which, on other grounds, have been identified as periods of social and economic transformation. The lack of metalworking evidence from the Chalcolithic, for example, makes it difficult to sustain any argument that conjures a rapid and dramatic 'industrial revolution' at the beginning of the Bronze Age. At the other end of the Bronze Age there is a significant decrease in the frequency and quantity of non-ferrous metalworking evidence from sites of the Earliest Iron Age. This mirrors the paucity of metal finds from this period: few hoards of Llyn Fawr date are known in comparison with the preceding Ewart Park phase. The rarity of hoards is therefore likely to reflect a decrease in the production of non-ferrous metalwork as well as changing depositional practices. Partly, this is likely to indicate a change in the social significance of the craft. Needham (2007) has argued that, from 800 BC on, the exchange, accumulation, and display of bronze was no longer the primary means of securing and maintaining social status; instead, control over agricultural production became increasingly important (see also Thomas 1989). Yet, non-ferrous metalworkers may have played a role in the introduction of iron: in the later Iron Age, at least, there is evidence to suggest that bronze smiths and iron workers may often have been one and the same individuals. There is less excavated evidence to suggest cross-craft interaction earlier in the period, though certain bronze artefact forms were copied in iron during the Earliest Iron Age (Boughton 2015). These were not always made in the same way, however: the loops on iron socketed axes, for example, were welded on unlike those on their visually similar bronze equivalents.

So too, the changing role of metalworking and its practitioners in the Late Iron Age casts light on social developments at the end of prehistory. In south-east England, the adoption of novel metalworking techniques and new kinds of metal artefacts – above all coins – was bound up with the emergence of new forms of political power and the recasting of social connections across the Channel. The appearance of possible metalworkers' graves in the Late Iron Age, and the depiction of metalworkers on coins, may suggest that the role of the smith took on a new significance, and can be seen as part of a wider pattern of increasing social differentiation in south-eastern England at this time (eg, Millett 1990; Eckardt & Crummy 2008). The fact that the production of coin pellets and associated precious metalworking was largely focused on the political centres known as oppida emphasises the links between metalworking and power at this time. Nevertheless, coin pellet moulds occur away from oppida and even within single oppida complexes the distribution of such moulds can be very dispersed, challenging the notion of 'mints' under close 'royal' control. The Roman conquest of southern Britain brought further major changes in metalworking practice, but there are significant elements of continuity across this transition. Handmade crucibles of Iron Age type, for example, continued to be used well beyond the conquest in parts of southern Britain, and indigenous metalwork forms ('Celtic art') continued to be produced, suggesting that some aspects of the practice and organisation of metalworking did not change.

Conclusion

Together, the evidence presented in this volume suggests significant variation in the social context of non-ferrous metalworking in later prehistory; in general, however, metalworkers appear to have been socially embedded members of the community who travelled at times both within their local areas and further afield. Most were not full-time specialists, although the technical skills displayed by certain individuals doubtless meant that they were regarded with admiration and respect and they may – in certain times and places – have been viewed as set apart. In many regions there is little to suggest that metalworkers were the clients of elite individuals or that the craft was subject to elite control. Sometimes, skilled master crafters may have joined others as they congregated at special places in the landscape such as hillforts, shrines, and timber platforms. Elsewhere, 'common craftspeople' made simple artefacts and repaired others between engaging in other activities. The selective deposition of metalworking debris suggests that the cultural meanings ascribed to these materials were important in determining how they were treated at the end of their lives. Metalworking did not only serve a practical purpose; instead, the cultural and symbolic significance of the craft – for this was an activity that made, transformed, and destroyed social relationships – meant that its residues could be employed in a variety of social and ritual practices such as rites of abandonment or the marking of boundaries. Elsewhere, though, metalworking debris was not treated in any special way and was deposited alongside a variety of other 'mundane' materials in domestic contexts.

There is, of course, further work to be done. A similar review of the depositional context of ironworking residues in Britain would be especially valuable and may provide a quite different perspective on the organisation and intensity of metalworking activities at some of the sites discussed in this book, while comparative work on other crafts could help to determine how different or special metalworking might have been. For practical purposes, our study has excluded the later centuries of the 'long' Scottish and Irish Iron Age, and it would be useful to assess how the organisation of non-ferrous metalworking changed after AD 100 in these regions. Likewise, future work should consider how the organisation of metalworking and the social roles of metalworkers were transformed by the incorporation of southern Britain into the Roman Empire.

Chemical or microscopic analysis of

refractory ceramics has been carried out at relatively few sites of Bronze Age or Iron Age date and work of this sort could shed light on regional and chronological variability in casting, alloying and recycling practices. Even at **Gussage All Saints** (Dorset) only a small sample of the crucibles and other metalworking residues from the site have been scientifically analysed (Craddock 1972; Kearn 2017). It will, however, be important to integrate such work with social archaeological approaches. Experimental bronze casting has rarely attempted to replicate and use different crucible forms or unusual objects such as bronze moulds. Geochemical analysis of buildings that have produced metalworking residues has been undertaken on only a handful of sites, so it is difficult to assess whether the craft was carried out in these structures or its debris redeposited from elsewhere. There has been little work on categories of artefact such as bone tools that may have been used to model clay moulds. Detailed comparative analysis at an intra-regional level of the distribution of metalwork and metalworking sites would be useful, as would further comparison of our dataset with the Continental evidence. Yet, we hope that by bringing together the significant numbers of new finds for which good contextual information is available we have been able to present a more sensitive and source-critical discussion of the organisation and social significance of non-ferrous metalworking in later prehistory and to point up the potential of this material to future research.

BIBLIOGRAPHY

Abbott., M. & Anderson Whymark, H. 2012. *Stonehenge Laser Scan: archaeological analysis report.* Swindon: English Heritage Research Report 32

Adams, S. 2013. *The First Brooches in Britain: from manufacture to deposition in the early and middle Iron Age.* Unpubl. PhD thesis, University of Leicester

Adams, S. 2017. The contents and context of the Boughton Malherbe Late Bronze Age hoard. *Archaeologia Cantiana* 138, 37–64

Adams, S., Martinón-Torres, M. & Webley, L. 2018. Diversity in Iron Age metalworking: a unique crucible from Westwood, Coventry. *Historical Metallurgy* 50 (2), 78–84

Adkins. L. & Needham, S. 1985. New research on a Late Bronze Age enclosure at Queen Mary's Hospital, Carshalton. *Surrey Archaeological Collections* 76, 11–50

Agache, R. 1968. Nord et Picardie. *Gallia Préhistoire* 11, 267–309

Ainslie, R. 1992. Excavations at Thrupp near Radley, Oxon. *South Midlands Archaeology* 22, 63–6

Aitken, G. M. & Aitken, G. N. 1991. Excavations at Whitcombe, 1965–1967. *Proceedings of the Dorset Natural History and Archaeological Society* 112, 57–94

Aldhouse-Green, M. 2002. Any old iron! Symbolism and ironworking in Iron Age Europe. In M. Aldhouse-Green & P. Webster (eds), *Artefacts and Archaeology. Aspects of the Celtic and Roman world*, 8–19. Cardiff: University of Wales Press

Aldhouse-Green, M. 2004. *An Archaeology of Images: iconology and cosmology in Iron Age and Roman Europe.* London: Routledge

Aldhouse-Green, M. & Aldhouse-Green, S. 2005. *The Quest for the Shaman: shape-shifters, sorcerers and spirit-healers of Ancient Europe.* London: Thames and Hudson

Alexander, D. 2000. Excavation of Neolithic pits, later prehistoric structures and a Roman temporary camp along the line of the A96 Kintore and Blackburn Bypass, Aberdeenshire. *Proceedings of the Society of Antiquaries of Scotland* 130, 11–75

Allen, C. 2009. *Exchange and Ritual at the Riverside: Late Bronze Age life in the lower Witham Valley at Washingborough, Lincolnshire.* Lincoln: Pre-Construct Archaeology

Allen, D. 1958. Belgic coins as illustrations of life in the late pre-Roman Iron Age of Britain. *Proceedings of the Prehistoric Society* 24, 43–63

Allen, M.J., Gardiner, J. & Sheridan, A. (eds), 2012. *Is there a British Chalcolithic? People, place and polity in the later third millennium.* Oxford: Prehistoric Society Research Papers 4

Allen, M.J., Leivers, M. & Ellis, C. 2008. Neolithic causewayed enclosures and later prehistoric farming: duality, imposition and the role of predecessors at Kingsborough, Isle of Sheppey, Kent, UK. *Proceedings of the Prehistoric Society* 74, 232–322

Allen, T. 1990. *An Iron Age and Romano-British Enclosed Settlement at Watkins Farm, Northmoor, Oxon.* Oxford: Oxford University Committee for Archaeology

Allen, T. 1991. Archaeological discoveries on the Banbury east–west link road. *Oxoniensia* 54, 25–44

Allen, T. 1999. Bogshole Lane, Broomfield, near Herne Bay. *Canterbury's Archaeology* 1998–1999, 12–13

Allen, T. & Robinson, M. 1993. *The Prehistoric Landscape and Iron Age Enclosed Settlement at Mingies Ditch, Hardwick-with-Yelford, Oxon.* Oxford: Oxford Archaeological Unit and Oxford University Committee for Archaeology

Allen, T., Cramp, K., Lamdin-Whymark, H. & Webley, L. 2010. *Castle Hill and its Landscape; archaeological investigations at the Wittenhams, Oxfordshire.* Oxford: Oxford Archaeology

Allen, T., Darvill, T., Green, L. & Jones, M. 1993. *Excavations at Roughground Farm, Lechlade, Gloucestershire: a prehistoric and Roman landscape.* Oxford: Oxford University Committee for Archaeology

Anderson, J. 1874. *Croydon: pre-historic and Roman.* Croydon

Anderson, J. & Black, G. 1888. Reports on local museums in Scotland, obtained through Dr. R. H. Gunning's jubilee gift to the Society. *Proceedings of the Society of Antiquaries of Scotland* 22, 331–422

Anderson, R. 1942. A cinerary urn from Sandmill Farm, Stranraer, Wigtownshire. *Proceedings of the Society of Antiquaries of Scotland* 76, 79–83

Anderson-Whymark, H., Garrow, D. & Sturt, F. (eds), 2015. *Continental Connections: cross-Channel relationships from the Mesolithic to the Iron Age.* Oxford: Oxbow Books

Andrews, P. 2004. *Weatherlees Wastewater Treatment Works, Ebbsfleet, Kent.* Salisbury: Wessex Archaeology. Unpubl. report

Andrews, P. & Clarke, P. 2015. *Iron Age Metalworking and Anglo-Saxon Settlement at Castleview Road, Slough.* Salisbury: Wessex Archaeology. Unpubl. report

Andrews, P., Jones, G. & Schuster, J. 2009. The hoards of the Ebbsfleet peninsula. In P. Andrews, K. Dinwiddy, C. Ellis, A. Hutcheson, C. Phillpotts, A. Powell & J. Schuster (eds), *Kentish Sites and Sites of Kent: a miscellany of four archaeological excavations*, 75–81. Salisbury: Wessex Archaeology Report 24

Andrews, P., Booth, P., Fitzpatrick, A. & Welsh, K. 2015. *Digging at the Gateway: archaeological landscapes of south Thanet. The archaeology of East Kent Access (Phase II).* Oxford and Salisbury: Oxford Wessex Archaeology Monograph 8

Annable, F. & Simpson, D. 1964. *Guide Catalogue of the Neolithic and Bronze Age Collections in Devizes Museum.* Devizes: Wiltshire Archaeological and Natural History Society

Anonymous 1913. Dwelling pits on Winterbourne Monkton Down. *Wiltshire Archaeological and Natural History Magazine* 38, 108–10

Anonymous 1980. Wiltshire archaeological register for 1976–7. *Wiltshire Archaeological Magazine* 72/73, 201–8

Anonymous 1988. The work of the Hereford and Worcester County Museum Archaeology Section, 1986–7. *Transactions of the Worcestershire Archaeological Society* 11, 59–70

Anthony, I. E. 1970. St Michael's, St Albans, Excavations, 1966. *Hertfordshire Archaeology* 2, 51–61

Antoni, B., Johnson, M. & McComish, J. 2009. *The University of York, Heslington East, York. assessment report.* York: York Archaeological Trust. Unpubl. report

ApSimon, A. & Greenfield, E. 1972. The excavation of the Bronze Age and Iron Age settlement at Trevisker Round, St. Eval, Cornwall. *Proceedings of the Prehistoric Society* 38, 302–81

Archaeological Institute 1846. Archaeological intelligence. *Archaeological Journal* 3, 255–70

Archaeological Institute 1850. *Memoirs Illustrative of the History and Antiquities of the County and City of Lincoln, Communicated to the Annual Meeting of the Archaeological Institute of Great Britain and Ireland, held at Lincoln, July 1848.* London: Archaeological Institute

Archaeological Institute 1851. *Memoirs Illustrative of the History and Antiquities of Norfolk and the City of Norwich, Communicated to the Annual Meeting of the Archaeological Institute of Great Britain and Ireland, held at Norwich, July 1847.* London: Archaeological Institute

Archaeological Institute 1852. Proceedings at the meeting of the Archaeological Institute, March 5, 1852. *Archaeological Journal* 9, 185–96

Archaeological Institute 1861. Antiquities and works of art exhibited. *Archaeological Journal* 18, 156–70

Armbruster, B. 2000. *Goldschmiedekunst und Bronzetechnik: Studien zum Metallhandwerk der Atlantischen Bronzezeit auf der Iberischen Halbinsel.* Montagnac: Monique Mergoil

Armbruster, B. 2006. Steingeräte des bronzezeitlichen Metallhandwerks. *Ethnographisch-Archäologische Zeitschrift* 47, 163–91

Armbruster, B. 2013. Gold and gold working of the Bronze Age. In Fokkens & Harding (eds), 454–68

Armbruster, B. 2017. Manufacturing processes of Atlantic Bronze Age annular gold ornaments: a case study of the Guînes gold hard (Pas-de-Calais, France). *Materials and Manufacturing Processes* 32, 728–39

Armit, I. 1997. Cultural landscapes and identities: a case study in the Scottish Iron Age. In Gwilt & Haselgrove 1997, 248–53

Armit, I. 2006. *Anatomy of an Iron Age Roundhouse: the Cnip wheelhouse excavations, Lewis.* Edinburgh: Society of Antiquaries of Scotland

Armit, I. 2007. Social landscapes and identities in the Irish Iron Age. In Haselgrove & Moore 2007, 130–9

Armit, I. & McKenzie, J. 2013. *An Inherited Place: Broxmouth hillfort and the south-east Scottish Iron Age.* Edinburgh: Society of Antiquaries of Scotland

Armit, I., Dunwell, A., Hunter, F. & Nelis, E. 2005. Traprain Law: archaeology from the ashes. *Past* 49, 1–4

Armstrong, E. 1917. On some associated finds of bronze celts discovered in Ireland. *Proceedings of the Royal Irish Academy, Section C* 33, 511–26

Arnold, D. 1985. *Ceramic Theory and Cultural Process.* Cambridge: Cambridge University Press

Arnoldussen, S. & Brusgaard, N. 2015. Production in deposition: structured deposition of Iron Age ironworking elements (The Netherlands). *Lunula Archaeologia Protohistorica* 23, 115–24

Ashbee, P. 1960. *The Bronze Age Round Barrow in Britain.* London: Phoenix House

Atkins, R. 2005. *Partney By-pass, Lincolnshire: post-excavation assessment and updated project design.* Cambridge: Cambridgeshire County Council Archaeological Field Unit. Unpubl. report

Atkins, R. 2011. *Multi-period Settlement and Funerary Evidence at Tithe Barn Farm, Chatteris: archaeological evaluation report.* Cambridge: Oxford Archaeology East. Unpubl. report

Atkins, R. 2013. *Iron Age to Roman Settlement at Low Park Corner, Chippenham, Cambridgeshire. Archaeological Excavation.* Cambridge: Oxford Archaeology East. Unpubl. report

Atkinson, M. & Preston, S. 2001. Prehistoric settlement and burials at Elms Farm, Heybridge. *Essex Archaeology and History* 32, 42–74

Atkinson, M. & Preston, S. 2015a. *Heybridge: A late Iron Age and Roman settlement. Excavations at Elms Farm 1993–5. Volume 1.* Chelmsford: East Anglian Archaeology 154

Atkinson, M. & Preston, S. 2015b. Heybridge: a late Iron Age and Roman settlement. Excavations at Elms Farm 1993–5. Volume 2. *Internet Archaeology* 40. http://dx.doi.org/10.11141/ia.40.1

Atkinson, R. 1953. The Neolithic long mound at Maiden Castle. *Proceedings of the Dorset Natural History and Archaeological Society* 74, 36–8

Avery, M., Sutton, J. & Banks, J. 1967. Rainsborough, Northants, England: excavations, 1961–5. *Proceedings of the Prehistoric Society* 33, 207–306

Bagwell, T. & Webster, C. 2006. Somerset archaeology, 2005. *Somerset Archaeology and Natural History* 149, 159–90

Baker, L., Sheridan, A. & Cowie, T. 2003. An early Bronze Age 'dagger grave' from Rameldry Farm, near Kingskettle, Fife. *Proceedings of the Society of Antiquaries of Scotland* 133, 85–123

Baldwin, A. & Joy, J. 2017. *A Celtic Feast: the Iron Age cauldrons from Chiseldon, Wiltshire.* London: British Museum

Barber, M. 2003. *Bronze and the Bronze Age.* Stroud: Tempus

Barford, P.M. 1982. Possible metalworking debris from Skeleton Green. *Hertfordshire Archaeology* 8, 200

Barnatt, J. 1982. *Prehistoric Cornwall: the ceremonial monuments.* Wellingborough: Turnstone Press

Barnes, B. 1982. *Man and the Changing Landscape: a study of occupation and palaeo-environment in the central Pennines.* Liverpool: Merseyside County Council

Barrett, J. 1980. The pottery of the later Bronze Age in lowland England. *Proceedings of the Prehistoric Society* 46, 297–319

Barrett, J. 1994. *Fragments from Antiquity: an archaeology of social life in Britain, 2900–1200 BC.* Oxford: Blackwell

Barrett, J. & Bradley, R. (eds), 1980. *Settlement and Society in the British Later Bronze Age.* Oxford: British Archaeological Report 83

Barrett, J. & Needham, S. 1988. Production, circulation and exchange: problems in the interpretation of Bronze Age bronzework. In J. Barrett & I. Kinnes (eds), *The Archaeology of Context in the Neolithic and Bronze Age: recent trends,* 127–40. Sheffield: Department of Archaeology and Prehistory, University of Sheffield

Barrett, J., Bradley, R. & Green, M. 1991. *Landscape, Monuments and Society: the prehistory of Cranborne Chase.* Cambridge: Cambridge University Press

Barrett, J., Freeman, P. & Woodward, A. 2000. *Cadbury Castle, Somerset: the later prehistoric and early historic archaeology.* London: English Heritage

Barrett, J., Downes, J., Macdonald, P., Northover, P., O'Connor, B., Salter, C. & Turner, L. 2000. The metalworking evidence, in Barrett *et al.* 2000, 291–301

Barrowclough, D. 2008. *Prehistoric Lancashire.* Stroud: History Press

Barrowclough, D. nd. *The Earliest Evidence for Lead Extraction in Northern Europe and Possible Lead Miners' Burials: Early Bronze Age lead mining dated to the second millennium BC.* https://www.academia.edu/8009014/The_Earliest_Evidence_for_Lead_Extraction_in_Northern_Europe_and_Possible_Lead_Miners_Burials_Early_Bronze_Age_Lead_Mining_dated_to_the_Second_Millennium_BC

Bartelheim, M. 2009. Elites and metals in the central European Early Bronze Age. In Kienlin & Roberts (eds), 2009, 34–46

Bartelheim, M., R. Krause & Pernicka, E. (eds), 2002. *The Beginnings of Metallurgy in the Old World.* Rahden: Marie Leidorf

Bartelheim, M., Peška, J. & Turek, J. (eds), 2013. *From Copper to Bronze:*

cultural and social transformations at the turn of the 3rd/2nd millennia B.C. in central Europe. Langenweissbach: Beier & Beran

Barton, K. 1964. Star Roman villa, Shipham, Somerset. *Proceedings of the Somersetshire Archaeological and Natural History Society* 108, 45–93

Bateman, T. 1855. *A Descriptive Catalogue of the Antiquities and Miscellaneous Objects Preserved in the Museum of Thomas Bateman, at Lomberdale House, Derbyshire*. Bakewell: privately published

Bates, S. 2000. Excavations at Quidney Farm, Saham Toney, Norfolk 1995. *Britannia* 31, 201–37

Bátora, J. 2002. Contribution to the problem of 'craftsmen' graves at the end of Aeneolithic and in the early Bronze Age in central, western and eastern Europe. *Slovenská Archeológia* 50, 179–228

Bátora, J. 2013. Metal founders' graves at the end of Aeneolithic and in the early Bronze Age in central and eastern Europe. In Bartelheim *et al.* (eds), 2013, 25–34

Bayley, J. 1983. *Crucibles and Clay Moulds from the Marlowes and Cakebread Robey Sites in Canterbury, Kent*, London: Ancient Monuments Laboratory Report 3862

Bayley, J. 1985. What's what in ancient technology: an introduction to high temperature processes. In P. Phillips (ed.), *The Archaeologist and the Laboratory*, 41–44. London: Council for British Archaeology Research Report 58

Bayley, J. 1992. *Non-ferrous Metalworking in England: Late Iron Age to Early Medieval*. Unpubl. PhD thesis, University College London

Bayley, J. 1994. *Non-ferrous Metalworking Debris from Yarnton Worton Rectory Farm, Oxon*. London: Ancient Monuments Laboratory Report 12/94

Bayliss, A. & Grogan, E. 2013. Chronologies for Tara and comparable royal sites of the Irish Iron Age. In M. O'Sullivan, C. Scarre & M. Doyle (eds), *Tara – From the Past to the Future. Towards a new research agenda*, 105–44. Dublin: Wordwell

Bayley, J. & Rehren, T. 2007. Towards a functional and typological classification of crucibles. In S. La Niece, D. Hook & P. Craddock (eds), *Metals and Mines: studies in archaeometallurgy*, 46–55. London: Archetype

Becker, K. 2008. Iron Age ring-headed pins in Ireland and Britain and on the Continent. *Archäologisches Korrespondenzblatt* 38(4), 513–20

Becker, K. 2010. *Rathgall, Co. Wicklow*. Dublin: Archaeology Ireland Heritage Guide 51

Becker, K. 2012. Iron Age Ireland: continuity, change and identity. In Moore & Armada 2012, 449–67

Becker, K. 2013. Transforming identities – new approaches to Bronze Age deposition in Ireland. *Proceedings of the Prehistoric Society* 79, 225–63

Becker, K., Ó Néill, J. & O'Flynn, L. 2008. *Iron Age Ireland: finding an invisible people. Report to the Heritage Council. 2008 Archaeology Grant Scheme, Project 16365*. Dublin: Unpubl. report to the Heritage Council

Bedwin, O. 1984. Excavations at Ounces Barn, Boxgrove, West Sussex. Rescue Archaeology in Sussex 1982. *Institute of Archaeology Bulletin* 20, 83–7

Bedwin, O. & Pitts, M. 1978. The Excavation of an Iron Age Settlement at North Bersted, Bognor Regis, West Sussex 1975–76. *Sussex Archaeological Collections* 116, 293–346

Bedwin, O. & Place, C. 1995. Late Iron Age and Romano-British occupation at Ounces Barn, Boxgrove, West Sussex; excavations 1982–83. *Sussex Archaeological Collections* 133, 45–101

Beesley, S. 2004. *Bronze Age Foundry Practice*. Part II thesis, Department of Materials, Oxford University

Bell, D. 2016. *Drilling Metal in the Bronze Age*. Unpubl. poster presented at the Metools conference, Belfast, 24–25 June 2016

Bendrey, R. 2010. The horse. In T. O'Connor & N. Sykes (eds), *Extinctions and Invasions: a social history of British fauna*, 10–16. Oxford: Windgather Press

Bennet, P., Couldrey, P. & Machperson-Grant, N. 2007. *Highstead, near Chislet, Kent. Excavations 1975–1977*. Canterbury: Canterbury Archaeological Trust

Bennett, W. 1953. Report on excavations near Burnley. *Transactions of the Lancashire and Cheshire Antiquarian Society* 62, 204–8

Benton, S., Childe, V.G. & Coghlan, H. 1952. Ancient Mining and Metallurgy Committee. *Man* 52, 89–90

Berridge, P. 1986. New light on the Chudleigh rapier moulds. *Devon Archaeological Society Proceedings* 44, 176–80

Bersu, G. 1940. Excavations at Little Woodbury, Wiltshire. *Proceedings of the Prehistoric Society* 6, 30–111

Bersu, G. 1977. *Three Round Houses on the Isle of Man*. Douglas: Manx Museum and National Trust

Bertemes, F. 2004. Frühe Metallurgen in der Spätkupfer und Frühbronzezeit. In H. Meller (ed.), *Der Geschmiedete Himmel*, 144–9. Stuttgart: Theiss

Bertemes, F. & Heyd, V. 2002. Der Übergang Kupferzeit/Frühbronzezeit am Nordwestrand des Karpatenbeckens – kulturgeschichtliche und paläometallurgische Betrachtungen. In Bartelheim *et al.* (eds), 2002, 185–229

Best, J., Woodward, A. & Tyler, K. 2013. *Late Bronze Age Pottery Production: evidence from a 12th to 11th century BC settlement at Tinney's Lane, Sherborne, Dorset*. Dorchester: Dorset Natural History and Archaeological Society

Best, J., Woodward, A., Allen, M.J., Cook, G., Dungworth, D., Gale, R., Hamilton, D., Higbee, L., Jones, J., Juleff, G., Lewis, M., Marshall, P., O'Connor, B., Riddler, I., Taylor, R., Tingle, M. & Tyler, K. 2012. Late Bronze Age pottery production: evidence from a 12th–11th century cal BC settlement at Tinney's Lane, Sherborne, Dorset. *Proceedings of the Prehistoric Society* 78, 207–61

Bevan, B. (ed.) *Northern Exposure: interpretative devolution and the Iron Ages in Britain*. Leicester: Leicester University Press

Bewley, R., Longworth, I., Browne, S., Huntley, J. & Varndell, G. 1992. Excavation of a Bronze Age cemetery at Ewanrigg, Maryport, Cumbria. *Proceedings of the Prehistoric Society* 58, 325–54

Bhreathnach, E. 1995. *Tara: a select bibliography*. Dublin: Royal Irish Academy for the Discovery Programme

Biddle, M. 1966. Excavations at Winchester, 1965 fourth interim report. *Antiquaries Journal* 46, 308–32

Biddulph, E. & Brady, K. 2015. *Excavations Along the M25: prehistoric, Roman and Anglo-Saxon activity between Aveley and Epping, Essex*. Colchester: Essex Society for Archaeology and History

Billard, C. 1991. L'habitat des Florentins à Val-de-Reuil (Eure). *Gallia Préhistoire* 33, 140–71

Binchy, E. 1967. Irish razors and razor-knives of the middle Bronze Age. In E. Rynne (ed.), *North Munster Studies. Essays in commemoration of Monsignor Michael Moloney*, 43–60. Limerick: Thomond Archaeological Society

Birbeck, V. 2006. Excavations on the Old Ditch linear earthwork, Breach Hill, Tilshead. *Wiltshire Archaeological and Natural History Magazine* 99, 79–103

Birch, S., Wildgoose, M. & Kozikowsi, G. 2010. *Uamh An Ard Achadh (High Pasture Cave). Kilbride, Strath, Isle of Skye. Archaeological deposits from a limestone cave on the island of Skye: a preliminary report*. West Coast Archaeological Services. Unpubl. report

Bird, D., Crocker, G., Maloney, C. & Saich, D. 1996. Archaeology in Surrey 1992–3. *Surrey Archaeological Collections* 83, 187–228

Bishop, B. 2006. *An Assessment of the Archaeological Excavations (Phase IV) at the Oliver Close Estate, Leyton, London Borough of Waltham Forest*. London: Pre-Construct Archaeology. Unpubl. report

Bishop, B. & Boyer, P. 2014. A Late Bronze Age enclosed settlement at the Oliver Close Estate, Leyton, London Borough of Waltham Forest. *Transactions of the London and Middlesex Archaeological Society* 65, 51–102

Bishop, M. 2012. Parrots Corner Park and Ride, Rossington, Doncaster. *Archaeology in South Yorkshire* 14, 88–90

Black, G. 1891. Report on the archaeological examination of the Culbin Sands, Elginshire, obtained under the Victoria Jubilee of His Excellency Dr R H Gunning, F.S.A. Scot. *Proceedings of the Society of Antiquaries of Scotland* 25, 484–511

Blake, B. 1960. Excavations of native (Iron Age) sites in Cumberland, 1956–58. *Transactions of the Cumberland and Westmoreland Antiquarian and Archaeological Society* 59, 1–14

Blin-Stoyle, A. 1959. Chemical composition of the bronzes. *Archaeometry* 2 (supplement), 1–24

Blockley, K., Blockley, M., Blockley, P., Frere, S. & Stow, S. 1995. *Excavations in the Marlowe Car Park and Surrounding Areas.* Canterbury: Archaeology of Canterbury 5

Boast, E. 2006. *Land to the Rear of 148 Minnis Road, Minnis Bay, Birchington, Kent: archaeological watching brief report.* Thanet Trust for Archaeology. Unpubl. report

Boden, D. 2005a. Ellington School, Ramsgate. *Canterbury's Archaeology* 2005–6, 27–9

Boden, D. 2005b. Holborough Quarry, Snodland. *Canterbury's Archaeology* 2005–6, 40–1

Boden, D. nd. *The Swordsmith of Snodland 900 BC.* Canterbury: Canterbury Archaeological Trust

Boden, D., Rady, J. and Allison, E. 2006. *Ellington School, Pysons Road, Ramsgate, Kent. Archaeological Excavation. Stratigraphic Report.* Canterbury: Canterbury Archaeological Trust. Unpubl. report

Bond, D. 1988. *Excavation at the North Ring, Mucking, Essex: a Late Bronze Age enclosure.* Chelmsford: East Anglian Archaeology 43

Boon, G. 1954. Some fragmentary flan-moulds in the Silchester collection at Reading Museum. *Antiquaries Journal* 34, 68–70

Boon, G. 1957. *Silchester: the Roman town of Calleva.* Newton Abbott: David and Charles

Booth, A. 2014. *Reassessing the Long Chronology of the Penannular Brooch in Britain: exploring changing styles, use and meaning across a millennium.* Unpubl. PhD thesis, University of Leicester

Boughton, D. 2015. *The Early Iron Age Socketed Axes in Britain.* Unpubl. PhD thesis, University of Central Lancashire

Bourhis, J. & Gomez, J. 1985. Déchets de fonderie de bronze des grottes du Queroy à Chazelles et des Perrats à Agris (Charente). In *Paléométallurgie de la France Atlantique, Âge du Bronze* 2, 111–17. Rennes: Laboratoire Anthropologie-Préhistoire-Protohistoire-Quaternaire Armoricains

Boutoille, L. 2009. Les dépôts de moules lithiques de fondeur de l'Âge du Bronze découverts en France. In S. Bonnardin, C. Hamon, M. Lauwers & B. Quilliec (eds), *Du Matériel au Spirituel: réalités archéologiques et historiques des «dépôts» de la préhistoire à nos jours*, 379–86. Antibes: Éditions APDCA

Boutoille, L. 2015a. Les techniques du dinandier de l'âge du Bronze: l'outillage en pierre spécifique à la déformation plastique des métaux. In S. Boulud-Gazo & T. Nicolas (eds), *Artisanats et Productions à l'âge du Bronze*, 83–96. Dijon and Paris: Association pour la Promotion des Recherches sur l'âge du Bronze and Société Préhistorique Française

Boutoille, L. 2015b. The coppersmith and the caster: initial thoughts on Irish stone casting mould hoards. *Ulster Journal of Archaeology* 71, 5–15

Boutoille, L. 2016. *The Metalworking Toolset Found at Upton Lovell G2a, Wiltshire, England.* Unpubl. poster presented at the Metools conference, Belfast, 24–25 June 2016

Bowden, M., Ford, S. & Gaffney, V. 1993. The excavation of a late Bronze Age artefact scatter on Weathercock Hill. *Berkshire Archaeological Journal* 74, 69–83

Bowen, E. & Gresham, C. 1967. *History of Merioneth. Volume 1.* Dolgellau: Merioneth Historical and Record Society

Bowman, S. & Needham, S. 2007. The Dunaverney and Little Thetford flesh-hooks: history, technology and their position within the late Bronze Age Atlantic zone feasting complex. *Antiquaries Journal* 87, 53–108

Boyd Dawkins, W. 1902. On Bigbury Camp and the Pilgrims' Way. *Archaeological Journal* 59, 211–18

Bradley, R. 1998. *The Passage of Arms: an archaeological analysis of prehistoric hoards and votive deposits* (2nd edn). Cambridge: Cambridge University Press

Bradley, R. 2005a. *The Moon and the Bonfire: an investigation of three stone circles in north-east Scotland.* Edinburgh: Society of Antiquaries of Scotland

Bradley, R. 2005b. *Ritual and Domestic Life in Prehistoric Europe.* Abingdon: Routledge

Bradley, R. 2013. Hoards and the deposition of metalwork. In Fokkens & Harding (eds), 2013, 121–39

Bradley, R. 2017. *A Geography of Offerings: deposits of valuables in the landscapes of ancient Europe.* Oxford: Oxbow Insights in Archaeology 2

Bradley, R. & Edmonds, M. 1993. *Interpreting the Axe Trade: production and exchange in Neolithic Britain.* Cambridge: Cambridge University Press

Bradley, R. & Gardiner, J. (eds), 1984. *Neolithic Studies: a review of some recent work.* Oxford: British Archaeological Report 133

Bradley, R., Green, C. & Watson, A. 2018. The placing of Early Bronze Age metalwork deposits: new evidence from Scotland. *Oxford Journal of Archaeology* 37, 137–45

Bradley, R., Haselgrove, C., Vander Linden, M. & Webley, L. 2015. *The Later Prehistory of Northwest Europe.* Oxford: Oxford University Press

Bradley, R., Lobb, S., Richards, J. & Robinson, M. 1980. Two Late Bronze Age settlements on the Kennet gravels: excavations at Aldermaston Wharf and Knight's Farm, Burghfield, Berkshire. *Proceedings of the Prehistoric Society* 46, 217–95

Bradley, R., Rogers, A., Sturt, F. & Watson, A. 2016. Maritime havens in earlier prehistoric Britain. *Proceedings of the Prehistoric Society* 82, 1–35

Brailsford, J. 1953. *Later Prehistoric Antiquities of the British Isles.* London: British Museum

Braithwaite, M. 1982. Decoration as ritual symbol: a theoretical proposal and an ethnographic study in southern Sudan. In I. Hodder (ed.), *Symbolic and Structural Archaeology*, 80–8. Cambridge: Cambridge University Press

Brandherm, D. 2009. The social context of early Bronze Age metalworking in Iberia: evidence from the burial record. In Kienlin & Roberts (eds), 2009, 172–80

Brandherm, D. 2014. Late Bronze Age casting debris and other base metal finds from Haughey's Fort. *Emania* 22, 59–68

Branigan, K. & Dearne, M. 1991. The Romano-British finds from Wookey Hole: a re-appraisal. *Somerset Archaeology and Natural History* 134, 57–80

Brannon, N. 1988. Archaeological excavations at Cathedral Hill, Downpatrick, 1987. *Lecale Miscellany* 6, 3–9

Bray, P. 2012. Before 29CU became copper: tracing the recognition and invention of metalleity in Britain and Ireland during the 3rd millennium BC. In Allen *et al.* (eds), 2012, 56–70

Bray, P. 2016. Metal, metalwork and specialization: the chemical composition of British Bronze Age swords in context. In Koch & Cunliffe 2016, 247–63

Bray, P. & Pollard, T. 2012. A new interpretive approach to the chemistry of copper-alloy objects: source, recycling and technology. *Antiquity* 86, 853–67

Bremer, W. 1926. A founder's hoard of the Copper Age at Carrickshedoge, Nash, Co. Wexford. *Journal of the Royal Society of Antiquaries of Ireland* 6 ser. 16, 88–91

Bremer, W. 1927. The Ballyliffin find. *Journal of the Royal Society of Antiquaries of Ireland* 17, 64

Brewster, T. 1963. *The Excavation of Staple Howe.* Wintringham: East Riding Archaeological Research Committee

Brewster, T. 1980. *The Excavation of Garton and Wetwang Slacks*, microfiche. Malton: East Riding Archaeological Research Committee

Briard, J. & Onee, Y. 1985. Le dépôt de moules de 'Pennavern' à Hanvec, Finistère (Bronze moyen). In *Paléométallurgie de la France Atlantique, Âge du Bronze.* 2, 119–36. Rennes: Laboratoire Anthropologie-Préhistoire-Protohistoire-Quaternaire Armoricains

Bridgford, S. 1998. British Late Bronze Age swords. The metallographic evidence. In Mordant *et al.* (eds), 1998, 205–17

Bridgford, S. 2000. *Weapons, Warfare and Society in Britain 1250–750 BC.* Unpubl. PhD thesis, University of Sheffield

Bridgford, S. 2011. *Bourton Business Park: assessment of the clay mould assemblage*. Gloucester: Gloucestershire County Council Archaeological Service. Unpubl. report

Briggs, S., Leahy, K. & Needham, S. 1987. The late Bronze Age hoard from Brough-on-Humber: a re-assessment. *Antiquaries Journal* 67, 11–28

Brindle, T. 2014. *The Portable Antiquities Scheme and Roman Britain*. London: British Museum

Brindley, A. & Lanting, J. 1992. Radiocarbon dates from wedge tombs. *Journal of Irish Archaeology* 6, 19–26

Britnell, W. 1989. The Collfryn hillslope enclosure, Llansantffraid Deuddwr, Powys: excavations 1980–1982. *Proceedings of the Prehistoric Society* 55, 89–134

Britnell, W. 1974. Beckford. *Current Archaeology* 4, 293–7

Britnell, W. 1975. An interim report upon excavations at Beckford, 1972–4. *Vale of Evesham Historical Society Research Papers* 5, 1–11

Britnell, W. 1989. The Collfryn hillslope enclosure, Llansantffraid Deuddwr, Powys: excavations 1980–1982. *Proceedings of the Prehistoric Society* 55, 89–134

Brittain, M., Evans, C. & Sharples, N. 2013. Excavations at Ham Hill, Stoke-sub-Hamdon. *Somerset Archaeology and Natural History* 156, 160–2

Britton, D. 1960a. The Isleham hoard, Cambridgeshire. *Antiquity* 38, 279–82

Britton, D. 1960b. *The Southall Hoard, Middlesex (England)*, Inventaria Archaeologica 8th Set, GB 51. London: British Museum

Britton, D. 1963. Traditions of metal-working in the later Neolithic and early Bronze Age of Britain: part 1. *Proceedings of the Prehistoric Society* 29, 258–325

Britton, D. 1971. The Heathery Burn cave revisited: an essay towards the reconstruction of a well-known archaeological discovery. In G. Sieveking (ed.), *Prehistoric and Roman Studies: commemorating the opening of the Department of Prehistoric and Romano-British Antiquities*, 20–38. London: British Museum Press

Britton, D. & Longworth, I. 1968. *Late Bronze Age Finds from the Heathery Burn Cave, Co. Durham*, Inventaria Archaeologica 9th set, GB 55. London: British Museum

Brodie, N. 1997. New perspectives on the Beaker culture. *Oxford Journal of Archaeology* 16, 297–314

Bronk Ramsey, C. 2009. Bayesian analysis of radiocarbon dates. *Radiocarbon* 51(1), 337–60

Brooks, R. 2013. *Long Melford Primary School, Long Melford. LMD 192. Post-excavation assessment report*. Bury St Edmonds Suffolk County Council Archaeology Service. Unpubl. report 2012/135

Brooks, R. 2016. *Long Melford Primary School, Long Melford, Suffolk. Archaeological excavation and analysis report vol. 1*. Bury St Edmonds Suffolk County Council Archaeology Service. Unpubl. report 2015/027

Brossler, A. 1999. *Leavesdon Aerodrome, Abbotts Langley, Watford, Hertfordshire: post-excavation assessment and research design*. Oxford: Oxford Archaeological Unit. Unpubl. report

Brossler, A., Laws, G. & Welsh, K. 2009. An Iron Age and Roman Site at Leavesden Aerodrome, Abbotts Langley. *Hertfordshire Archaeology and History* 16, 27–56

Brown, C. & Hugo, T. 1983. Prehistoric and Romano-British finds from Mount Batten, Devon: 1979–1983. *Devon Archaeological Society Proceedings* 41, 69–74

Brown, G. 1967. Harpole. *Excavations Annual Report* 1966, 6

Brown, J. 2012. Middle Iron Age marginal settlement at Newton Leys, Newton Longville, Milton Keynes. *Records of Buckinghamshire* 52, 33–73

Brown, M. & Blin-Stoyle, A. 1959. A sample analysis of British middle and late Bronze Age material, using optical spectrometry. *Proceedings of the Prehistoric Society* 25, 188–208

Brown, N. & Medlycott, M. 2013. *The Neolithic and Bronze Age Enclosures at Springfield Lyons, Essex: Excavations 1981–1991*. Chelmsford: East Anglian Archaeology 149

Brown, R. 1986. The Iron Age and Romano-British settlement at Woodcock Hall, Saham Toney, Norfolk. *Britannia* 17, 1–58

Brück, J. 1995. A place for the dead: the role of human remains in Late Bronze Age Britain. *Proceedings of the Prehistoric Society* 61, 245–77

Brück, J. 1999a. Ritual and rationality. Some problems of interpretation in European archaeology. *European Journal of Archaeology* 2, 313–44

Brück, J. 1999b. Houses, lifecycles and deposition on Middle Bronze Age settlements in southern England. *Proceedings of the Prehistoric Society* 65, 245–77

Brück, J. 1999c. What's in a settlement? Domestic practice and residential mobility in early Bronze Age southern England. In J. Brück & M. Goodman (eds), *Making Places in the Prehistoric World*, 52–75. London: UCL Press

Brück, J. 2000. The Early–Middle Bronze Age transition in southern England. *Oxford Journal of Archaeology* 19(3), 273–300

Brück, J. 2001. Body metaphors and technologies of transformation in the English middle and late Bronze Age. In Brück (ed.) 2001, 149–60

Brück, J. (ed.) 2001. *Bronze Age Landscapes: tradition and transformation*. Oxford: Oxbow Books

Brück, J. 2004. Material metaphors. The relational construction of identity in early Bronze Age burials in Ireland and Britain. *Journal of Social Archaeology* 4, 307–33

Brück, J. 2006. Fragmentation, personhood and the social construction of technology in middle and late Bronze Age Britain. *Cambridge Archaeological Journal* 16, 297–315

Brück, J. 2007. The character of Late Bronze Age settlement in southern Britain. In Haselgrove & Pope (eds), 2007, 24–38

Brück, J. 2019. *Personifying Prehistory: relational ontologies in Bronze Age Britain and Ireland*. Oxford: Oxford University Press

Brück, J. & Fontijn, D. 2013. The myth of the chief: prestige goods, power and personhood in the European Bronze Age. In Fokkens & Harding (eds), 2013, 197–215

Brudenell, M. 2012. *Pots, Practice and Society: an investigation of pattern and variability in the post-Deverel Rimbury ceramic tradition of East Anglia*. Unpubl. PhD thesis, University of York

Brudenell, M. & Cooper, A. 2008. Post-middenism: depositional histories on later Bronze Age settlements at Broom, Bedfordshire. *Oxford Journal of Archaeology* 27, 15–36

Bruhns, K. & Stothert, K. 1999. *Women in Ancient America*. Norman OK: University of Oklahoma Press

Brumfiel, E. & Earle, T. 1987. *Specialization, Exchange and Complex Societies*. Cambridge: Cambridge University Press

Brysbaert, A. & Gorgues, A. 2017. *Artisans versus Nobility? Multiple Identities of Elites and 'Commoners' Viewed though the Lens of Crafting from the Chalcolithic to the Iron Ages in Europe and the Mediterranean*. Leiden: Sidestone Press

Bucher, J., Nagy, P., Osimitz, S. & Schäppi, K. 2011. Auf den Spuren der keltischen Münzmeister. Untersuchungen zur Herstellung spätlatènezeitlicher subaerater Münzen – Ein interdisziplinäres Forschungsprojekt. *Experimentelle Archäologie in Europa, Bilanz 2011*, 120–9.

Buchsenschutz, O. & Ralston, I. 2007. Dépôts et fortifications à l'âge du Fer. In P. Barral, A. Daubigney, C. Dunning, G. Kaenel & M.-J. Roulière-Lambert (eds), *L'Âge du Fer dans l'Arc Jurassien et ses Marges: dépôts, lieux sacrés et territorialité à l'âge du Fer*, 757–76. Besançon: Presses Universitaires de Franche-Comté

Buckley, D., Hedges, J. & Priddy, D. 1987. *Excavation of a Cropmark Enclosure Complex at Woodham Walter, Essex, 1976 and an Assessment of Excavated Enclosures in Essex Together with a Selection of Cropmark Sites*. Chelmsford: East Anglian Archaeology 33

Budd, P. & Gale, D. (eds), 1997. *Prehistoric Extractive Metallurgy in Cornwall*, 23–33. Truro: Cornwall County Council

Budd, P. & Taylor, T. 1995. The faerie smith meets the bronze industry:

magic versus science in the interpretation of prehistoric metal-making. *World Archaeology* 27, 133–43

Budd, P., Gale, D., Ixer, R. & Thomas, R. 1994. Tin sources for prehistoric bronze production in Ireland. *Antiquity* 68, 518–24

Bull, R. 2015. An early Bronze Age Beaker domestic site: excavations at 105–109 New Road, Rainham, London Borough of Havering. *Transactions of the Essex Society for Archaeology and History* 4 ser. 5, 1–18

Bulleid, A. & Gray, H. St G. 1911. *The Glastonbury Lake Village: a full description of the excavations and the relics discovered, 1892–1907. Volume 1*. Glastonbury: Glastonbury Antiquarian Society

Bulleid, A. & Gray H. St G. 1917. *The Glastonbury Lake Village: a full description of the excavations and the relics discovered, 1892–1907. Volume 2*. Glastonbury: Glastonbury Antiquarian Society

Bunnefeld, J.-H. 2016. Crafting swords: the emergence and production of full-hilted swords in the Early Nordic Bronze Age. *Prähistorische Zeitschrift* 91, 379–430

Burgess, C. 1968. *Bronze Age Metalwork in Northern England, c. 1000 to 700 BC*. Newcastle: Oriel Press

Burgess, C. 1976. The Gwithian mould and the forerunners of South Welsh axes. In C. Burgess & R. Miket (eds), *Settlement and Economy in the Third and Second Millennia BC*, 69–79. Oxford: British Archaeological Report 33

Burgess, C. 1980. *The Age of Stonehenge*. London: Dent

Burgess, C. & Church, M. 1995. Uig Sands to Aird Uig, Isle of Lewis (Uig parish), survey. *Discovery and Excavation in Scotland* 1995, 111

Burgess, C. & Coombs, D. (eds), 1979. *Bronze Age Hoards: some finds old and new*. Oxford: British Archaeological Report 67

Burgess, C. & Gerloff, S. 1981. *The Dirks and Rapiers of Great Britain and Ireland*. Munich: Prähistorische Bronzefunde IV.7

Burgess, C., Gilmour, S. & Church, M. 1996. Guinnerso (Uig parish), relict landscape. *Discovery and Excavation in Scotland* 1996, 111–112

Burgess, C., Church, M., Heald, A. & Gilmour, S. 1997. Guinnerso (Uig parish), relict landscape. *Discovery and Excavation in Scotland* 1997, 85–86

Burley, E. 1956. A catalogue and survey of the metal-work from Traprain Law. *Proceedings of the Society of Antiquaries of Scotland* 89, 118–226

Burnham, B. & Burnham, H. 2004. *Dolaucothi-Pumsaint: survey and excavations at a Roman gold-mining complex 1987–1999*. Oxford: Oxbow Books

Bushe-Fox, J. 1915. *Excavations at Hengistbury Head, Hampshire in 1911–12*. London: Society of Antiquaries

Büster, L. & Armit, I. 2014. *The Covesea Caves Project, Excavations and Associated Fieldwork 2014. Data structure report*. University of Bradford. Unpubl. report

Butcher, C. 1922. A hoard of bronze discovered at Grays Thurrock. *Antiquaries Journal* 2, 105–8

Butler, J. & van der Waals, J. 1967. Bell Beakers and early metal-working in the Netherlands. *Palaeohistoria* 12, 41–139

Byrnes, E. 1999. Recent excavations at Richardstown, Co. Louth. *Archaeology Ireland* 13(2), 33

Cahill, M. 1996. Later BA goldwork from Ireland – form, function and formality. In Shee Twohig & Wadell 1996, 63–72

Cahill, M. 2009. Working with wire – the functional and decorative uses of gold wire in Bronze Age Ireland, 2200–700 BC. In Cooney et al. (eds), 2009, 91–105

Cahill, M. 2016. A stone to die for. *Archaeology Ireland* 30(3), 26–9

Callander, J. 1904. Notice of a stone mould for casting flat bronze axes and bars found in the parish of Insch, Aberdeenshire; with notes on the occurrence of flat axe moulds in Europe. *Proceedings of the Society of Antiquaries of Scotland* 38, 487–505

Callander, J. 1906. A stone mould for casting flat bronze axes and bars found at Pitdoulzie. *Proceedings of the Society of Antiquaries of Scotland* 40, 35–6

Callander, J. 1923. Scottish Bronze Age hoards. *Proceedings of the Society of Antiquaries of Scotland* 57, 123–66

Callander, J. & Grant, W. 1934. The broch of Midhowe, Rousay, Orkney. *Proceedings of the Society of Antiquaries of Scotland* 68, 444–516

Card, N. & Downes, J. 2003. Mine Howe – the significance of space and place in the Iron Age. In J. Downes & A. Ritchie (eds), *Sea Change: Orkney and northern Europe in the later Iron Age AD 300–800*, 11–9. Balgavies: Pinkfoot Press

Carey, C., Jones, A., Allen, M.J. & Juleff, G. 2019. The social organisation of metalworking in southern England during the Beaker period and Bronze Age: absence of evidence or evidence of absence? *Internet Archaeology* 52. https://doi.org/10.11141/ia.52.4

Carlin, N. 2018. *The Beaker Phenomenon? Understanding the character and context of social practices in Ireland, 2500–2000 BC*. Leiden: Sidestone

Carlin, N. & Brück, J. 2012. Searching for the Chalcolithic: continuity and change in the Irish final Neolithic/early Bronze Age. In Allen et al. (eds), 2012, 193–210

Carlyle, S. 2011. *Rutland Water Habitat Creation, Lagoon B: an Iron Age enclosure and Romano-British shrine near Egleton, Rutland*. Northampton: Northamptonshire Archaeology. Unpubl. report

Carlyle, S. 2012. *Glenfield Park Western Employment Area, Glenfield, Leicestershire: archaeological evaluation*. Cirencester: Cotswold Archaeology. Unpubl. report

Carreck, N. 2008. Are honey bees (*Apis mellifera* L.) native to the British Isles? *Journal of Apicultural Research* 47, 318–22

Carter, S., Hunter, F. & Smith, A. 2010. A 5th century BC Iron Age chariot burial from Newbridge, Edinburgh. *Proceedings of the Prehistoric Society* 76, 31–74

Cartwright, C. 1992. Excavations of a Romano-British Iron Working Site at Broadfield, West Sussex. *Sussex Archaeological Collections* 131, 22–59

Carver, M. 2004. *Sutton Hoo Research Project 2001*. http://archaeologydataservice.ac.uk/archives/view/suttonhoo_var_2004/ and http://dx.doi.org/10.5284/1000266

Carver, M. 2005. *A Seventh Century Princely Burial Ground and its Context*. London: British Museum Press

Caswell, E. & Roberts, B. 2018. Reassessing community cemeteries: cremation burials in Britain during the Middle Bronze Age (*c.* 1600–1150 BC). *Proceedings of the Prehistoric Society*, 329–57

Cavers, G. 2010. *Crannogs and Later Prehistoric Settlement in Western Scotland*. Oxford: British Archaeological Report 510

Chadburn, A. 2006. *Aspects of the Iron Age Coinages of Northern East Anglia with Especial Reference to Hoards*. Unpubl. PhD thesis, University of Nottingham

Chadwick, A. 2012. Routine magic, mundane ritual: towards a unified notion of depositional practice. *Oxford Journal of Archaeology* 31, 283–315

Chadwick, A. 2015. Doorways, ditches and dead dogs: material manifestations of practical magic in Iron Age and Roman Britain. In C. Houlbrook & N. Armitage (eds), *The Materiality of Magic: an artefactual investigation into ritual practices and popular beliefs*, 37–64. Oxford: Oxbow Books

Champion, T. 1980. Settlement and environment in later Bronze Age Kent. In Barrett & Bradley (eds), 1980, 223–46

Champion, T. 2011. Later prehistory. In A. Smith (ed.), *On Track: the archaeology of High Speed 1 Section 1 in Kent*, Oxford: Oxford Wessex Archaeology Monograph 4

Chapman, A. 1998. Rugby, Coton Park, Iron Age settlement, *West Midlands Archaeology* 41, 95–7

Chapman, A. 2000. *Excavation of an Iron Age Settlement at Coton Park, Rugby, Warwickshire, 1998: interim report*. Northampton: Northamptonshire Archaeology. Unpubl. report

Chapman, A. 2001. Excavation of an Iron Age settlement and a Middle Saxon cemetery at Great Houghton, Northampton, 1996. *Northhamptonshire Archaeology* 29, 1–41

Chapman, A. 2019. *A Middle Iron Age Settlement, with Copper Alloy Casting, at Coton Park, Rugby, Warwickshire*. Oxford: Archaeopress

Chapman, A. & Atkins, R. 2004. Iron Age and Roman settlement at

Mallard Close, Earls Barton, Northamptonshire. *Northamptonshire Archaeology* 32, 23–55

Chapman, H., Fletcher, W., Fenwick, H., Lillie, M. & Thomas, G. 2000. The archaeological survey of Hull valley. In R. Van de Noort & S. Ellis (eds), *Wetland Heritage of the Hull Valley: an archaeological survey*, 105–73. Hull: University of Hull

Charles, B., Parkinson, A. and Foreman, S. 2000. A Bronze Age ditch and Iron Age settlement at Elms Farm, Humberstone, Leicester. *Transactions of the Leicestershire Archaeological and Historical Society* 74, 113–220

Charlton, E. 1855. On an enamelled bronze cup, and a celt and ring mould, in the possession of Sir W. Calverley Trevelyan, Baronet; with observations on the use of metals by the ancient British and the Romans. *Archaeologia Aeliana* 4, 102–8

Chenery, C. & Evans, J. 2011. A summary of the strontium and oxygen isotope evidence for the origins of Bell Beaker individuals found near Stonehenge. In Fitzpatrick 2011, 185–90

Childe, V. 1930. *The Bronze Age*. Cambridge: Cambridge University Press

Childe, V. 1935. Excavation of the vitrified fort of Finavon, Angus. *Proceedings of the Society of Antiquaries of Scotland* 69, 49–80

Childe, V. 1936. *Man Makes Himself*. London: Watts

Childe, V. 1940. *Prehistoric Communities of the British Isles*. London: Chambers

Childe, V. 1948. A bronze worker's anvil and other tools recently acquired by the Inverness Museum, with a note on another Scottish anvil. *Proceedings of the Society of Antiquaries of Scotland* 80, 8–11

Childe, V. 1954. *What Happened in History* (2nd edn). Harmondsworth: Penguin

Childe, V. 1958. *The Prehistory of European Society*. Harmondsworth: Penguin

Childs, S. & Killick, D. 1993. Indigenous African metallurgy: nature and culture. *Annual Review of Anthropology* 22, 317–37

Chirikure, S. 2007. Metals in society. Iron production and its position in Iron Age communities of southern Africa. *Journal of Social Archaeology* 7, 72–100

Chirikure, S. 2015. *Metals in Past Societies: a global perspective on indigenous African metallurgy*. Cham: Springer

Chowne, P., Cleal, R. & Fitzpatrick, A. 2001. *Excavations at Billingborough, Lincolnshire, 1975–8: a Bronze-Iron Age settlement and salt-working site*. Salisbury: East Anglian Archaeology 94

Church, M. & Gilmour, S. 1998. Guinnerso (Uig parish), relict landscape. *Discovery and Excavation in Scotland* 1998, 106–7

Clark, A. 1993. *Excavations at Mucking. Volume 1: the site atlas. Excavations by Margaret and Tom Jones*, London: English Heritage Archaeological Report 20

Clark, E. 1905. Report as local secretary for Yorkshire. *Proceedings of the Society of Antiquaries of London* 2 ser. 20, 258–63

Clark, P. 2004. The Dover Boat ten years after its discovery. In P. Clark (ed.), *The Dover Bronze Age Boat in Context: society and water transport in prehistoric Europe*, 1–12. Oxford: Oxbow Books

Clark, P. (ed.) 2009. *Bronze Age Connections: cultural contact in prehistoric Europe*. Oxford: Oxbow Books

Clarke, D. 1970. *Beaker Pottery of Great Britain and Ireland*. Cambridge: Cambridge University Press

Clarke, D., Cowie, T. & Foxon, A. 1985. *Symbols of Power at the Time of Stonehenge*. Edinburgh: HMSO

Clarke, J. 1873. Notes on objects in the Meyer collection relating to Essex. *Transactions of the Historic Society of Lancashire and Cheshire* new ser. 13, 271–84

Claughton, P. 2011. Mineral resources. In J. Crick & E. van Houts (eds), *A Social History of England, 900–1200 AD*, 56–65. Cambridge: Cambridge University Press

Claughton, P. & Rondelez, P. 2013. Early silver mining in western Europe: an Irish perspective. *Journal of the Mining Heritage Trust of Ireland* 13, 1–8

Clay, P. & Mellor, J. 1985. *Excavations in Bath Lane, Leicester*. Leicester: Leicestershire Museums, Art Galleries and Records Service

Clay, R. 1925. An inhabited site of La Tène I date on Swallowcliffe Down. *Wiltshire Archaeological and Natural History Magazine* 43, 59–93

Cleal, R. & Pollard, J. 2012. The revenge of the native: monuments, material culture, burial and other practices in the third quarter of the 3rd millennium BC in Wessex. In Allen *et al.* (eds), 2012, 318–32

Clifford, E. 1961. *Bagendon: a Belgic oppidum. A record of the excavations of 1954–56*. Cambridge: Heffer

Clinch, G. 1901. Early man. In H. Doubleday (ed.), *The Victoria History of the County of Norfolk. Volume 1*, 253–78. London: Archibald Constable

Cody, P. 1863. Mould from Ballydagh. *Journal of the Kilkenny and South-East of Ireland Archaeological Society* new ser. 4, 307–8

Coffey, G. 1901. Irish copper celts. *Journal of the Anthropological Institute of Great Britain and Ireland* 31, 265–79

Coffey, G. 1907. Moulds for primitive spear-heads found in the County Tyrone. *Journal of the Royal Society of Antiquaries of Ireland* 5 ser. 37, 181–6

Coffey, G. 1913. Recent prehistoric finds acquired by the Academy. *Proceedings of the Royal Irish Academy, Section C* 30, 83–93

Coffey, G. 1913. *The Bronze Age in Ireland*. Dublin: Hodges, Figgis and Co

Coghlan, H. 1975. *Notes on the Prehistoric Metallurgy of Copper and Bronze in the Old World* (2nd edn). Oxford: Oxford University Press

Coghlan, H. & Case, H. 1957. The early metallurgy of copper in Ireland and Britain. *Proceedings of the Prehistoric Society* 23, 91–123

Coghlan, H. & Raftery, J. 1961. Irish prehistoric casting moulds. *Sibrium* 6, 223–44

Coles, J. 1962. Scottish late Bronze Age metalwork: typology, distribution and chronology. *Proceedings of the Society of Antiquaries of Scotland* 93, 16–134

Coles, J. 1965. Bronze Age metalwork in Dumfries and Galloway. *Transactions of the Dumfriesshire and Galloway Natural History and Antiquarian Society* 42, 61–98

Coles, J. 1966. Scottish middle Bronze Age metalwork. *Proceedings of the Society of Antiquaries of Scotland* 97, 82–156

Coles, J. 1971. Scottish early Bronze Age metalwork. *Proceedings of the Society of Antiquaries of Scotland* 101, 1–110

Coles, J. 1987. *Meare Village East: the excavations of A. Bulleid and H. St. George Gray 1932–1956*. Exeter: Somerset Levels Project

Coles, J. & Minnit, S. 1995. *Industrious and Fairly Civilized: the Glastonbury lake village*. Taunton: Somerset Levels Project and Somerset County Museums Service

Collard, M., Darvill, T. & Watts, M. 2006. Ironworking in the Bronze Age? Evidence from a 10th century BC settlement at Hartshill Copse, Upper Bucklebury, West Berkshire. *Proceedings of the Prehistoric Society* 72, 367–421

Collins, A. 1970. Bronze Age moulds in Ulster. *Ulster Journal of Archaeology* 33, 23–36

Collins, A. & Seaby, W. 1960. Structures and small finds discovered at Lough Eskragh, Co. Tyrone. *Ulster Journal of Archaeology* 3rd ser. 23, 25–37

Colquhoun, I. & Burgess, C. 1988 *The Swords of Britain*. Munich: Prähistorische Bronzefunde IV.5

Colt Hoare, R. 1812. *The Ancient History of Wiltshire*. London: W. Miller

Cook, G., Dixon, T., Russell, N., Naysmith, P., Xu, S. & Andrian, B. 2010. High-precision radiocarbon dating of the construction phase of Oakbank Crannog, Loch Tay, Perthshire. *Radiocarbon* 52, 346–55

Cook, J., Guttmann, E. & Mudd, A. 2005. Excavations of an Iron Age site at Coxwell Road, Faringdon. *Oxoniensia* 69, 181–285

Cooke, N. & Mudd, A. 2014. *A46 Nottinghamshire: the archaeology of the Newark to Widmerpool Improvement Scheme, 2009*. Salisbury: Cotswold/Wessex Archaeology

Cooke, N., Brown, F. & Phillpots, C. 2008. *Hunter Gatherers to Huntsmen. A history of the Stansted landscape*. Oxford and Salisbury: Framework Archaeology

Coombs, D. 1971. *Late Bronze Age metalwork in the south of England: typology, chronology and industrial traditions*. Unpubl. PhD thesis, University of Cambridge

Coombs, D. 2001. Metalwork. In Pryor (ed.) 2001, 255–98

Coombs, D., Northover, P. & Maskall, J. 2003. Tower Hill axe hoard. In Miles *et al.* (eds), 2003, 203–25

Cooney, G. 1998. Breaking stones, making places: the social landscapes of axe production sites. In Gibson & Simpson (eds), 1998, 108–19

Cooney, G. 2000. *Landscapes of Neolithic Ireland.* London: Routledge

Cooney, G., Becker, K., Coles, J., Ryan, M. & Sievers, S. (eds), 2009. *Relics of Old Decency: archaeological studies of later prehistory.* Dublin: Wordwell

Cooper, A. & Edmonds, M. 2007. *Past and Present: excavations at Broom, Bedfordshire 1996–2005.* Cambridge: Cambridge Archaeological Unit

Cooper, G. 1862. An account of some British antiquities found at Wilmington. *Sussex Archaeological Collections* 14, 171–5

Copley, M., Berstan, R., Straker, V., Payne, S. & Evershed, R. 2005. Dairying in antiquity II. Evidence from absorbed lipid residues dating to the British Bronze Age. *Journal of Archaeological Science* 32, 505–21

Copley, M., Berstan, R., Mukherjee, A., Dudd, S., Straker, V., Payne, S. & Evershed, R. 2005. Dairying in antiquity III. Evidence from absorbed lipid residues dating to the British Neolithic. *Journal of Archaeological Science* 32, 523–46

Corlett, C. & Potterton, M. (eds), 2012. *Life and Death in Iron Age Ireland in the Light of Recent Archaeological Excavations.* Dublin: Wordwell

Corney, M. 1984. A field survey of the extra-mural region of Silchester. In M. Fulford (ed.), *Silchester Defences 1974–80,* 239–97. London: *Britannia* Monograph Series 5

Costin, C. 1991. Craft specialization: issues in defining, documenting and explaining the organisation of production. In Schiffer, M. (ed.), 1–56. Tuscon AZ: *Archaeological Method and Theory* 3

Cotswold Archaeology 2012. *Land at Recreation Way, Mildenhall, Suffolk. Post-Excavation Assessment and Updated Project Design. Vol. 1: text and figures. CA Project No. 9100, Report 12114.* Cirencester: Cotswold Archaeology. Unpubl. report

Cottam, G. 2001. Plated Iron Age coins: official issues or contemporary forgeries? *Oxford Journal of Archaeology* 20, 377–90

Cotter, C. 2012. *The Western Stone Forts Project: excavations at Dún Aonghasa and Dún Eoghanachta.* Dublin: Wordwell

Cotton, J. 2010 *Prehistoric and Roman Settlement at Tothill Street, Minster in Thanet, Kent.* London: Museum of London Archaeology. Unpubl. report

Cowell, M. & Tite, M. 1982. Examination of the coin moulds. *Hertfordshire Archaeology* 8, 57

Cowie, T. 1988. *Magic Metal: early metalworkers in the north-east.* Aberdeen: Anthropological Museum, University of Aberdeen

Cowie, T. 2000. An early Bronze Age stone mould for casting flat axeheads from Glenhead Farm, Carron Bridge, near Denny. *Calatria* 14, 97–107

Cowie, T. 2002. Galmisdale, Eigg. *Discovery and Excavation in Scotland* 2001, 63

Cowie, T. 2003. Galmisdale, Isle of Eigg. *Discovery and Excavation in Scotland* 2002, 78

Cowie, T. 2004. Special places for special axes? Early Bronze Age metalwork from Scotland in its landscape setting. In Shepherd & Barclay (eds), 2004, 247–61

Cowie, T. & O'Connor, B. 2009. Some early Bronze Age stone moulds from Scotland. In Kienlin & Roberts (eds), 2009, 313–27

Cox, P. & Hearne, C. 1991. *Redeemed from the Heath: the archaeology of the Wytch Farm oilfield (1987–1990).* Dorchester: Dorset Natural History and Archaeological Society Monograph 9

Cracknell, S. & Smith, B. 1984. Archaeological investigations at Mavis Grind, Shetland. *Glasgow Archaeological Journal* 10, 13–39

Craddock, P. 1972. *British Museum Research Laboratory file no. 3309, 1/11/1972.* London: British Museum. Unpubl. report

Craddock, P. 1994. Recent progress in the study of early mining and metallurgy in the British Isles. *Historical Metallurgy* 28, 69–83

Craddock, P. & Tite, M. 1981. Report on the scientific examination of coin moulds from Gatesbury. In Partridge (ed.) 1981, 326

Craddock, P., Cowell, M. & Stead, I. 2004. Britain's first brass. *Antiquaries Journal* 84, 339–46

Crane, P. 2010. The excavation of a coastal promontory fort at Porth y Rhaw, Solva, Pembrokeshire, 1995–98. *Archaeologia Cambrensis* 159, 53–98

Craven, J. 2004. *Extension to Ingham Quarry, Fornham St Genevieve FSG 017: a report on the archaeological evaluation, 2004.* Bury St Edmonds Suffolk County Council Archaeological Service. Unpubl. report 2004/122

Crawford, O.G.S. 1912. The distribution of early Bronze Age settlements in Britain. *Geographical Journal* 40, 184–97 and 304–17

Cree, J. & Curle, A. 1922. Account of the excavations on Traprain Law during the summer of 1921. *Proceedings of the Society of Antiquaries of Scotland* 56, 189–259

Creighton, J. 2000. *Coins and Power in Late Iron Age Britain.* Cambridge: Cambridge University Press

Cressey, M. & Anderson, S. 2011. *A Later Prehistoric Settlement and Metalworking Site at Seafield West, near Inverness, Highland.* Edinburgh: Scottish Archaeological Internet Report 47

Crew, P. & Rehren, T. 2002. High-temperature workshop residues from Tara: iron, bronze and glass. *Discovery Programme Reports* 6, 83–102

Cromarty, A., Barclay, A., Lambrick, G. & Robinson, M. 2006. *Late Bronze Age Ritual and Habitation on a Thames Eyot at Whitecross Farm, Wallingford. The archaeology of the Wallingford bypass, 1986–92.* Oxford: Oxford Archaeology

Crowe, K. 2003. Two late Bronze Age hoards from south-east Essex. *Essex Archaeology and History* 34, 1–18

Cruickshanks, G. & Hunter, F. nd. *Metalworking Debris and other Vitrified Material from High Pasture Cave.* Edinburgh: National Museum of Scotland. Unpubl. specialist report

Crumley, C. 1995. Heterarchy and the analysis of complex societies. *Archeological Papers of the American Anthropological Association* 6, 1–5

Cunliffe, B. 1984. *Danebury: an Iron Age hillfort in Hampshire. Volume 2. The excavations 1969–1978: the finds.* London: Council for British Archaeology Research Report 52

Cunliffe, B. 1987. *Hengistbury Head, Dorset. Volume 1: the prehistoric and Roman settlement, 3500 BC–AD 500.* Oxford: Oxford University Committee for Archaeology

Cunliffe, B. 1988. *Mount Batten, Plymouth: a prehistoric and Roman port.* Oxford: Oxford University Committee for Archaeology

Cunliffe, B. 1992. Pits, preconceptions and propitiation. *Oxford Journal of Archaeology* 11, 69–83

Cunliffe, B. 1995a. *Danebury: an Iron Age hillfort in Hampshire. Volume 6. A hillfort community in perspective.* York: Council for British Archaeology Research Report 102

Cunliffe, B. 1995b. The Celtic chariot: a footnote. In Raftery *et al.* (eds), 1995, 31–40

Cunliffe, B. 2005. *Iron Age Communities in Britain* (4th edn). Abingdon: Routledge

Cunliffe, B. & Phillipson, D. 1968. Excavations at Eldon's Seat, Encombe, Dorset. *Proceedings of the Prehistoric Society* 34, 191–237

Cunliffe, B. & Poole, C. 1991. *Danebury: an Iron Age hillfort in Hampshire. Volume 5. The excavations 1979–1988: the finds.* London: Council for British Archaeology Research Report 73

Cunliffe, B. & Poole, C. 2000. *The Danebury Environs Project. Volume 2 – part 2: Bury Hill, Upper Clatford, Hants, 1990.* Oxford: Oxford University School of Archaeology

Cunliffe, B. & Poole, C. 2008. *The Danebury Environs Roman Programme. Volume 2 – part 5: Rowbury Farm, Wherwell, Hants, 2003.* Oxford: Oxford University School of Archaeology

Cunnington, B. & Cunnington, M. 1913. Casterley Camp. Being an account of excavations carried out by Mr and Mrs B.H. Cunnington. *Wiltshire Archaeological and Natural History Magazine* 38, 53–105

Cunnington, M. 1909. Notes on a late Celtic rubbish heap near Oare. *Wiltshire Archaeological and Natural History Magazine* 36, 125–39

Cunnington, M. 1912. Bronze Age barrows on Arn Hill, Warminster. *Wiltshire Archaeological and Natural History Magazine* 37, 538–41

Cunnington, M. 1920. Notes on objects from an inhabited site on the Worms Head, Glamorgan. *Archaeologia Cambrensis* 6 ser. 20, 251–6

Cunnington, M. 1923. *The Early Iron Age Inhabited Site at All Cannings Cross Farm, Wiltshire*. Devizes: George Simpson

Cunnington, M. & Goddard, E. 1934. *Catalogue of Antiquities in the Museum of the Wiltshire Archaeological and Natural History Society at Devizes*. Part II (2nd edn). Devizes: George Simpson

Cunnington, W. 1806. Account of tumuli opened in Wiltshire. *Archaeologia* 15, 122–9

Curle, A. 1932. Interim report on the excavation of a Bronze Age dwelling at Yarlshof, Shetland, in 1931. *Proceedings of the Society of Antiquaries of Scotland* 66, 113–28

Curle, A. 1933. Accounts on further excavation in 1932 of the prehistoric township at Jarlshof, Shetland, on behalf of HM officer of works. *Proceedings of the Society of Antiquaries of Scotland* 67, 82–136

Curle, A. 1934. An account of further excavation at Jarlshof, Sumburgh, Shetland, in 1932 and 1933. *Proceedings of the Society of Antiquaries of Scotland* 68, 224–319

Curle, A. 1935. An account of the excavation, on behalf of HM Office of Works, of another prehistoric dwelling (no. V) at Jarlshof, Sumburgh, Shetland, in the summer of 1934. *Proceedings of the Society of Antiquaries of Scotland* 69, 85–107

Currás, B.X. & Sastre, I. (eds), 2019. *Alternative Iron Ages: social theory from archaeological analysis*. Abingdon: Routledge.

Curwen, E. 1954. *The Archaeology of Sussex* (2nd edn). London: Methuen

Curwen, E. & Curwen, E.C. 1927. Excavations in the Caburn, near Lewes. *Sussex Archaeological Collections* 68, 1–56

Dalland, M. 2014. Boynds Farm, Inverurie. Excavation (Aberdeenshire). *Discovery and Excavation in Scotland* 2014, 29

Dalland, M. & Cox, S. 2014. *Results of an Archaeological Excavation at Boynds Farm, Inverurie*. Edinburgh: Headland Archaeology. Unpubl. draft report

Darbyshire, G. 1995. *Pre-Roman Iron Tools for Working Metal and Wood in Southern Britain*. Unpubl. PhD thesis, University of Wales, Cardiff

Darvill, T. 2000. *Billown Neolithic Landscape Project, Isle of Man. Fifth report: 1999*. Bournemouth and Douglas: Bournemouth University and Manx National Heritage

Darvill, T. 2001. *Billown Neolithic Landscape Project, Isle of Man. Sixth report: 2000*. Bournemouth and Douglas: Bournemouth University and Manx National Heritage

Darvill, T. 2002. White on blonde: quartz pebbles and the use of quartz at Neolithic monuments in the Isle of Man and beyond. In Jones & MacGregor (eds), 2002, 73–91

Darvill, T. 2004. *Billown Neolithic Landscape Project, Isle of Man. Eighth report: 2003*. Bournemouth and Douglas: Bournemouth University and Manx National Heritage

Davey, C. 2009. The early history of lost-wax casting. In J. Mei & T. Rehren (eds), *Metallurgy and Civilisation: Eurasia and beyond*, 147–54. London: Archetype

Davey, P. 1973. Bronze Age metalwork from Lincolnshire. *Archaeologia* 104, 51–127

Davey, P. 1978. Bronze Age metalwork from the Isle of Man. In P. Davey (ed.), *Man and the Environment in the Isle of Man*, 219–32. Oxford: British Archaeological Report 54

Davies, O. 1939. Excavations at the Giant's Grave, Loughash. *Ulster Journal of Archaeology* 3rd ser 2, 254–68

Davis, M. & Gwilt, A. 2008. Material, style and identity in first century AD metalwork, with particular reference to the Seven Sisters hoard. In Garrow *et al.* (eds), 2008, 145–83

Davis, R. 2006. *Basal-looped Spearheads: typology, chronology, context and use*. Oxford: British Archaeological Report S1497

Davis, R. 2012. *The Early and Middle Bronze Age Spearheads of Britain*. Stuttgart: Prähistorische Bronzefunde V.5

Davis, R. 2015. *The Late Bronze Age Spearheads of Britain*. Stuttgart: Prähistorische Bronzefunde V.7

De'Athe, R. 2013. Early Iron Age metalworking and Iron Age/early Romano-British settlement evidence along the Barton Stacey to Lockerley Gas Pipeline. *Proceedings of the Hampshire Field Club and Archaeological Society* 68, 29–63

Dent, J. 1984. *Wetwang Slack. An Iron Age Cemetery on the Yorkshire Wolds*. Unpubl. MPhil thesis, University of Sheffield

Dent, J. 2010. *The Iron Age in East Yorkshire: an analysis of the later prehistoric monuments of the Yorkshire Wolds and the culture which marked their final phase*. Oxford: British Archaeological Report 508

Denyer, S. 1978. *African Traditional Architecture: an historical and geographical perspective*. London: Heinemann

de Jersey, P. 2009. Some experiments in Iron Age coin production, and some implications for the production of Gallo-Belgic E. In J. van Heesch & I. Heeren (eds), *Coinage in the Iron Age: essays in honour of Simone Scheers*, 257–69. London: Spink

de Jersey, P. 2014. *Coin Hoards in Iron Age Britain*. London: Spink

de Salis, J. 1863. A moiety of a stone mould for casting spearheads. *Archaeological Journal* 20, 170–1

Dietrich, O. 2012. Travelling or not? Tracing individual mobility patterns of late Bronze Age metalworkers in the Carpathian Basin. In L. Marta (ed.), *The Gáva Culture in the Tisa Plain and Transylvania*, 211–29. Satu Mare: Muzeul Judeţean Satu Mare

Dinn, J. & Evans, J. 1990. Aston Mill Farm, Kemerton: excavation of a ring-ditch, Middle Iron-Age enclosure and a Grubenhaus. *Transactions of the Worcestershire Archaeological Society* 12, 5–66

Dixon, T. 2003. Oakbank Crannog (Kenmore Parish). Crannog (Perth and Kinross). *Discovery and Excavation in Scotland* 2003, 108–110

Dixon, T. & Cavers, M. 2001. Oakbank Crannog, Loch Tay (Kenmore Parish). Excavation (Perth and Kinross). *Discovery and Excavation in Scotland* 2001, 78–9

Dixon, T., Cook, G., Andrian, B., Garety, L., Russell, N. & Menard, T. 2007. Radiocarbon dating of the crannogs of Loch Tay, Perthshire (Scotland). *Radiocarbon* 49(2), 673–84

Dolan, B. 2012. *The social and technological context of iron production in Iron Age and Early Medieval Ireland c. 600 BC–AD 900*. Unpubl. PhD thesis, University College Dublin

Dolan, B. 2014. Beyond elites: reassessing Irish Iron Age society. *Oxford Journal of Archaeology* 33, 361–77

Doody, M. 2008. *The Ballyhoura Hills Project*. Dublin: Wordwell

Doonan, R. 1999. *The Mould Fragments and Slag from Huntsmans Quarry, Kemerton*. London: Ancient Monuments Laboratory Report 71/1999

Dorling, P. 2014. *Eaton Camp, Ruckhall, Eaton Bishop, Herefordshire: a report on excavations in May 2012 and June 2013*. Hereford: Herefordshire Archaeology. Unpubl. report

Dowling, G. 2014. Landscape and settlement in late Iron Age Ireland: some emerging trends. In J. Cahill Wilson (ed.), *Late Iron Age and 'Roman' Ireland*, 151–74. Dublin: Wordwell

Drenth, E. & Williams, G. 2011. Het geheim van de smid? Een opmerkelijk depot van de Klokbekercultuur uit Hengelo (Gld.). In H. van der Velde, N. Jaspers, E. Drenth & H. Scholte Lubberink (eds), *Van Graven in de Prehistorie en Dingen die Voorbijgaan*, 87–113. Leiden: Sidestone Press

Drenth, E., Freudenberg, M. & Hartz, S. 2009. Een depot van stenen werktuigen afkomstig van een smid van de Klokbekercultuur? In G. Williams (ed.), *Van Onder de Es: een archeologische opgraving aan de Elderinkweg te Hengelo, gemeente Bronckhorst*, 42–87. Amersfoort: ADC Rapport 1576

Drenth, E., Freudenberg, M. & van Os, B. 2013. Prehistoric stone tools for metal-working from the Netherlands: an overview. In Bartelheim *et al.* (eds) 2013, 41–51

Drescher, H. 1957. Bronzeguß in Formen aus Bronze. *Die Kunde, Neue Folge* 8, 52–75

Dubreucq, E. 2017. The artisans of metal and the elite in the western Hallstatt zone (630–450 BC). In Brysbaert & Gorgues (eds), 2017, 161–90

Dungworth, D. 1996. The production of copper alloys in Iron Age Britain. *Proceedings of the Prehistoric Society* 62, 399–421

Dungworth, D. 1997. Iron Age and Roman copper alloys from northern Britain. *Internet Archaeology* 2. doi: 10.11141/ia.2.2

Dungworth, D. 2000. A note on the analysis of crucibles and moulds. *Historical Metallurgy* 34 (2), 83–6

Dungworth, D. 2001. *Metal Working Debris from Elms Farm, Heybridge, Essex.* London, unpubl. Centre for Applied Archaeology Report 69/2001

Dunning, G. 1934. The swan's-neck and ring-headed pins of the Early Iron Age in Britain. *Archaeological Journal* 91, 269–95

Dunning, G. 1976. Salmonsbury, Bourton-on-the-Water, Gloucestershire. In Harding (ed.) 1976, 75–118

Dunwell, A. 1999. Edin's Hall fort, broch and settlement, Berwickshire (Scottish Borders): recent fieldwork and new perceptions. *Proceedings of the Society of Antiquaries of Scotland* 129, 303–57

Dutton, A., Fasham, P., Jenkins, D., Caseldine, A. & Hamilton-Dyer, S. 1994. Prehistoric copper mining on the Great Orme, Llandudno, Gwynedd. *Proceedings of the Prehistoric Society* 60, 245–86

du Noyer, G. 1847. Bronze celts, and celt moulds of stone and bronze. *Archaeological Journal* 4, 327–37

Earle, T. 2002. *Bronze Age Economics: the beginnings of political economies.* Cambridge: Westview

Earle, T. & Kristiansen, K. 2010. *Organising Bronze Age Societies: the Mediterranean, central Europe, Scandinavia compared.* Cambridge: Cambridge University Press

Earle, T. Ling, J., Uhnér, C., Stos-Gale, Z. & Melheim, L. 2015. The political economy and metal trade in Bronze Age Europe: understanding regional variability in terms of comparative advantages and articulations. *European Journal of Archaeology* 18, 633–57

Eckardt, H. & Crummy, N. 2008. *Styling the Body in Late Iron Age and Roman Britain: a contextual approach to toilet instruments.* Montagnac: Monographies Instrumentum 36

Edwardson, A. 1970. *Bronze Age Metalwork in Moyse's Hall Museum, Bury St Edmunds, Suffolk.* Bury St Edmunds: Moyse's Hall Museum

Ehrenberg, M. 1981. The anvils of Bronze Age Europe. *Antiquaries Journal* 61, 14–28

Ehrenberg, M. & Caple, C. 1983. Excavations at Fimber, Yorkshire. Interim report on 1st season, 1982. *Prehistory Research Section Bulletin* 20, unpaginated

Ehrenberg, M. & Caple, C. 1985. Excavations at Fimber, Yorkshire. Interim report on 2nd season, 1983. *Prehistory Research Section Bulletin* 22, unpaginated

Ehrenreich, R. 1985. *Trade, Technology and the Ironworking Community in the Iron Age of Southern Britain.* Oxford: British Archaeological Report 144

Ehrenreich, R. 1991. Metalworking in Iron Age Britain: heterarchy or hierarchy? In R. Ehrenreich (ed.), *Metals in Society: theory beyond analysis*, 69–80. Philadelphia: MASCA

Ehrenreich, R. 1995. Early metalworking: a heterarchical analysis of industrial organization. *Archeological Papers of the American Anthropological Association* 6, 34–9

Ehser, A., Borg G. & Pernicka, E. 2011. Provenance of the gold of the early Bronze Age Nebra Sky Disk, central Germany: geochemical characterization of natural gold from Cornwall. *European Journal of Mineralogy* 23, 895–910

Elgee, F. 1930. *Early Man in North-east Yorkshire.* Gloucester: John Bellows

Eliade, M. 1971. *The Forge and the Crucible: the origins and structure of alchemy.* New York: Harper and Row

Elliott, R., Clarke, L. & Ginn, V. 2008. *M3 Clonee-North of Kells. Contract 1: Clonee-Dunshaughlin. Report on the archaeological excavation of Pace 1, Co. Meath.* Drogheda, Co. Louth: Archaeological Consultancy Services. Unpubl. report

Ellis, C. 2004. *A Prehistoric Ritual Complex at Eynesbury, Cambridgeshire.* Salisbury: East Anglian Archaeology Occasional Paper 17

Ellis, C. 2012. The excavation of a Late Bronze Age/Early Iron Age-Middle Iron Age settlement at Home Field, Down Farm, Sixpenny Handley, Dorset. *Proceedings of the Dorset Natural History and Archaeological Society* 133, 77–97

Ellis, C. & Rawlings, M. 2001. Excavations at Balksbury Camp, Andover 1995–97. *Proceedings of the Hampshire Field Club and Archaeological Society* 56, 21–94

Ellis, P. 1990. Norton Fitzwarren hillfort: a report on the excavations by Nancy and Philip Langmaid between 1968 and 1971. *Somerset Archaeology and Natural History* 133, 1–74

Ellis, P. 1993. *Beeston Castle, Cheshire: a report on the excavations 1968–85.* London: English Heritage

Ellis, S., Fenwick, H., Lillie, M. & Van de Noort, R. 2001. *Wetland Heritage of the Lincolnshire Marsh: an archaeological survey.* Hull: University of Hull

Ellison, A. 1980. Deverel-Rimbury urn cemeteries: the evidence for social organisation. In Barrett & Bradley (eds), 1980, 115–26

Ellison, A. 1981. Towards a socioeconomic model for the Middle Bronze Age in southern England. In I. Hodder, G. Isaac & N. Hammond (eds), *Pattern of the Past: studies in honour of David Clarke*, 413–38. Cambridge: Cambridge University Press

Elsden, N. 1996. *Cranford Lane, Harlington, London Borough of Hillingdon: post excavation report.* London: Museum of London Archaeology Service. Unpubl. report

Elsdon, S. 1997. *Old Sleaford Revealed.* Oxford: Oxbow Books

Eogan, G. 1965. *Catalogue of Irish Bronze Swords.* Dublin: The Stationary Office

Eogan, G. 1983. *The Hoards of the Irish Later Bronze Age.* Dublin: University College Dublin

Eogan, G. 1986. *Knowth and the Passage Tombs of Ireland.* London: Thames and Hudson

Eogan, G. 1993. Aspects of metal production and manufacturing systems during the Irish Bronze Age. *Acta Praehistorica et Archaeologica* 25, 87–110

Eogan, G. 1994. *The Accomplished Art: gold and gold-working in Britain and Ireland during the Bronze Age (c. 2300–650 BC).* Oxford: Oxbow Books

Eogan, G. 2000. *The Socketed Bronze Axes in Ireland.* Stuttgart: Prähistorische Bronzefunde IX.22

Essex County Council, 2015. *Elms Farm Portfolio Project.* http:// archaeologydataservice.ac.uk/archives/view/elmsfarm_eh_2013/ index.cfm

Evans, C. 2003. *Power and Island Communities: excavations at the Wardy Hill ringwork, Coveney, Ely.* Cambridge: East Anglian Archaeology 103

Evans, C. & Knight, M. 1997. *The Barleycroft Paddocks Excavations, Cambridgeshire.* Cambridge: Cambridge Archaeological Unit. Unpubl. report

Evans, C. & Knight, M. 2000. A Fenland delta: later prehistoric land-use in the lower Ouse reaches. In M. Dawson (ed.), *Prehistoric, Roman and Post-Roman Landscapes of the Great Ouse Valley*, 89–106. York: Council for British Archaeology Research Report 119

Evans, C. & Patten, R. 2011. An inland Bronze Age: excavations at Striplands Farm, West Longstanton. *Proceedings of the Cambridge Antiquarian Society* 100, 7–45

Evans, C., Appleby, G., Lucy, S., Appleby, J. & Brudenell, M. 2015. *Lives in Land. Mucking Excavations by Margaret and Tom Jones, 1965–1978: prehistory, context and summary.* Oxford: Oxbow Books

Evans, J. 1881. *The Ancient Bronze Implements, Weapons, and Ornaments, of Great Britain and Ireland.* London: Longmans, Green and Co

Evens, E., Grinsell, L., Piggot, S. & Wallis, F. 1962. Fourth report of the sub-committee of the South-Western Group of Museums and Art Galleries on the petrological identification of stone axes. *Proceedings of the Prehistoric Society* 28, 209–66

Evens, E., Smith, I. & Wallis, F. 1972. The petrological identification of stone implements from south-western England: fifth report of the sub-committee of the South-Western Federation of Museums and Art Galleries. *Proceedings of the Prehistoric Society* 38, 235–75

Fairhurst, H. 1984. *Excavations at Crosskirk Broch, Caithness.* Edinburgh: Society of Antiquaries of Scotland

Farley, J. 2012. *At the Edge of Empire: Iron Age and early Roman metalwork in the East Midlands.* Unpubl. PhD thesis, University of Leicester

Farley, J. & Hunter, F. 2015. *Celts: art and identity.* London: British Museum Press

Fasham, P. 1985. *The Prehistoric Settlement at Winnall Down, Winchester: excavations of MARC3 site R17 in 1976 and 1977.* Winchester: Hampshire Field Club and Archaeological Society Monograph 2

Fasham, P. 1987. *A 'Banjo' Enclosure in Micheldever Wood, Hampshire: MARC3 site R27.* Winchester: Hampshire Field Club and Archaeological Society Monograph 5

Fell, C. 1937. The Hunsbury hill-fort, Northants: a new survey of the material. *Archaeological Journal* 93, 57–100

Fell, D. 2017 Scotch Corner: a crossroads on the Roman frontier. *British Archaeology* 154, 14–21

Fell, D. & Hunn, J. 2005. Kings Sutton, 16–18 Wales Street. *South Midlands Archaeology* 35, 33–4

Fell, V. 1988. Iron Age metalworking tools from Gussage All Saints, Dorset. *Proceedings of the Dorset Natural History and Archaeological Society* 110, 73–6

Fell, V. 1990. *Pre-Roman Iron Age Metalworking Tools from England and Wales: their use, technology, and archaeological context.* Unpubl. PhD thesis, University of Durham

Fell, V. 1993. Examination of four Iron Age ferrous hammer heads from Bredon Hill (Hereford and Worcester), England. *Historical Metallurgy* 27, 60–70

Fell, V. 1997. Iron Age iron files from England. *Oxford Journal of Archaeology* 16, 79–98

Fell, V. 1998. Iron Age ferrous hammerheads from Britain. *Oxford Journal of Archaeology* 17, 207–25

Fenton, P. 1996. *An Interim Statement on the Archaeological Excavations at Church Farm, Bierton, Aylesbury, Buckinghamshire.* Oxford: Tempus Reparatum. Unpubl. report

Field, D. & Needham, S. 1986. Evidence for Bronze Age settlement on Coombe Warren, Kingston Hill. *Surrey Archaeological Collections* 77, 127–51

Field, N. 1966. Romano-British settlement at Studland, Dorset. *Proceedings of the Dorset Natural History and Archaeological Society* 87, 142–207

Field, N. & Parker Pearson, M. 2003. *Fiskerton: an Iron Age timber causeway with Iron Age and Roman votive offerings: the 1981 excavation.* Oxford: Oxbow Books

Figuier, L. 1870. *L'Homme Primitif.* Paris: Hachette

Fitzpatrick, A. 1997. *Archaeological Excavations on the Route of the A27 Westhampnett Bypass, West Sussex, 1992.* Salisbury: Wessex Archaeology Report 12

Fitzpatrick, A. 2009. In his hands and in his head: the Amesbury Archer as a metalworker. In Clark (ed.) 2009, 176–88

Fitzpatrick, A. 2011. *The Amesbury Archer and the Boscombe Bowmen. Bell beaker burials on Boscombe Down, Amesbury, Wiltshire.* Salisbury: Wessex Archaeology Report 27

Fitzpatrick, A. 2015a. Great Britain and Ireland in 2200 BC. In H. Meller, H. Arz, R. Jung & R. Risch (eds), *2200 BC – ein Klimasturz als Ursache für den Zerfall der Alten Welt?,* 805–32. Halle: Landesamt für Denkmalpflege und Archäologie Sachsen-Anhalt and Landesmuseum für Vorgeschichte Halle

Fitzpatrick, A. 2015b. The Kirkhaugh cairn: an old find and a new tale. *Past* 79, 4–6

Fitzpatrick, A. 2019. Mining, making and stone tools: the earliest metal objects in Britain and Ireland. In D. Brandherm (ed.), *Aspects of the Bronze Age in the Atlantic Archipelago and Beyond: proceedings from the Belfast Bronze Age Forum, 9–10 November 2013,* 177–202. Hagen: Archæologia Atlantica – Monographiæ III

Fitzpatrick, A., Barnes, I. & Cleal, R. 1995. An early Iron Age settlement at Dunston Park, Thatcham. In I. Barnes, W. Boismier, R. Cleal, A. Fitzpatrick & M. Roberts (eds), *Early Settlement in Berkshire: Mesolithic–Roman occupation in the Thames and Kennet Valleys,* 65–92. Salisbury: Wessex Archaeology Report 6

Fitzpatrick, M. 1997. *1997:615 – Johnstown South, Wicklow.* http://www.excavations.ie/report/1997/Wicklow/0003164/

Fitzpatrick, M. 1998. *Preliminary Report, Archaeological Excavation at Johnstown South, Arklow, Co. Wicklow.* Castlecomer, Co. Kilkenny: Valerie J. Keeley. Unpubl. report

Flanagan, L. 1979. Industrial resources, production and distribution in earlier Bronze Age Ireland. In Ryan (ed.) 1979, 145–63

Flanagan, L. 1991. Metal production. In Ryan (ed.) 1991, 78–82

Flanagan, L. 1998. *Ancient Ireland. Life before the Celts.* Dublin: Gill and Macmillan

Flower, J. 1874. Notice of a hoard of bronze implements found at Beddington, Surrey. *Surrey Archaeological Collections* 6, 125–6

Fokkens, H. 2012. Dutchmen on the move? A discussion of the adoption of the Beaker package. In Allen *et al.* (eds), 2012, 115–25

Fokkens, H. & Harding, A. (eds), 2013. *The Oxford Handbook of the European Bronze Age.* Oxford: Oxford University Press

Foltz, E. 1980. Guss in verlorener Form mit Bleimodellen? *Archäologisches Korrespondenzblatt* 10, 345–9

Fontijn, D. 2001. Rethinking ceremonial dirks of the Plougrescant-Ommerschans type: some thoughts on the structure of metalwork exchange. In Metz *et al.* (eds), 2001, 263–280

Fontijn D. 2002. *Sacrificial Landscapes: cultural biographies of persons, objects and 'natural' places in the Bronze Age of the Netherlands c. 2300–600 BC.* Leiden: *Analecta Praehistorica Leidensia* 33/34

Fontijn, D. 2005. Giving up weapons. In M. Parker Pearson (ed.), *Warfare, Violence and Slavery in Prehistory,* 145–54. Oxford: British Archaeological Report S1374

Forster, A. & Turner, V. (eds), 2009. *Kleber: Shetland's oldest industry. Shetland soapstone since prehistory.* Lerwick: Shetland Amenity Trust

Foster, J. 1980. *The Iron Age Moulds from Gussage All Saints.* London: British Museum Occasional Paper 12

Foster, J. 1995. Metalworking in the British Iron Age: the evidence from Weelsby Avenue, Grimsby. In Raftery *et al.* (eds), 1995, 49–60

Fournet, J. 1862. *Du Mineur, son Rôle et son Influence sur les Progrès de la Civilisation, d'après les Données Actuelles de l'Archéologie et de la Géologie.* Lyon: Rey et Sézanne

Fowler, C. 2005. Identity politics: personhood, kinship, gender and power in Neolithic and Early Bronze Age Britain. In E. Casella & C. Fowler (eds), *The Archaeology of Plural and Changing identities: beyond identification,* 109–34. New York: Plenum

Fowler, C. 2013. *The Emergent Past. A Relational Realist Archaeology of Early Bronze Age Mortuary Practices.* Oxford: Oxford University Press

Fowler, P. 1960. Excavations at Madmarston Camp, Swalcliffe, 1957–8. *Oxoniensia* 25, 3–48

Fox, A. 1957. Excavations on Dean Moor, in the Avon valley, 1954–1956. The late Bronze Age settlement. *Reports and Transactions of the Devonshire Association for the Advancement of Science, Literature and Art* 89, 18–77

Fox, C. 1923. *The Archaeology of the Cambridge region.* Cambridge: Cambridge University Press

Fox, C. 1947. *A Find of the Early Iron Age from Llyn Cerrig Bach, Anglesey.* Cardiff: National Museum of Wales

Fox, C. 1958. *Pattern and Purpose: a survey of early Celtic art in Britain.* Cardiff: National Museum of Wales

Framework Archaeology, 2009. *The Stansted Framework Project.* http://archaeologydataservice.ac.uk/archives/view/stansted_framework_2009/downloads.cfm?type=gis. doi:10.5284/1000029

Frazer, W. 1889. On a mould of micaceous sandstone for casting a celt with a double loop, lately found in the south of Ireland, with observations. *Journal of the Royal Historical and Archaeological Association of Ireland* 19, 289–92

Fregni, E. 2014. *The Compleat Metalsmith: craft and technology in the British Bronze Age*. Unpubl. PhD thesis, University of Sheffield

Frei, K., Mannering, U., Kristiansen, K., Allentoft, M., Wilson, A., Skals, I., Tridico, S., Nosch, M.-L., Willerslev, E., Clarke, L. & Frei, R. 2015. Tracing the dynamic life story of a Bronze Age female. *Nature Scientific Reports* 5, 10431. doi: 10.1038/srep10431

Frei, K., Villa, C., Jørkov, M., Allentoft, M., Kaul, F., Ethelberg, P., Reiter, S., Wilson, A., Taube, M., Olsen, J., Lynnerup, N., Willerslev, E., Kristiansen, K. & Frei, R. 2017. A matter of months: high precision migration chronology of a Bronze Age female. *PLoS One* 12(6), 1–20

Frere, S. 1941. A Claudian site at Needham, Norfolk. *Antiquaries Journal* 21, 40–55

Frere, S. 1983. *Verulamium Excavations. Volume 2*. London: Report of the Research Committee of the Society of Antiquaries of London 41

Freudenberg, M. 2010. Stone Age or Bronze Age? Cushion stones and other stone tools used for early metalworking in Schleswig-Holstein. In B. Eriksen (ed.), *Lithic Technology in Metal-using Societies*, 23–32. Højbjerg: Jutland Archaeological Society

Frieman, C. & Hofmann, D. 2019. Present pasts in the archaeology of genetics, identity, and migration in Europe: a critical essay. *World Archaeology*. DOI: 10.1080/00438243.2019.1627907

Fulford, M. & Timby, J. 2000. *Late Iron Age and Roman Silchester: excavations on the site of the Forum-Basilica 1977, 1980–86*. London: *Britannia* Monograph 15

Fulford, M., Clarke, A., Durham, E. & Pankhurst, N. 2018. *Late Iron Age Calleva: the pre-conquest occupation at Silchester Insula IX*. London: *Britannia* Monograph 32

Furholt, M. 2018. Massive migrations? The impact of recent aDNA studies on our view of third millennium Europe. *European Journal of Archaeology* 21, 159–91

Gabillot, M. & Lagarde, C. 2008. Voluntary destructions of objects in middle and late Bronze Age hoards in France. In Hamon & Quilliec (eds), 2008, 59–65

Garrow, D. 2012. Odd deposits and average practice. A critical history of the concept of structured deposition. *Archaeological Dialogues* 19, 85–115

Garrow, D. & Gosden, C. 2012. *Technologies of Enchantment? Exploring Celtic art: 400 BC to AD 100*. Oxford: Oxford University Press

Garrow, D., Gosden, C. & Hill, J. (eds), 2008. *Rethinking Celtic art*. Oxford: Oxbow Books

Garrow, D., Gosden, C., Hill, J. & Bronk Ramsey, C. 2010. Dating Celtic art: a major radiocarbon dating programme of Iron Age and early Roman metalwork in Britain. *Archaeological Journal* 166, 79–123

Garstki, K. 2017. *Production and Technological Change: ironworking in prehistoric Ireland*. Unpubl. PhD, University of Wisconsin Milwaukee

Garstki, K. 2019. The social production of iron in first millennium BC Ireland. *Oxford Journal of Archaeology* 38, 443–63

Gebhard, R., Lehrberger, G., Morteani, G., Raub, C., Wagner, F. & Wagner, U. 1995. Coin moulds and other ceramic material: a key to Celtic precious metal working. In G. Morteani & J.P. Northover (eds), *Prehistoric Gold in Europe: mines, metallurgy and manufacture*, 273–301. Dordrecht: Kluwer

Gell, A. 1998. *Art and agency: an anthropological theory*. Oxford: Oxford University Press

Gelling, P. 1958. Close ny Chollagh: an Iron Age fort at Scarlett, Isle of Man. *Proceedings of the Prehistoric Society* 24, 85–100

Gelling, P. 1977. Excavations on Pilsdon Pen, Dorset, 1964–71. *Proceedings of the Prehistoric Society* 43, 263–86

George, T. 1917. Early man in Northamptonshire, with particular reference to the late Celtic period as illustrated by Hunsbury Camp. *Northamptonshire Natural History Society and Field Club Journal* 18, 1–40

Gerloff, S. 2010. *Atlantic Cauldrons and Buckets of the Late Bronze and Early Iron Ages in Western Europe*. Stuttgart: Prähistorische Bronzefunde II.18

Giazzon, D. 2013. *Mathieu (Calvados), 'Le Clos des Châtaigniers'. Une semi-enceinte du Bronze final lll*. Where: Inrap Grand-Ouest. Unpubl. report

Gibson, A. 1994. Excavations at the Sarn-y-bryn-caled cursus complex, Welshpool, Powys, and the timber circles of Great Britain and Ireland. *Proceedings of the Prehistoric Society* 60, 143–223

Gibson, A. & Simpson, D.D.A. (eds), 1998. *Prehistoric Ritual and Religion*. Stroud: Sutton

Gibson, D. 1996. Death of a salesman: Childe's itinerant craftsman in the light of present knowledge of late prehistoric European craft production. In B. Wailes (ed.) *Craft Specialization and Social Evolution: in memory of V. Gordon Childe*, 107–19. Philadelphia PA: University of Pennsylvania Museum of Archaeology and Anthroplogy

Gibson, D. 2016. Chalcolithic beginnings and ecological change spanning 1,000 years as glimpsed from a doline in the Burren, Co. Clare. *Proceedings of the Royal Irish Academy, Section C* 116, 1–59

Gibson, D. & Knight, M. 2006. *Bradley Fen Excavations 2001–2004, Whittlesey, Cambridgeshire. An archaeological assessment report*. Cambridge: Cambridge Archaeological Unit. Unpubl. report

Gibson-Hill, J. 1975. Crawley, Sussex: Roman Bloomery Site at Broadfields (TQ 258353). Bulletin 96, April 1973. Extracts from the Bulletins of 1973. *Surrey Archaeological Collections* 70, 149–50

Giles, M. 2007. Making metal and forging relations: ironworking in the British Iron Age. *Oxford Journal of Archaeology* 26, 395–413

Giles, M. 2012. *A Forged Glamour: landscape, identity and material culture in the Iron Age*. Oxford: Windgather Press

Giles, M. & Joy, J. 2007. Mirrors in the British Iron Age: performance, revelation and power. In M. Anderson (ed.), *The Book of the Mirror. An Interdisciplinary Collection Exploring the Cultural Story of the Mirror*, 16–31. Newcastle: Cambridge Scholars Press

Giles, M. & Parker Pearson, M. 1999. Learning to live in the Iron Age: dwelling and praxis. In Bevan (ed.) 1999, 217–32

Gillies, W. 1981. The craftsmen in early celtic literature. *Scottish Archaeological Forum* 11, 70– 85

Gingell, C. 1982. Excavation of an Iron Age enclosure at Groundwell Farm, Blunsdon St Andrew, 1976–7. *Wiltshire Archaeological and Natural History Magazine* 76, 33–75

Gingell, C. 1992. *The Marlborough Downs: a later Bronze Age landscape and its origins*. Devizes: Wiltshire Archaeological and Natural History Society and the Trust for Wessex Archaeology

Ginn, V. 2016. *Mapping Society: settlement structure in Later Bronze Age Ireland*. Oxford: Archaeopress

Ginn, V. & Rathbone, S. 2012. *Corrstown: a coastal community. Excavations of a Bronze Age village in Northern Ireland*. Oxford: Oxbow Books

Ginnever, M. 2015. *Results of an Archaeological Excavation at Portstown, Inverurie*. Edinburgh: Headland Archaeology. Unpubl. report

Glover, G., Flintoft, P. & Moore, R. 2016. *'A mersshy contree called Holdernesse'. Excavations on the route of a National Grid pipeline in Holderness, East Yorkshire*. Oxford: Archaeopress

Goddard, E. 1912. Notes on implements of the Bronze Age found in Wiltshire, with a list of all known examples found in the county. *Wiltshire Archaeological and Natural History Magazine* 37, 92–158

Goddard, E. 1917. Bronze implements of the Bronze Age found in Wiltshire, not previously recorded. *Wiltshire Archaeological and Natural History Magazine* 39, 477–84

Goldhahn, J. 2007. *Dödens Hand: en essä om brons- och hällsmed*. Gothenburg: Gotarc Serie C/Arkeologiska Skrifter 65

Goldhahn, J. 2013. Rethinking Bronze Age cosmology: a north European perspective. In Fokkens & Harding (eds), 2013, 248–65

Gomez de Soto, J. 1996. *La Grotte des Perrats à Agris (Charente). Étude préliminaire 1981–1994*. Angoulême: Société d'Archéologie et d'Histoire de Chauvigny

Gomez de Soto, J. & Kerouanton, I. 1991. La grotte du Quéroy à Chazelles (Charente): le Bronze final III b. *Bulletin de la Société Préhistorique Française* 88, 341–92

Goody, J. 2012. *Metals, Culture and Capitalism: an essay on the origins of the modern world*. Cambridge: Cambridge University Press

Gordon, D. 2012. *Quarrywood Henge, Elgin: archaeological investigation*. Kilwinning: Rathmell Archaeology. Unpubl. report

Gossip, J. in press. Life outside the round: Bronze Age and Iron Age settlement at Higher Besore and Truro College, Threemilestone, Truro. In A. Jones (ed.) Prehistoric Settlement in Cornwall. Truro: Cornwall Archaeological Unit.

Gowen, M. 1988. *Three Irish Gas Pipelines: new archaeological evidence in Munster*. Dublin: Wordwell

Graham, A., Hinton, D. & Peacock, D. 2002. The excavation of an Iron Age and Romano-British settlement in Quarry Field, south of Compact Farm, Worth Matravers, Dorset. In D. Hinton (ed.), *Purbeck Papers*, 1–83. Oxford: Oxbow Books

Gray, H. St G. 1927. Excavations at Ham Hill, South Somerset. Part III. *Proceedings of the Somersetshire Archaeological and Natural History Society* 72, 55–68

Gray, H. St G. & Bulleid, A. 1953. *The Meare Lake Village. Volume 2*. Taunton: Privately published

Gray, H. St G. & Cotton, M. 1966. *The Meare Lake Village. Volume 3*. Taunton: Privately published

Green, C. 1987. *Excavations at Poundbury, Dorchester, Dorset, 1966–1982. Vol I: The settlements*. Dorchester: Dorset Natural History and Archaeological Society Monograph 7

Green, H. 1985. A Bronze Age stone mould from New Mills, Newtown, Powys. *Bulletin of the Board of Celtic Studies* 32, 273–4

Green, M. 1973. A late Bronze Age socketed axe-mould from Worthing. *Sussex Archaeological Collections* 111, 87–92

Green, M. 1987. Excavations in Home Field, Down Farm, Gussage St Michael. *Proceedings of the Dorset Natural History and Archaeological Society* 108, 171–3

Greenwell, W. 1894. Antiquities of the Bronze Age found in the Heathery Burn Cave, County Durham. *Archaeologia* 54, 87–114

Greenwell, W. & Brewis, W. 1909. The origin, evolution, and classification of the bronze spear-head in Great Britain and Ireland. *Archaeologia* 61, 439–72

Greenwell, W. & Clinch, G. 1905. Early man. In W. Page (ed.), *The Victoria History of the County of Durham. Volume 1*, 199–209. London: Archibald Constable

Greenwood, P. 1997. Uphall Camp, Ilford – an up-date. *London Archaeologist* 9, 207–16

Gregory, R. 1807. Antiquities discovered in Ireland. *Archaeologia* 15, 394

Gregory, T. 1991. *Excavations in Thetford, 1980–1982, Fison Way*. Gressenhall: East Anglian Archaeology 53

Greig, J. 1970. Excavations at Castle Point, Troup, Banffshire. *Aberdeen University Review* 43, 274–83

Greig, J. 1971. Excavations at Cullykhan, Castle Point, Troup, Banffshire. *Scottish Archaeological Forum* 3, 15–22

Greig, J. 1972. Cullykhan. *Current Archaeology* 32, 227–31

Grenter, S. 1989. Gwernymynydd axe hoard. *Archaeology in Wales* 29, 46

Grogan, E. 2005. *The North Munster Project, Volume 1. The prehistoric landscape of south-east Clare*. Dublin: Discovery Programme Monograph 6

Grogan, E. & Eogan, G. 1987. Lough Gur excavations by Seán P. Ó Ríordáin: further Neolithic and Beaker habitations on Knockadoon. *Proceedings of the Royal Irish Academy, Section C* 87, 299–506

Guilbert, G. 1996. The oldest artefact of lead in the Peak: new evidence from Mam Tor. *Mining History* 13, 12–18

Guttman, E. 1996. *Excavation of a Late Bronze Age Settlement at South Hornchurch, Greater London. Interim report*. Hertford: Hertfordshire Archaeological Trust. Unpubl. report 194

Guttman, E. & Last, J. 2000. A Late Bronze Age Landscape at South Hornchurch, Essex. *Proceedings of the Prehistoric Society* 66, 319–59

Gwilt, A. & Haselgrove, C. (eds), 1997. Reconstructing Iron Age Societies. Oxford: Oxbow Books

Gwilt, A. & Lodwick, M. 2006. Continuing fieldwork at Llanmaes, Vale of Glamorgan. *Morgannwg* 50, 187–9

Gwilt, A., Lodwick, M. & Deacon, J. 2006. Excavation at Llanmaes, Vale of Glamorgan, 2006. *Archaeology in Wales* 46, 42–8

Gwilt, A., Lodwick, M., Deacon, J., Wells, N., Madgwick, R. & Young, T. 2016. Ephemeral abundance at Llanmaes: exploring the residues and resonances of an Earliest Iron Age midden and its associated archaeological context in the Vale of Glamorgan. In Koch & Cunliffe (eds), 2016, 294–329

Haaland, R. 2004. Technology, transformation and symbolism: ethnographic perspectives on European iron working. *Norwegian Archaeological Review* 37, 1–19

Halkon, P., Millett, M. & Woodhouse, H. 2015. *Hayton, East Yorkshire: archaeological studies of the Iron Age and Roman landscapes*. Leeds: Yorkshire Archaeological Report 7

Halpin, E. 1998. 1998:115 – *Cathedral Hill, Downpatrick, Down*. http://www.excavations.ie/report/1998/Down/0003288/

Hamilton, J. 1956. *Excavations at Jarlshof, Shetland*. Edinburgh: HMSO

Hamilton, J. 1968. *Excavations at Clickhimin, Shetland*. Edinburgh: HMSO

Hamilton, S. & Manley, J. 2001. Hillforts, monumentality and place: a chronological and topographic review of first millennium BC hillforts in south-east England. *European Journal of Archaeology* 4(1), 7–42

Hamilton, W.D. 2010. *The Use of Radiocarbon and Bayesian Modelling to (Re)write Later Iron Age Settlement Histories in East-Central Britain*. Unpubl. PhD thesis, University of Leicester

Hamilton, W.D., Sayle, K., Boyd, M., Haselgrove, C. & Cook, G. 2019. 'Celtic cowboys' reborn: application of multi-isotopic analysis (δ^{13}C, δ^{15}N, and δ^{34}S) to examine mobility and movement of animals within an Iron Age British society. *Journal of Archaeological Science* 101, 189–98

Hamon, C. & Quilliec, B. (eds), 2008. *Hoards from the Neolithic to the Metal Ages*. Oxford: British Archaeological Report S1758

Hansen, S. 1991. *Studien zu den Metalldeponierungen während der Urnenfelderzeit im Rhein-Main-Gebiet*. Bonn: Universitätsforschungen zur prähistorischen Archäologie 5

Hansen, S. 2016. A short history of fragments in hoards of the Bronze Age. In H. Baitinger (ed.), *Materielle Kultur und Identität im Spannungsfeld zwischen mediterraner Welt und Mitteleuropa*, RGZM-Tagungen 27, 185–208. Mainz: Römisch-Germanisches Zentralmuseum

Harbison, P. 1968. Catalogue of Irish Early Bronze Age associated finds containing copper or bronze. *Proceedings of the Royal Irish Academy* 67C, 35–91

Harbison, P. 1973. The earlier Bronze Age in Ireland. Late 3rd millennium–*c*. 1200 B.C. *Journal of the Royal Society of Antiquaries of Ireland* 103, 93–152

Harding, A. & Young, R. 1986. Pictures of an exhibition: new discoveries concerning the Heathery Burn hoard. *Durham Archaeological Journal* 2, 1–5

Harding, D. (ed.) 1976. *Hillforts: later prehistoric earthworks in Britain and Ireland*. London: Academic Press

Harding, D. 1987. *Excavations in Oxfordshire, 1964–66*. Edinburgh: University of Edinburgh

Harding, D. 2004. Dunagoil, Bute, re-instated. *Transactions of the Buteshire Natural History Society* 26, 3–19

Harding, D. 2012. *Iron Age Hillforts in Britain and Beyond*. Oxford: Oxford University Press

Harding, J. 1964. Interim report on the excavation of a Late Bronze Age homestead in Weston Wood, Albury. *Surrey Archaeological Collections* 61, 10–7

Harris, D., Pearce, S., Miles, H. & Irwin, M. 1977. Bodwen, Lanlivery: a multi-period occupation. *Cornish Archaeology* 16, 43–59

Harrison, A. 1991. Excavation of a Belgic and Roman site at 50–54 High Street, Rochester. *Archaeologia Cantiana* 109, 41–50

Harrison, S. & Card, N. 2005. *Mine Howe. Fieldwork and excavation 2000–2005*. Kirkwall: Friends of the Orkney Archaeological Trust

Hartridge, R. 1978. Excavations at the prehistoric and Romano-British site on Slonk Hill, Shoreham, Sussex. *Sussex Archaeological Collections* 116, 69–141

Harvey, J. 2010. *Archaeological Excavations on Land between Leicester Road and Dalby Road, Melton Mowbray, Leicestershire.* Leicester: University of Leicester Archaeological Services. Unpubl. report

Haselgrove, C. 1999. The development of Iron Age coinage in Belgic Gaul. *Numismatic Chronicle* 159, 111–68

Haselgrove, C. 2000. The character of oppida in Iron Age Britain. In V. Guichard, S. Sievers & O. Urban (eds), *Les Processus d'Urbanisation à l'Âge du Fer*, 103–10. Glux-en-Glenne: Centre Archéologique Européen du Mont Beuvray

Haselgrove, C. 2016. *Cartimandua's Capital? The late Iron Age royal site at Stanwick, North Yorkshire: fieldwork and analysis 1981–2011.* York: Council for British Archaeology Research Report 175

Haselgrove, C. & Hingley, R. 2006. Iron deposition and its significance in pre-Roman Britain. In G. Bataille & J.-P. Guillaumet (eds), *Les Dépôts Métalliques au Second Âge du Fer en Europe Tempérée*, 147–63. Glux-en-Glenne: Bibracte Centre Archéologique Européen

Haselgrove, C. & McCullagh, R. 2000. *An Iron Age Coastal Community in East Lothian: the excavation of two later prehistoric enclosure complexes at Fishers Road, Port Seton, 1994–5.* Edinburgh: Scottish Trust for Archaeological Research

Haselgrove, C. & Moore, T. (eds), 2007. *The Later Iron Age in Britain and Beyond.* Oxford: Oxbow Books

Haselgrove, C. & Pope, R. (eds), 2007. *The Earlier Iron Age in Britain and the near Continent.* Oxford: Oxbow Books

Haselgrove, C. & Webley, L. 2016. Lost purses and loose change? Coin deposition on settlements in Iron Age Europe. In C. Haselgrove & S. Krmnicek (eds), *The Archaeology of Money*, 85–114. Leicester: Leicester University Press

Haslam, R. 2012. Iron Age and Roman settlement and burial activity at Old Kempshott Lane, Basingstoke. *Proceedings of the Hampshire Field Club and Archaeological Society* 67, 79–141

Hastings, F. 1965. Excavation at an Iron Age Farmstead at Hawk's Hill, Leatherhead. *Surrey Archaeological Collections* 62, 1–43

Haustein, M., Gillis, C. & Pernicka, E. 2010. Tin isotopy: a new method for solving old questions. *Archaeometry* 52, 816–32

Hawkes, C. & Crummy, P. 1995. *Camulodunum 2.* Colchester: Colchester Archaeological Report 11

Hawkes, C. & Fell, C. 1943. The early Iron Age settlement at Fengate, Peterborough. *Archaeological Journal* 100, 188–223

Hawkes, C. & Hull, M. 1947. *Camulodunum: first report on the excavations at Colchester 1930–1939.* London: Report of the Research Committee of the Society of Antiquaries of London 14

Hawkes, C. & Smith, M. 1955. *The Thorndon Hoard (Suffolk).* London: British Museum Inventaria Archaeologica GB 11

Hawkes, C. & Smith, M. 1957. On some buckets and cauldrons of the Bronze and Early Iron Age. *Antiquaries Journal* 37, 131–98

Hayman, G. 1996. Iron Age discoveries in Tongham. *Surrey Archaeological Society Bulletin* 281

Heald, A. 2005. *Non-ferrous Metalworking in Iron Age Scotland c. 700BC to AD 800.* Unpubl. PhD thesis, University of Edinburgh

Hearne, C. 1994. Sandwich Bay Wastewater Treatment Scheme: interim note of discoveries. *Archaeologia Cantiana* 114, 435–6

Hearne, C. & Heaton, M. 1994. Excavations at a late Bronze Age settlement in the Upper Thames Valley at Shorncote Quarry near Cirencester, 1992. *Transactions of the Bristol and Gloucestershire Archaeological Society* 112, 17–57

Hearne, C., Perkins, D. & Andrews, P. 1995. The Sandwich Bay Wastewater Treatment Scheme Archaeological Project, 1992–1994. *Archaeologia Cantiana* 115, 239–354

Helm, R. 2001. Bogshole Lane, Broomfield. *Canterbury's Archaeology* 2000–2001, 23–4

Helm, R. 2004. *Archaeological Evaluation of the Cornfield, Holborough Quarry, Snodland.* Canterbury: Canterbury Archaeological Trust. Unpubl. report

Helms, M. 1988. *Ulysses' Sail: an ethnographic odyssey of power, knowledge, and geographical distance.* Princeton NJ: Princeton University Press

Helms, M. 1993. *Craft and the Kingly Ideal: art, trade, and power.* Austin TX: University of Texas Press

Helms, M. 2012. Nourishing a structured world with living metal in Bronze Age Europe. *World Art* 2, 105–18

Hencken, T.C. 1938. The excavation of the Iron Age camp on Bredon Hill, Gloucestershire, 1935–1937. *Archaeological Journal* 95, 1–111

Henderson, J. 1987. The archaeology and technology of glass at Meare Village East. In J. Coles (ed.), *Meare Village East. The Excavations of A. Bulleid and H. St. George Gray 1932–1956*, 170–82. Cambridge: Somerset Levels Papers 13

Henderson, J. 1989. The scientific analysis of ancient glass and its archaeological interpretation. In J. Henderson (ed.), *Scientific Analysis in Archaeology and its Interpretation*, 30–62. Oxford and Los Angeles: Oxford University Committee for Archaeology and UCLA Institute for Archaeology

Henderson, J. 1991. Industrial specialization in late Iron Age Britain and Europe. *Archaeological Journal* 148, 104–48

Henig, M. 1972. The origin of some ancient British coin types. *Britannia* 3, 209–23

Henning, J. 1991. Schmiedegräber nördlich der Alpen. *Saalburg Jaarbuch* 46, 65–82

Henshall, A. 1979. Artefacts from the Quanterness cairn. In C. Renfrew (ed.), *Investigations in Orkney*, 75–93. London: Report of the Research Committee of the Society of Antiquaries of London 38

Herbert, E. 1984. *Red Gold of Africa: copper in precolonial history and culture.* Madison WI: University of Wisconsin Press

Herbert, E. 1994. *Iron, Gender and Power: rituals of transformation in African societies.* Bloomington IN: Indiana University Press

Herity, M. & Eogan, G. 1977. *Ireland in Prehistory.* London: Routledge and Kegan Paul

Heslop, D. 1987. *The Excavation of an Iron Age Settlement at Thorpe Thewles, Cleveland, 1980–1982.* London: Council for British Archaeology Research Report 65

Heslop, M. & Langdon, M. 1996. Excavations at West Huntspill, 1993. *Somerset Archaeology and Natural History* 139, 89–97

Hey, G. 1995. Iron Age and Roman settlement at Old Shifford Farm, Standlake. *Oxoniensia* 60, 93–175

Hey, G., Booth, P. & Timby, J. 2011. *Yarnton: Iron Age and Romano-British settlement and landscape. Results of excavations 1990–98.* Oxford: Thames Valley Landscape Monograph 35

Hey, G., Laws, G. & Hayden, C. 2006. Cassington, Cassington West Extension, Cassington Pit. *South Midlands Archaeology* 36, 45

Hill, J.D. 1995a. *Ritual and Rubbish in the Iron Age of Wessex: a study on the formation of a specific archaeological record.* Oxford: British Archaeological Report 242

Hill, J.D. 1995b. How should we understand Iron Age societies and hillforts? A contextual study from southern Britain. In J. D. Hill & C. Cumberpatch (eds), *Different Iron Ages: studies on the Iron Age in temperate Europe*, 45–66. Oxford: British Archaeological Report S602

Hill, J.D. 2012. How did British Middle and Late pre-Roman Iron Age societies work (if they did)? In Moore & Armada (eds), 2012, 242–63

Hill, S. 2002. *Interim Report: archaeological work at Westwood Running Track, University of Warwick, Coventry, SP 2690 7660.* Coventry: University of Warwick. Unpubl. report

Hingley, R. 1980. Excavations by R.A. Rutland on an Iron Age site at Wittenham Clumps. *Berkshire Archaeological Journal* 70, 21–55

Hingley, R. 1990. Iron Age 'currency bars': the archaeological and social context. *Archaeological Journal* 147, 91–117

Hingley, R. 1997. Iron, ironworking and regeneration: a study of the symbolic meaning of metalworking in Iron Age Britain. In Gwilt & Haselgrove (eds), 1997, 9–18

Hingley, R. 1999. The creation of later prehistoric landscapes and the context of the reuse of Neolithic and earlier Bronze Age monuments in Britain and Ireland. In Bevan (ed.) 1999, 233–51

Hoad, S., Knight, H. & Elsden, N. 2010. *Home Farm, Harmondsworth Lane, Sipson, London UB7*. London: Museum of London Archaeology. Unpubl. report

Hodges, H. 1954. Studies in the late Bronze Age in Ireland: 1. Stone and clay moulds, and wooden models for bronze implements. *Ulster Journal of Archaeology* 3rd ser. 17, 62–80

Hodges, H. 1955. A palstave adze from Pusey, Berkshire. *Oxoniensia* 20, 93–5

Hodges, H. 1957. Studies in the late Bronze Age in Ireland 3. The hoards of bronze implements. *Ulster Journal of Archaeology* 3rd ser. 20, 51–63

Hodges, H. 1959. The Bronze Age moulds of the British Isles, part 1: Scotland and northern England – moulds of stone and clay. *Sibrium* 4, 129–37

Hodges, H. 1960. The Bronze Age moulds of the British Isles, part 2: England and Wales – moulds of stone and bronze. *Sibrium* 5, 153–62

Hogg, A. 1977. Castle Ditches, Llancarfan, Glamorgan. *Archaeologia Cambrensis* 125, 13–39

Hooley, R. 1931. Excavation of an early Iron Age village on Worthy Down, Winchester. *Proceedings of the Hampshire Field Club and Archaeological Society* 10, 178–92

Horn, J. 2015. Tankards of the British Iron Age. *Proceedings of the Prehistoric Society* 81, 311–41

Howard, H. 1983. *The Bronze Casting Industry in Later Prehistoric Southern Britain: a study based on refractory debris*. Unpubl. PhD thesis, University of Southampton

Howarth, E. 1899. *Catalogue of the Bateman Collection of Antiquities in Sheffield Museum*. London: Dulau and Co

Hughes, G. 1996. Old Oswestry hillfort: excavations by W.J. Varley 1939–1940. *Archaeologia Cambrensis* 143, 46–91

Hughes, G. 1998. *The Excavation of an Iron Age Settlement at Covert Farm (DIRFT East), Crick, Northamptonshire*. Birmingham: Birmingham University Field Archaeology Unit. Unpubl. report

Hughes, G. & Woodward, A. 2015. *The Iron Age and Romano-British Settlement at Crick Covert Farm. Excavations 1997–1998 (DIRFT volume 1)*. Oxford: Archaeopress

Hummler, M. 2005. Before Sutton Hoo: the prehistoric settlement (*c*. 3000 BC to *c* AD 550). In M. Carver (ed.), *Sutton Hoo: a seventh-century princely burial ground and its context*, 391–458. London: Trustees of the British Museum and the Society of Antiquaries of London

Hunn, J. & Richmond, A. 2004. *16–18 Wales Street, Kings Sutton, Northamptonshire: archaeological watching brief and salvage excavation*. Bedford: Phoenix Consulting. Unpubl. report

Hunn, J.R. 2007. *Remedial Excavation: River Rib, Ford Bridge, Braughing, Hertfordshire*. Milton Keynes: Archaeological Services and Consultancy. Unpubl. report

Hunter, F. 2000. Excavation of an Early Bronze Age cemetery and other sites at West Water Reservoir, West Linton, Scottish Borders. *Proceedings of the Society of Antiquaries of Scotland* 130, 115–82

Hunter, F. 2006. *Excavations at Birnie, Moray, 2005*. Edinburgh: National Museums Scotland. Unpubl. report

Hunter, F. 2007. *Excavations at Birnie, Moray, 2006*. Edinburgh: National Museums Scotland. Unpubl. report

Hunter, F. 2008. Celtic art in Roman Britain. In Garrow *et al*. (eds), 2008, 129–45

Hunter, F. 2010. *Excavations at Birnie, Moray, 2009*. Edinburgh: National Museums Scotland. Unpubl. report

Hunter, F. 2011. *Crucibles and Moulds, Culduthel*. Edinburgh: National Museums Scotland. Unpubl. draft specialist report

Hunter, F. 2015. Craft in context: artefact production in later prehistoric Scotland. In F. Hunter & I. Ralston (eds), *Scotland in Later Prehistoric Europe*, 225–46. Edinburgh: Society of Antiquaries of Scotland

Hunter, F. 2018. The Blair Drummond (UK) gold torc hoard: regional styles and international connections in the later Iron Age. In Schwab *et al*. (eds), 2018, 431–9

Hunter, F. & Davis, M. 1994. Early Bronze Age lead – a unique necklace from southeast Scotland. *Antiquity* 68, 824–30

Hurcombe, L. 2000. Time, skill and craft specialisation as gender relations. In M. Donald & L. Hurcombe (eds), *Gender and Material Culture in Archaeological Perspective*, 88–109. Basingstoke: Palgrave Macmillan

Hurl, D. 1995. Killymoon: new light on the late Bronze Age. *Archaeology Ireland* 9 (4), 24–7

Hurl, D., Nelis, E. & Murray, B. 1995. *Excavations at Killymoon, Co. Tyrone*. Belfast: Centre for Archaeological Fieldwork, Queen's University Belfast. Unpubl. report

Hurst, J. & Jackson, R. 2007. *Assessment and Updated Project Design for the Bredon Hillfort (Worcestershire) Archive – 1935–7 excavations by Thalassa Cruso Hencken*. Worcester: Worcestershire Historic Environment and Archaeology Service. Unpubl. report

Hurst, J. & Wills, J. 1987. A 'horn cap' mould from Beckford, Worcestershire. *Proceedings of the Prehistoric Society* 55, 492–3

Ialongo, N. 2018. The earliest balance weights in the West: towards an independent metrology for Bronze Age Europe. *Cambridge Archaeological Journal* 29(1), 103–24

Iles, L. 2018. Forging networks and mixing ores: rethinking the social landscapes of iron metallurgy. *Journal of Anthropological Archaeology* 49, 88–99

Inglis, J. & Inglis, R. 1983. An early metalworker's mould from Corseight, New Deer. *Proceedings of the Society of Antiquaries of Scotland* 113, 634–6

Jackson, D. & Dix, B. 1987. Late Iron Age and Roman settlement at Weekley, Northants. *Northamptonshire Archaeology* 21, 41–93

Jackson, D. & Ambrose, T. 1978. Excavations at Wakerley, Northants, 1972–75. *Britannia* 9, 115–242

Jackson, J. 1979. Metallic ores in Irish prehistory: copper and tin. In Ryan (ed.) 1979, 107–25

Jackson, J. 1991. The geology and raw materials of the Bronze Age. In Ryan (ed.) 1991, 73–5

Jackson, R. 2015. *Huntsman's Quarry, Kemerton: a Late Bronze Age settlement and landscape in Worcestershire*. Oxford: Oxbow Books

Jackson, R. & Napthan, M. 1998. Interim report on salvage recording of a Neolithic/Beaker and Bronze Age settlement and landscape at Huntsmans Quarry, Kemerton 1994–6. *Transactions of the Worcestershire Archaeological Society* 16, 57–68

Jackson, R. & Potter, T. 1996. *Excavations at Stonea, Cambridgeshire, 1980–85*. London: British Museum Press

James, S. 2008. The economic, social and environmental implications of faunal remains from the Bronze Age copper mines at Great Orme, North Wales. In N. Sykes, C. Newton & H. Cool (eds), *Food and Drink in Archaeology* 2, 57–63. Nottingham: University of Nottingham

Jantzen, D. 2008. *Quellen zur Metallverarbeitung im Nordischen Kreis der Bronzezeit*. Stuttgart: Prähistorische Bronzefunde XIX.2

Jennings, D., Muir, J., Palmer, S. & Smith, A. 2004. *Thornhill Farm, Fairford, Gloucestershire: an Iron Age and Roman pastoral site in the Upper Thames Valley*. Oxford: Thames Valley Landscapes Monograph 23

Jessup, R. 1930. *The Archaeology of Kent*. London: Methuen

Jessup, R.G. 1933. Bigberry Camp, Harbledown, Kent. *Archaeological Journal* 89, 87–115

Jobey, G. 1973. A native settlement at Hartburn and the Devil's Causeway, Northumberland. *Archaeologia Aeliana* 5th ser. 1, 11–53

Jobey, G. 1977. Iron Age and later farmsteads on Belling Law, Northumberland. *Archaeologia Aeliana* 5th ser. 5, 1–38

Jochum Zimmermann, E., Künzler Wagner, N. & Kunnert, U. 2003. Zurück zur Gussform. Zum Einfluss des Gussformmaterials auf die Mikrostruktur eines gegossenen Bronzeobjektes. *Experimentelle Archäologie in Europa, Bilanz 2002*, 79–91

Jockenhövel, A. 1980. *Die Rasiermesser in Westeuropa*. Munich: Prähistorische Bronzefunde VIII.3

Johnson, B. 1975. *Archaeology and the M25*. Aldershot: Surrey Archaeological Society

Johnson, M. 2014. A Bronze Age flat axe mould from Gunnerside, Swaledale. *Prehistoric Yorkshire* 51, 66–7

Johnston, R. 2008. Later prehistoric landscapes and inhabitation. In J. Pollard (ed.), *Prehistoric Britain*, 268–87. Oxford: Blackwell

Johnston, S. & Wailes, B. 2007. *Dún Ailinne: excavations at an Irish royal site, 1968–1975*. Philadelphia PA: University of Pennsylvania Museum of Archaeology and Anthropology

Jones, A. 2002. A biography of colour: colour, material histories and personhood in the Early Bronze Age of Britain and Ireland. In Jones & MacGregor (eds), 2002, 159–174

Jones, A. 2006. Animated images: images, agency and landscape in Kilmartin, Argyll, Scotland. *Journal of Material Culture* 11, 211–25

Jones, A. 2012. *Prehistoric Materialities: becoming material in prehistoric Britain and Ireland*. Oxford: Oxford University Press

Jones, A. 2015a. Rock art and the alchemy of bronze. Metal and images in early Bronze Age Scotland. In P. Skoglund, J. Ling & U. Bertilsson (eds), *Picturing the Bronze Age*, 79–88. Oxford: Oxbow Books

Jones, A. 2015b. Ritual, rubbish or everyday life? Evidence from a Middle Bronze Age settlement in mid-Cornwall. *Archaeological Journal* 172(1), 30–51

Jones, A. 2016. *Preserved in the Peat: an extraordinary Bronze Age burial on Whitehorse Hill, Dartmoor, and its wider context*. Oxford: Oxbow Books.

Jones, A. & MacGregor, G. (eds), 2002. *Colouring the Past: the significance of colour in archaeological research*. Oxford: Berg

Jones, A. & Quinnell, H. 2014. *Lines of Archaeological Investigation along the North Cornwall Coast*. Oxford: British Archaeological Report 594

Jones, A., Gossip, J. & Quinnell, H. 2015. *Settlement and Metalworking in the Middle Bronze Age and Beyond. New evidence from Tremough, Cornwall*. Leiden: Sidestone Press

Jones, A., Marley, J., Quinnell, H. & Hartgroves, S. 2011. On the beach: new discoveries at Harlyn Bay, Cornwall. *Proceedings of the Prehistoric Society* 77, 88–109

Jones, C. 2002. Axe mould. In H. Armitage (ed.), *The Hunt Museum Essential Guide*, 164. London: Scala

Jones, C. & Chapman, A. 2012. *Archaeological Trial Trench Evaluation at Castleview Road, Slough, June 2012*. Northampton: Northamptonshire Archaeology. Unpubl. report

Jones, E. 1945. Mould for socketed chisel found at Abermâd. *Archaeologia Cambrensis* 98, 146

Jones, M. & Bond, D. 1980. Later Bronze Age settlement at Mucking, Essex. In Barrett & Bradley (eds), 1980, 471–82

Jones, M., Kent, J., Musty, J. & Biek, L. 1976. Celtic coin moulds from Old Sleaford, Lincolnshire. *Antiquaries Journal* 56, 238–41

Jones, S. 1999. Great Orme, Bronze-Age smelting site, Llandudno. *Archaeology in Wales* 39, 79

Jope, E. 1971. The Witham shield. *British Museum Quarterly* 35, 61–9

Jope, E. 2000. *Early Celtic Art in the British Isles*. Oxford: Oxford University Press

Joy, J. 2010. *Iron Age Mirrors: a biographical approach*. Oxford: British Archaeological Report 518

Joy, J. 2014. 'Fire burn and cauldron bubble': Iron Age and early Roman cauldrons of Britain and Ireland. *Proceedings of the Prehistoric Society* 80, 327–62

Joy, J. 2015. Connections and separation? Narratives of Iron Age art in Britian and its relationship with the Continent. In Anderson-Whymark et al. (eds), 2015, 145–65

Joy, J. 2017. The Chiseldon cauldrons in context. In Baldwin & Joy (eds), 2017, 97–119

Juleff, G. & Bray, L. 2007. Minerals, metal, colours and landscape: Exmoor's Roman Lode in the early Bronze Age. *Cambridge Archaeological Journal* 17, 285–96

Kamash, Z., Gosden, C. & Lock, G. 2012. The Vale and Ridgeway Project: excavations at Marcham/Frilford 2011, interim report. *South Midlands Archaeology* 42, 77–83

Karl, R. 2006. *Altkeltische Sozialstrukturen*. Budapest: Archaeolingua main series 18

Kearn, O. 2017. *An Examination of Non-ferrous Alloying Practices at the Iron Age Site of Gussage All Saints, Dorset, UK*. Unpubl. BSc dissertation, University College London

Kearns, T., Martinón-Torres, M. & Rehren, T. 2010. Metal to mould: alloy identification in experimental casting moulds using XRF. *Historical Metallurgy* 44 (1), 48–58

Keeley, V. 1999. Iron Age discoveries at Ballydavis. In P. Lane & W. Nolan (eds), *Laois: history and society*, 25–34. Dublin: Geography Publications

Keeley, V. nd. *Preliminary Report, Archaeological Excavations, Ballydavis Td., Portlaoise By-pass, Co. Laois*. Castlecomer, Co. Kilkenny: Valerie J. Keeley. Unpubl. report

Kenyon, K. 1950. Excavations at Breedon-on-the-Hill, 1946. *Transactions of the Leicestershire Archaeological Society* 26, 17–82

Kenyon, K. 1954. Excavations at Sutton Walls, Herefordshire, 1948–1951. *Archaeological Journal* 110, 1–87

Kiely, J. & O'Callaghan, N. 2010. *Archaeological Excavation Report. 02E0055 – Ballydowny, Killarney, Co. Kerry*. Cork: Eachtra Archaeological Projects. Unpubl. report

Kienlin, T. 2007. Von den Schmieden der Beile: zu Verbreitung und Angleichung Praehistorische Angleichung metallurgischen Wissens im Verlauf der Frühbronzezeit. *Prähistorische Zeitschrift* 82, 1–22

Kienlin, T. 2008. *Frühes Metall im Nordalpinen Raum. Eine Untersuchung zu technologischen und kognitiven Aspekten früher Metallurgie anhand der Gefüge frühbronzezeitlicher Beile*. Bonn: Habelt

Kienlin, T. & Roberts, B. (eds), 2009. *Metals and Societies: studies in honour of Barbara S. Ottaway*. Bonn: Rudolf Habelt

Kienlin, T. 2010. *Traditions and Transformations: approaches to Eneolithic (Copper Age) and Bronze Age metalworking and society in eastern central Europe and the Carpathian Basin*. Oxford: British Archaeological Report S2184

Kienlin, T. 2013. Copper and bronze: Bronze Age metalworking in context. In Fokkens & Harding (eds), 2013, 414–36

Kilbride-Jones, H. 1936. Late Bronze Age cemetery: being an account of the excavations of 1935 at Loanhead of Daviot, Aberdeenshire, on behalf of HM Office of Works. *Proceedings of the Society of Antiquaries of Scotland* 70, 278–310

Kinnes, I., Cameron, F., Trow, S. & Thomson, D. 1998. *Excavations at Cliffe, Kent*. London: British Museum Occasional Paper 69

Kinory, J. 2012. *Salt Production, Distribution and Use in the British Iron Age*. Oxford: British Archaeological Report 559

Kipling, R. 2008. Bath Lane (former Merlin Dye Works). *Transactions of the Leicestershire Archaeological and Historical Society* 82, 275–8

Kirwan, R. 1870. Notes on the pre-historic archaeology of east Devon. Part III. *Transactions of the Devonshire Association* 4, 295–304

Koch, J. & Cunliffe, B. (eds), 2016. *Celtic from the West 3. Atlantic Europe in the Metal Ages: questions of shared languages*. Oxford: Oxbow Books

Knight, D. 1988. An Iron Age hillfort at Castle Yard, Farthingstone, Northamptonshire. *Northamptonshire Archaeology* 21, 31–40

Knight, D. 1993. Excavations of an Iron Age settlement at Gamston, Nottinghamshire. *Transactions of the Thoroton Society of Nottinghamshire* 96, 16–90

Knight, M. 2014. Masters of mysteries or haphazard handymen? An assessment of the evidence for metalworkers at Bronze Age settlements in Cornwall and Devon, south-western England. *Trowel* 15, 29–41

Knight, M. 2018. *The Intentional Destruction and Deposition of Bronze Age Metalwork in South West England*. Unpubl. PhD thesis, University of Exeter

Knight, M., Ormrod, T. & Pearce, S. 2015. *The Bronze Age Metalwork of South Western Britain*. Oxford: British Archaeological Report 610

Knight, M., Ballantyne, R., Robinson, I. & Gibson, D. 2019. The Must Farm pile-dwelling settlement. *Antiquity* 93, 645–63

Kristiansen, K. 1998. *Europe before History*. Cambridge: Cambridge University Press

Kristiansen, K. 2002. The tale of the sword: swords and swordfighters in Bronze Age Europe. *Oxford Journal of Archaeology* 21(4), 319–32

Kristiansen, K. & Larsson, T. 2005. *The Rise of Bronze Age Society*. Cambridge: Cambridge University Press

Kuijpers, M. 2008. *Bronze Age Metalworking in the Netherlands (c. 2000–800 BC)*. Leiden: Sidestone Press

Kuijpers, M. 2017. *An Archaeology of Skill: metalworking skill and material specialization based on Late Copper Age and Early Bronze Age axes from central Europe*. Abingdon: Routledge

Kuijpers, M. 2018. The Bronze Age, a world of specialists? Metalworking from the perspective of skill and material specialization. *European Journal of Archaeology* 21(4), 550–71

Lachenal, V., Rinalducci de Chassey, K., Georges, K. & Sargiano, J.-P. 2010. Une tuyère du Bronze ancien à la Bastide Neuve II (Velaux, Bouches-du-Rhône). Un témoin d'activité métallurgique en contexte domestique en Provence occidentale? Remarques sur les tuyères en céramique d'Europe occidentale, *Bulletin de la Société Préhistorique Française* 107, 549–65

Ladle, L. & Woodward, A. 2009. *Excavations at Bestwall Quarry, Wareham 1992–2005. Volume 1: the prehistoric landscape*. Dorchester: Dorset Natural History and Archaeological Society Monograph 19

Lake, W. 1867. *A Complete Parochial History of the County of Cornwall. Volume 1*. London: J.B. Nichols and Son

Lambrick, G. & Allen, T. 2004. *Gravelly Guy, Stanton Harcourt: the development of a prehistoric and Romano-British community*. Oxford: Thames Valley Landscapes Monograph 21

Lamdin-Whymark, H., Brady, K. & Smith, A. 2009. Excavation of a Neolithic to Roman landscape at Horcott Pit near Fairford, Gloucestershire, in 2002 and 2003. *Transactions of the Bristol and Gloucestershire Archaeological Society* 127, 45–131

Landon, M. 2009. *The Puckeridge Coin Mould Assemblage: an interim report*. Braughing: Braughing Archaeological Society. Unpubl. report

Landon, M. 2010. *The Ford Bridge Coin Mould Assemblage*. Braughing: Braughing Archaeological Society. Unpubl. report

Landon, M. 2016. *Making a Mint: comparative studies in late Iron Age coin mould*. Oxford: Archaeopress

Langmaid, N. 1976. *Bronze Age Metalwork in England and Wales*. Princes Risborough: Shire

Lauermann, E. & Pany-Kucera, D. 2013. Grab 3 aus dem Aunjetitzer Gräberfeld von Geitzendorf. Der erste Nachweis einer Metallverarbeiterin in der Frühbronzezeit Niederösterreichs, *Slovenská Archeológia* 61, 93–106

Lavelle, C. 2012. *The Non-destructive Qualitative pXRF Compositional Analysis of the Copper-alloy Whitchurch Miniature Axes, Manufacturing Waste, Tools and Weapons*. Unpubl. MSc thesis, University of Cardiff

Lawrence, D. 1996. *Archaeological Investigations at Oliver Close, Leyton, LE OC 95*. London: Newham Museums Service. Unpubl. report

Lawson, A. 1980. A late Bronze Age hoard from Beeston Regis, Norfolk. *Antiquity* 54, 217–9

Lawson, A. 1999. The Bronze Age hoards of Hampshire. In A. Harding (ed.), *Experiment and Design: archaeological studies in honour of John Coles*, 94–107. Oxford: Oxbow Books

Lawson, A. 2000. *Potterne 1982–5: animal husbandry in later prehistoric Wiltshire*. Salisbury: Wessex Archaeology Report 17

Lawson, A. 2013. *Three Late Bronze Age Hoards from North East Norfolk*, hbsmrgateway2.esdm.co.uk/norfolk/DataFiles/Docs/AssocDoc38554.pdf

La Niece S. & Cartwright, C. 2009. Bronze Age gold lock-rings with wores of wax and wood. In Kienlin & Roberts (eds), 2009, 307–12

La Niece, S., Farley, J., Meeks, N. & Joy, J. 2018. Gold in Iron Age Britain. In Schwab *et al.* (eds), 2018, 407–29

Leah, M. & Young, C. 2001. A Bronze-Age burnt mound at Sandy Lane, Charlton Kings, Gloucestershire: excavations in 1971. *Transactions of the Bristol and Gloucestershire Archaeological Society* 119, 59–82

Leahy, K. 1977. *A Survey of Casting Moulds from the Middle and Late Bronze Age in Great Britain and Ireland*. Unpubl. BA thesis, University of Leicester

Leary, J. (ed.) 2014. *Past Mobilities: archaeological approaches to movement and mobility*. Farnham: Ashgate

Leechman, M. H. 1962. *The Vitrified Fort of Dunagoil*. Unpubl. MA dissertation, Department of Archaeology, University of Edinburgh

Leeds, E. 1927. Excavations at Chûn Castle, in Penwith, Cornwall. *Archaeologia* 76, 205–40

Leins, I. 2012. *Numismatic Data Reconsidered: coin distributions and interpretation in studies of late Iron Age Britain*. Unpubl. PhD thesis, University of Newcastle

Leivers, M. 2008. Prehistoric pottery. In N. Cooke, F. Brown & C. Phillpots (eds), *Hunter Gatherers to Huntsmen: a history of the Stansted landscape*, 17.1–17.46. Oxford and Salisbury: Framework Archaeology

Lenerz-de Wilde, M. 1995. Prämonetäre Zahlungsmittel in der Kupfer- und Bronzezeit Mitteleuropas. *Fundberichte aus Baden-Württemberg* 20, 229–327

Lewis, A. 2015. *Iron Age and Roman-era Vehicle Terrets from Western and Central Britain: an interpretive study*. Unpubl. PhD thesis, University of Leicester

Lewis, C. 1998. The Bronze Age mines of the Great Orme and other sites in the British Isles and Ireland. In Mordant *et al.* (eds), 1998, 45–58

Lewis-Williams, J. & Dowson, T. 1990. Through the veil: San rock paintings and the rock face. *South African Archaeological Bulletin* 45, 5–16

Le Carlier de Veslud, C., Edme, L. & Fily, M. 2014. Lingots et déchets de fonderie dans les dépôts de l'horizon de l'épée à pointe en langue de carpe (Bronze final IIIb): proposition de typologie. *Bulletin de la Société Préhistorique Française* 111, 509–22

Le Roux, C. 1975. Bretagne. *Gallia Préhistoire* 18, 511–39

Lineen, J. 2017. *Spearheads in the Landscape: a contextual analysis*. Unpubl. MA thesis, University College Cork

Ling, J., Stos-Gale, Z., Grandin, L., Billström, K., Hjärthner-Holdar, E. & Persson, P.-O. 2014. Moving metals II: provenancing Scandinavian Bronze Age artefacts by lead isotope and elemental analyses. *Journal of Archaeological Science* 41, 106–32

Linton, R. & Bayley, J. 1982. *Technological Samples from Beckford, Herefordshire [sic]*. London: Ancient Monuments Laboratory Report 3762

Liversage, G. 1968. Excavations at Dalkey Island, Co. Dublin, 1956–1959. *Proceedings of the Royal Irish Academy Section C* 66, 53–233

Lock, G., Gosden, C. & Daly, P. 2005. *Segsbury Camp. Excavations in 1996 and 1997 at an Iron Age hillfort on the Oxfordshire Ridgeway*. Oxford: Oxford University School of Archaeology

Lodwick, M. & Gwilt, A. 2004. Cauldrons and consumption: Llanmaes and Llyn Fawr. *Archaeology in Wales* 44, 77–81

Longley, D. 1977. *Runnymede Bridge 1976: excavations on the site of a late Bronze Age settlement*. Farnham: Research Volume of the Surrey Archaeological Society 6

Longworth, I. & Kinnes, I. 1980. *Sutton Hoo Excavations 1966, 1968–70*. London: British Museum

Longworth, I., Herne, A., Varndell, G. & Needham, S. 1991. *Excavations at Grimes Graves, Norfolk, 1972–1976. Fascicule 3. Shaft X: Bronze Age flint, chalk and metal working*. London: British Museum

Lort, M. 1779. Observations on celts. *Archaeologia* 5, 106–18

Lowe, C. 1990. St Boniface (Papa Westray parish). Broch, cliff section, farm, mound. *Discovery and Excavation in Scotland* 1990, 45–7

Lowe, C. 1993. Preliminary results of the excavation assessment at Munkerhoose cliff-section and farm mound, St Boniface Church, Papa Westray, Orkney. *Scottish Society for Northern Studies* 30, 19–33

Lowe, C. & Boardman, S. 1998. *Coastal Erosion and the Archaeological Assessment of an Eroding Shoreline at St Boniface Church, Papa Westray, Orkney*. Stroud and Edinburgh: Sutton Publishing and Historic Scotland

Lucas, A. 1968. National Museum of Ireland: archaeological acquisitions in the year 1965. *Journal of the Royal Society of Antiquaries of Ireland* 98, 93–159

Lucas, A. 1973. National Museum of Ireland Archaeological Acquisitions in the Year 1970. *Journal of the Royal Society of Antiquaries of Ireland* 103, 177–213

Lynch, F. 1970. *Prehistoric Anglesey*. Llangefni: Anglesey Antiquarian Society

Lynch, F. 1998. Colour in prehistoric architecture. In Gibson & Simpson (eds), 1998, 62–7

Lynch, F. 2001. Axes or skeuomorphic cushion stones: the purpose of certain 'blunt' axes. In Metz *et al.* (eds), 2001, 399–404

Lynch, P. 2011. *M3 Clonee-North of Kells Motorway Scheme. E3158: Cakestown Glebe 2, final report*. Kilcoole, Co.Wicklow: Irish Archaeological Consultancy. Unpubl. report

Lynch, R. 2012. *M1 Northern Motorway Gormanston-Monasterboice (Drogheda Bypass) Platin to Oldbridge Chainage: 21600-24800 Contract 7. Final Report*. Kilcoole, Co.Wicklow: Irish Archaeological Consultancy. Unpubl. report

Lyne, E. 2009. *N18 Gort to Crusheen Road Scheme: Rathwilladoon 2 and 3. Final report on behalf of Galway County Council*. Kilcoole, Co.Wicklow: Irish Archaeological Consultancy. Unpubl. report

Lyne, E. 2012. Multiphase prehistoric settlement at Rathwilladoon. In S. Delaney, D. Bayley, E. Lyne, S. McNamara, J. Nunan & K. Molloy (eds), *Borderlands. Archaeological excavations on the route of the M18 Gort to Crusheen road scheme*. Dublin: NRA Scheme Monographs 9

Lynn, C. 1977. Trial excavation at the King's Stables, Tray townland, County Armagh. *Ulster Journal of Archaeology* 40, 42–62

Macalister, R. 1921. *Ireland in Pre-Celtic Times*. Dublin: Maunsel and Roberts

Macdonald, P. 2007a. *Llyn Cerrig Bach: a study of the copper alloy artefacts from the insular La Tène assemblage*. Cardiff: University of Wales Press

Macdonald, P. 2007b. Perspectives on insular La Tène art. In Haselgrove & Moore (eds), 2007, 329–38

Macdonald, P. & Ó Néill, J. 2009. Investigation of the find-spot of the Tamlaght hoard, Co. Armagh. In Cooney *et al.* (eds), 2009, 167–79

MacGregor, A. 2004. Re-presenting John Evans. *The Ashmolean* 47, 17–9

Mackay, A. 1906. Notes on a slab with incised crescentic design, stone mould for casting spear-heads, a cup-marked stone, holy-water stoup, and other antiquities in Strathnaver, Sutherlandshire. *Proceedings of the Society of Antiquaries of Scotland* 40, 128–33

Mackie, D. 1993. Prehistoric ditch systems at Ketton and Tixover, Rutland. *Transactions of the Leicestershire Archaeological and Historical Society* 67, 1–14

MacKie, E. 1969. Radiocarbon dates and the Scottish Iron Age. *Antiquity* 43, 15–26

MacKie, E. 2002. *The Roundhouses, Brochs and Wheelhouses of Atlantic Scotland* c. *700BC–AD500: architecture and material culture. Part 1 – The Orkney and Shetland Isles*. Oxford: British Archaeological Report 342

MacKie, E. 2007. *The Roundhouses, Brochs and Wheelhouses of Atlantic Scotland* c. *700BC – AD500: architecture and material culture. Part 2 – The northern and southern mainland and the Western Isles*. Oxford: British Archaeological Report 444

MacKie, E. 2015. Excavations on Sheep Hill, West Dunbartonshire, 1966–69: A late Bronze Age timber-framed dun and a small Iron Age hillfort. *Scottish Archaeological Journal* 36–7, 65–137

Machling, T. & Williamson, R. 2018. 'Up close and personal': the later Iron Age torcs from Newark, Nottinghamshire and Netherurd, Peebleshire. *Proceedings of the Prehistoric Society* 84, 387–403

Madgwick, R. & Mulville, J. 2015. Feasting on fore-limbs: conspicuous consumption and identity in later prehistoric Britain. *Antiquity* 89 (345), 629–44

Mahé-le Carlier, C., Lulzac, Y. & Giot, P.-R. 2001. Etude des déchets de réduction provenant de deux sites d'exploitation d'étain armoricain de l'Age du Bronze et du Moyen Age. *Revue Archéologique de l'Ouest* 18, 45–56

Mahr, A. 1939. *Ancient Irish Handicraft*. Limerick: Thomond Archaeological Society and Field Club

Malham, A. 2010. *The Classification and Interpretation of Tin-smelting Remains from South-west England*. Unpubl. PhD thesis, University of Bradford

Malim, T. 2010. The environmental and social context of the Isleham hoard. *Antiquaries Journal* 90, 73–130

Mallory, J. 1995. Haughey's Fort and the Navan complex in the late Bronze Age. In Shee Twohig & Wadell (eds), 1995, 73–86

Malrain, F. & Pinard, E. 2006. *Les Sites Laténiens de la Moyenne Vallée de l'Oise du Ve au 1er s. avant notre ère*. Senlis: Revue Archéologique de Picardie Numéro Spécial 23

Manby, T. 1966. The Bodwrdin mould, Anglesey. *Proceedings of the Prehistoric Society* 32, 349

Manby, T. 1980. Bronze Age settlement in eastern Yorkshire. In Barrett & Bradley (eds), 1980, 307–70

Manby, T. 1983. Thwing excavation 1982. *Yorkshire Archaeological & Historical Society Prehistory Research Section Bulletin* 20, unpaginated

Manby, T. 2007. Continuity of monumental traditions into the late Bronze Age? Henges to ring-forts, and shrines. In C. Burgess, P. Topping & F. Lynch (eds), *Beyond Stonehenge. Essays on the Bronze Age in Honour of Colin Burgess*, 403–24. Oxford: Oxbow Books

Manby, T., King, A. & Vyner, B. 2003. The Neolithic and Bronze Ages, a time of early agriculture. In T. Manby, S. Moorhouse & P. Ottaway (eds), *The Archaeology of Yorkshire: an assessment at the beginning of the 21st century*, 35–113. Leeds: Yorkshire Archaeological Society

Mann, F. 1939. Roman Britain in 1938, Norfolk. *Journal of Roman Studies* 29, 214

Mann, L. 1923. Discoveries in north-western Wigtownshire: cinerary and incense-cup urns and perforated axe-hammer; mould for bronze winged chisel; whetstone for stone axes; cup-marked rocks and boulder; apron of moss fibres. *Proceedings of the Society of Antiquaries of Scotland* 57, 98–107

Mann, L. 1925. Note on the results of the Exploration of the Fort at Dunagoil. *Transactions of the Buteshire Natural History Society* 9, 56–60

Manning, A. & Moore, C. 2011. Excavations at Lea Farm, Hurst, 1998. *Berkshire Archaeological Journal* 80, 31–71

Manning, W. 1980. Blacksmiths' tools from Waltham Abbey, Essex. In W. Oddy (ed.), *Aspects of Early Metallurgy*, 87–96. London: British Museum

Manning, W. 1985. *Catalogue of the Romano-British Iron Tools, Fittings and Weapons in the British Museum*. London: British Museum

Maraszek, R. 2007. *Spätbronzezeitliche Hortfundlandschaften in Atlantischer und Nordischer Metalltradition*. Halle: Landesamt für Denkmalpflege und Archäologie Sachsen-Anhalt, Landesmuseum für Vorgeschichte

Marcigny, C., Colonna, C., Ghesquière, E. & Verron, G. 2005. *La Normandie à l'Aube de l'Histoire: les découvertes archéologiques de l'âge du Bronze, 2300–800 av. J.-C*. Paris: Somogy

Marshall, A. 2004. *Farmstead and Stronghold: development of an Iron Age and Roman settlement complex at The Park-Bowsings, near Guiting Power, Glos. (UK)*. Guiting Power: Guiting Power Amenity Trust

Marshall, D. 1964. Report on excavations at Little Dunagoil. *Transactions of the Buteshire Natural History Society* 16, 3–69

Marshall, P. & Parker Pearson, M. 2012. Excavations of an Iron Age islet settlement in Upper Loch Bornish. In M. Parker Pearson (ed.), *From Machair to Mountains. Archaeological survey and excavation in South Uist*, 259–70. Oxford: Oxbow Books

Marshall, P., Mulville, J., Parker Pearson, M., Smith, H. & Ingram, C. 2000. Cladh Hallan. *Discovery and Excavation in Scotland* 1999, 91–3

Martin, E. 1988. *Burgh, the Iron Age and Roman Enclosure*. Bury St Edmonds East Anglian Archaeology 40

Martin, K. 2014. Was bleibt … Der Metallurg und sein Handwerk im archäologischen Befund. In H. Meller, R. Risch & E. Pernicka (eds),

Metalle und Macht: frühes gold und silber, 309–19. Halle: Landesmuseum für Vorgeschichte Halle

Martinón-Torres, M. & Uribe-Villegas, M. 2015. Technology and culture in the invention of lost-wax casting in South America: an archaeometric and ethnoarchaeological perspective. *Cambridge Archaeological Journal* 25, 377–90

Maryon, H. 1936. Excavation of two Bronze Age barrows at Kirkhaugh, Northumberland. *Archaeologia Aeliana* 4th ser. 13, 207–17

Maryon, H. 1938. The technical methods of the Irish smiths in the Bronze and early Iron Ages. *Proceedings of the Royal Irish Academy. Section C* 44, 181–228

Mathiot, D. 2012. La structuration spatiale de l'économie à l'Âge du fer en Gaule du Nord: une organisation originale au coeur des campagnes. In A. Esposito & G. Sanidas (eds), *Quartiers Artisanaux en Grèce Ancienne: une perspective méditeranée*, 387–405. Villeneuve d'Ascq: Presses Universitaires du Septentrion

Matthews, S. 2013. The Boughton Malherbe hoard, Kent. Un dépôt du groupe de l'épée en langue de carpe français en Angleterre? *Bulletin de l'Association pour la Promotion des Recherches sur l'Age du Bronze* 11, 56–60

Mattusch, C. 2008. Metalworking and tools. In J. Olesen (ed.), *The Oxford Handbook of Engineering and Technology in the Classical World*, 418–38. Oxford: Oxford University Press

May, J. 1996. *Dragonby. Report on excavations at an Iron Age and Romano-British settlement in north Lincolnshire.* Oxford: Oxbow Books

May, J. 2006. An Iron Age coin weight from Rotherwick, Hampshire. In P. de Jersey (ed.), *Celtic Coinage: new discoveries, new discussion*, 243–8. Oxford: British Archaeological Report S1532

McCarthy, C. 2010. *Final Archaeological Report, Hotel Development Ballynakelly and Rathcreedan, Newcastle, Co. Dublin.* Dublin: Arch-Tech. Unpubl. report

McDonald, T. 1999. *Excavations at Turner's Hall Farm and Sandridge, Hertfordshire: interim site narrative.* Hertford: Hertfordshire Archaeological Trust. Unpubl. report 574

McDonnell, G. 2014. *Assessment of the Slags Recovered from Turing College, University of Kent. Site code: K3 UKC-EX-13.* Canterbury: Canterbury Archaeological Trust. Unpubl. report

McKeon, J. & O'Sullivan, J. 2014. *The Quiet Landscape: archaeological investigations on the M6 Galway to Ballinasloe national road scheme.* Dublin: NRA Scheme Monographs 15

McKinley, J. 2011. Human remains (grave 1236 and 1289). In Fitzpatrick 2011, 77–87

McKinley, J., Leivers, M., Schuster, J., Marshall, P., Barclay, A. & Stoodley, N. 2014. *Cliffs End Farm, Isle of Thanet, Kent: a mortuary and ritual site of the Bronze Age, Iron Age and Anglo-Saxon period with evidence for long-distance maritime mobility.* Salisbury: Wessex Archaeology Report 31

McNally, L. 1997. Experimenting in metal: discovering the skill of the prehistoric bronzesmith. *Archaeology Ireland* 11(1), 10–12

McOmish, D. 1996. East Chisenbury: ritual and rubbish at the British Bronze Age–Iron Age transition. *Antiquity* 70, 68–76

McOmish, D., Field, D. & Brown, G. 2010. The late Bronze Age and early Iron Age midden site at East Chisenbury, Wiltshire. *Wiltshire Archaeological and Natural History Magazine* 103, 35–101

McQuade, M. 2007. *Final Report at Ballylegan, N8 Cashel to Mitchelstown Road Improvement Scheme.* Dublin: Margaret Gowen. Unpubl. report

McQuade, M., Molloy, B. & Moriarty, C. 2009. *In the Shadow of the Galtees: archaeological excavations along the N8 Cashel to Mitchelstown road scheme.* Dublin: NRA Scheme Monograph 4

Meadows, I. 2006. *Tarmac Quarry Maxey: assessment report for phases 1–3.* Northampton: Northamptonshire Archaeology. Unpubl. report

Meeks, N. 1986. Tin-rich surfaces on bronze – some experimental and archaeological considerations. *Archaeometry* 28, 133–62

Megaw, B. & Hardy, E. 1938. British decorated axes and their diffusion during the earlier part of the Bronze Age. *Proceedings of the Prehistoric Society* 4, 272–307

Megaw, J.V.S., Thomas, A. & Wailes, B. 1961. The Bronze Age settlement at Gwithian, Cornwall: preliminary report on the evidence for early agriculture. *Proceedings of the West Cornwall Field Club* 2(5), 200–15

Megaw, M.R. & Megaw, J.V.S. 1989. *Celtic Art from its Beginnings to the Book of Kells.* London: Thames and Hudson.

Melheim, L. 2015. *Recycling Ideas: Bronze Age metal production in southern Norway.* Oxford: British Archaeological Report S2715

Melheim, L. & Horn, C. 2014. Tales of hoards and swordfighters in early Bronze Age Scandinavia: The brand new and the broken. *Norwegian Archaeological Review* 47, 18–41

Mercer, R. 1981. *Grimes Graves, Norfolk. Excavations 1971–1972.* Southampton: HMSO

Mercer, R. 1985. Everley Water Meadow, Iwerne Stepleton, Dorset. *Dorset Natural History and Archaeological Society Proceedings* 106, 110–11

Mercer, R. & Healy, F. 2008. *Hambledon Hill, Dorset, England: excavation and survey of a Neolithic monument complex and its surrounding landscape.* London: English Heritage

Metz, W., van Beek, B. & Steegstra, H. (eds), 2001. *Patina: essays presented to Jay Jordan Butler on the occasion of his 80th birthday.* Groningen: privately published

Mighall, T., Timberlake, S., Singh, S. & Bateman, M. 2008. Records of palaeo-pollution from mining and metallurgy as recorded by three ombrotrophic peat bogs in Wales, UK. In S. La Niece, D. Hook & P. Craddock (eds), *Metal and Mines: studies in archaeometallurgy*, 56–64. London: British Museum Press

Mighall, T., Timberlake, S., Foster, I., Krupp, E. & Singh, S. 2009. Ancient copper and lead pollution records from a raised bog complex in central Wales, UK. *Journal of Archaeological Science* 36, 1504–15

Mighall, T., Martínez Cortizas, A., Silva Sánchez, N., Foster, I., Singh, S., Bateman, M. & Pickin, J. 2014. Identifying evidence for past mining and metallurgy from a record of metal contamination preserved in an ombrotrophic mire near Leadhills, SW Scotland, UK. *The Holocene* 24, 1719–30

Miles, D., Palmer, S., Lock, G., Gosden, C. & Cromarty, A.-M. 2003. *Uffington White Horse and its Landscape: Investigations at White Horse Hill, Uffington, 1989–95, and Tower Hill, Ashbury, 1993–4.* Oxford: Thames Valley Landscapes Monograph 18

Miles, H. 1975. Barrows on the St Austell granite, Cornwall. *Cornish Archaeology* 14, 5–81

Miles, H. & Miles, T. 1969. Settlement sites of the late pre-Roman Iron Age in the Somerset Levels. *Somerset Archaeology and Natural History* 113, 17–55

Millett, M. 1990. *The Romanization of Britain: an essay in archaeological interpretation.* Cambridge: Cambridge University Press

Millett, M. & Russell, D. 1984. An Iron Age and Romano-British site at Viables Farm, Basingstoke. *Proceedings of the Hampshire Field Club and Archaeological Society* 40, 49–60

Milligan, S. 1886. Notes and queries. *Journal of the Royal Historical and Archaeological Association of Ireland* 4th ser. 7(67), 538

Milligan, S. 1911. Some recent archaeological finds in Ulster. *Journal of the Royal Society of Antiquaries of Ireland* 6th ser. 1, 380–4

Mitchell, A. 1866. Stone moulds. *Proceedings of the Society of Antiquaries of Scotland* 6, 48

Mitchell, A. 1898. Note regarding a mould used in the making of bronze axes. *Proceedings of the Society of Antiquaries of Scotland* 32, 39–41

Modarressi-Tehrani, D. 2009. *Untersuchungen zum Früheisenzeitlichen Metallhandwerk im Westlichen Hallstatt- und Frühlatènegebiet.* Rahden: Bochumer Forschungen zur ur- und frühgeschichtlichen Archäologie 2

Mohen, J.-P. 1978. Moules en bronze de l'Age du Bronze. *Antiquités Nationales* 10, 23–32

Mohen, J.-P. 1984. Nouvelles decouvertes de vestiges métallurgiques de l'âge du Bronze à Fort-Harrouard - Sorel-Moussel (Eure et Loire). In Université de Rennes (ed.), *Paléométallurgie de la France Atlantique*, 181–91. Rennes: Université de Rennes

Mohen, J.-P. 1989. Ateliers métallurgiques dans l'habitat protohistorique du Fort-Harrouard. *Bulletin de la Société Préhistorique Française* 86, 404–8

Mohen, J.-P. & Bailloud, G. 1987. *La Vie Quotidienne, les Fouilles du Fort-Harrouard*. Paris: L'Age du Bronze en France 4

Moloney, C., Holbrey, R., Wheelhouse, P. & Roberts, I. 2003. *Catterick Racecourse, North Yorkshire: the reuse and adaptation of a monument from prehistoric to Anglian times*. Leeds: Archaeological Services WYAS Publication 4

Mordant, C., Pernot M. and Rychner V. (eds), 1998. *L'Atelier du Bronzier en Europe du XXe au VIIIe Siècle Avant Notre Ère. Tome II*. Paris: CTHS

Moore, C. 1978. The South Welsh axe: its origins and distribution. *Archaeological Journal* 135, 57–66

Moore, C. 2008. Old Routes to New Research: the Edercloon wetland excavations in County Longford. In J. O'Sullivan & M. Stanley (eds), *Roads Rediscovery and Research*, 1–12. Dublin: National Roads Authority

Moore, C. & Rowlands, M. 1972. *Bronze Age Metalwork in Salisbury Museum*. Salisbury: Salisbury and South Wiltshire Museum

Moore, J. & Jennings, D.1992. *Reading Business Park: a Bronze Age landscape*. Oxford: Oxford Archaeological Unit

Moore, R., Byard, A., Mounce, S. & Thorpe, S. 2007. A4146 Stoke Hammond and Linslade Western Bypass: archaeological excavations 2005. *Records of Buckinghamshire* 47, 1–62

Moore, T. 2006. *Iron Age Societies in the Severn-Cotswolds: developing narratives of social and landscape change*. Oxford: British Archaeological Report 421

Moore, T. 2012. Beyond the oppida: polyfocal complexes and Late Iron Age societies in southern Britain. *Oxford Journal of Archaeology* 31(4), 391–417

Moore, T., 2017. Beyond Iron Age 'towns': Examining oppida as examples of low-density urbanism. *Oxford Journal of Archaeology* 36, 287–305

Moore, T. & Armada, X.-L. (eds), 2012. *Atlantic Europe in the First Millennium BC: crossing the divide*. Oxford: Oxford University Press

Morris, E. 1989. The Iron Age occupation at Dibble's Farm, Christon. *Somerset Archaeology and Natural History* 132, 23–81

Morris, E. 1996. Artefact production and exchange in the British Iron Age. In T. Champion & J. Collis (eds), *The Iron Age in Britain and Ireland: recent trends*, 41–65. Sheffield: JR Collis Publications

Morris, E. & Gelling, P. 1991. A note on The Berth. *Transactions of the Shropshire Archaeological and Historical Society* 67, 58–62

Mortimer, J. 1905. *Forty Years' Researches in British and Saxon Burial Mounds of East Yorkshire*. London: A. Brown and Sons

Mörtz, T. 2014. Erz und Erzeugnis. Bemerkungen zu den Gießformen für Schwerter der späten Bronzezeit Großbritanniens. In B. Nessel, I. Heske & D. Brandherm (eds), *Ressourcen und Rohstoffe in der Bronzezeit. Nutzung – Distribution – Kontrolle*, 61–73. Wünsdorf: Brandenburgisches Landesamt für Denkmalpflege und Archäologisches Landesmuseum

Moucha, V. 1989. Böhmen am Ausklang des Äneolithikums und am Anfang der Bronzezeit. In M. Buchvaldek & E. Pleslová-Štiková (eds), *Das Äneolithikum und die Früheste Bronzezeit (C14 3000–2000 BC) in Mitteleuropa: kulturelle und chronologische Beziehungen*, 213–18. Prague: Praehistorica 15

Mount, C. 1994. Aspects of ritual deposition in the late Neolithic and Beaker periods at Newgrange, Co. Meath. *Proceedings of the Prehistoric Society* 60, 433–43

Moyler, S. 2007. *Life on the Cutting Edge: interpreting patterns of wear on Scottish early Bronze Age axes*. Unpubl. PhD thesis, University of Southampton

Moyler, S. 2008. Doing away with dichotomies? Comparative use-wear analysis of early Bronze Age axes from Scotland. In Hamon & Quilliec (eds), 2008, 79–90

Mudd, A., Williams, R. & Lupton, A. 1999. *Excavations Alongside Roman Ermin Street, Gloucestershire and Wiltshire*. Oxford: Oxford Archaeological Unit

Muldowney, M. 2015. *Archaeological Excavation at Humberston Avenue, Humberston, North-East Lincolnshire, June to July 2014*. Northampton: MOLA Northampton. Unpubl. report

Müller, J. 1982. Die späte Aunjetizer Kultur des Saalegebietes im Spannungsfeld des Südostens Europas. *Jahresschrift für mitteldeutsche Vorgeschichte* 65, 107–27

Muñiz-Pérez, M., Bermingham, N. & O'Sullivan, J. 2011. A multiperiod landscape in Treanbaun, East Galway: archaeological excavations on the M6 Galway to Ballinasloe motorway scheme. *Journal of the Galway Archaeological and Historical Society* 63, 1–21

Murdock, G. & Provost, C. 1973. Factors in the division of labor by sex: a cross-cultural analysis. *Ethnology* 12, 203–25

Murgia, A., Roberts, B. & Wiseman, R. 2014. What have metal-detectorists ever done for us? Discovering Bronze Age gold in England and Wales. *Archäologisches Korrespondenzblatt* 44(3), 353–67

Murray, R. 2006a. Culduthel Farm, Inverness. *Discovery and Excavation in Scotland* 7 (new ser.), 94–5

Murray, R. 2006b. Culduthel: an Iron Age smelting site near Inverness. *Historical Metallurgy Society News* 64, 3

Murray, R. 2007. *Culduthel Mains Farm, Inverness, Phase 5. Excavation of a later prehistoric settlement: assessment report*. Edinburgh: Headland Archaeology. Unpubl. report

Murray, R. 2011. Beads, brooches and blacksmiths: the Iron Age craftsmen of Culduthel. *The Archaeologist* (summer issue), 22–23

Murray, R. 2012. *Bellfield Farm, North Kessock, Area 2 and 3 archaeological excavation for Tulloch Homes Ltd*. Edinburgh: Headland Archaeology. Unpubl. report

Musson, C. 1991. *The Breiddin Hillfort: a later prehistoric settlement in the Welsh Marches*. London: Council for British Archaeology Research Report 76

Musson, C. & Northover, J.P. 1989. Llanymynech hillfort, Powys and Shropshire: observations on construction work, 1981. *Montgomeryshire Collections* 77, 15–26

Musson, C., Britnell, W., Northover, J.P. & Salter, C. 1992. Excavations and metal-working at Llwyn Bryn-dinas hillfort, Llangedwyn, Clwyd. *Proceedings of the Prehistoric Society* 58, 265–83

Mytum, H. 2013. *Monumentality in Later Prehistory: building and rebuilding Castell Henllys hillfort*. New York: Springer

Nash-Williams, V. 1933. An early Iron Age hill-fort at Llanmelin, near Caerwent, Monmouthshire. *Archaeologia Cambrensis* 88, 237–346

National Museum of Ireland 1971. Archaeological acquisitions in the year 1968. *Journal of the Royal Society of Antiquaries of Ireland* 101, 184–244

Neal, D.S., Wardle, A. & Hunn, J. 1990. *Excavation of the Iron Age, Roman and Medieval Settlement at Gorhambury, St Albans*, London: Historic Buildings and Monuments Commission for England Archaeological Report 14

Nebelsick, L. 2000. Rent asunder: ritual violence in late Bronze Age hoards. In C. Pare (ed.), *Metals Make the World go Round: the supply and circulation of metals in Bronze Age Europe*, 160–75. Oxford: Oxbow Books

Needham, S. 1980a. An assemblage of late Bronze Age metalworking debris from Dainton, Devon. *Proceedings of the Prehistoric Society* 46, 177–215

Needham, S. 1980b. The Bronzes. In Longley, D. (ed), *Runnymede Bridge 1976: excavation on the site of a Late Bronze Age settlement*. Guildford: Surrey Archaeological Society Research Volume 6. 13–27

Needham, S. 1981. *The Bulford-Helsbury Manufacturing Tradition: the production of Stogursey socketed axes during the later Bronze Age in southern Britain*. London: British Museum Occasional Paper 13

Needham, S. 1988. Selective deposition in the British early Bronze Age. *World Archaeology* 20, 229–48

Needham, S. 1990a. Middle Bronze Age ceremonial weapons: new finds from Oxborough, Norfolk, and Essex/Kent. *Antiquaries Journal* 70, 239–52

Needham, S. 1990b. *The Petters Late Bronze Age Metalwork: an analytical study of Thames Valley metalworking in its settlement context*. London: British Museum Occasional Paper 70

Needham, S. 1990c. The clay mould assemblage. In Ellis (ed.) 1999, 24–9

Needham, S. 1992a. The structure of settlement and ritual in the Late Bronze Age of south-east Britain. In C. Mordant & A. Richard (eds), *L'Habitat et l'Occupation du Sol à l'Âge du Bronze en Europe*, 49–69. Paris: Editions du Comité des Travaux historiques et scientifiques

Needham, S. 1992b. *Excavation and Salvage at Runnymede Bridge, 1978. The Late Bronze Age Waterfront Site.* London: British Museum Press/ English Heritage

Needham, S. 1993a. A Bronze Age goldworking anvil from Lichfield, Staffordshire. *Antiquaries Journal* 73, 125–32

Needham, S. 1993b. The Beeston Castle Bronze Age metalwork and its significance. In P. Ellis (ed.), *Beeston Castle, Cheshire: a report on the excavations 1968–85*, 41–50. London: English Heritage

Needham, S. 2002. Analytical implications for Beaker metallurgy in north-west Europe In Bartelheim *et al.* (eds), 2002, 98–13

Needham, S. 2004. Migdale-Marnoch: sunburst of Scottish metallurgy. In I. Shepherd & G. Barclay (eds), *Scotland in Antiquity: the Neolithic and early Bronze Age of Scotland in their European context*, 217–45. Edinburgh: Society of Antiquaries of Scotland

Needham, S. 2007. 800 BC, the great divide. In Haselgrove & Pope (eds), 2007, 39–64

Needham, S. 2014. *Metalworking in the Wilburton Tradition at Holborough Quarry.* Canterbury: Canterbury Archaeological Trust. Unpubl. report

Needham, S. 2011a. 'Cushion' stone. In Fitzpatrick 2011, 113–17

Needham, S. 2011b. Gold basket-shaped ornaments from graves 1291 (Amesbury Archer) and 1236. In Fitzpatrick 2011, 129–38

Needham, S. & Bridgford, S. 2013. Deposits of clay refractories for casting bronze swords. In N. Brown & M. Medlycott, *The Neolithic and Bronze Age Enclosures at Springfield Lyons, Essex: excavations 1981–1991*, 47–74. Chelmsford: East Anglian Archaeology 149

Needham, S. & Cowie, T. 2012. The halberd pillar at Ri Cruin cairn, Kilmartin, Argyll. In A. Cochrane & A. Jones (eds), *Visualising the Neolithic*, 89–110. Oxford: Oxbow Books

Needham, S. & Hook, D. 1988. Lead and lead alloys in the Bronze Age – recent finds from Runnymede Bridge. In Slater & Tate (eds), 1988, 259–74

Needham, S. & Sheridan, A. 2014. Chalcolithic and early Bronze Age goldwork from Britain: new finds and new perspectives. In H. Meller, R. Risch & E. Pernicka (eds), *Metalle der Macht: frühes gold und silber*, 903–41. Halle: Landesmuseum für Vorgeschichte Halle

Needham, S. & Spence, T. 1996. *Refuse and Disposal at Area 16 East, Runnymede. Runnymede Bridge research excavations, volume 2.* London: British Museum Press

Needham, S. & Woodward, A. 2008. The Clandon barrow finery: a synopsis of success in an Early Bronze Age world. *Proceedings of the Prehistoric Society* 74, 1–52

Needham, S., Cowell, M. & Howard, H. 1989. A technological study of the Ham Hill stone moulds. *Somerset Archaeology and Natural History* 132, 15–21

Needham, S., Lawson, A. & Woodward, A. 2010. 'A noble group of barrows': Bush Barrow and the Normanton Down Early Bronze Age cemetery two centuries on. *Antiquaries Journal* 90, 1–39

Needham, S., Parham, D. & Frieman, C. 2013. *Claimed by the Sea: Salcombe, Langdon Bay, and other marine finds of the Bronze Age.* York: Council for British Archaeology Research Report 173

Needham, S., Woodward, A. & Hunter, J. 2015. Items of personal adornment II: gold and the regalia from the Bush Barrow. In A. Woodward and J. Hunter (eds), *Ritual in Early Bronze Age Grave Goods*, 209–60. Oxford: Oxbow Books

Needham, S., Leese, M., Hook, D. & Hughes, M. 1989. Developments in the Early Bronze Age metallurgy of southern Britain. *World Archaeology* 20(3), 383–402

Needham, S., Davis, M., Gwilt, A., Lodwick, M., Parkes, P. & Reavill, P. 2015. A hafted halberd excavated at Trecastell, Powys: from

undercurrent to uptake – the emergence and contextualisation of halberds in Wales and north-west Europe. *Proceedings of the Prehistoric Society* 81, 1–41

Neipert, M. 2006. *Der Wanderhandwerker. Archäologisch-ethnographische Untersuchungen.* Rahden: Tübinger Texte zur Ur- und Frühgeschichtlichen Archäologie 6

Nessel, B. 2010. Bronzene Sägeblätter – Handhabung und Konzeption im Lichte experimentalarchäologischer Versuche. *Apulum* 47, 41–56

Nessel, B. 2012. Hervorgehobene oder verborgene Identität? Zu Ausstattungsmustern von Metallhandwerkergräbern. In I. Heske & B. Horejs (eds), *Bronzezeitliche Identitäten und Objekte*, 55–74. Bonn: Rudolf Habelt

Network Archaeology 2003. *Willington to Steppingley 900mm Gas Pipeline: archaeological evaluation, excavation and watching brief 2002.* Lincoln: Network Archaeology. Unpubl. report

Nevell, M. & Redhead, N. 2005. *Mellor: living on the edge.* Manchester: University of Manchester Field Archaeology Centre

Newton, A. & Mustchin, A. 2015. Archaeological excavations at Ingham Quarry, Fornham St Genevieve. *Proceedings of the Suffolk Institute of Archaeology and History* 43, 337–69

Ní Líonáin, C. 2008. *Final Excavation Report. Site of hotel development, Stamullin, Co. Meath.* Dublin: Arch-Tech. Unpubl. report

Niblett, R. 1985. *Sheepen: an early Roman industrial site at Camulodunum.* London: Council for British Archaeology Research Report 57

Niblett, R. 1993. Verulamium since the Wheelers. In S. J. Greep (ed.), *Roman Towns: the Wheeler inheritance.* York: Council for British Archaeology Research Report 93

Niblett, R. 1999. *The Excavation of a Ceremonial Site at Folly Lane, Verulamium.* London: *Britannia* Monograph 14

Niblett, R. & Thompson, I. 2005. *Alban's Buried Towns: an assessment of St Albans' Archaeology up to AD 1600.* Oxford: Oxbow Books

Nicholson, K. 2006a. An Iron Age site at South Witham Quarry, Lincolnshire. *Lincolnshire History and Archaeology* 41, 22–40

Nicholson, K. 2006b. *Excavations at South Witham Quarry, Lincolnshire.* Ware: Archaeological Solutions. Unpubl. report

Nisbet, H. 1996. Craigmarloch Hillfort, Kilmacolm. In D. Alexander (ed.), *Prehistoric Renfrewshire: papers in honour of Frank Newall*, 43–58. Edinburgh: Renfrewshire Local History Forum

Nixon, S., Rehren, T. & Guerra, M. 2011. New light on the early Islamic West African gold trade: coin moulds from Tadmekka, Mali. *Antiquity* 85, 1353–68

Norfolk Museums Service 1977. *Bronze Age Metalwork in Norwich Castle Museum.* Norwich: Norfolk Museums Service

Nørgaard, H.W. 2014. The Bronze Age smith as individual. In V. Ginn, R. Enlander & R. Crozier (eds), *Exploring Prehistoric Identity in Europe: our construct or theirs?*, 97–102. Oxford: Oxbow Books

Nørgaard, H.W. 2018. *Bronze Age Metalwork Techniques and Traditions in the Nordic Bronze Age 1500–1100 BC.* Oxford: Archaeopress

Northamptonshire Archaeology 2004. *A421 Great Barford Bypass, Bedfordshire: trial trench evaluation, interim report (part 1) zones 1 and 2, February and March 2004.* Northampton: Northamptonshire Archaeology. Unpubl. report

Northover, J.P. 1980. The analyses of Welsh Bronze Age metalwork, in Savory, H. *Guide Catalogue of the Bronze Age Collections*, 229–43. Cardiff: National Museum of Wales

Northover, J.P. 1982a. The exploration of the long-distance movement of bronze in Bronze and Early Iron Age Europe. *Bulletin of the Institute of Archaeology* 19, 45–71

Northover, J.P. 1982b. The metallurgy of the Wilburton hoards. *Oxford Journal of Archaeology* 1, 69–109

Northover, J.P. 1984. Iron Age bronze metallurgy in central southern England. In B. Cunliffe & D. Miles (eds), *Aspects of the Iron Age in Central Southern Britain*, 126–45. Oxford: Oxford University Committee for Archaeology

Northover, J.P. 1988a. The analysis and metallurgy of British Bronze Age swords. In I. Colquhoun & C. Burgess, *The Swords of Britain*, 130–46. Munich: Prähistorische Bronzefunde IV.5

Northover, J.P. 1988b. Copper, tin, silver and gold in the Iron Age. In Slater & Tate (eds), 1988, 223–33

Northover, J.P. 1991. Non-ferrous metalwork and metallurgy, in B. Cunliffe and C. Poole *Danebury: an Iron Age hillfort in Hampshire. Volume 5. The excavations 1979–1988: the finds*, 407–12. London: Council for British Archaeology Research Report 73

Northover, J.P. 1992. Materials issues in Celtic coinage. In M. Mays (ed.), *Celtic Coinage: Britain and beyond*, 235–99. Oxford: British Archaeological Report 222

Northover, J.P. 1995a. Late Bronze Age drawplates in the Isleham hoard. In B. Schmid-Sikimic & P. Della Casa (eds), *Trans Europam. Beiträge zur Bronze- und Eisenzeit Zwischen Atlantik und Altai. Festschrift für Margarita Primas*, 15–22. Bonn: Rudolf Habelt

Northover, J.P. 1995b. The technology of metalwork: bronze and gold. In M. Green (ed.), *The Celtic World*, 285–309. London: Routledge

Northover, J.P. 1999. The earliest metalworking in southern Britain. In A. Hauptmann, E. Pernicka, T. Rehren & Ü. Yalçin (eds), *The Beginnings of Metallurgy*, 211–25. Bochum: Vereinigung der Freunde von Kunst und Kultur im Bergbau

Northover, J.P. 2004a. Ross Island and the physical metallurgy of the earliest Irish copper. In W. O'Brien (ed.), *Ross Island: mining, metal and society in early Ireland*, 525–38. Galway: National University of Ireland, Galway

Northover, J.P. 2004b. Composition of non-ferrous metalwork of Iron Age and Roman date, in G. Lambrick, G. & Allen, T., *Gravelly Guy, Stanton Harcourt: the development of a prehistoric and Romano-British community*, 346–57. Oxford: Oxford Archaeology

Northover, J.P. 2013. Metal analyses. In S. Needham, D. Parham and C. Frieman, *Claimed by the Sea: Salcombe, Langdon Bay and other marine finds of the Bronze Age*, 101–11 York: Council for British Archaeology Research Report 173

Northover, J.P. 2015. Analysis and metallography of ingots and metalworking waste, in Mckinley *et al.* 2015, 182–7

Northover, J.P. nd. *Analysis and Microscopy of Metallurgical Debris from Bourton Business Park*. Gloucester: Gloucestershire County Council Archaeological Service. Unpubl. report

Northover, J.P. & Palk, N. 2000. Metallurgical debris: catalogue and analysis. In Fulford & Timby (eds), 2000, 395–421

Northover, J.P., O'Brien, W. & Stos, S. 2001. Lead isotopes and metal circulation in Beaker/Early Bronze Age Ireland. *Journal of Irish Archaeology* 10, 25–47

Nowakowski, J. 1991. Trethellan Farm, Newquay: the excavation of a lowland Bronze Age settlement and Iron Age cemetery. *Cornish Archaeology* 30, 5–242

Nowakowski, J. 2001. Leaving home in the Cornish Bronze Age: insights into planned abandonment processes. In Brück (ed.) 2001, 161–9

Nowakowski, J. & Quinnell, H. 2011. *Trevelgue Head, Cornwall: the importance of C K Croft Andrew's 1939 excavations for prehistoric and Roman Cornwall*. Truro: Cornwall Council

Nowakowski, J., Quinnell, H., Sturgess, J., Thomas, C. & Thorpe, C. 2007. Return to Gwithian: shifting the sands of time. *Cornish Archaeology* 46, 13–82

Ó Faoláin, S. 2004. *Bronze Artefact Production in Late Bronze Age Ireland: a survey*. Oxford: British Archaeological Report 382

Ó Faoláin, S. & Northover, J. 1998. The technology of late Bronze Age sword production in Ireland. *Journal of Irish Archaeology* 9, 69–88

Ó h-Iceadha, G. 1946. The Moylisha megalith, Co. Wicklow. *Journal of the Royal Society of Antiquaries of Ireland* 76, 119–28

Ó Maoldúin, R. 2014. *Exchange in Chalcolithic and Early Bronze Age Ireland: connecting people, objects and ideas*. Unpubl. PhD thesis, NUI Galway

Ó Néill, J. 2009. *Burnt Mounds in Northern and Western Europe: a study of prehistoric technology and society*. Saarbrücken: Müller

Ó Nualláin, S. 1975. The stone circle complex of Cork and Kerry. *Journal of the Royal Society of Antiquaries of Ireland* 105, 83–131

Ó Ríordáin, S. 1935. Recent acquisitions from County Donegal in the National Museum. *Proceedings of the Royal Irish Academy, Section C* 42, 145–91

Ó Ríordáin, S. 1946. Prehistory in Ireland, 1937–46. *Proceedings of the Prehistoric Society* 12, 142–71

Ó Ríordáin, S. 1954. Lough Gur excavations: Neolithic and Bronze Age houses on Knockadoon. *Proceedings of the Royal Irish Academy, Section C* 56, 297–459

Ó Ríordáin, S. & Ó h-Iceadha, G. 1955. Lough Gur excavations: the megalithic tomb. *Journal of the Royal Society of Antiquaries of Ireland* 85, 34–50

O'Brien, W. 1994. *Mount Gabriel: Bronze Age copper mining in Ireland*. Galway: National University of Ireland, Galway

O'Brien, W. 1999. *Sacred Ground: megalithic tombs in coastal south-west Ireland*. Galway: National University of Ireland, Galway

O'Brien, W. 2004. *Ross Island: mining, metal and society in early Ireland*. Galway: National University of Ireland, Galway

O'Brien, W. 2012. The Chalcolithic in Ireland: a chronological and cultural framework. In Allen *et al.* (eds), 2012, 211–25

O'Brien, W. 2015. *Prehistoric Copper Mining in Europe 5500–500 BC*. Oxford: Oxford University Press

O'Brien, W. & O'Driscoll, J. 2017. *Hillforts, Warfare and Society in Bronze Age Ireland*. Oxford: Archaeopress

O'Brien, W., Northover, J. & Cameron, E. 1990. An early Bronze Age metal hoard from a wedge tomb at Toormore, Co. Cork. *Journal of Irish Archaeology* 5, 9–17

O'Carroll, F. 2012. The crucible assemblage. In C. Cotter, *The Western Stone Forts Project: excavations at Dún Aonghasa and Dún Eoghanachta. Volume 2*, 42–6. Dublin: Wordwell

O'Connell, M. 1986. *Petters Sports Field, Egham: excavation of a Late Bronze Age/Early Iron Age site*. Guildford: Surrey Archaeological Society Research Volume 10

O'Connor, B. 1980. *Cross-Channel Relations in the Later Bronze Age: relations between Britain, northeast France and the Low Countries during the Later Bronze Age and the Early Iron Age, with particular reference to the metalwork*. Oxford: British Archaeological Report S91

O'Connor, B. 1991. Bronze Age metalwork from Cranborne Chase: a catalogue. In J. Barrett, R. Bradley & M. Hall (eds), *Papers on the Prehistoric Archaeology of Cranborne Chase*, 231–41. Oxford: Oxbow Books

O'Flaherty, R. 1995. An analysis of Irish early Bronze Age hoards containing copper or bronze objects. *Journal of the Royal Society of Antiquaries of Ireland* 125, 10–45

O'Flaherty, R. 2002. *The Early Bronze Age Halberd in Ireland*. Unpubl. PhD thesis, University College Dublin

O'Kelly, M. 1969. A stone mould for axeheads from Doonour, Bantry, Co. Cork. *Journal of the Royal Society of Antiquaries of Ireland* 99, 117–24

O'Kelly, M. 1975. An axe mould from Lyre, Co. Cork. *Journal of the Cork Historical and Archaeological Society* 75, 25–8

O'Kelly, M. & Shell, C. 1979. Stone objects and a bronze axe from Newgrange, Co. Meath. In Ryan 1979, 127–44

O'Kelly, M., Cleary, R. & Lehane, D. 1983. *Newgrange, Co. Meath, Ireland. The late Neolithic/Beaker period settlement*. Oxford: British Archaeological Report S190

O'Sullivan, A. 1997. Interpreting the archaeology of Late Bronze Age lake settlements. *Journal of Irish Archaeology* 8, 115–121

Olalde, I., Brace, S., Allentoft, M., Armit, I., Kristiansen, K., Rohland, N., Mallick, S. *et al.* 2018. The Beaker phenomenon and the genomic transformation of northwest Europe. *Nature* 555, 190–6

Oliver, M. & Applin, B. 1979. Excavation of an Iron Age and Romano-British settlement at Ructstalls Hill, Basingstoke, Hampshire, 1972–5. *Proceedings of the Hampshire Field Club and Archaeological Society* 35, 41–92S

Ord, J. 1846. *The History and Antiquities of Cleveland*. London: Simpkin and Marshall

Oswald, A. 1969. Excavations for the Avon/Severn Research Committee at Barford, Warwickshire. *Birmingham Archaeological Society Transactions and Proceedings* 83, 1–64

Ottaway, B. & Roberts, B. 2008. The emergence of metalworking. In A. Jones (ed.), *Prehistoric Europe: theory and practice*, 193–225. Chichester: Wiley-Blackwell

Ottaway, B. & Seibel, S. 1998. Dust in the wind: experimental casting of bronze in sand moulds. In M.-C. Frère-Sautot (ed.), *Paléométallurgie des Cuivres*, 59–63. Montagnac: Monographies Instrumentum 5

Ottaway, B. & Wang, Q. 2004. *Casting Experiments and Microstructure of Archaeologically Relevant Bronzes*. Oxford: British Archaeological Report S1331

Owen, O.A. 1992. Eildon Hill North, Roxburghshire, Borders. In J.S. Rideout, O.A. Owen & E. Halpin (eds), *Hillforts of Southern Scotland*. Edinburgh: AOC Scotland and Historic Scotland, monograph 1

Owen, W. 1999. *13th Green, Llanymynech Golf Club, Powys: archaeological assessment*. Welshpool: Clwyd-Powys Archaeological Trust. Unpubl. report

Owoc, M.-A. 2002. Munselling the mound: the use of soil colour as metaphor in British Bronze Age funerary ritual. In Jones & MacGregor (eds), 2002, 127–40

Oxford Archaeological Unit 2003. *Beechbrook Wood Post Excavation Assessment Report. Channel Tunnel Rail Link*. Oxford: Oxford Archaeological Unit. Unpubl. report

Oxford Archaeology 2015. *The Foreland School, Newlands Lane, Ramsgate, Kent: interim excavation report*. Oxford: Oxford Archaeology. Unpubl. report

Oxford Wessex Archaeology 2013. *East Kent Access (Phase II), Thanet, Kent: draft publication report*. Oxford: Oxford Wessex Archaeology Joint Venture. Unpubl. report

Page, N., Hughes, G., Jones, R. & Murphy, K. 2012. Excavations at Erglodd, Llangynfelyn, Ceredigion: prehistoric/Roman lead smelting site and medieval trackway. *Archaeologia Cambrensis* 161, 285–356

Pailler, Y., Gandois, H. & Tresset, A. 2008. *Beg ar Loued: un habitat en pierres sèches campaniforme*. Rennes: Programme Archéologique Molénais report 11

Pailler, Y., Stéphan, P., Gandois, H., Nicolas, C., Sparfel, Y., Tresset, A., Donnart, K., Dréano, Y., Fichaut, B., Suanez, S., Dupont, C., Audouard, L., Marcoux, N., Mougne, C., Salanova, L., & Dietsch-Sellami, M.-F. 2014. Landscape evolution and human settlement in the Iroise Sea (Brittany, France) during the Neolithic and Bronze Age. *Proceedings of the Prehistoric Society* 80, 105–39

Palk, N. 1991. *Metal Horse Harness of the British and Irish Iron Ages*. Unpubl. PhD thesis, University of Oxford

Pare, C. 1999. Weights and weighing in Bronze Age central Europe. In Römisch-Germanisches Zentralmuseum (ed.), *Eliten in der Bronzezeit*, 421–514. Mainz: Römisch-Germanisches Zentralmuseum

Pare, C. (ed.) 2000. *Metals Make the World Go Round. The Supply and Circulation of Metals in Bronze Age Europe*. Oxford: Oxbow Books

Pare, C. 2013. Weighing, commodification and trade. In Fokkens & Harding (eds), 2013, 508–27

Parenteau, F. 1868. Découverte du Jardin des Plantes de Nantes. *Bulletin de la Société Archéologique de Nantes et du Département de la Loire-Inférieure* 8, 19–46

Parker Pearson, M., Sharples, N. & Symonds, J. 2004. *South Uist: archaeology and history of a Hebridean island*. Stroud: Tempus

Parker Pearson, M., Marshall, P., Mulville, J. & Smith, H. 2001. Cladh Hallan, South Uist. *Discovery and Excavation in Scotland* 2000, 97–8

Parker Pearson, M., Marshall, P., Mulville, J. & Smith, H. 2002. Cladh Hallan. *Discovery and Excavation in Scotland* 2001, 103–4

Parker Pearson, M., Sheridan, A., Jay, M., Chamberlain, A., Richards, M. & Evans, J. (eds), 2019. T*he Beaker People: isotopes, mobility and diet in prehistoric Britain*. Oxford: Prehistoric Society Research Papers 7

Parker, J. 2005. Foxrush Farm excavations 2004: an interim report. *Teesside Archaeological Society Bulletin* 10, 21–8

Parker, J. 2006. Foxrush Farm 2005: a brief summary of work by the Teesside Archaeological Society. *Teesside Archaeological Society Bulletin* 11, 40–2

Parker, J. 2007. Foxrush Farm excavations 2006: a final update? *Teesside Archaeological Society Bulletin* 12, 36–8

Parrington, M. 1978. *The Excavation of an Iron Age Settlement, Bronze Age Ring-Ditches and Roman Features at Ashville Trading Estate, Abingdon (Oxfordshire) 1974–76*. London: Oxfordshire Archaeological Unit and Council for British Archaeology Research Report 28

Parsons, J. 1996. Stone mould from the Derwent Valley, Derbyshire. *Derbyshire Archaeological Journal* 116, 60–7

Partridge, C. 1979a. Excavations at Puckeridge and Braughing, 1975–79. *Hertfordshire Archaeology* 7, 28–131

Partridge, C. 1979b. Excavations at Puckeridge and Braughing 1975–79: Gatesbury Track 1979. *Hertfordshire Archaeology* 7, 97–132

Partridge, C. 1981. *Skeleton Green. A Late Iron Age and Romano-British Site*. London: *Britannia* Monograph 2

Partridge, C. 1982. Braughing, Wickham Kennels 1982. *Hertfordshire Archaeology* 8, 40–59

Passmore, A. 1931. A hoard of bronze implements from Donhead St. Mary, and a stone mould from Bulford, in Farnham Museum, Dorset. *Wiltshire Archaeological Magazine* 45, 373–6

Pattison, S. 1849. A celt mould found at Altarnun. *Annual Report of the Royal Institution of Cornwall* 31, 57–8

Paynter, S. 2000. *Metalworking Waste from Canterbury Road, Hawkinge, Kent. Centre for Archaeology*. London:: Archaeology South-East. Unpubl. report

Peacock, D. 1981. Archaeology, ethnology and ceramic production. In H. Howard & E. Morris (eds), *Production and Distribution: a ceramic viewpoint*, 187–94. Oxford: British Archaeological Report S120

Peake, R., Séguier, J.-M. & Gomez de Soto, J. 1999. Trois exemples de fléaux de balances en os de l'âge du Bronze. *Bulletin de la Société Préhistorique Française* 96, 643–4

Pearce, I. 2006. The Bronze Age hoard. In I. Pearce (ed.), *Roseberry Topping: geology, landscape, history, heritage*, 47–53. Great Ayton: Great Ayton Community Archaeology Project

Pearce, M. 2013. The spirit of the sword and spear. *Cambridge Archaeological Journal* 23, 55–67

Pearce, S. 1974. Finds of Bronze Age material from Kent's Cavern, Torquay. *Transactions and Proceedings of the Torquay Natural History Society* 16 (4), 176–94

Pearce, S. 1983. *The Bronze Age Metalwork of South Western Britain*. Oxford: British Archaeological Report 120

Pearce, S. 1984. *Bronze Age Metalwork in Southern Britain*. Princes Risborough: Shire

Peltenburg, E. 1982. Excavations at Balloch Hill, Argyll. *Proceedings of the Society of Antiquaries of Scotland* 112, 142–214

Pendleton, C. 1999. *Bronze Age Metalwork in Northern East Anglia*. Oxford: British Archaeological Report 279

Penhallurick, R. 1986. *Tin in Antiquity*. London: Institute of Metals

Penhallurick, R. 1997. The evidence for prehistoric mining in Cornwall. In Budd & Gale (eds), 1997, 23–33.

Percival, S. 2017a. *Clay Refractory Debris*. Cambridge: Oxford Archaeology East. Unpubl. specialist report

Percival, S. 2017b. *Clifton Hills Field, Girton, Nottinghamshire: refractory clay moulds, pottery and baked clay*. Nottingham: Trent and Peak Archaeology. Unpubl. specialist report

Perkins, D. 1992. Archaeological evaluations at Ebbsfleet in the Isle of Thanet. *Archaeologia Cantiana* 110, 269–311

Perkins, D. 1993. *Additional Evaluation Work at Dumpton Park Drive, Broadstairs, Kent, 1993*. Birchington: Trust for Thanet Archaeology. Unpubl. report

Perkins, D. 1995a. *Overall Assessment of the Pottery and other Finds from* the 1907–9 South Cliff Parade, 1971–2 and 1974 Dumpton Gap and 1992–1994 South Dumpton Downs Excavations. Birchington: Trust for Thanet Archaeology. Unpubl. report

Perkins, D. 1995b. Report on Work by the Trust for Thanet Archaeology. *Archaeologia Cantiana* 115, 468–70

Perkins, D., Macpherson-Grant, N. & Healey, E. 1994. Monkton Court Farm Evaluation, 1992. *Archaeologia Cantiana* 114, 237–316

Pernicka, E., Lutz, J. & Stöllner, T. 2016. Bronze Age copper produced at Mitterberg, Austria, and its distribution. Archaeologia Austriaca 100, 19–55

Peška, J. 2016. Graves of metallurgists in the Moravian Beaker cultures. In E. Guerra Doce & C. Liesau von Lettow-Vorbeck (eds), *Analysis of the Economic Foundations Supporting the Social Supremacy of the Beaker Groups*, 1–18. Oxford: Archaeopress

Phillips, T. 2011. *Late Iron Age and Roman Settlement at Land off Broadway, Yaxley, Peterborough: post-excavation assessment and updated project design.* Cambridge: Oxford Archaeology East. Unpubl. report

Pickin, J. & Worthington, T. 1989. Prehistoric mining hammers from Bradda Head, Isle of Man. *Bulletin of the Peak District Mines Historical Society* 10, 274–5

Piggott, C. 1946. The Late Bronze Age razors of the British Isles. *Proceedings of the Prehistoric Society* 12, 121–41

Piggott, C. 1947. A Late Bronze Age spearhead mould from Campbeltown. *Proceedings of the Society of Antiquaries of Scotland* 81, 171–2

Piggott, C. & Seaby, W. 1937. Early Iron Age site at Southcote, Reading. *Proceedings of the Prehistoric Society* 3, 43–57

Piggott, S. 1939. The Badbury barrow, Dorset, and its carved stone. *Antiquaries Journal* 19 (3), 291–9

Piggott, S. 1962. From Salisbury Plain to south Siberia. *Wiltshire Archaeological and Natural History Magazine* 58, 93–7

Piggott, S. 1973. The later Neolithic: single-graves and the first metallurgy, *c.* 2000–*c.* 1500 BC. In E. Crittall (ed.), *A History of Wiltshire. Volume 1*, 333–75. Oxford: Oxford University Press

Pine, J. 2013. Iron Age and Roman settlement at Manor Cottage, Temple Lane, Bisham, Berkshire. In S. Preston (ed.), *Iron Age Iron Production Sites in Berkshire: excavations 2003–2012*, 61–95. Reading: Thames Valley Archaeological Services

Pine, J. & Preston, S. 2004. *Iron Age and Roman settlement and Landscape at Totterdown Lane, Horcott, near Fairford, Gloucestershire.* Reading: Thames Valley Archaeological Services

Piper, L. 2008. *Pinden Quarry, Longfield, Kent: metal detecting and test pitting survey and RCHME survey report.* Oxford: Oxford Archaeological Unit. Unpubl. report

Pitts, M. 1976a. A field survey of Oving and District with a trial excavation of an Iron Age site at North Bersted, West Sussex. Rescue Archaeology in Sussex, 1975. *Institute of Archaeology Bulletin* 13, 75–7

Pitts, M. 1976b. North Bersted, Hazel Road S931010. *Sussex Archaeological Society Newsletter* 18, 81

Pitts, M. 2010. Re-thinking the southern British oppida: networks, kingdoms and material culture. *European Journal of Archaeology* 13 (1), 32–63

Platt, L. & Jones, H. 2009. *Clifton Hills Field, Girton, Nottinghamshire: interim report on excavation of a Romano-British settlement.* Nottingham: Trent and Peak Archaeology. Unpubl. report

Ponting, M. 2018. *Pretia victoriae* or just an occasional bonus? Analysis of Iron Age lead artefacts from the Somerset lake villages. *Oxford Journal of Archaeology* 37, 185–99

Porteus, S. 2010. *Geoarchaeological and Archaeological Evaluation and Watching Brief at 12 North Street, Worthing, West Sussex.* London: Archaeology South-East. Unpubl. report

Powell, A. 2008. *Excavations South-East of Park Farm, Ashford, Kent. Part 1 and Part 2.* Salisbury: Wessex Archaeology. Unpubl. report

Powell, A., Jones, G. & Mepham, L. 2008. An Iron Age and Romano-British settlement at Cleveland Farm, Ashton Keynes, Wiltshire. *Wiltshire Archaeological and Natural History Magazine* 101, 18–50

Powell, A., Barclay, A., Mepham, L. & Stevens, C. 2015. *Imperial College Sports Ground and RMC Land, Harlington: the development of prehistoric and later communities in the Colne Valley and on the Heathrow Terrace.* Salisbury: Wessex Archaeology Report 33

Powell, K., Laws, G. & Brown, L. 2009. A late Neolithic/early Bronze Age enclosure and Iron Age and Romano-British settlement at Latton Lands, Wiltshire. *Wiltshire Archaeological and Natural History Magazine* 102, 22–113

Powell, K., Smith, A. & Laws, G. 2010. *Evolution of a Farming Community in the Upper Thames Valley: excavation of a prehistoric, Roman and post-Roman landscape at Cotswold Community, Gloucestershire and Wiltshire.* Oxford: Oxford Archaeology

Powell-Cotton, P. & Pinfold, G. 1939. The Beck find. Prehistoric and Roman site on the foreshore at Minnis Bay. *Archaeologia Cantiana* 51, 191–203

Power, P. 1931. Some recent antiquarian finds in Munster. *Journal of the Royal Society of Antiquaries of Ireland* 7 ser. 1, 55–60

Prendergast, E. 1958. Stone mould for flat axes. *Journal of the Royal Society of Antiquaries of Ireland* 88, 139–43

Preston-Jones, A. 2007. *Kynance Gate, Cornwall: scrub clearance and interpretation.* Truro: Cornwall County Council. Unpubl. report

Price, E. 2000. *Frocester: a Romano-British settlement, its antecedents and successors.* Stonehouse: Gloucester and District Archaeological Research Group

Price, N. 2011. Shamanism. In T. Insoll (ed.), *The Oxford Handbook of the Archaeology of Ritual and Religion*, 983–1003. Oxford: Oxford University Press

Priestley-Bell, G. 2000a. *Post-Excavation Assessment of Archaeological Investigations at Land at Canterbury Road, Hawking, Kent: project No. 1091.* London: Archaeology South-East. Unpubl. report

Priestley-Bell, G. 2000b. *The Excavation of a Multi-Period Site at Canterbury Road, Hawkinge, Kent, 2000.* Where: Archaeology South-East. Unpubl. report

Primas, M. 1997. Bronze Age economy and ideology: central Europe in focus. *Journal of European Archaeology* 5(1), 115–30

Probert, L. 1976. Twyn-y-Gaer hill-fort, Gwent: an interim assessment. In G. Boon & J. Lewis (eds), *Welsh Antiquity*, 105–19. Cardiff: National Museum of Wales

Proudfoot, V.B. 1954. Excavations at the Cathedral Hill, Downpatrick, Co. Down. *Ulster Journal of Archaeology* 17, 97–102

Proudfoot, V.B. 1955. *The Downpatrick Gold Find.* Belfast: HMSO

Proudfoot, V.B. 1957. A second gold find from Downpatrick. *Ulster Journal of Archaeology* 20, 70–2

Pryor, F. 1980. *Excavation at Fengate, Peterborough, England: the third report.* Northampton and Toronto: Northamptonshire Archaeological Society and Royal Ontario Museum

Pryor, F. 1984. *Excavation at Fengate, Peterborough, England: the fourth report.* Northampton and Toronto: Northamptonshire Archaeological Society and Royal Ontario Museum

Pryor, F. 2001. *The Flag Fen Basin: archaeology and environment in a fenland landscape.* London: English Heritage

Qualmann, K., Rees, H., Scobie, G. & Whinney, R. 2004. *Oram's Arbour: the Iron Age enclosure at Winchester. Volume 1: investigations 1950–1999.* Winchester: Winchester Museums Service

Queixalos, I., Menu, M. & Mohen, J.-P. 1987. Creusets pour la fonte des alliages à base de cuivre du Bronze final au Fort-Harrouard à Sorel-Moussel (Eure-et-Loir). *Bulletin de Société Préhistorique Française* 84(1), 22–30

Quilliec, B. 2007. *L'Épée Atlantique: échanges et prestige au Bronze final.* Paris: Société Préhistorique Française

Quinnell, H. 1986. Cornwall during the Iron Age and the Roman period. *Cornish Archaeology* 25, 111–34

Quinnell, H. 2017. Dartmoor and prehistoric to Early Medieval tinworking. In P. Newman (ed.), *The Tinworking Landscape of Dartmoor in a European context – prehistory to 20th century*, 19–26. Exeter: Dartmoor Tinworking Research Group

Quinnell, H. & Harris, D. 1985. Castle Dore: the chronology reconsidered. *Cornish Archaeology* 24, 123–40

Racket, T. 1840. Antiquities found in the counties of Dorset, Devon and Somerset. *Archaeologia* 28, 450–1

Radford, C. 1951. Report on the excavations at Castle Dore. *Journal of the Royal Institution of Cornwall* new ser. 1 (appendix), 1–119

Radivojević, M., Roberts, B., Pernicka, E., Stos-Gale, Z., Martinón-Torres, M., Rehren, T., Bray, P., Brandherm, D., Ling, J., Mei, J., Vandkilde, H., Kristiansen, K., Shennan, S. & Broodbank, C. 2018. The provenance, use, and circulation of metals in the European Bronze Age: the state of debate. *Journal of Archaeological Research* 26, 1–55

Raftery, B. 1970. The Rathgall hillfort, County Wicklow. *Antiquity* 44, 51–4

Raftery, B. 1971. Rathgall, Co. Wicklow: 1970 excavations. *Antiquity* 45, 296–8

Raftery, B. 1976. Rathgall and Irish hillfort problems. In Harding (ed.) 1976, 339–57

Raftery, B. 1983. *A Catalogue of Irish Iron Age Antiquities*. Marburg: Druckerei Kempkes

Raftery, B. 1994. *Pagan Celtic Ireland*. London: Thames and Hudson

Raftery, B., Megaw, V. & Rigby, V. (eds), 1995. *Sites and Sights of the Iron Age*. Oxford: Oxbow Books

Raftery, B. & Becker, J. forthcoming. *The Excavations at Rathgall, County Wicklow*. Bray: Wordwell

Raftery, J. 1945. Contributions to the study of western archaeology: notes on recent finds from Co. Galway. *Journal of the Galway Archaeological and Historical Society* 21, 107–27

Raftery, J. 1951. *Prehistoric Ireland*. London: Batsford

Raftery, J. 1960. A hoard of the Early Iron Age. *Journal of the Royal Society of Antiquaries of Ireland* 90, 2–5

Rahmstorf, L. 2019. Scales, weights and weight-regulated artefacts in Middle and Late Bronze Age Britain. *Antiquity*. https://doi.org/10.15184/aqy.2018.257

Rahtz, P. & Brown, J. 1959. Blaise Castle Hill, Bristol. 1957. *Proceedings of the University of Bristol Spelaeological Society* 8 (3), 147–71

Ralston, I. 1996. Four short cists from north-east Scotland and Easter Ross. *Proceedings of the Society of Antiquaries of Scotland* 126, 121–55

Randall, N. & Poulton, R. 2014. *An Archaeological Excavation at the Planned Cranmere School Site, Arran Way, Esher, Surrey*. Woking: Surrey County Archaeological Unit. Unpubl. report

RCAHMW 1921. *An Inventory of the Ancient Monuments of Wales and Monmouthshire. VI: County of Merioneth*. London: HMSO

RCAHMW 1960. *An Inventory of the Ancient Monuments in Caernarvonshire. Volume II: central*. London: HMSO

RCHMS 2008. *Argyll: an inventory of the ancient monuments. Volume 6*. Edinburgh: Royal Commission on the Ancient and Historical Monuments and Constructions of Scotland

Read, C. 1897. Hoard from Southall, Middlesex. *Proceedings of the Society of Antiquaries of London* 2nd ser. 16, 328–30

Read, C. 1904. *A Guide to the Antiquities of the Bronze Age in the Department of British and Mediæval Antiquities*. London: British Museum

Rees, H. 1993. Later Bronze Age and early Iron Age settlements in the lower Test Valley: evidence from excavations and finds 1981–9. *Proceedings of the Hampshire Field Club and Archaeological Society* 49, 19–46

Reid, M. & Marriott, J. 2010. *Old Oswestry Hillfort Conservation Plan*. London: English Heritage. Unpubl. report

Rhodes, D. 2009. *Druimsdale Machair, South Uist: summary report*. Edinburgh: AOC Archaeology. Unpubl. report no. 4385/32

Richards, C. & Thomas, J. 1984. Ritual activity and structured deposition in later Neolithic Wessex. In Bradley & Gardiner (eds), 1984, 189–218

Richards, D. 2000. Iron-working and other miscellaneous metal-working residues. In Fulford & Timby 2000, 421

Richardson, J. 2011. Bronze Age cremations, Iron Age and Roman settlement and early medieval inhumations at the Langeled Receiving Facilities, Easington, East Riding of Yorkshire. *Yorkshire Archaeological Journal* 83, 59–100

Richmond, I. 1968. *Hod Hill. Volume 2: excavations carried out between 1951 and 1958 for the trustees of the British Museum*. London: British Museum

Rigby, V. 2004. *Pots in Pits: the British Museum East Yorkshire settlements project 1988–1992*. Hull: East Riding Archaeologist 11

Rigby, V. 2013. The making of Iron-Age horse harness mounts: a catalogue of the fired clay mould fragments found at Waldringfield, Suffolk. *Proceedings of the Suffolk Institute of Archaeology and History* 43 (1), 24–37

Robbins, K. 2013. Balancing the scales: exploring the variable effects of collection bias on data collected by the Portable Antiquities Scheme. *Landscapes* 14 (1), 54–72

Roberts, B. 2009. Production networks and consumer choice in the earliest metal of western Europe. *Journal of World Prehistory* 22, 461–81

Roberts, B. & Frieman, C. 2012. Drawing boundaries and building models: investigating the concept of the 'Chalcolithic frontier' in north-west Europe. In Allen *et al.* (eds), 2012, 27–39

Roberts, B. & Ottaway, B. 2003. The use and significance of socketed axes during the late Bronze Age. *European Journal of Archaeology* 6, 119–40

Roberts, B. & Veysey, C, 2011. Trading places. *British Museum Magazine* 70, 44–5

Roberts, B., Boughton, D., Dinwiddy, M., Doshi, N., Fitzpatrick, A., Hook, D., Meeks, N., Mongiatti, A., Woodward, A. & Woodward, P. 2015. Collapsing commodities or lavish offerings? Understanding massive metalwork deposition at Langton Matravers, Dorset during the Bronze Age-Iron Age transition. *Oxford Journal of Archaeology* 34, 365–95

Roberts, E. 2002. Great Orme: Bronze Age mining and smelting site. *Current Archaeology* 181, 29–32

Roberts, I. 2005. *Ferrybridge Henge: the ritual landscape*. Morley: Archaeological Services WYAS

Roberts, I., A. Burgess and D. Berg 2001. *A New Link to the Past: the archaeological landscape of the M1–A1 link road*. Morley: West Yorkshire Archaeology Service

Robinson, I. 2007. *Middle Bronze Age Cremation Practice in East Anglia: continuity and change in cemetery form and development*. Unpubl. MPhil thesis, University of Cambridge. https://www.academia.edu/6980998/Middle_Bronze_Age_cremation_practice_in_East_Anglia_Continuity_and_change_in_cemetery_form_and_development

Roche, H. 1998. Rath na Ríogh (Tara), Castleboy. In I. Bennett (ed.), *Excavations 1997: summary accounts of archaeological excavations in Ireland*, 139. Bray: Wordwell

Roche, H. 1999. Late Iron Age activity at Tara, Co. Meath. *Ríocht na Midhe* 10, 18–30

Roche, H. 2002. Excavations at Ráith na Ríg, Tara, Co. Meath, 1997. *Discovery Programme Reports* 6, 19–82

Roe, F. 1987. *Report on Worked Stone from Beckford, Worcestershire*. London: Ancient Monuments Laboratory Report 154/87

Rohl, B. & Needham, S. 1998. *The Circulation of Metal in the British Bronze Age: the application of lead isotope analysis*. London: British Museum Press

Roseff, R. 1996. *Church Farm, Bierton, Bucks: archaeological evaluation*. Aylesbury: Buckinghamshire County Museum Archaeological Service. Unpubl. report

Rowlands, M. 1971. The archaeological interpretation of prehistoric metalworking. *World Archaeology* 3, 210–24

Rowlands, M. 1976. *The Production and Distribution of Metalwork in the Middle Bronze Age in Southern Britain*. Oxford: British Archaeological Report 31

Rowley, G. 1977. The excavation of a barrow at Woodhouse End,

Gawsworth, near Macclesfield. *Journal of the Chester Archaeological Society* 60, 1–34

Royal Society of Antiquaries of Ireland 1899. Proceedings. *Journal of the Royal Society of Antiquaries of Ireland* 5th ser. 9, 80–92

RPS Consultants 2001. *SeaClean Wight Pipelines: archaeological assessment report*. Abingdon: RPS Consultants. Unpubl. report

Rudling, D. 2002. Excavations Adjacent to Coldean Lane. In Rudling (ed.) 2002, 141–201

Rudling, D. (ed.) 2002. *Downland Settlement and Land-use: the archaeology of the Brighton bypass*. London: Archetype and English Heritage

Rudd, C. 2014. Was Britain's first coin die a forgery? *Treasure Hunting* July, 37–9

Russell, I. 2004. *Final Report on the Archaeological Excavation at Kilsharvan 5, Co. Meath*. Kilcoole, Co. Wicklow: Irish Archaeological Consultancy. Unpubl. report

Russell, M. 2002. Excavations at Mile Oak Farm. In Rudling (ed.) 2002, 5–81

Russell, M. & Cheetham, P. 2016. Finding Duropolis: a new kind of Iron Age settlement. *Current Archaeology* 313, 12–8

Rutter, J. 1956. *The Scarborough Museum: the archaeology of Scarborough and district*. Scarborough: Scarborough Libraries Committee

Ryan, M. (ed.) 1979. *The Origins of Metallurgy in Atlantic Europe*. Dublin: Stationary Office

Ryan, M. (ed.) 1991.*The Illustrated Archaeology of Ireland*. Dublin: Country House

Rynne, E. 1963. Notes on some antiquities in Co. Kildare. *Journal of the Kildare Archaeological Society* 13, 458–62

Sahlén, D. 2011. *Ceramic Technology and Technological Traditions: the manufacture of metalworking ceramics in late prehistoric Scotland*. Unpubl. PhD thesis, University of Glasgow

Sahlén, D. 2013. Selected with care? – the technology of crucibles in late prehistoric Scotland. A petrographic and chemical assessment. *Journal of Archaeological Science* 40, 4207–21

Salisbury Museum 1864. *Descriptive Catalogue of the Salisbury and South Wilts Museum*. Salisbury: Bennett

Salter, C. 1997. A note on tin slags from Caerloggas Down, Cornwall and the Upper Merrivale blowing-house, Devon. In Budd & Gale (eds), 1997, 45–50

Samson, A. 2006. Offshire finds from the Bronze Age in north-west Europe: the shipwreck scenario revisited. *Oxford Journal of Archaeology* 25 (4), 371–88

Sandeman, E. 1910. Excavation discoveries in the Derwent valley. *Journal of the Derbyshire Archaeological and Natural History Society* 32, 73–5

Saunders, A. & Harris, D. 1982. Excavation at Castle Gotha, St Austell. *Cornish Archaeology* 21, 109–53

Saunders, N. 2002. The colours of light: materiality and chromatic cultures of the Americas. In Jones & MacGregor (eds), 2002, 209–226. Oxford: Berg

Saville, A. 1983. *Uley Bury and Norbury Hillforts: rescue excavations at two Gloucestershire Iron Age sites*. Bristol: Western Archaeological Trust

Saville, A. 1984. The Iron Age in Gloucestershire: a review of the evidence. In A. Saville (ed.), *Archaeology in Gloucestershire: from the earliest hunters to the industrial age*, 140–78. Cheltenham: Cheltenham Art Gallery and Museums and Bristol and Gloucestershire Archaeology Society

Savory, H. 1954. The excavation of an early Iron Age fortified settlement on Mynydd Bychan, Llysworney (Glam.), 1949–50. Part I. *Archaeologia Cambrensis* 103, 85–108

Savory, H. 1955. The excavation of an early Iron Age fortified settlement on Mynydd Bychan, Llysworney (Glam.), 1949–50. Part II. *Archaeologia Cambrensis* 104, 14–51

Savory, H. 1974. An early Iron Age metalworker's mould from Worms Head. *Archaeologia Cambrensis* 123, 170–4

Savory, H. 1980. *Guide Catalogue of the Bronze Age Collections*. Cardiff: National Museum of Wales

Savory, H. & Nash-Williams, V. 1946. Current work in Welsh archaeology. A: excavations and discoveries. *Bulletin of the Board of Celtic Studies* 12, 56–66

Schletter, H.-P. 2011. Eine befestigte Siedlung des 1. Jahrhunderts v. Chr. in Rees-Haldern. *Archäologie in Rheinland* 2010, 87–9

Schmidt, P. 1980. Beile als Ritualobjekte in der Altbronzezeit der Britischen Inseln. *Jahresbericht des Instituts für Vorgeschichte der Universität Frankfurt a. M.* 1978–9, 311–20

Schmidt, P. & Burgess, C. 1981. *The Axes of Scotland and northern England*. Munich: Prähistorische Bronzefunde IX.7

Schmidt, R. (ed.) 1996. *The Culture and Technology of African Iron Production*. Gainesville FL: University Press of Florida

Schot, R. 2018. Forging life amid the dead: crafting and kingship at Iron Age Tara. *Discovery Programme Reports* 9, 107–28

Schwab, R., Milcent, P.-Y., Armbruster, B. & Pernicka, E. (eds), 2018. *Early Iron Age Gold in Celtic Europe: society, technology and archaeometry*. Rahden: Marie Leidorf

Score, V. 2011. *Hoards, Hounds and Helmets: a conquest-period ritual site at Hallaton, Leicestershire*. Leicester: University of Leicester Archaeological Services

Shand, G. 2000. Eddington Farm, Herne Bay, *Canterbury's Archaeology* 1999–2000, 18–23

Sharples, N. 1990. Late Iron Age society and continental trade in Dorset. In A. Duval, J.-P. Le Bihan & Y. Menez (eds), *Les Gaulois d'Armorique: la fin de l'age du fer en Europe tempérée*. Rennes: Revue Archeologique de l'Ouest Supplément 3, 299–304

Sharples, N. 1991. *Maiden Castle: excavations and field survey 1985–6*. London: English Heritage

Sharples, N. 2010. *Social Relations in Later Prehistory: Wessex in the first millennium BC*. Oxford: Oxford University Press

Sharples, N. & Parker Pearson, M. 1997. Why were brochs built? Recent studies in the Iron Age of Atlantic Scotland. In Gwilt & Haselgrove (eds), 1997, 254–65

Shee Twohig & Wadell, J. (eds), 1996. *Ireland in the Bronze Age*. Dublin: Stationary Office

Shell, C. 2000. Metalworker or shaman: Early Bronze Age Upton Lovell G2a burial. *Antiquity* 74, 271–2

Shepherd, I. & Barclay, G. (eds), 2004. *Scotland in Ancient Europe: the Neolithic and early Bronze Age of Scotland in their European context*. Edinburgh: Society of Antiquaries of Scotland

Sheppard, T. 1900. On a bronze mould and a hoard of bronze axes found at Hotham Carrs, East Yorkshire. *Transactions of the Hull Scientific and Field Naturalists' Club* 1 (3), 120–2

Sheppard, T. 1923. Bronze-Age mould for casting palstaves. *The Naturalist* 795, 141–2

Sheppard, T. 1930. Clay moulds for Bronze Age implements. *The Naturalist* 1930, 347–50

Sheridan, A. 2012. A Rumsfeld reality check: what we know, what we don't know and what we don't know we don't know about the Chalcolithic in Britain and Ireland. In Allen *et al.* (eds), 2012, 40–55

Sheridan, A. & Shortland, A. 2004. '… beads which have given rise to so much dogmatism, controversy and rash speculation': faience in early Bronze Age Britain and Ireland. In Shepherd & Barclay (eds), 2004, 263–79

Sheridan, A., Parker Pearson, M., Jay, M., Richards, M. & Curtis, N. 2006. Radiocarbon dating results from the Beaker People Project: Scottish samples. *Discovery and Excavation in Scotland* 7, 198–201

Sherlock, S. 2004. Initial excavations at Foxrush Farm, Redcar. *Teesside Archaeological Society Bulletin* 9, 4–10

Sherlock, S. 2012. *Late Prehistoric Settlement in the Tees Valley and North-East England*. Hartlepool: Tees Archaeology

Sherriff, J. 1997. A possible early Bronze Age metalworker's mould from Angus. *Tayside and Fife Archaeological Journal* 3, 55–7

Sillon, C. 2015. Des coins monétaires du Nord-Ouest de la Gaule découverts en Bretagne insulaire. *Bulletin de la Société Francaise de Numismatique* 70 (7), 173–9

Sills, J. 1981. Grimsby, Weelsby Avenue. *Lincolnshire History and Archaeology* 16, 71

Sills, J. & Kinsley, G. 1978. Grimsby, Weelsby Avenue. *Lincolnshire History and Archaeology* 13, 77–8

Sills, J. & Kinsley, G. 1990. An Iron Age bronze foundry at Weelsby Avenue, Grimsby. *Lincolnshire History and Archaeology* 25, 49–50

Silvester, R. 1980. The prehistoric open settlement at Dainton, south Devon. *Devon Archaeological Society Proceedings* 38, 17–48

Silvester, R. 1986. The later prehistoric and Roman material from Kent's Cavern, Torquay. *Devon Archaeological Society Proceedings* 44, 9–38

Silvester, R. & Northover, J.P. 1991. An Iron Age pit at Holmebrink Farm, Methwold. *Norfolk Archaeology* 41 (2), 214–18

Simmonds, A. 2016. *East-West Rail Phase 1: Bicester to Oxford improvements. Post-excavation assessment and updated project design.* Oxford: Oxford Archaeology. Unpubl. report

Simpson, D., Murphy, E. & Gregory, R. 2006. *Excavations at Northton, Isle of Harris.* Oxford: British Archaeological Report 408

Skowranek, C. 2007. *Random Places or Organized Industry? The middle to late Bronze Age metalworking sites in south-west England.* Unpubl. MA thesis, University of Bristol

Slater, A. & Brittain, M. 2012. *Excavations at Ham Hill, Somerset (2011).* Cambridge: Cambridge Archaeological Unit. Unpubl. report

Slater, E. & Tate, J. (eds), 1980. *Proceedings of the 16th International Symposium on Archaeometry and Archaeological Prospection, Edinburgh 1976.* Edinburgh: National Museum of Antiquities of Scotland

Slater, J. & Doonan, R. 2014. Envaluing past practice: a framework for the spatial analysis of metal production in first millennium BC Britain. In R. Scott, D. Braekmans, M. Carremans & P. Degryse (eds), *Proceedings of the 39th International Symposium for Archaeometry, 28 May–1 June 2012, Leuven, Belgium*, 113–19. Leuven: Centre for Archaeological Sciences, KU Leuven

Smith, A, 2001. *The Differential Use of Constructed Sacred Space in Southern Britain from the Late Iron Age to the 4th century AD.* Oxford: British Archaeological Report 318

Smith, A., Allen, M., Brindle, T., Fulford, M., Lodwick, L. & Rohnbogner, A. 2018. *Life and Death in the Countryside of Roman Britain.* London: Britannia Monograph 31

Smith, G. 1991. Excavations at Ham Hill, 1983. *Somerset Archaeology and Natural History* 134, 27–45

Smith, G. 2015. Rescue excavation at the Bronze Age copper smelting site at Pentrwyn, Great Orme, Llandudno, Conwy, 2011. *Archaeology in Wales* 54, 53–71

Smith, G. & Williams, R.A. 2012. *Pentrwyn Copper Smelting Site Excavation, 2011, Great Orme, Llandudno, Conwy.* Bangor: Gwynedd Archaeological Trust. Unpubl. report

Smith, I.M. & Taylor, J. 2000. Excavations on an Iron Age and Medieval earthwork at the Dod, Borders Region, 1979–81. *Archaeological Journal* 157, 229–353

Smith, K. 1977. The excavation of Winklebury Camp, Basingstoke, Hampshire. *Proceedings of the Prehistoric Society* 43, 31–129

Smith, M. 1956. *Isle of Harty hoard, Isle of Sheppey (Kent)*, Inventaria Archaeologica 3rd set, GB 18. London: British Museum

Smith, M. 1958. *Wickham Park Hoard, Croydon (Surrey)*, Inventaria Archaeologica 6th set, GB 39. London: British Museum

Smith, R. 1928. Pre-Roman remains at Scarborough. *Archaeologia* 77, 179–200

Smith, S. 1984. An Iron Age settlement at Maddison Street, Southampton. *Proceedings of the Hampshire Field Club and Archaeological Society* 40, 35–47

Society of Antiquaries of London 1829. Appendix. *Archaeologia* 22, 405–30

Society of Antiquaries of Scotland 1855. February 14, 1855. *Proceedings of the Society of Antiquaries of Scotland* 2, 32–5

Society of Antiquaries of London 1855. Thursday, March 8th, 1855. *Proceedings of the Society of Antiquaries of London* 3, 158–64

Society of Antiquaries of London 1864. Thursday, 5th June, 1862. *Proceedings of the Society of Antiquaries of London* 2nd Series, 2, 126–35

Society of Antiquaries of London 1873. Thursday, January 30th, 1873. *Proceedings of the Society of Antiquaries of London* 2nd Series, 5, 420–35

Society of Antiquaries of Scotland 1865. *Catalogue of Antiquities in the National Museum of the Society of Antiquaries of Scotland.* Edinburgh: Society of Antiquaries of Scotland

Society of Antiquaries of Scotland 1873. Monday, 12th June 1871. *Proceedings of the Society of Antiquaries of Scotland* 9, 238–49

Society of Antiquaries of Scotland 1892. *Catalogue of the National Museum of Antiquities of Scotland.* Edinburgh: Society of Antiquaries of Scotland

Society of Antiquaries of Scotland 1909. Meeting minutes. *Proceedings of the Society of Antiquaries of Scotland* 43, 1–23

Society of Antiquaries of Scotland 1929. Meeting minutes. *Proceedings of the Society of Antiquaries of Scotland* 63, 1–28

Society of Antiquaries of Scotland 1930. Meeting minutes. *Proceedings of the Society of Antiquaries of Scotland* 64, 1–24

Society of Antiquaries of Scotland 1956. Donations to and purchases for the museum, 1955–6. *Proceedings of the Society of Antiquaries of Scotland* 89, 458–63

Sommerfeld, C. 1994. *Gerätegeld Sichel. Studien zur monetären Struktur bronzezeitlicher Horte im nördlichen Mitteleuropa.* Berlin: De Gruyter

Sørensen, M. 1996. Women as/and metalworkers. In A. Devonshire & B. Wood (eds), *Women in Industry and Technology from Prehistory to the Present Day*, 45–51. London: Museum of London

Sörman, A. 2017. A place for crafting? Late Bronze Age metalworking in southern Scandinavia and the issue of workshops. In Brysbaert & Gorgues 2017, 53–78. Leiden: Sidestone Press

Sörman, A. 2018. *Gjutningens Arenor: metallhantverkets rumsliga, sociala och politiska organisation i södra Skandinavien under bronsåldern.* Stockholm: Stockholm Studies in Archaeology 75

Sotheby 1924. *Catalogue of the Well-known Collection of Pre-historic Antiquities etc., Chiefly from Ireland, formed by W.J. Knowles.* London: Sotheby, Wilkinson and Hodge

Spielmann, K.A. 2002. Feasting, craft specialisation, and the ritual mode of production in small-scale societies. *American Anthropologist* 104, 195–207.

Spratling, M. 1972. *Southern British Decorated Bronzes of the Late Pre-Roman Iron Age.* Unpubl. PhD thesis, University of London

Spratling, M. 1979. The debris of metalworking. In Wainwright 1979, 125–53

Spratling, M., Tylecote, R., Kay, P., Jones, L., Wilson, C., Pettifer, K., Osborne, G., Craddock, P. & Biek, L 1980. An Iron Age bronze foundry at Gussage All Saints, Dorset: preliminary assessment of technology. In Slater & Tate (eds), 1980, 268–92

Standish, C., Dhuime, B., Hawkesworth, C. & Pike, A. 2015. A non-local source of Irish Chalcolithic and Early Bronze Age gold. *Proceedings of the Prehistoric Society* 81, 149–77

Stanford, S. 1974. *Croft Ambrey.* Hereford: Privately published

Stanford, S. 1981. *Midsummer Hill: an Iron Age hillfort on the Malverns.* Leominster: Privately published

Staniaszek, B. & Northover, J.P. 1983. The properties of leaded bronze alloys. In A. Aspinall & S. Warren (eds), *The Proceedings of the 22nd Symposium on Archaeometry held at the University of Bradford, Bradford, UK, 30th March–3rd April 1982*, 262–72. Bradford: University of Bradford

Stansby, A. 1984. *The Production and Finishing of Wrought Bronze Tools and other Objects.* Unpubl. Part II thesis, Faculty of Physical Sciences, Oxford University

Starley, D. 1995. *Examination of Slag and other Metalworking Debris from Westhampnett Bypass, Chichester, West Sussex.* London: Ancient Monuments Laboratory Report 34/95

Starley, D. 1997. *An Assessment of Metalworking Debris from Uphall Camp, Ilford, Essex.* London: Ancient Monuments Laboratory Report 4/97

Starley, D. & Tulp, C. 1998. *The Assessment of Metalworking Debris from Covert Farm (DIRFT East), Crick, Northamptonshire.* London: Ancient Monuments Laboratory Report 54/98

Stead, I. 1980. *Rudston Roman Villa.* Leeds: Yorkshire Archaeological Society

Stead, I. 1991. *Iron Age Cemeteries in East Yorkshire.* London: English Heritage

Stead, I. 2006. *British Iron Age Swords and Scabbards.* London: British Museum Press

Stead, I. & Rigby, V. 1986. *Baldock: the excavation of a Roman and Pre-Roman settlement, 1978–72.* London: Britannia Monograph 7

Stead, I. & Rigby, V. 1989. *Verulamium: the King Harry Lane Site.* London: English Heritage and the British Museum

Steadman, S. & Thomas, A. 1998. Stotfold, Groveland Way. *South Midlands Archaeology* 28, 13

Steadman, S. 2005. *Iron Age, Roman and Saxon Settlement at Stotfold, Bedfordshire: the early to middle Iron Age phases at Groveland Way, Stotfold.* Bedford: Albion Archaeology. Unpubl. draft publication excerpts

Stebbing, W. 1934. Miscellaneous notes: an Early Iron Age site at Deal. *Archaeologia Cantiana* 46, 207–9

Steele, P. 2012. *Llyn Cerrig Bach: treasure from the Iron Age.* Llangefni: Oriel Ynys Môn

Stewart, D.S. 1985. Turnford Half Hide Lane. Hertford: *Hart Archaeological Unit Newsletter* (autumn issue)

Stewart, M. 1955. Note on the association between metallurgy and archaeology with particular reference to the Scottish early Bronze Age. *Bulletin of the Institution of Metallurgists* 5 (8), 4–12

Stewart, M., Close-Brooks, J., McKerrell, H. & Thomas, L. 1985. The excavation of a henge, stone circles and metal working area at Moncrieffe, Perthshire. *Proceedings of the Society of Antiquaries Scotland* 115, 125–50

Stokes, M. 1995. Archaeology in Shrewsbury Museum Service 1994. *Transactions of the Shropshire Archaeological and Historical Society* 70, 217

Stukeley, W. 1776. *Itinerarium Curiosum* (2nd edn). London: Baker and Leigh

Surrey County Archaeological Unit. 2015 online news item. http://www.bajrfed.co.uk/bajrpress/late-bronze-age-smelters-hoard-excavation/

Swan, V. 1975. Oare reconsidered and the origins of Savernake ware in Wiltshire. *Britannia* 6, 36–61

Swift, D. 2004. *Hunts Hill Farm: a post-excavation assessment. Site code UP-HH89.* London: Museum of London Archaeology Service. Unpubl. report

Swift, D. 2008. *A Post-Excavation Assessment and Updated Project Design on the Former Syngenta Chemical Works, Hampstead Lane, Yalding, Kent.* London: Archaeology South-East. Unpubl. report

Tabor, R. 2002. The fieldwork. In R. Tabor (ed.), *South Cadbury Environs Project: interim fieldwork report, 1998–2001,* 57–122. Bristol: University of Bristol, Centre for the Historic Environment

Tabor, R. 2008. *Cadbury Castle: the hillfort and landscapes.* Stroud: History Press

Tabor, R. & Johnson, P. 2002. Sigwells, Charlton Horethorne: the identification, interpretation and testing of Bronze Age to early Medieval landscapes by geophysical survey and excavation. *Somerset Archaeology and Natural History* 144, 1–24

Talbot, J. 2017. *Made for Trade: a new view of Icenian coinage.* Oxford: Oxbow Books

Tarlow, S. 1992. Each slow dusk a drawing down of blinds. *Archaeological Review from Cambridge* 11 (1), 125–140

Taylor, E. 2010. *An Iron Age settlement at Tattenhoe Park, Bletchley, Milton Keynes, Buckinghamshire.* Northampton: Northamptonshire Archaeology. Unpubl. report

Taylor, J. 1980. *Bronze Age Goldwork of the British Isles.* Cambridge: Cambridge University Press

Taylor, M. 1884. On the discovery of stone moulds for spearheads at Croglin, Cumberland, and on the process of casting in bronze. *Transactions of the Cumberland and Westmoreland Antiquarian and Archaeological Society* 7, 279–88

Taylor, R. 1993. *Hoards of the Bronze Age in Southern Britain: analysis and interpretation.* Oxford: British Archaeological Report 228

Taylor, S.R. forthcoming. *Down the Bright Stream: the prehistory of Woodcock Corner and the Tregurra Valley.* Oxford: Archaeopress

Teesside Archaeological Society 2003. Foxrush Farm excavations 2002. *Teesside Archaeological Society Bulletin* 8, 17–20

Telfer, A. 2004. *Uphall Camp, Uphall Road, Ilford: a post-excavation assessment.* London: Museum of London Archaeology Services. Unpubl. report

Thelin, V. 2007. *Were Burnt Moulds Derived from Prehistoric Copper Production Activities?* Unpubl. MPhil thesis, University of Durham

Thévenot, J.-P. 1998. Un outillage de bronzier: le dépôt de La Petite Laugère, à Génelard (Saône-et-Loire, France). In Mordant *et al.* (eds), 1998, 123–44

Thomas, A. & Enright, D. 2003. Excavation of an Iron Age settlement at Wilby Way, Great Doddington. *Northamptonshire Archaeology* 31, 15–69

Thomas, D. 1995. *Llanymynech Hillfort, Powys: archaeological evaluation.* Welshpool: Clwyd-Powys Archaeological Trust. Unpubl. report

Thomas, I. 1957. Kynance Gate. *The Lizard* 1 (1), 10–11

Thomas, I. 1960. The excavations at Kynance 1953–1960. *The Lizard* 1 (4), 5–16

Thomas, J. 1991. Reading the body: Beaker funerary practice in Britain. In P. Garwood, D. Jennings, R. Skeates & J. Toms (eds), *Sacred and Profane: proceedings of a conference on archaeology, ritual and religion, Oxford, 1989,* 33–42. Oxford: Oxford University Committee for Archaeology Monograph 32

Thomas, J. 2011. *Two Iron Age 'Aggregated' Settlements in the Environs of Leicester. Excavations at Beaumont Leys and Humberstone.* Leicester: University of Leicester Archaeological Services

Thomas, N. 1972. An early Bronze Age stone axe-mould from the Walleybourne below Longden Common, Shropshire. In F. Lynch & C. Burgess (eds), *Prehistoric Man in Wales and the West: essays in honour of Lily F. Chitty,* 161–6. Bath: Adams and Dart

Thomas, N. 2005. *Conderton Camp, Worcestershire: a small middle Iron Age hillfort on Bredon Hill.* York: Council for British Archaeology Research Report 143

Thomas, R. 1989. The Bronze Age-Iron Age transition in southern England. In R. Thomas & M. L. S. Sørensen (eds), *The Bronze Age-Iron Age Transition in Europe: aspects of continuity and change in European societies c. 1200–500 BC,* 263–86. Oxford: British Archaeological Report S483

Thomas, R., Robinson, M., Barrett, J. & Wilson, B. 1986. A late Bronze Age riverside settlement at Wallingford, Oxfordshire. *Archaeological Journal* 143, 174–200

Thompson, F. 1983. Excavations at Bigberry, near Canterbury, 1978–80. *Antiquaries Journal* 63 (2), 237–78

Thorpe, I.J. & Richards, C. 1984. The decline of ritual authority and the introduction of Beakers into Britain. In Bradley & Gardiner (eds), 1984, 67–84

Threipland, L. 1957. An excavation at St. Mawgan-in-Pydar, north Cornwall. *Archaeological Journal* 113, 33–81

Tierney, M. & Johnston, P. 2009. *Final Excavation Report, N25 Harristown to Rathsillagh, Harristown Big, Co. Wexford.* Cork: Eachtra Archaeological Projects. Unpubl. report

Tilley, C. 2004. *The Materiality of Stone: explorations in landscape phenomenology.* Oxford: Berg

Timberlake, S. 2003. Early mining research in Britain: the developments of the last ten years. In P. Craddock & J. Lang (eds), *Mining and Metal Production throughout the Ages,* 22–42. London: British Museum Press

Timberlake, S. 2004. Pwll Roman mine, Tre Taliesin. *Archaeology in Wales* 44, 142–3

Timberlake, S. 2009. Copper mining and production at the beginning of the British Bronze Age. In Clark (ed.) 2009, 94–121

Timberlake, S. 2017. New ideas on the exploitation of copper, tin, gold, and lead ores in Bronze Age Britain: the mining, smelting, and movement of metal. *Materials and Manufacturing Processes* 32, 709–27

Timberlake, S. & Driver, T. 2006. Excavations at Darren Camp and Darren mine (opencuts), Banc-y-Darren, Trefeurig, Ceredigion. *Archaeology in Wales* 45, 98–102

Timberlake, S. & Hartgroves, S. 2018. New evidence for Bronze Age tin/ gold mining in Cornwall: the date of the antler pick from the Carnon Valley streamworks, Devoran, near Truro, *Cornish Archaeology* 57, 107–122

Timberlake, S. & Prag, A. 2005. *The Archaeology of Alderley Edge: survey, excavation and experiment in an ancient mining landscape*. Oxford: British Archaeological Report 396

Timby, J. 1998. *Excavations at Kingscote and Wycomb, Gloucestershire*. Cirencester: Cotswold Archaeological Trust

Timby, J., Biddulph, E., Hardy, A. & Powell, A. 2007. *A Slice of Rural Essex: archaeological discoveries from the A120 between Stansted Airport and Braintree*. Oxford and Salisbury: Oxford Wessex Archaeology Monograph 1

Timby, J., Brown, R., Hardy, A., Leech, S., Poole, C. & Webley, L. 2007. *Settlement on the Bedfordshire Claylands: archaeology along the A421 Great Barford Bypass*. Oxford: Oxford Archaeology

Tite, M., Pradell, T. & Shortland, A. 2008. Discovery, production and use of tin-based opacifiers in glasses, enamels and glazes from the late Iron Age onwards: a reassessment. *Archaeometry* 50, 67–84

Todd, M. 2007. *Roman Mining in Somerset. Charterhouse on Mendip: excavations 1993–5*. Exeter: Mint Press

Tol, A. 2015. *Erven uit de Bronstijd en Ijzertijd op een Dekzandrug te Tilburg-Zuid: een opgraving in plangebied Tradepark-Noord te Tilburg*. Leiden: Archol Rapport 176

Tournaire, J., Buchsenschutz, O., Henderson, J. & Collis, J. 1982. Iron Age coin moulds from France. *Proceedings of the Prehistoric Society* 48, 417–35

Trow, S. 1982. The Bagendon project 1981–1982: a brief interim report. *Glevensis* 16, 26–9

Trow, S. 1988. Excavations at Ditches hillfort, North Cerney, Gloucestershire, 1982–3. *Transactions of the Bristol and Gloucestershire Archaeological Society* 106, 19–85

Trow, S., James, S. & Moore, T. 2009. *Becoming Roman, being Gallic, staying British: research and excavations at Ditches 'hillfort' and villa 1984–2006*. Oxford: Oxbow Books

Tschen-Emmons, J. 2016. *Buildings and Landmarks of Medieval Europe: the Middle Ages revealed*. Santa Barbara CA: Greenwood

Turek, J. 2004. Craft symbolism in the Bell Beaker burial customs. Resources, production and social structure at the end of Eneolithic period. In M. Besse & J. Desideri (eds), *Graves and Funerary Rituals during the Late Neolithic and the Early Bronze Age in Europe (2700–2000 BC)*, 147–56. Oxford: British Archaeological Report S1284

Turnbull, A.L. 1984. *From Bronze to Iron: the occurrence of iron in the British later Bronze Age*. Unpubl. PhD thesis, University of Edinburgh

Turner, C. 2002. *A10 Wadesmill Bypass: Phase 2, Haul Road. HN361. Archaeological evaluation report, report no. 161*. Letchworth: The Heritage Network. Unpubl. report

Turner, L. 2010. *A Re-interpretation of the Later Bronze Age Metalwork Hoards of Essex and Kent*. Oxford: British Archaeological Report 507

Tylecote, R. 1969. Bronze melting remains and artifacts from Caistor-by-Norwich. *Bulletin of the Historical Metallurgy Group* 3 (2), 46–47

Tylecote, R. 1986. *The Prehistory of Metallurgy in the British Isles*. London: Institute of Metals

Uckelmann, M. 2012. *Die Schilde der Bronzezeit in Nord-, West- und Zentraleuropa*. Stuttgart: Prähistorische Bronzefunde III.4

Vacher, S. & Bernard, V. 2003. Un site en zone inondable: Le Grand Aunay à Yvré-l'Evêque. *Revue Archéologique de l'Ouest* 10, 189–212

Valentin, J. 1994. An Early Iron Age hilltop settlement at Heron Grove, Sturminster Marshall, Dorset: first excavation report. *Proceedings of the Dorset Natural History and Archaeological Society* 115, 63–70

Valentin, J. 1995. Heron Grove, Sturminster Marshall – Area C. *Proceedings of the Dorset Natural History and Archaeological Society* 116, 126

Vallancey, C. 1786. *Collectanea de Rebus Hibernicis. Volume 4*. Dublin: Luke White

Vandkilde, H. 1996. *From Stone to Bronze: the metalwork of the Late Neolithic and Earliest Bronze Age in Denmark*. Aarhus: Jutland Archaeological Society

Van Arsdell, R. 1986. An industrial engineer (but no papyrus) in Celtic Britain. *Oxford Journal of Archaeology* 5, 205–21

Van Arsdell, R. 1989. *Celtic Coinage of Britain*. London: Spink

Van Arsdell, R. 1993. Coin scales in late pre-Roman Iron Age Britain. *Oxford Journal of Archaeology* 12, 361–5

Van de Noort, R. 2004. An ancient seascape: the social context of seafaring in the early Bronze Age. World Archaeology 35 (3), 404–15

van den Broeke, P. 2012. *Het Handgevormde Aardewerk uit de Ijzertijd en de Romeinse tijd van Oss-Ussen: studies naar typochronologie, technologie en herkomst*. Leiden: Sidestone Press

van der Leeuw, S. 1984. Dust to dust: a transformational view of the ceramic cycle. In S. van der Leeuw & A. Pritchard (eds), *The Many Dimensions of Pottery*, 707–73. Amsterdam: University of Amsterdam

van Heeringen, R. 1987. The Iron Age in the western Netherlands II: site catalogue and pottery description map sheet I, *Berichten van de Rijksdienst voor het Oudheidkundig Bodemonderzoek* 37, 39–121

van Renswoude, J. & van Kerckhove, J. 2009. *Opgravingen in Geldermalsen-Hondsgemet: een inheemse nederzetting uit de late Ijzertijd en Romense tijd*. Amsterdam: Zuidnederlandse Archeologische Rapporten 35

Vauterin, C.-C., Chanson, K., Zaour, N., Féret, L. & Le Forestier, S. 2011. La culture matérielle de l'âge du Fer: un outil de réflexion sur les sites d'habitat de Basse-Normandie. In P. Barral, B. Dedet, F. Delrieu, P. Giraud, I. Le Goff, S. Marion & A. Villard-Le Tiec (eds), *L'Âge du Fer en Basse-Normandie*, 203–29. Besançon: Presses Universitaires de Franche-Comté

Vince, A. 2006. *Characterisation Studies of an Iron Age Crucible from Partney, Lincolnshire*. Lincoln: Alan Vince Archaeological Consultancy. Unpubl. report

Voce, E. 1951. Bronze castings in ancient moulds. In H. Coghlan (ed.), *Notes on the Prehistoric Metallurgy of Copper and Bronze in the Old World*, 112–15. Oxford: Oxford University Press

von Nicolai, C. 2009. Pour une «contextualisation» des dépôts du deuxième âge du Fer en Europe tempérée. *Revista d'Arqueologia de Ponent* 19, 75–90

Waddell, J. 1990. *The Bronze Age Burials of Ireland*. Galway: Galway University Press

Waddell, J. 2010. *The Prehistoric Archaeology of Ireland* (revised edn). Dublin: Wordwell

Waddington, K. 2009. *Reassembling the Bronze Age: exploring the southern British midden sites*. Unpubl. PhD thesis, University of Cardiff

Waddington, K. & Sharples, N. 2011. *The Excavations at Whitchurch 2006–2009: an interim report*. Cardiff: Cardiff Studies in Archaeology Specialist Report 31

Waddington, K., Bayliss, A., Higham, T., Madgwick, R. & Sharples, N. 2019. Histories of deposition: creating chronologies for the Late Bronze Age-Early Iron Age transition in southern Britain. *Archaeological Journal* 176, 84–133

Wailes, B. (ed.) 1996. *Craft Specialization and Social Evolution*. Philadelphia PA: University of Pennsylvania Press

Wainwright, G. 1969. The excavation of Balksbury Camp, Andover, Hants. *Proceedings of the Hampshire Field Club and Archaeological Society* 26, 21–55

Wainwright, G. 1970. An Iron Age promontory fort at Budbury, Bradford-on-Avon, Wiltshire. *Wiltshire Archaeological and Natural History Magazine* 65, 108–66

Wainwright, G. 1971. The excavation of a fortified settlement at Walesland Rath, Pembrokeshire. *Britannia* 2, 48–108

Wainwright, G. 1979. *Gussage All Saints: an Iron Age settlement in Dorset*. London: HMSO

Wainwright, G. & Davies, S. 1995. *Balksbury Camp, Hampshire: excavations 1973 and 1981*. London: English Heritage

Wainwright, G. & Spratling, M. 1973. The Iron Age settlement at Gussage All Saints – a chronology. *Antiquity* 47, 109–30

Wait, G. 1985. *Ritual and Religion in Iron Age Britain*. Oxford: British Archaeological Report 149

Wakeman, W. 1895. On a recently-discovered pagan sepulchral mound in the grounds of Old Connaught, Co. Dublin. *Journal of the Royal Society of Antiquaries of Ireland* (5th ser. 5, 106–14

Walford, T. 1803. An account of a Roman military way, in Essex, and of Roman antiquities, found near it. *Archaeologia* 14, 61–74

Walker, D. 1992. An investigation of a late Iron Age site at Sewell Lane, near Dunstable, Bedfordshire. *Bedfordshire Archaeology* 20, 2–17

Walker, G., Thomas, A. & Bateman, C. 2004. Bronze-Age and Romano-British sites south-east of Tewkesbury: evaluations and excavations 1991–7. *Transactions of the Bristol and Gloucestershire Archaeological Society* 122, 29–94

Walker, I. 1974. The counties of Nairnshire, Moray and Banffshire in the Bronze Age, Part II. *Proceedings of the Society of Antiquaries of Scotland* 104, 71–120

Wallace, A. & Anguilano, L. 2010. Iron smelting and smithing: new evidence emerging on Irish road schemes. In M. Stanley, E. Danher & J. Eogan (eds), *Creative Minds: production, manufacturing and invention in ancient Ireland*, 69–84. Dublin: National Roads Authority Monograph 7

Walsh, A. 2011. Clay mould pieces from Bourton-on-the-Water, Gloucestershire. *HMS News* 77, 3

Wang, Q., Strekopytov, S. & Roberts, B. 2018. Copper ingots from a probable Bronze Age shipwreck off the coast of Salcombe, Devon: composition and microstructure. *Journal of Archaeological Science* 97, 102–17

Wang, Q., Strekopytov, S., Roberts, B. & Wilkin, N. 2016. Tin ingots from a probable Bronze Age shipwreck off the coast of Salcombe, Devon: composition and microstructure. *Journal of Archaeological Science* 67, 80–92

WANHS 1980. Wiltshire archaeological register for 1976–7. *Wiltshire Archaeological and natural history Magazine* 72/73, 201–8

WANHS 1990. Wiltshire archaeological registers for 1987 and 1988. *Wiltshire Archaeological and Natural History Magazine* 83, 224–35

Warner, R. 2014. The gold fragments from Haughey's Fort, Co. Armagh: description and XRF analysis. *Emania* 22, 69–76

Warner, R. & Cahill, M. 2012. The Downpatrick hoards: an analytical reconsideration. In J. Trigg (ed.), *Of Things Gone but not Forgotten: essays in archaeology for Joan Taylor*, 95–108. Oxford: British Archaeological Report S2434

Warner, R., Moles, N. & Chapman, R. 2010. Evidence for early Bronze Age tin and gold extraction in the Mourne Mountains, Co. Down. *Journal of the Mining Heritage Trust of Ireland* 10, 29–36

Warrilow, W., Owen, G. & Britnell, W. 1986. Eight ring-ditches at Four Crosses, Llandysilio, Powys, 1981–85. *Proceedings of the Prehistoric Society* 52, 53–87

Waterman, D. & Lynn, C. 1997. *Excavations at Navan Fort 1961–71*. Belfast: Stationary Office

Way, A. 1856. Notices of bronze celts and of celt-moulds found in Wales. *Archaeologia Cambrensis* 3rd ser. 2, 120–31

Webley, L. 2007. Using and abandoning roundhouses: a reinterpretation of the evidence from Late Bronze Age-Early Iron Age southern England. *Oxford Journal of Archaeology* 26, 127–44

Webley, L. 2015. Rethinking Iron Age connections across the Channel and North Sea. In Anderson-Whymark *et al.* (eds), 2015, 122–44

Webley, L. & Adams, S. 2016. Material genealogies: bronze moulds and their castings in later Bronze Age Britain. *Proceedings of the Prehistoric Society* 82, 323–340.

Webley, L., Timby, J. & Wilson, M. 2007. *Fairfield Park, Stotfold, Bedfordshire: later prehistoric settlement in the eastern Chilterns*. Oxford: Oxford Archaeological Unit and Bedfordshire Archaeological Council

Webster, C. & Croft, R. 1995. Somerset archaeology 1994. *Somerset Archaeology and Natural History* 138, 165–85

Wedlake, W. 1958. *Excavations at Camerton, Somerset*. Camerton: Camerton Excavation Club

Welfare, A. 2011. Great Crowns of Stone: the recumbent stone circles of Scotland. Edinburgh: Royal Commission on the Ancient and Historical Monuments of Scotland

Wessex Archaeology 2006. *Cliffs End Farm, Ramsgate, Kent: archaeological assessment report*. Salisbury: Wessex Archaeology. Unpubl. report

Wessex Archaeology 2010. *Margetts Pit, Margetts Lane, Burham, Kent: post-excavation assessment report*. Salisbury: Wessex Archaeology. Unpubl. report

Wessex Archaeology and CgMS, 2008. *Former Queen Mary's Hospital, Carshalton, London: archaeological evaluation report*. Salisbury: Wessex Archaeology and CgMS. Unpubl. report

West, A. 2014. A Late Bronze Age hoard from Feltwell. In S. Ashley & A. Marsden (eds), *Landscapes and artefacts: studies in East Anglian archaeology presented to Andrew Rogerson*, 11–25. Oxford: Archaeopress

West, S. 1989. *West Stow, Suffolk: the prehistoric and Romano-British occupations*. Bury St Edmonds: East Anglian Archaeology 48

Wheeler, R.E.M. 1931. Prehistoric Scarborough. In A. Rowntree (ed.), *The History of Scarborough*, 9–33. London: Dent

Wheeler, R.E.M. 1943. *Maiden Castle, Dorset*. London: Report of the Research Committee of the Society of Antiquaries of London 12

Wheeler, R.E.M. 1954. *The Stanwick Fortifications*. London: Report of the Research Committee of the Society of Antiquaries of London 17

Wilde, W. 1863. *A Descriptive Catalogue of the Antiquities in the Museum of the Royal Irish Academy. Volume 1: articles of stone, earthen, vegetable and animal materials; and of copper and bronze*. Dublin: Royal Irish Academy

Williams, B. 1980. Bronze Age stone moulds from Sultan, County Tyrone. *Ulster Journal of Archaeology* 3rd ser. 43, 102–3

Williams, B. & Gormley, S. 2002. *Archaeological Objects from County Fermanagh*. Belfast: Northern Ireland Archaeological Monographs 5

Williams, B. & Pilcher, J. 1978. Excavations at Lough Eskragh, County Tyrone. *Ulster Journal of Archaeology* 3rd ser. 41, 37–48

Williams, D. 2008. A hoard of late Bronze Age ingots. *Surrey Archaeological Society Bulletin* 410, 2

Williams, H. 1924. A flat celt mould from the Lledr valley. *Archaeologia Cambrensis* 7th ser. 4, 212–3

Williams, J., Burnett, A., La Niece, S. & Cowell, M. 2007. A new Gallo-Belgic B coin die from Hampshire. In C. Gosden, H. Hamerow, P. de Jersey & G. Lock (eds), *Communities and Connections: essays in honour of Barry Cunliffe*, 357–66. Oxford: Oxford University Press

Williams, M. 2003. Growing metaphors. The agricultural cycle as metaphor in the later prehistoric period of Britain and north-western Europe. *Journal of Social Archaeology* 3, 223–55

Williams, R.A. 2013. Linking Bronze Age copper smelting slags from Pentrwyn on the Great Orme to ore and metal. *Historical Metallurgy* 47, 93–110

Williams, R.A. & Le Carlier de Veslud, C. 2019. Boom and bust. Major copper production in Bronze Age Britain from the Great Orme mine and European trade *c.* 1600–1400 BC. *Antiquity* 93, 1178–96

Williams, R.J. & Zeepvat, R. 1994. *Bancroft: the Late Bronze Age and Iron Age settlements and Roman temple-mausoleum*. Aylesbury: Buckinghamshire Archaeological Society

Willis, S. 2007. Sea, coast, estuary, land, and culture in Iron Age Britain. In Haselgrove & Moore (eds), 2007, 107–29

Wills, J. 1976. Beckford, Hereford and Worcester. *West Midlands Archaeological News Sheet* 20, 35

Wills, J. 1978. Beckford 1978. *West Midlands Archaeological News Sheet* 21, 43–5

Wilmott, T. & Rahtz, S. 1985. An Iron Age settlement outside Kenchester, (*Magnis*), Herefordshire. Excavations 1977–1979. *Transactions of the Woolhope Naturalists Field Club* 45 (1), 36–185

Wilson, D. 1863. *The Prehistoric Annals of Scotland*. London: Macmillan

Wilson, F. 2004. Field studies: excavations at Chapel Garth, Arram. *East Riding Archaeological Society News* 59, 4–6

Wilson, F. 2006. *The Significance of Copper-alloy Metalworking in Iron Age East Yorkshire*. Unpubl. BA dissertation, University of Hull

Wilson, F. 2007. An update on excavations at Arram. *East Riding Archaeological Society News* 66, 10–4

Wilson, F. 2009. Excavations at Chapel Garth, Arram. *East Riding Archaeologist* 12, 167–71

Wilthew, P. 1985. *Examination and Analysis of Coin Pellet Moulds from Rochester, Kent.* London: Ancient Monuments Laboratory Report 4541

Wilthew, P. 1986. *Examination of Crucibles and Moulds from Wetwang Slack, Humberside*. London: Ancient Monuments Laboratory Report 4873

Windell, D. 1980. A45 new road archaeological project. *Council for British Archaeology Group 9 Newsletter* 10, 23–8

Wirth, M. 2003. *Rekonstruktion Bronzezeitlicher Gießereitechniken mittels Numerischer Simulation, Gießtechnologischer Experimente und Werkstofftechnischer Untersuchungen an Nachguss und Original*. Aachen: Shaker

Wiseman, R. 2018. Random accumulation and breaking: the formation of Bronze Age scrap hoards in England and Wales. *Journal of Archaeological Science* 90, 39–49

Woodcock, A. 1999. A Late Bronze Age waterlogged site at Shinewater Park near Eastbourne, East Sussex. *NewsWARP* 25, 2–4

Woodham, A. & Mackenzie, J. 1957. Two Cists as Golspie, Sutherland. *Proceedings of the Society of Antiquaries Scotland* 90, 234–238

Woodman, P. 1988. Bay (Carnlough). *Journal of Irish Archaeology* 4, 66

Woodward, A. 2000. *British Barrows: a matter of life and death*. Stroud: Tempus

Woodward, A. & Hughes, G. 2007. Deposits and doorways: patterns within the Iron Age settlement at Crick Covert Farm, Northampton-shire. In Haselgrove & Pope (eds), 2007,185–203

Woodward, A. & Hunter, J. (eds), 2015. *Ritual in Early Bronze Age Grave Goods*. Oxford: Oxbow Books

Woolls, C. 1839. *The Barrow Diggers*. London: Whittaker

Worrell, S. 2007. Detecting the Later Iron Age: a view from the Portable Antiquities Scheme. In Haselgrove & Moore (eds), 2007, 371–88

Worsaae, J. 1866. Om nogle mosefund fra Broncealderen. *Aarbøger for Nordisk Oldkyndighed og Historie* 1866, 313–26

Worsaae, J. 1872. Ruslands og det skandinaviske Nordens bebyggelse og ældste kulturforhold. *Aarbøger for Nordisk Oldkyndighed og Historie* 1872, 309–430

Worsfold, F. 1943. A report on the Late Bronze Age Site excavated at Minnis Bay, Birchington, Kent, 1938–40. *Proceedings of the Prehistoric Society* 9, 28–47

Wymer, J. 1987. A pair of bronze palstave moulds from Harling. *Norfolk Archaeology* 40, 122–6

Yates, D. 2007. *Land, Power and Prestige: Bronze Age field systems in southern England*. Oxford: Oxbow Books

Yates, D. 2012. Connecting and disconnecting in the Bronze Age. *Transactions of the Essex Society for Archaeology and History* 3, 26–36

Yates, D. & Bradley, R. 2010a. The siting of metalwork hoards in the Bronze Age of south-east England. *Antiquaries Journal* 90, 41–72

Yates, D. & Bradley, R. 2010b. Still water, hidden depths: the deposition of Bronze Age metalwork in the English Fenland. *Antiquity* 84, 405–15

Yates, J. 1849. Use of bronze celts in military operations. *Antiquaries Journal* 6, 363–92

York, J. 2002. The life cycle of Bronze Age metalwork from the Thames. *Oxford Journal of Archaeology* 21, 77–92

Young, T. 2008. *Archaeometallurgical Residues from Richard Lander School (RLS04) and Truro College (TCF05)*. Caerphilly: GeoArch. Unpubl. report

Young, T. 2011a. *Evaluation of Possible Archaeometallurgical Residues from Bourton Business Park (34301/35138)*. Caerphilly: GeoArch. Unpubl. report

Young, T. 2011b. *Archaeometallurgical Residues from Platin/Lagavooren 1 (01E0822), Co. Meath, Northern Motorway (J2009)*. Caerphilly: GeoArch. Unpubl. report

Young, T. 2013. *Assessment of Bronze Casting Debris from Banwell, North Somerset*. Caerphilly: GeoArch. Unpubl. report

Young, T. 2015. *Assessment of Archaeometallurgical Residues from Truro EDC (2014)*. Caerphilly: GeoArch. Unpubl. report

Young, T. 2019. Archaeometallurgical residues. In T. Havard, M. Alexander & R. Holt, Iron Age Fortification beside the River Lark: Excavations at Mildenhall, Suffolk. *East Anglian Archaeology Report* 169, 53–55

Zaour, N., Lepaumier, H., Berranger, M. & Fluzin, P. 2014. Les activités métallurgiques dans les établissements ruraux enclos du second âge du Fer en Basse-Normandie: l'exemple du site des 'Pleines' à Orval (Manche). *ArcheoSciences* 38, 165–81

Zvelebil, M. & Parker Pearson, M. 2014. *Excavations at Cill Donnain: a Bronze Age settlement and Iron Age wheelhouse in South Uist*. Oxford: Oxbow Books

APPENDICES

APPENDIX 1

Excavated sites of Bronze Age and Iron Age date that have produced metalworking tools and residues

England (by modern administrative area)

Bath & Northeast Somerset:
Peasedown St John: Wedlake 1958

Bedford:
Great Barford Bypass site 2: Northamptonshire Archaeology 2004; Timby *et al.* 2007

Brighton:
Downsview (adjacent to Coldean Lane), Brighton: Rudling 2002
Mile Oak Farm, Portslade: Russell 2002

Bristol:
Blaise Castle Hill: Rahtz & Brown 1959

Buckinghamshire:
A4146 Stoke Hammond & Linslade Western Bypass site F, Soulbury: Moore *et al.* 2007
Church Farm, Bierton: Fenton 1996; Roseff 1996

Cambridgeshire:
Barford Road, Eynesbury: Ellis 2004
Barleycroft Farm, Needingworth: Evans & Knight 1997; 2000
Bradley Fen, Whittlesey: Gibson & Knight 2006
Broadway, Yaxley: Phillips 2011
Low Park Corner, Chippenham: Atkins 2013
Stonea Grange: Jackson & Potter 1996
Striplands Farm, Longstanton: Evans & Patten 2011

Tithe Barn Farm, Chatteris: Atkins 2011
Wardy Hill, Coveney: Evans 2003
Witchford Fen: Percival 2017a

Central Bedfordshire:
Broom: Cooper & Edmonds 2007
Fairfield Park, Stotfold: Webley *et al.* 2007
Groveland Way, Stotfold: Steadman & Thomas 1998; Steadman *et al.* 2005
Sewell Lane, Houghton Regis: Walker 1992
Willington to Steppingley Gas Pipeline Site 52, Steppingley: Network Archaeology 2003

Cheshire East:
Woodhouse End, Gawsworth: Rowley 1977; Bewley *et al.* 1992

Cheshire West & Chester:
Beeston Castle: Howard 1983; Ellis 1993; Needham 1993b

Cornwall:
Caerloggas Down: Miles 1975; Salter 1997; Malham 2010
Castle Dore: Radford 1951; Quinnell & Harris 1985; Quinnell 1986
Castle Gotha: Saunders & Harris 1982
Chûn Castle: Leeds 1927
Gwithian: Megaw *et al.* 1961; Burgess 1976; Needham 1991; Pearce 1993; Nowakowski *et al.* 2007
Higher Besore and Truro College, Threemilestone: Young 2008; Knight *et al.* 2015; Gossip in press

Kynance Gate: Thomas 1957; 1960; Pearce 1983; Preston-Jones 2007; Knight *et al.* 2015
Sennen: Carey *et al.* 2019; A. Jones pers. comm.
St Mawgan-in-Pydar: Threipland 1957
Tremough: Jones *et al.* 2015
Trethellan Farm, Newquay: Nowakowski 1991
Trevalga: Jones & Quinnell 2014
Trevelgue Head: Nowakowski & Quinnell 2011
Trevisker: ApSimon & Greenfield 1972
Woodcock Corner (EDC), Truro: Young 2015; Taylor forthcoming

Cumbria:
Ewanrigg: Bewley *et al.* 1992; Craddock 1994
Wolsty Hall: Blake 1960

Derbyshire:
Mam Tor: Guilbert 1996

Devon:
Dean Moor: Fox 1957; Malham 2010
Gittisham: Kirwan 1870
Stoneycombe Quarry, Dainton: Needham 1980a; Silvester 1980; Pearce 1983

Doncaster:
Parrots Corner, Rossington: Bishop 2012

Dorset:
Bestwall Quarry: Ladle & Woodward 2009
Down Farm, Gussage St Michael: Barrett *et al.* 1991; O'Connor 1991
Down Farm (Home Field), Gussage St Michael: Green 1987; Ellis 2012
Eldon's Seat, Encombe: Cunliffe & Phillipson 1968; Howard 1983
Everley Water Meadow, Iwerne Stepleton: Howard 1983; Mercer 1985; Mercer & Healy 2008
Gussage All Saints: Wainwright 1979; Foster 1980; Spratling *et al.* 1980; Howard 1983; Fell 1988; 1990; 1997; Garrow *et al.* 2010; Garrow & Gosden 2012
Hengistbury Head: Bushe-Fox 1915; Cunliffe 1987
Heron Grove, Sturminster Marshall: Valentin 1994; 1995
Maiden Castle: Wheeler 1943; Atkinson 1953; Howard 1983; Fell 1990; Sharples 1991; Slater & Doonan 2014
Ower Peninsula: Cox & Hearne 1991
Pilsdon Pen: Gelling 1977
Poundbury: Green 1987
Tinney's Lane, Sherborne: Best *et al.* 2012; 2013
Whitcombe: Aitken & Aitken 1991
Winterborne Kingston: Russell & Cheetham 2016
Woodhouse Hill, Studland: Field 1966
Worth Matravers, Quarry Field: Graham *et al.* 2002

East Riding of Yorkshire:
Burnby Lane, Hayton: Halkon *et al.* 2015
Burton Constable: Glover *et al.* 2016
Chapel Garth, Arram: Wilson 2004; 2006; 2007; 2009
Garton Slack: Brewster 1980; Fell 1990; Darbyshire 1995
Gilcross: Glover *et al.* 2016
Hanging Cliff, Kilham: Rigby 2004
Kelk: Chapman *et al.* 2000
Lady Graves, Fimber: Mortimer 1905; Sheppard 1930; Burgess 1968; Schmidt & Burgess 1981; Ehrenberg & Caple 1983; 1985; Howard 1983
Langeled Receiving Facilities, Easington: Richardson 2011
Makeshift, Rudston: Fell 1990; 1998; Stead 1991; Darbyshire 1995
New York, Burstwick: Glover *et al.* 2016
Out Newton Road, Skeffling: Glover *et al.* 2016
Paddock Hill, Thwing: Manby 1980; 1983; 2007; Manby *et al.* 2003
Rudston villa: Stead 1980
Scorborough Hill: Glover *et al.* 2016
Tuft Hill, Burton Agnes: Rigby 2004
Wetwang Slack: Dent 1984; Wilthew 1986; Giles 2000; 2004; Wilson 2006

East Sussex:
The Caburn, Lewes: Curwen & Curwen 1927

Essex:
Heybridge: Dungworth 2001; Atkinson & Preston 2001; 2015a; 2015b; Essex County Council 2015
Greenfields (A120 Stansted to Braintree): Timby *et al.* 2007; Yates 2012
Passingford Bridge (M25): Biddulph & Brady 2015
Sheepen (*Camulodunum*), Colchester: Hawkes & Hull 1947; Niblett 1985; Hawkes & Crummy 1995
Springfield Lyons: Brown & Medlycott 2013
Stansted Airport, MTCP & M11: Leivers 2008; Cooke *et al.* 2008; Framework Archaeology 2009

Gloucestershire:
Bagendon: Clifford 1961; Trow 1982; Fell 1990; Darbyshire 1995
Bourton Business Park, Bourton-on-the-Water: Bridgford 2011; Walsh 2011; Young 2011a; Northover nd
Ditches, North Cerney: Trow 1988; Trow *et al.* 2009
Ermin Farm, Preston: Mudd *et al.* 1999
Frocester Court: Price 2000
Horcott Pit/Totterdown Lane, Horcott: Pine & Preston 2004; Lamdin-Whymark *et al.* 2009
Ireley Farm, Stanway: Saville 1984; Morris 1996
Roughground Farm, Lechlade: Allen *et al.* 1993
Salmonsbury: Dunning 1976; Howard 1983
Sandy Lane, Charlton Kings: Leah & Young 2001

Shorncote/Cotswold Community: Hearne & Heaton 1994;
Powell *et al.* 2010
Tewkesbury: Walker *et al.* 2004
The Park, Guiting Power: Marshall 2004
Thornhill Farm, Fairford: Jennings *et al.* 2004
Uley Bury: Saville 1983

Greater London:
Cranford Lane, Harlington: Elsden 1996; HER ref
MLO65693
Home Farm, Harmondsworth Lane, Sipson: Hoad *et al.*
2010
Hunts Hill Farm, Aveley Road, Upminster: Swift 2004;
HER ref MLO63020
Imperial College Sports Ground and RMC Land,
Harlington: Powell *et al.* 2015
Oliver Close, Leyton: Lawrence 1996; Bishop 2006; Bishop
& Boyer 2014
South Hornchurch, Havering: Guttman 1996; Guttman
& Last 2000
Uphall Camp, Ilford: Greenwood 1997; Starley 1997; Telfer
2004

Hampshire:
Balksbury Camp: Wainwright 1969; Wainwright & Davies
1995; Ellis & Rawlings 2001
Barton Stacey to Lockerley Gas Pipeline Site 8, Michelmersh:
D'Athe 2013
Bury Hill: Cunliffe & Pool 2000
Church Lane, Nursling: Rees 1993
Danebury: Cunliffe 1984; 1995a; Cunliffe & Poole 1991
Old Kempshott Lane, Basingstoke: Haslam 2012
Oram's Arbour, Winchester: Biddle 1966; Qualmann *et
al.* 2004
Rowbury Farm, Wherwell: Cunliffe & Poole 2008
Ructstalls Hill, Basingstoke: Oliver & Applin 1979
Silchester: Boon 1954; 1957; Corney 1984; Fulford &
Timby 2000; Fulford *et al.* 2018
Viables Farm, Basingstoke: Millett & Russell 1984
Winklebury Camp: Smith 1977
Winnall Down: Fasham 1985
Worthy Down: Hooley 1931; Fell 1990

Herefordshire:
Croft Ambrey: Stanford 1974; 1981; Darbyshire 1995
Eaton Camp: Dorling 2014
Kenchester: Wilmott & Rahtz 1985
Midsummer Hill: Stanford 1981; Fell 1990; 1997; 1998;
Darbyshire 1995
Sutton Walls: Kenyon 1954; Howard 1983

Hertfordshire:
13 Wick Avenue, Wheathampstead: Curteis 2001; Simon
West pers. comm.

Baldock: Stead & Rigby 1986
Ford Bridge, Braughing: Hunn 2007; Landon 2010
Gatesbury and Gatesbury Track, Braughing: Partridge
1979a; 1979b; Craddock & Tite 1981
Gorhambury: Neal *et al.* 1990
Halfhide Lane, Broomfield Avenue, Turnford: Stewart
1985; Quilliec 2007; HER ref 6484; Stuart Needham notes
King Harry Lane, St Albans: Stead & Rigby 1989
Leavesden Aerodrome, Abbotts Langley: Brossler 1999;
Brossler *et al.* 2009
Moles Farm, A10, Haul Road, Wadesmill Bypass: Turner
2002
Puckeridge: Landon 2009
Skeleton Green, Puckeridge: Partridge 1981; Barford 1982
Turnershall Farm (also known as Turner's Hall Farm),
Wheathampstead: McDonald 1999
Verlamion, St Albans: Anthony 1970; Frere 1983; Niblett
1993; 1999; Niblett & Thompson 2005
Wickham Kennels, Braughing: Partridge 1982

Hull:
Salthouse School, Hull: Wilson 2006

Isle of Wight:
SeaClean Wight Pipeline Site 32, Havenstreet: RPS
Consultants 2001

Kent:
Beechbrook Wood, CTRL, near Ashford: Oxford
Archaeological Unit 2003; Champion 2011
Bigbury Hillfort (Bigberry Camp), Harbledown, near
Canterbury: Boyd Dawkins 1902; Jessup 1933; Thompson
1983
Bogshole Lane, Broomfield: Allen 1999; Helm 2001
Canterbury Road, Hawkinge: Paynter 2000; Priestley-Bell
200a; b;
Cliffe: Kinnes *et al.* 1998
Cliffs End Farm, Ramsgate: Wessex Archaeology 2006;
Leivers *et al.* 2015
Dumpton, Broadstairs: Perkins 1993; 1995a; 1995b
East Kent Access, Thanet: Oxford-Wessex Archaeology
2013; Andrews *et al.* 2015; Robinson 2015
Eddington Farm, Herne Bay: Shand 2000
Ellington School, Pysons Rd, Ramsgate: Boden 2005a;
Boden *et al.* 2006; Oxford Archaeology 2015; John Rady,
pers. comm.
Hampstead Lane (Former Syngenta Chemical Works),
Yalding: Swift 2008
Highstead, near Chislet, Canterbury: Bennet *et al.* 2007
Holborough Quarry, Snodland: Helm 2004; Boden 2005b;
2006; nd.; Needham 2014
Margetts Pit, Margetts Lane, Burham: Wessex Archaeology
2010
Marlowe Theatre and Car Park, Canterbury: Bayley 1983;

Blockley *et al.* 1995
Mill Hill, Deal: Stebbing 1934; Champion 1980; Turnbull 1984
Milner's Gravel Pit, Sturry, Canterbury: Turnbull 1984
Monkton Court Farm, Thanet: Perkins *et al.* 1994
Park Farm, Ashford: Powell 2008
Turing College, University of Kent, Canterbury: McDonnell 2014

Lancashire:
Cliviger Laithe, Cliviger: Barnes 1982; Barrowclough 2008
Mosley Height, Cliviger: Barnes 1982; Bennett 1953; Barrowclough 2008

Leicester:
Bath Lane/Blackfriars Street/Merlin Works, Leicester: Clay & Mellor 1985; Kipling 2008; Landon 2016
Elms Farm/Manor Farm, Humberstone: Charles *et al.* 2000; Thomas 2011

Leicestershire:
Breedon-on-the-Hill: Kenyon 1950
Hallaton: Score 2011
Glenfield Park: Carlyle 2012
Leicester Road/Dalby Road, Melton Mowbray: Harvey 2010

Lincolnshire:
Billingborough: Chowne *et al.* 2001
Fiskerton: Field & Parker Pearson 2003
Old Sleaford: Jones *et al.* 1976; Elsdon 1997
Partney bypass: Atkins 2005; Vince 2006
South Witham Quarry: Nicholson 2006a; 2006b
Washingborough: Allen 2009

Medway:
50–54 High Street, Rochester: Wilthew 1985; Harrison 1991
Cliffe: Kinnes *et al.* 1998

Milton Keynes:
Bancroft: Williams & Zeepvat 1994
Newton Leys: Brown 2012
Tattenhoe Park: Taylor 2010

Norfolk:
Fison Way, Thetford: Gregory 1991
Grimes Graves, near Brandon: Mercer 1981; Longworth *et al.* 1991
Holmebrink Farm, Methwold: Silvester & Northover 1991
Needham: Frere 1941
Quidney Farm, Saham Toney: Bates 2000
Woodcock Hall, Saham Toney: Brown 1986
Caistor St Edmund (Caistor-by-Norwich/*Venta Icenorum*/Caistor Castle): Mann 1939; Tylecote 1969

North Lincolnshire:
Dragonby: May 1996

North Somerset:
Banwell: Young 2013
Dibble's Farm, Christon: Morris 1989

North Yorkshire:
Castle Hill, Scarborough: Smith 1928; Wheeler 1931; Dungworth 1997
Catterick Racecourse: Moloney *et al.* 2003
Scorton Grange: Sherlock 2012
Scotch Corner, M1/A1: Fell 2017
Stanwick: Haselgrove 2016
Staple Howe: Brewster 1963; Dungworth 1997

Northamptonshire:
Castle Yard: Knight 1988; Fell 1990; Darbyshire 1995
Clay Lane, Earls Barton: Windell 1980
Covert Farm (DIRFT East), Crick: Starley & Tulp 1998; Hughes & Woodward 2015
Harpole: Brown 1967
Hunsbury: George 1917; Fell, C. 1937; Howard 1983; Fell, V. 1990; 1997; 1998; Darbyshire 1995
Mallard Close, Earls Barton: Chapman & Atkins 2004
Rainsborough Camp: Avery *et al.* 1967; Fell 1990; Darbyshire 1995
Wakerley: Jackson & Ambrose 1978
Wales Street, Kings Sutton: Hunn & Richmond 2004; Fell & Hunn 2005
Wilby Way, Great Doddington: Thomas & Enright 2003
Weekley: Jackson & Dix 1987

North East Lincolnshire:
Humberston Avenue, Humberston: Muldowney 2015
Weelsby Avenue, Grimsby: Sills & Kinsley 1978; 1990; Sills 1981; Howard 1983; Fell 1990; Foster 1995; Dungworth 1997; Ellis *et al.* 2001

Northumberland:
Belling Law: Jobey 1977
Hartburn: Jobey 1973
Kirkhaugh: Maryon 1936; Needham 2011; Fowler 2013; Fitzpatrick 2015b; 2018; Linda Boutoille pers. comm.

Nottinghamshire:
Clifton Hills Field, Girton: Platt & Jones 2009; Percival 2017b
Gamston: Knight 1993
High Thorpe, Cropwell Butler: Cooke & Mudd 2014

Oxfordshire:
Ashville Trading Estate, Abingdon: Parrington 1978
Cassington Pit West Extension, Cassington: Hey *et al.* 2006

Coxwell Road, Faringdon: Cook *et al.* 2005
Gravelly Guy, Stanton Harcourt: Lambrick & Allen 2004
Grimsbury House, Banbury: Allen 1991
Madmarston Camp: Fowler 1960; Fell 1990; Darbyshire 1995
Mingies Ditch, Hardwick-with-Yelford: Allen & Robinson 1993
Oddington Crossing (South of), East-West Rail Phase 1: Simmonds 2016
Old Shifford Farm, Standlake: Hey 1995
Segsbury Camp: Lock *et al.* 2005
Thrupp, Radley: Ainslie 1992
Tower Hill, Ashbury: Miles *et al.* 2003
Trendles Field, Marcham/Frilford: Kamash *et al.* 2010
Watkins Farm, Northmoor: Allen 1990
Whitecross Farm, Wallingford: Thomas *et al.* 1986; Cromarty *et al.* 2006
Wittenham Clumps, Little Wittenham: Hingley 1980; Allen *et al.* 2010
Woodeaton: Harding 1987; Fell 1990; 1997; Darbyshire 1995
Worton Rectory Farm/Cresswell Field, Yarnton: Bayley 1994; Hey *et al.* 2011

Peterborough:
Fengate Gravel Pits, Fengate: Hawkes & Fell 1943
Maxey Quarry: Meadows 2006; Needham & Bridgford 2013
Newark Road, Fengate: Pryor 1980
Storey's Bar Road, Fengate: Pryor 1984

Plymouth:
Mount Batten: Brown & Hugo 1983; Cunliffe 1988

Reading:
Reading Business Park: Moore & Jennings 1992
Southcote: Piggott & Seaby 1937; Fell 1990

Redcar & Cleveland:
Foxrush Farm, Redcar: Teeside Archaeological Society 2003; Sherlock 2004; Parker 2005; 2006; 2007
Kilton Thorpe, Brotton: Sherlock 2012

Rutland:
Egleton: Carlyle 2011
Ketton: Mackie 1993

Shropshire:
Old Oswestry: Hughes 1996; Reid & Marriott 2010
The Berth: Morris & Gelling 1991

Slough:
Castleview Road: Jones & Chapman 2012; Andrews & Clarke 2015

Somerset:
Alstone: Miles & Miles 1969; Heslop & Langdon 1996
Glastonbury Lake Village: Bulleid & Gray 1911; 1917; Howard 1983; Fell 1990; 1997; 1998; Coles & Minnitt 1995; Darbyshire 1995
Ham Hill: Gray 1927; Needham *et al.* 1989; Fell 1990; 1998; Smith 1991; Darbyshire 1995; Webster & Croft 1995; Slater & Brittain 2012
Meare East: Coles 1987; Howard 1983; Fell 1990
Meare West: Gray & Bulleid 1953; Gray & Cotton 1966; Howard 1983; Fell 1990
Norton Fitzwarren: Ellis 1990; Needham 1990c
Sigwells, Charlton Horethorne: Webster & Croft 1995; Tabor 2002; 2008; Tabor & Johnson 2002; Knight *et al.* 2015
South Cadbury/Cadbury Castle: Fell 1990; Barrett *et al.* 2000a
Star: Barton 1964

Southampton:
Maddison Street, Southampton: Smith 1984

Stockport:
Mellor: Nevell & Redhead 2005

Stockton-on-Tees:
Castle Hill, Kirklevington: Sherlock 2012
Thorpe Thewles: Heslop 1987

Suffolk:
Burgh: Martin 1988
Ingham Quarry, Fornham St Genevieve: Craven 2004; Newton & Mustchin 2015
Long Melford Primary School, Long Melford: Brooks 2013; 2016
Recreation Way, Mildenhall: Cotswold Archaeology 2012; Young 2019
Sutton Hoo, near Woodbridge: Longworth & Kinnes 1980; Carver 2004; 2005; Hummler 2005
Waldringfield: Rigby 2013
West Stow: West 1989

Surrey:
Cranmere School, Arran Way, Esher: Randall & Poulton 2014; Surrey County Archaeological Unit 2015
Hawk's Hill, Fetcham: Hastings 1965
Petters Sports Field, Egham: Johnson 1975; Needham 1981; 1990b; O'Connell 1986
Runnymede Bridge: Longley 1980; Needham 1980b; 1992b; Needham & Spence 1996; Waddington 2009
Tongham Nurseries, Guildford: Bird *et al.* 1996; Hayman 1996
Weston Wood, Albury: Harding 1964

Swindon:
Burderop Down: Howard 1983; Gingell 1992
Groundwell Farm, Blunsdon St Andrew: Gingell 1982; Fell 1990

Thurrock:
Mucking Iron Age settlement: Clark 1993; Evans *et al.* 2015
Mucking North Ring: Bond 1988; Evans *et al.* 2015
Mucking South Rings: Jones & Bond 1980; Evans *et al.* 2015

Wakefield:
Ferrybridge: Roberts 2005

Warwickshire:
Coton Park, Rugby: Chapman 1998; 2000; 2019
Westwood Campus, University of Warwick: Hill 2002; Adams *et al.* 2018
Whitchurch: Waddington 2009; Waddington & Sharples 2011; Lavelle 2012

West Berkshire:
Aldermaston Wharf: Bradley *et al.* 1980
Dunston Park, Thatcham: Fitzpatrick *et al.* 1995
Weathercock Hill, Lambourn: Bowden *et al.* 1993

West Sussex:
12 North Street, Worthing: Porteus 2010
Goffs Park & Southgate West: Gibson-Hill 1975; Cartwright 1992
Hazel Road, North Bersted: Pitts 1976a; 1976b; Bedwin & Pitts 1978
Ounces Barn, Boxgrove: Bedwin 1984; Bedwin & Place 1995
Slonk Hill, Shoreham: Hartridge 1978
Westhampnett Bypass: Starley 1995; Fitzpatrick 1997

Wiltshire:
All Cannings Cross: Cunnington 1923; Howard 1983
Amesbury Archer, Amesbury, Boscombe Down: Fitzpatrick 2011
Arn Hill, Warminster: Cunnington 1912; Shell 2000
Bishops Cannings Down: Gingell 1992
Breach Hill, Tilshead: Birbeck 2006
Budbury: Wainwright 1970; Darbyshire 1995
Casterley Camp: Cunnington & Cunnington 1913; Fell 1998
Cleveland Farm, Ashton Keynes: Powell *et al.* 2008
East Chisenbury: McOmish 1996; McOmish *et al.* 2010
Latton Lands: Powell *et al.* 2009
Potterne: Lawson 2000
South Lodge Camp: Barrett *et al.* 1991; O'Connor 1991
Swallowcliffe Down: Clay 1925
Upton Lovell: Cunnington 1806; Annable & Simpson 1964; Piggott 1973; Shell 2000

Winterbourne Monkton: Anon. 1913
Withy Copse, Oare: Cunnington 1909; Swan 1975; Fell 1998

Windsor & Maidenhead:
Manor Cottage, Bisham: Pine 2013

Wokingham:
Lea Farm, Hurst: Manning & Moore 2011

Worcestershire:
Aston Mill Farm, Kemerton: Dinn & Evans 1990
Beckford: Britnell 1974; 1975; Wills 1976; 1978; Linton & Bayley 1982; Howard 1983; Hurst & Wills 1987; Roe 1987; Anon. 1988; Fell 1990
Bredon Hill (Kemerton Camp): Hencken 1938; Fell 1990; 1993; 1997; 1998; Darbyshire 1995; Moore 2006; Hurst & Jackson 2007
Conderton Camp: Thomas 2005
Huntsman's Quarry, Kemerton: Jackson & Napthan 1998; Doonan 1999; Jackson 2015

York:
Heslington East: Antoni *et al.* 2009

Isle of Man

Ballacagen Lough: Bersu 1977
Ballanorris: Bersu 1977
Billown Quarry: Darvill 2000; 2001; 2004
Close ny Chollagh: Gelling 1958

Scotland

Aberdeenshire:
Covesea Cave 2, Moray: Büster & Armit 2014
Cullykhan: Greig 1970; 1971; 1972; Tylecote 1986; Heald 2005
Deer's Den, Kintore: Alexander 2000
Loanhead of Daviot: Kilbride-Jones 1936
Osprey Heights, Boynds Farm, Uryside, Inverurie: Dalland 2014; Dalland & Cox 2014; Ginnever 2015

Angus:
Finavon: Childe 1935; MacKie 1969; Heald 2005

Argyll & Bute:
Balloch Hill: Peltenburg 1982
Dunagoil: Mann 1925; Leechman 1962; Harding 2004; Boughton 2016
Little Dunagoil: Marshall 1964; Schmidt & Burgess 1981; Harding 2004

East Lothian:
Broxmouth: Armit & McKenzie 2013
Fishers Road East, Port Seton: Haselgrove & McCullagh 2000
Traprain Law: Cree & Curle 1922; Burley 1956; Armit *et al.* 2005; Sahlén 2011

Highland:
Bellfield Farm, North Kessock: Murray 2012
Crosskirk Broch, Caithness: Fairhurst 1984
Culduthel Farm, Inverness: Murray 2006a; b; 2007; 2011; Hunter 2011
Galmisdale, Eigg: Cowie 2002; 2003; Sahlén 2011
Golspie: Woodham & Mackenzie 1957; Sheridan *et al.* 2006
High Pasture Cave (Uamh an ard Achadh), Skye: Birch *et al.* 2010; Cruickshanks & Hunter nd.
Ness: Mackie 2007
Seafield West: Cressey & Anderson 2011

Inverclyde:
Craigmarloch hillfort, Craigmarloch Wood, Kilmacolm: Nisbet 1996

Moray:
Birnie: Hunter 2006; 2007; 2010; Sahlén 2011; 2013
Covesea Cave 2, Moray: Büster & Armit 2014

Orkney:
Bu 'Navershaw' or 'Navershough': Mackie 2002; Canmore Site Number HY20NE 11: http://canmore.org.uk/site/1483
Midhowe, Rousay: Callander & Grant 1934
Mine Howe: Card & Downes 2003; Harrison & Card 2005
St Boniface Church, Papa Westray: Lowe 1990; 1993; Lowe & Boardman 1998

Perth & Kinross:
Moncrieffe: Stewart *et al.* 1985
Oakbank Crannog, Loch Tay: Dixon & Cavers 2001; Dixon 2003; Dixon *et al.* 2007; Cook *et al.* 2010

Scottish Borders:
Eildon Hill North: Owen 1992
The Dod: Smith & Taylor 2000

Shetland:
Clickhimin: Hamilton 1968
Jarlshof: Curle 1932; 1933; 1834; 1935; Hamilton 1956; MacKie 2002; Heald 2005; Mörtz 2014

West Dumbartonshire:
Sheep Hill: McKie 2015

Comhairle nan Eilean Siar:
Cill Donnain: Zvelebil & Parker Pearson 2014
Cladh Hallan: Marshall *et al.* 2000; Parker Pearson *et al.* 2001; 2002; 2004; Sahlén 2011; 2013
Cnip 1: Armit 2006
Druimsdale Machair/Drimsdale, South Uist: Rhodes 2009
Dun Bharabhat (Loch Baravat/Dun Baravat 1), Lewis: Mackie 2007
Guinnerso, Uig, Lewis: Burgess & Church 1995; Burgess *et al.* 1996; 1997; Church & Gilmour 1998; Canmore: http://canmore.org.uk/site/109409
Northton: Simpson *et al.* 2006
Upper Loch Bornish, South Uist: Marshall & Parker Pearson 2012

Wales

Conwy:
Pentrwyn: Jones 1999; Roberts 2002; Smith & Williams 2012; Williams 2013; Smith 2015

Monmouthshire:
Llanmelin: Nash-Williams 1933

Pembrokeshire:
Castell Henllys: Mytum 2013
Pill Rath: Savory & Nash-Williams 1946
Porth y Rhaw: Crane 2010
Walesland Rath: Wainwright 1971

Powys:
Sarn-y-bryn-caled, Welshpool: Gibson 1994
Four Crosses: Warrilow *et al.* 1986
Collfryn: Britnell 1989
The Breiddin: Howard 1983; Fell 1990; Musson 1991; Darbyshire 1995; Needham & Bridgford 2013
Llanymynech: Musson & Northover 1989; Thomas 1995; Owen 1999
Llwyn Bryn-dinas: Musson *et al.* 1992
Twyn y Gaer: Probert 1976; Fell 1990; Darbyshire 1995

Vale of Glamorgan:
Castle Ditches, Llancarfan: Hogg 1977
Llanmaes: Lodwick & Gwilt 2004; Gwilt & Lodwick 2006; Gwilt *et al.* 2006
Mynydd Bychan: Savory 1954; 1955; Fell 1990; Darbyshire 1995

Ireland

Co. Antrim:
Bay, Carnlough: Woodman 1988; Ó Faoláin 2004
Corrstown: Ginn & Rathbone 2012

Co. Armagh:
Haughey's Fort: Mallory 1995; Bradherm 2014; Warner 2014
King's Stables: Lynn 1977
Navan: Waterman & Lynn 1997

Co. Clare:
Mooghaun South: Grogan 2005

Co. Cork:
Toormore: O'Brien *et al.* 1990

Co. Down:
Cathedral Hill, Downpatrick: Halpin 1998

Co. Dublin:
Ballynakelly: McCarthy 2010
Dalkey Island: Liversage 1968; Eogan 1965; 2000; Ó Faoláin 2004
Oldconnaught: Wakeman 1895

Co. Fermanagh:
Boho: Royal Society of Antiquaries of Ireland 1899; Hodges 1954; Coghlan & Raftery 1961; Williams & Gormley 2002; Ó Faoláin 2004

Co. Galway:
Cross: McKeon & O'Sullivan 2014
Dún Aonghasa: Cotter 2012
Rathwilladoon: Lyne 2009; 2012

Co. Kerry:
Ross Island: O'Brien 2004

Co. Kildare:
Knockaulin: Johnston & Wailes 2007; Bayliss & Grogan 2013

Co. Kilkenny:
Baysrath: Dowling 2014

Co. Laois
Ballydavis: Keeley 1999; nd

Co. Limerick
Lough Gur (Knockadoon) sites C, D, F & K: Ó Ríordáin 1954; Coghlan & Raftery 1961; Grogan & Eogan 1984; Ó Faoláin 2004 Lough Gur wedge tomb: Ó Ríordáin, Ó h-Iceadha 1955
Raheen: Gowen 1988

Co. Louth:
Richardstown: Byrnes 1999

Co. Meath:
Cakestown Glebe: Lynch 2011
Kilsharvan: Russell 2004
Newgrange: O'Kelly & Shell 1979; O'Kelly *et al.* 1983
Pace: Elliott *et al.* 2008
Platin/Lagavooren 1: Young 2011b; Lynch 2012
Ráith na Ríg, Tara: Roche 1998; 1999; 2002; Crew & Rehren 2002; Bayliss & Grogan 2013
Stamullin: Ní Líonáin 2008

Co. Sligo:
Rathtinaun: Coghlan & Raftery 1961; Raftery 1994; O'Sullivan 1998; 2004

Co. Tipperary
Ballylegan: McQuade 2007; McQuade *et al.* 2009
Chancellorsland: Doody 2008

Co. Tyrone:
Killymoon: Hurl 1995; Hurl *et al.* 1995
Lough Eskragh: Hodges 1954; Collins & Seaby 1960; Eogan 1965; 2000; Collins 1970; Williams & Pilcher 1978
Loughash: Davies 1939

Co. Wicklow:
Harristown Big: Tierney & Johnston 2009
Johnstown South: Fitzpatrick 1997; 1998; Ó Faoláin 2004
Labbanasigha, Moylisha: Ó h-Iceadha 1946; Brindley & Lanting 1992
Rathgall: Raftery 1970; 1971; 1976; Eogan 2000; Ó Faoláin 2004; Becker 2010; Raftery & Becker forthcoming

Appendix 2
One-piece stone moulds of Early Bronze Age date

ENGLAND

Locality	Administrative area	Find context	Matrices	Condition	Stone	References	Museum (accession no.)
Hurbuck, Lanchester	Co. Durham	Unknown	Flat axe × 3, ?awl	Complete	Sandstone	Callander 1904, 492; Greenwell & Clinch 1905; Brailsford 1953, fig. 12; Britton 1963, 320; Schmidt & Burgess 1981, 54 & pl. 26B	BM (WG 2267)
Hurbuck, Lanchester	Co. Durham	Unknown	Flat axe × 3	?	Sandstone	Callander 1904, 492; Greenwell & Clinch 1905; Britton 1963, 320; Schmidt & Burgess 1981, 54	–
Altarnun	Cornwall	'In the meadow below the vicarage-house at Altarnun' (Pattison 1849, 57); 'found in a tin work, near the church village' (Lake 1867, 20)	Flat axe	Complete	Probably polyphont	Pattison 1849; Lake 1867; Britton 1963, 319 & fig. 6; Pearce 1983, 399, pls 1 & 122	Royal Cornwall
Barf End, Gunnerside	North Yorkshire	Garden wall, SD959986; on steep slope overlooking Swaledale, at limit of agricultural land	Flat axe	Complete	Sandstone	Johnson 2014	Hawes
Scarborough	North Yorkshire	Unknown	Flat axe	Complete	Yellowish stone with grey surface	Rutter 1956; Britton 1963, 321; Schmidt & Burgess 1981, 54, pl. 26	Scarborough (184.38)
Cambo, Wallington	Northumberland	In a field to the north of Cambo	Flat axe × 2, ring, knife blade	Complete	Sandstone	Charlton 1855; Hodges 1960, pl. I; Britton 1963, 320; Schmidt & Burgess 1981, 54, pl. 26A	BM (1852, 10-4, 1)
Walleybourne Brook, Longden Common	Shropshire	SJ 435043; 'More or less midstream' in Walleybourne Brook in a 'miniature gorge'	Flat axe × 5	Complete	Carboniferous grit	Thomas 1972	Shrewsbury (M1)
'Suffolk Fens'	Suffolk?	Unknown; provenance to Suffolk has been questioned	Flat axe, bar, ring, knife blade	Complete	Orange–yellow stone	Tylecote 1962, 112; Britton 1963, 276, 320–1 & fig. 7	Manchester (O.6923)

IRELAND

Locality	Administrative area	Find context	Matrices	Condition	Stone	References	Museum (accession no.)
'Lough Gall'	'Co. Antrim'	Unknown; could mean Lough Guile in Co. Antrim or Loughgall, Co. Armagh	Flat axe × 4, bar × 2	Complete	Sandstone	Crawford 1912, 317 (as 'Loughcal'); Collins 1970, 25, fig. 2	Lost? Formerly Pitt-Rivers Museum, Farnham
?	?	Unknown	Flat axe × 3, tanged dagger	Complete	Mica schist	Society of Antiquaries of Scotland 1865, 94; Megaw & Hardy 1938, pl. 53; Harbison 1973, pl. 13a; Schmidt 1980, fig. 3	NMS (CN1)
Ballymena	Co. Antrim	Unknown; ex Evans collection	Flat axe	Complete	Micaceous sandstone	Evans 1881, 428, fig. 515	Ashmolean (1927.2733)
Ballyglisheen	Co. Carlow	Found during ploughing in Ballyglisheen townland	Flat axe × 8	Near-complete	Millstone grit, possibly from local glacial drift	Prendergast 1958; Coghlan & Raftery 1961, 226, fig. 3; Harbison 1973, pl. 13b	NMI (1957: 342)
Doonour	Co. Cork	Found in field close to present coast (<150m)	Flat axe × 5, chisel × 2	Complete	Old red sandstone, 'could be immediately local'	O'Kelly 1969	NMI (1966: 33)
Kilcronat, near Ballynoe	Co. Cork	Unknown	Flat axe	Complete	Old red sandstone	Power 1931; Coghlan & Raftery 1961, 226, fig. 2	NMI (P. 1948: 157)
Lyre	Co. Cork	Found in farmyard at northern end of Lyre townland; gently sloping ground down to River Glashanabrack (c. 150 m away)	Flat axe x 2	Complete	Sandstone	O'Kelly 1975	Cork (G.680)
Ballynahinch	Co. Down	Unknown	Flat axe × 4 (1 unfinished)	Complete	Sandstone	du Noyer 1847, 335, pl. 6; Wilde 1863, 392–3, fig. 307; Collins 1970, 24–5, fig. 1; Flanagan 1979, pl. 1b; 1991, 79; 1998, pl. 7	Ulster (1911.1121)
Lough Scur	Co. Leitrim	Later Bronze Age crannóg	Flat axe × 2; later reused for bivalve palstave mould	Complete	Grit	Wilde 1863, 91, fig. 72; Coghlan & Raftery 1961, 225, fig. 1	NMI (W.83)
?	?	Unknown	Flat axe × 3	Complete	?	C. Jones 2002	Hunt Museum, Limerick (HCA 212)

SCOTLAND

Locality	Administrative area	Find context	Matrices	Condition	Stone	References	Museum (accession no.)
'Burreldales, Fyvie' or 'Pitdoulzie'	Aberdeenshire	Unknown	Flat axe, bar × 2, ?knife blade, plate with rounded ends	Complete	Sandstone	Callander 1906; Stewart 1955, 8, fig. 2; Society of Antiquaries of Scotland 1956; Hodges 1959, pl. y; Britton 1963, 321–3, fig. 10; Schmidt & Burgess 1981, 53, pl. 23	NMS (CM 42)
Burgh Muir (Borough Moor), Kintore	Aberdeenshire	'Found in a cairn', location not recorded	Flat axe, ?bar × 2, knife blade	Complete	Sandstone	Society of Antiquaries of Scotland 1855, 33; Britton 1963, 322; Schmidt & Burgess 1981, 53, pl. 25	NMS (CM 1)
East Cruchie, Drumblade	Aberdeenshire	NJ 5889 4249; 'to the SE of the farm buildings in an arable field sloping down to the Drumblade Burn & it is likely that the stone had been dragged downslope by ploughing'	Flat axe	Complete. Possibly reused saddle quern	Light grey schistose stone	Cowie & O'Connor 2009, 317, fig. 3	Aberdeen University (37856)
Foudland, Insch	Aberdeenshire	'On a small farm on the south face of the Hill of Foudland', the highest hill in the local area	Flat axe × 4, bar × 2, ?knife blade × 3	Complete	Sandstone	Callander 1904; Britton 1963, 321–2; Schmidt & Burgess 1981, 53, pl. 24; Jones 2015, fig. 7.5	Aberdeen University (18237)
Mains of Corsegght	Aberdeenshire	On a low eastward sloping flank of a low hill (NJ 845 499); undated enclosure nearby	Flat axe	Complete	Old Red Sandstone	Inglis & Inglis 1983; Cowie & O'Connor 2009, 315–17, fig. 2	Aberdeen University (15503)
Mains of Corsegght	Aberdeenshire	Close to other Mains of Corsegght mould, probably at NJ 849 499	Flat axe	Complete	Sandstone	Cowie & O'Connor 2009, 315–17, fig. 2; Fitzpatrick 2015, fig. 8a	Aberdeen University (15947)
Marnoch	Aberdeenshire	Unknown	Flat axe, bar, ring	Complete	Sandstone	Anderson & Black 1888, 369; Callander 1904, 492; Britton 1963, 323; Walker 1974; Schmidt & Burgess 1981, 53, pl. 25	Banff
New Deer	Aberdeenshire	Unknown	Flat axe × 2, bar × 2	Complete	Sandstone	Callander 1904, 492; Britton 1963, 322; Schmidt & Burgess 1981, 53, pl. 24	NMS (CM 27)

Locality	Administrative area	Find context	Matrices	Condition	Stone	References	Museum (accession no.)
Ferintosh	Highland	Unknown	Flat axe × 2, possible further matrix	Complete	Sandstone	Society of Antiquaries of Scotland 1929, 12; Britton 1963, 324; Schmidt & Burgess 1981, 54, pl. 26	NMS (CM 32)
Strathconon	Highland	Peat bog between Blair-na-Bithe & Loch Scardroy, in remote glen	Flat axe, triangular casting	Complete	Greyish brown stone	Mitchell 1898; Britton 1963, 324, fig. 11; Schmidt & Burgess 1981, 54, pl. 26	NMS (CM 26)
'Cutties Hillock', Quarrywood, near Elgin	Moray	Interior of Late Bronze Age enclosure & possible stone circle (Gordon 2012), located on southern crest of hill with wide view to south	Flat axe	Complete	Fine-grained buff stone	Benton *et al.* 1952; Britton 1963, 324; Walker 1974; Schmidt & Burgess 1981, 54	Elgin (1945, 2)
Culbin Sands	Moray	Coastal sand dunes; possible Bronze Age 'maritime haven' (Bradley *et al.* 2016)	Flat axe × 3, ?awl	Complete	Micaceous sandstone	Black 1891; Megaw & Hardy 1938, pl. 53; Britton 1963, 323, pl. 26; Walker 1974; Schmidt & Burgess 1981, 53–4, pl. 26; Barber 2003, fig. 33	NMS (CM 18)
Culbin Sands	Moray	As above	Flat axe × 2	Frag.	Micaceous sandstone	Black 1891; Britton 1963, 324; Walker 1974; Schmidt & Burgess 1981, 54	NMS (CM 19)
Glenrinnes House, Dufftown	Moray	'Found in a drystone dyke, about 200 yards from Glenrinnes House'	Flat axe × 3, bar × 2	Complete	Grey fine-grained stone	Society of Antiquaries of Scotland 1930, 14; Britton 1963, 323, pl. 26; Walker 1974; Schmidt & Burgess 1981, 53, pl. 25; Needham 2004, fig. 19.9; this volume, Fig. 2.10	NMS (CM 33)
Easter Clunie, Abernethy	Perth and Kinross	In an arable field, *c.* NO 21 17	Flat axe × 2, small axe or chisel, ?large dagger blade (matrix incomplete), bars × 2	Broken (appears old break)	Sandstone	Cowie & O'Connor 2009, 317–19, fig. 4	–
'Rubers Law or The Dunion'	Scottish Borders	Unknown; Rubers Law & the Dunion are both prominent hills	Flat axe x 2 (1 unfinished), small axe or chisel	Complete	Sandstone	Cowie 2000; Cowie & O'Connor 2009, 321–2, figs 6–7	–

Locality	Administrative area	Find context	Matrices	Condition	Stone	References	Museum (accession no.)
			WALES				
Glenhead Farm, Carron Bridge	Stirling	NS 757 850; above steep slope down to River Carron	Flat axe	Near complete	Sandstone	Cowie 2000; Cowie & O'Connor 2009, 319–20, fig. 5	Falkirk (1998-37)
Bwlch-y-Maen, near Betws-y-Coed	Conwy	Slope overlooking Lledr river valley	Flat axe	Complete	Fine-grained, blue–grey quartz-grit; origin in N Wales possible	Williams 1924; Britton 1963, 321, fig. 8	–
New Mills	Powys	At edge of grass field at junction with steep valley side down to Rhiw river	Halberd blank × 2, unidentified × 1, possible further matrix. 1 matrix unfinished	Complete	Sandstone	Green 1985; Needham et al. 2015	NMW (79.26H)

Uncertain and spurious moulds

Site	Administrative area	Matrices	Comments	References	Museum (accession no.)
			ENGLAND		
Derwent Dam	Derbyshire	Ring × 2 (plus 1 unfinished), circular ?ingot × 2, bar × 2	More likely Iron Age or Romano-British on typological grounds (Parsons 1996)	Sandeman 1910; Britton 1963, 324–5; Parsons 1996	-
			IRELAND		
near Carrickfergus	Co. Antrim	Trapezoidal matrices × 3	Would have cast trapezoidal objects, 7.5 cm, 6 cm, and 3.8 cm long, with rounded underside. Described by Bateman as 'for casting the earliest type of celt'. It is perhaps possible that the larger matrices were intended for casting blanks for small broad-butted axes, but it seems more likely that this is an ingot mould of uncertain date	Bateman 1855, 78	NMI (1893.31)

Site	Administrative area	Matrices	Comments	References	Museum (accession no.)
Dunbeacon North, near Schull	Co. Cork	Bar; circular depression	EBA date suggested by Cahill, but later date may be more likely as circular matrix is not paralleled on any certain BA moulds	Lucas 1973, 202, fig. 19; Cahill 2006, 275	NMI (1970:14)
Chancellorsland	Co. Tipperary	'Flat axe'	Broken mudstone object suggested to be unfinished flat axe mould, from excavation of a MBA enclosure. V. questionable	Doody 2008	–
ISLE OF MAN					
Maughold	Isle of Man	'Flat axe, bar'	Does not exist	Pickin & Worthington 1989	–
SCOTLAND					
Ledmore	Angus	'Flat axe' x 2	Identification questioned by Cowie & O'Connor; may not be a mould	Sherriff 1997; Cowie & O'Connor 2009	–
Kilmallie (Kilmailie)	Highland	Ring; further possible disc or ring	Early Bronze Age date possible but unproven	Society of Antiquaries of Scotland 1873, 248; Britton 1963, 325	NMS (CM 9)

Appendix 3

Bivalve stone moulds *c.* 1700–600 BC

Date	Locality	Administrative area	Find context	Matrices	Condition	Stone	References	Museum (accession no.)
ENGLAND								
M–LBA	Downsview, Brighton	Brighton & Hove	Excavated; house platform	Annular object (possible bracelet or quoit-headed pin)	2 frags	Oolitic limestone	Rudling 2002	–
MBA	Bodwen, Lanlivery	Cornwall	On sloping ground at edge of what is now moorland	Rapier	2 non-joining frags of 1 valve	Greenstone	Evens *et al.* 1972; Harris *et al.* 1977; Pearce 1983, 413, pl. 9	Royal Cornwall (1971/5)
LBA	Gwithian	Cornwall	Excavated; 2 round-houses	Socketed axe × 2	2 frags of 1 valve	Chlorite-talc schist	Megaw *et al.* 1961; Burgess 1976; Needham 1981; Pearce 1983, 409, pl. 6; Nowakowski *et al.* 2007	–
LBA	Helsbury Quarry, Michaelstow	Cornwall	'Cave' in valley of River Camel	Socketed axe	Both valves	Chlorite schist	Hodges 1960, pl. 2; Evens *et al.* 1962; Fox 1964, pl. 52; Needham 1981; Pearce 1983, 419, pl. 13	Royal Cornwall
LBA	Helsbury Quarry, Michaelstow	Cornwall	As above	Socketed axe	Both valves	Chlorite schist	Hodges 1960, pl. ii; Evens *et al.* 1962; Fox 1964, pl. 52; Needham 1981; Pearce 1983, 419, pls 13 & 147	Royal Cornwall
LBA	Helsbury Quarry, Michaelstow	Cornwall	As above	Socketed axe	Both valves	?	Needham 1981; Pearce 1983, 419	–
Late EBA	Herodsfoot	Cornwall	Unknown	Tanged chisel	1 valve	Greenstone	Pearce 1983, 551–2, pl. 118	–
LBA	Linkinhorne	Cornwall	Unknown	Socketed chisel	?	?	Hodges 1960, 160	–
LBA	St Keverne	Cornwall	SW7872722706	Socketed axe	Frag.	Greisen	PAS: CORN-031000; Knight 2015, 33, fig. 1	–
MBA	Tremough	Cornwall	Excavated; round-house	Socketed tool	Frag.	Elvan	Jones *et al.* 2015	–
MBA	Tremough	Cornwall	As above	Pin shaft	Frag.	Elvan	As above	–
MBA	Tremough	Cornwall	As above	Ring-headed pin; pin shaft	Frag.	Elvan	As above	–
MBA	Tremough	Cornwall	As above	Socketed axe	1 valve	Greenstone	As above	–
MBA	Tremough	Cornwall	As above	Pin shaft	1 valve, near complete	Elvan	As above	–

Date	Locality	Administrative area	Find context	Matrices	Condition	Stone	References	Museum (accession no.)
MBA	Tremough	Cornwall	As above	Pin shaft	1 valve, near complete	Elvan	As above	–
MBA	Tremough	Cornwall	As above	Ring-headed pin	1 valve, near complete	Elvan	As above	–
MBA	Tremough	Cornwall	As above	Tanged chisel × 2	1 valve	Probably volcanic tuff	As above	–
MBA	Tremough	Cornwall	As above	Bladed implement?	Frag.	Elvan	As above	–
MBA	Trethellan Farm, Newquay	Cornwall	Excavated; hollow/round-house	Chisel? × 2	Frag.; possibly reused as whetstone	Mica	Nowakowski 1991	Royal Cornwall
MBA	Trevalga	Cornwall	Excavated; round-house	Racloir; chisel?; unfinished matrix	1 valve	Elvan	Jones & Quinnell 2014	–
MBA	Croglin	Cumbria	Found on wasteland	Spearhead; probable ferrule	Both valves, both broken	Sandstone	Taylor 1884; Davis 2012, 164.	Tullie House (1889.49)
MBA	Burgh Island, Bigbury	Devon	Offshore island	Palstave?	Frag.	Mica-schist	Pearce 1983, 433, pl. 23	Plymouth (38.5)
MBA	Hennock	Devon	Close to River Teign; 2 moulds found 20 ft apart, each with matrices fitted together, 1 placed horizontally the other vertically.	Rapier; ornamental strip or bracelet	Both valves; some damage, not clear if sustained when recovered	'Light green micaceous schist' (=?Greenstone)	Archaeological Institute 1852; Hodges 1960, pl. i; Fox 1964, pl. 48; Pearce 1983, 447; Berridge 1986	Casts in BM, Ashmolean, Exeter & NMS
MBA	Hennock	Devon	As above	Rapier	Both valves; some damage, not clear if sustained when recovered	'Light green micaceous schist' (= ?Greenstone)	Archaeological Institute 1852; Hodges 1960, pl. i; Fox 1964, pl. 49; Pearce 1983, 447; Berridge 1986	As above
MBA	Holsworthy	Devon	Unknown; found during drainage works	Dirk; ornamental strip	Both valves. 'A double groove (?sharpening) is in one mould, adjacent and parallel to the blade recess'	Greenstone	Pearce 1983, 443–4, pls 31 & 133; 1984, pl. 6	Holsworthy
MBA	Alland's Quarry, Marnhull	Dorset	Low ridge	Palstave	Frag.	Glauconitic quartzite	Evens et al. 1962; Pearce 1983, 476	–

Date	Locality	Administrative area	Find context	Matrices	Condition	Stone	References	Museum (accession no.)
LBA	Everley Water Meadow, Iwerne Stepleton	Dorset	Roman or later palaeochannel deposit close to MBA burnt mound	Socketed axe	Frag.	Syenite	Howard 1983; Mercer & Healy 2008	–
LBA	Firtree Field, Gussage St Michael	Dorset	SU00142; axe blade found nearby but not in association	Socketed axe	Frag.	?	Knight et al. 2015, 53	–
LBA	Milton or Ansty	Dorset	Unknown	Socketed axe	1 valve	'A composite stone' (Woolls 1839)	Woolls 1839, 75–6, fig. 10; Racket 1840; Hodges 1960, pl. iii; Pearce 1983, 477, pls 54 & 146	Dorset County (1902/1/9)
LBA	Washingborough	Lincolnshire	Excavated; peat deposits by timber platform	Pin heads (multiple)	3 frags, not clear if same mould	Sandstone?	Allen 2009	–
LBA	Coombe Warren, Kingston Hill	London	'Close to the junction of Combe Lane with the road from London to Kingston, at the gravel pits of the estate of H.R.H. Duke of Cambridge and at the west side of Coombe Wood'	Implement base/socket?	Frag.	'Fine-grained stone'	*Journal of the British Archaeological Association* 37, 1881, 188; Field & Needham 1986	–
MBA	Kames (Kaims?) near Bamburgh	Northumberland	Unknown	Rapier	Frag.	'Sandstone (?)'	Burgess & Gerloff 1981, 116, pl. 125	–
ErIA	Ham Hill	Somerset	Unstratified from contemporary hillfort	Socketed axe	Frag.	Greisen	Hodges 1960, pl. 3; Pearce 1983, 532, pls 90 & 153; Needham et al. 1989	Somerset (A954)
ErIA	Ham Hill	Somerset	Unstratified from contemporary hillfort	Socketed axe	Frag.	Greisen	As above	Somerset (A955)
LBA	Petters Sports Field, Egham	Surrey	Excavated; pit with pottery & bone	Socketed axe	Frag.	Keratophyre	Johnson 1975; Needham 1981	Guildford (AS 680)
LBA	Burderop Down	Swindon	Unstratified, between M–LBA settlement & barrow	Socketed axe	3 fitting pieces from 1 valve	Syenite or keratophyre	Gingell 1992	Wiltshire (DZSWS:19 76.52.2)

Date	Locality	Administrative area	Find context	Matrices	Condition	Stone	References	Museum (accession no.)
LBA	Nine Mile Water, Bulford	Wiltshire	'Near Nine Mile Water, in the parish of Bulford, almost opposite the 10th milestone from Salisbury to Marlborough, but on the opposite (north) side of the stream' (Salisbury Museum 1864, 38–9). Woolls' earlier attribution to Chidbury (now Sidbury) Hill appears to be wrong	Socketed axe × 2	1 valve	Probably Keratophyre	Woolls 1839, 77–80, figs 17–18; Yates 1849; Salisbury Museum 1864, 38–9; Evans 1881, 432; Passmore 1931; Moore 1978, pl. 1; Needham 1981	Salisbury (SBYWM:1 C3B.1)
late EBA to MBA	Beckford	Worcester-shire	Excavated; unstratified. River valley	Razor × 2. Possibly a one-piece mould	Broken	Peloidal limestone or oolite marl	Roe 1987	–
			IRELAND					
MBA	?	?	Unknown; ex John Evans collection	Spearhead	1 valve	Sandstone	Evans 1881, 435; Eogan 1993; Lineen 2017	Ashmolean (1927:2897)
MBA	?	?	Unknown	Spearhead	1 valve, damaged	Steatite	Hodges 1954, fig. 2.5; Coghlan & Raftery 1961, 238, fig. 32; Eogan 1993; Ó Faoláin 2004, 169, pl. 6A; Davis 2006, 198, pl. 44; Lineen 2017	NMI (1903:236)
MBA	?	?	Unknown	Spearhead	Frag.	Steatite?	National Museum of Ireland 1971, 215; Ó Faoláin 2004, fig. 34C, pl. 6B; Lineen 2017	NMI (1968:379)
MBA	?	?	Unknown	Spearhead	Both valves	Micaceous grit	Coghlan & Raftery 1961, 238–9, fig. 33; Eogan 1993; Lineen 2017	NMI (P.1173–4)
MBA	?	?	Unknown	Rapier	Both valves	Aplite	Worsae 1872, 376; Coghlan & Raftery 1961, 240, fig. 36; Burgess & Gerloff 1981, appx 2; Eogan 1993	NMI (P.1882:88)
MBA	?	?	Unknown	Palstave; blade or knife	Both valves	Metamorphic rock	?Du Noyer 1847, pl. 4; Armstrong 1917, 523; Coghlan & Raftery 1961, 230–1, fig. 14; Eogan 1993	NMI (P.1882:89)
MBA	?	?	Unknown	Palstave	1 valve	Siliceous grit	Armstrong 1917, 523; Coghlan & Raftery 1961, 229–30, fig. 12; Eogan 1993	NMI (1000:1884 AKA P.2)

Date	Locality	Administrative area	Find context	Matrices	Condition	Stone	References	Museum (accession no.)
MBA	?	?	Unknown	Palstave; possible matrix for triangular object	1 valve	Steatite	Armstrong 1917, 523; Coghlan & Raftery 1961, 230, fig. 13; Eogan 1993; Ó Faoláin 2004, 168–9	NMI (P.438)
EtIA	?	?	Unknown	Socketed axe	1 valve	?	Wilde 1863, fig. 73; Figuier 1870, fig. 227; Coghlan & Raftery 1961, 231–2, fig. 16; Eogan 1993; 2000; Ó Faoláin 2004, 173, pl. 9A. Probably Worsaae 1872, 376	NMI (W.85)
MBA	?	?	Unknown	Spearhead; razor	1 valve	?	Binchy 1967, 60, fig. 4; Collins 1970, 27, fig. 12; Jockenhövel 1980, 52, pl. 5; Eogan 1993; Lineen 2017	Ulster (3785/6.54)
MBA	?	?	Unknown	Spearhead	1 valve	Chlorite schist	Collins 1970, 32, fig. 19; Eogan 1993; Lineen 2017	Ulster (3787/6.53)
MBA	?	?	Unknown	Palstave	1 valve	Chlorite schist	Collins 1970, 25–7, fig. 8; Eogan 1993	Ulster (3788/11.55)
MBA	?	?	Unknown	Spearhead; razor	1 valve	Chlorite schist	Collins 1970, 27–30, fig. 13; Jockenhövel 1980, 53, pl. 7; Eogan 1993; Lineen 2017	Ulster (Raphael collection)
MBA	?	?	Unknown	Spearhead	1 valve, damaged	Chlorite schist	Collins 1970, 32–4, fig. 22; Eogan 1993; Lineen 2017	Ulster (Raphael collection)
M–LBA	?	?	Unknown; ex George Roots collection	Socketed chisel	1 valve	?	–	BM (1891,0514.3)
MBA	?	?	Unknown	Spearhead	1 valve	?	Lineen 2017	Ulster (AYM346.1974)
MBA	?	?	Unknown; ex-Kearney collection	Palstave	1 valve	Steatite	–	NMI (1999 C1:115)
MBA	?	?	Unknown	Spearhead	?	?	Lineen 2017	NMI (E186:11–12). Not clear if these 2 valves belong to same mould; not seen by authors

Date	Locality	Administrative area	Find context	Matrices	Condition	Stone	References	Museum (accession no.)
MBA	? ('near Ballymena')	?	Unknown	Spearhead	1 valve	Chlorite schist	Sotheby 1924, 44, pl. 4 (no. 668); Collins 1970, 30, fig. 14; Eogan 1993; Lineen 2017	Ulster (533:1924)
MBA	? ('near Ballymena')	?	Unknown	Spearhead	1 valve, damaged	Chlorite schist	Sotheby 1924, 44, pl. 4 (no. 669); Collins 1970, 30, fig. 15; Eogan 1993; Lineen 2017	Ulster (534:1924)
MBA	? ('near Ballymena')	?	Unknown	Spearhead; triangular chisel or ingot?	1 valve	Chlorite schist	Sotheby 1924, 44, pl. 4 (no. 669); Collins 1970, 30, fig. 17; Eogan 1993; Lineen 2017	Ulster (535:1924)
MBA	? ('near Ballymena')	?	Unknown	Spearhead	1 valve	Chlorite schist	Collins 1970, 27, fig. 11; Eogan 1993; Lineen 2017	Ulster (536:1924)
MBA	? ('near Ballymena')	?	Unknown	Spearhead; razor (unfinished)	1 valve	Chlorite schist	Collins 1970, 30–2, fig. 18; Jockenhövel 1980, 52, pl. 6; Eogan 1993; Lineen 2017	Ulster (537:1924)
MBA	? ('near Ballymena')	?	Unknown	Spearhead	Frag.	Chlorite schist	Collins 1970, 34, fig. 24; Eogan 1993; Lineen 2017	Ulster (539:1924)
MBA	? ('near Ballymena')	?	Unknown	Razor x 2; tanged blade; ring x 5	1 valve	Steatite	Sotheby 1924, 44, pl. 4 (no. 671); Piggott 1946, 141, fig. 10; Binchy 1967, 52, fig. 10; Collins 1970, 32, fig. 20; Jockenhövel 1980, 53, pl. 6; Eogan 1993	Ulster (540:1924)
MBA	? ('near Ballymena')	?	Unknown	Spearhead	Frag.	Biotite granite	Sotheby 1924, 44; Collins 1970, 27, fig. 10; Eogan 1993; Lineen 2017	Ulster (543:1924)
MBA	River Bann	?	Unknown	Palstave	1 valve	Steatite	Evans 1881, 431; Leahy 1977; Eogan 1993	BM (78.1–25.1)
MBA	Armoy	Co. Antrim	Unknown	Spearhead	1 valve	?	Evans 1881, 435; Eogan 1993	Supposedly in BM (from Greenwell collection), cannot be traced. Possibly an alias of the Little Ballymena mould?

Date	Locality	Administrative area	Find context	Matrices	Condition	Stone	References	Museum (accession no.)
MBA	Ballycastle	Co. Antrim	Unknown	Palstave	Both valves	Sandstone	Evans 1881, fig. 516; Armstrong 1917, 523; Coghlan & Raftery 1961, 227, fig. 5; Eogan 1993; Ó Faoláin 2004, 161	NMI (R140)
MBA	Ballymoney (near)	Co. Antrim	Unknown	Tanged knife or blade	1 valve	Sandstone	Evans 1881, 433, fig. 518; Eogan 1993	Ashmolean (1927.2896)
Late EBA	Broughshane	Co. Antrim	Unknown	Dirk; small flat axe/chisel; trunnion chisel; curved band (unfinished?)	1 valve	Mica slate	Evans 1881, 433, fig. 519; Leahy 1977; Burgess & Gerloff 1981, appx 2, pl. 125; Eogan 1993	Ashmolean (1927.2898)
MBA	Corrstown	Co. Antrim	Excavated; settlement	Palstave	1 valve	Dolerite	Ginn & Rathbone 2012	–
MBA	Corrstown	Co. Antrim	Excavated; settlement	Chisel; tapering rod/pin shank × 3	1 valve	Dolerite	As above	–
MBA	Corrstown	Co. Antrim	Excavated; settlement	Chisel?; uncertain object	Frag.	Dolerite	As above	–
MBA	Corrstown	Co. Antrim	Excavated; settlement	Gouge?	Frag.	Dolerite	As above	–
MBA	Killymaddy	Co. Antrim	Hoard, found close to a stream, on a ridge overlooking the Bann valley	Spearhead; dirk; razor. Core former on edge face?	Both valves	Chlorite schist	Milligan 1911; Coffey 1913a; 1913b; Coghlan & Raftery 1961, 232, fig. 17; Binchy 1967, 54; Jockenhövel 1980, 53, pl. 6; Burgess & Gerloff 1981, appx 2; Eogan 1993; Lineen 2017	NMI (1911.73–4)
MBA	Killymaddy	Co. Antrim	As above	Spearhead; tanged razor	Both valves	Chlorite schist	Milligan 1911; Coffey 1913a; 1913b; Coghlan and Raftery 1961, 232–3, fig. 18; Binchy 1967, 54; Jockenhövel 1980, 52–3, pls 5–6; Eogan 1993; Lineen 2017	NMI (1911.75–6)
MBA	Killymaddy	Co. Antrim	As above	Rapier	1 valve	Sandstone	Milligan 1911; Coffey 1913a; 1913b; Coghlan & Raftery 1961, 239, fig. 34; Burgess & Gerloff 1981, appx 2; Eogan 1993	NMI (1911.77)
MBA	Killymaddy	Co. Antrim	As above	Spearhead; knife?	1 valve	Sandstone	Milligan 1911; Coffey 1913a; 1913b; Coghlan & Raftery 1961, 233, fig. 19; Binchy 1967, 54; Eogan 1993; Lineen 2017	NMI (1911.78)

Date	Locality	Administrative area	Find context	Matrices	Condition	Stone	References	Museum (accession no.)
MBA	Killymaddy	Co. Antrim	As above	Leaf-shaped blade (razor?)	1 valve	Sandstone	Milligan 1911; Coffey 1913a; 1913b; Coghlan & Raftery 1961, 241, fig. 41; Binchy 1967, 54; Eogan 1993	NMI (1911.79)
MBA	Killymaddy	Co. Antrim	As above	Tanged sickle	Both valves, both broken & 1 slightly incomplete	Sandstone	Milligan 1911; Coffey 1913a; 1913b; Coghlan & Raftery 1961, 240-1, figs 37-9; Eogan 1993; Boutoille 2015; this vol Fig. 4.2	NMI (1911.80-5)
MBA	Little Ballymena, Skerry	Co. Antrim	Unknown	Spearhead; unfinished spearhead?; v-shaped bar	1 valve	Steatite	Greenwell & Brewis 1909, fig. 85; Eogan 1993; Lineen 2017. See also the 'Armoy' mould above	BM (WG 1639)
MBA?	Mistyburn	Co. Antrim	Unknown	Socketed chisel?	1 valve	Chlorite schist	Hodges 1954, fig. 2.4; Collins 1970, 34, fig. 23; Eogan 1993	Ulster (538.1934)
MBA	Rasharkin	Co. Antrim	Unknown	Spearhead	1 valve	Steatite	Hodges 1954, 77; Collins 1970, 30, fig. 16; Eogan 1993; Lineen 2017	Ulster (542.1924)
MBA	Whitepark Bay	Co. Antrim	'Lying on surface on the summit of ridge between stone circle and the Causeway end'	Palstave; unidentified implement	1 valve, damaged	Sandstone	Hodges 1954, 77; Collins 1970, 27, fig. 9; Eogan 1993	Ulster (644.30)
MBA	?	Co. Carlow	Unknown	Palstave	Both valves	Aplite	Du Noyer 1847, pl. 5; Wilde 1863, 91-2; Coghlan & Raftery 1961, 227; Eogan 1993. Probably also Worsaae 1872, 376	NMI (1936:W84)
MBA	Lough Ramor	Co. Cavan	Unknown	Spearhead; tanged leaf-shaped blade/razor; blade. Part of an earlier spearhead matrix on edge face	1 valve	Sandstone	Wilde 1863, fig. 74; Coghlan & Raftery 1961, 233-4, fig. 20; Binchy 1967, 54; Jockenhövel 1980, 52, pl. 6; Eogan 1993; Ó Faoláin 2004, 164-5; Lineen 2017	NMI (W.90)
MBA	Gragan West	Co. Clare	Found during levelling of EBA barrow	Palstave	1 valve	Sandstone	Excavations.ie 1988; Eogan 1993	NMI (E458:40)

Date	Locality	Administrative area	Find context	Matrices	Condition	Stone	References	Museum (accession no.)
Late EBA	Inchnagree (AKA Inchnogue)	Co. Cork	Unknown	Rapier × 3; dirk; tanged razor (1 valve); pin (1 valve)	Both valves	Aplite	Hodges 1954, 77; Coghlan & Raftery 1961, 239–40, fig. 35; Binchy 1967, 54; Jockenhövel 1980, 53, pl. 7; Burgess & Gerloff 1981, appx 2; Eogan 1993; Ó Faoláin 2004, 156	NMI (1916:25)
MBA	Maghera	Co. Derry	Unknown	Spearhead	Both valves	Steatite	Society of Antiquaries of London 1873, 427; Evans 1881, 435, fig. 522; Greenwell & Brewis 1909, fig. 84; Brailsford 1953, 34, fig. 12.3; Leahy 1977; Eogan 1993	BM (WG.1640)
MBA	Maghera	Co. Derry?	Unknown	Spearhead	1 valve	Chlorite schist	Collins 1970, 32, fig. 21; Eogan 1993; Lineen 2017	Ulster (Raphael collection)
MBA	Ardvarnock Glebe, Raphoe	Co. Donegal	Unknown	Palstave	1 valve	Steatite	Ó Ríordáin 1935, 156, pl. 17; Coghlan & Raftery 1961, 228, fig. 7; Eogan 1993	NMI (1932:7038)
MBA	Ballyliffin	Co. Donegal	Hoard, under a shelving ledge of rock	Palstave	Both valves	Steatite	Bremer 1927; Ó Ríordáin 1935; Mahr 1939, pl. 5; Coghlan & Raftery 1961, 228, fig. 8; Collins 1970, 25, figs 3–4; Eogan 1993; Ó Faoláin 2004, 158–9	NMI (SA 1925:27)
MBA	Ballyliffin	Co. Donegal	As above	8 × unfinished moulds (13 valves); also 2 other complete moulds reportedly found but in private possession (NMI catalogue)		Steatite	Bremer 1927; Ó Ríordáin 1935; Coghlan & Raftery 1961, 242–3; Collins 1970, 25, figs 5–7; Eogan 1993	NMI (1925:28–32 & 1941:474) & Ulster (Swan Collection)
MBA	Ballyliffin	Co. Donegal	As above	Palstave	Both valves	Steatite	Bremer 1927; Ó Ríordáin 1935	–
MBA	Ballyshannon	Co. Donegal	Unknown	Spearhead	1 valve	?	Coghlan & Raftery 1961, 234, fig. 21; Eogan 1993; Lineen 2017	NMI (1959:405)
Late EBA	Inch Island	Co. Donegal	Unknown	Spearhead; trunnion chisel	1 valve	Sandstone	Hodges 1954, 77; Coghlan & Raftery 1961, 234, fig. 22; Eogan 1993; Ó Faoláin 2004, 156–7, pl. 4; Lineen 2017	NMI (1926:4)

Date	Locality	Administrative area	Find context	Matrices	Condition	Stone	References	Museum (accession no.)
MBA	Maghera	Co. Donegal	Unknown	Spearhead	1 valve	Micaceous rock	Hodges 1954, 77; Coghlan & Raftery 1961, 234–5, fig. 23; Eogan 1993; Lineen 2017	NMI (1916:25)
MBA	Dromore	Co. Down	Unknown	Palstave	1 valve	Steatite	Armstrong 1917, 523; Coghlan & Raftery 1961, 228, fig. 9; Eogan 1993; Ó Faoláin 2004, 166	NMI (1876:1257)
MBA	Culfin	Co. Galway	Hoard	Spearhead	1 valve	Steatite	Raftery 1945; Coghlan & Raftery 1961, 235, fig. 24; Eogan 1993; Lineen 2017	NMI (1942:1841)
MBA	Culfin	Co. Galway	As above	Spearhead	1 valve, tip broken off	Steatite	Raftery 1945; Coghlan & Raftery 1961, 235, fig. 24; Eogan 1993; Lineen 2017	NMI (1942:1842)
MBA	Culfin	Co. Galway	As above	Palstave × 2	1 valve	Steatite	Raftery 1945; Coghlan & Raftery 1961, 229, fig. 10; Eogan 1993	NMI (1942:1843)
MBA	Knock Gerrane Bane, Clarinbridge	Co. Galway	Near a cahir	Spearhead; other spearhead(s)? (not illustrated)	Both valves	Steatite	Gregory 1807; Eogan 1993	–
EtIA	Ballydaw (AKA Ballydag(h))	Co. Kilkenny	Found when reclaiming a bog	Socketed axe	Both valves	Steatite	Cody 1863; Coghlan & Raftery 1961, 231, fig. 15; Eogan 1993; 2000; Ó Faoláin 2004, 172, pls 7–8A; Boutoille 2015, pl. 2	NMI (1901:56)
MBA	Moonbaun Bog, Mountrath	Co. Laois	Bog	Palstave; blade; thin bar or pin shank	Both valves	Micaceous grit	Armstrong 1917, 523; Coghlan & Raftery 1961, 227, fig. 4; Eogan 1993	NMI (1900:54)
MBA	Lough Scur	Co. Leitrim	Crannog	Palstave (on reused flat axe mould)	1 valve	Grit	Wilde 1863, 91, fig. 72; Coghlan & Raftery 1961, 225, fig. 1; Eogan 1993	NMI (W.83)
Late EBA	Lough Gur	Co. Limerick	Unknown	Spearhead × 4; flat pointed object × 2	1 valve	Steatite	de Salis 1863; Leahy 1977; Eogan 1993; Lineen 2017	BM (1862,1206.1)
MBA	Lough Gur site D	Co. Limerick	Excavated; associated with later BA house	Palstave	Frag.	Sandstone	Ó Ríordáin 1954; Coghlan & Raftery 1961, 229, fig. 11; Eogan 1993; Ó Faoláin 2004, 173–4, pl. 9B	NMI (E252)
MBA–LBA	Lough Gur wedge tomb	Co. Limerick	Excavated; adjacent to wedge tomb	Spearhead	Frag.	Schistose stone	Ó Ríordáin & Ó h-Iceadha 1955; Ó Faoláin 2004, 174, fig. 37A, pl. 10	NMI (E73:102)
MBA	Raheen	Co. Limerick	Excavated; gully	Palstave	Frag.	Granite rhyolite	Gowan 1988; Eogan 1993	Limerick (E385:11)

Date	Locality	Administrative area	Find context	Matrices	Condition	Stone	References	Museum (accession no.)
MBA	Dundalk (near)	Co. Louth	Unknown	Adze	1 valve	Steatite	Wilde 1863, 93; Evans 1881, fig. 517; Coghlan & Raftery 1961, 241, fig. 40; Eogan 1993	NMI (W.96)
MBA	Farney Barony (?)	Co. Mayo	Unknown; ex Shirley collection	Spearhead	1 valve	Steatite	Lucas 1968, 116–18; Eogan 1993	NMI (1965:177)
MBA	Toorglass, Kilcommon	Co. Mayo	Hoard; c. 300ft from shoreline at estuary in Trawmore Bay (NMI catalogue)	Spearhead	1 valve	Steatite	Mahr 1939, pl. 7; Raftery 1951, fig. 118; Coghlan & Raftery 1961, 235–6, fig. 25; Eogan 1993; Davis 2006, 198, pl. 67; Boutoille 2015, pl. 1; Lineen 2017	NMI (1931: 338)
MBA	Toorglass, Kilcommon	Co. Mayo	As above	Spearhead; tanged razor	1 valve	Steatite	Mahr 1939, pl. 7; Raftery 1951, fig. 118; Coghlan & Raftery 1961, 235–6, fig. 26; Binchy 1967, 58; Jockenhövel 1980; Eogan 1993; Davis 2006, 198, pl. 67; Boutoille 2015, pl. 1; Lineen 2017	NMI (1931: 339)
MBA	Kilsharvan	Co. Meath	Excavated; round-house	Spearhead	Both valves, broken but near complete	Sandstone	Russell 2004	–
MBA	Loughash	Co. Tyrone	Excavated; interior of wedge tomb	Palstave	Frag.	Hydrolysed dolerite	Davies 1939; Eogan 1993	Ulster
Late EBA	Omagh (near)	Co. Tyrone	Hoard	Spearhead socket	Both valves	Muscovite-hornfels	Coffey 1907; Greenwell & Brewis 1909, pl. 81 (cast?); Coghlan & Raftery 1961, 236, fig. 27; Eogan 1993; Lineen 2017, fig. 5.1	NMI (1956: 416–7)
Late EBA	Omagh (near)	Co. Tyrone	As above	Spearhead; spearhead blade	Both valves, 1 broken	Muscovite-hornfels	Coffey 1907; Greenwell & Brewis 1909, pl. 81 (cast?); Coghlan & Raftery 1961, 236–7, fig. 28; Eogan 1993; Lineen 2017	NMI (1956: 420–1)
Late EBA	Omagh (near)	Co. Tyrone	As above	Spearhead; dagger. Spearhead matrices are cut on to ground down ?spearhead blade/dagger matrices	Both valves	Muscovite-hornfels	Coffey 1907; Greenwell & Brewis 1909, pl. 81 (cast?); Coghlan & Raftery 1961, 237, fig. 29; Eogan 1993; Lineen 2017	NMI (1956: 422–3)
Late EBA	Omagh (near)	Co. Tyrone	As above	Pin; half of an earlier spearhead socket matrix	1 valve	Muscovite-hornfels	Coffey 1907; Coghlan & Raftery 1961, 238, fig. 30; Eogan 1993; Lineen 2017	NMI (1956:424)

Date	Locality	Administrative area	Find context	Matrices	Condition	Stone	References	Museum (accession no.)
Late EBA	Omagh (near)	Co. Tyrone	As above	Dagger or spearhead blade; anvil; thin bar; flat strip with rivet hole	Both valves	Muscovite-hornfels	Coffey 1907; Greenwell & Brewis 1909, pl. 81 (cast?); Coghlan & Raftery 1961, 241-2, fig. 42; Eogan 1993; Lineen 2017	NMI (1956: 418-19)
MBA	Sultan	Co. Tyrone	Hoard originally containing more moulds	Palstave	1 valve	Chlorite schist	Williams 1980; Eogan 1993	–
MBA	Sultan	Co. Tyrone	As above	Palstave	1 valve	Chlorite schist	As above	–
MBA	Sultan	Co. Tyrone	As above	Palstave	Frag.	Chlorite schist	As above	–
MBA	Sultan	Co. Tyrone	Presumably hoard as above	Spearhead	Both valves, 1 missing tip end	?	-	Ulster (Belu.A6433 & Belu.A6434)
MBA	Fethard	Co. Wexford	Unknown	Spearhead	1 valve	?	Lineen 2017, fig. 5.16	BM (1899, 0523.1)
EtIA	Innyard Hill, Fethard	Co. Wexford	Unknown	Socketed axe	1 valve	Mica schist	Frazer 1889; Leahy 1977; Eogan 1993; 2000, 220	BM (1900, 0619.1)
MBA	Moylisha	Co. Wicklow	Wedge tomb	Spearhead	Both valves	Aplite	Ó h-Iceadha 1946; Coghlan & Raftery 1961, 238, fig. 31; Eogan 1993; Ó Faoláin 2004, pl. 5; Boutoille 2015, pl. 3; Lineen 2017	NMI (1938: 8572-3)
SCOTLAND								
MBA	?	Aberdeenshire	Unknown	Spearhead; leaf-shaped blade or knife	1 valve	Talc schist	PSAS 60 (1925-6), 19; Hodges 1959, pl. B2; Coles 1962, 89; 1966, 147; Davis 2012, 164	NMS (CM 31)
MBA	Culter	Aberdeenshire	Unknown	Spearhead	1 valve?	Sandstone	Hodges 1959, pl. B1; Coles 1962, 89; Coles 1966, 147 (as 'Culter or Cromar'); MacGregor 2004	Ashmolean (1927/2723) Cast in NMS (CM 22)
MBA	Campbeltown	Argyll & Bute	Unknown	Spearhead	Both valves	Amphibolite	Mitchell 1866; Coles 1962, 89; 1966, 147; Barber 2003, fig. 33; Davis 2012, 164	NMS (CM 2-3)
MBA	Campbeltown	Argyll and Bute	Unknown	Spearhead; razor	Both valves	Talc schist	Mitchell 1866; Piggott 1947; Coles 1962, 89; 1966, 147; Jockenhövel 1980, pl. 7; Davis 2012, 164	NMS (CM 5-6)

Date	Locality	Administrative area	Find context	Matrices	Condition	Stone	References	Museum (accession no.)
MBA	Low (now Little) Glengyre, Kirkcolm	Dumfries and Galloway	Unknown	Palstave-like implement or anvil?	1 incomplete valve	Sandstone	Mann 1923; Childe 1948; Coles 1962, 89; 1966, 120, 147; Schmidt & Burgess 1981, 171, pl. 70	Cast in NMS (CM 29). Original supposedly in Hunterian, Glasgow, but cannot be traced
EtIA	Stittenham, Rosskeen	Highland	100 yds NE of office houses of Stittenham Farm	Socketed axe	Both valves	Steatite	Wilson 1863, 345–6, fig. 48; Hodges 1959; Coles 1962, 89; Schmidt & Burgess 1981, 243, pl. 102	Ashmolean (1927.2725)
EtIA	Stittenham, Rosskeen	Highland	As above	Socketed axe	Both valves	Steatite	Wilson 1863, 345–6, fig. 49; Hodges 1959; Coles 1962, 89; Schmidt & Burgess 1981, 243 and pl. 102; Barber 2003, fig. 33; this vol. Fig. 2.11	NMS (CM 51–52)
MBA?	Strathnaver (between Langdale and Skail)	Highland	Between foot of Langdale and head of Skail	Tanged spearhead or razor	1 valve	Talc schist	Mackay 1906; Coles 1966, 118, 147	NMS (CM 39)
MBA	Culbin Sands	Moray	Unknown	Spearhead or razor	1 valve	Sandstone	Walker 1974, 101; Coles 1966, 118, 147	NMS (CM 21)
MBA	?	Orkney?	Unknown	Palstave?	Frag.	Amphibolite	Society of Antiquaries of Scotland 1909; Hodges 1959, pl. C1; Coles 1962, 89; 1966, 147; Schmidt & Burgess 1981, pl. 70	NMS (CM 25)
MBA	Eildon Camp (=Eildon Hill North?)	Scottish Borders	Eildon Hill North is a hillfort possibly constructed in LBA & certainly with LBA occupation, on a commanding hill visible 40 km away. Hunterian catalogue also gives Strathpeffer (Highland) as provenance	Palstave	Frag.	Steatite	Callander 1923; Coles 1962, 89	Hunterian, Glasgow (A.1912.5)

WALES

Date	Locality	Administrative area	Find context	Matrices	Condition	Stone	References	Museum (accession no.)
LBA	Abermâd, Llanilar	Ceredigion	From the bed of a stream (Afon Fâd) close to its confluence with the River Ystwyth	Socketed chisel	1 valve	Grit	Jones 1945; Leahy 1977; Savory 1980, fig. 40	NMW
Late EBA	Bodwrdin	Isle of Anglesey	'Between Bodwrdin and Tre Ddafydd'	Spearhead × 3 (1 unfinished); 'groove'	1 valve, near complete but broken in 2 during recovery	Sandstone	Archaeological Institute 1846; Greenwell & Brewis 1909, fig. 83; Britton 1963; Manby 1966; Lynch 1970, fig. 62; Davis 2012, 164.	Gwynedd, on loan from Tolson (A.63.60)

Possible fakes (Ireland)

Date	Locality	Administrative area	Find context	Matrices	Condition	Stone	References	Museum (accession no.)
MBA?	Lough Corrib	Co. Galway	Unknown	Palstave	1 valve	Sandstone	Society of Antiquaries of Scotland 1865, 94; Hodges 1954, 77; Eogan 1993. V. likely fake according to Eogan	NMS (CN 2–3)
LBA?	? (near Ballymena')	?	Unknown	Miniature socketed axe	1 valve	Sandstone	Sotheby 1924, 44, pl. 4 (no. 671); Collins 1970, 23–4; Eogan 2000, 220. Rejected as fake by Collins but accepted by Eogan	Ulster (541:1924)
MBA?	?	?	Unknown	Socketed chisel	1 valve	Steatite	Hodges 1954, fig. 2.3. Rejected as fake by Collins 1970, 23–4	Ulster (3786/6.54)
MBA?	?	?	Unknown; ex Lord Antrim collection	Palstave. Sharpness of matrix could suggest fake	1 valve	Steatite	Hodges 1954, 77; Leahy 1977, fig. 67; Eogan 1993. May not be genuine according to Eogan	Ashmolean (1886:5765)
MBA?	?	?	Unknown; ex Lord Antrim collection	Spearhead	1 valve	Steatite	Leahy 1977, fig. 77; Eogan 1993. May not be genuine according to Eogan	Ashmolean (1886:5766)
LBA?	?	?	Unknown	Spearhead	Both valves	Chlorite-amphibole-schist	Society of Antiquaries of Scotland 1865, 94; Eogan 1993. Difficult to say if genuine according to Eogan	NMS (CN 4–5)
MBA?	?	?	Unknown	Palstave	1 valve	Serpentenite	Society of Antiquaries of Scotland 1892, 124; Eogan 1993. Difficult to say if genuine according to Eogan	NMS (CN 7)

Spurious provenances

Date	Locality	Administrative area	Matrices	References
				ENGLAND
MBA	Yorkshire Moors	?	Spearhead; palstave adze	Hodges 1954; 1955, citing BM no. 99.5-23.1, which is actually provenanced to Fethard Castle, Wexford. The stone type (steatite) is more compatible with an Irish provenance
				SCOTLAND
MBA	Cromar	Aberdeenshire	Spearhead	Hodges 1954; 1959, pl. A3, citing NMS accession no. CM 22. Actually a plaster cast of the Ashmolean Culter mould
LBA	Ardrossan	North Ayrshire	Socketed axe	Hodges 1954; Coles 1962. Described by Coles as similar to the Rosskeen moulds. However both give the Ashmolean accession no 1927.2725, which is ascribed to Rosskeen in the Ashmolean catalogue

Appendix 4
Bronze Age bronze moulds from Britain and Ireland

Locality	County	Context	Date*	Matrix	Condition	Exterior decoration	References	Museum (accession no.)
Isleham	Cambridgeshire	Hoard	LBA	Palstave	Frag.	No	Britton 1960a; Edwardson 1970; Coombs 1971, fig. 48; O'Connor 1980, 366; Pearce 1984, pl. 12; Taylor 1993, M2:C5, pl. 70b; Beesley 2004, fig. 9d	West Stow (X21.1)
New Street, Cambridge	Cambridgeshire	Single find	LBA	Socketed axe	Both valves	Yes	Fox 1923, 58, pl. 9; Hodges 1960, pl. 6B	Cambridge MAA (1905.6)
Spinkhill	Derbyshire	Dispersed hoard	LBA	Axe	Frag.	Yes	PAS: DENO-6C81A3	–
White Edge, Froggatt	Derbyshire	Single find	LBA	Socketed axe	1 valve	No	*East Midlands Archaeological Bulletin* 3, 1; Leahy 1977	Derby Silk Mill (471.60)
Heathery Burn, Stanhope	Durham	Cave with other artefacts	LBA	Socketed axe	1 valve	Knobs only	Society of Antiquaries of London 1864; Greenwell 1894; Greenwell & Clinch 1905; Hodges 1960, pl. 7C; Britton & Longworth 1968; Britton 1971; Schmidt & Burgess 1981, 232, pl. 95	BM (1911.10-21.9)
Wilmington	East Sussex	Hoard	LBA	Socketed axe	Both valves	No	Cooper 1862; Curwen 1954, fig. 59; Hodges 1960, pl. 6A; Coombs 1971, fig. 441	Lewes
Brough on Humber	East Riding of Yorkshire	Hoard, with the below	LBA	Socketed axe	Both valves	Yes	Lort 1779, pl. 7; du Noyer 1847, pl. 3; Brailsford 1953, fig. 12 (as 'Quantock Hills'); Hodges 1960, pl. 8A–B (ditto); Schmidt & Burgess 1981, 209, nos 1254 & 1255 (as 'Yorkshire'); Briggs *et al.* 1987	BM (OA 116 & 117)
Brough on Humber	East Riding of Yorkshire	Hoard, with the above	LBA	Socketed axe	Both valves	Knobs only	Stukeley 1776, pl. 96; du Noyer 1847, pl. 2; Leahy 1977 (as 'South Wiltshire'); Briggs *et al.* 1987	BM (T.43.a-b)
Hotham Carrs, Hotham	East Riding of Yorkshire	Hoard	MBA	Palstave	Both valves	Yes	Society of Antiquaries of London 1873, 426; Evans 1881, 440, fig. 527; Sheppard 1900; Hodges 1960, pl. 4A; Burgess 1968, fig. 3; Schmidt & Burgess 1981, 169 and pl. 69	BM (WG 1851)
Arkesden	Essex	Hoard	LBA	Socketed axe	1 valve	No	Clarke 1873; Fox 1923, 324	–
Barling	Essex	Dispersed hoard	LBA	Socketed axe	Frag.	Yes	Crowe 2003	–

Locality	County	Context	Date*	Matrix	Condition	Exterior decoration	References	Museum (accession no.)
Blackwater valley, near Maldon	Essex	Hoard	LBA	Axe	Frag.	Knob only	PAS: ESS-F8865B	–
Hafod Mountain, Gwernymynydd	Flintshire	Hoard	LBA	Socketed axe	Both valves (fused)	Yes	Grenter 1989	Flintshire (CLWMS HQA 1989.1/1)
Beddington Park	Greater London	Hoard	LBA	Socketed axe	Frag.	?	Anderson 1874, pl. 2; Flower 1874	–
'London'	Greater London?	Unknown; provenance uncertain	MBA	Palstave	Both valves	No	Sheppard 1923; Hodges 1960, pl. 5D	Hull (KINCM:1980.6 66.1-2)
Southall	Greater London	Hoard	LBA	Socketed axe	Both valves (1 broken during recovery)	No	Read 1897; Britton 1960b; Hodges 1960, pl. 7A–B (pl. 7A erroneously labelled as 'Beddington')	BM (1897.4-10.1)
Wickham Park, West Wickham	Greater London	Hoard	LBA	Socketed axe	Frag.	No	Anderson 1874, 11; Smith 1958; Hodges 1960, pl. 7D lower	BM (1855.2-27.14)
Deansfield (AKA Danesfield), Glan-Adda, Bangor	Gwynedd	With the below & 1 palstave	MBA	Palstave	Both valves	Yes	Yates 1849; Way 1856; Hodges 1960, pl. 4; RCAHMW 1960, li-lii	1 valve in BM (1849,0521.5), other in Cambridge MAA
Deansfield	Gwynedd	With the above & 1 palstave	MBA	Palstave	Both valves (1 broken)	Yes	as above	as above
Llwyn-mawr, Llanycil	Gwynedd	Single find	LBA	'Late' palstave	1 valve	No	RCAHMW 1921, 148; Hodges 1960, pl. 4B; Bowen & Gresham 1967, fig, 46; Burgess 1968, fig, 5; Leahy 1977	BM (1913.5-28.1)
Hayling Island	Hampshire	Hoard	MBA	Socketed punch	Both valves	Yes	Lawson 1999 & pers. comm.; S. Needham pers. comm.	–
Boughton Malherbe	Kent	Hoard, with other Boughton Malherbe moulds	LBA	End-winged axe	1 valve	Yes	Adams 2017	Maidstone (260)

Locality	County	Context	Date*	Matrix	Condition	Exterior decoration	References	Museum (accession no.)
Boughton Malherbe	Kent	Hoard, with the above	LBA	End-winged axe	Frag.	Yes	Adams 2017	Maidstone (246)
Boughton Malherbe	Kent	Hoard, with the above	LBA	End-winged axe	Frag.	Knobs only	Adams 2017	Maidstone (247)
Boughton Malherbe	Kent	Hoard, with the above	LBA	Axe?	Frag.? part of #25 or different mould	No	Adams 2017	Maidstone (218)
Crundale	Kent	Hoard	LBA	Socketed axe	Frag.	No	PAS: KENT-7C3863	Canterbury
Isle of Harty	Kent	Hoard, with other Isle of Harty moulds	LBA	Socketed gouge	Both valves	No	Society of Antiquaries of London 1873, 424; Evans 1881, 441–6 and fig. 532; Smith 1956; Leahy 1977; Pearce 1984, pl. 15	Ashmolean (AN1927.2507)
Isle of Harty	Kent	Hoard, with the above	LBA	Socketed axe	Both valves	Knobs only	Society of Antiquaries of London 1873, 424; Evans 1881, 441–5, fig. 530; Smith 1956; Leahy 1977; Pearce 1984, pl. 15	Ashmolean (AN1927.2490)
Isle of Harty	Kent	Hoard, with the above	LBA	Socketed axe	Both valves	Knobs only	Society of Antiquaries of London 1873, 424; Evans 1881, 441–5, fig. 531; Smith 1956; Leahy 1977; Pearce 1984, pl. 15	Ashmolean (AN1927.2498)
Isle of Harty	Kent	Hoard, with the above	LBA	Socketed axe	1 valve	No	Society of Antiquaries of London 1873, 424; Evans 1881, 441–5; Smith 1956; Leahy 1977; Pearce 1984, pl. 15; this volume, Fig. 4.25	Ashmolean (AN1927.2501)
Stoke, Hoo	Kent	Hoard	LBA	Axe	Frag.	Yes	Jessup 1930, 108 (as 'Rochester'); Hodges 1960, pl. 7D upper (erroneously labelled as 'Wickham Park'); Maraszek 2007, 440, pl. 8.27; Turner 2010	BM (1893.2-5.27)
Beacon Hill, Woodhouse	Leicestershire	Single find	LBA	Socketed axe	1 valve	No	Clark 1905; Hodges 1960, pl. 6C (as 'Charnwood Forest, Notts.'); Leahy 1977	Charnwood
Rothley	Leicestershire	Hoard	LBA	Socketed axe	Both valves	Yes	PAS: LEIC-A6BB51	Charnwood
Washingborough Fen	Lincolnshire	Hoard	LBA	Socketed axe	Both valves	Knobs only	Archaeological Institute 1850, xxviii; Archaeological Institute 1861, 166; Davey 1973, 98, fig. 23; Leahy 1977	Lincoln (10-55)

Locality	County	Context	Date*	Matrix	Condition	Exterior decoration	References	Museum (accession no.)
Beeston Regis	Norfolk	Hoard	LBA	Socketed axe	1 valve	No	Lawson 1980; 2013; Taylor 1993, M2:D10	Norwich Castle (1981.79.19)
Harling	Norfolk	Single find	MBA	Palstave	Both valves	Yes	Wymer 1987	Norwich Castle (1986.58)
Hempnall	Norfolk	Found with the below	MBA	Palstave	Both valves, 1 broken	Yes	PAS: SF-2D55E2	Norwich Castle (2014.16)
Hempnall	Norfolk	Found with the above	MBA	Palstave	Both valves	Yes	PAS: SF-2D55E2	Norwich Castle (2014.16)
Hevingham	Norfolk	Hoard	LBA	Socketed axe	Both valves	No	Lawson 2013; Norfolk HER no. 36973	Norwich Castle (2003.71)
North Tuddenham	Norfolk	Hoard	LBA	Axe	Frag.	Yes	PAS: NMS2464; Norfolk HER no. 36081	–
Oxnead, Brampton	Norfolk	Hoard	LBA	Axe	Frag.	Yes	Norfolk HER no. 24343	–
Unthank Road, Norwich	Norfolk	Hoard	LBA	Socketed axe	Both valves	Yes	Society of Antiquaries of London 1829, 424; Archaeological Institute 1851, xxvi; Hodges 1960, pl. 6D; Coombs 1971, fig. 334; Langmaid 1976, fig. 26; Norfolk Museums Service 1977, 35, fig. 93; Taylor 1993, M2:F12, pl. 89b	Norwich Castle (1946.161.1)
Barnetby le Wold	North Lincolnshire	Single find	LBA	Socketed axe	1 valve	Yes	North Lincolnshire HER no. 20024	N. Lincolnshire (1995:119)
Roseberry Topping	North Yorkshire	Hoard	LBA	Socketed axe	Both valves	No	Ord 1846, 126-8; Evans 1881, 447 (as 'Cleveland Hills'); Howarth 1899, 86-7; Clark 1905; Elgee 1930, pl. 24; Hodges 1960, pl. 8C; Leahy 1977; Schmidt & Burgess 1981, 243, pl. 102; Pearce 2006	Weston Park, Sheffield (J93.514)
Blewbury	Oxfordshire	Hoard	LBA	Socketed axe	Both valves	Yes	PAS: BERK-56BD17	–
Chinnor	Oxfordshire	Single find	MBA	Palstave	Both valves	Knobs only	PAS: BUC-7E5EA8	–
Sutton Courtenay	Oxfordshire	Single find	MBA	Palstave-chisel	Both valves	Yes	–	BM (1998,0501.1)
Oakhurst, Gobowen	Shropshire	With 1 axe	LBA	Socketed axe	Both valves	No	Shropshire HER no. 04253	Shrewsbury (E.01701.002)

Locality	County	Context	Date*	Matrix	Condition	Exterior decoration	References	Museum (accession no.)
Marton	Shropshire	Single find	MBA?	Palstave	1 valve	?	Stokes 1995; Shropshire HER no. 30983	–
East Pennard	Somerset	Single find	MBA	Socketed spear-head	1 valve	Yes	Davis 2006; 2012; Knight *et al.* 2015, 65, pl. 27, fig. 9	Somerset (TTNCM 63/1994)
Arwarton	Suffolk	Single find	LBA	Axe	Frag.	Yes	PAS: SF2231	–
Levington	Suffolk	Hoard	LBA	Socketed axe	Frag.	Knob only	Coombs 1971, fig. 388; Taylor 1993, M3:B1, pl. 111a; Pendleton 1999, 208	Ipswich (1961.103)
Sutton	Suffolk	Single find	LBA	Socketed axe	1 valve	Knobs only	PAS: SF-839555	–
Penderry	Swansea	Single find	MBA	Palstave	Frag.	Yes	PAS: NMGW-9883F6	–
Grays Thurrock	Thurrock	Hoard	LBA	Socketed axe	Frag.	Yes	Butcher 1922; Coombs 1971, fig. 128; Turner 2010	Colchester
Castle Road, Worthing	West Sussex	Single find	LBA	Socketed axe	Both valves	No	Green 1973	Worthing
near Devizes	Wiltshire	Single find	MBA	Palstave	1 valve	Yes	PAS: WILT-FFC218	–
Donhead Clift, Donhead St Mary	Wiltshire	Hoard	LBA	Socketed axe	Both valves	No	Goddard 1912, 138; Passmore 1931; Hodges 1960, pl. 8D; Taylor 1993, M1:G9, pl. 50	Salisbury (1C5A1 & 1C5A6)
"South Wiltshire"	Wiltshire	Unknown	MBA	Palstave	Both valves	Yes ('cords')	Society of Antiquaries of London 1855; Evans 1881, 440–1; Brailsford 1953, fig. 12; Hodges 1960, pl. 5; Leahy 1977	BM (1855.5–3.1)
"Ireland" (?)	?	Unknown	MBA	Palstave	1 valve	Knobs only	Vallancey 1786, 59–60 and pl. 10 (?); Burgess 1980, pl. 16; Ó Faoláin 2004, 175–6, pl. 11	NMI

Possible lost mould

Locality	County	Context	Date*				Comments	
Heathery Burn, Stanhope	Durham	Cave, as #5	LBA				A 19th century photograph of objects from the Heathery Burn cave shows a possible second axe mould, now lost (Harding & Young 1986), but the image is too unclear for certainty.	

Spurious moulds

Locality	County	Comments
Carbrooke	Norfolk	A record of a socketed axe mould from Carbrooke (Clinch 1901, 276; Norfolk HER no. 8814) derives from confusion with the mould from Unthank Road, Norwich (A. Lawson pers. comm.).
Stow Bedon	Norfolk	A small bronze fragment is identified in Norfolk HER (no. 55139) as part of a mould, but this seems unlikely on the evidence of the accompanying photograph.
Quantock Hills	Somerset	Spurious provenance for 1 of the Brough on Humber moulds (see above).
Coate	Wiltshire	Initially identified as a possible axe mould fragment (Goddard 1917; Anonymous 1980) but actually a medieval cauldron foot (Wiltshire Museum catalogue no. 1977.08 and L. Brown pers. comm.).

Abbreviations: BM = British Museum; HER = Historic Environment Record; LBA = Late Bronze Age; MBA = Middle Bronze Age; PAS = Portable Antiquities Scheme.
* For moulds found in hoards, date of hoard deposition is given.

Appendix 5
Coin pellet mould finds

Site	County	Context	Context date (century)	References
Colchester, Sheepen	Essex	Territorial oppidum	Early & late 1st AD	Hawkes & Hull 1947; Hawkes & Crummy 1995
Bagendon	Gloucestershire	Territorial oppidum (Bagendon-Ditches)	Early 1st AD	Clifford 1961; Trow 1982; Landon 2016
Ditches	Gloucestershire	Territorial oppidum (Bagendon-Ditches)	Late Iron Age-mid-1st AD	Trow 1988; Trow & Moore 2009
Silchester	Hampshire	Oppidum	15 BC-AD 40/50 & early Roman	Boon 1954; Corney 1984; Fulford & Timby 2000; Fulford *et al.* 2018
Winchester, Cathedral Green	Hampshire	Oppidum?	Residual	Biddle 1966
Braughing/Puckeridge/Standon	Hertfordshire	Oppidum	AD 25-70 (Wickham Kennels)	Landon 2016
Verlamion	Hertfordshire	Oppidum	Late Iron Age & early Roman	Frere 1983; Thompson 2005
Wheathampstead, Turners Hall Farm	Hertfordshire	Settlement	Mid-1st-2nd AD	Landon 2016
Canterbury, Marlowe Theatre & Car Park	Kent	Oppidum?	Late 1st BC-AD 70/80	Blockley *et al.* 1995
Rochester, High Street	Kent	Settlement	Late Iron Age	Withew 1985; Harrison 1991
Leicester, Bath Lane/Blackfriars Street	Leicestershire	Oppidum	Mid-late 1st AD	Clay & Mellor 1985; Kipling 2008
Old Sleaford	Lincolnshire	Oppidum	First half of 1st AD	Elsdon 1997; Landon 2016
Scotton	Lincolnshire	Unstratified	–	Whitwell 1982, 15; Landon 2016
Torksey	Lincolnshire	Unstratified	–	PAS: LIN-155F48
Needham	Norfolk	Early Roman settlement	Mid-late 1st AD	Frere 1941
Saham Toney, Woodcock Hall	Norfolk	Unstratified from unexcavated Late Iron Age & Roman settlement or ritual site		Brown 1986
Thetford, Fison Way	Norfolk	Ritual site	40s-70s AD	Gregory 1991
Scotch Corner	North Yorkshire	Early Roman settlement	Late 1st AD	Fell 2017
Haverhill, Place Farm	Suffolk	Unstratified	–	Walford 1803, 72-3
Boxgrove, Ounces Barn	Sussex	Territorial oppidum? (Chichester Dykes)	Late Iron Age-late 1st AD	Bedwin & Place 1995

INDEX

Numbers in *italic* denote pages with images, numbers followed by 't' indicate pages with tables. All materials and objects are copper alloy/bronze unless stated otherwise